Handbook of Aviation Neuropsychology

Handbook of Aviation Neuropsychology

A Practical Guide for the Clinician

Edited by
Robert Bor
Carina Eriksen
Randy J. Georgemiller
Alastair L. Gray

hogrefe

Library of Congress Cataloging in Publication information for the print version of this book is available via the Library of Congress Marc Database under the LC Control Number 2024945048

Library and Archives Canada Cataloguing in Publication
Title: Handbook of aviation neuropsychology : a practical guide for the clinician / edited by Robert Bor, Carina Eriksen, Randy J. Georgemiller, Alastair L. Gray.
Names: Bor, Robert, editor. | Eriksen, Carina, editor | Georgemiller, Randy J. (Randy James), 1953- editor | Gray, Alastair L., editor.
Description: Includes bibliographical references.
Identifiers: Canadiana (print) 20240449746 | Canadiana (ebook) 20240450701 | ISBN 9780889376397 (softcover) | ISBN 9781616766399 (PDF) | ISBN 9781613346396 (EPUB)
Subjects: LCSH: Aviation psychology—Handbooks, manuals, etc. | LCSH: Neuropsychology—Handbooks, manuals, etc. | LCSH: Aeronautics—Safety measures—Handbooks, manuals, etc. | LCGFT: Handbooks and manuals.
Classification: LCC RC1085 .H36 2024 | DDC 155.9/65—dc23

http://www.hogrefe.com

Cover image based on illustrations by cherezoff, Viks_jin, and German Ovchinnikov (Adobe Stock)

PUBLISHING OFFICES
USA: Hogrefe Publishing Corporation, 44 Merrimac St., Newburyport, MA 01950
Phone 978 255 3700; E-mail customersupport@hogrefe.com
EUROPE: Hogrefe Publishing GmbH, Merkelstr. 3, 37085 Göttingen, Germany
Phone +49 551 99950 0, Fax +49 551 99950 111; E-mail publishing@hogrefe.com
SALES & DISTRIBUTION
USA: Hogrefe Publishing, Customer Services Department,
30 Amberwood Parkway, Ashland, OH 44805
Phone 800 228 3749, Fax 419 281 6883; E-mail customersupport@hogrefe.com
EUROPE: Hogrefe Publishing, Merkelstr. 3, 37085 Göttingen, Germany
Phone +49 551 99950 0, Fax +49 551 99950 111; E-mail publishing@hogrefe.com
OTHER OFFICES
CANADA: Hogrefe Publishing, 82 Laird Drive, East York, Ontario, M4G 3V1
SWITZERLAND: Hogrefe Publishing, Länggass-Strasse 76, 3012 Bern

Printed and bound in the Czech Republic

ISBN 978-0-88937-639-7 (print) • ISBN 978-1-61676-639-9 (PDF) • ISBN 978-1-61334-639-6 (EPUB)
https://doi.org/10.1027/00639-000

Contents

Foreword

It's time. The moment is right for a volume like handbook of aviation neuropsychology. This book not only chronicles the significant contribution that aviation neuropsychology has made to aviation safety but, unlike some books that are dated at the time of publication, the editors have drawn from the progressive thinkers in the discipline who are charting the way forward for the field. We are at a critical juncture in global aviation where we are highly sensitized to the health and well-being of aviators and the personnel who support our ability to safely traverse the airways. This book tackles many of the issues facing the aviation industry as it relates to human operators, such as normal and abnormal aging, mental health conditions, stress and fatigue, and the various medical and neurological conditions that can compromise pilot performance. The book offers cutting-edge perspectives for addressing these concerns based on aviation neuropsychological assessment techniques with a nod to prevention, health promotion, and remediation strategies. In my role as the US Federal Air Surgeon, I take particular pride in the editorial and scholarly contribution represented in this book by my Federal Aviation Administration colleagues who serve as aeromedical review officers, neuropsychologists, and human factors psychologists. Their expertise, passion, and dedication to the field are apparent in the chapters they have contributed. Their work is integrated with a panel of international experts with incredible credentials so that the book is able to offer a wraparound global perspective as it pertains to aviation neuropsychology. Anyone with even tangential interest in the field of aviation neuropsychology will find many chapters of value in the book, given the editors' devotion to material that is both relevant and accessible to a broad readership. And for the professional with more direct regulatory, academic, or clinical interest in aviation neuropsychology, this book will assuredly be a top-shelf addition to their professional resources. I commend the editors for their vision in expanding our understanding of the concepts and skills, and also practice dilemmas, in aviation neuropsychology. I congratulate them for bringing together such an expert panel of contributors, all of whom work to improve aerospace and aviation safety and promote the physical and mental health and wellness of all who work in aviation.

Susan E. Northrup, MD, MPH

US Federal Air Surgeon, Office of Aerospace Medicine, Federal Aviation Administration

Introduction

Rob Bor, Carina Eriksen, Randy J. Georgemiller, and Alastair Lewis Gray

Neuropsychology is the gateway to understanding and improving human performance and safety in the aerospace industry. Research and the applications of findings and insights in neuropsychology, as well as clinical experience, are core to improving our understanding of human behavior in safety-critical settings, and specifically in this context, to include pilots, air traffic controllers, engineers, and other professional groups who collectively manage risks in their everyday work.

Neuropsychology is the branch of psychology that focuses on the relationship between brain and behavior. When applied to aviation, the subspecialty of aviation neuropsychology has a common thread that knits together the various applications within the field, despite diverse international origin or application to civil or military flight, and that is *safety*. Whether it is the safety of the estimated 300,000+ commercial pilots or the 4.5 billion passengers they transport yearly worldwide, safety is what has been the impetus for the origins of the field and what will propel the nascent field of aviation neuropsychology into the future. This edited book, with contributions from a range of experts in the field and specialisms, seeks to describe the background, aims, principles, challenges, and associated practice skills and research themes of aviation neuropsychology, with a main emphasis on operational staff and safety.

While a range of health-care professionals are the primary intended audience for this book – including neuropsychologists, clinical psychologists, aviation psychologists, aviation medical examiners, neurologists, and human factors and flight safety specialists as well as physiologists, researchers, and aviation regulators, among others – we were mindful that many others, both inside and outside of aviation, would likely be interested in some or all of the topics covered here, including human resources and selection specialists, crew managers, other health-care professionals, air accident investigators, pilots, cabin crew, air traffic controllers, aviation lawyers, crew scheduling teams, and aircraft designers as well as related professionals and similar specialists in other safety-critical sectors.

The early days of aviation were characterized by a need for pilots to understand both the mechanics of flight and the mechanical contraptions that they placed their trust in. Modern aviation is far from those embryonic early years and pilots need to be able to not only fly an aircraft, but also manage a team, problem solve quickly, be the public face of the airline, and cope with the stresses of spending sometimes extended periods away from home, family, and friends. In a military context, such stresses and strains are compounded by the addition of performing in the theater of combat, often flying at the extremes of what airframes and human beings can stand. Pressures from either the commercial or military perspective can have neuropsychological consequences that can significantly impact upon an individual's ability to safely perform their duties. Aviation neuropsychology is key to identifying the effects of such pressures and underlying medical conditions that may pose a significant risk to aviation safety.

The *Handbook of Aviation Neuropsychology* is a comprehensive textbook for clinicians, practitioners, managers, and researchers working in the increasingly important specialty of aviation neuropsychology. We endeavored to provide clinicians and related colleagues with an up-to-date summary of the neuropsychological and psychological issues that form part of the essential considerations and components of effective, valid, and comprehensive neuropsychological evaluations of flight crew personnel working in both civil and military settings. The *Handbook of Aviation Neuropsychology* starts from a "first principle" viewpoint, describing the relevance and importance of neuropsychology to the aviation industry – from the selection of trainee pilots through to the evaluation of complex psychological presentations that could impact upon flight safety. Readers will find insights, theory, research, and case studies that detail the neuropsychological assessment of specific conditions through to case studies detailing air accidents where neuropsychological assessment could have pinpointed issues before the aircraft left the runway.

Using a practical, "hands-on" format, this book provides an opportunity for clinicians in this rapidly developing specialty to advance their continuing professional development. We have aimed to deliver a guide for neuropsychology in modern aviation where key specialist areas are covered in chapters written by international leaders in their respective fields. Ideally, a book of this scope and with related ambition would cover every facet of the field, the full range of neurocognitive deficits and conditions of interest in aviation, the most complete review of assessment tools and related clinical skills and therapeutic approaches, and a review of all relevant research in the field. As editors, our engagement in this project, in addition to our collective career experience, has only heightened our awareness of how complex and diverse the field and specialism are. Likewise, our involvement with this project has helped to identify gaps in knowledge and improved awareness of dilemmas and debates in assessments and clinical standards. Future editions of the book will hopefully develop and refine the relevant domains of interest as well as the approaches to assessment and research in the field, among other topics. While previously published books, such as the comprehensive and well-received *Aeromedical Psychology* by our colleagues Kennedy and Kay (2013), have included aviation neuropsychology as one of several main foci, no single text has brought together current international thinking that reflects current policies, procedures, practices, and standards in what is an international industry. This book expands upon areas of aviation neuropsychology that previously published works were only able to introduce and provides a comprehensive resource that focuses on the very specific needs of aviation neuropsychological assessment.

We are also only too aware that just like aviation neuropsychology, the book reflects an inequity in neuropsychological practice, resources, and standards globally. All four of us as editors, and most contributors, come from resource-rich countries and regions where support and infrastructure for neuropsychology generally, and aviation psychology specifically, are developed. We recognize that neuropsychological expertise is underdeveloped in some countries, and the application of the specialism to aviation may be nonexistent. This book hopefully sends a message of encouragement to aviation regulators, health-care professionals, and airline managers to give more attention to the insights and advantages of neuropsychology expertise in safety-critical work settings.

In addition to neuropsychological expertise, safety-critical work settings – as this handbook reflects – also depend on a range of operator and professionals' actions and work practices. Psychologists working in aviation have a track record in augmenting safety through their training and skills, and specifically in assisting with (a) selecting the most suitable employees (and screening out those where higher levels of risk may present); (b) improving awareness of human factors principles generally and of work-specific risks; (c) ensuring that physical and psychological work conditions are conducive to safe practice and operations; (d) being clear about acceptable and unacceptable errors and deviations from operating procedures; (e) inculcating a just and fair work culture where mistakes, errors, and slips can be addressed openly without fear of recrimination; (f) reducing or eliminating jeopardy associated with self-assessment with respect to fitness to operate; (g) ensuring employees have rapid access to peer support and more specialist technical, managerial, or professional support; (h) ensuring thorough review and remedy of practices postincident; and (i) having an effective input of the above into a responsive safety management system.

Recent tragic accidents have highlighted the vital role that neuropsychological assessment has in aviation safety. The murder–suicide crash of Germanwings Flight 9525 initiated a broadening of emphasis on pilot selection, ongoing assessment, and evaluation, whereby ability to fly an aircraft became insufficient reason to be deemed fit for duty. Consequently, new emphasis on mental health and neuropsychological functioning has become a vital focus of aviation regulatory authorities worldwide. However, to date, no single neuropsychological text has brought together the wealth of knowledge that has accumulated since and has been triggered by research and development in aviation neuropsychology, following the Germanwings tragedy.

For both the general psychologist and the specialist aviation neuropsychologist, applying neuropsychological principles to the unique world of commercial and military aviation is a challenge. Infections such as HIV and COVID-19, as well as medical and mental health conditions that may not be considered relevant in many ground-based occupations, take on a new significance in the air. The neuropsychological effects of pressurization are negligible for the flying public but become a more important consideration for the pilot; stress and burnout are more manageable in an office environment than in a cockpit, where multiple sources of information need to be assimilated, communicated, and actioned at the right time and in the right order to ensure the ongoing safety of the aircraft, its crew, and its passengers. Common mental health conditions such as depression have been shown to significantly impact upon an individual's ability to perform complex multitasking, while commonly used medications can also radically impact upon ability to function. Even the neuropsychological assessment process sometimes differs in aviation, where specific pilot-derived normative data compete with general population norms and specific "aviation-developed" neuropsychological assessments vie for attention, competing with established cognitive evaluations. Clinical diagnoses and "caseness" in general neuropsychology can have different meanings and implications for safety in aviation psychology.

Each chapter in this book offers unique insight into different areas of aviation neuropsychology, and we therefore suggest our audience take the time to read the whole book. As you can see from the table of contents, the book is divided into five parts. The first theme captures the development of aviation neuropsychology, touching on the history as well as the role of neuropsychology in personnel selection and psychiatry. The second category focuses on prevention and resilience, giving readers modern insight into the importance of strengthening airline workers' cognitive and mental functioning to reduce the risk of human errors and aircraft accidents. The third section looks at assessments across areas including pilot medical certification, neuropsychological testing, and cultural considerations in neuropsychological evaluations. This is followed by an investigative theme capturing the importance of learning from past errors but also taking stock of what the airline industry is doing well to capture and build on existing strengths. The final category offers excellent insight into the specialist aspects of aviation neuropsychology including common conditions, symptoms of COVID-19, and report writing in aviation. The five sections will allow neuropsychologists, aviation medical examiners, pilots, air traffic controllers, aviation military personnel, selection and recruitment departments, occupational health doctors, psychologists, human resources specialists, academic professionals, neurologists, human factor specialists, aviation managers, and other professionals to gain new insight as well as to build on their existing knowledge of aviation neuropsychology.

If you are unfamiliar with the historical development of neuropsychology, Georgemiller offers a thorough outline of significant benchmark events in the development of US civil aviation neuropsychology in Chapter 1. In Chapter 2, Vink gives an overview of the history of the techniques, methods, and practices of neuropsychology, whereas Newman focuses on the implication of neurological conditions for crew licensing and safety in Chapter 3. King and Caretta's description of neuropsychology's role in personnel selection in Chapter 4 is followed by Pavel and Green's outline of the principles and practices in military aeromedical neuropsychology in Chapter 5. Butt and Padua in Chapter 6 describe the role of psychiatry in aviation, with Van Dillen et al. introducing aerospace neuropsychological modeling of pilot resources in Chapter 7.

In Chapter 8, Sharma et al. offer a fresh perspective on how to develop positive mental health and well-being in aviation. This is followed by Ackland and Molesworth's insights into vulnerability and protective factors in pilot mental health and well-being in Chapter 9. Chapter 10 by Milanovich highlights the possibility of structured cognitive training in pilots to boost cognitive functioning, a model that could easily be used across safety-critical professions, while Snyder describes substance use disorders in Chapter 11.

Fercho's perspective on the role of cognitive screening for pilot medical certification in Chapter 12 gives readers an up-to-date understanding of the challenges presented in Class 1 pilot medical certification. In Chapter 13, Belser and Oubaid highlight the cognitive challenges of aviation, and in Chapter 14, Kane et al. take readers through the challenges of test results in neuropsychological aeromedical testing. Boudreau and Totten introduce us to a systematic review of neuropsychological tests in aviation in Chapter 15. Chafetz, in Chapter 16, takes this further and discusses the importance of a systemized interpretation for the pilot neuropsychological examination, whereas Irani et al. consider cultural and language factors in neuropsychological evaluations in Chapter 17. In Chapter 18, Vink calls for the definition of real-time computational human performance, while Chapter 19 by Basner et al. introduces the reader to the cognitive assessment of astronauts.

Bor et al. describe the process of air accident investigations focusing on both examining and learning from human errors and strength to enhance safety in Chapter 20. Wiggins describes piloting and cognitive functioning in the context of incidents in Chapter 21, which is followed by the data-driven approaches of Norris et al. for flight safety and pilot well-being in Chapter 22. In Chapter 23, Mackenzie Ross discusses the health and safety risks associated with toxic fumes in airplane cabins.

Drag, in Chapter 24, describes the common conditions in aviation and their neuropsychological implications, which is then taken further by Hesselbrock's insightful perspective on neurological conditions with aeromedical relevance in Chapter 25. Flynn, in Chapter 26, offers fresh knowledge on the initial and chronic neuropsychological symptoms of COVID-19, and Levine discusses neurocognitive functioning in HIV for aviators and air traffic controllers in Chapter 27. King and Da Silva, in Chapter 28, talk readers through ADHD in aviation neuropsychology offering a comprehensive understanding of ADHD and its implications for medical licensing. In Chapter 29, Gray presents a series of ADHD and ASD case studies to highlight the practical aspects of neuropsychological evaluations in aviation. Da Silva and King, in Chapter 30, offer unique insights into learning disability in aviation neuropsychology, which is followed by a description of the impact of age on cognitive performance in pilots and air traffic controllers in Chapter 31 by Causse et al. Finally, in Chapter 32 Gray gives readers a thorough understanding of neuropsychological report writing in aviation.

Every chapter was written for your benefit, but we recognize that not every professional reading this book is as experienced as others in the field. We therefore thought you may want to start with Chapter 25, Hesselbrock's great outline of neurological factors that may impact pilot performance and therefore flight safety. Newman, in Chapter 3, outlines a range of neurological conditions that may cause temporary or permanent loss of crew license. Those with a specific interest in recruitment and selection would benefit from reading Chapter 4, where King and Carretta share their wisdom on the role of neuropsychology in personnel selection.

Those readers who wish to further their knowledge in pilot selection may consult the book *Pilot Selection: Psychological Principles and Practice* edited by Bor, Eriksen, Hubbard, and King (Bor et al., 2020). We also suggest reading Chapter 24 by Drag and Chapter 8 by Sharma et al., which highlight the importance of identifying, assessing, and treating mental health issues to enhance pilot performance and flight safety. Readers who wish to gain more insight to aviation mental health should refer to the text *Pilot Mental Health and Support: A Practitioners Guide* edited by Bor, Eriksen, Oakes, and Scragg (Bor et al., 2017).

If you have an interest in any aspects of either aviation or neuropsychology, this book is for you, regardless of your occupation or background. We hope the knowledge will continue to grow via dialogue, research, and communication from specialists in the field and those who have a passion for or interest in the topic. We very much welcome readers' thoughts and comments, hoping this will prompt the growth of knowledge in this important and fascinating topic. Since this is the first handbook in aviation neuropsychology, we hope it can be used as a springboard for many more to come. With more research, communication, dialogue, and shared professional experiences, we can generate new knowledge, techniques, and robust instruments to improve crew and air traffic controllers' cognitive performance, resilience, and well-being. This will ultimately strengthen flight safety and reduce the risk of near or fatal aviation accidents.

The process of working with so many talented authors has been truly rewarding. Each chapter has taught us something new, given us a different perspective, and offered fresh insight into a specific area of aviation neuropsychology. The knowledge and the wisdom of each author are truly impressive, as illustrated throughout the respective chapters. They are the true creators of this book, and we are very grateful for their time, efforts, and willingness to share their expertise. Thank you to each one of you for taking the time to read the book. We are humbled by your interest and hope you enjoy the authors' contribution as much as we do.

References

Bor, R., Eriksen, C., Hubbard, T., & King, R. (2020). *Pilot selection: Psychological principles and practice*. CRC/Taylor Francis Press.

Bor, R., Eriksen, C., Oakes, M., & Scragg, P. (2017). *Pilot mental health assessment and support*. Routledge.

Kennedy, C., & Kay, G. (2013). *Aeromedical psychology*. Ashgate.

Section I

The History and Development of Aviation Psychology

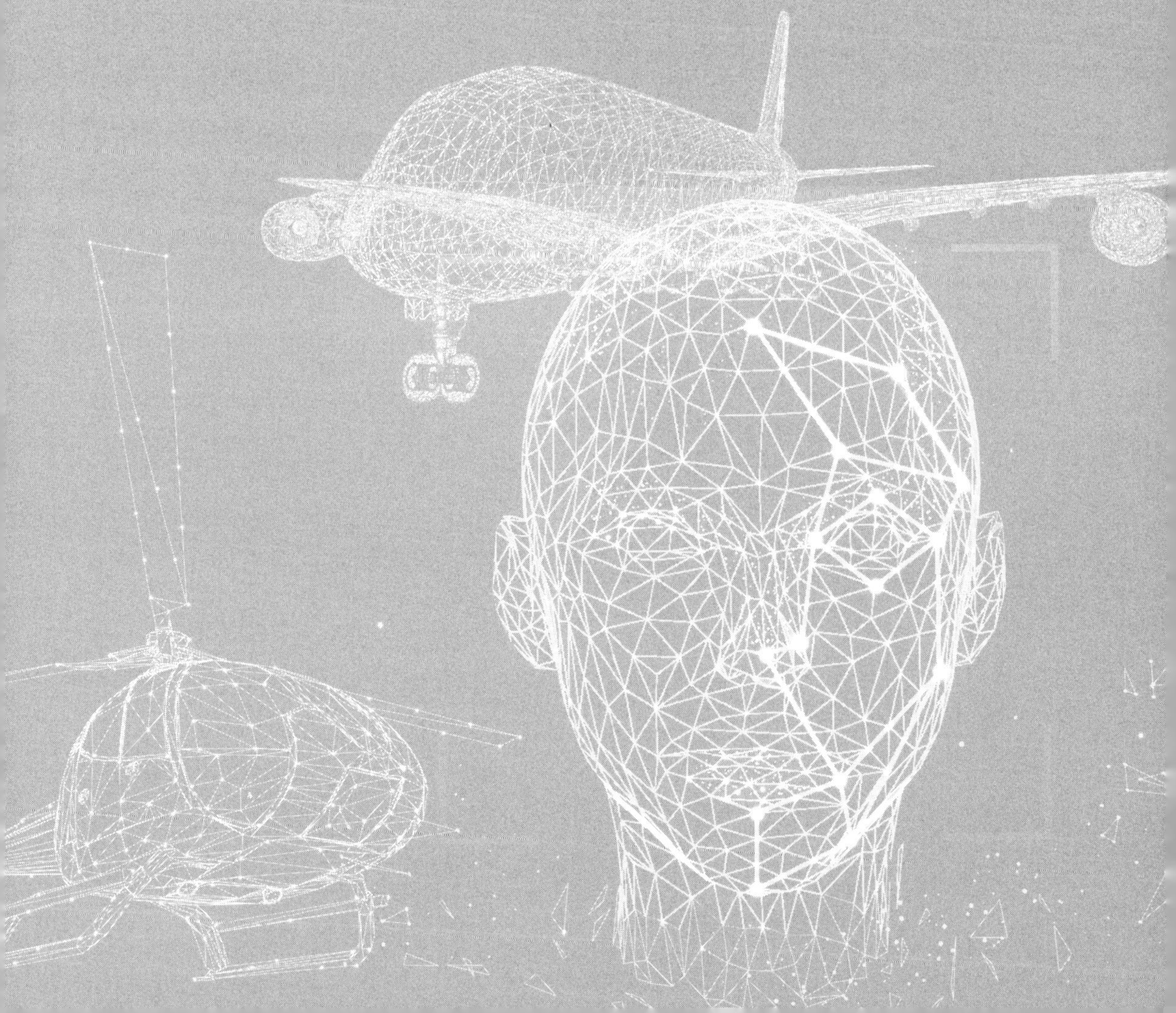

Chapter 1
Practicing Aviation Neuropsychology in a Civilian Regulatory Environment

Randy J. Georgemiller

Benchmark Events in the Development of US Civilian Aviation Neuropsychology

Federal regulation of the United States National Airspace System (NAS) began in the mid-1920s with the Air Commerce Act in 1926 (Kraus, 2008). With advances in aviation technology, increased air traffic, and a series of midair collisions, these factors led to the passage of the Federal Aviation Act (August 23, 1958), marking the beginning of the Federal Aviation Administration (FAA; Kraus, 2008). The simplicity and brevity of the FAA's mission mask the complexity of the endeavor: "Our continuing mission is to provide the safest, most efficient aerospace system in the world" (FAA, n.d.-b). On a daily basis the FAA oversees more than 45,000 flights and the transport of 2.9 million airline passengers spanning the 29 million miles of the US NAS (FAA, n.d.-a).

The contribution of aviation neuropsychology to the FAA safety mission began many years after the agency's inception. One of the earliest formal entries into the aviation regulatory environment was the inclusion of psychology in the Human Intervention Motivational Study (HIMS). HIMS (n.d.) began in 1974 and is a joint undertaking by the FAA, airlines, and airline pilot unions to address the issue of substance dependence and abuse among airline transportation pilots. Regarding substance dependence, previously a permanently disqualifying condition for medical certification leading to job termination, the HIMS program was designed to reduce the risk to flight safety posed by alcohol and drug dependence among pilots and return them to the cockpit by offering special issuance authorization/medical waivers based on identification, treatment, and monitoring. HIMS set the standard for other professional programs such as state medical board impaired professional programs. (For more information about HIMS, refer to Chapter 11 by Quay Snyder.) The process of evaluation and monitoring included psychologists who assessed psychological and cognitive factors in collaboration with psychiatrists. Psychology's unique contribution to HIMS was the ability to identify potential neurocognitive deficits by way of standardized neuropsychological measures associated with substance dependence and other coexisting conditions from the time of pilot identification, into treatment, and the monitoring phase as needed. For psychology's involvement in the program, the only requirements were to tag-team with a psychiatrist in performing the evaluations, be licensed, and complete an introductory HIMS training designed for select medical professionals, airline personnel, and airline union representatives.

Another turning point for neuropsychologists was when the FAA solicited a proposal from the American Medical Association (AMA) in 1977 "for an authoritative document concerning the current state of knowledge about selected neurological and neurosurgical conditions" (FAA Office of Aerospace Medicine, 1981, p. i). Expert panels that included representatives from the American Academy of Neurology (AAN) and American Association of Neurological Surgeons (AANS) provided a report that was designed to inform FAA "regulatory standards, examination procedures, and decisions about medical certification of airman applicants" (FAA, 1981, p. i). While outlining diagnostic and treatment requirements for various potentially disqualifying conditions to include cardiovascular disease, intracranial tumors, head injuries, demyelinating and degenerative diseases, extrapyramidal disorders, neuromuscular disorders, injuries to the peripheral and cranial nerves and spinal cord, seizure disorders and disturbances of consciousness, migraine and other headaches, and dizziness and disorders of equilibrium, throughout the document the need for "psychometrics, psychological testing, and neuropsychological examination" for specified conditions is highlighted. Linking these diagnostic procedures, there is reference to various cognitive abilities associated with neurological conditions that would jeopardize aviation safety to include intellectual skills, mental processing speed, memory, verbal skills, and executive abilities – cognitive domains that clinical neuropsychology is particularly well suited to assess. In the AMA document there is even an outline of a standardized neuropsychological protocol for the assessment of head injury in pilots (FAA Office of Aerospace Medicine, 1981, p. 56), which 40 years later still includes some procedures that are in use by the FAA to assist with making medical certification determinations.

Shortly afterward, the FAA again contracted with the AMA (AMA, 1984) to review medical standards for civilian aviation per Part 67 of the Federal Aviation Regulations (FAR; Code of Federal Regulations, 2023). The two-volume technical report is summarized and analyzed by Engelberg et al. (1986). As it pertains to neuropsychology, the AMA report offered a series of changes to the Aviation Medical Examination to include "Mini-mental status" (AMA, 1984, p. II-9). A brief four-item test was outlined, which included word repetition and recall, serial sevens, figure drawing from memory, and digit span. (AMA, 1984, p. III-16). If failed, the full Mini-Mental State Examination was to be administered (Folstein et al., 1975). Standards for medical certification for a variety of mental and behavioral disorders included psychiatric evaluation in conjunction with psychological testing. Neuropsychological evaluation protocols were discussed in detail as pertaining to the assessment of dementia.

The report went on to recommend adoption of the five-question Mini-Mental State Examination with further study as to its acceptance by aviation medical examiners (AMEs) as well as research into its utility in detecting cognitive impairment among pilots. This was followed by a recommendation for development of a computerized test of cognitive function to be administered and scored at the AME's office. The goal of such a measure "would be a screening test that would detect significant cognitive impairments that may otherwise go unrecognized during a routine physical examination" (AMA, 1984, p. V-2).

In response to the AMA study results, Banich et al. (1989) challenged the recommendation of adopting a mini-mental status examination (Folstein et al., 1975) as part of the AME flight physical. The authors indicated that the screening tests were designed to differentiate clinical from normal populations and make determinations regarding capacity for self-care, not the cognitive skills necessary to pilot an aircraft. They went on to review the literature based on job analysis to define the critical cognitive skills required for aviation: "perceptual-motor abilities; spatial abilities; working memory; attentional performance; processing flexibility; and planning or sequencing abilities (Banich et al., 1989, p. 362). Their recommendation was to incorporate extant neuropsychological tests into a cognitive screening device.

Associated with the issue of screening pilot cognitive status as part of medical certification, the FAA embarked on an 8-year study to develop a comprehensive, computer-administered and scored cognitive screening test designed to detect subtle potentially disqualifying cognitive deficits in aviators. This resulted in the development of CogScreen–Aeromedical Edition (CogScreen-AE; Kay, 1995, 2013). In the final phase of the project, 403 commercial airline pilots provided the basis for the initial normative database. A series of aviation-relevant cognitive skills are tapped by the test: "attention, immediate- and short-term memory, visual-perceptual functions, sequencing functions, logical problem solving, calculation skills, reaction time, simultaneous information processing abilities, and executive functions" (Kay, 1995, p. 1). The test has been applied to a civilian pilot population but also to military aviators (Chee et al., 2021; King et al., 2012) and has assisted with informing policy decisions, such as changing the Age 60 Rule that advanced the retirement age for air carrier captains and pilots to 65 (Georgemiller, 2013), as well as decisions related to a variety of medical conditions and medication treatments that may be associated with aeromedically significant cognitive impairment (see Chapter 22 by Norris et al. regarding research using CogScreen-AE to examine neuropsychological changes associated with use of selective serotonin reuptake inhibitors[SSRIs], multiple sclerosis, Parkinson's disease, and human immunodeficiency virus [HIV]). Relevant to current FAA practice, CogScreen-AE is an integral part of most of the psychological and neuropsychological specifications for assessing pilots for possible subtle cognitive incapacitation. (See Chapter 12 by Fercho for a discussion of cognitive screening in aviation neuropsychology.)

The Role of Civilian Aviation Neuropsychology in Medical Clearance and Certification Determination

To facilitate its mission, the FAA is structured around various organizations. Aviation Safety (AVS) is an organization within the FAA that in part is responsible for pilot certification (FAA, n.d.-c). Within Aviation Safety, the Office of Aerospace Medicine is responsible for a broad range of medical programs to include (FAA, n.d.-d):

- Aerospace medical education
- Aerospace medical and human factors research
- Aviation industry drug and alcohol testing
- Employee health awareness program
- FAA employee drug and alcohol testing
- Medical clearance of air traffic control specialist (ATCS) and other FAA employees required to meet medical standards to perform safety-sensitive duties
- Occupational health
- Pilot medical certification

In this regard, neuropsychology is one of the medical specialties assisting the Federal Air Surgeon in determining medical clearance of ATCSs and other FAA employees required to meet medical standards to perform safety-sensitive duties as well as pilot medical certification.

Currently, neuropsychology is responsible for assisting with the assessment of a range of potentially disqualifying conditions as outlined in the *Guide for Aviation Medical Examiners* (FAA, 2023a).

There are a series of six standardized examination protocols that neuropsychologists in the field are expected to comply with when an evaluation is requested by the FAA:

- Attention-deficit/hyperactivity disorder (ADHD)
- HIV
- SSRIs
- HIMS substance abuse and dependence
- Neuropsychological disorder
- Potential neurocognitive impairment

The American structure for aviation regulatory neuropsychological evaluations is different to civil aviation administrations in other countries, which do not have specified neuropsychological test batteries. This may reflect in part the American tradition of neuropsychological assessment with its emphasis on a laboratory-based, quantitative, test battery approach as opposed to a "qualitative syndrome-analysis scheme of clinical investigation" as found in other countries (Luria & Majovski, 1977, p. 959). Also, some countries do not rely as heavily on neuropsychological assessment, or in some cases not at all. For example, the Australian Civil Aviation Safety Authority allows for certification of aviators with a diagnosis of ADHD after rigorous record review and completion of a standardized reporting form by a treating physician and flight instructor, which inquires about ADHD-relevant behaviors that may be observed in and out of the cockpit. Neuropsychological evaluation is not required but is included in the review if it was conducted as part of the pilot's evaluation and ongoing treatment plan for ADHD (Australian Government Civil Aviation Safety Authority, n.d.).

The aforementioned neuropsychological test protocols grew out of the specific need for the thorough evaluation of potentially disqualifying medical conditions. In each case the testing protocol is reflective of the research in the field at the time of implementation. Before final approval by the Office of Aerospace Medicine Policy Branch, the test battery is reviewed and commented upon by a panel of neuropsychology consultants chosen by the FAA Office of Aerospace Medicine Director of Medical Specialties. Subject matter experts in the field may also be consulted. Besides being informed by the literature, criteria for including tests are that they are generally accepted by clinicians and available to community-based neuropsychologists who conduct the evaluations. Also, there must be an adequate representation of tests to be able to assist with making a medical certification determination without creating an evaluation process that is excessive in terms of time demands and costs to the pilot or ATCS undergoing examination (Knippa & Georgemiller, 2022). Appropriate population norms must be available, and when possible, there is a preference for including tests with pilot norms. Test batteries are updated based on developments in the field as well as internal FAA research conducted by the FAA Civil Aerospace Medical Institute (CAMI). (Please refer to Chapter 22 by Norris et al. for a discussion of FAA data-driven policy-making.)

Some other factors come into play as it pertains to FAA neuropsychological evaluation protocols. While there are doubtless differences across neuropsychological evaluators based on their training, experience, and practices, the standardization of test protocols allows for some semblance of uniformity and fairness. Regardless of where the testing is done, there is a basic understanding that any pilot or ATCS seen for evaluation will undergo similar testing. Standardization of test batteries and the supporting documentation that accompanies all evaluation reports also lend themselves to independent review by an FAA neuropsychologist, who may be asked to advise the Federal Air Surgeon in making a final medical certification determination. Lastly, sufficient data in support of the neuropsychological findings must be present in cases where a pilot seeks an appeal from the National Transportation Safety Board (National Transportation Safety Board, n.d.).

FAA neuropsychological evaluations are a high-stakes venture. The findings may prevent someone from pursuing their passion or even maintaining their livelihood. There is a natural tendency to want to maximize performance on these tests to increase the likelihood of securing a positive outcome, in this case medical certification. Also, part of the aviation ethos is to anticipate risk and develop a plan for mitigation, as found with concepts like aeronautical decision-making (ADM). “ADM is a systematic approach to the mental process used by aircraft pilots to consistently determine the best course of action in response to a given set of circumstances” (FAA, 1991, p. 4). The need for preparedness and anticipation of situations flies in the face of the need for examinees to be naïve to the tests used to grade performance when conducting a neuropsychological evaluation. Neuropsychological measures of cognitive performance were standardized and validated with participants who had no prior knowledge of or exposure to their content. This conflict heightens the need for test security in conducting FAA neuropsychological evaluations. “Test security refers to the broad and clear expectation that in order to maintain valid use and effectiveness, the contents and key operational characteristics of psychological and neuropsychological tests must be protected from inappropriate disclosure to non-psychologists” (American Academy of Clinical Neuropsychology [AACN], 2021). The 2021 position statement of the AACN outlines threats to test security as jeopardizing the effectiveness and validity of the tests and ultimately as possibly being detrimental to society. The statement even specifies the impact to public safety and cites FAA neuropsychological evaluations in support of this effort. One only needs to scan on-line discussion forums to see specific test item information being shared that potentially undermines test validity and reliability. In personal communications with community-based neuropsychologists, I have learned of multiple examples of threats to test security by pilots having advanced knowledge of test material.

Consistent with the AACN (2021) statement and other professional organizations such as the American Psychological Association (APA, 2017), American Educational Research Association (2014), and International Test Commission (2014), the FAA has instituted several practices in recognition of the importance of test security in support of NAS safety.

1. References to specific neuropsychological and psychological tests have been deleted in publications of the *Guide for Aviation Medical Examiners* (FAA, 2023a) since 2019. The guide is publicly accessible on the Internet and details all of the medical protocols and conditions assessed during flight physicals conducted by AMEs. Since 2019, whenever neuropsychological or psychological testing is referred to in the guide, the reader is given an email link where they may make inquiries about testing. Emails are monitored by an FAA neuropsychologist and responded to with the intention of assisting with the completion of the evaluation process while maintaining test security.
2. A secure website houses the FAA neuropsychological test protocols (FAA, n.d.-e) and only authorized personnel are granted access. The site is overseen by an FAA neuropsychologist.

3. FAA personnel have presented on the topic of test security to constituent groups to heighten awareness of the threat posed by inappropriate disclosure of test material in an attempt to decrease coaching.
4. Neuropsychologists conducting ATCS and pilot evaluations requested by the FAA are discouraged from providing advance knowledge about test names or materials to examinees and to delete the names of tests in the narrative reports provided to test-takers.
5. All FAA sponsored educational presentations restrict disclosure or dissemination of specific information about neuropsychological and psychological instruments used in the assessment of ATCSs and pilots as part of FAA medical clearance and certification.
6. The FAA has identified and recommended alternate tests that community-based neuropsychologists may employ when specific tests within the protocols have been compromised by advanced exposure to test stimuli. Guidelines for identifying potential threats to test security have also been disseminated by the FAA (FAA, n.d.-e).
7. Despite the increased prevalence and acceptance of remote test administration reliant on live videoconferencing, especially with health precautions put in place during the COVID-19 pandemic (APA, n.d.-a; Inter Organizational Practice Committee, 2020), the FAA allows only face-to-face fully proctored test administration (Giovanetti, 2020). There have been advances in improving the validity and reliability of remote testing, but the increased threats with surreptitious methods employed by highly motivated examinees limit this option within a regulatory environment.

Future Directions and Opportunities for Civilian Aviation Neuropsychology

While still rudimentary and not reflective of a certification, the more formalized current FAA eligibility requirements for neuropsychologists to participate in the HIMS evaluation process were initiated in 2019 (P. Giovanetti, personal communication, January 12, 2018):

1. State licensure as a psychologist
2. Board certification in clinical neuropsychology or documentation from a board that eligibility criteria have been fulfilled for board certification in clinical neuropsychology
3. Attendance at a HIMS basic seminar
4. Licensing for CogScreen-AE and training in the interpretation of this test

Based on these criteria, the FAA Office of Aerospace Medicine at the last count has 113 neuropsychologists around the country and internationally to conduct evaluations (Georgemiller, 2022). They are dispersed around the country with typical clustering around major metropolitan centers. All major airline hubs are covered and there is an effort to recruit interested neuropsychologists in areas that are underserved, that is, parts of the United States that have a concentration of pilots who are remote from a HIMS neuropsychologist. Geographic diversity and availability are the goal, and outreach to current HIMS neuropsychologists to co-locate offices to meet the need has also been pursued. There are also 58 HIMS psychologists available to provide evaluations. These professionals meet all of the aforementioned HIMS eligibility criteria except for neuropsychology board certification or eligibility for neuropsychology board certification. HIMS psychologists provide many of the evaluations that may include cognitive screening and initial assessment but not in-depth neuropsychological examination of underlying brain-related disorders. Ultimately, all of the psychologists and neuropsychologists are expected to provide services within the scope of their license and within the limits of their training and experience. The number of neuropsychologists and psychologists seeking addition to the eligibility list and completing the requirements has steadily grown over the years since the initiation of the updated eligibility criteria in 2019.

As such, clinical neuropsychology has been recognized as a specialty since 1996 by the APA Commission for the Recognition of Specialties and Subspecialties in Professional Psychology (CRSSPP; APA, n.d.-b):

> A specialty is a defined area of professional psychology practice characterized by a distinctive configuration of competent services for specified problems and populations. Practice in a specialty requires advanced knowledge and skills acquired through an organized sequence of formal education, training, and experience in addition to the broad and general education and core scientific and professional foundations acquired through an APA or CPA accredited doctoral program. (p. 2)

What is lacking is recognition of aviation neuropsychology as a subspecialty – "a concentrated area of knowledge, skills, and attitudes that exists within at least one recognized specialty" (APA, n.d.-b). To advance the field of aviation neuropsychology's integrity and secure its ongoing role in the ever-evolving field of aviation, resources and efforts will need to be expended to accomplish this goal.

While FAA neuropsychology is not engaged in a formal process to achieve subspecialty status for aviation neuropsychology as practiced in the civilian arena, it has invested significant resources to support the "knowledge, skills, and attitudes" that are unique to this subspecialty. The FAA Office of Aerospace Medicine has been an ongoing participant in the Aerospace Psychology Seminar (APS), now in its 10th year, and has been its sole sponsor since 2021 (FAA, 2023b). The seminar was originally designed to supplement the training of neuropsychologists who attended the annual HIMS basic seminar. Under the leadership of a group of FAA neuropsychology consultants and FAA staff psychologist (Dr. Chris Front) with corporate sponsorship from Dr. Gary Kay and CogScreen, the seminar has represented the sole recurring venue for training community-based psychologists and neuropsychologists to conduct pilot and ATCS examinations required by the FAA. Some stand-alone introductory education has been initiated in professional settings (Elliott, 2023; Georgemiller, 2021, 2022; King et al., 2021), but APS is the only ongoing multiday educational event of its kind in the United States. In its current format the APS was designed to orient and educate psychology and neuropsychology providers regarding FAA policies and procedures pertaining to the conduct of pilot and ATCS examinations; to provide a venue for conferring about relevant clinical matters; to disseminate research pertinent to aerospace psychology and neuropsychology; and to conduct required training on the administration, scoring, and interpretation of the FAA-mandated cognitive screening test, CogScreen-AE. Additionally, eligibility training for psychologists to conduct FAA-required ATCS psychological evaluations takes place during the seminar.

Of the attendees at the 2022 APS, approximately one half of the psychologists and neuropsychologists reported that it was the first seminar they had attended. Given the unique characteristics and demands of practicing clinical neuropsychology and psychology in this specialized realm and the influx of newer less experienced professionals familiar with this subspecialty, the FAA adopted the "Aerospace Neuropsychology and Psychology Mentorship Program" (FAA, 2023c). Mentoring has been recognized as an effective tool for career development (APA, 2012). Spearheaded by a workgroup chaired by Drs. Lauren Drag, Richard Berg, Ciaran Considine, Laurence Levine, and Allison Waterworth, the FAA-sponsored program is designed to provide mentorship to neuropsychologists and psychologists early in their experience of conducting aviation neuropsychological and psychological evaluations. Based on participation in voluntary individual and group training sessions held virtually and in-person, the goal of the program is to orient and assist newer members of this professional community with the goal of fostering the FAA mission of promoting the safety of the NAS. Potential topics for training as outlined by the work group are: important components of the neuropsychological/psychological report, the evaluation process from start to finish, coordinating with FAA evaluators from other specialties, building referrals, sample case reviews, review of the individual test protocols, addressing the needs of challenging cases and/or pilots, second opinions, alternatives to required tests, and the mechanics of processing a case for submission to the FAA.

If aviation neuropsychological examinations wish to continue to make a valuable contribution to ensuring the safety of the NAS, evaluation methods and the expertise and background of the neuropsychologists engaged in this practice will need to adapt in general to changing population demographics and in particular to shifts in the aviation community. The AACN (2022) sounded the alarm in its "Relevance 2050 Initiative" in which it challenged the field to address demographic racial, ethnic, and language diversity in its assessment strategies or face possible irrelevance. In Kay's (2013) discussion of aviation neuropsychology, he described the impact of the changing cohort of commercial airline pilots from ex-military aviators to civilian trained pilots on the application of existing aviation neuropsychological test norms. A field that was almost exclusively the domain of White males is now emerging as increasingly accessible to women and ethnic and racial minorities. There is an incremental but steady increase in the number of pilot certificates held by women in the United States, but still only less than 5% of air transport pilots are women (Lutte, 2021). The prospect of continued expansion of female pilots in the field is found in the statistic that female student pilot certificate holders account for more than 14% of the total certificates. There is an overall increase in both women and minority admissions to aviation college programs. When reviewing statistics for the period 1996–2007, Ison (2009) found a statistically significant rise in the student population for women, Blacks, Hispanics, Asians, and American Indians. In the development of future aviator norms for neurocognitive performance, these changing demographics will need to be addressed for aviation neuropsychology to retain its relevance. In an informal survey of members of the FAA Aerospace Neuropsychology KSN site and attendees at the 2021 APS, Drag et al. (2021) found that respondents were somewhat dissimilar to the general characteristics of US psychologists and neuropsychologists by being more represented by males (51.8% vs. 39.4%). Otherwise, racial representation appeared reflective of the field. Overall, 37% reportedly speak, read, or write another language, spanning a total of 14 languages. In response to a series of questions pertaining to comfort and training in dealing with cultural, linguistic, and diversity issues, respondents provided a range of answers indicating the need for additional training and experience around these issues and the need for consultation and flexible examination strategies to adapt to these factors when applicable.

The graying of aviation poses challenges and opportunities to the field of aviation neuropsychology. The average age of general aviation pilots has been increasing over the years, with a figure of 60,763 at the age of 70 and above as of the end of 2022 (FAA, 2022). Age restriction for airline pilots was raised from 60 to 65 in 2007 with the passage of the Fair Treatment for Experienced Pilots Act (2007). Aviation neuropsychology weighed in on this regulatory, political, and scientific debate as society grappled with the perceived safety concerns (Georgemiller, 2013). Aviation neuropsychology will again need to be there in an attempt to inform legislation and policy as the United States confronts the current airline pilot shortage and a proposed solution to the problem by increasing the retirement age of commercial pilots to age 67 (Skores, 2023).

Conclusion

As a nascent specialized field within neuropsychology, aviation neuropsychology has developed a solid foundation within the civilian regulatory realm and is fueled by senior professionals and a cadre of next-generation neuropsychologists looking to expand and enrich the field and by governmental agency support, all in the service of maintaining a safe NAS. Unlimited ceiling and visibility conditions prevail for the future of aviation neuropsychology.

References

American Academy of Clinical Neuropsychology. (2021). Official position of the American Academy of Clinical Neuropsychology (AACN): Disclosure of neuropsychological test data. *The Clinical Neuropsychologist, 35*(4), 709–729. https://doi.org/10.1080/13854046.2021.2022214

American Academy of Clinical Neuropsychology. (2022). *Relevance 2050*. https://theaacn.org/relevance-2050/

American Educational Research Association, American Psychological Association, & National Council on Measurement in Education. (2014). *Standards for educational and psychological testing*. American Educational Research Association. https://www.apa.org/science/programs/testing/standards

American Medical Association. (1984). *Review of Part 67 of the Federal Aviation Regulation and the medical certification of airmen*. (Vols. 1 and 2, DTFA01-83-C-20066). FAA Headquarters. https://apps.dtic.mil/sti/citations/ADA166465

American Psychological Association. (n.d.-a). *How to do psychological testing via telehealth*. APA Services. https://www.apaservices.org/practice/reimbursement/health-codes/testing/prsychological-telehealth

American Psychological Association. (n.d.-b). *Specialties, subspecialties, and proficiencies*. https://www.apa.org/ed/graduate/specialize

American Psychological Association. (2012, January 1). *Introduction to mentoring: A guide for mentors and mentees*. https://apa.org/education-career/grad/mentoring

American Psychological Association. (2017). *Ethical principles of psychologists and code of conduct*. https://www.apa.org/ethics/code/

Australian Government Civil Aviation Safety Authority. (n.d.). *Attention deficit hyperactivity disorder (ADHD). Designated aviation medical examiner's clinical practice guidelines*. https://www.casa.gov.au/licences-and-certificates/medical-professionals/dames-clinical-practice-guidelines/attention-deficit-hyperactivity-disorder-adhd

Banich, M., Stokes, A., & Elledege, V. (1989). Neuropsychological screening of aviators: A review. *Aviation, Space, & Environmental Medicine, 60*(4), 361–366.

Chee, S., Bigornia, V., & Logson, D. (2021). The application of a computerized cognitive screening tool to naval aviators. *Military Medicine, 186*, 198–204. https://doi.org/10.1093/milmed/usaa333

Code of Federal Regulations. (2023). *Title 14 (aeronautical and space), Chapter 1 (Federal Aviation Administration, Department of Transportation), Subchapter D (airmen), Part 67 (medical standards and certification)*. https://www.ecfr.gov/cgi-bin/text-idx?tpl=/ecfrbrowse/Title14/14cfr67_main_02.tpl

Drag, L., Irani, F., Mi-Yeoung, J., & Silva, D. (2021, October 8–10). *Cultural diversity considerations in neuropsychological evaluations with aviators* [Seminar session]. Ninth Annual Aerospace Psychology Seminar [Virtual].

Elliott, R. (2023, October 26). *Aviation neuropsychology: Where regulation meets clinical practice* [Conference session]. National Academy of Neuropsychology Annual Conference, Philadelphia, PA, USA.

Engelberg, A., Gibbons, H., & Doege, T. (1986). A review of the medical standards for civilian airmen. *JAMA, 12*(12), 1589–1599. https://doi.org/10.1001/jama.1986.03370120067025

Fair Treatment for Experienced Pilots Act, H.R. 4343, 110 Cong. (2007). https://www.govtrack.us/congress/bills/110/hr4343

Federal Aviation Administration. (n.d.-a). *Air traffic by the numbers.* https://www.faa.gov/air_traffic/by_the_numbers

Federal Aviation Administration. (n.d.-b). *Mission.* https://www.faa.gov/about/mission

Federal Aviation Administration. (n.d.-c). *Aviation safety (AVS).* https://www.faa.gov/about/office_org/headquarters_offices/avs

Federal Aviation Administration. (n.d.-d). Office of aerospace medicine. https://www.faa.gov/about/office_org/headquarters_offices/avs/offices/aam

Federal Aviation Administration. (n.d.-e). *Aerospace neuropsychology.* https://avssp.faa.gov/avs/aam/HQ/AAM200/AAM220/NP/SitePages/Neuropsychology.aspx

Federal Aviation Administration. (1991). *Aeronautical decision making* (Advisory Circular No. 60–22). https://www.faa.gov/regulations_policies/advisory_circulars/index.cfm/go/document.information/documentid/22624

Federal Aviation Administration. (2022). *US civil airmen statistics.* https://www.faa.gov/data_research/aviation_data_statistics/civil_airmen_statistics

Federal Aviation Administration. (2023a). *Guide for aviation medical examiners.* http://www.faa.gov/about/office_org/headquarters_offices/avs/offices/aam/ame/guide/

Federal Aviation Administration. (2023b). *Tenth annual aerospace psychology seminar.* https://na.eventscloud.com/ehome/index.php?eventid=752680&

Federal Aviation Administration. (2023c). *Aerospace neuropsychology and psychology mentorship program.* https://avssp.faa.gov/avs/aam/HQ/AAM200/AAM220/NP/Resource%20Library/Mentorship%20Program/mentorship%20program%20final%2025%20jul%202023.pdf

Federal Aviation Administration Office of Aerospace Medicine. (1981). *Neurological and neurosurgical conditions associated with aviation safety* (Report No. DOT/FAA/AM-81/3). https://www.faa.gov/data_research/research/med_humanfacs/oamtechreports/1980s/1981/198103

Folstein, M., Folstein, S., & McHugh, P. (1975). Mini Mental State: A practical method for grading the cognitive state of patients for the clinician. *Journal of Psychiatric Research, 12*, 189–198. https://doi.org/10.1016/0022-3956(75)90026-6

Georgemiller, R. (2013). The aging aviator. In C. Kennedy & G. Kay (Eds.), *Aeromedical psychology* (pp. 269–286). Ashgate Publishing.

Georgemiller, R. (Guest). (2021, August). *Aerospace neuropsychology. Navigating neuropsychology* [Audio podcast]. The International Neuropsychological Society. https://www.navneuro.com/76/[Virtual]

Georgemiller, R. (2022). *Neuropsychology and medical certification considerat*ions. Ninth Annual Aerospace Psychology Seminar [Seminar session]. Federal Aviation Administration in conjunction with the American College of Professional Neuropsychology, Washington, DC, USA.

Georgemiller, R. (2022, November). *Introduction to civilian aviation neuropsychology.* US Army Aeromedical Psychology Training Course, School of Army Aviation Medicine, Ft. Rucker, AL.

Giovanetti, P. (2020). *Guidance for the conduct of neuropsychological evaluations during the COVID-19 pandemic.* Federal Aviation Administration. https://avssp.faa.gov/avs/aam/HQ/AAM200/AAM220/NP/SitePages/Neuropsychology.aspx

Human Intervention Motivational Study (HIMS). (n.d.). *Program development.* https://himsprogram.com/

International Test Commission. (2014). *International guidelines on the security of tests, examinations, and other assessments.* https://www.intestcom.org

Inter Organizational Practice Committee. (2020, May). *Inter Organizational Practice Committee recommendations/guidance for teleneuropsychology (TeleNP) in response to the COVID-19 pandemic.* https://iopc.online/teleneuropsychology-guidelines

Ison, D. (2009). Have we made progress? Trends in minority participation in postsecondary aviation education. *Collegiate Aviation Review, 27*(1), 53–64. https://commons.erau.edu/ww-graduate-studies/5

Kay, G. (1995). *CogScreen-Aeromedical Edition professional manual.* Psychological Assessment Resources.

Kay, G. (2013). Aviation neuropsychology. In C. Kennedy & G. Kay (Eds.), *Aeromedical psychology* (pp. 239–268). Ashgate Publishing.

King, J., Georgemiller, R., & Kay, G. (2021, June 9–12). *Introduction to aviation neuropsychology* [Conference session]. 19th Annual American Academy of Clinical Neuropsychology Conference. [Virtual].

King, R., Retzlaff, P., Barto, E., Ree, M., Teachout, M., & Caretta, T. (2012). *Pilot cognitive functioning and training outcomes* (AFRL-SA-WP-TR-2012-0004). Wright-Patterson AFB. https://doi.org/10.21236/ADA566316

Knippa, J., & Georgemiller, R. (2022, October). *Introduction to the FAA protocols: Strengths, weaknesses & considerations* [Seminar session]. Ninth Annual Aerospace Psychology Seminar.

Kraus, T. (2008). *The Federal Aviation: A historical perspective, 1903–2008.* US Department of Transportation, Federal Aviation Administration.

Luria, A., & Majovski, L. (1977). Basic approaches used in American and Soviet clinical neuropsychology. *The American Psychologist, 32*(11), 959–968. https://doi.org/10.1037//0003-066x.32.11.959

Lutte, R. (2021). *Women in aviation: A workforce report.* Aviation Institute, University of Nebraska at Omaha.

National Transportation Safety Board. (n.d.). *Airman appeal process.* https://www.ntsb.gov/legal/alj/Pages/process.aspx

Skores, A. (2023, June). Upping the retirement age for pilots to 67 is facing fierce opposition – from pilots. *Dallas Morning News.* https://www.dallasnews.com/business/airlines/2023/06/19/upping-the-retirement-age-for-pilots-to-67-is-facing-fierce-opposition-from-pilots/

Chapter 2
A History of the Techniques, Methodologies, and Practices of Neuropsychology for Operational Support in Airline Operations and Air Traffic Management

Lea Sophie Vink

Introduction

Don't Let Me Interrupt, but on a Scale of 1 to 5, How Busy Are You?

Many aviators and operators are taught a crucial acronym: *ANCA* (or variations of it), which stands for *aviate (operate), navigate, communicate,* and *administrate*. The acronym is taught for times where there is heightened activity or crisis in the cockpit or operational environment. It is extremely useful because in times like this, pilots will fall back on their training and experience and rely upon these key skills to successfully solve an issue (Katerinakis, 2014). This was one of the contributing factors to the Boeing 737 Max accidents in Nigeria and Indonesia. The pilots in both cases acted according to their learned patterns of operating due to high levels of stress, but this conflicted with what the autopilots were programmed to do, which led to confusion and ultimately to the pilots working against the aircraft to resolve a situation (Appicharla, 2023; Spielman & Le Blanc, 2021). ANCA helps pilots to strip it back to the essentials. Fundamentally, when all the systems fail, or workload is too high, they still know how to fly (operate) an aircraft. The next step is always to be able to locate themselves geographically to understand what options they might have. Once they have the mental resources to continue, they should communicate their plans and intentions and then, finally, administrate by recording as much as they can about the issues.

This acronym usefully contains much of the scientific wisdom of neuropsychology, work and organizational psychology, teamwork, leadership, and human factors within one key phrase. This is because at the root of it lies the understanding of the limitations of human neural processing and capabilities. When stress sets in due to heightened workload, pilots know that their ability to concentrate and solve problems will decrease the longer the stressor continues (Tsang & Vidulich, 2002). The other key thing about this acronym is that is distils what is most likely to happen when things do go wrong. This is to say that despite over 50 years of developments in psychology and human factors and their contributions to aviation, when things get busy the operators will sometimes make decisions that in hindsight might seem “unsupported by evidence” or “psychologically unsound.” In a nutshell, the acronym might best be described as the “current” contribution to operational support from the field of neuropsychology. This is because although we can use the tools with great precision to recruit, select, train, provide trauma and clinical support, and analyze post-operations from the confines of the laboratory or the office, ultimately the need to operate and navigate has meant that invasive and distracting neuropsychological tools had to take a backseat.

Understanding the current limitations of neuropsychology, particularly when it comes to deploying and integrating tools and techniques into the operating environment, reveals why even today – with the rapid roll-out of artificial intelligence and automation – powerful techniques are not more widely deployed and why operators still need to fall back on things like ANCA to support them. But this is not to say that neuropsychological advances have not already transformed the general *concepts of operation*, whether that be through legislative and regulatory frameworks, crew resource management techniques and training, biomedical feedback and fatigue management, or improvements in investigation procedures. This chapter outlines these contributions and bring us up to date on the key evidentiary findings and techniques deployed or primed to be deployed in the years ahead in the key areas that concern us in the operational environment. This chapter focuses on two main areas: (a) the contribution to legislation and regulations including the infrastructure that humans operate in and (b) a survey of the day-to-day critical human factors of operating.

First, we consider the contributions of neuropsychology within the legislative approach. This is most recently driven by one of the cornerstones of European legislation in aviation: EU 2017/373 (European Union Aviation Safety Agency [EASA], 2017). Within this legislation are three key “human factors” that need to be managed in the aviation context: *fatigue risk management*, *stress reduction and management*, and *psychoactive substance abuse*. The legislation argues that these elements are the most important for minimizing human error and maximizing performance and should be governed by the European States within their aviation safety legalization (EASA, 2017).

The EU’s position is supported by the International Civil Aviation Organization (ICAO) in their 2021 manual on human performance for regulators (ICAO, 2021). But ICAO goes further and recommends that the day-to-day human factors that contribute most when operating an aircraft or managing air traffic are attention, concentration and monotony aversion, decision-making, and human error analysis and investigation (ICAO, 2021). When ANCA needs to be deployed by a pilot, these are the elements that will come into play.

We should note the sizable contribution of neuropsychology to the field of cognitive ergonomics and the design of aviation infrastructure (cockpits, radar screens, towers etc.). Much of this is covered in International Organization for Standardization (ISO) Document 9241 and other associated design style guides and resources. Most modern legislation requires that aviation organizations provide safety assurance for their infrastructure, and this increasingly requires human factors assurances (e.g., EASA, 2017), but as this is not operationally time critical, it will not be discussed in this chapter.

This chapter is primarily a historical survey of the literature, techniques, and methodologies and what they have provided for the modern operation to bring us up to date on usage for direct operational support. What neuropsychology has not done yet for the most part is to break into the actual cockpits or air traffic control towers and operations rooms and start running minute-by-minute support for the operators. The chapter explores why this is and offers hope that just around the corner there may soon be an enhanced integration and deployment of tools such as complex algorithms for assessing real-time workload and fatigue risk (Vink & Walzl, 2024) or predicting human error before it happens (Vink, 2022).

Neuropsychological Contributions to Legislation Covering Operations

At first glance, within the realm of aviation regulations and requirements for aviation operations, the integration of neuropsychological contributions may not be readily apparent. However, beneath the surface of the regulatory landscape lies a rich tapestry of the history of neuropsychology insights and findings that have made their way into safety and human performance standards. This section delves into the intriguing intersection of neuropsychology and aviation regulations. By examining the role of neuropsychological assessments, considerations of cognitive performance, and psychological factors, the vital role that neuropsychology plays in the development and implementation of regulations that safeguard the aviation industry is illuminated.

Aviation legislation is governed globally by the ICAO. This is a specialized agency of the United Nations (UN) and allows non-UN member states to become members of the organization. Because of the importance of global standards on aviation management, ICAO membership is almost universal despite many countries not being members of the UN (ICAO, 2023). Most national legislation begins by referencing or at least adopting ICAO recommended guidelines. The prevailing document concerning the performance of human operators within aviation is the recently issued ICAO Document 10151, the *Manual on Human Performance for Regulators* first published in 2021 (ICAO, 2021). This document brought together and replaced several previous documents related to human factors, and this was a distinctive shift away from the "factors" and more toward the idea that human cognitive success is dependent on a sociotechnical system in which the person can perform with support from tools and procedures (Vink & Walzl, 2024). This is important to note because these documents are the blueprint for most individual state legislations globally. Their history also shows the history of the evolution of neuropsychological contributions to managing human performance.

According to Document 10151, the chief aim is to highlight the importance of integrating human performance and all associated human factors into national regulations. The goal is to "make it easy for people in the aviation system to do the right thing and avoid negative safety consequences" (ICAO, 2021, p. v, paragraph 1 in the foreword). A survey of neuropsychological contributions to regulations must begin by understanding the primary purposes of this kind of legislation:

1. Rules exist to maximize safety enhancement.
2. Best practices help to optimize performance.
3. Recommend the best practices to manage key well-being factors like fatigue and stress.
4. Assist in developing the most optimal human–machine interfaces to support Items 1–3.
5. Allow for the oversight of these areas to ensure compliance.
6. Enable continuous improvements as and when new findings and recommendations are provided.

ICAO Document 10151 provides the blueprint for all nations to provide their detailed regulations. Some of the largest and most comprehensive sets of regulations cover the most complex operations on earth. For example, FAA Order 9550.8 covers the United States Human Factors Policy (Federal Aviation Authority [FAA], 1993). In the European Union, the primary laws can be seen across many bits of legislation but are compiled by the EASA into the "Easy Access Rules for Air Operations" (EASA, 2012) and "Easy Access Rules for Air Traffic Management" (EASA, 2017). In the United Kingdom, the Civil Aviation Authority (CAA) has issued several civil aviation publications (CAP) covering human factors and human performance including the 2002 "Fundamental Human Factors Concepts" (CAP 719; CAA, 2002), the 2016 "Air Traffic Management Automation: Guidance on Human Technology Integration" (CAP 1377; CAA, 2016), and the latest "Guidance Material for the Psychological Assessment of Pilots" (CAP 1938; CAA, 2020). The Canadian government has issued the "Canadian Aviation Regulations SOR/96-433," which extensively covers human factors (Transport Canada, 2021). Australia similarly with Advisory Circular 119-12 V1.0 presents the Australian CAA "Human Factors Principles and Non-technical Skills Training and Assessment for Air Transport Operations" (Civil Aviation Safety Authority, 2020).

The previous paragraph represents a brief collection of some of the major pieces of national legislation that covers human operators. Because much of this legislation is so comprehensive, it is often difficult to know where to begin in terms of identifying the key contributions. To make it easier to understand what contributions exist, an artificial intelligence (AI)-assisted word analysis was conducted of global legislation. All of the aforementioned legislation was included, plus a number of additional legislation taken from across Europe, Asia/Pacific, and North America. Legislation was analyzed prior to 2010 and after 2010 to understand how human factors requirements have evolved. Tables 2.1 and 2.2 show the predominant recommended scope of human factors legislation in aviation prior to 2010 (Table 2.1) and after 2010 (Table 2.2).

Table 2.1. Consolidated human factors/psychological requirements globally before 2010

Primary legislation features	Detail or specific requirements
1. Human factors importance	Taught to pilots Introduced to air traffic controllers
2. Pilot crew resource management	Communication Teamwork Decision-making
3. Fatigue risk management	Pilot rest hours Air traffic controller shifts
4. Human error reduction	Accident and occurrence investigations
5. Safety management systems	Human element and safety culture

Table 2.2. Consolidated human factors/psychological requirements globally after 2010

Primary legislation	Details	Subdetails
Human performance management	Measurement	
	Monitoring	
	Performance	Human error reduction
		Situational awareness
		Workload management
	Improvements and maturity	
Safety management systems	Safety culture	
	Just culture	
	Sociotechnical systems view	
Resource management	Team resource management for air traffic management	
	Crew resource management in all air crew	Pilot regular training and simulator exercises
		Cabin crew
		Ground staff
	Team resource management in ground crew and technical services	
Fatigue risk management	Regulated for all air crew	
	Pilot-focused long-haul solutions	Duty time limitations
		Rest requirements
	Focused monitoring	
	Improvement system	
	Air traffic controller Rostering enhancements	Duty time limitations
		Rest requirements
	Importance for maintenance and technical staff	
Cognitive ergonomics and human–machine interface designs	Usability	
	Acceptability	
	Training and practice	
	Common style guides	
	Automation attentiveness	
Well-being and occupational health	Stress management	Critical incident stress response
		Mental health screening
	Psychoactive substances	

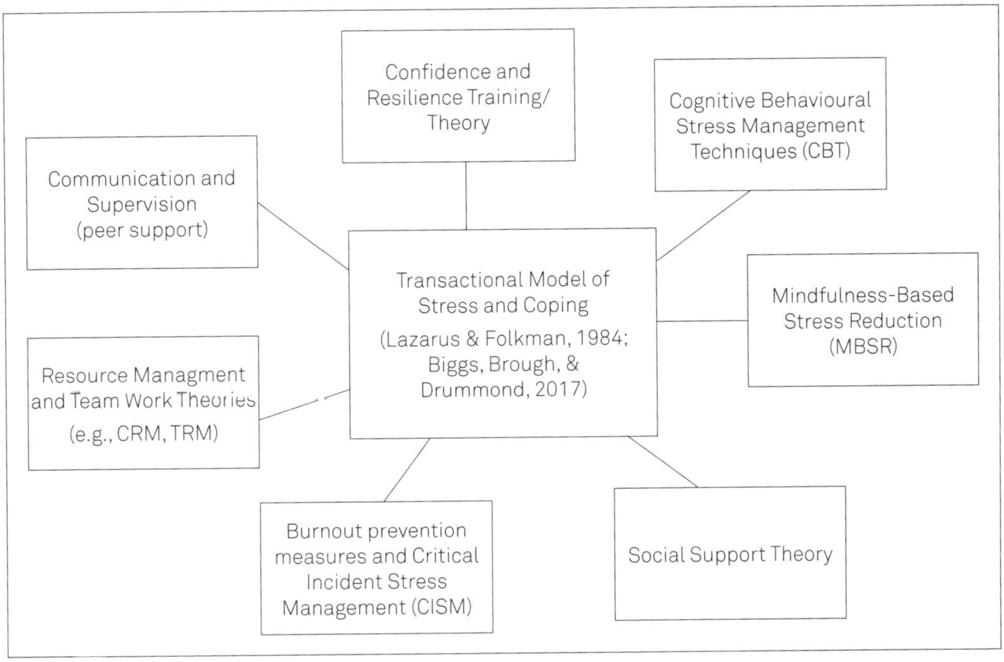

Figure 2.1. Most cited systems and solutions for stress management in aviation.

Table 2.1 and Table 2.2 show a dramatic evolution in the contribution of neuropsychological contributions via human factors and human performance regulations. Prior to 2010, the topics discussed and recommended included only basic human factors importance, crew resource management focused mainly on pilots, fatigue risk management focused again mainly on pilot crew rest, and human error reduction but conducted primarily through occurrence investigations and safety management systems that had a human element. These topics were mainly developed out of a surge in interest in human factors through the late 1980s and 1990s, which demonstrated the importance of the topics. As can be seen in Figure 2.1, the subelements of these regulations focused on mainly social psychological concepts such as teamwork, communication, and training. The neuropsychological elements were mainly aimed at fatigue management and decision-making. Some forms of safety management and human error analysis were also developed.

In the late 1990s and early 2000s several major air accidents resulted in the crucial incorporation of neuropsychological tools to human factors. Specifically, American Airlines Flight 587 (2001), the Milan Linate Airport disaster (2001), the Überlingen disaster (2002), and Air France Flight 447 (2009) each contributed major advances in human factors understanding. American Airlines Flight 587 resulted in developments in pilot training and crew resource management as well as a refocus on hands-on flying techniques (Fraher, 2015). In Milan, the Linate disaster revealed major flaws in ground-based air traffic management and resulted in major overhauling of tower operations incorporating new concepts of attention and decision-making with technological support during low visibility (Catino, 2008). The Überlingen disaster was the second major air traffic management disaster that demonstrated the extent to which safety culture, maintenance procedures, single-person operations, stress, fatigue, and confusion can contribute to catastrophe (Rodgers, 2017). Überlingen also revealed major issues when conflicting laws such as interpreting traffic collision avoidance system (TCAS) alarms in a cockpit can lead to pilots behaving in opposite ways (Masys, 2005). Finally, Air France 447 prompted a refocus on fatigue risk management, maintenance, and training for pilots as well as deeper research into attention, cognition, and decision-making under pressure (Kharoufah et al., 2018). More recently, Germanwings Flight 9525 that crashed due to a deliberate suicidal action by the copilot prompted the European Union to issue stronger screening of mental health and support to aircrew, which was then adopted more globally (Pasha & Stokes, 2018). Finally, the two recent accidents involving Boeing 737 Max aircraft in Indonesia (2018) and Ethiopia (2019) prompted a larger focus on the design of systems, coding, and automation and the limitations of pilot command of aircraft when the aircraft perform contrary to the pilots' instinctive training (Spielman & Le Blanc, 2021).

These accidents have resulted in the evolution of human factors and human performance requirements since 2010, as can be seen in Table 2.2. One of the largest shifts has been toward the concept of human performance management as a larger concept than individual human factors. These principles are outlined carefully by ICAO (10151) and Civil Air Navigation Services Organization (CANSO, 2019), and the basic premise is that all human factors combine to produce human performance that can be monitored, manipulated, and improved by designing and altering various elements of human factors (Vink & Walzl, 2024). Neuropsychological contributions to human performance increasingly look toward active workload management and human error reduction via real-time feedback of machine interactions (Vink & Walzl, 2024). Safety management systems now mandate safety culture and just culture programs that cover the importance of social psychology to how the larger sociotechnical system works (e.g., EASA, 2017). In fact, as was evident in the Boeing 737 Max story, the importance of safety culture across the world has never been more important as the rise of automation- and software-driven aircraft are requiring a broader group of engineers, pilots, and regulators to engage in closer cooperation (Naor et al., 2020).

Resource management is now required for pilots, air crew, air traffic controllers, and increasingly ground operations such as maintenance or air traffic management technicians (Mizrak & Mizrak, 2020). This is because of the importance of "shared situational awareness" and increasingly remote communication and digital landscapes that require cooperation on a large geographical scale. The Miracle on the Hudson River accident of 2009 showed the power of training entire aircrew (not just pilots) in cooperating as a team. All the crew were trained in psychological concepts, and this led to everyone surviving when the Airbus A320 performed an emergency water landing (Martin, 2019). The more recent contributions of well-being, mental health, and long-term burnout prevention have led to the mandating of various systems such as critical incident stress management and mental health screening alongside other medical checks for pilots and air traffic controllers (Bor et al., 2019).

The contribution of neuropsychology to legislation cannot be overstated. Since 2010, as has been shown, the scope of rules concerning the safety operation of aircraft and air traffic management has been driven by advances in techniques and methodologies not only for retrospective improvements learned because of accidents, but increasingly in proactive measures to develop better systems. These measures consider the limitations of human operators and especially their interactions both with technical systems that are increasingly automated and also in advanced and ever more sophisticated (and remote) teams (Vink, 2021).

Day-to-Day Human Factors That Matter When Flying Becomes Tricky

If legislation and regulations provide the blueprints for what is vital for human operators in day-to-day operations, then it is important to take a survey of the academic neuropsychological contributions to operations. Specifically, this section focuses on the idea of a pilot actively flying the plane, an air traffic controller plugged into a controller working position (radar station), or maintenance technicians conducting their work. This is considered *live operations* and, as suggested earlier, legislation is trending toward the eventual active monitoring of neuropsychological indicators to help the operator work more efficiently and safely in real time (Vink & Walzl, 2024).

So, what human factors matter? Table 2.2 shows the rules that have been reported to be the most important for active control of aircraft or air traffic management. Here, we focus on the traditional concepts of neuropsychology and show the link to the legislation described earlier. When we think about ANCA, discussed in the Introduction, we can identify the psychological areas in terms of most time-critical through to least time-critical when it comes to operating, and for this reason the order is deliberately chosen as follows:

1. Workload, attention, perception, vigilance, and monotony aversion
2. Situational awareness
3. Stress reduction and coping
4. Fatigue risk management
5. Communication and team work
6. Psychoactive substances

For this survey, we take a broader view that focuses on two key areas: first the "usefulness" or "validity" of certain tools versus the cost, time, and difficulty of use in live operations. Figure 2.2 presents these contributions as an illustration to show the state of neuropsychology contributions to live traffic up to the present day. For our purpose in this chapter, we will not include communication and teamwork that focusses mainly on social psychology contributions, although it should be noted that the concept of *shared situational awareness* is increasingly important in crew resource management and is linked to Item 2 above. Also discounted from the survey is psychoactive substances because the effect on operations is considered negligible given the prohibited nature of the substances for operators.

Workload, Attention, Perception, Vigilance and Monotony Aversion: The Big Five for Operating an Aircraft or Managing Air Traffic

Attention is often defined by, "a state or condition of *selective awareness* or perceptual receptivity, by which specific stimuli are selected for enhanced processing" (Breedlove & Watson, 2017, p. 146). In terms of operating an aircraft or managing air traffic, these are the most time-critical elements of human performance. When attention and vigilance slip, then the reaction times to respond decrease and, conversely, if people are in a bored or monotonous state for too long, their fatigue levels increase, and the risk of overload can sometimes be more dangerous than stressful situations (Breedlove & Watson, 2017).

To have attention, we need to have something to focus on. In aviation operations this is usually given to us by workload or tasks. Usually, a human will direct sensors and perception overtly toward the same targets. For example, when reading this sentence, your eyes are focusing on the text and the subject of the text is selected by your brain for focus. However, in 1962, Hermann von Helmholtz demonstrated that humans are quite capable of shifting the focus of our attention covertly while maintaining overt behavior toward something else (Breedlove & Watson, 2017). Another way to understand attention and the importance in operations is the *cocktail party effect*. At a noisy cocktail party, we can focus on an individual conversation despite the overwhelming stimulus provided by the environment. In the cockpit, pilots demonstrate this all the time, for example, listening to air traffic control through their headsets over all the other noises, alarms, visual stimulants, and sensory information (Breedlove & Watson, 2017). There are major limitations on attention, however, and they are usually understood in terms of the Yerkes–Dodson stress curve and other resource theories (Wickens et al., 2021). Because attention, vigilance, and monotony are based on using effort, this can lead to energy depletion that can increase the risk of human error and of decreased human performance. This is why in the operation, they are the areas of human performance that are most needed for active monitoring (Wickens et al., 2021).

Traditional Measures

The traditional measures of operator human performance usually begin with capturing workload. Workload is the combination of task load and a perception of how it feels (Wickens et al., 2021). Therefore, studies normally also collect task load that is more generic and then apply workload measures by asking operators how they perceive the task load. Task load is usually either counted by tasks (e.g., how many planes an air traffic controller is currently controlling) or using an instantaneous self-assessment, which might ask, "On a scale of 1 to 5, how busy are you right now?" This is repeated at preset times (usually 3 or 5 min; Tattersall & Foord, 1996). Workload scales such as the Bedford Workload Rating Scale (Roscoe, 1987) or the NASA Task Load Index (NASA-TLX; Hart & Staveland, 1988) are then used additionally to understand perceived workload. Sometimes there are digital versions, for example, NASA have released their TLX on a digital device format. In the cockpit or operations room, the NASA-TLX and other tasks can now be done relatively easily and quickly without much disruption to operations, but they are inherently biased by user experience, backgrounds, and perceptions and therefore victim to the usual subjective errors (Devos et al., 2020).

More expansive batteries of tests have been created that are computer-based cognitive assessments such as the Cambridge Neuropsychological Test Automated Battery (CANTAB; Robbins et al., 1994) or the CNS Vital Signs neurocognitive function technology (Gualtieri & Johnson, 2006). Both provide more valid and expansive sets of neuropsychological data related to these elements. For example, the CNS Vital Signs can look closely at memory, pain, sleep, and attention deficits. But these two batteries of tests are more often used for clinical assessments, and due to the cost and need to have highly trained technicians to administer and interpret them, they cannot be used in live operations in any meaningful way.

Traditional measures have got us quite far with regard to designing the system and evaluating expected performance. However, in human performance research there are several issues pertaining to the validity of measures such as workload and situational awareness (Helmke et al., 2018). The overwhelming majority of evidence presented continues to be with subjective measures such as the NASA-TLX. The issue with using subjective measures falls into three broad categories:

1. Scales are prone to lower validity and individual differences. Subjective measures are highly variable and not very reliable (Ayres, 2006; Gawron, 2019).
2. They are usually prone to simulator bias as well as sterile and often not realistic operational conditions. Participant sample size is usually low, which does not counteract the effects in Point 1 (Reynolds et al., 2017).
3. The tests are often filled out by hand, which requires postexperimental data input that can be time consuming and expensive and also requires a large effort by the experts.

The problems are especially compounded if practitioners are attempting to gather information from live operations, where the preparation and interjection from researchers is not only distracting to controllers but can bias results further as controllers adjust to researcher presence (Gawron, 2019). Each of these three problems are factors in multiple on-going research in both European multinational research programs and in the United States (e.g., SESAR, n.d.). In these projects, human factors evaluations are usually completed alongside industrial research but still rely heavily on subjective measures. Even when novel approaches are taken to elicit more data from limited simulator runs, the conclusions of this research remain consistent: not enough participants, not enough runs, not enough validity (Gawron, 2019; Helmke et al., 2018). The traditional measures have a very good utility as far as "back-room" research is concerned, but their use in live operations is limited by the processing time, the need for distraction, and their lower validities.

Physiological and Biofeedback Measures

If the use of traditional measures can only get us so far in terms of supporting live operations, then what about the other end of the scale of cost and validity? There is growing excitement around several technological breakthroughs in biofeedback. With every generation of technology, the devices are becoming smaller, wireless, and more usable in live operations (LaRocco et al., 2020). Research to capture the Big Five primary human performance indicators has focused on biofeedback technologies. Tao et al. (2019) conducted an extensive review of physiological measures and identified 78 different types from 91 studies. Interestingly, only 16% of studies were found to have been published before the year 2000 with over 50% occurring in the last 10 years, which indicates the over-reliance on traditional measures up to the early 2000s. Tao et al. list seven categories of physiological measures (Table 2.3).

Overall, Tao et al. (2019) found that cardiovascular, electroencephalographic (EEG), and eye-tracking measures are the most widely used. Of these three measures, heart rate variability (HRV) appears to be the most reliable measure of mental workload, which is consistent with other studies (Charles & Nixon, 2019), but there is almost as good evidence for EEG and eye-tracking measures.

Table 2.3. Summary overview of biofeedback tools

Physiological types		Cited measurement techniques
1	Cardiovascular measures	Frequency-domain HRV Time-domain HRV Electrocardiography Interbeat interval Blood pressure Blood oxygenation
2	Eye movement measures	Blink rate Pupil diameter Blink duration Fixation duration Saccade velocity
3	EEG measures	Majority of studies have focused on: α power θ power β power Time-domain P300 N100
4	Respiration measures	Respiration rate
5	Skin measures	Skin conduction
6	EMG measures	EMG amplitude
7	Neuroendocrine measures	Plasma cortisol Adrenaline excretion Dopamine Noradrenaline

Note. EEG = electroencephalography; EMG = electromyography; HRV = heart rate variability.

Practical Use of Cardiovascular Measures

Despite the promising power of cardiovascular measures found by many studies, including the usage of HRV not only in workload but also in concentration, attention, and boredom, the practical use of these measures remains tricky in a live operational environment. For example, Hughes et al. (2019) point out that there is no "best cardiac" measure for human performance indicators, which means it is difficult for an untrained expert to know which to use and when. Cardiac measures are also dependent on the physical health of the operator and are thus highly individualized. Many studies have been conducted in highly controlled environments, which does not allow them to capture broader standard deviations and to assess wider population effects. The capturing of heart rate measures is also difficult, normally requiring individual calibration and export to an external system, although wearable devices such as digital watches are quickly overcoming this. Another issue highlighted by Straeter (2020) is that HRT is only a "half-way-valid" psychophysiological indicator because if an operator is experiencing physically demanding tasks or is highly stressed then the HRT cannot be used.

Cardiovascular measures demonstrate the strong power of monitoring and predicting human performance metrics, but their practical usage in live operations still requires expertise to capture, interpret, and aggregate in order to understand the "so what" element of using the data for immediate support to the operations. The confounding of cardiovascular measures by physical load cannot be overcome yet (Straeter, 2020)

Practical Use of Eye-Tracking Measures

There has been much excitement around the use of eye-tracking measures for neuropsychological support to operations. A lot of research has been focused on the benefits for human performance when using eye-tracking solutions. Peißl et al. (2018) conducted a literature review of 79 studies, and their findings were in line with Tao et al. (2019) that eye-tracking could be useful in measuring workload, cognitive processes, human error reduction, stress, and fatigue management and even hypoxia or spatial disorientation. Ayiei (2020) similarly found strong evidence particularly in the use of eye-tracking for attention, which is most linked to human error risk and loss of human performance as operators become either overstressed or underloaded.

However, of the three main areas (cardiovascular, eye-tracking, and EEG), eye-tracking is perhaps the most difficult to implement into a live environment. There are three types of video eye-tracking: mobile eye-tracking, remote eye-tracking systems, and tower-based systems. All these systems use infrared illumination and some sort of camera to monitor eye movements. Mobile eye-tracking systems usually require an intrusive headset or wearable contact lenses, which can be irritating. Furthermore, they are not so useful in bright environments like a cockpit, and they have trouble tracking eye movements to the periphery. Remote systems do not touch a user and are hard mounted and often cannot be used outside of a particular range of motion in the shoulders and head (in other words, users still have to remain fixed on a set of screens). This means that although they are not intrusive, they can only be used in a limited working area – although this may make them quite suitable in a cockpit, which is a smaller working area (Martinez-Marquez et al., 2021).

The biggest practical challenges to using eye-tracking, however, is the individual calibration required every time a different user sits down. This makes these systems almost impossible to deploy in an operational environment where time margins are already quite short and operators often have to relieve each other quite quickly. Despite their promise, manufacturers of aircraft and infrastructure designers for air traffic management are often reluctant to redesign entire working areas just to facilitate the inclusion of hardware like this that does not have enough demand. Until the issue of individual calibration is overcome, most likely using an integrated software solution relying on machine learning of large data sets, they are very promising in a laboratory or simulator setting but not so suitable for live operational support.

Practical Use of EEG

Of the three physiological measures, EEG measures are quickly becoming the most promising. Chikhi et al. (2022) conducted a meta-analysis of 24 studies to investigate the use of power spectral analysis for measurement of cognitive workload and other human performance indicators. Their findings, however, alluded to one of the limitations of EEG, which is that studies still need to overcome the individual issue of other factors influencing spectral power such as emotional load. There have been ergonomic issues with the usage of EEG in the past. Traditional use of EEG has remained in a clinical setting because of the sheer number of electrodes and types of head caps that needed to be worn. For EEG to become useful in live operations, it needs to be highly portable, comfortable, and wireless as well as to use dry sensors (Ayaz & Dehais, 2021). But this is quickly becoming viable, as LaRocco et al. (2020) showed that portable EEG devices were becoming increasingly more sophisticated and capable of producing usable and valid results, especially for attention, vigilance, and drowsiness (related to monotonous situations).

However, one of the key differences with EEG data is that they can be averaged, and the individual differences can be controlled statistically much faster to show trends and focus points. The use of EEG data to fill a larger neural network is perhaps the fastest way to create a predictive machine-learning-driven system that can calculate predicted human performance outcomes. This is because EEG data can provide large data sets in ways that are much easier to correlate with other types of big data, unlike cardiovascular and eye-tracking data that require several more layers or expert interpretation and pre-processing. It is for this reason that EEG is inching ahead in terms of being able to provide not live operational support but assistance in building systems that can offer the kind of live data support needed.

Practical Issues With Other Physiological Measures

The predominant issue with the remaining four physiological measures investigated by Tao et al. (2019) is the way data are collected. There are very few portable devices outside of clinical settings that can capture them. They therefore would not meet the immediate time-critical factor required for supporting live operations. They are also highly individual, and so far, very few studies have gathered the kind of big data required to find population trends that could be used as guidance in systems for covering all pilots or air traffic controllers. Individually they show promise but have required far too much investment and expertise and are difficult to use in operations. The same can be said of advanced imagine techniques such as functional magnetic resonance imaging (fMRI) or other clinical neuroimaging tools. Their usage would be impractical in a live operational setting.

Situational Awareness and Decision-Making

In the previous section, we discussed the Big Five human performance indicators that have a time-critical function. In the ANCA, they represent the *aviate/operate* element of live operations. Workload drives attention, perception, vigilance, and boredom, and measuring and capturing these in real time is a crucial step in using neuropsychological tools to support live operations. Once information is perceived in the brain, it forms a situational awareness that in turn allows for decision-making to occur (Wickens, 2008).

Situational Awareness

There are a myriad of situational awareness (SA) concepts, but they tend to build on one of the prevailing concepts that was introduced by Endsley in 1995. The SA model describes the process through which individuals gather, interpret, and utilize information from their environment to understand the current situation. It consists of three levels: perception, comprehension, and projection. The main idea is that in the brain, perception and attention give rise to a mental model, which can also be shared in a team setting whereby several members of the team hold a shared mental model (Endsley, 1995). Endsley conducted a meta-review of measures for SA in 2021 and discussed the objective and subjective types. As mentioned earlier, some of the biophysical measures such as eye-tracking can give objective insight into SA but there is still limited validation evidence. Instead, SA measures are normally subjective measures including the Situational Awareness Rating Technique (SART), the Situational Awareness Global Assessment Technique (SAGAT), and the Situation Present Assessment Test (SPAM). The subjective tests tend to be strong predictors of human performance and can indicate human error risk and decision-making risks, but they tend to have several limitations including that they are intrusive, are memory dependent, have sampling biases, and require an expert to be present to conduct them (Endsley, 2021). Above all, the SAGAT shows the best usage, but entails something called the "freeze" technique that requires operators to stop what they are doing to capture SA. This is obviously impractical in a live setting, but SA as a concept has still shown strong correlations with workload and decision-making, which means it is a useful construct in the understanding of human performance. SA will remain a vital research topic in the years ahead, especially with the interaction of more automation that can lead to periods of monotony and inattention when SA might decrease. A key question will be, how much SA do you need to intervene with a system?

Decision-Making

Decision-making is one of the most written about subjects in psychology. But the contribution to aviation and in particular to the neuropsychological concepts is of vital importance in the achievement of high human performance and reduction of human error. Furthermore, decision-making is a vital part of the investigation process when operators are often grilled on why they made certain decisions (Vink, 2022). Several key theories remain embedded in the training material and are used in operational support contexts. It is sufficient in this chapter simply to list them, and the reader is encouraged to consider them for their own needs (Table 2.4).

Table 2.4. Most widely used decision-making theories and frameworks

Decision-making theory	Reference	Brief description
Multiple-resource theory	Wickens, 2008	The brain allocates resources to multiple processes simultaneously. Decisions require long-term memory, short-term perception, and attention and situational awareness as well as action execution and feedback.
Dual-process theory	Kahneman, 2011	Decision-making involves two distinct cognitive processes; a fast and automatic (subconscious) System 1 and a slow and conscious System 2. Decisions are normally biased and scripted to preserve energy and be fast enough for survival.
Naturalistic decision-making model (NDM)	Klein, 2008	The NDM model focuses on decision-making in real-world, dynamic, and time-pressured situations.
Information processing theory	Simon, 1978	Examines how individuals acquire, process, store, and retrieve information to make decisions.
Decision field theory	Busemeyer & Townsend, 1993	Decision field theory is a computational model of decision-making that combines elements of cognition and perception. It posits that decision-making involves a competition between alternatives based on their subjective values and probabilities.
Hierarchy of effects model	Bye et al., 1999	The hierarchy of effects model suggests that decision-making and situation assessment are influenced by different levels of cognitive processes, ranging from perception and recognition to comprehension and projection.

Stress Reduction and Coping Mechanisms

Stress is a medical term that follows the Yerkes–Dodson curve (Breedlove & Watson, 2017). Human performance typically follows the Yerkes–Dodson curve in a particular way, as proposed by de Waard and Brookhuis (1996). Fundamentally, in low-arousal or high-arousal situations, human performance tends to be limited. The optimum balance is when workload is managed to keep operators primed, attentive, and working at a comfortable pace. But as the multiple-resource theory of Wickens (2008) shows that as an individual descends the Yerkes–Dodson curve and energy is consumed to the point of exhaustion, human performance decreases rapidly. This can cause dangerous situations such as overload in air traffic controllers or an inability for pilots to continue operating their aircraft.

Many theories have been advanced to assist operators with stress reduction and coping. The leading theory that dominates much of the aviation industry is the transactional model of stress and coping, introduced by Lazarus and Folkman (1984). Figure 2.1 shows the most prevailing coping strategies and systems employed by aviation to help operators cope with stress. Above all other neuropsychological contributions to live operations, it is perhaps the body of literature dedicated to clinical solutions for stress management and coping that has been the most used and implemented. As shown in the legislation section of this chapter, stress mitigation is a requirement by most nations these days and the contribution of the clinical world to this topic is extensively covered elsewhere in this book.

Fatigue Risk Management

Fatigue has become a prominent subject, evident through the increasing number of scientific papers and regulations addressing this topic. However, fatigue is often regarded as the problem and the result at the same time, whereas it should be viewed as an umbrella term encompassing different phenomena (Eurocontrol, 2023). Mental fatigue can be examined from a temporal perspective, distinguishing between acute and chronic fatigue.

Chronic fatigue pertains to a persistent and prolonged state of weariness that extends beyond the usual recovery period. It presents normally as longer-term physical and mental health issues and sometimes as burnout. It is often protected by occupational health and safety and working time rules. Acute fatigue refers to a temporary state of reduced vigilance and attention resulting from prolonged wakefulness or extended mental exertion. Acute fatigue is a true safety risk for aviation because it usually presents as reduced reaction time, cognitive impairment, and sometimes behavioral issues (Rangan et al., 2020; Rudin-Brown & Filtness, 2023). These can lead directly to impaired performance at the workstation. Once individuals are already suffering from chronic fatigue, this can further exacerbate acute fatigue. The difference between these two types of fatigue is significant because the approaches to managing and counteracting them should be different.

Most countries today employ a fatigue risk management system (FRMS) of some kind and they usually involve a combination of rostering, rest periods, training, and holidays (Eurocontrol, 2023; Rudin-Brown & Filtness, 2023). There are four primary methods to measure fatigue: observational studies, surveys, cognitive tests, and neuroimaging/biofeedback data (Eurocontrol, 2023). However, increasingly sophisticated attempts to capture fatigue as a long term risk associated with burnout involve studying employee human resource data such as sick leave, overtime hours, and holiday usage (Rudin-Brown & Filtness, 2023).

The five most widely used and valid cognitive tests for fatigue are the following:

1. The Psychomotor Vigilance Test (Wilkinson & Houghton, 1982): This task is usually completed using a computer, and it times how quickly a participant can respond to a given task. For a normal person who is not fatigued, the signaling time usually takes between 150 and 220 ms for eyesight to register something, process it, and relay a signal to a finger to click a button. Values higher than 250 ms indicate increased acute fatigue as reaction times begin to decrease (Breedlove & Watson, 2017).
2. The Stroop Test: This test measures selective attention and the ability to suppress irrelevant information. It shows the effects of sleep deprivation on cognitive performance (Jensen, 1965).
3. The Wisconsin Card Sorting Test (or various other secondary task techniques): These tests usually involve a participant conducting a secondary task alongside their primary task (like flying a plane or air traffic control), and their ability to succeed demonstrates cognitive flexibility that decreases as they become fatigued (Grant & Berg, 1948).
4. The Visual Analogue Scales – Fatigue (Lee et al., 1991): They are a set of five scales related to energy and 13 related to fatigue where a participant responds on a Likert scale.
5. The Karolinska Sleepiness Scale (Åkerstedt & Gillberg, 1990): It is a basic set of Likert-scale responses to how fatigued and sleepy a participant is.

These are the measures most widely used today. However, all five of the methods discussed are intrusive in that they require the participant to actively engage, which can be quite distracting during operating tasks. Usually, they are conducted in simulator studies where safety is not so much of an issue, but this has the problem of inducing simulator biases to the results, which means that findings are often less valid or less representative of "real life" (Bendak & Rashid, 2020). As noted earlier, increasingly, biofeedback tools are being sought to measure fatigue in real time.

Summary of the Available Tools for Assisting Human Performance in Live Operations

Figure 2.2 lists a summary of the tools that have been used for human and neuropsychological performance measures, indicators, and predictors in aviation. They are grouped according to their validity as measurements and predictors of the cost, the time needed to conduct them, and the practicality of use in live operations. The grouped area in the middle of Figure 2.2 represents a set of human performance measures that have not been discussed in this chapter. They are collectively the big data measures that could be used in the future with a combination of algorithms and weak-signal style analysis.

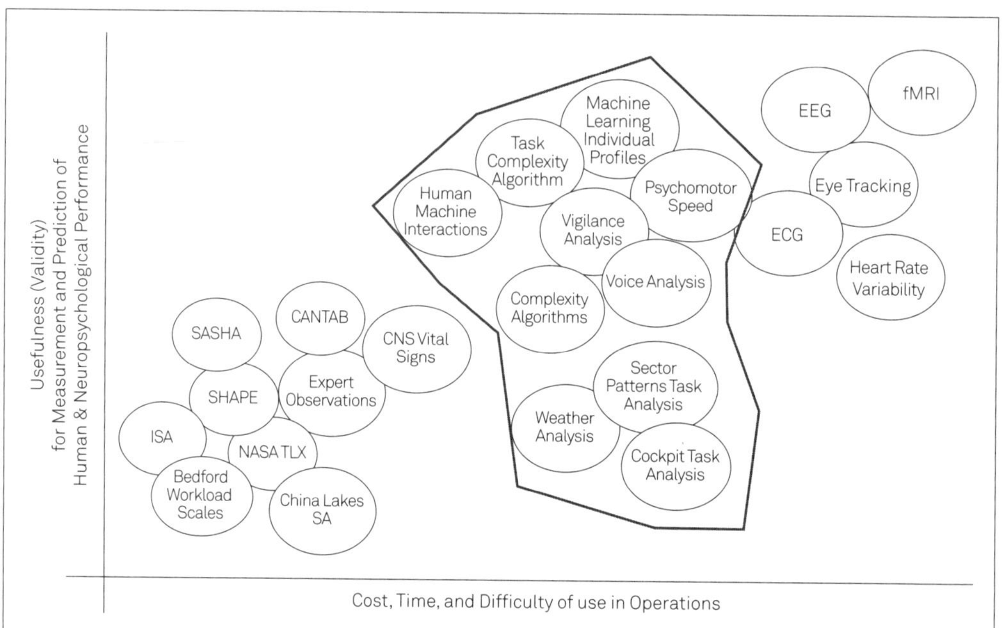

Figure 2.2. Summary of techniques and methods from neuropsychology to support operations in aviation.

Conclusion

In this chapter, we have looked at traditional measures (shown in the lower left side of Figure 2.2) and the biophysical and neuroimaging concepts (shown in the top right side). As can be seen in Figure 2.2, these two categories of research have benefits but also costs and their deployment in live operations is often marked by impracticalities or a lack of validity.

As of 2024, it is still not common for aviation organizations to employ neuropsychological support in live operations on a routine basis. As is widely discussed in the rest of this book, neuropsychological techniques, methodologies, and assessments may be conducted during the medical certification process for pilots and air traffic controllers, but these assessments primarily focus on identifying any preexisting conditions or impairments that may affect flight safety. They are also predominantly used in selection, recruitment, and postincident treatment. Furthermore, they are used for specific cases involving pilots with suspected cognitive impairments or neurologic conditions. In these instances, neuropsychological evaluations may be conducted to assess the pilot's cognitive abilities and determine their fitness to fly. In terms of safety design and assurance, techniques are also still used mainly in controlled simulations and research settings.

But with rapid improvements to technology in terms of wearable devices, with smaller less intrusive cameras and headsets, the opportunity for deploying neuropsychological tools is soon to become viable in direct live operations. Combined with big data and machine learning approaches where these types of data can be included, we may soon have the solution at hand to utilize neuropsychological support live in the cockpit or control room.

References

Åkerstedt, T., & Gillberg, M. (1990). Subjective and objective sleepiness in the active individual. *International Journal of Neuroscience, 52*(1–2), 29–37. https://doi.org/10.3109/00207459008994241

Appicharla, S. (2023). The Boeing 737 Max 8 crashes: System-based approach to safety – a different perspective. *Safety-Critical Systems, 2*(1), 1–6.

Ayaz, H., & Dehais, F. (2021). Neuroergonomics. In H. Ayas & F. Dehais (Eds.), *Handbook of human factors and ergonomics* (pp. 816–841). Academic Press.

Ayiei, A. (2020). The use of eye tracking in assessing visual attention. *Journal of Aircraft and Spacecraft Technology, 4*(1), 117–124. https://doi.org/10.3844/jastsp.2020.117.124

Ayres, P. (2006). Using subjective measures to detect variations of intrinsic cognitive load within problems. *Learning and Instruction, 16*(5), 389–400. https://doi.org/10.1016/j.learninstruc.2006.09.001

Bendak, S., & Rashid, H.S. (2020). Fatigue in aviation: A systematic review of the literature. *International Journal of Industrial Ergonomics, 76*, 102928. https://doi.org/10.1016/j.ergon.2020.102928

Biggs, A., Brough, P., & Drummond, S. (2017). Lazarus and Folkman's psychological stress and coping theory. In C.L. Cooper & J.C. Quick (Eds.), *The handbook of stress and health: A guide to research and practice* (pp. 349–364). Wiley-Blackwell.

Bor, R., Eriksen, C., Hubbard, T., & King, R. (2019). Pilot selection: Psychological principles and practices. In R. Bor, C. Eriksen, T. Hubbard, & R. King (Eds.), *Pilot mental health assessment and support: A practitioner's guide* (pp. 55–76). CRC Press.

Breedlove, M., & Watson, N.V. (2017). *Behavioural neuroscience* (8th ed.). Oxford University Press.

Busemeyer, J.R., & Townsend, J.T. (1993). Decision field theory: A dynamic-cognitive approach to decision making in an uncertain environment. *Psychological Review, 100*(3), 432. https://doi.org/10.1037/0033-295X.100.3.432

Bye, A., Hollnagel, E., & Brendeford, T.S. (1999). Human-machine function allocation: A functional modelling approach. *Reliability Engineering & System Safety, 64*(2), 291–300. https://doi.org/10.1016/S0951-8320(98)00069-6

CANSO. (2019). *Human performance management standards of excellence.* https://canso.org/publication/canso-standard-of-excellence-in-human-performance-management/

Catino, M. (2008, July 10–12). *The Linate air disaster. A multilevel model of accident analysis* [Paper presentation]. 24th Colloquium EGOS, Upsetting Organisations, Amsterdam, the Netherlands.

Charles, R.L., & Nixon, J. (2019). Measuring mental workload using physiological measures: A systematic review. *Applied Ergonomics, 74*, 221–232. https://doi.org/10.1016/j.apergo.2018.08.028

Chikhi, S., Matton, N., & Blanchet, S. (2022). EEG power spectral measures of cognitive workload: A meta-analysis. *Psychophysiology, 59*(6), e14009. https://doi.org/10.1111/psyp.14009

Civil Aviation Authority. (2002). *Fundamental human factors concepts (CAP 719).* https://www.caa.co.uk/our-work/publications/documents/content/cap-719/

Civil Aviation Authority. (2016). *Air traffic management automation: Guidance on human technology integration (CAP 1377).* https://www.caa.co.uk/our-work/publications/documents/content/cap1377/

Civil Aviation Authority. (2020). *Psychological assessment of pilots (CAP 1938).* https://www.caa.co.uk/our-work/publications/documents/content/cap1938/

Civil Aviation Safety Authority. (2020). *AC 119-12 v1.0: Human factors principles and non-technical skills training and assessment for air transport operations.* https://www.google.com/url?sa=t&rct=j&q=&esrc=s&source=web&cd=&ved=2ahUKEwih1_nIja6HAxU5S_EDHXxmBRQQFnoECBMQAQ&url=https%3A%2F%2Fwww.casa.gov.au%2Fhuman-factors-principles-and-non-technical-skills-training-and-assessment-air-transport-operations&usg=AOvVaw3XF-mxa03PMurDalI2aMdm&opi=89978449

Devos, H., Gustafson, K., Ahmadnezhad, P., Liao, K., Mahnken, J.D., Brooks, W.M., & Burns, J.M. (2020). Psychometric properties of NASA-TLX and index of cognitive activity as measures of cognitive workload in older adults. *Brain Sciences, 10*(12), 994. https://doi.org/10.3390/brainsci10120994

de Waard, D., & Brookhuis, K.A. (1996). *The measurement of drivers' mental workload.* University of Groningen.

European Union Aviation Safety Agency. (2012). *Commission regulation (EU) No. 965/2012 – easy access rules: Air operations.* https://www.easa.europa.eu/en/document-library/easy-access-rules/easy-access-rules-air-operations-regulation-eu-no-9652012

European Union Aviation Safety Agency. (2017). *Commission implementing regulation (EU) 2017/373 – ATM/ANS common requirements. Easy access rules.* https://www.easa.europa.eu/en/document-library/easy-access-rules/easy-access-rules-air-traffic-managementair-navigation-services

Endsley, M.R. (1995). Measurement of situational awareness in dynamic systems. *Human Factors, 37*(1), 65–84. https://doi.org/10.1518/001872095779049499

Endsley, M.R. (2021). A systematic review and meta-analysis of direct objective measures of situational awareness: a comparison of SAGAT and SPAM. *Human Factors, 63*(1), 124–150. https://doi.org/10.1177/0018720819875376

Eurocontrol. (2023, May). *Guidelines on fatigue management in ATC rostering systems* (Document NMD/SAF/2611). https://skybrary.aero/sites/default/files/bookshelf/34421.pdf

Federal Aviation Authority. (1993). *Order 9550.8 – human factors policy.* https://www.faa.gov/documentLibrary/media/Order/9550.8.pdf

Fraher, A. (2015). A dark side case study of American Airlines Flight 587: The paradox of advanced technology. *Academy of Management Proceedings, 1*, 11127.

Gawron, V.J. (2019). *Human performance, workload, and situational awareness measures handbook.* CRC Press.

Grant, D.A., & Berg, E.A. (1948). A behavioral analysis of degree of reinforcement and ease of shifting to new responses in a Weigl-type card-sorting problem. *Journal of Experimental Psychology, 38*(4), 404–411. https://doi.org/10.1037/h0059831

Gualtieri, C.T., & Johnson, L.G. (2006). Reliability and validity of a computerized neurocognitive test battery, CNS Vital Signs. *Archives of Clinical Neuropsychology, 21*(7), 623–643. https://doi.org/10.1016/j.acn.2006.05.007

Hart, S.G., & Staveland, L.E. (1988). Development of NASA-TLX (Task Load Index): Results of empirical and theoretical research. In P.A. Hancock & N. Meshkati (Eds.), *Advances in psychology* (Vol. 52, pp. 139–183). Elsevier.

Helmke, H., Slotty, M., Poiger, M., Herrer, D.F., Ohneiser, O., Vink, N., & Pérez, M.B. (2018, September). *Ontology for transcription of ATC speech commands of SESAR 2020 solution PJ. 16-04*. IEEE/AIAA 37th Digital Avionics Systems Conference (pp. 1–10). IEEE.

Hughes, A.M., Hancock, G.M., Marlow, S.L., Stowers, K., & Salas, E. (2019). Cardiac measures of cognitive workload: a meta-analysis. *Human Factors, 61*(3), 393–414. https://doi.org/10.1177/0018720819830553

International Civil Aviation Organization. (2021). *Document 10151 manual on human performance (HP) for regulators*. https://www.icao.int/safety/OPS/OPS-Section/Documents/Advance-unedited.Doc.10151.alltext.en.pdf

International Civil Aviation Organization. (2023, June 16). *About ICAO*. https://www.icao.int/about-icao/Pages/default.aspx#:~:text=The%20International%20Civil%20Aviation%20Organization,policies%20for%20international%20civilian%20flight

Jensen, A.R. (1965). Scoring the Stroop test. *Acta Psychologica, 24*(5), 398–408. https://doi.org/10.1016/0001-6918(65)90024-7

Kahneman, D. (2011). *Thinking, fast and slow*. Machmillan.

Katerinakis, T. (2014). *Aviate, navigate, communicate: Silence, voice and situational awareness in aviation safety*. [Unpublished doctoral dissertation]. Drexel University.

Kharoufah, H., Murray, J., Baxter, G., & Wild, G. (2018). A review of human factors causations in commercial air transport accidents and incidents: From 2000-2016. *Progress in Aerospace Sciences, 99*, 1–13. https://doi.org/10.1016/j.paerosci.2018.03.002

Klein, G. (2008). Naturalistic decision making. *Human Factors, 50*(3), 456–460. https://doi.org/10.1518/001872008X288385

LaRocco, J., Le, M.D., & Paeng, D.G. (2020). A systemic review of available low-cost EEG headsets used for drowsiness detection. *Frontiers in Neuroinformatics, 42*, Article 553352.

Lazarus, R.S., & Folkman, S. (1984). *Stress, appraisal, and coping*. Springer Publishing Company.

Lee, K.A., Hicks, G., & Nino-Murcia, G. (1991). Validity and reliability of a scale to assess fatigue. *Psychiatry Research, 36*(3), 291–298. https://doi.org/10.1016/0165-1781(91)90027-M

Martin, W. (2019). Crew resource management and individual resilience. In B.G. Kanki, J. Anca, & T.R. Chidester (Eds.), *Crew resource management* (3rd ed., pp. 207–226). Elsevier Academic Press. https://doi.org/10.1016/B978-0-12-812995-1.00007-5

Martinez-Marquez, D., Pingali, S., Panuwatwanich, K., Stewart, R.A., & Mohamed, S. (2021). Application of eye tracking technology in aviation, maritime, and construction industries: A systematic review. *Sensors, 21*(13), 4289. https://doi.org/10.3390/s21134289

Masys, A. (2005). A systemic perspective of situational awareness: An analysis of the 2002 mid-air collision over Überlingen, Germany. *Disaster Prevention and Management, 14*(4), 548–557. https://doi.org/10.1108/09653560510618375

Mizrak, K.C., & Mizrak, F. (2020). The impact of crew resource management on reducing the accidents in civil aviation. *Journal of Aviation Research, 2*(1), 1–25.

Naor, M., Adler, N., Pinto, G.D., & Dumanis, A. (2020). Psychological safety in aviation new product development teams: Case study of 737 MAX airplane. *Sustainability, 12*(21), 8994. https://doi.org/10.3390/su12218994

Pasha, T., & Stokes, P.R. (2018). Reflecting on the Germanwings disaster: A systematic review of depression and suicide in commercial airline pilots. *Frontiers in Psychiatry, 9*, 86. https://doi.org/10.3389/fpsyt.2018.00086

Peißl, S., Wickens, C.D., & Baruah, R. (2018). Eye-tracking measures in aviation: A selective literature review. *The International Journal of Aerospace Psychology, 28*(3–4), 98–112. https://doi.org/10.1080/24721840.2018.1514978

Rangan, S., Riedy, S.M., Bassett, R., Klinck, Z.A., Hagerty, P., Schek, E., Belenky, G., &, Van Dongen, H.P. (2020). Predictive and proactive fatigue risk management approaches in commercial aviation. *Chronobiology International, 37*(9–10), 1479–1482. https://doi.org/10.1080/07420528.2020.1803902

Reynolds, H.D., DeLaura, R., & Soulliard, B. (2017). 'How good is good enough?' Exploring validation for serious gaming in air traffic control. In J. Kantola, T. Barath, S. Nazir, & T. Andre (Eds.), *Advances in human factors, business management, training and education* (Vol. 498). Springer. https://doi.org/10.1007/978-3-319-42070-7_64

Robbins, T.W., James, M., Owen, A.M., Sahakian, B.J., McInnes, L., & Rabbitt, P. (1994). Cambridge Neuropsychological Test Automated Battery (CANTAB): A factor analytic study of a large sample of normal elderly volunteers. *Dementia and Geriatric Cognitive Disorders, 5*(5), 266–281. https://doi.org/10.1159/000106735

Rodgers, M. (2017). *Human factors impacts in air traffic management*. Routledge. https://doi.org/10.4324/9781315253015

Roscoe, A.H. (1987). In-flight assessment of workload using pilot ratings and heart rate. The practical assessment of pilot workload. *AGARDograph, 282*, 78–82.

Rudin-Brown, C.M., & Filtness, A.J. (Eds.). (2023). *The handbook of fatigue management in transportation: Waking up to the challenge*. CRC Press. https://doi.org/10.1201/9781003213154

SESAR. (n.d.). *Delivering the Digital European Sky. SESAR joint undertaking*. https://www.sesarju.eu

Simon, H.A. (1978). Information-processing theory of human problem solving. *Handbook of Learning and Cognitive Processes, 5*, 271–295.

Spielman, Z., & Le Blanc, K. (2021). Boeing 737 MAX: Expectation of human capability in high automated systems. *Proceedings of the AHFE 2020 Virtual Conference on Human Factors in Robots, Drones and Unmanned Systems* (pp. 64–70). Springer International Publishing.

Straeter, O. (2020). An objective measure for detecting workload and errors in monotone, repetitive or fatigue-causing environments using pupil variation. *Human mental workload: Models and applications: 4th International Symposium, H-WORKLOAD 2020, Granada, Spain. Proceedings 4* (pp. 3–12). Springer International Publishing. https://doi.org/10.1007/978-3-030-62302-9_1

Tao, D., Tan, H., Wang, H., Zhang, X., Qu, X., & Zhang, T. (2019). A systematic review of physiological measures of mental workload. *International Journal of Environmental Research and Public Health, 16*(15), Article 2716.

Tattersall, A.J., & Foord, P.S. (1996). An experimental evaluation of instantaneous self-assessment as a measure of workload. *Ergonomics, 39*(5), 740–748. https://doi.org/10.1080/00140139608964495

Transport Canada. (2021). *Canadian aviation regulations (SOR/96-433)*. https://tc.canada.ca/en/corporate-services/acts-regulations/list-regulations/canadian-aviation-regulations-sor-96-433

Tsang, P.S., & Vidulich, M.A. (Eds.). (2002). *Principles and practice of aviation psychology*. CRC Press. https://doi.org/10.1201/b12466

Vink, L.-S. (2021). The effect to human performance and wellbeing of air traffic management operational staff through the COVID-19 pandemic. In *Proceedings of the 91st International Symposium on Aviation Psychology* (p. 370). Wright State University.

Vink, L.-S. (2022). A new methodology for assessing human contributions to occurrences (MAHCO) in air traffic management utilising a Bayesian hierarchical predictive coding approach to the brain, and the benefits for just culture. *Transportation Research Procedia, 66*, 201–213. https://doi.org/10.1016/j.trpro.2022.12.021

Vink, L.-S., & Walzl, B. (2024). A framework to redefine human performance in complex socio-technical systems. *Journal of Aviation Psychology and Applied Human Factors*. Manuscript submitted for publication.

Wickens, C. (2008). Multiple resources and mental workload. *Human Factors, 50*(3), 449–455. https://doi.org/10.1518/001872008X288394

Wickens, C.D., Helton, W.S., Hollands, J.G., & Banbury, S. (2021). *Engineering psychology and human performance*. Routledge. https://doi.org/10.4324/9781003177616

Wilkinson, R.T., & Houghton, D. (1982). Field test of arousal: A portable reaction timer with data storage. *Human Factors, 24*(4), 487–493. https://doi.org/10.1177/001872088202400409

Chapter 3
Neurological Conditions and Their Implications for Crew Licensing and Safety

David G. Newman

Introduction

Flying an aircraft is a complex technical activity. It takes hundreds of hours to learn the fundamentals of flying an aircraft, depending on the type, and years of experience to become highly proficient. The flying task requires good hand–eye coordination and knowledge of aircraft systems, aerodynamics, and physics as well as of the regulations and rules that govern safe operation of the aircraft in an increasingly busy airspace. Flying requires not only physical health, but also good cognitive and neurological health. In the modern era, aircraft are not as physically demanding as they used to be, largely driven by the increasing use of automation and technology. Military aviation remains a physically demanding activity, not only due to the nature of the high-risk operations being undertaken, but also as a consequence of the physical demands of the environment. These include high altitude, high +Gz forces, and thermal extremes and of course the stresses involved in combat operations.

In the modern airline environment, the nature of the flying task is now largely a cognitive one. As such, pilots need to be able to demonstrate good clear cognitive processes. Situational awareness, risk assessment, threat detection, error management, judgment, and decision-making are all imperative to the pilot task. In turn, these elements are based on accurate perception and interpretation of the operating environment, good memory function (at all levels, such as working, short-term, and long-term memory) and good reasoning ability. Being able to plan ahead, to objectively assess risk, to have alternative courses of actions prepared depending on changing circumstances, and to recall and deploy highly proficient technical flying skills when needed, based on standard operating procedures, are all critical cognitive tasks that are necessary for a safe flight to occur. Clearly then, any neurological condition that affects cognitive function at any level can potentially threaten the safety of a flight. Such conditions can adversely affect a pilot's ability to continue to exercise the privileges of their license, either temporarily or permanently. This critical determination is the role of the aeromedical certification process.

The purpose of this chapter is to examine the aeromedical certification and flight safety issues involved in neurological conditions that may occur in pilots. To do this, the chapter examines various neurological conditions and how they impact on flight safety and aeromedical certification. A full and exhaustive assessment of all known neurological conditions is clearly well beyond the scope of a single textbook chapter. With that in mind, the general principles relating to aeromedical certification of any neurological disorder are considered.

For the purposes of this chapter, the discussion is necessarily limited to the more common neurological conditions that might affect a pilot. These consist of the following:

- Head injury
- Epilepsy
- Headache
- Cerebrovascular accidents
- Degenerative neurological illnesses
- Neuropathies
- Effects of aging

The Aeromedical Certification Process

All pilots are required by law to undertake a regular medical examination by a licensed aviation medical examiner (AME). They may also need a medical examination following injury or illness in order to determine their fitness to return to flying. An AME is a medical doctor who has received specialized training in aviation medicine from a recognized institution. In general terms the AME effectively conducts the medical examination of the pilot as a delegate of the regulatory authority of the nation who issued the license to the pilot being examined. The medical standards that need to be met for each class of license are stipulated as *standards and recommended practices* (SARPs) in Annex 1 (Personnel Licensing) of the Convention on International Civil Aviation (the Chicago Convention). Each signatory nation to the International Civil Aviation Organization generally adopts these aeromedical standards into their own national legislation relating to civil aviation regulations. Exceptions to this are permitted, and nations can publish these as differences based on specific circumstances and alternative approaches taken by that particular nation to the certification requirements of a given medical condition. It is important to note here that, in general, aeromedical regulation often tends to lag behind advances in best clinical practice.

The fundamental purpose of the aeromedical certification process is to ensure that pilots are medically and psychologically fit to exercise the privileges of their license. This is particularly important for air transport pilots, who are responsible for the safety of hundreds of passengers on board their aircraft.

The frequency of aviation medical examinations for pilots depends on the nature of the license held by the pilot as well as on their age. In general terms, the complexity and frequency of the medical examination increase with the level of license held and with age. Advancing age generally comes with a higher risk of developing an illness. An older professional pilot will generally need to have more tests done in concert with the medical examination to ensure that illnesses typical of that age group are not present. For example, the likelihood of cardiovascular disease increases with age, and therefore the examination of older pilots requires more investigative tests to be done to determine whether significant cardiovascular disease is present. Electrocardiograms (ECGs) are more frequently used for older pilots, as well as more advanced testing (echocardiograms, exercise testing, etc.).

A professional pilot holding a commercial pilot's or air transport pilot's license (Class 1) requires an annual medical examination, moving to every 6 months beyond a certain age (usually 60 years). A private pilot typically needs a Class 2 license medical examination every 4–5 years (depending on jurisdiction) until the age of 40, after which it becomes every 2 years.

The underlying rationale at the heart of the medical examination of an aviation license holder is to ensure that there is a low likelihood of incapacitation due to the presence of a medical condition. Where the risk of incapacitation is deemed to be unacceptably high, the pilot may be temporarily or permanently considered unfit and thus not be able to exercise their license privileges. In the event of a temporary suspension of license, successful treatment and resolution of the illness should reduce the aeromedical risk and allow re-certification of the individual and a return to flight duties.

An incapacitation event compromises the safety of the flight and puts the crew and passengers at risk. Quantifying the potential risk of incapacitation in a pilot with a known medical condition is a challenge, and this is particularly true of complex neurological conditions. The so-called 1% rule is based on the risk of a cardiovascular event, and represents the annual medical incapacitation risk limit in multi-crew commercial air transport operations. It has since become more widely applied to all clinical conditions in order to give some guidance as to level of risk. While a comprehensive analysis of the 1% rule is beyond the scope of this chapter, it is sufficient to say that there is ongoing discussion as to whether this rule is overly conservative, especially given its inherent assumptions and limitations (Mitchell & Evans, 2004).

In terms of outcomes, the medical certification process can either lead to a pilot being certified (since they meet the medical standards required of their license), suspended (either permanently or for a specified temporary period), or certified with restrictions. These restrictions take into account various issues relating to the condition and may include multi-crew-only restrictions. For Class 1 pilots this is known as an *operational multi-pilot limitation* (OML), and for Class 2 pilots this is known as an *operational safety pilot limitation* (OSL). In either case, solo flying operations are not permitted.

Neurological Conditions and Flight Safety

While it accounts for only 2% of body weight, the human brain consumes 20% of the oxygen supplied to the body (Bullmore & Sporns, 2012; Clark & Sokoloff, 1999; Raichle & Gusnard, 2002). The brain is arguably the least understood and the most complicated of the major organs. As a result, neurological conditions are often complex. Some neurological conditions are well known, with established diagnostic criteria and treatment regimes that are in widespread and effective use. Epilepsy and stroke are examples. However, there are almost innumerable syndrome complexes involving constellations of various neurological symptoms and signs, many of which are rare. A significant number have genetic origins or are related to exposure to specific toxins, while some have origins and causes that are currently unknown.

Illnesses such as cardiovascular disease are in relative terms easy to test for, easy to resolve, and have well-established protocols for determining safe return to flying. While this is common for many illnesses, neurological conditions are often problematic and less easy to resolve. As a case in point, even a headache is not as simple as it might seem. There are many different types of headache, ranging from a simple tension or stress-induced headache through to complex multi-symptom migraine headaches. Diagnosing the type of headache accurately is important, especially in pilots and air traffic controllers. Dismissing a persistent headache as simply being stress-related may mean an underlying brain tumor remains undetected, delaying potentially life-saving treatment.

Neurological conditions often present with some form of physical or cognitive impairment that can limit a person's overall function and ability to work. This is particularly relevant to pilots and air traffic controllers, where good cognitive function is particularly critical. A neurological condition occurring in a pilot is a potentially life-changing and career-limiting issue. This requires careful clinical investigation in order to make an informed decision with regard to aeromedical disposition that does not lead to any adverse outcome on flight safety.

From an aeromedical certification standpoint, any condition that can lead to incapacitation of a pilot, whether it be subtle or sudden, is a cause for concern. In many cases, neurological conditions can lead to functional impairment and potential incapacitation of a pilot. Were this to occur at a critical stage of flight, such as taking off or landing, the safety of the aircraft and the occupants can be imperiled. Clearly, such incapacitation can be immediately obvious, were it to occur. A sudden loss of consciousness due to a stroke is obvious, as is major fitting from an epileptic seizure. Airlines usually have well-established protocols for the crew to follow in the case of an incapacitated pilot. Of more concern is the pilot who suffers a subtle form of incapacitation due to a neurological condition that may not be obvious to other crew members. A neurological event at a critical stage of flight that results in physical incoordination (e.g., sudden onset of paralysis affecting the limbs), sudden loss of memory, impaired decision-making and judgment, speech difficulties, loss of vision, or an altered state of consciousness that is not readily apparent represents a serious existential threat to the safety of the aircraft if none of these symptoms and signs are recognized by other crew members.

On the other hand, a pilot with a known neurological condition may not be able to continue to work as a pilot given the nature of the condition and the adverse impact it could have on the flight. For example, a pilot with a known fitting tendency due to epilepsy would not be allowed to continue flying.

Many studies have examined the prevalence and nature of in-flight incapacitation events (DeJohn et al., 2006; Evans & Radcliffe, 2012; James & Green, 1991; Newman, 2007). The most common cause of incapacitation events is acute gastrointestinal illness (James & Green, 1991). Neurological conditions leading to an in-flight incapacitation event have a remarkably low prevalence (Newman, 2007). This reflects the overall success and effectiveness of the aeromedical certification process, which ensures that only those pilots who are fit to do so are allowed to fly aircraft. The risks of incapacitation, while not eliminated entirely, are thus minimized.

It is also important to note that the treatment must also be considered in the fitness-to-fly decision, as any medication side effects can be almost as problematic as the condition for which the treatment is given. Known side effects of many medications can include impairment of cognitive functions (such as memory, attention, and decision-making), sedation and drowsiness, altered states of arousal and alertness, mood alterations, sensory impairment (affecting vision, hearing, and balance), allergic reactions, and gastrointestinal upset. These types of side effects represent an obvious threat to flight safety.

The Flight Environment

The flight environment can have an adverse neurological effect on an otherwise completely fit and well pilot. For example, operations at altitude in a hypoxic environment can impact on the neurological performance of a pilot, leading to deterioration over time (which gets worse as altitude increases) and if untreated leads to total incapacitation and unconsciousness. Pilots of high-performance aircraft can become incapacitated and unconscious due to the application of high +Gz loads that can overwhelm the ability of the cardiovascular system to ensure adequate cerebral perfusion (Newman, 2017). Spatial disorientation can affect any pilot and is known to affect every single pilot at some stage if they fly long enough (Newman, 2017). The disorienting potential of flight is very well established, particularly in bad weather and/or at night when visual cues are absent or degraded. Vision contributes 80 % of our orientation information, and in the absence of this information less accurate cues such as vestibular inputs and proprioception become relatively more prominent. This can result in well-known spatial disorientation illusions, which in many cases can lead to accidents if unresolved. High workload, stress, temperature extremes, fatigue, and circadian dysrhythmia can also have an effect. All of these physiological challenges can lead to neurological performance impairment in an otherwise fit and well pilot.

From a flight safety perspective, then, the presence of a known neurological disease in a pilot is a significant issue. How that condition might affect the ability of a pilot to safely operate the aircraft, with the known influences of the flight environment potentially acting as aggravating factors, makes a careful approach to aeromedical certification crucial.

General Principles

In considering the aeromedical certification implications of a given neurological condition, there are a number of general principles to consider. Many of these relate to understanding the natural history of the condition and the extent of any associated risk of incapacitation or functional impairment.

Time Course

It is important to understand the time course of the neurological condition. In many cases this is based on what is known of the natural history of the condition in general, but it also needs to take into account the particular clinical circumstances of the affected individual. It is important to understand whether the condition is stable or is likely to progressively worsen. Does the condition involve a single, isolated event, or is it likely to be a recurrent issue? How frequent are these recurrences? Is the time interval between these recurrences stable and predictable, or variable and unpredictable? How quickly does any associated impairment develop (is it acute or does it gradually appear?). Are there any warning signs or symptoms (e.g., a visual aura associated with migraine) that might indicate the onset of the problem? How much lead time is given by these warning signs and symptoms?

Assessment needs to be based on the nature of this time course and the risk of sudden (but perhaps transient) impairments, the frequency of recurrent events, and the known natural history of the condition.

Nature of Impairment

Given the inherent complexity of the nervous system, there are different types of functional impairment that can occur with neurological conditions. Motor problems can include paralysis (which may be full or partial), tremor, and weakness, which can directly affect a pilot's ability to manipulate the aircraft controls throughout the entire flight envelope of the aircraft. Switches and buttons may be difficult to operate in the absence of adequate fine motor control. Motor problems may also affect ingress and egress, particularly in an emergency situation. Sensory impairments include those affecting vision and proprioception (which are important for accurate orientation – impaired function can lead to an increased likelihood of spatial disorientation) as well as hearing (which can adversely affect communications). Multiple cognitive problems can occur, as detailed earlier. Emotional problems may be seen, manifesting in mood disorders, behavioral disturbances, and personality changes.

Extent of Impairment

As far as possible, the criteria for determining the extent of any neurological impairment should be objective, relevant, and reproducible. Understanding the degree of functional impairment is crucial to making a fully informed aeromedical disposition decision. Neurocognitive testing can be useful. Arguably the most appropriate way to assess functional impairment is by testing the individual's actual flight performance. Proficiency checks, using either an appropriate type-specific flight simulator or an aircraft flight, provide an objective method of assessing functional impairment against a known standard of technical performance (Hastings, 2022; Verde et al., 2022). This is especially so when the assessment is conducted by an instructor pilot or type rating examiner. The outcome of such proficiency checks can contribute significantly to the determination of aeromedical disposition. Where the impairment is significant enough that safe flight cannot be demonstrated, the affected pilot will in most cases recognize this themselves through their own less-than-satisfactory performance. This makes the decision to restrict or permanently disqualify easier for the affected pilot to understand and accept.

Treatment

Issues with medication have been highlighted earlier. Surgical treatments can also be problematic. Invasive cranial surgery for a tumor, blood clot, or vascular malformation may be effective in dealing with the underlying problem, but it carries with it a risk of postsurgical epilepsy. Indeed, from a pilot certification process, any penetration of the skull vault due to injury or surgery is likely to lead to a significant period of grounding due to this risk of post-traumatic epilepsy (PTE).

In summary, any neurological condition that is progressive, unpredictable, acute, and recurrent, with a known natural history of increased deterioration over time, is likely to lead to permanent aeromedical disqualification of the pilot. This is especially so if there is no known effective treatment, or if the treatment is just as aeromedically problematic as the condition being treated.

In the next section, specific neurological conditions are considered from an aeromedical disposition and flight safety perspective.

Neurological Conditions

Head Injury

Injury to the head, from whatever cause, can be particularly problematic for the ongoing certification of a pilot. The evaluation of the injury and the potential for secondary problems is often extensive and complicated. What needs to be remembered is that even a relatively trivial head injury can lead to an extended period of loss of aeromedical certification.

Head injuries, for the purposes of aeromedical certification, are graded according to specific criteria into five categories – minimal, mild, moderate, severe, and very severe. In general terms, a very severe head injury is likely to be incompatible with ongoing certification. The key to determining the aeromedical disposition of a pilot with a head injury is understanding the severity of the injury, the actual impairment arising as a result, and the likelihood of secondary problems developing that could be problematic for certification.

The diagnostic criteria for evaluating a head injury are as follows:

- Symptoms of concussion
- The initial Glasgow Coma Score (GCS) at time of injury
- Loss of consciousness (LOC)
- Posttraumatic amnesia (PTA)
- The presence and extent of any focal neurological impairments
- The presence of a skull fracture (and the type of fracture)
- Bleeding on or in the brain
- The presence of a seizure within the first 7 days postinjury

For some of these criteria, such as PTA and LOC, the duration is also important. The longer the period of PTA and/or LOC, the higher the injury classification. A thorough evaluation of the injury can be time-consuming and involves a multitude of investigations, including computed tomography (CT) or magnetic resonance imaging (MRI) scans, neurocognitive testing, and specialist assessments.

In general terms, the more severe the head injury classification, the longer the period of grounding. A minimal head injury (LOC and PTA less than 30 min) typically involves a minimum of 6 weeks of grounding. Class 1 pilots will then be given a multi-crew limitation for 12 months. A very severe head injury, on the other hand, is usually regarded as permanently unfit for flying duties. This disqualification applies to commercial pilots, private pilots, and air traffic controllers. To be classified as very severe, the head injury may involve penetration of the brain, actual structural damage to the brain matter, persisting neurological impairment, and the presence of early seizures. This set of symptoms clearly represents a significant injury to the brain with a high risk of PTE and ongoing functional impairment (Annegers & Coan, 2000). Traumatic brain injuries such as these can also lead to various neuropsychiatric symptoms, including cognitive impairments, behavioral disturbances, and deficits in executive function leading to poor planning, reasoning, and impulse control (Fiedler et al., 2001). Such injuries represent too high a risk for the pilot to be subsequently returned to flight duties (Verde et al., 2022).

In some cases, the treatment required to deal with a head injury can also lead to long-term disqualification from flight duties. Where a head injury leads to a neurosurgical intervention, such as for elevation of a depressed skull fracture, removal of a blood clot, or to stop intracerebral bleeding, the injury is then categorized as severe, which for commercial pilots and air traffic controllers leads to a 2-year period of grounding. For injuries other than very severe, the subsequent return to flight duties once the period of grounding has elapsed requires extensive evaluation. This evaluation needs to demonstrate either full recovery without symptoms or stable symptoms that are non-incapacitating. This decision is typically the responsibility of aviation medicine specialists at the relevant national regulatory authority. The decision is based on the results of investigative tests such as CT or MRI scans and neurocognitive testing. Functional evaluation via a flight test or demonstration of safe operation and proficiency in a simulator is, as we have seen, particularly useful.

Epilepsy

Epilepsy is a complex clinical syndrome. Diagnosis requires two or more unprovoked seizures occurring more than 24 hr apart. The presence of a seizure tendency in pilots is of significant aeromedical concern. A fitting episode can interfere with the pilot's ability to control the aircraft, potentially leading to an adverse safety outcome. Postseizure symptoms such as loss of consciousness also can have safety implications. As a result, a pilot with a history of epilepsy or seizures warrants careful clinical and aeromedical evaluation to determine whether they are able to safely exercise the privileges of their license.

A single seizure may be caused by many different factors, including infantile febrile conditions, pre-eclampsia in pregnancy, use or abuse of drugs or alcohol, or a head injury, as discussed earlier. While the cause of a single seizure is important to determine for the purposes of aeromedical certification, the risk of recurrence is also of paramount importance. Determining this recurrence risk can be problematic. After a single seizure, the risk of recurrence is highly variable. However, on average, prospective studies demonstrate a 2-year recurrence risk of around 40 %, and 80 %–90 % of individuals who do have a recurrence will do so within 2 years (Berg, 2008).

The risk of PTE following either head injury or cranial surgery depends on several factors, including the extent of surgical interference, the site of the injury or surgical intervention, whether early posttraumatic seizures were seen (in the first 7 days postinjury), PTA greater than 24 hr, depressed skull fracture with laceration of the dura, and intracranial bleeding. In those who will get late PTE, 50 % will have a seizure within 1 year and 80 % within 2 years (Verellen & Cavazos, 2010). The risk of PTE declines over time. In one study the overall risk of postcraniotomy seizures was found to be 17 % (Foy et al., 1981).

In considering aeromedical certification, understanding the nature of the seizure event is important. The key question is whether the seizure was provoked or unprovoked. Where the seizure is considered unprovoked, a recurrence more than 24 hr later satisfies the diagnostic criteria for epilepsy. Such a diagnosis is aeromedically disqualifying. In the case of a provoked seizure, the emphasis is on understanding the precipitating factors that provoked the seizure. These include drug or alcohol use or withdrawal, neonatal febrile illness, or simple head injury. If the cause is fully understood and appropriately managed, aeromedical certification may be possible. This is particularly true if the seizure is historical and sufficient time has elapsed without a recurrence and there is no suggestion of any continued predisposition to epilepsy. The UK Civil Aviation Authority specifies a time period free from recurrence and not on treatment of at least 10 years. It is important to note that the treatment for epilepsy is also problematic, given the risk of aeromedically significant side effects.

Seizure events in pilots are uncommon. In a 1990 Air France study examining in-flight incapacitation events in their flight crews over a 20-year period, only two cases of epileptic seizure events were reported, out of a population of some 1,800 personnel (Martin-Saint-Laurent et al., 1990).

Headache

There are many different types of headache, ranging from the common headache through to migraine. Simple headaches that are easily resolved with typical over-the-counter medication and are not associated with any neurological impairment are not aeromedically concerning. However, a migraine headache is potentially incapacitating. It can result in acute headache, nausea, vomiting, and sensitivity to light. Medication for migraine can contribute to impairment, with drowsiness often seen as a side effect.

Migraine headaches tend to be chronic with a multifactorial cause (Ferrari et al., 2022; Goadsby et al., 2002). There are two basic types of migraine. Migraine with aura (previously known as "classic migraine") accounts for around 15 % of cases and is characterized by the appearance of transient focal neurological symptoms before the onset of the headache (Rasmussen & Olesen, 1992). These are mostly visual in nature. This aura serves as a warning to sufferers that the full suite of migraine headache symptoms is developing. Migraine without aura is as the name suggests devoid of these warning neurological symptoms.

As with all neurological conditions, the severity and frequency of any functional impairments due to migraine are important determinants in the aeromedical certification outcome. The side effect profile of any medication used is also important in making this decision. After diagnosis, a period of episode-free grounding is usually required (2–6 months depending on nature of the first episode), and then a return to flying (with OML for Class 1) can be allowed. The restriction may be lifted after 1 year with no further episodes. Disabling migraines may require a significant period of Class 1 OML restriction (10 years). If the migraine headache is disabling, unpredictable in occurrence, frequent, associated with significant neurological impairments, and requiring medication that has a side effect profile incompatible with flight duties, certification of the individual will be unlikely.

Cerebrovascular Accidents

Also known more colloquially as a "stroke," a cerebrovascular accident (CVA) has been defined clinically as "the abrupt onset of symptoms of focal neurological dysfunction that last more than 24 hours (or lead to earlier death) and are caused by acute vascular injury to part of the brain" (Hankey & Blacker, 2015, p. 1, based on Warlow et al., 2008, p. 39). The causative injury is either ischemia (the vast majority of cases) or hemorrhage within the vascular supply of the brain. In either case, affected brain areas are deprived of adequate oxygen delivery, leading to neurological impairment. This impairment may be temporary or permanent in duration and focal or global in terms of extent. A CVA may be immediately fatal if the vascular insult is severe. In other cases, it can produce a sudden, severe headache and neurological symptoms related to the affected area of the brain. These can include paralysis (which may be limited to one side of the body only), visual problems, and speech difficulties (e.g., slurring of words). Neuropsychiatric problems involving cognitive, behavioral, and personality disturbances can also occur (Chemerinski & Robinson, 2000) as can almost any other neurological symptom.

Diagnosis of a stroke leads to an immediate and extended period of grounding (at least 12 months). Aeromedical certification is generally not considered until after this period of grounding and the individual has recovered to a stable end point. The period of grounding can be significant, depending on the speed and extent of recovery. The certification decision is then based on a thorough evaluation and risk assessment of the affected individual, to determine the extent of neurological damage present (if any), the risk of any recurrence, and the risk of epilepsy. The treatment used for a CVA can complicate this decision – neurosurgical intervention to clip a bleeding aneurysm or to evacuate a blood clot in order to relieve pressure on the brain increases the risk of postevent epilepsy.

Where the CVA was caused by other conditions, such as diabetes mellitus or cardiovascular disease (e.g., atherosclerosis or atrial fibrillation), the aeromedical certification decision may be based on the extent of the precipitating disease as well as any functional impairment from the CVA. Indeed, in the case of severe cardiovascular disease the aeromedical risk associated with this may be much more significant.

Degenerative Illnesses

By their very nature, degenerative neurological diseases are problematic for ongoing aeromedical certification. They are typically associated with a progressively worsening clinical picture. However, the rate at which a given individual's disease will progress varies widely, making a case-by-case decision in relation to aeromedical certification a much fairer and defensible approach.

There are many different types of degenerative neurological diseases, but for the purposes of this chapter two relatively common ones will be considered – Parkinson's disease and multiple sclerosis.

Parkinson's disease is a slowly progressive neurodegenerative condition affecting specific areas of the brain involved with motor control. The disease manifests in movement and gait disorders, with tremors, rigidity, bradykinesia (slow movements), and even akinesia (inability to move). Soft speech (hypophonia) is a common presentation. Many nonmotor symptoms are also often present, including neurobehavioral disorders, cognitive disturbances, and even dysfunction of the autonomic nervous system leading to postural hypotension (Beitz, 2014; Bloem et al., 2021). Some individuals may experience anxiety and depression related to the diagnosis and the impact it has on their daily lives and employment. Treatments are available and are variably effective. However, they do tend to have side effects that are in general incompatible with aeromedical certification.

An applicant for an initial pilot certification who has Parkinson's disease will not typically be certified. Where a pilot develops Parkinson's, a careful clinical neurological evaluation will be required. Any cognitive dysfunction, motor control deficits, or tremor will make aircraft control problematic, thus representing a potential flight safety hazard.

The slowly progressive nature of the condition means that any aeromedical certification granted will most likely be removed at some point in the future. Typically, pilots with mild symptoms that are considered aeromedically acceptable may be given certification to fly, but with a multi-crew limitation and more frequent review by a neurologist and the aviation medicine specialists at the national regulatory authority. A low dose of some medications may also be considered acceptable, but with regular review. Aeromedical certification is often made on a case-by-case basis, given the wide variation in symptom expression and disease progression with this condition.

Multiple sclerosis (MS) is a chronic autoimmune disease that leads to demyelination of nerve cells in the central nervous system. It is a complex illness with an uncertain cause and no known cure, although available treatments can lead to variable degrees of symptom improvement (Dobson & Giovannoni, 2019). It is an unpredictable disease that affects individuals differently. It is typically diagnosed on the basis of at least two clinical episodes separated in time and location. The symptoms of MS are highly variable, with almost all neurological functions potentially affected. Symptoms include motor control issues, weakness and fatigue, eye problems such as optic neuritis and internuclear ophthalmoplegia (disordered conjugate gaze), sensory disturbances, vertigo, cognitive impairment, and mood disorders (McGinley et al., 2021). There can be worsening of symptoms with exercise or heat, known as Uhthoff's phenomenon (Frohman et al., 2013).

In general, a diagnosis of MS is incompatible with certification. However, depending on the nature of the illness in a given individual, particularly where the disease symptoms are mild and infrequent, with periods of remission, certification may be possible. Several cases have been published with successful return to flying albeit with operational restrictions (Belletrutti et al., 2004; Zinger et al., 2011). The process is complicated, and for a Class 1 pilot requires regular specialist medical surveillance and simulator proficiency checks as well as possible certification restrictions to multi-crew only. In the event of any clinical deterioration, certification is likely to be revoked.

Neuropathies

There are several different types of neuropathy, but the more common form is peripheral neuropathy. This is nerve damage affecting nerves outside the brain. Symptoms can be varied but may involve sensory changes (e.g., pain, pins and needles), muscle weakness, and limitations on the range of movement of an affected limb. From an aeromedical perspective, the issues relate to the symptoms experienced, their severity, and the degree of any functional impairment, but also to the nature of the underlying cause. Fitness to fly will be based on a careful consideration of these aspects.

Peripheral neuropathy can be due to a number of underlying problems. These include diabetes, injury, infection, vitamin deficiency (especially B_{12}), alcohol use, or the effect of some toxins. Degenerative changes in the spine, particularly the cervical and lumbar regions, can lead to peripheral nerve impingement. Neck injuries due to repetitive +Gz force exposure are a frequent problem in pilots of high-performance aircraft (Newman, 2017). These injuries can lead to a neuropathy, with pain and restricted movement that makes ongoing exposure to that environment problematic without definitive treatment.

Where a causative problem has been identified, definitive treatment may relieve the neuropathy and allow unrestricted aeromedical certification. If the cause relates to a significant issue such as diabetes or alcohol abuse, the aeromedical certification decision will be driven largely by the considerations relevant to the underlying cause. Degenerative spinal column changes brought on by osteoarthritis, intervertebral disc prolapse, or acute injury may require surgical intervention to relieve pressure on the affected nerves. Where this is successful, and no functional impairment remains, full aeromedical certification can be expected. The Royal Australian Air Force published a case study dealing with cervical intervertebral disc protrusion in the pilot of an F-111C aircraft, which led to significant right arm neurological symptoms. Following successful treatment, he was allowed to return to fast jet flying (Newman, 1996).

Effects of Aging

Cognitive aging is a fact of life. It is associated with multiple symptoms and signs. These include a decline in fluid intelligence (e.g., adaptive thinking, critical reasoning), slower information processing, memory impairment, visual ability deterioration (affecting visual acuity, color discrimination, and depth perception), and hearing impairment. Cognitive ability is, as we have seen, crucial for pilots. Uneventful, routine flight operations might be fine, but what about a sudden time-critical emergency?

There is a fundamental trade-off between the adverse effects of aging and the operational benefits of years of experience. Everyone of course ages in different ways and at different rates. The level of visual, cognitive, and psychomotor impairment that precludes safe aircraft operation can be readily determined in pilots using either an actual flight test or a flight simulator, where their performance against a known proficiency standard is measured.

In any discussion of the neurological effects of aging, dementia must be considered. Dementia is a neurological condition whose prevalence increases with advancing age. There are many types of dementia, including Alzheimer's disease and vascular dementia. Dementia may sometimes be secondary to other pathologies, which when treated can often lead to full recovery of cognitive function. Signs and symptoms include memory loss; behavioral changes; difficulties with planning, judgment, and problem solving; and behavioral changes. The performance decrements associated with early dementia might not be recognized by a pilot, and indeed may not manifest themselves in activities of daily living, but can become of critical significance to flight safety. Symptoms of dementia, such as cognitive deficits and behavioral disturbances, can be unpredictable. Where symptoms are severe enough that they impact on normal function, disqualification from pilot or air traffic control duties can be considered an inevitable outcome.

Conclusion

Neurological conditions can lead to significant functional impairment in pilots and air traffic controllers. Careful assessment and evaluation of the condition in a pilot is essential to making an appropriate decision in relation to aeromedical certification. The nature, extent, and progression of any functional impairment is a key element in this decision. Where necessary, the use of an actual aircraft flight test or flight simulator assessment can determine performance against known proficiency standards and help lend weight to any aeromedical certification decision. In most cases, expert neurological opinion and aviation medicine assessment will be needed. It is not always possible to allow pilots and air traffic controllers to continue to exercise the privileges of their license, due to the impairments associated with some serious neurological conditions. However, accurate assessment, careful evaluation, and regular medical surveillance can permit many of them to regain certification, even with some operational restrictions.

References

Annegers, J.F., & Coan, S.P. (2000). The risks of epilepsy after traumatic brain injury. *Seizure, 9*(7), 453–457. https://doi.org/10.1053/seiz.2000.0458

Beitz, J.M. (2014). Parkinson's disease: A review. *Frontiers in Bioscience-Scholar, 6*(1), 65–74. https://doi.org/10.2741/S415

Belletrutti, P.J., Courchesne, C.E., & Gray, G.W. (2004). Seizure as the manifestation of relapse of multiple sclerosis in a military pilot. *Aviation Space and Environmental Medicine, 75*(4), 367–369.

Berg, A.T. (2008). Risk of recurrence after a first unprovoked seizure. *Epilepsia, 49*, 13–18. https://doi.org/10.1111/j.1528-1167.2008.01444.x

Bloem, B.R., Okun, M.S., & Klein, C. (2021). Parkinson's disease. *The Lancet, 397*(10291), 2284–2303. https://doi.org/10.1016/S0140-6736(21)00218-X

Bullmore, E., & Sporns, O. (2012). The economy of brain network organization. *Nature Reviews Neuroscience, 13*(5), 336–349. https://doi.org/10.1038/nrn3214

Chemerinski, E., & Robinson, R.G. (2000). The neuropsychiatry of stroke. *Psychosomatics, 41*(1), 5–14. https://doi.org/10.1016/S0033-3182(00)71168-6

Clark, D.D., & Sokoloff, L. (1999). Circulation and energy metabolism of the brain. In G.J. Siegel, B.W. Agranoff, R.W. Albers, S.K. Fisher, & M.D. Uhler (Eds.), *Basic neurochemistry: Molecular, cellular and medical aspects* (pp. 637–670). Lippincott.

DeJohn, C.A., Wolbrink, A.M., & Larcher, J.G. (2006). In-flight medical incapacitation and impairment of airline pilots. *Aviation Space and Environmental Medicine, 77*(10), 1077–1079.

Dobson, R., & Giovannoni, G. (2019). Multiple sclerosis – a review. *European Journal of Neurology, 26*(1), 27–40. https://doi.org/10.1111/ene.13819

Evans, S., & Radcliffe, S.A. (2012). The annual incapacitation rate of commercial pilots. *Aviation Space and Environmental Medicine, 83*(1), 42–49. https://doi.org/10.3357/ASEM.3134.2012

Ferrari, M.D., Goadsby, P.J., Burstein, R., Kurth, T., Ayata, C., Charles, A., Ashina, M., Van Den Maagdenberg, A.M.J.M., & Dodick, D.W. (2022). Migraine. *Nature Reviews Disease Primers, 8*(1), 1–20. https://doi.org/10.1038/s41572-021-00328-4

Fiedler, E.R., Orme, D.R., Millis, W., & Patterson, J.C. (2001). *Assessment of head-injured aircrew: Comparison of FAA and USAF procedures* (No. DOT/FAA/AM-01/11). United States Department of Transportation, Federal Aviation Administration. https://rosap.ntl.bts.gov/view/dot/40330

Foy, P.M., Copeland, G.P., & Shaw, M.D. M. (1981). The incidence of postoperative seizures. *Acta Neurochirurgica, 55*, 253–264. https://doi.org/10.1007/BF01808441

Frohman, T.C., Davis, S.L., Beh, S., Greenberg, B.M., Remington, G., & Frohman, E.M. (2013). Uhthoff's phenomena in MS – clinical features and pathophysiology. *Nature Reviews Neurology, 9*(9), 535–540. https://doi.org/10.1038/nrneurol.2013.98

Goadsby, P.J., Lipton, R.B., & Ferrari, M.D. (2002). Migraine – current understanding and treatment. *New England Journal of Medicine, 346*(4), 257–270. https://doi.org/10.1056/NEJMra010917

Hankey, G., & Blacker, D. (2015). Is it a stroke? *BMJ, 350*, Article h56. https://doi.org/10.1136/bmj.h56

Hastings, J. (2022). The evaluation of traumatic brain injury: A call to action. *Aerospace Medicine and Human Performance, 93*(10), 758–759. https://doi.org/10.3357/AMHP.6090.2022

James, M., & Green, R. (1991). Airline pilot incapacitation survey. *Aviation Space and Environmental Medicine, 62*(11), 1068–1072.

McGinley, M.P., Goldschmidt, C.H., & Rae-Grant, A.D. (2021). Diagnosis and treatment of multiple sclerosis: A review. *JAMA, 325*(8), 765–779. https://doi.org/10.1001/jama.2020.26858

Martin-Saint-Laurent, A., Lavernhe, J., Casano, G., & Simkoff, A. (1990). Clinical aspects of inflight incapacitations in commercial aviation. *Aviation Space and Environmental Medicine, 61*(3), 256 260.

Mitchell, S.J., & Evans, A.D. (2004). Flight safety and medical incapacitation risk of airline pilots. *Aviation Space and Environmental Medicine, 75*(3), 260–268.

Newman, D.G. (1996). Cervical intervertebral disc protrusion in an RAAF F-111C pilot: A case report. *Aviation Space and Environmental Medicine, 67*(4), 351–353.

Newman, D.G. (2007). *Pilot incapacitation: Analysis of medical conditions affecting pilots involved in accidents and incidents.* Australian Transport Safety Bureau.

Newman, D.G. (2017). *Flying fast jets: Human factors and performance limitations.* CRC Press. https://doi.org/10.1201/9781315582542

Raichle, M.E., & Gusnard, D.A. (2002). Appraising the brain's energy budget. *Proceedings of the National Academy of Sciences, 99*(16), 10237–10239. https://doi.org/10.1073/pnas.172399499

Rasmussen, B.K., & Olesen, J. (1992). Migraine with aura and migraine without aura: An epidemiological study. *Cephalalgia, 12*(4), 221–228. https://doi.org/10.1046/j.1468-2982.1992.1204221.x

Verde, P., Guadagno, A.G., D'Angelo, A., Vitalone, R., Di Vita, A., & Piccardi, L. (2022). A controversial assessment of fitness to fly after a traumatic brain injury. *Aerospace Medicine and Human Performance, 93*(2), 116–122. https://doi.org/10.3357/AMHP.5978.2022

Verellen, R.M., & Cavazos, J.E. (2010). Post-traumatic epilepsy: An overview. *Therapy, 7*(5), 527. https://doi.org/10.2217/thy.10.57

Warlow, C.P., Van Gijn, J., Dennis, M.S., Wardlaw, J.M., Bamford, J.M., Hankey, G.J., Sandercock, P.A., Rinkel, G., Langhorne, P., Sudlow, C., & Rothwell, P. (2008). *Stroke: Practical management* (3rd ed.). Blackwell Publishing. https://doi.org/10.1002/9780470696361.ch3

Zinger, H., Grossman, A., Assa, A., Barel, O., Barenboim, E., & Levite, R. (2011). Return to flight with multiple sclerosis: Aeromedical considerations. *Aviation Space and Environmental Medicine, 82*(1), 61–64. https://doi.org/10.3357/ASEM.2774.2011

Chapter 4
Neuropsychology's Role in Personnel Selection

Raymond E. King and Thomas R. Carretta

Introduction

Does neuropsychology have a role in personnel selection? Neuropsychology is, after all, typically considered to be in the medical realm rather than a part of industrial/organizational psychology. Let us consider the flavors of selection. In selection, an organization can employ one of two (or both) strategies. The focus can be *select out* – which can be a medical function. Here the goal is to eliminate candidates (1) do not have the minimal knowledge, skills, or abilities deemed necessary to perform or learn the task, (2) have a personality profile indicative of poor person-job fit or likelihood to engage in counterproductive work behaviors, or (3) a neuropsychological disability, such as attention-deficit/hyperactivity disorder or autistic spectrum disorder, as described by the *Diagnostic and Statistical Manual of Mental Disorders, Fifth Edition, Text Revision* (American Psychiatric Association, 2022). Disqualifying conditions are listed in Federal Aviation Administration (FAA) Order 3930.3C (Air Traffic Control Specialist Health Program) for FAA air traffic control specialists and Medical Standards and Certification (FAR Part 67) for aviators (pilots and contract controllers).

The other approach is *select in*. Here the goal is to identify the aptitude requirements for a particular job, rank order candidates from highest to lowest based on aptitude, then use top-down selection until the desired number of applicants have been selected. The danger here is that too much of a good thing is not necessarily ideal. For example, an extremely bright candidate may become bored and find themself unfulfilled and eventually attrite. A better approach would be to recruit and select candidates whose aptitudes match job requirements (e.g., cognitive complexity, work preferences, physical requirements) to ensure good person-job fit. On the other hand, it is a good idea to recruit some high-aptitude candidates who are likely to learn quickly, get promoted steadily, and become leaders. In the United States, the select-in function must be performed first, in accordance with the Americans With Disabilities Act (Pub L. 101-336; ADA, 1990). It may also be a good idea to cognitively baseline newly hired employees when they are onboarded (King & Flynn, 1995; King et al., 2011). The purpose here is not selection, but rather to archive cognitive information for future cognitive assessments. As such, this information is in the medical realm and needs to be safeguarded under the Health Insurance Portability and Accountability Act (HIPPA; https://www.hhs.gov/hipaa/for-professionals/privacy/laws-regulations). Such safeguarding is also required under the Privacy Act of 1974 (1974; Public Law 93-579, as codified at 5 U.S.C. 552a). HIPPA applies to "defined entities," such as health plans, health care clearinghouses, and health care providers. So while an organization may not be a health organization and thus may not be covered by HIPPA, they still have an obligation to protect personally identifiable information.

In practice, some assessments serve both a select-out and select-in function (e.g., Armed Services Vocational Aptitude Battery [ASVAB]). The Armed Forces Qualification Test (AFQT) is a composite of the ASVAB verbal and math subtests. The AFQT has been shown to be a measure of premorbid intelligence, demonstrating a correlation of .66 with the Multidimensional Aptitude Battery full-scale IQ composite (Orme, Brehm, & Ree, 2001). The Department of Defense has set a minimum qualifying score of the ninth percentile for enlistment eligibility (United States Department of Defense, 2015). In practice, each US military service sets its own AFQT minimum (the Air Force and Navy use AFQT ≥ 31). Each service also sets minimum aptitude requirements for each training specialty using composites of ASVAB subtests. The content of the composites and minimum requirements are based on job analyses of the training courses (i.e., course content and cognitive complexity).

Murphy (2019) notes that cognitive ability tests are used in high-stakes situations, including personnel selection. The predictive utility of these tests is largely based on their measurement of general mental ability (*g*; see Gottfredson, 1997; Jensen, 1998; Murphy, 2019; Ree & Carretta, 2022). G is a general mental capability involving reasoning, abstract thinking, complex idea comprehension, planning, problem solving, and learning from experience (Gottfredson, 1997; Jensen, 1998). The widespread use of cognitive assessments in personnel selection is due to their demonstrated predictive utility for a variety of educational and occupational settings (Jensen, 1998; Makransky & Glas, 2013; Salgado et al., 2003). Morgan (2014) notes that it may be better to use tests that do not result in a single score, as adverse impact is reduced. Adverse impact is defined as a substantially different rate of selection in hiring, promotion, or other employment decision that works to the disadvantage of members of a race, sex, or ethnic group (EEOC Uniform Employee Selection Guidelines Questions and Answers; https://www.uniformguidelines.com). While multiple aptitude cognitive ability tests measure several specific domains (e.g., verbal, math, perceptual speed, spatial), most of the predictive utility comes from their measurement of *g* (Jensen, 1998; Ree & Carretta, 2022) as opposed to specific cognitive abilities. It may be best, however, to ensure that candidates meet minimum qualifications to satisfy requirements for an occupation and to be sure that a higher score on one area of functioning does not compensate for weaker abilities.

As noted above, in the United States, medical assessments, to include tests that ask questions about medical conditions, cannot be conducted until after a tentative job offer has been extended, in accordance with the Americans With Disabilities Act (ADA, 1990; Pub L. 101-336). Neuropsychology, however, is concerned with the cognitive functioning of an individual as well as other qualities that can be measured and compared with other individuals. Cognitive skills can be considered part of a medical assessment but can also be considered part of KSAOs, which comprise the factors considered in personnel selection, when they are relevant to the job at hand. Individuals obviously vary in their cognitive abilities and KSAOs. The measurement afforded by neuropsychology can gauge cognitive ability and other KSAOs in a job applicant. Thus, the skills of the neuropsychologist can be used to assess desirable qualities within the range of the normal (nonpathological) spectrum. Practitioners are cautioned, however, to be sure that the neurological instruments used for personnel selection are linked to the job-related tasks of the job at hand and provide fair discrimination between job candidates (American Psychological Association, 2018).

Setting an appropriate range of item difficulty for a cognitive assessment is critical to ensure its utility for the target population (i.e., discriminability). Little information about ability level is provided by very easy items, as nearly everyone answers the item correctly. If an item is very difficult, again it provides little information about relative aptitude, as nearly everyone answers it incorrectly. These situations would occur if a test designed for a general population with a wide range on the underlying ability were used in a targeted group that is well above or below the general population on the latent ability. An example is provided by Carretta et al. (2016), who examined cognitive performance for a large sample (N=25,514) of US Air Force pilot candidates who tested on the Multidimensional Aptitude Battery (MAB). The MAB is designed to be used in the broad adult population, where the full-scale composite has a mean of 100 and a standard deviation (*SD*) of 15. The mean and *SD* for the pilot candidate sample were 120 and 6.19, respectively. The pilot candidate mean was about 1.33 *SD*s above the adult population value and the variance was only about 17% that of the adult population. Thus, the MAB has less discriminability for the pilot sample than for the adult population, which will affect the psychometric properties of the scores including predictive validity (King et al., 2013). There are a couple of ways to address this situation. One would be to use a different test that is more appropriate for the target group. Another approach would be to develop sample-specific norms (Carretta et al., 2016) and perform corrective statistical procedures when conducting validation studies (e.g., corrections for reliability and range restriction of the scores; see Carretta & Ree, 2001).

Diversity and Inclusion

Adverse impact is a matter to always be considered and is defined as occurring when a selection process has a disproportionally negative effect in a protected group, even though the adverse impact may have been unintentional. The four-fifths rule is a statistical guideline established by the Equal Employment Opportunity Commission (1978) to measure adverse impact. The rule states that if the selection rate for a certain group is less than 80% of the group with the highest selection rate, there is adverse impact for that group. The rule applies to hiring, promotion, and other employment decisions that affect protected groups, such as ethnic groups, genders, age groups, and sexualities. The US Supreme Court (*Griggs v. Duke Power Co.*, 401 U.S. 424, 1971), ruled that under Title VII of the Civil Rights Act of 1964 (1964, Pub. L. 88-352) tests that disparately affect racial or ethnic minorities (protected groups) must be reasonably related to the job for which the test is required (i.e., demonstrate criterion-related validity). Protections based on gender are also afforded. The US military has launched several initiatives to qualify a larger more diverse pool of military applicants while maximizing prediction of training success. These initiatives are in line with the US Secretary of Defense (2020) recommendations on diversity and inclusion.

One way to deal with adverse impact is to use tests that consider more than cognitive abilities, such as situational judgment tests (Morgan, 2014) or personality tests (Shewach et al., 2023; Woolley et al., 2023). According to the US Office of Personnel Management (Situational Judgment Tests, https://www.opm.gov), "situational judgment tests (SJTs) present applicants with a description of a work problem or critical situation related to the job they are applying for and ask them to identify how they would handle it. SJTs are not the same as personality tests. SJTs can measure effectiveness in social functioning dimensions such as conflict management, cultural awareness, facilitating teamwork, interpersonal skills, negotiation skills, and problem solving. SJTs are particularly effective measures of managerial and leadership competencies."

The US Air Force is exploring the use of an SJT as a potential addition to the Air Force Officer Qualifying Test (Barron et al., 2021; Sizemore et al., 2022) to assess officership. SJTs are frequently used to assess complex relational skills, such as interpersonal skills and leadership (e.g., Christian et al., 2010). See Sullivan et al. (2019) for a discussion of best practices in SJT development.

Because applicants are not placed in a simulated work setting and are not asked to perform the task or behavior (as would be the case in an assessment center or a work sample), SJTs are classified as low-fidelity simulations. Regardless of what method is used, the practitioner should be able to demonstrate "business necessity," meaning that the measures used have a demonstrable correlation to the job-related tasks.

Shewach et al. (2023) examined the utility of predictive success models (PSMs) based on cognitive subtests and personality facets to qualify US Space Force enlisted and officer applicants for several training specialties. A Pareto optimization approach was used that optimally combined scores on a cognitive aptitude test (ASVAB for enlisted; Air Force Officer Qualifying Test [AFOQT] for officers) and personality assessment (Tailored Adaptive Personality Assessment System [TAPAS] for enlisted; Self-Description Inventory [SDI] for officers) to maximize training success and improve diversity. The PSMS for enlisted personnel demonstrated improvement in both predictive validity and qualification rates compared to cognitive (ASVAB-only) aptitude composites. The PSMs for officers demonstrated less improvement than those for the enlisted personnel. Woolley et al. (2023) used a regression-based approach to examine aptitude composites for officers attending aircrew training (piloted aircraft pilot, remotely piloted aircraft pilot, combat systems officer, and air battle manager). The models using both cognitive (AFOQT) and personality (SDI) scores showed modest increases in predictive validity over the baseline cognitive composites (AFOQT only). The impact on diversity and inclusion varied by career field and sometimes benefited one minority group (e.g., African Americans) but not another (e.g., women).

Population Versus Subgroup Norms

Another potential concern for neuropsychology when involved with personnel selection is the use of population versus subgroup norms (e.g., age-related norms, race, gender). There is a saying in aviation (the attribution of this common wisdom is not known): "There are no age-adjusted runways!" While age-related norms are typical in neuropsychology, such a practice could run afoul of the Age Discrimination in Employment Act of 1967 (ADEA; Pub. L. 90–202), which prohibits age discrimination in hiring, promotion, and other human relations practices in the United States and applies to those over 40 years of age and employers who employ at least 20 employees. The ADEA was subsequently amended in 1986 (Age Discrimination in Employment Amendments of 1986, Pub. L. 99–592) and specifically exempted firefighters and law enforcement officers. The best defense under ADEA is to use age-related norms when there is a bona fide occupational qualification. Matters of mandatory retirement ages are not addressed in this chapter, as the focus of this chapter is personnel selection. Readers interested in the aging aviator are referred to Georgemiller (2013).

When dealing with the assessment of cognitive abilities for personnel selection, the assessing psychologist is afforded the luxury of being unconcerned with positive impression management. A person either has the ability or does not. The test-taker is motived to do the best that their cognitive ability allows them to do. This is a case where the goal is to have the job candidate put their best foot forward. What about negative impression management? Unlike clinical neuropsychology, which sometimes deals with individuals who are invested in being seen as having a disability, in the personnel selection realm we can only assume that the person wants to be seen as competent. Typically, a test-taker is not motivated to feign incompetence, unless the goal is to *not* get selected for an occupational opportunity. On the other hand, examinees may engage, either purposely or inadvertently, in careless responding on all or portions of a test. For example, someone who takes the AFOQT to get commissioned but is not interested in applying for aircrew training may try to perform well on the officer commissioning subtests but put little effort into the aircrew-related subtests. Another example could be US Air Force officers taking the MAB during medical flight screening. Since they have already been selected for training, some examinees may put little effort into doing well on the test. There may even be an attempt to do poorly with the objective of appearing less impaired during a future assessment.

What about strategies that give an unfair advantage, commonly termed "cheating?" These strategies include practice and coaching schemes, especially when these opportunities are not available to the entire pool of candidates. While it is encouraging that a candidate would put forth the effort to do better on an assessment and that superior motivation is desirable, the skills that are measured may not translate to the actual job (Heil et al., 2002) and not be indicative of the applicant's aptitude. Eyde et al. (2010) provide useful guidance for those who wish to provide assistance to test-takers. They advocate that those who administer tests provide guidance on what type of assistance is appropriate to familiarize test-takers with the questions they will be asked. During the actual testing session, they emphasize that test manuals must provide administration directions that are formally scripted and read to test-takers exactly as they appear.

Testing Methodology

There are two basic test designs – fixed form, or static testing, and adaptive. In a fixed-form test, every examinee receives the same items that can be delivered via paper or computer. In static testing, different versions of the test can be created to combat practice effects if re-testing is allowed. Computerized adaptive tests (CAT), on the other hand, are dynamic and use examinee response patterns to tailor the test content to match examinee latent ability level (Thissen, 2014). Adaptive testing has several advantages over static assessments. While the initial development costs are greater (e.g., development of large item banks, calibration of test items), in the long run it is more cost-effective especially if large numbers of assessments are to be performed (e.g., college entrance, military enlistment). Other benefits include reduction in test administration time, more precise measurement of aptitude, reduced threat of cheating since examinees do not receive the same items, and a better overall experience for the examinees. It should be noted that CAT has been applied to the assessment of personality with similar benefits of improved measurement, reduced test administration time, and lower susceptibility to faking than static tests (Drasgow et al., 2023; Stark et al., 2012).

These highly correlated cognitive domains (e.g., verbal, math, spatial, technical knowledge) are usually assessed one at a time. Braecken and Paap (2020) and Segall (2010) advocate for the use of multidimensional computerized adaptive testing (MCAT), which explores the relationships between the subdomains that are measured; it also affords the ability to have shorter tests with increased selection utility compared to more traditional testing methods.

Conclusion

Thus, it can be demonstrated that neuropsychology does indeed have a role in personnel selection. Tests that are based on neuropsychology can be used during both the select-in and select-out phases of assessment. The practitioner must be careful, however, to not assess medical conditions before a conditional job offer is extended, at least in the United States. Whenever possible, noncognitive assessments (e.g., situational judgment, personality, work interests) should be used to broaden the measurement of occupation-relevant KSAOs. In personnel selection, tests must be used that have a demonstrated relationship to the tasks of the job.

Acknowledgments

The views expressed are those of the authors and do not necessarily reflect those of the US Government, Federal Aviation Administration, Department of Defense, or Department of the Air Force. Send correspondence to the first author at skykingray321@gmail.com.

References

Age Discrimination in Employment Act of 1967. (1967). U.S. Equal Employment Opportunity Commission. https://www.eeoc.gov/laws/statutes/adea.cfm

Age Discrimination in Employment Amendments of 1986. (1986). U.S. Equal Employment Opportunity Commission. https://www.eeoc.gov/history/age-discrimination-employment-amendments-1986

American Psychiatric Association. (2022). *Diagnostic and statistical manual of mental disorders* (5th ed., text rev.).

American Psychological Association. (2018). *Principles for the validation and use of personnel selection procedures* (5th ed.). Society for Industrial and Organizational Psychology.

Americans With Disabilities Act of 1990, Pub. L. No. 101-336, 104 Stat. 328 (1990).

Barron, L.G., Aguilar, I.D., Rose, M.D., & Carretta, T.R. (2021). Development of a situational judgment test to supplement current US Air Force measures of officership. *Military Psychology, 36*(1), 33–48. https://doi.org/10.1080/08995605.2021.1997500

Braecken, J., & Paap, M.C.S. (2020). Making fixed-precision between-item multidimensional computerized adaptive tests even shorter by reducing the asymmetry between selection and stopping rules. *Applied Psychological Measurement, 44* (7–8), 531–547. https://doi.org/10.1177/0146621620932666

Carretta, T.R., King, R.E., Ree, M.J., Teachout, M.S., & Barto, E. (2016). Compilation of cognitive and personality norms for military aviators. *Aerospace Medicine and Human Performance, 87*, 764–771. https://doi.org/10.3357/AMHP.4545.2016

Carretta, T.R., & Ree, M.J. (2001). Pitfalls of ability research. *International Journal of Selection and Assessment, 9*, 325–335. https://doi.org/10.1111/1468-2389.00184

Christian, M.S., Edwards, B.D., & Bradley, J.C. (2010). Situational judgment tests: Constructs assessed and a meta-analysis of their criterion-related validities. *Personnel Psychology, 63*, 83–117. https://doi.org/10.1111/j.1744-6570.2009.01163.x

Civil Rights Act of 1964 § 7, 42 U.S.C. § 2000e et seq (1964).

Drasgow, F., Chernyshenko, O.S., Stark, S., & Nye, C.D. (2023). *Tailored Adaptive Personality Assessment System (TAPAS): Pre-implementation documentation* (AFRL-RH-WP-TR- 2023-0014). 711 Human Performance Wing, Airman Systems Directorate, Airman Biosciences Division, Performance Optimization Branch.

Equal Employment Opportunity Commission. (1978). *Uniform guidelines on employment selection procedures* (43FR; August 25, 1978). EEOC.

Eyde, L.D., Robertson, G.L., & Krug, S.E. (2010). *Responsible test use: Case studies for assessing human behavior* (2nd ed.). American Psychological Association.

Georgemiller, R. (2013). The aging aviator. In G.G. Kay & C.H. Kennedy (Eds.), *Aeromedical psychology* (pp 269–286). Ashgate.

Gottfredson, L.S. (1997). Why g matters: The complexity of everyday life. *Intelligence, 24,* 79–132. https://doi.org/10.1016/S0160-2896(97)90014-3

Griggs v. Duke Power Co., 401 U.S. 424 (1971).

Heil, M.C., Detwiler, C.A., Agen, R.A., Williams, C.A., Agnew, B.O., & King, R.E. (2002). *The effects of practice and coaching on the Air Traffic Selection and Training Battery* (DOT/FAA/AM-02/24). FAA Office of Aerospace Medicine.

Jensen, A.R. (1998). *The g factor.* Praeger.

King, R.E., Barto, E., Ree, M.J., Teachout, M.S., & Retzlaff, P. (2011). *Compilation of pilot cognitive ability norms* (AFRL-SA-WP-2012-0001). 711 Human Performance Wing, USAF School of Aerospace Medicine.

King, R.E., Carretta, T.R., Retzlaff, P.D., Barto, E., Ree, M.J., & Teachout, M.S. (2013). Standard cognitive psychological tests predict military pilot training outcomes. *Aviation Psychology and Applied Human Factors, 3,* 28–38. https://doi.org/10.1027/2192-0923/a000040

King, R.E., & Flynn, C.F. (1995). Defining and measuring the "right stuff:" Neuropsychiatrically Enhanced Flight Screening (N-EFS). *Aviation, Space, and Environmental Medicine, 66,* 951–956.

Makransky, G., & Glas, C.A.W. (2013). The applicability of multidimensional computerized adaptive testing for cognitive ability measurement in organization assessment. *International Journal of Testing, 13*(2), 123–139. https://doi.org/10.1080/15305058.2012.672352

Morgan, K.E. (2014). Rethinking intelligence tests: Using multidimensional item response theory to access ability. *Dissertation Abstracts International: Section B: The Sciences and Engineering, 76.*

Murphy, K.R. (2019). Cognitive ability: Psychometric perspectives on the important of general mental ability. In D.J. McFarland (Ed.), *General and specific mental abilities* (pp. 59–79). Cambridge Scholars Publishing.

Orme, D.R., Brehm, W., & Ree, M.J. (2001). Armed Forces Qualification Test as a measure of premorbid intelligence. *Military Psychology, 13,* 187–197. https://doi.org/10.1207/S15327876MP1304_1

Privacy Act of 1974, 5 U.S.C. 552a (1974).

Ree, M.J., & Carretta, T.R. (2022). Thirty years of research on general and specific abilities: Still not much more than g. *Intelligence, 91,* Article 101617. https://doi.org/10.1016/j.intell.2021.101617

Salgado, J.F., Anderson, N., Moscoso, S., Bertua, C., de Fruyt, F., & Rolland, J.P. (2003). A meta-analytic study of general mental ability validity for different occupations in the European community. *Journal of Applied Psychology, 88,* 1068–1081. https://doi.org/10.1037/0021-9010.88.6.1068

Segall, D.O. (2010). Principles of multidimensional adaptive testing. In W.J. van der Linden & C.A.W. Glas (Eds.), *Elements of adaptive testing* (pp. 57–75). Springer.

Shewach, O.R., Ingerich, M., Butterfuss, R., Gunther, K., Carretta, T.R., & Persing, K. (2023). *Optimizing qualification to US Space Force spacepower disciplines* (AFREL-RH-WP-TR-2023-0049). 711 Human Performance Wing, Airman Systems Directorate, Airman Biosciences Division, Performance Optimization Branch.

Sizemore, S.J., Wilson, R., Mann, K.J., & Carretta, T.R. (2022, December). *Air Force Officer Qualifying Test (AFOQT): Situational Judgment Test (SJT) revision* (AFRL-RH-WP-TR-2022-0076). 711 Human Performance Wing, Airman Biosciences Division, Performance Optimization Branch.

Stark, S., Chernyshenko, O.S., Drasgow, F., & White, L.A. (2012). Adaptive testing with multidimensional pairwise preference items: Improving the efficiency of personality an other noncognitive assessments. *Organizational Research Methods, 15,* 463–487. https://doi.org/10.1177/1094428112444611

Sullivan, T.S., Burgoyne, T.C., McCloy, R.A., & Whetzel, D.L. (2019). *Review of situational judgment test (SJT) prototype development process and materials* (AFRL-RH-WP-TR-2019-0018). 711 Human Performance Wing, Airman Systems Directorate, Warfighter Interface Division, Collaborative Interfaces and Teaming Branch.

Thissen, D. (Ed.) (2014). *Computerized adaptive testing: A primer* (2nd ed.). Routledge.
United States Department of Defense. (2015). *Qualification standards for enlistment, appointment and inclusion* (DODI 1304.26).
United States Secretary of Defense. (2020). *Memorandum for senior Pentagon leadership commanders of the Combatant Commands Defense Agency and Department of Defense (DoD) field activity directors.*
Woolley, M. R., Walsh, J. L., Carretta, T. R., Moulon, A. N., & Deregla, A. R. (2023). *Development and psychometric evaluation of predictive success models for US Air Force rated career fields* (AFRL-RH-WP-TR-2023-0007). 711 Human Performance Wing, Airman Systems Directorate, Airman Biosciences Division, Performance Optimization Branch.

Chapter 5
Principles and Practices in Military Aeromedical (Neuro)Psychology

Ryan Green and Forest Pavel

Introduction

In the complex environment of military aviation, where split-second decisions can influence mission success or mission failure, the significance of neurocognitive and psychological fitness cannot be overstated. The demanding and complex tasks faced by military aviation personnel often require levels of cognitive and psychological ability that exceed the demands placed on other military specialties. The high-stakes environment of aviation combat, aviation-based medical evacuation, and aviation-based logistical movements has solidified the pivotal role of the neuropsychologist in assessing the cognitive abilities and psychological well-being of military aviators, non-piloted aerial vehicle (UAV) operators, and those who operate as aviation ground support. Neuropsychological expertise in brain–behavior relationships is a critical cornerstone in ensuring the overall safety and success of aviation missions.

This chapter addresses the vital role played by neuropsychologists and how they interface with clinical psychologists in military aviation in the United States, where cognitive and psychological fitness are not merely desirable traits but absolute imperatives. As we navigate through the unique challenges of military aviation, we will explore how neuropsychologists contribute to aeromedical assessment, their role in fitness for duty determinations, and the challenges they face.

Basic Overview of Military Aviation Standards for Flight Duty

Before specifically addressing the neuropsychologist's role in military aviation, it is important to understand the context in which neuropsychologists operate in military aviation. A brief introduction to military aviation standards for flight duty and the associated governing documents will be given followed by a more detailed review of the aeromedical processes, procedures, and training programs for each branch of the United States Armed Forces. (For additional information about these topics, see Graver et al., 2020; Kennedy & Kay, 2013; and the *Med Standards* mobile application available on Android and Apple Doc Apps, LLC, 2016.)

To safeguard the physical and mental health of military aviation personnel and to help return them to duty when they fail to meet physical and mental health standards, the United States Military provides written guidelines for aeromedical providers. Although these guidelines are similar in many respects to those written for civilian flight standards codified in the United States by the Federal Aviation Administration (FAA), they also differ in many ways and are tailored to the unique needs of each branch of service. For example, The United States Army publishes aeromedical policy letters (APLs) and aeromedical technical bulletins (ATBs) to give:

> Aeromedical providers guidance in regards to examinations and procedures to determine the fitness for flying duties, and the interim aeromedical disposition of disqualifying conditions ... Policy letters recommend Army-wide standardization of aeromedical evaluation, treatment, and disposition for a variety of common clinical problems. They provide continuity of aeromedical care for aeromedical providers and aircrew members world-wide and ensure the optimum quality of care. They ensure the safe return of countless aircrew members to flying duties once effective treatment has been achieved ... Technical bulletins recommend Army-wide standardization of aeromedical testing and administration. They ensure consistency in the completion of administrative requirements and the proper use of testing equipment and testing procedures throughout the Army's medical system. (United States Army Aeromedical Activity, 2021, p. 2)

The United States Navy provides aeromedical guidance in the US Navy Aeromedical Reference and Waiver Guide (ARWG; United States Department of the Navy, 2023b). The introduction to the ARWG states:

> Aviation physical standards ensure the most qualified personnel are accepted and retained by Naval Aviation. The intent is to prevent medical, physical, or psychological conditions from adversely affecting flight performance, safety, or mission. Standards differ between applicants and designated personnel, and among different flying classes based on risk assessment. Applicant standards are the most rigorous to ensure candidates are capable of training completion and continued performance as a designated Naval Aviator in the demanding environment. Designated aviation standards ensure consistent flight performance, safety, and mission completion. Disqualification removes an individual based on risks associated with a medical condition, while waivers of policy allow retaining an individual based on careful risk assessment, risk control measures, and mission requirements. All conditions may be considered for waiver to preserve the aviator in the mission; however, certain conditions, treatments, and medications are generally not conducive to aviation service due to a likely adverse impact on health, safety, or mission completion. (Aviation Physical Standards – 1)

The United States Air Force provides aeromedical guidance in their Medical Standards Directory (MSD; United States Department of the Air Force, 2023b) and their Aerospace Medicine Waiver Guide (AMWG; United States Department of the Air Force, 2023a) stating:

> The Aerospace Medicine Waiver Guide provides guidance for waivers relating to flying class and special duty personnel medical standards ... [The AMWG provides] guidance to be used by flight surgeons for aeromedical decision-making. It does not replace individualized clinical judgment, nor does it limit options for aeromedical disposition. (MSD p. 1, AMWG PDF p. 2)

Although the different branches of the military have developed unique standards for their specific aeromedical needs as detailed below, they all generally include the following four areas:

1. **Medical Standards**
   Military aviation has stringent medical standards to assess an individual's physical health. These standards cover most aspects of medicine, including specific disorders in most medical specialties. Periodic aeromedical evaluations are conducted to assess an aviator's physical and mental fitness.

2. **Psychological/Psychiatric Standards**
   Military aviation also has stringent mental health standards that cover most psychological and psychiatric disorders. Psychological and psychiatric assessments are conducted to evaluate an individual's mental health and ensure they are mentally fit for aviation duties. These assessments may include tests for cognitive abilities, stress management, and overall psychological well-being. This includes strict rules governing substance and alcohol use, which can include regular toxicological testing to ensure that individuals involved in aviation duties are free from impairing substances.
3. **Duty Restrictions**
   Depending on physical/mental health diagnosis, treatment, and symptom presentation, duty restrictions may be imposed on individuals. For example, an aviator may be restricted from certain types of flights or duties based on their medical or psychological status (e.g., may include complete grounding from flight duty or restriction to simulator flight until full fitness for duty can be achieved).
4. **Waivers and Exceptions to Policy**
   In some cases, depending on the severity/nature of the condition and specific aviation specialty, waivers may be granted for specific medical or psychological conditions that are otherwise disqualifying for aviation duty. These waivers can be granted on a case-by-case basis often after multiple echelons of review have been undertaken to consider the risks and likelihood of flight safety (e.g., medical provider review, board/panel review, approval authority review). In the parlance of the FAA, these waivers would be akin to special issuances.

Specific Review of Aeromedical Processes, Procedures, and Training Programs

United States Air Force

The United States Air Force (USAF) developed the first formalized training program focusing on collaboration between psychologists and flight surgeons in 1985 (Saitzyk et al., 2013; Saitzyk et al., 2017). This program formalized a model where the two clinical fields supported each other in maintaining safe flying operations, and enabled Air Force psychologists to be placed at most Air Force bases. The Air Force subsequently created a course of training specific for the education of aeromedical psychologists. Unfortunately, this program was terminated only 2 years later in 1987, leading to Air Force embedded aeromedical psychologists being much less utilized over the next few decades.

Following 20 years of continuous combat vis-à-vis the Global War on Terror, and a recognition that Air Force aviation personnel need, yet have by and large been avoiding, mental health care (Tirpak, 2023), the United States Air Force has once again recognized the need for trained aeromedical psychologists and the importance of their role as embedded aviation health assets (Hoffman et al., 2022; Lee, 2022; Reichhardt, 2009; Roza, 2023). Currently there are three methods by which Air Force psychologists and neuropsychologists may be recognized as aeromedical psychologists (Saitzyk et al., 2013; Saitzyk et al., 2017; Wright, 2022).

The first path to becoming an Air Force aeromedical psychologist requires on-the-job training, which is fulfilled through a (generally) 3-year tour of duty with the Air Force's Aeromedical Consultation Service at the USAF School of Aviation Medicine (USAFSAM), USAF Special Operations Command, or other designated position that the Air Force deems qualifying. The second path involves completion of a competitive year-long Aviation Psychology Fellowship conducted through the Air Force Institute of Technology. This fellowship, started in 2013, accepts no more than two applicants per year and has a primary focus on human factors and error analysis in the prevention of aviation mishaps. The third path is through attending the Aviation Psychology Introductory Course (APIC). The APIC was launched in 2022 to expand the pool of trained aeromedical psychologists serving in the Air Force. The course is held at Columbus Air Force Base in Mississippi and comprises 14 days of training focused on understanding behavioral factors involved in aviation, associated human factors, and orientation to aviation culture. The APIC provides a similar experience as the United States Army Aeromedical Psychology Training Course (APTC), which was initiated when the Air Force discontinued its initial course in 1987.

All three paths to becoming an Air Force aeromedical psychologist provide a thorough background on the service's psychological standards, disqualifying conditions, and waiver process. The United States Air Force regulates these medical certification standards and processes through the *Department of the Air Force Manual* (DAFMAN; United States Department of the Air Force, 2020) 48-123, Medical Examinations and Standards, which is further supplemented by the Medical Standards Directory (MSD; United States Department of the Air Force, 2023b) and the Aerospace Medicine Waiver Guide (AMWG; United States Department of the Air Force, 2023a).

The DAFMAN 48-123 outlines overall medical standards for the Air Force, and provides specific guidance regarding the jobs that various flying classes fall under (see Table 5.1 for an organizational breakdown of all flying classes). The MSD provides guidance on what standards apply for each flying class and for which specific conditions (including Section Q: psychiatric, and Section L: neurologic conditions). The AMWG provides specific guidance on the waiver submission process and evaluative procedures for each delineated condition. Several medical conditions necessitate neuropsychological evaluation (such as multiple sclerosis, traumatic brain injury [TBI], and stroke) with a stipulation that the Aeromedical Consultation Service (ACS) Neuropsychology at USAFSAM needs to be contacted for guidance on what tests should comprise the test battery. Psychiatric conditions listed in the AMWG include specific guidance on what must be submitted as part of the waiver consideration and submission process, the period of clinical stability required prior to waiver consideration, records that must be reviewed, laboratory test results, commander's letter of endorsement, flight surgeon aeromedical summary (AMS), and mental health evaluation by a doctoral-level provider. Evaluation by a psychiatrist is preferred if the aviation asset is taking psychotropic medication (certain psychotropic medications as monotherapies have been allowed since 2013; Celexa, Lexapro, Prozac, Wellbutrin SR/XL, and Zoloft depending on the condition). Some conditions require psychological or neuropsychological evaluation, and a list of specific tests required or recommended are provided by ACS. The AMWG indicates that consultation with ACS psychiatry and neuropsychology is recommended if clarification is needed on the waiver process, and should be utilized if specific tests are unavailable by the evaluating psychologist or neuropsychologist.

Air Force operational needs, often requiring shortened timeframes, dictate much of the decision-making when it comes to balancing aeromedical risk, aviation safety, and mission requirements. When these needs are combined with the limited number of neuropsychologists in military service, and a small pool of trained aeromedical psychologists/neuropsychologists, the Air Force realized that forcing aviation personnel to undergo evaluation only by aeromedically trained (neuro)psychologists created an untenable backlog of grounded personnel. Therefore, balancing mission needs, and aeromedical safety, resulted in the Air Force allowing non-aeromedically trained psychologists/neuropsychologists and psychiatrists to perform psychiatric waiver evaluations, albeit with appropriate consultation from the ACS.

United States Space Force

Established in December 2019, the United States Space Force (USSF) is the newest component of the United States Armed Forces. As of November 2023, the United States Space Force remains part of the Department of the Air Force, in a similar fashion to how the United States Marine Corps falls under the Department of the Navy (United Sates Space Force, n.d.). Due to this organizational structure, Air Force Medical Standards Directory and Aerospace Medicine Waiver Guide are applied to Space Force personnel, including those pertaining to the psychological and neuropsychological evaluation of personnel who operate in the aerospace environment. Additionally, as with all military personnel who seek to become manned astronauts, NASA Spaceflight Human–System Standards may also apply to Space Force Astronauts (NASA 2023a, 2023b).

United States Army

Following the closure of the Air Force's first aeromedical psychology training program in 1987, the Army took the concept of the course and started implementing it at Fort Novosel (formerly Fort Rucker), AL. The course now known as the Aeromedical Psychology Training Course (APTC) was trialed in 1992 before becoming formalized in 1998 (Bowles, 1994; Saitzyk, et al., 2017). The APTC is a 3-week course comprising "topics in clinical aviation psychology, flight safety, aerospace physiology, and aviation medicine," with a "curriculum focused on aviation psychology, assessment and treatment of aviators, and the medical waiver and review process" (Durham, 2021, p. 1). Most Army psychology students completing predoctoral clinical psychology internships and postdoctoral clinical psychology residency programs are provided with opportunities to attend the APTC. All Army psychologists who primarily work in aviation at one of the 12 combat aviation brigades, or in special operations organizations, must attend this course. Psychologists from all other branches of the US Armed Forces may attend this course to gain formalized training in aeromedical psychology; however, spaces in the course are limited. The APTC is offered twice per year and graduates between 20 and 25 students per iteration. Following completion of the course, Army uniformed psychologists receive the N7 Additional Skill Identifier (ASI), denoting them as aeromedical psychologists. Uniformed providers who complete the course, and are assigned to an aviation unit while on flight status, may earn the Army Aviation Badge (formerly Army Aircrew Wings), in accordance with Army Regulation (AR) 600-8-22, Military Awards (US Department of the Army, 2019a). Completion of this course is required for credentialing an Army psychologist to perform aeromedical psychological evaluations. A majority of all uniformed Army psychologists and neuropsychologists complete this course, in addition to uniformed and civilian counterparts in sister services, resulting in the bulk of all formally trained military aeromedical psychologists being APTC graduates.

Similar to other uniformed services, the Army applies both general and specific medical standards to Army aviation personnel. Basic medical standards for fitness, as well as general guidance on medical fitness for aviation personnel, are provisioned by AR 40-501, Standards of Medical Fitness, AR 40-8, Temporary Flying Restrictions due to Exogenous Factors Affecting Aircrew Efficiency, AR600-106, Flying Status for Nonrated Army Aviation Personnel, AR 600-105, Aviation service of Rated Army Officers (US Department of the Army, 2019b; US Department of the Army, 2020; US Department of the Army, 2022a; US Department of the Army, 2022b). Chapter 4 of AR 40-501, Medical Fitness Standards for Flying Duty, provides definitions for the various flight classes as well as conditions that are disqualifying for flight duties. As noted above, the APLs and ATBs (2021), published by the US Aeromedical Activity (USAAMA) at Fort Novosel, AL, "recommend Army-wide standardization of aeromedical evaluation, treatment, and disposition for a variety of common clinical problems ... [that] ensure the safe return of countless aircrew members to flying duties once effective treatment has been achieved" (United States Army Aeromedical Activity, 2021, p. 2).

The waiver process is initiated when an aviation asset is requesting initial flight status or resumption of flight status after a medically disqualifying condition (psychiatric, neurologic, or otherwise) is discovered. The Army defines approval for Class 1 flight status after a disqualifying medical condition is discovered to be an "exception to policy," and reserves the term "waiver" for all other flight classes. While the terms are colloquially interchangeable, it is important for a psychologist/neuropsychologist to recognize the difference when working with Army aviation assets and flight surgeons.

The APLs for various conditions may prescribe psychological or neuropsychological evaluation as part of a packet for consideration of medically approved flight status. Some conditions require a neuropsychological evaluation, whereas most do not. Similar to the Air Force, the Army also allows aviators to fly while taking certain psychotropic medication (e.g., monotherapy for treatment of mood or anxiety conditions with selective serotonin reuptake inhibitor [SSRI]/serotonin-norepinephrine reuptake inhibitor [SNRI] medication, with possible adjunctive Bupropion to combat psychosexual side effects; non-stimulant psychotropic medication for treatment of attention-deficit/hyperactivity disorder [ADHD], such as Atomoxetine or Bupropion) if on a stable dose for approved period of time, symptoms are well managed with the medication, and other waiver conditions are met.

Where the Army differs greatly, is that APLs rarely dictate specific psychological/neuropsychological tests, and at most may provide guidance on broad categories of tests that can be utilized in an aeromedical psychological evaluation (i.e., requiring continuous performance testing for ADHD vs. stipulating a Conners Continuous Performance Test 3rd Edition (CPT-3) over a Test of Variables of Attention (TOVA), or indicating personality testing is required without providing guidance on which test to utilize). This occurs, in large part, because Army psychologists do not have access to a standardized test battery at all duty stations. Many Army psychologists are forced to work within the confines of limited access to psychological tests. They must tolerate onerous processes for obtaining new testing supplies and materials, and institutional difficulties in installing testing software on government computers. Furthermore, given that regulations necessitate that an aviator is formally terminated from flight duties after 1 year of grounding, psychological/neuropsychological evaluations may be completed with limited resources in order to meet mission needs. Mission needs within the Army, like all the other Armed Forces, dictate a balance between aeromedical safety and application of gold standard best practices.

Furthermore, while neuropsychological testing may be recommended or required for a given aeromedical psychological evaluation, the Army does not require in all instances that the neuropsychological testing must be done by a neuropsychologist. Understanding that the

Army lacks a large number of neuropsychologists, they have reasonably allowed clinical/counseling psychologists who are trained to administer neuropsychological tests to utilize those measures in aeromedical psychological evaluations. The Army requires that clinical/counseling psychologists seek consultation and supervision from a neuropsychologist if they are unfamiliar with these tests and defer to ethical standards of performing within one's comfort zone when engaging in less familiar practices during times of need (American Psychological Association, 2017).

United States Navy

The United States Navy differs from the Air Force and the Army in that they do not have a training program with a specific goal toward psychological assessment of aviation personnel for medical certification. Those who desire to become Navy Aerospace Clinical Psychologists can, however, attend the same 6-month training as Aerospace Experimental Psychologists (AEP), and earn their "wings of gold" (Saitzyk, et al., 2017).

Navy AEPs are commissioned officers who are master's-level or PhD scientists with expertise in human factors and the behavioral sciences. Until 2008, AEPs were drawn from those with a focus in "non-clinical areas of psychology such as cognitive, experimental, and industrial/organizational psychology, neuroscience, or an interdisciplinary program emphasizing human factors or behavioral science" (Naval Aerospace Experimental Psychology, 2023). Training consists of 6 weeks of introductory flight training, 10 weeks of fixed wing flight training, 10 weeks of advanced rotary flight training, and 6 weeks of aeromedical officer training. During the aeromedical officer training phase, psychologists develop skills in aerospace psychology, with an emphasis on those "pertinent to the aviation environment: vision, human performance, human factors engineering, research and development, test and evaluation techniques, training systems, systems acquisition, and human research requirements" (Naval Aerospace Experimental Psychology, 2023).

Prior to 2008, only neuropsychologists (civilian and uniformed) assigned to the Naval Aviation Medical Institute (NAMI) leveraged institutional and experiential knowledge in their role as consultants on aeromedical psychological evaluation and waiver recommendation. NAMI psychologists either conducted evaluations themselves or provided supervision and consultation to fleet psychologists and psychiatrists who provided the actual evaluations in accordance with the US Navy ARWG.

In 2008, the Navy accepted its first clinical neuropsychologist as an AEP. Over the next 15 years, the Navy graduated a total of four clinical psychologists as AEPs (Naval Aerospace Experimental Psychology, 2023), and formally designated them as *Navy aerospace clinical psychologists*. This comprehensive training allows Navy aerospace clinical psychologists to be utilized as NAMI psychologists, where they conduct psychological and neuropsychological evaluations and consult with flight surgeon and aviation squadron commanders throughout the fleet (Bowles & Bartone, 2017).

All naval aviation personnel must meet the medical standards of the Navy, in accordance with the *Manual of the Medical Department* (MANMED), NAVMED P-117 (United States Department of the Navy, 2023a), in addition to the ARWG (United States Department of the Navy, 2023b). The ARWG is developed by NAMI, and serves as the framework for ensuring all naval aviation assets (Navy and Marine Corps) meet aviation physical standards. The ARWG provides guidance on the evaluation and waiver recommendations for a multitude of aeromedically significant psychiatric conditions (ARWG, United States Department of the Navy, 2023b), but encourages flight surgeons to contact NAMI for guidance if specific assistance is needed. Unlike the Air Force and Army, the Navy does not allow aviators to fly on any psychotropic medication. Several conditions, such as ADHD, TBI, and obstructive sleep apnea, necessitate evaluation with a specific battery of neuropsychological tests by a credentialed neuropsychologist. For the majority of other aeromedically significant psychiatric conditions (e.g., depression, anxiety, psychotic disorders, trauma-related disorder, etc.), however, the Navy states that only "a current psychiatric evaluation is required" (US Navy Aeromedical Reference and Waiver Guide, United States Department of the Navy, 2023b), and that it may be done by a clinical psychologist or even a licensed clinical social worker. The Navy, like all other military services, understood the lack of feasibility of requiring a neuropsychologist for all aeromedical psychological evaluations, as mission needs exceeded the number of available resources (i.e., neuropsychologist manpower, and lack of unified psychological testing libraries within the fleet).

United States Marine Corps

By Title 10 statute of the United States Code, the United States Marine Corps is a constituent Armed Force organized under the Department of the Navy. Therefore, the United States Marine Corps utilizes Department of Navy medical personnel and medical standards, to include aviation medical standards. Marine aviation assets are considered naval aviation personnel for all procedures and standards that require neuropsychological and/or psychological evaluation. As such the *Manual of the Medical Department* (MANMED), NAVMED P-117 (United States Department of the Navy, 2023a), and US Navy Aeromedical Reference and Waiver Guide both apply for the Marine Corps. Psychological and neuropsychological evaluations for aeromedical purposes are similarly conducted in accordance with these standards.

United States Coast Guard

Although one of the eight uniformed services, the United States Coast Guard uniquely falls under the Department of Homeland Security when not in times of war; and during war they are considered constituent to the Department of the Navy. Similar to the Space Force and the Marine Corps, the Coast Guard relies upon another uniformed service to provide medical care. Nearly all medical officers in the Coast Guard are members of the United States Public Health Service (USPHS) Commissioned Corps, and all psychologists are USPHS officers detailed to the Coast Guard.

Coast Guard aviation medical standards are outlined in the *Coast Guard Medical Manual* (COMDTINST M6000.1F; United States Coast Guard, 2022), and *Coast Guard Aviation Medicine Manual* (COMDTINST M6410.3A; United States Coast Guard, 2012). These regulations delineate the specific classes of Coast Guard aviation personnel for medical certification. These standards also establish the roles of the flight surgeon, aeromedical physician's assistant, as well as psychologists. The Coast Guard does not, however, specify a role for an aeromedical or aerospace psychologist, nor do they have any specific training in this regard. USPHS psychologists detailed to the Coast Guard have attended the Army's APTC in order to establish their knowledge base for aeromedical psychological evaluations.

Prior to 2023, the Coast Guard utilized their own regulations for the guidance of establishing medication certification of aviation assets. USCG APLs (n.d.) and Coast Guard AERO

ATBs (2010) were adapted from similar Army guidance, and remained doctrine for over a decade. This guidance, however, only addressed the psychological/psychiatric "conditions" of alcohol abuse or dependence and aeromedical adaptability (i.e., behavioral or personality-based issues that are not diagnosable but are determined to be at an unacceptable high risk for the aviation environment). They also indicated that a Coast Guard aviation asset required grounding, and a medical recommendation for flying duty, if they were "interviewed for or entered into a drug/alcohol treatment program," or were "evaluated by mental/behavioral health (include Employee Assistance Program [EAP], private marital counseling, or other civilian related services)" (*Coast Guard Aviation Medicine Manual* [COMDTINST M6410.3A], United States Coast Guard, 2012). No information was provided for how a psychological evaluation would be conducted to determine fitness from an aeromedical perspective or how to address the presence or history of other psychological conditions beyond grounding due to unsatisfactory aeromedical adaptability.

Aeromedical cases considered to be "unusual, complicated, or controversial" per the *Coast Guard Aviation Medicine Manual* (COMDTINST M6410.3A; United States Coast Guard, 2012) were referred to Aeromedical Consultation Advisory Boards, or were referred for consultation and evaluation by Army aeromedical psychologists or NAMI psychologists. These consultation psychologists were often selected based on geographic location and availability, with aeromedical waiver evaluation standards being applied based upon the service branch of the evaluator. In an effort to curtail this lack of standardization, in October 2023 the Coast Guard adopted the Navy's standards for aeromedical certification and waiver procedures (Pavel & Gracey, 2023).

The Reality of the (Neuro)Psychologist in Military Aviation

Although these fitness-for-duty standards have been codified for military aviation personnel, and the importance of the neuropsychologist in assessing cognitive fitness for aviation duty cannot be overstated, the reality of military operations often does not allow for the traditional role of the neuropsychologist to be fully utilized. The limitations placed on neuropsychologists in military operations are in large part due to environmental constraints (e.g., military operations often happen in austere and harsh environments), budget constraints (e.g., accessing funding for neuropsychological test batteries), and personnel constraints (e.g., there are often not enough trained neuropsychologists working in the United States Armed Forces as Department of Defense civilian employees or uniformed service members).

Given the dynamic and challenging milieu of military aviation, which includes the formidable constraints of austere operational environments, limited budgets and access to resources, and staffing shortages, neuropsychologists are required to confront these limitations and still achieve mission success. Neuropsychologists help overcome these obstacles by strategically approaching the problems.

Firstly, uniformed and civilian neuropsychologists provide invaluable supervision and consultation to other psychologists by leveraging their expertise to enhance the overall effectiveness of the aeromedical assessment process. For this reason, neuropsychologists have been placed in key billets across the military enterprise to ensure access to these supervi-

Table 5.1. Comparison of flight medical certificate classes

Component	Class 1	Class 2	Class 3	Class 4
FAA	Class 1 medical certificates are required for airline transport pilots (ATPs) operating as a pilot-in-command, pilots aged 60+ serving as required aircrew, and airline pilots operating as second in command on an aircraft requiring three or more pilots	Class 2 medical certificates are required for commercial pilots, and airline transport pilots (ATPs) operating as a second in command	Class 3 medical certificates are required for private pilots, recreational pilots, student pilots, certified flight instructors (CFIs), required flight crew members (aside from those requiring a 1st class medical), and pilot examiners (minimum required medical certification for performance of this duty)	N/A
Army	Applies to all candidates seeking initial medical certification as a rated (piloted) aviator, prior to beginning training at aircraft controls	Class 2: all rated aviators who have started pilot training Class 2F and 2P: All current flight surgeons, and physicians, medical students, nurse practitioners, and physician assistants who are seeking enrollment in the Flight Surgeon Primary Course	All army personnel who are considered non-rated, and perform duties aboard aircraft aloft, nonrated medical personnel selected for aeromedical training	Unmanned aerial systems (UAS) operators and air traffic control specialists (ATC)
Navy/Marine Corps	Naval aviators and student naval aviators Medical Service Group 1: aviators qualified for unlimited or unrestricted flight duty Medical Service Group 2: aviators restricted from shipboard duties (including V/STOL) except helicopters	Aviation personnel other than naval aviators, including naval flight officers (NFO), technical observers, naval flight surgeons (NFS), aeromedical physician assistant (APA), aerospace physiologist (AP), aerospace experimental psychologist (AEP), naval aerospace optometrists, all aeromedical evacuation personnel, naval aircrew (NAC), and other ordered to duty involving flying/or will fly on a regular basis	Those in aviation related duty requiring them to personally be airborne, including air traffic controllers (ATCs), flight deck, and flight line personnel	Those in aviation-related duty not requiring them to be airborne, including non-piloted aerial vehicle (UAV) operators

Table 5.1. continued

Component	Class 1	Class 2	Class 3	Class 4
	Medical Service Group 3: aviators restricted to operating aircraft equipped with dual controls and accompanied on all flights by a pilot or copilot of Medical Service Group 1 or 2, qualified in the model of aircraft operated. A waiver to medical Service Group 3 includes pilot-in-command (PIC) authority unless PIC authority is specifically restricted			
Air Force/ Space Force	Initial Flying Class I: all pilot applicants for any airframe Initial Flying Class IA: All applicants seeking entry to undergraduate combat system officers, navigator, and special operations combat system officer	Initial Flying Class II: all applicants for Flight Surgeon training Flying Class II: all manned aviators who have completed aviation training, and all flight surgeons upon completion of their training	Flying Class III: all non-rated aviator positions Initial RPA (remotely piloted aircraft): Applicants RPA training must hold a current FAA Class 3 medical certificate, in addition to meeting GBO standards	The USAF does not have Class 4 medical certification; however, air traffic controller (ATC), ground-based operator (GBO)*, and Special Warfare Airmen (SWA) have separate medical certification guidelines outside of Classes I, IA, II, and III *RPA pilots fall under GBO, and were formally Flying Class IIU. Personnel who are ground-based controllers of spacecraft/ satellites also fall under GBO
Coast Guard	All pilots, including initial entrance (accession) pilots, and current (rated) aviators	All flight surgeons (FS), flight surgeon trainees (FST), and aeromedical physician's assistants	All other crew members authorized to fly in Coast Guard aircraft	N/A

sion and consultation services. These supervision and consultation processes take place in garrison as well as in deployed/combat environments. Military neuropsychologists offer specialized guidance to ensure assessment procedures align with the unique challenges faced by military aviation personnel, whose cognitive requirements often differ from specialty to specialty. Examples of differing requirements include the neuropsychological requirements of a single- or dual-seat fighter aircraft, crewed transport aircraft, and air traffic controllers. Neuropsychologists therefore tailor their supervision and consultation practices with other psychologists to encompass the most important aspects of a neuropsychological assessment for a specific individual who is presenting with a specific duty-limiting difficulty. This becomes particularly important when access to full neuropsychological assessment batteries is not possible (see below for more on this issue).

As noted, in environments where limited resources are the norm, optimizing available resources and access to neuropsychological test instruments becomes paramount. This often includes a beg-and-borrow approach in which aeromedical providers share resources ensuring that mission requirements are met. Neuropsychological consultation provided to leadership is often required to help commanders, and others in the chain of command, appreciate and understand the importance of allocating funding to purchase assessment materials required to maintain flight safety standards.

The unfortunate reality is that sometimes appropriate standardized test batteries are not available. This requires out-of-the-box problem solving akin to A. R. Luria's battlefield assessments (Ardila, 1992). In these instances, neuropsychologists can help aeromedical providers develop observational strategies to "assess" various aspects of cognition. For example, in a simulated or supervised flight environment an aviation asset can be given an increasing list of task demands during which the psychologist observationally assesses their ability to shift attention, detect problems, and regulate their emotion/stress levels.

In worst-case scenarios, where immediate access to neuropsychological resources is logistically unfeasible, solutions involve relocating military aviation personnel to places where the services of a neuropsychologist or at least the requisite neuropsychological assessment materials can be accessed. This relocation strategy helps transcend geographical constraints when neuropsychologists or the assessment materials required for an adequate aeromedical assessment are not geographically available. However, while this relocation strategy offers a viable solution to address geographical constraints, its implementation often entails a substantial increase in costs associated with the movement of personnel and the use of other logistical resources. The financial burden associated with relocating military aviation personnel is a notable drawback, which can result in diverting resources that could be allocated to other critical aspects of military operations. Moreover, the economic considerations of frequent relocations may impact the overall budget allocated for cognitive health initiatives, prompting a need for more cost-effective alternatives to ensure sustained neuropsychological support.

As implied, oftentimes a hybrid approach to solving these unique military challenges is required. For example, conducting an adequate aeromedical assessment may require that a psychologist receive supervision or consultation with a neuropsychologist, geographically relocating an aviation asset, and/or borrowing or buying testing material to meet mission requirements. Despite these limitations, maximizing the impact of neuropsychologists involves collaborative efforts, creative solutions, and a commitment to prioritizing cognitive health and aviation safety within military aviation operations.

Aspirations for Standardized Neuropsychological Assessment Batteries

Despite Luria's battlefield approach and focus on individualized neurocognitive assessment strategies (Ardila, 1992), standardized assessment batteries, which include normative data sets and standardized administration procedures, are the currently accepted model for understanding individual differences in neuropsychological test performance. These norm-based assessment procedures are used to determine fitness for duty in military aviation as well as civilian aviation. However, the difference between military aviation fitness-for-duty determinations and civilian aviation fitness-for-duty determinations is that standardized neuropsychological assessment batteries can be prescribed for neuropsychologists to use in the civilian context. That is, neuropsychologists wanting to conduct civilian neuropsychological aviation evaluations must follow the standardized testing batteries prescribed by the FAA.

By contrast, in most military environments, prescribing standardized test batteries is not operationally feasible and is often impractical because of the lack of standardized resourcing across behavioral health clinics; some clinics, through supportive leadership, timing, budgeting, and convincing argument, have adequately resourced neuropsychological assessments, whereas others have been less successful, resulting in little to no access to neuropsychological test materials. (The most well-resourced neuropsychological clinics are often the larger military treatment facilities [MTF] rather than the smaller clinics found in deployed environments.) Therefore, prescribing standardized test batteries in some military contexts would be unreasonable and immediately met with mission failure because the requisite resources would not always be available.

In many instances when prescriptions are made for the neuropsychological evaluation of certain disorders, they are left purposefully vague in order to allow aeromedical providers to meet the intent of the mission requirement without being tied down by specific requirements. For example, in the United States Army APLs the information required for initial waiver or exception to policy for the diagnosis and treatment of ADHD includes but is not limited to the following:

1. Detailed interview by a clinical psychologist/psychiatrist to include developmental, academic, employment, social, substance use, legal, medication, and concomitant behavioral health history.
2. Neuropsychological assessment to include cognitive domains, IQ, and achievement testing is required. If medication(s) is required, this assessment should be conducted both on and off medication.
3. Continuous performance testing (e.g., Conners, Integrated Visual and Auditory Continuous Performance Test, TOVA) is required.

Multiple aspects of the assessment requirements are left intentionally unspecified. For example, the neuropsychological assessment should include "cognitive domains, IQ, and achievement testing." However, the cognitive domains required to be tested are not prescribed, and there is no prescription for the specific tests that should be used. The closest thing to a specific requirement is for continuous performance testing, and examples of acceptable tests are given. Nevertheless, it is up to the neuropsychologist to determine most of the assessment battery. Additionally, some aspects of the "requirements" are determined to not be necessary when overly impractical. For example, the APL for ADHD states that, when medication is required, it is necessary to have two neuropsychological assessments: one off and one on the medication. This can be useful when stimulant medications are the medication in question because they have relatively short half-lives and test-retest on/off medications can be done within a rather short timeframe. However, the United States Army also allows aviation assets with ADHD diagnoses to be prescribed Strattera and Wellbutrin, both of which have much longer half-lives. Testing individuals both on and off Strattera or Wellbutrin poses at least two problems: (1) The evaluations would have to be separated by weeks to months to allow therapeutic effects of the medications to wear off (tapering off) or become clinically meaningful (titrating up), which means that the aviation asset will be mission incapable for a much longer period than would be desired; and (2) when medications are being tapered off or titrated up, the aviation asset is put at increased psychological risk because their level of psychological stability may be compromised by medication side effects or other undesired psychological phenomena when the psychotropic chemicals are not stabilized in their bodies.

Graver et al. (2020), most likely in response to the intentional lack of prescription in the APLs for neuropsychological assessments, provided a suggested test battery but acknowledge that there is flexibility regarding which assessment measures are used in aeromedical evaluations, so long as they are appropriately validated. These authors also note that specific cognitive domains of functioning should be assessed: intellectual functioning, premorbid estimate of cognitive functioning, basic attention, sustained attention, processing speed, phonemic fluency, semantic fluency visual scanning, abstract reasoning, visuomotor ability, mental flexibility, impulse control, mental stamina, problem-solving, and achievement testing. It should be further noted that, depending on the nature of the evaluation and reason for referral, additional domains of cognitive functioning may also need to be assessed (e.g., sensation; perception; motor; verbal learning, memory, and recognition; visual learning, memory, and recognition; and concentration/working memory; see Harvey, 2019, for a brief review of ways of understanding and assessing domains of cognitive functioning).

Just as in civilian aviation contexts, it is important that standardized psychological assessments are used in military aviation evaluations (Graver et al., 2020). When choosing standardized psychological assessments, well-developed measures that include validity indicators (particularly measures that assess "faking good" or under-reporting approaches to test-taking) need to be used by military aeromedical providers. The Minnesota Multiphasic Personality Inventory (MMPI) family of tests, the Millon Clinical Multiaxial Inventory (MCMI)-IV, and the Personality Assessment Inventory (PAI) all provide research-supported validity measures that help military psychologists and neuropsychologists understand an individual's approach to test taking (i.e., Did they attend/understand/respond consistently? Did they under-report? Did they over-report?). Although over-reporting is rarely seen in military neuropsychological aviation evaluations, some individuals do "fake bad," or over-report, either consciously or unconsciously to avoid continuing their aviation duties. More commonly observed are aviation personnel who under-report symptoms in order to continue their aviation duties despite having duty-limiting symptoms and conditions (Hoffman, et al., 2022; Reichhardt, 2009; Roza, 2023).

Conclusion

To help commanders manage risk while also meeting mission requirements with flight safety as a top priority, military neuropsychologists (uniformed and civilian) provide cognitive and psychological assessments that help maintain the health of uniformed aviation assets. Neuropsychologists are trained in aeromedical policy, including disqualifying conditions and the waiver processes, to help aviation personnel return to flight duty after having limitations placed upon them.

Despite the codification of fitness-for-duty standards, disqualifying conditions, and waiver processes across the various Armed Forces, neuropsychologists working with military aviation assets are often met with constraints. These constraints include the austere and harsh locations where military operations take place, fiscal constraints, and personnel shortages; all of which pose formidable impediments that often keep neuropsychologists from operating in their traditional capacities. Nevertheless, the judicious methodologies employed by neuropsychologists, coupled with collaboration with fellow psychologists, help optimize the impact of their expertise to overcome the challenges endemic to military aviation. As aspirations for standardized neuropsychological assessment batteries persist, creative solutions are often required to balance meeting mission requirements and maintaining flight safety.

References

American Psychological Association. (2017, January 1). *Ethical principles of psychologists and code of conduct.* https://www.apa.org/ethics/code

Ardila, A. (1992). Luria's approach to neuropsychological assessment. *International Journal of Neuroscience, 66*(1–2), 35–43.

Bowles, S.V. (1994). Military aeromedical psychology training. *International Journal of Aviation Psychology, 4*(2), 167–173. https://doi.org/10.1207/s15327108ijap0402_4

Bowles, S.V., & Bartone, P.T. (2017). *Handbook of military psychology clinical and organizational practice.* Springer International Publishing.

Doc Apps, LLC. (2016). *Med standards* (Version: 1.4.60.5) [Mobile application]. Google Play Store and Apple App Store.

Durham, T.L. (2021). *Aeromedical psychology training course* (6H-F27). US Army Aeromedical Activity.

Graver, C.J., Armistead-Jehle, P., & Fritch, A.M. (2020). Neuropsychologist's guide to aeromedical examinations in the military. *Military Behavioral Health, 9*(1), 89–100. https://doi.org/10.1080/21635781.2020.1742823

Harvey, P.D. (2019). Domains of cognition and their assessment. *Dialogues in Clinical Neuroscience, 21*(3), 227–237. https://doi.org/10.31887/DCNS.2019.21.3/pharvey

Hoffman, W.R., Aden, J.K., Barbera, D., & Tvaryanas, A. (2022). Self-reported health care avoidance behavior in U.S. military pilots related to fear for loss of flying status. *Military Medicine, 188*(3–4), 446–450. https://doi.org/10.1093/milmed/usac311

Kennedy, C.H., & Kay, G.G. (2013). *Aeromedical psychology.* Ashgate.

Lee, A.J. (2022). Building trust between military pilots and flight surgeons. *Military Medicine, 188*(3–4), 92–94. https://doi.org/10.1093/milmed/usac314

National Aeronautics and Space Administration. (2023a). *NASA spaceflight human-system standard (Vol. 1). Crew health.* (NASA-STD-3001). https://standards.nasa.gov/sites/default/files/standards/NASA/C//nasa-std-3001-vol-1-rev-c-signature.pdf

National Aeronautics and Space Administration. (2023b). *NASA spaceflight human-system standard (Vol. 2). Human factors, habitability, and environmental health.* (NASA-STD-3001). https://standards.nasa.gov/sites/default/files/standards/NASA/D//nasa-std-3001-vol-2-rev-d-signature.pdf

Naval Aerospace Experimental Psychology. (2023, May 19). *NavyAEP.com – Where service and science combine.* https://navyaep.com/#home

Pavel, F., & Gracey, S. (2023, November 11). *Information gleaned from interview of CDR Sherry Gracey, PsyD (USPHS) regarding USCG adoption of USN aeromedical standards.* 10th Annual Aerospace Psychology Seminar, Washington, DC.

Reichhardt, T. (2009, August 27). Who's depressed? Not military pilots. *Smithsonian*. https://www.smithsonianmag.com/air-space-magazine/whos-depressed-not-military-pilots-115099111/
Roza, D. (2023, March 27). Military pilots avoid health care to keep flying, study confirms. *Air & Space Forces Magazine*. https://www.airandspaceforces.com/military-pilots-medical-exam/
Saitzyk, A.R., Alfonzo, C.A., Greydanus, T.P., Reaume, J.R., & Parsa, B.B. (2013). US military standards and aeromedical waivers for psychiatric conditions and treatments. In C.H. Kennedy & G.G. Kay (Eds.), *Aeromedical psychology* (pp. 125–158). Ashgate Publishing Company.
Saitzyk, A.R., Mayfield, T.E., Sharkey, L.M., & Cox Coleman, C.E. (2017). Aeromedical Psychology. In S.V. Bowles & P.T. Bartone (Eds.), *Handbook of military psychology* (pp. 19–31). Springer International Publishing.
Tirpak, J. (2023, February 23). Air Force has to "get our house in order" on pilot retention red tape, Slife says. *Air & Space Forces Magazine*. https://www.airandspaceforces.com/air-force-has-to-get-our-house-in-order-on-pilot-retention-red-tape-slife-says/
United States Army Aeromedical Activity. (2021). *Aeromedical policy letters and aeromedical technical bulletins.* (revision date December 2021)
United States Coast Guard. (n.d.). *Aeromedical policy letters*. Office of Operational Medicine and Quality Improvement Division (CG-1121). https://www.dcms.uscg.mil/Portals/10/CG-1/cg112/cg1121/docs/pdf/USCG_Aeromedical_Policy_Letters.pdf
United States Coast Guard. (2010). *Aeromedical technical bulletins*. Office of Operational Medicine and Quality Improvement Division (CG-1121). https://www.dcms.uscg.mil/Portals/10/CG-1/cg112/cg1121/docs/pdf/AeromedicalTechnicalBulletins.pdf
United States Coast Guard. (2012). *Coast Guard aviation medicine manual* (COMDTINST M6410.3A). https://media.defense.gov/2022/Dec/20/2003135402/-1/-1/0/CIM_6410_3A.PDF
United States Coast Guard. (2022). *Coast guard medical manual* (COMDTINST M6000.1F). https://media.defense.gov/2022/Sep/14/2003076969/-1/-1/0/CIM_6000_1F.PDF
United States Department of the Air Force. (2020). *DAFMAN 48-123: Medical examinations and standards*. https://static.e-publishing.af.mil/production/1/af_sg/publication/dafman48-123/dafman48-123.pdf
United States Department of the Air Force. (2023a). *Air Force waiver guide*. https://kx.health.mil/kj/kx7/waiverguide/Pages/home.aspx
United States Department of the Air Force. (2023b). *Medical standards directory (MSD)*. https://kx.health.mil/Pages/default.aspx
United States Department of the Army. (2019a). *AR 600-8-22: Military awards*. Army Publishing Directorate. https://armypubs.army.mil/ProductMaps/PubForm/Details.aspx?PUB_ID=1003738
United States Department of the Army. (2019b). *AR 40-501: Standards of medical fitness*. Army Publishing Directorate. https://armypubs.army.mil/ProductMaps/PubForm/Details.aspx?PUB_ID=1004688
United States Department of the Army. (2020). *AR 600-105: Aviation service of rated army officers*. Army Publishing Directorate. https://armypubs.army.mil/ProductMaps/PubForm/Details.aspx?PUB_ID=1007445
United States Department of the Army. (2022a). *AR 40-8: Temporary flying restriction due to exogenous factors affecting aircrew efficiency*. Army Publishing Directorate. https://armypubs.army.mil/ProductMaps/PubForm/Details.aspx?PUB_ID=1020677
United States Department of the Army. (2022b). *AR 600-106: Flying status for nonrated army aviation personnel*. Army Publishing Directorate. https://armypubs.army.mil/ProductMaps/PubForm/Details.aspx?PUB_ID=1021076
United States Department of the Navy. (2023a). *Manual of the Medical Department (MANMED), NAVMED P-117*. https://www.med.navy.mil/Directives/MANMED/
United States Department of the Navy. (2023b). *US Navy aeromedical reference and waiver guide*. https://www.med.navy.mil/Navy-Medicine-Operational-Training-Command/Naval-Aerospace-Medical-Institute/Aeromedical-Reference-and-Waiver-Guide/
United Sates Space Force. (n.d.). *About the space force*. https://www.spaceforce.mil/About-Us/About-Space-Force/
Wright, K. (2022, August 6). *Inaugural aviation training proves success for air force psychologists*. https://www.af.mil/News/Article-Display/Article/3115179/inaugural-aviation-training-proves-success-for-air-force-psychologists/

Chapter 6
The Role of the Psychiatrist in Mental Health and Neuropsychiatric Assessments in Aviators

Asha Pook and Raymond Padua

Introduction

The culture of flight safety within the aviation industry is of paramount importance. A great deal of time, effort, and expense is spent analyzing errors and improving the many components on which safe aviation relies, including the human element, whether they be the pilots, air traffic controllers, cabin crew, or flight engineers. This chapter addresses all the various roles that have an air-safety-critical aspect to their work; however, for brevity, we will refer to pilots/aircrew. The role of aviation medical risk management is to ensure that these operators are as medically fit as can be and to reduce the possibility of illness compromising overall flight safety through distraction, impairment, or incapacitation. Not only must the medical symptoms and treatment be evaluated, but the specific challenges of the aviation environment must also be taken into consideration, for example, pressurization/hypoxia, night shifts, layovers, and access to medication. In order to be licensed as pilots, candidates must reach and maintain certain medical standards. Most commercial and military pilots have annual medicals, but this can vary according to their age and role. Aviation medical examiners (AME) are usually family physicians or general practitioners (GP) with specialist training in aviation and are regulated by the relevant aviation regulatory authorities. At certain points, all regulations rely on pilots consulting a GP or AME if their health status changes in any way.

Depending on the aviation authority, most mental health conditions are usually disqualifying for aircrew. Where there is irreversibility or a high rate of relapse, such as schizophrenia and bipolar disorder, permanent disqualification from flying is indicated. However, pilots with common mental health conditions such as depression, anxiety, adjustment disorders, and posttraumatic stress disorder (PTSD), depending on their severity and risk of recurrence, may be returned to flying once treated with either psychotherapy, medications (usually an antidepressant), or both.

The tragedy of the Germanwings murder–suicide in 2016 became the catalyst in highlighting the importance of mental health within the aviation industry (Bureau d'Enquetes et d'Analyses [BEA], 2016). The impact of the COVID-19 pandemic on this sector appears to have led to an increase in a wide range of mental health symptoms and disorders (Flynn et al., 2022). To what extent these represent new cases, or a tipping point reached by those previously putting up with or concealing symptoms finally coming forward for help, is not clear.

Although flying is a job or a hobby, many pilots see flying as defining who they are as people rather than merely something they do. This taps into a lifelong determination and ambition to achieve their wings, into the professionalism and high standards they hold themselves accountable to, and into their ultimate commitment to flight safety. Not only does flying provide their income and status, it also is a source of reward and achievement. Therefore, aircrew are very wary of anyone who may have the potential to take this away, including aviation medicine specialists. For this reason, unlike other clinical situations, it is useful to bear in mind that there are specific challenges in assessing the mental health of aircrew. The fear of being grounded (unfit from flying duties) – not only due to practicalities like income, but the perceived stigma of being seen to be "weak" – can mean they avoid or delay seeking health care, which ultimately can result in symptoms becoming worse and treatment taking longer (Hoffman, 2023). This under-reporting and continuing to fly while symptomatic represents the greatest risk to air safety. Dispelling the stigma around seeking help relies on better health promotion for aircrew and a culture that makes self-reporting the norm. For the majority, treatment for the most common mental health disorders is successful and leads to a return to flying.

In this chapter we consider the area of neuropsychiatry, outlining some of the complexity around this specialty in general and how this relates to the area of aviation medicine. Furthermore, we illustrate some of the clinical principles through a case vignette.

Neuropsychiatry as a Speciality

What is mind? No matter – What is matter? Never mind.
(George Berkeley)

The debate about the relationship between the brain and the mind is an ongoing one. Cartesian mind-body dualism drew a distinction between the mind as a nonphysical, "mental" concept and the brain as the physical, "biological" structure. The influence of this philosophy has shaped the development of medical thinking about diseases and the development of services. The medical specialty of neurology is concerned with the structure, function, and diseases of the brain (central) and peripheral nervous system. By contrast, the branch of medicine known as psychiatry covers diseases of the "mind." While neurological conditions were thought of as physical, that is, with a clear link to underlying medical pathology, psychiatric disorders were seen as functional, that is, having no identified biological basis. Developments in neuroscience, and in particular in functional neuroimaging, have allowed us to update this old-fashioned dualistic thinking. We now better understand the components of the brain and how the anatomy and physiology are linked to certain patterns of behaviour and emotion (Henderson et al., 2020). Equally, we also know that our stressful experiences and our environment can also directly change our neural pathways. A more modern view of the relationship between the mind and the brain is that the mind is the product of an embodied nervous system, including the brain.

Neuropsychiatry, which is a subspeciality of psychiatry, seeks to deliver a more integrated medical approach to the cognitive, emotional, and behavioral symptoms of psychiatric disorders arising in the context of a neurological disorder. Neuropsychiatric symptoms can arise in most of the major categories of neurological disorders: movement disorders, cerebrovascular disease, epilepsy and head injury, infections (encephalitis), and brain tumors (Butler & Zeman, 2005). The genetic-based Huntington's disease can present with depression, abnormal movements, and difficulty in concentrating with memory lapses. In traumatic brain injury (TBI), damage to the temporal lobes can lead to memory difficulties and emotional dysregulation. When the frontal lobes are damaged, symptoms of impaired concentration, fatigue, and depression can also be seen. In some circumstances there may be more than one illness occurring concurrently; for example, there are higher rates of depression and PTSD in TBI cases and these require treatment in their own right as comorbid conditions. Trying to tease out the overlap and origins of symptoms can be challenging, but it has significant implications for treatment. For example, bacterial encephalitis can cause inflammation of the brain leading to a variety of symptoms including headache, confusion, hallucinations, and memory problems. The correct treatment is antibiotics, not psychotropic medication, and once the infection is controlled the psychiatric issues will resolve.

Features that may suggest that the psychiatric symptoms are secondary to a physical condition include evidence of cerebral or physical disease, a temporal relationship between the development of the psychiatric symptoms and the illness, and also the disappearance of symptoms once the medical condition is treated. Additionally, there should not be any evidence suggesting a primary psychiatric disorder such as a prior personal history of mood disorder, a positive family psychiatric history, or recent life events/stressors etc. Thus, if a person presented with a history of indecisiveness, not being able to concentrate at work, or forgetting things, but the history revealed their spouse had recently passed away, then you might suspect and wish to exclude a primary depressive disorder before considering screening for dementia.

The opposite of physical disease causing psychological/behavioral symptoms can also be found, where patients present with very convincing physical symptoms but no physical pathology is found, and thus the cause is presumed to be in the mind. The terms functional illness, somatoform disorder (now disorders of bodily distress or experience in International Classification of Disease, 11th Revision [ICD-11]), or medically unexplained symptoms are used in this context. An example of this is someone presenting with seizures, who is examined for epilepsy but the neurologists exclude a physical basis for the symptoms; instead, the cause is confirmed as psychological and a psychotherapeutic approach is used to address the "pseudo-seizures."

There are also neurocognitive syndromes associated with alcohol and illicit substances. The increased consumption of alcohol among some aircrew is partly personality driven but also amplified by lifestyle factors of layovers and work social functions based in the bar. A recent European Union Aviation Safety Agency (EASA) report estimated that risky alcohol use might affect between 5% and 20% of pilots and controllers (EASA, 2022). The range of presentations arising from excessive use of alcohol in the short term include acute intoxication (lability of mood, disinhibited behavior, and memory blackouts) and withdrawal (anything from mild tremor and anxiety to delirium tremens with clouding of consciousness, disorientation, and perceptual disturbances). Longer-term alcohol dependency can lead to brain damage (ranging from mild cognitive impairment to Wernicke's encephalopathy) and psychiatric symptoms (depression, suicidal behavior, or pathological jealousy).

And lastly, there is the category of neurodevelopmental disorders (NDDs) to consider within this discussion, the most prominent being autism spectrum disorder (ASD) and attention-deficit/hyperactivity disorder (ADHD). These are multifaceted conditions characterized by impairments in cognition, communication, and behavior arising during development and they have a mixed etiology. The changes in both the Diagnostic and Statistical Manual of Mental Disorders, Fifth Edition (DSM-5) and ICD-11 from a categorical approach to a dimensional one now describes ASD/ADHD along a continuum of symptoms rather than according to the impact on functioning (mild, moderate, or severe). In society, the term neurodiversity has gained traction, as a more socially acceptable and nonmedical approach, which emphasizes differences rather than deficits, and recognizes both strengths and challenges. This is a rapidly evolving area, with a surge in these presentations in the general population, both in children and adults (who have sought late diagnosis), which has implications for recruitment into the aviation sector as these are still usually disqualifying conditions for training. In trained aircrew, if the diagnosis is made at a later stage, then with or without medication they are likely to be grounded. This means the quality of the diagnostic assessment is critical. The challenge for the regulators is to develop a nuanced tailor-made approach based on time-consuming thorough neuropsychological assessments, to ascertain whether there are cases where specific air safety roles may be undertaken safely (Laukkala et al., 2017).

Aeromedical Implications

Many of the conditions in neurology and psychiatry, and hence neuropsychiatry, can be unpredictable and involve significant disturbances to cognition (including poor concentration and diminished information-processing, decision making and problem-solving) and behaviour (slow reaction time, poor coordination, risk-taking behaviour and mood changes). Some medication (steroids or chemotherapy) prescribed for physical disease can also affect the brain, leading to some of these presentations. From an aviation medicine perspective, these symptoms have clear potential to cause incapacitation and, once they are diagnosed, the risk to flight safety may lead to the removal of flying privileges. However, many of these conditions can start off insidiously, causing subtle and intermittent changes in performance before enough evidence of an underlying disorder is found. Older pilots may be showing some age-appropriate decline in cognitive function whilst others could be at the early stages of a dementing illness, or they may be experiencing behavioural or mood changes due to advance physical illness. In this way, the AME needs to be alert to early or low-level signs, or changes to prior functioning, and consider whether extra precautions or limitations, or a period of grounding, are necessary whilst further investigations are made.

Guiding principles for good decision-making when it comes to treating aircrew include, as much as possible, evaluating the successes and risks of the treatment itself; looking at the research for recurrence rates; and attempting to fine-tune the period of grounding by considering each case individually to allow for the variation in symptoms, functioning, and the specific context of the flying role. For example, the medical standards for certification are the most stringent for military aviators, especially when in single-seat or instructor roles, and on the civilian side, commercial/Class 1 licenses require much higher medical standards than licenses for flying recreationally. Also, most civilian and military regulators retain the ability to grant waivers or special issuances in certain cases where flight safety is felt to be preserved.

Case Vignette

Maverick is a 61-year-old airline pilot who has been flying for over 40 years. He has been with the same airline for 27 years and has been a captain for the last 20 years. Over the past year, Maverick has noticed he has been having difficulties with his memory and performance. He finds he is forgetful both at home and work. He is concerned that on a couple of occasions he has made small errors during flight, but this has been quickly caught and addressed. Additionally, Maverick has also lost interest in activities he used to enjoy, including going to his golf club. In a crew resource management review, Maverick's crew have raised concerns about the changes they have noticed in their colleague (seems less upbeat than before and not attending work socials), and therefore it was recommended that he consult his AME.

At the AME's office, a full history is gathered, which includes the patient's history of presenting illness, past psychiatric history, family psychiatric history, developmental history, medical history, medications, substance use history, and forensic history. For aircrew, other pertinent information may include total flying hours, flying hours for that year, current flying status, any incidents or accidents, and what air frames they have flown and are currently flying.

Aircrew patients are no different to other patients when conducting an assessment and examination. A standard structured clinical approach, starting with a good history, will usually lead to the most likely diagnosis, which will then inform the most appropriate treatment plan. However, unlike with non-aircrew patients, AME physicians need to be cognizant of how an aircrew's symptoms can impact on flight safety. In all occupational medical settings where the examiner is assessing fitness for work, there is an extra dynamic within the consultation, which is probably the most pronounced in mental health. A descriptive cross-sectional study published in 2016 by Wu et al. using an anonymous web-based survey showed that hundreds of pilots currently flying are managing depressive symptoms without the possibility of treatment due to the fear of negative career impacts. This study found 233 (12.6%) airline pilots met the depression threshold and 75 (4.1%) pilots reported having suicidal thoughts. We know that pilots are very resourceful and thus they will try to treat their distressing symptoms on their own for as long as they can, for example, using caffeine, alcohol, and over-the-counter medications or herbal remedies for sleep. Sometimes they can end up taking illicit drugs (such as cannabis for mood and anxiety). Not only does this represent considerable "hidden" risk of the underlying condition that is not being treated properly, but also there are the direct side effects of these medications that may encroach on performance, for example, excess caffeine can cause dizziness, dehydration, and anxiety symptoms. Longer-term self-medicating can cause additional mental health issues, for example, alcohol is a depressant.

Thus, alongside the fact-finding history, there is a simultaneous process of forming an impression of the pilot's attitude, demeanor, and openness regarding their psychological functioning. Effort made in communication skills and creating rapport will put them at ease, build trust, and tiny clues may appear from a more relaxed conversation, which can then be probed a little further with open questions. Nonverbal cues may be the only sign of uneasiness or emotion and could be missed if the examiner is scribbling notes or filling in forms. Despite making this extra effort in paying attention to these aspects of the presentation, the pilot may still withhold how they are truly feeling. However, it is our clinical experience that most clients have spoken of their relief when an AME or health professional took enough time or showed sufficient interest to allow them an opportunity to identify any particular work pressure or interpersonal issues that may be a source of stress.

Bearing in mind our introduction and the wide range of diagnostic possibilities that can present with neurocognitive symptoms, a thorough history of all the presenting symptoms is critical, including speed of onset, triggering events, precise symptoms and anything that exacerbates or relieves them, duration, and whether symptoms are continuous or intermittent, getting worse or better. Ask about any recent physical symptoms and whether they are taking any over-the-counter medication or any new medication has been prescribed by the GP. As with any mental health condition, it is also important to capture the level of distress and disruption to their daily lives and functioning that the symptoms are causing. Perhaps more than other conditions, when dealing with memory issues having an informant present can be useful, and they may be able to provide more objective or detailed observations. In this case, having feedback from work colleagues or line managers can also be useful.

While conducting the mental state examination it is important to identify any possible comorbidities such as anxiety, mania, psychosis, obsessive-compulsive disorder (OCD), eating disorders, substance use, personality disorders, sleep disorder, and PTSD using a systematic approach. Questionnaires such as the Patient Health Questionnaire (PHQ)-9, Hamilton Depression Scale, Mood Disorder Questionnaire, PTSD Checklist (PCL)-5, and Generalized Anxiety Disorder (GAD)-7 can be provided to the patient before or during the interview to help guide the interview. Columbia suicide rating scales or other tools can also inform a risk assessment. Risk factors in this case include depression, alcohol use, financial stress, loneliness, age, and sex.

> The history reveals that Maverick recently divorced from his second wife after 7 years of marriage. He has three children from his first marriage, who were raised by their mother and are not close to him. The divorce has taken both an emotional and financial toll on Maverick. He has had a lot of personal administration to do, which he has fallen behind on, and so sometimes takes it to work. He is worried about finances now, as his older children are approaching college. At times he feels some of his younger copilots make barbed comments about his age. This has made him concerned that if he were to become ill, his company may offer him early retirement. His recent lapses of attention at work have knocked his confidence and he dwells on these in the evenings and sometimes thinks he is no longer at the top of his game. Maverick admits that in the past month things have felt worse and he has been consistently feeling low for more days than not. He feels sluggish during the day and eats only one meal in the evening. He describes feelings of guilt and failure in his work and relationship and a mild hopelessness for the future. He denies any suicidal ideation.
>
> With regard to cognition, over the past year, Maverick has noticed occasional lapses in attention and memory both at home and in the cockpit. He reports not always paying attention to conversations, has forgotten birthdays, and on a handful of occasions has misplaced his phone and keys. In the cockpit, he is able to function by following standard operating procedures; however, at times his mind drifts and he has to be reminded by his copilot if he misses a procedure. In addition, Maverick reports to having a family history of Alzheimer's dementia on the maternal side of the family. His medical

history also shows he had multiple mild concussions as a teenager playing hockey, with no obvious sequelae. Maverick reports he is not on any regular medications except for the occasional ibuprofen for muscle pain.

Maverick's AME also conducts a mental status examination for his patient. He finds Maverick to be pleasant and chatty but looks tired, and his shirt has a stain on it. His mood is dysphoric. Maverick reported feeling sluggish but his thought process seemed linear and logical. His thought content revolved around his worries about losing his pilot's license, financial stress from the divorce, and his forgetfulness. He denied any perceptual abnormalities and did not appear to be responding to internal stimuli. It was felt that he did not express anything that would suggest he was a risk to himself or others. He was orientated in person, place, and time and his memory for his history was reasonable. He was not sure what was wrong with him and was worried that he might be developing dementia. Maverick's AME then conducts a thorough medical examination to identify any underlying medical conditions contributing to cognitive decline or depression. While a physical examination is best practice for all patients, where there is suspicion of cognitive problems, a careful and thorough assessment of the central and peripheral nervous system is mandatory. Maverick's blood pressure is mildly elevated (139/90) as is his heart rate at 92 bpm. Otherwise, the physical examination is unremarkable with no focal neurological findings.

Because of Maverick's description of memory problems plus his family history of Alzheimer's dementia, Maverick's AME performs a basic neurocognitive assessment. There are a number of options but on this occasion he uses the Mini-Mental State Examination (MMSE), which is a standardized test to assess cognitive functions, including memory, attention, and orientation Maverick scores 25/30, losing some points for attention and short-term memory, placing him just below the normal cognitive range. As such, the AME decides to refer him to a neuropsychologist at a memory clinic. Further investigations for neurocognitive disorders would be guided by the history and examination. Structural brain imaging such as computed tomography (CT) scans or magnetic resonance imaging (MRI) are first-line tools for ruling out stroke and brain tumors or for identifying any structural changes in specific lobes. If these results are equivocal, then it may be considered helpful to proceed with functional brain imaging such as single-photon emission CT (SPECT) or positron emission tomography (PET). An electroencephalogram (EEG) may be indicated to rule out epilepsy.

Maverick also reports a history of drinking two to three glasses of wine daily on his own, sometimes more than six if he socializes. He reports he has been having a "night cap" prior to bed to help him relax and sleep. He states he never drinks 8 hr before he has to fly but he does not wake up well rested in the morning. This prompts Maverick's AME to conduct a more thorough alcohol assessment. Maverick's tolerance for alcohol has increased in that he is now drinking up to four glasses of red wine every evening to get the same effect. He does not report hangover symptoms in the morning, or ever being tempted to have an "eye-opener" and he is able to have periods of 3–4 days without a drink if his shift pattern requires this. Maverick denies alcohol has interfered with his work performance, with his duties at home, or with his usual recreational activities, including driving.

Psychometric questionnaires such as the Alcohol Use Disorder Identification Test (AUDIT) and Severity of Alcohol Dependence Questionnaire (SADQ) can be helpful in understanding the full extent of his alcohol use and whether or not there are features of alcohol dependency. Blood tests including liver function tests and vitamin B12 levels to assess for potential alcohol-related issues or deficiencies are also relatively easy to do. In addition, the AME orders other blood tests such as a complete blood count, electrolytes, renal function tests, thyroid-stimulating hormone, and fasting blood glucose to rule out any medical abnormalities that may make Maverick susceptible to depressive symptoms. Once the results are completed, Maverick's AME finds the results of the laboratory tests to be all normal with the exception of a mild elevation in gamma-glutamyl transferase (GGT), alanine aminotransferase (ALT), and aspartate transaminase (AST), likely due to chronic alcohol use.

Pulling together the history and information from the examination and investigations, his AME decides that the most likely diagnosis for Maverick is a major depressive disorder (MDD) and an alcohol use disorder, mild possibly moderate, but not dependency. There is clear evidence that these symptoms are of a significant severity, frequency, and duration to cause Maverick considerable distress and affect his performance at work and his social life. In this case it seems that the divorce was the trigger to his depression developing; however, the additional worry about his cognitive symptoms and possible impact on his performance and career added to this. To what degree his chronic alcohol use may be contributing to his mood and memory problems is unknown. His worsening mood and social withdrawal appear to have led to an increase in his drinking alone. And what about the issue of his memory loss? His age, chronic use of alcohol, mild hypertension, and family history are risk factors for early dementia and thus it seems reasonable to further investigate this with a more detailed neuropsychological assessment. However, the other consideration is that his cognitive symptoms are a feature of his MDD. A key diagnostic criterion for depression is "a diminished ability to think or concentrate or indecisiveness" (DSM-5), and emerging research shows that up to 40% of people with a diagnosis of depression have evidence of some cognitive impairment and this may persist even after remission, although the cause of this is uncertain (Mokhtari et al., 2023). Additionally, concentration and attention can be affected by other depressive features such as poor sleep and fatigue. In clinical practice, if the cognitive symptoms resolve with the treatment of the depression, then it is probably unlikely to be a separate condition. A meta-analysis in 2014 found that antidepressant monotherapy can have beneficial effects on cognitive function in depression (Keefe et al., 2014), which should encourage clinicians to treat the depression actively.

On managing Maverick's depression and alcohol use disorder, his AME decides on a safety, biological, and psychosocial approach. From a safety perspective: Maverick's AME feels the patient can be safely treated as an outpatient in the community. However, due to the risk of distraction and impairment at work due to his neurocognitive and fatigue/motivation problems, Maverick's AME recommends the patient refrain from piloting duties (grounding) and depending on the patient's local aviation medical regulations, his condition is reported to the aviation medical authority. Psychosocial treatment: Maverick is then offered psychotherapy, such as cognitive-behavioral therapy (CBT), to address his depression. Maverick is also offered support for alcohol cessation, which may include addiction counseling and referral to a Human Intervention Motivational Study (HIMS) program. With regard to Maverick's social stressors, he was directed to his pilot's union to see whether there were resources for financial counseling. Maverick was also encouraged to connect with his local pilot peer support network for support while he is away from work during treatment. Biological treatment: Maverick's AME decides that due to the severity of his depressive symptoms, the patient may benefit from a trial of medication. In this case Maverick is offered monotherapy with sertraline starting at 50 mg oral daily with an adjustment of the dose depending on the clinical efficacy and side effect profile.

There are strict thresholds and regulations, based on the available current evidence and research, concerning the safe use of prescribed medication for all medical conditions in aircrew. Psychotropic medication, that is, medication that can affect psychological functioning, often has significant side effects including sedation. For this reason, most of these medications are disqualifying for flying or air safety critical work. Moreover, there are very few research studies looking at the use of psychotropic medication in a working and highly skilled population, such as aircrew, which means that many existing policies have inherent wide margins for error, which can be perceived as overly harsh when aircrew are prevented from flying for long periods of time.

Options of psychotropic medications for mood disorders include antidepressants, mood stabilizers, and antipsychotics. However, mood stabilizer medications (such as valproic acid and lamotrigine) and antipsychotics (such a quetiapine and risperidone) are incompatible for aircrew duties due to their adverse side effects on cognition and sedation. By contrast, depending on the aeromedical authority, certain antidepressant medications are allowed to be prescribed and are generally either selective serotonin reuptake inhibitors (SSRIs) or serotonin-norepinephrine reuptake inhibitors (SNRIs; venlafaxine) or norepinephrine-dopamine reuptake inhibitors (NDRI; bupropion) due to their relatively safe and low side effect profile. The most common side effects of the SSRI medications (citalopram, escitalopram, sertraline, fluoxetine) are gastrointestinal and sexual dysfunction, although insomnia or sedation, dizziness, and akathisia can be experienced (Hamon & Bourgoin, 2006; Paul et al., 2007). The use of antidepressant medication to treat depression, anxiety, and other related disorders (PTSD) in aircrew has been common practice for the past 10–15 years. A key study published in Australia, looking at safety outcomes in aircrew flying and air traffic controllers working while taking medication, led the way for other countries to follow. This study found no evidence of adverse safety outcomes arising from permitting individual to operate as commercial or private aircrew or air traffic controllers while using antidepressants, provided specific criteria are met and maintained (Ross et al., 2007).

Some overarching guiding principles exist to maximize air safety even when using authorized medications. These include no return to flying will be considered until the patient has been clinically in remission, on a medication dose that is stable (maintenance dose), for a period of several continuous months without any side effects that would be aeromedically significant. If a dose change is required or when ceasing the medication, there is a short period of grounding to allow for possible discontinuation side effects. Only single medications (monotherapy) can be used at one time, and if there is a return to flying/controlling while taking medication, then certain limitations or restrictions may be required (such as operational multipilot limitation [OML], suitably qualified pilot on type) and there is regular follow-up in the psychiatry clinic. The actual medications and timescales vary slightly between countries and are also regularly updated. We would advise the reader to check with the relevant regulatory authority for the most up-to-date information.

> Maverick was signed off on sick leave and stabilized on 100 mg sertraline daily. Within a few weeks he had started to play golf again and noticed that with more time outdoors, light exercise, and company his mood improved as did his sleep. He decided to sell his house and downsize to ease his financial pressures. His treating psychiatrist reviewed him after 6 months and felt he had been in remission for a couple of months and was ready to be weaned off the medication. At the 1-year point, having been off sertraline for over 3 months, his full medical category/license was restored and he was authorized by his airline authority to start a return to flying package of SIMS and

supervised flights. His work performance reports were all satisfactory and stated there was no evidence of errors or lapse in concentration or attention. At his final review 3 months after that, he remained well, reported no further memory problems, and was discharged from the psychiatrist.

Conclusion

Hopefully this chapter and the clinical vignette have either introduced or reinforced some of the principles of aviation medicine as applied to mental health and specifically the interface between psychiatry, neuropsychiatry, and physical health. Ultimately, the aim of the aviation medical examiner and aviation specialist is to correctly diagnose and treat the clinical condition while keeping in mind the impact on flight safety – before, during, and following an episode of mental illness. The process is no different to any other clinical scenario except for being aware of the regulations regarding treatment and certification. There is a wide variation between medical policy and the level of access for aircrew to aviation-trained specialists globally, and therefore we emphasize that professionals must familiarize themselves with their local regulatory authority for guidance. Finally, through promoting better mental health awareness and therapeutic optimism that most of these conditions can be treated successfully and a return to flying will be possible, the burden of symptoms and stigma can hopefully be lifted for many.

References

Bureau d'Enquetes et d'Analyses. (2016). *Final report, Germanwings Airbus A320-211 (D-AIPX), accident 24 March 2015* (BEA2015-0125).

Butler, C., & Zeman, A. Z. J. (2005). Neurological syndromes which can be mistaken for psychiatric conditions. *Journal of Neurology, Neurosurgery & Psychiatry, 76*, 131–138. https://doi.org/10.1136/jnnp.2004.060459

European Union Aviation Safety Agency. (2022). *MESAFE: Mental health for aviation safety. D-3.1: Report on the analysis of the suitability of screening and confirmation tests for misuse of alcohol and drugs* (EASA.2022.C07).

Flynn, C. F., King, R. E., Bor, R., & Tvaryanas, A. (2022). Mental health implications for aviators from COVID-19. *REACH, 27–28*, 100050. https://doi.org/10.1016/j.reach.2022.100050

Hamon, M., & Bourgoin, S. (2006). Pharmacological profile of antidepressants: A likely basis for their efficacy and side effects? *European Neuropharmacology, 16*, 5625–5632. https://doi.org/10.1016/S0924-977X(06)70008-6

Henderson, T. A., Van Lierop, M. J., McLean, M., Uszler, J. M., Thornton, J. F., Siow, Y. H., Pavel, D. G., Cardaci, J., & Cohen, P. (2020). Functional neuroimaging in psychiatry – aiding in diagnosis and guiding treatment. What the American Psychiatric Association does not know. *Frontiers in Psychiatry, 11,* Article 276. https://doi.org/10.3389/fpsyt.2020.00276

Hoffman, W. (2023). Aircraft pilot healthcare avoidance due to fear of aeromedical certificate loss and implications for neurology care of the pilot patient (P4-7.004). *Neurology, 100*(17, Suppl. 2), Article 2142. https://doi.org/10.1212/WNL.0000000000202343

Keefe, S. E., McClintock, S. M., Roth, R. M., Doraiswamy, M., Tiger, S., & Madhoo, M. (2014). Cognitive effects of pharmacotherapy for major depressive disorder: A systematic review. *Journal of Clinical Psychiatry, 75*(8), 864–876. https://doi.org/10.4088/JCP.13r08609

Laukkala, T., Bor, R., Budowle, B., Sajantila, A., Navathe, P., Sainio, M., & Vuorio, A. (2017). Attention-deficit/hyperactivity disorder and fatal accidents in aviation medicine. *Aerospace Medicine and Human Performance, 88*(9), 871–875. https://doi.org/10.3357/AMHP.4919.2017

Mokhtari, S., Mokhtari, A., Bakizadeh, F., Moradi, A., & Shalbafari, M. (2023). Cognitive rehabilitation for improving cognitive functions and reducing the severity of depressive symptoms in adult patients with Major Depressive Disorder: A systematic review and meta-analysis of randomised controlled clinical trials. *BMC Psychiatry, 23*(1), Article 77. https://doi.org/10.21203/rs.3.rs-2075769/v1

Paul, M.A., Gray, G.W., Love, R.J., & Lange, M. (2007). SSRI effects on psychomotor performance: Assessment of citalopram and escitalopram on normal subjects. *Aviation, Space and Environmental Medicine, 78*, 693–697.

Ross, J., Griffiths, K., Dear, K., Emonson, D., & Lambeth, L. (2007). Antidepressant use and safety in civil aviation: A case-control study of 10 years off Australian data. *Aviation, Space, and Environmental Medicine, 78*, 749–755.

Wu, A.C., Donnelly-McLay, D., Weisskopf, M.G., McNeely, E., Betancourt, T.S., & Allen, J.G. (2016). Airplane pilot mental health and suicidal thoughts: A cross-sectional descriptive study via anonymous web-based survey. *Environmental Health, 15*(1), Article 121. https://doi.org/10.1186/s12940-016-0200-6

Further Reading on Civilian Aviation Authorities

Civil Aviation Authority:
Mental health guidance material. UK CAA Flow Chart for depression and related disorder https://www.caa.co.uk/media/00lbz5lx/20230202-v5-0-depression-flow-chart.pdf

Civil Aviation Safety Authority:
https://www.casa.gov.au/resources-and-education/publications-and-resources/aviation-medicine-fact-sheets-and-case-studies/depression-and-anxiety-safety-fact-sheet#Effectsofflyingondepression

Transport Canada:
Handbook for civil aviation medical examiners. https://tc.canada.ca/en/aviation/publications/handbook-civil-aviation-medical-examiners-tp-13312#psychiatry-ssris

Federal Aviation Administration website:
Guide for aviation medical examiners: Decision considerations – Aerospace medical dispositions. Item 47. Psychiatric conditions – Use of antidepressant medications. https://www.faa.gov/ame_guide/app_process/exam_tech/item47/amd/antidepressants

Chapter 7
Aerospace Neuropsychological Modeling of Pilot Resources

Thomas A. Van Dillen, Robert L. Kane, Anthony P. Tvaryanas, Hunter T. Klevgard, Tammy T. Ho, Kelene A. Fercho, Brett S. Torrence, and Sarah V. Ligda

Introduction and Background

The mission of civil aviation authorities (CAAs) is to ensure that the global airspace is safe and efficient. Safety is, and will always be, the number one priority of the FAA and CAAs globally. To this end, the FAA is a signatory member state of the International Civil Aviation Organization safety goals. The FAA functions within a Safety Management System (SMS) framework (FAA, 2020). This framework seeks to describe, measure, and manage risk within the National Airspace (NAS).

By viewing the core functions of the FAA within a risk management framework, we can better understand systematic goals and how clinical assessment operates as a risk assessment subsystem. The FAA's Medical Standards and Certification for Airmen are published as a federal regulation in Title 14, Code of Federal Regulations, Part 67. The standards are a regulatory structure upon which a rules-based approach is layered for risk assessment and certification decision making. To obtain a medical certification, the pilot must undergo a physical examination given by an FAA-approved aviation medical examiner (AME).

From a medical perspective fitness is related to risk of failure. The risks may be subtle or of sudden onset. In either case a risk factor can lead to incapacitation or off nominal flight performance sufficient to produce a safety hazard. A heart condition becomes an aeromedically significant issue if a pilot is at risk of a heart attack or malfunction that could affect their ability to competently operate the aircraft. Cognitive limitations or vulnerabilities can constitute risks to safe operator performance. The challenge in medical certification is to define the capacities needed for safe operator performance and to determine when a limitation in these abilities results in aeromedically significant risk. This chapter focuses on the conceptualization of aeromedically significant cognitive risk and presents models that have been employed in this endeavor. In this context we will also present general systems performance theory (GSPT) as an approach that could compliment current modeling approaches.

There are three classes of FAA medical certificate a pilot can apply for, each with a more restrictive set of medical standards (see Appendix A). Each consecutive class of medical certificate is associated with increasing medical standards across vision, hearing, balance, and cardiovascular health. Pilots who do not initially meet the set requirements may be deferred to the Aeromedical Certification Division (AAM-300) and, in some cases, are required to provide additional supporting materials regarding aspects of the pilot's physical, cognitive, or psychological health.

If a pilot has a static defect that is unlikely to change (e.g., limb amputation), they may be granted a statement of demonstrated ability (SODA). Medical flight tests can also be conducted to demonstrate that a pilot with a static defect can safely operate the aircraft. For nonstatic medical conditions that are well controlled and unlikely to acutely or subtly degrade pilot performance, the pilot may be approved for a time-limited special issuance (14 C.F.R. § 67, 1996).

This rule-based approach to aeromedical decision-making is dependent on prescriptive processes and procedures and does not routinely include objective criteria that may inform on the applicant's capability to perform the duties authorized by the class of medical certificate (A. P. Tvaryanas, personal communication, August 11, 2023). By contrast, pilot certificates and ratings may be issued once an applicant has satisfied the required training and testing and has demonstrated the knowledge and skill in tasks and standards identified by the FAA. The ultimate predictive judgment of interest is simple and relates to the question of whether the pilot being evaluated presents greater than normal risk to the safety of the NAS. While medical certification is not the same as flight proficiency assessment, it is important to make medical criteria as objective as possible when relating medical capabilities to flight standards.

In this chapter we examine through models of performance how we may be able to identify human factors thought to be vital and necessary for safe and efficient flying; how modeling of performance may be able to inform performance-based medical standards, away from a rule-based process; and finally, how shifting the process of assessment can impact the current systems approach to medical certification and therefore culture of safety.

Models of Human Performance and Limitations

Neuropsychologists who evaluate pilots must have a clear understanding of what pilots do when flying. A range of human factors and cognitive functions critical for flying efficacy have been identified (see Appendix B). Prior support is documented by Fleishman and Ornstein (1960), in which the authors detail a factor analysis of human performance in various flying maneuvers, including control precision, spatial orientation (judgment/response), multilimb coordination, response orientation, rate control, and kinesthetic discrimination. In modern day, the range of knowledge, skills, and cognitive abilities identified to be vital for safe and efficient flying has become extensive and includes neuropsychological processes such as mental flexibility/processing speed, working memory, spatial perception, math processing, and executive functioning/problem solving.

Neuropsychologists must also have an appreciation of the rigors that flying imposes on pilots and conditions that can change and create even higher unique demands on the pilot. Some situations like flying over extreme terrains, such as mountains and hills during difficult weather conditions, increase the hazards that can interfere with safe flight. White-outs and illusions caused by the environment can decrease visibility causing spatial disorientation. In such situations it may be necessary to fly by instrumentation thereby increasing stress and fatigue due to required sustained alertness. Extended operations can lead to fatigue that in turn impacts concentration, communication, attention, and judgment. There is a need to have data-based decision-making models both for assessment and safety of flight/pilots. Although the current models inform on factors contributing to the pilot's presumed performance, they are limiting in scope and provide a narrow view of the pilot's overall capacity.

Capturing the Capacity for Flying Safely

Various approaches have been used to assess underlying cognitive capabilities needed for successful flight performance under normal and challenging conditions. Some involve a direct measurement of cognitive skills, others use physiological metrics to help evaluate stress and workload. Correlation and regression-based statistical methods are the most frequently used approaches to evaluate capabilities against performance. Examples of these approaches are given next. We also provide a brief presentation of general systems performance theory (GSTP) developed by Kondraske in 2011 (Kondraske, 2011). GSPT has emerged as a potential method for modeling specific capabilities related to safe and effective flight performance.

Several published studies have explored the best methods for measuring cognitive function in pilots and other personnel in aviation occupations. In this instance, test batteries are generally used to inform decision-making when selecting best-fit pilot candidates. The most widely used cognitive assessments include the Cog Screen-Aeromedical Edition, Micro-cog, MAB-II, and Wechsler Adult Intelligence Test (Carretta, 2011; Ozdil Arikan et al., 2018; Yesavage et al., 2011). These cognitive test batteries typically consist of separate subtests assessing cognitive skills such as attention, memory, visual processing, reasoning, multitasking, and multilimb coordination. Often, existing neurocognitive tests also include Digit Span, Stroop Color, and Automated Neuropsychological Assessment Metrics Switching Task to measure for individual functions. Specifically, the FAA Neuropsychological Assessment involves one-on-one assessment of skills that are considered important for the cognitive demands of flight including attention, focus, sustained attention, distractibility, memory, visual–spatial skills, auditory perception, perceptual speed, rapid motor responses, decision-making, and the ability to rapidly process information (FAA, 2023).

Borghini et al. (2022) investigated the use of neurophysiological data such as electroencephalograms (EEG) and electrocardiograms (ECG), as an index for mental effort, to indirectly measure the operator expertise and performance capacity of pilots. This study primarily focused on the neurophysiological differences between novice pilots (those with an average of 37 flight hours) and expert pilots (those with an average of 467 flight hours) when preforming flight simulations scenarios. Using a high-fidelity flight simulator, pilots were tasked with recovering aircraft control from unusual attitude and solving for electrical failures. Findings suggest that although performance quality was equivalent among both pilot groups, novices required more mental effort than experts to complete identical tasks as indicated by an EEG-based mental effort index. When compared with the results from the EEG-based mental effort index, subjective measures of mental effort did not accurately capture the cognitive demands of the pilots' performance in flying tasks. Although the results from this study introduced novel measures to assess pilots' performance progress, the measure itself is limited in scope and does not capture specific aspects of performance resources.

Similarly, Causse et al. (2011) developed an assessment to measure pilots' executive functions, reasoning skills, and psychomotor reaction time and their relationship to crash risk and flight performance. Participants were assessed using the Barratt Impulsiveness Scale and a neuropsychological assessment battery that includes Target Hitting, 2-Back Test of Working Memory, Deductive Reasoning, Computerized Wisconsin Card Sorting Test, and Spatial Stroop Test. Participants performed navigation tasks and crosswind landing decision tasks on a PC-based flight simulator that has been configured by flight instructors for realism and relevant difficulty. The results of this study show that the cognitive tests were able to reliably predict both piloting and decision-making performance; namely, reasoning performance was most predictive of the factors measured to predict pilot performance abilities. Reasoning abilities are often linked to fluid intelligence and abstract problem-solving skill (Causse et al., 2011). This suggests that those scoring higher in reasoning abilities were able to better perform piloting tasks, as they were able to adapt to novel and complex problems such as unpredicted flight errors. The results from this study highlight the potential of developing neuropsychological assessment software that could aid in pilot certification; however, this study's method of assessing performance may be better suited for early detection of subtle cognitive declines using individual archived performance data rather than forecasting an individual's full range of performance capabilities. In this case, cognitive performance data can be archived and later used to detect early signs of fatigue, substance conception, and stress or to track piloting performance during recovery from the onset of diseases. Currently, the results of this study fall short in supporting the effort to identify and forecast pilot performance capabilities.

One of the more recent studies to update our understanding of pilots' performance abilities comes from Chira et al. (2020). In their study, Chira et al. (2020) aimed to develop a performance envelope for pilots based on the influences of certain factors (i.e., situational awareness, mental workload, stress, and attention) on an individual's physiological measures. Physiological parameters such as heart rate, respiratory rate, pupil diameter, blink frequency, and self-reported questionnaires were then used to shape the human performance envelope model. This study was able to develop an accurate human performance envelope for pilots without the need to incorporate additional psychological factors such as communication and teaming. This could suggest that physiological factors are predictors of human performance and provide adequate data for the development of an individual performance envelope.

Model-Based Performance Assessment

Within the context of the existing measures and their limitations, there is a need to develop a model-based performance assessment that not only calculates an individual's performance range but also forecasts potential performance based on current abilities and incorporates environmental (situational) demands. The pilot performance envelope model by Chira et al. (2020) aimed to inform decision-makers on whether or not an individual has the basic performance resources required to satisfy the demands of piloting an aircraft. This decision is based on individual assessment of physiological parameters and factors during intense piloting simulations. Individual performance resource data can also be retrospectively examined to identify changes in abilities following adverse experience (e.g., injury, health crisis).

The Fitness for Duty Assessment by Kennedy et al. (1988) used archived performance data of nuclear power plant personnel to detect subtle changes relating to shift work, stress, and toxic agents without the need for repeated intrusive measures. Another way performance assessment modeling can optimize task operations is by identifying courses or training to update based on performance demand–resource trends. The military demand–resource model (Bates et al., 2013) identified areas of improvements in leadership and training by identifying and addressing common gaps found in an individual's performance resource envelope. Finally, assessment of performance can help identify necessary updates to system design and task interface to aid in performance resource demands. In a report discussing human performance models and their potential use in system design and evaluation, the National Research Council points out the use for performance models in improving functions of human-machine systems (1990). Performance resource data and the resulting capacity envelope can highlight system configurations necessary for optimal human-machine performance.

As noted above, a promising approach to quantifying aspects of human performance and forecasting performance is the *general systems performance theory* (GSTP; Kondraske, 2011). Inspired by concepts found in resource economics, the GSPT framework models human attributes of performance in a system during task operations. At its core, GSPT demonstrates that all tasks require performance resources and can only be successfully accomplished when the system, in this case the human, has sufficient resource availability in order to meet or exceed the resource demand. In this framework, the resource demands of a particular task are observed and the essential attributes of available performance resources or basic performance resources (BPRs) are quantified and predicted. Considering principles of resource economics, an individual's BPRs can either contribute to or limit the performance of more challenging tasks. In addition, more complex tasks are referred to as *high-level tasks* (HLTs), and they require additional resources to be successfully completed. The complex operations involved in piloting an aircraft summarily place it in the category of HLTs because it requires more performance resources.

Early studies of GSPT demonstrate the ability of nonlinear causal resource analysis (NCRA) as an alternative to regression analysis for predicting human performance and identifying limiting performance resources. That is, the unique factor of the GSPT is the performance prediction methodology of NCRA (Kondraske, 2011). NCRA helps identify the minimal basic performance resources necessary to perform an HLT. This directly sets GSPT and the practical method of NCRA apart from existing performance prediction models. With this threshold-based analysis, the NCRA can predict the highest level of performance in a task given a set of resources available. Recent studies, namely, those by Beller (2022), Fischer et al. (2002), Johnson et al. (2004), Dillon et al. (2000), Innes et al. (2011), Kondraske et al. (1997), and Taranto (2020), aim to optimize task operations assessment by leveraging the GSPT framework and NCRA to predict performance by using an individualized approach of identifying a performance capacity envelope.

A recent application of performance modeling in aviation, specifically utilizing the GSPT and NCRA framework, was used in a study conducted by Taranto (2020) investigating the predictive performance of 64 participants without prior piloting experience. A total of 17 BPRs were developed by reviewing relevant tasks, skills, and abilities listed in O*NET (https://www.dol.gov/agencies/eta/onet) and Fleishman and Reilly's *Handbook of Human Abilities* (1992; see Appendix B). Following the BPR measures, participants performed piloting tasks on an X-plane 11 and their HLT performance was quantified using a modified FAA-referenced scorecard. Inputs for the study were the 17 measured BPRs and outputs were the HLT performance (HLTp) measured during piloting tasks. The performance model was then validated via a technique in which each BPR was multiplied by n-1 participants until individual models were gathered. Taranto (2020) found 97% agreement between median predicted scores and median actual performance scores. In addition to agreement between scores, the results also demonstrate that NCRA performs well in the domain of aviation by predicting piloting performance in high-level and low-level tasks. Overall, the study conducted by Taranto (2020) could be a relevant reference when developing a performance-based applied assessment for pilots, as it is among the first to relate GSPT and NCRA to pilot performance.

The current research on human performance modeling, task-specific resource demands, and accepted testing instruments can inform current researchers by providing recommendations for best practices and requirements for performance assessments. A performance resource-demand model, such as Kondraske's (2011) GSPT and Taranto's (2020) model-based human systems integration, is best suited within the reviewed literature for performance modeling of complex tasks, as it forecasts performance based on an individual's performance rather than on standardized assessments. In terms of recommended instruments for assessing individual abilities, many of the studies used industry-standard neuropsychological tests.

Resilience Associated With General Systems Performance Theory

Because we are evaluating the performance of pilots and the environment with which aviation demands vary, we need to consider resilience, since much of the construct overlaps with that of GSPT. However, there is no universally accepted scientific definition of *resilience* (Curtis & Cicchetti, 2003; Masten, 2001; Newman, 2005): It is a dynamic term that incorporates a holistic perspective of the human or pilot. Ultimately, resilience is a multidimensional construct that is best understood in the context of the environment. Each area of adversity needs to be considered in relation to the individual because resilience can be different things in different environments. By specifying the dynamics of the individual and his or her situation, the construct of what is protective and resilient will be better defined. The focus of this construct is on those elements that make pilots better at what they do and how they do it within a given extreme environment or environments.

The neuropsychological demand–resource model (NMDR; Van Dillen & Fujimoto, 2010) was an attempt at evaluating the factors that make up psychological fitness and resilience. The NMDR is seen as a component of resilience in the theoretical sense and defines *resilience* as the bidirectional interaction of psychological fitness, which is comprised of cognitive emotional factors and information-processing abilities within the context of the environment. It is the degree to which an individual has the capacity to maximally and effectively interact within his or her environment as well as adapt to changing environments. Depending on the environment and its demands as well as on one's abilities and experiences, a continuum and range of effectiveness and functionality develops.

Essentially, NMDR utilizes a demand–resource modeling approach, as it examines the HLTs and BPRs of a task demand and determines whether the individual has the *minimum* resources to effectively meet the demand. Critical is the dynamic relationship between the human resources and the environmental demand. As the demands change, do the resources of the human effectively meet those new demands and do so efficiently and safely?

Risk Modeling Integral to GSPT

Risk modeling is integral to GSPT decision-making. The FAA have used risk assessments to aid decision-making and resource allocation. Psychological and medical health factors have not traditionally been included in these risk assessments, because there are no working models in use. Ideally, modeling would highlight psychological and medical health influences on the pilot's capacity to fly safely, which could be used in decision-making (i.e., fly/no-fly decisions for a given situation). This approach will more likely reduce the elimination of someone just because they have a medical risk factor (e.g., heart disease) but rather identifying the specific health condition to flying safely.

As integral to overall flight planning, pilots could utilize in the future readiness to perform assessments of their current resources in relationship to flight plan demands and subsequent risk to fly safely and efficiently. This could mean choosing not to fly given the demands of the flight pattern, weather, etc., or perhaps determining another way/means to meet the need, for example, call up another pilot or change the route, or cancel all together. Using a functional approach to examine the current needs with that of individual factors (e.g., psychological health and resilience) could perpetuate a cultural shift to protective factors and building those into the model to mitigate risk, thereby enhancing safety of the NAS.

Research Inquiries

The landscape of today's assessment of pilots/aviators raises many critical questions upon which it would be advantageous to gain insight. The following research questions are just a few examples of the type of knowledge needed to succeed with pilot assessment, which a functional assessment/GSPT model may help answer:

- Can pilots adapt in the most extreme conditions and even excel?
- What are the characteristics of pilots that allow them to effectively adapt to different environments with different demands?
- Are those pilots who show the capacity to adapt in extreme environments also capable of switching between different environments?
- What set of characteristics of pilots show the greatest resilience to frequent flights and fatigue?
- Do the number and type of flights (conditions) supersede the most adaptable characteristics for pilots?

Conclusion

This chapter discussed models for evaluating pilot performance capabilities as related to medical certification. Although medical certification is different from flight performance assessment, medical certification attempts to mitigate risks to safety by identifying cognitive limitations that may affect operator performance in complex and demanding environments. The process is challenging and involves the investigation of different models to determine the method or combination of methods that can best capture neurocognitive parameters of safe pilot performance. The models that emerge may involve making use of regression-based methods and computational models derived from cognitive test scores; they may incorporate GSPT or they may incorporate physiological measures of stress and workload. Since human beings do not perform consistently at every point in time, resilience models may help capture critical aspects of performance.

Aerospace is rapidly expanding and evolving to include a wide range of environments, new and emerging technologies, and differential demands on pilots and technical operations. It is prime time for the advancement and development of new measures, methods, and approaches. Common to most areas in psychology is the utilization of assessment methods to gather information and analyze data. Depending on the examiners' input and outcomes desired, assessment instruments vary widely for the specific purposes intended. Utilizing the GSPT model will contribute to the assessment methodology and in the development of assessment instruments.

The fields of aerospace psychology and neuropsychology would likely benefit from this approach as it is holistic in nature and uses a wide array of test instruments from both the information processing and cognitive emotional domains. In addition, the goals of this type of assessment are to characterize the individual pilot's functioning in the context of the environment, therefore assuring functioning capabilities are optimal to the demands of the flight plan, ultimately assigning accountability to the pilot in the moment.

Additionally, the impact of a functional approach would improve informed decisions concerning the qualities of personnel needed for certain situations and, possibly, even the way a situation needs to be managed and staffed to maximize performance in any given circumstance. Demonstrating a proactive rather than reactive solution set will likely help the mission of the FAA to assure everything is being done in the name of safe and secure operations.

References

Bates, M.J., Fallesen, J.J., Huey, W.S., Packard, G.A., Ryan, D.M., Burke, C.S., Smith, D.G., Watola, D.J., Pinder, E.D., Yosick, T.M., Estrada, A.X., Crepeau, L., & Bowles, S.V. (2013). Total force fitness in units, part 1: Military demand-resource model. *Military Medicine, 178*(11), 1164–1182. https://doi.org/10.7205/MILMED-D-12-00519

Beller, T. (2022). *The application of general systems performance theory to improve flight safety* [Unpublished doctoral dissertation]. Embry-Riddle Aeronautical University.

Borghini, G., Aricò, P., Flumeri, G.D., Ronca, V., Giorgi, A., Sciaraffa, N., & Babiloni, F. (2022). Air force pilot expertise assessment during unusual attitude recovery flight. *Safety, 8*(2), Article 38. https://doi.org/10.3390/safety8020038

Carretta, T.R. (2011). Pilot candidate selection method: Still an effective predictor of US Air Force pilot training performance. *Aviation Psychology and Applied Human Factors, 1*(1), 3–8. https://doi.org/10.1027/2192-0923/a00002

Causse, M., Dehais, F., & Pastor, J. (2011). Executive functions and pilot characteristics predict flight simulator performance in general aviation pilots. *The International Journal of Aviation Psychology, 21*(3), 217–234. https://doi.org/10.1080/10508414.2011.582441

Chira, A.I., Dumitrescu, A., Moisoiu, C.S., & Tanase, C.A. (2020). Human performance envelope model study using pilot's measured parameters. *INCAS Bulletin, 12*(4), 49–61. https://doi.org/10.13111/2066-8201.2020.12.4.5

Curtis, W.J., & Cicchetti, D. (2003). Moving research on resilience into the 21st century: Theoretical and methodological considerations in examining the biological contributors to resilience. *Development and Psychopathology, 15*(3), 773–810. https://doi.org/10.1017/s0954579403000373

Dillon, W.E., Kondraske, G.V., Everett, L.J., & Volz, R.A. (2000). Performance theory based outcome measurement in engineering education and training. *IEEE Transactions on Education, 43*(2), 92–99. https://doi.org/10.1109/13.848059

Federal Aviation Administration (FAA). (2020, June). *Order 8000.369C safety management system.* https://www.faa.gov/documentLibrary/media/Order/Order_8000.369C.pdf

Federal Aviation Administration (FAA). (2023). *Recommended practices for human space flight occupant safety.* https://www.faa.gov/media/71481

Fischer, C.A., Kondraske, G.V., & Stewart, R.M. (2002). Prediction of driving performance using nonlinear causal resource analysis. Proceedings of the second joint 24th annual conference and the annual fall meeting of the Biomedical Engineering Society. *Engineering in Medicine and Biology, 3*, 2473–2474. IEEE. https://doi.org/10.1109/IEMBS.2002.1053382

Fleishman, E.A., & Ornstein, G.N. (1960). An analysis of pilot flying performance in terms of component abilities. *Journal of Applied Psychology, 44*(3), 146–155. https://doi.org/10.1037/h0043480

Fleishman, E.A., & Reilly, M.E. (1992). *Handbook of human abilities: Definitions, measurements, and job task requirements*. Consulting Psychologists Press.

Innes, C.R., Lee, D., Chen, C., Ponder-Sutton, A.M., Melzer, T.R., & Jones, R.D. (2011). Do complex models increase prediction of complex behaviors? Predicting driving ability in people with brain disorders. *Quarterly Journal of Experimental Psychology, 64*(9), 1714–25. https://doi.org/10.1080/17470218.2011.555821

Johnson, D.B., Kondraske, G.V., Wilhelm, D.M., Jacomides, L., Ogan, K., Pearle, M.S., & Cadeddu, J.A. (2004). Assessment of basic human performance resources predicts the performance of virtual ureterorenoscopy. *The Journal of Urology, 171*(1), 80–84. https://doi.org/10.1097/01.ju.0000100167.92139.cb

Kennedy, R.S., Turnage, J.T., & Lane, N.E. (1988, June). Application of a portable microcomputer mental acuity battery for fitness-for-duty assessment in power plant operations. In *Conference Record for 1988, IEEE Fourth Conference on Human Factors and Power Plants*, (pp. 551–558). Institute of Electrical and Electronics Engineering (IEEE).

Kondraske, G.V. (2011). General systems performance theory and its application to understanding complex system performance. *Information Knowledge Systems Management, 10*(1–4), 235–259. https://doi.org/10.3233/IKS-2012-0195

Kondraske, G.V., Johnston, C., Pearson, A., & Tarbox, L. (1997). Performance prediction and limiting resource identification with nonlinear causal resource analysis. *Proceedings of the 19th Annual International Conference of the IEEE Engineering in Medicine and Biology Society* (Cat. No. 97CH36136). https://doi.org/10.1109/iembs.1997.757081

Masten, A.S. (2001). Ordinary magic: Resilience processes in development. *American Psychologist, 56*(3), 227–238. https://doi.org/10.1037/0003-066X.56.3.227

Medical Standards and Certification, 14 C.F.R. § 67 (1996). https://www.ecfr.gov/current/title-14/chapter-I/subchapter-D/part-67

National Research Council. (1990). *Quantitative modeling of human performance in complex, dynamic systems*. The National Academies Press. https://doi.org/10.17226/1490

Newman, R. (2005). APA's resilience initiative. *Professional Psychology: Research and Practice, 36*(3), 227–229. https://doi.org/10.1037/0735-7028.36.3.227

Ozdil Arikan, Z., Ertemir, D., & Keskinkilic, C. (2018). A norm study of a neuropsychological test battery for evaluating cognitive functions in commercial airline pilots. *Dusunen Adam: The Journal of Psychiatry and Neurological Sciences, 31*(4), 375–388. https://doi.org/10.5350/dajpn2018310406

Taranto, M.T. (2020). *Model-based human systems integration* [Unpublished doctoral dissertation]. Naval Postgraduate School, Monterey, California.

Van Dillen, T. & Fujimoto, A. (2010, July). *Neuropsychological military demand resource model (NMDR): In support of the integrated Total Force Fitness (TFF) Approach*. Unpublished whitepaper for Defense Centers of Excellence (DCoE) for Psychological Health & Traumatic Brain Injury.

Yesavage, J.A., Jo, B., Adamson, M.M., Kennedy, Q., Noda, A., Hernandez, B., & Taylor, J.L. (2011). Initial cognitive performance predicts longitudinal aviator performance. *Journals of Gerontology Series B: Psychological Sciences and Social Sciences, 66*(4), 444–453. https://doi.org/10.1093/geronb/gbr031

Appendix A

Pilots can apply for three classes of FAA medical certificate.

First Class Medical Certificate

Those looking for a career as an airline transportation pilot (ATP) and looking to fly for airline companies.

Requirements:
20/20 vision with or without correction
Must meet mental and neurological standards
ECG required at age 35 and annually after 40 years old

Limitations:
Must be renewed every 12 months (6 months for over age 40)
Not recognized by the military

Second Class Medical Certificate

For pilots who are looking to carry passengers or cargo for hire and other commercial uses. Similar to 3rd Class certificate but with higher standards in certain areas including vision.

Requirements:
20/20 vision with or without correction
Must pass color vision test
Must pass all health standards

Limitations:
Must be renewed every year
Not able to fly for transportation airlines

Third Class Medical Certificate

For private, recreational, and student pilots to obtain.

Requirements:
Must meet eye, ear, nose, throat, and other standards in examination
Must meet mental health standards
Must disclose health history

Limitations:
Must be renewed every 5 years if under 40, every 2 years if over 40
Pilots must fly recreationally, not for hire
Not for commercial or airline pilots

Appendix B

Comparison of aviation pilots' performance resources and abilities in the literature (basic performance resources listed here are not in order of priority)

Taranto (2020)	Beller (2022)	Fleishman & Ornstein (1960)	O*NET OnLine
Visual motion tracking accuracy	Multilimb coordination speed	Control precision	Control precision
Visual motion prediction accuracy	Multilimb coordination accuracy	Spatial orientation (judgment/response)	Vision acuity (near/far)
Multilimb coordination speed	Multilimb coordination throughput	Multilimb coordination	Problem sensitivity
Multilimb coordination accuracy	Short-term memory capacity	Response orientation	Response orientation
Multilimb coordination throughput	Multichoice reaction speed	Rate control	Reasoning (inductive/deductive)
Multichoice reaction speed	Math processing speed	Kinesthetic discrimination	Depth perception
Spatial orientation response speed	Math processing accuracy		Information ordering
Spatial orientation response accuracy	Math processing throughput		Oral comprehension and expression
Spatial orientation response throughput	Spatial orientation response speed		Perceptual speed
Perceptual integration capacity (concealed word)	Spatial orientation response accuracy		Speech clarity and recognition
Perceptual integration capacity (snowy pictures)	Spatial orientation response throughput		Multilimb coordination
Math processing speed	Switching response speed		Reaction time
Math processing accuracy	Switching response accuracy		Selective attention
Math processing throughput	Switching response throughput		Written comprehension
Switching response speed	Perceptual integration capacity (concealed word)		Flexibility and speed of closure
Switching response accuracy	Perceptual integration capacity (snowy pictures)		Manual dexterity
Switching response throughput	Spatial disorientation knowledge		Rate control
	Change detection throughput		Spatial orientation
	Spatial awareness accuracy		Time sharing
	Total flight experience		Arm–hand steadiness

Taranto (2020)	Beller (2022)	Fleishman & Ornstein (1960)	O*NET OnLine
	Flight time in the preceding 90 days		Hearing sensitivity
	Total simulated instrument experience		Written expression
	Total actual instrument experience		Finger dexterity
	Instrument experience in the preceding 90 days		Glare sensitivity
			Visual color discrimination
			Visualization
			Auditory attention
			Category flexibility
			Fluency of ideas

Section II

Prevention and Resilience

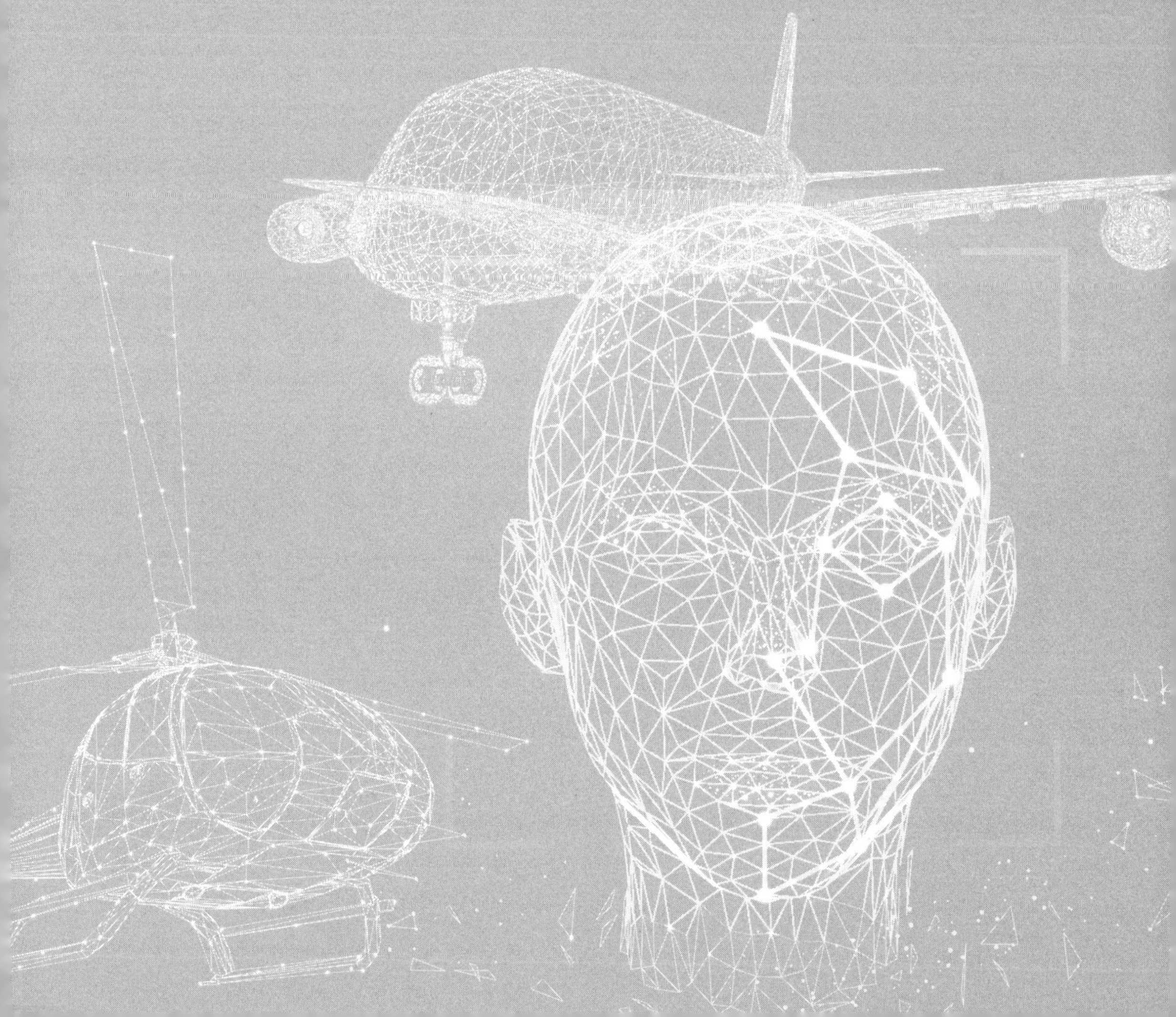

Chapter 8
Salutogenic Approach to Mental Health and Well-Being in Aviation

Sanjiv Sharma, Laurie Shaw, and Anthony Carter

Introduction

As human beings, we remain exposed to stresses – personal, social, and environmental – each of which could impact one's sense of mental wellness. Our social-media-dependent lifestyle increasingly isolates and alienates us, and more individuals seek to cope with their personal stresses without adequate family/social support. This could partly be because of the stigma that still exists for "mental illness" and the adverse effects it has on all aspects of a person's life.

The harsh realities of the socioeconomic impact of the recent COVID-19 pandemic further exposed our vulnerabilities and its adverse effects on mental health. In the context of aviation, this is complicated by an individual's own fears about whether they may be unable to regain medical certification to undertake safety-sensitive duties and the risk to their employment and career.

Inability to cope with stress – coupled with the stigma about mental illness and its implications for employability – leaves pilots, air traffic controllers, maintenance personnel, cabin crew, and other aviation staff vulnerable. The need for timely intervention and help is compromised by their reluctance to speak about it or seek professional help. Therefore, there is a need to look beyond the disease-/diagnosis-based regulatory approach to mental illness.

This is possible when we recognize that humans remain in a "health ease/dis-ease continuum" (Antonovsky, 1990, p. 76) dependent on their prevailing state of health/well-being and, in turn, requires a bold approach to replace the prevailing pathogenic paradigm with a salutogenic approach to health promotion.

Mental health issues, in particular, need to be addressed collaboratively by all the aviation stakeholders: aviation medical certificate holders, airlines/employers, and aviation regulators. With this in mind, this chapter discusses a salutogenic approach to the health of aviation professionals, specifically focusing on mental health and well-being. It further proposes that peer support embodies a salutogenic approach to enable an affected individual to remain productive and safe with adequate support from their employer and appropriate regulatory oversight.

The structure of the chapter progresses from discussing mental health and its impact on aviation and safety; defining salutogenesis, including its core concept of *sense of coherence* (SOC); describing the usefulness of peer support and the need for applying salutogenesis for mental well-being among aviation personnel; and finally, proposing inclusion of a salutogenic approach to mental well-being in the *safety management system* (SMS) of aviation operators/airlines as part of the regulatory approach.

This chapter is a distinct departure from the traditional disease model discussed elsewhere in this book. Instead of focusing on pathology, including the prevailing deficit model within the context of neuropsychology with inherent focus on human limitations, the salutogenic approach focuses on the individual within their environmental context (Mittelmark et al., 2017). This, in turn, removes the dichotomy between health and disease to promote health as a continuum (Antonovsky, 1996). It must be added that this chapter has drawn heavily from *The Handbook of Salutogenesis* (Mittelmark et al., 2022), and the same has been quoted repeatedly. Even though salutogenesis is practiced elsewhere in different ways, including in nonmedical fields, our focus throughout this chapter remains on how salutogenesis is applicable in the context of aviation.

Mental Health and Its Impact on Aviation and Safety

Aviation regulators screen for mental health conditions for aeromedical certification purposes to ensure that pilots' and controllers' mental well-being translates into aviation safety with their ability to perform optimally despite usual aviation stresses: physical, physiological, and psychological. The biggest barrier in such an approach is a lack of a complete history due to the prevalent perception among the majority of aviation professionals that a disclosed history of mental illness will adversely affect their employability. However, without the complete psychiatric history being known to aviation regulators, fitness for flying privileges may be based on an inadequate risk assessment.

The Germanwings tragedy of March 24, 2015 was a grim reminder of the potential consequences of mental illness on the safety of air operations. The copilot on that flight had a mental health disorder and was taking antidepressant and sleeping aid medications (Bureau d'Enquêtes et d'Analyses, 2016). Both his medical condition and treatment with psychotropic medication would have prevented him flying if that had been known to the safety regulator and his employer. Due to the privacy protections in relation to medical records in Germany at the time, this vital information was not disclosed. Mulder and de Rooy (2018) reported that there have been at least nine accidents most likely attributed to mental illness, resulting in 576 fatalities. Over a period of 20 years, it was estimated that 24 out of 7,244 (0.33%) fatal aircraft accidents were likely to be aircraft-assisted suicides in the United States (Vuorio et al., 2014). Similarly, there were three suicides out of 1,000 (0.3%) consecutive aircraft accidents over 40 years in the United Kingdom (Cullen et al., 1997). In Germany, this was also estimated at around 0.3% per year (Schwark et al., 2008).

Despite the likelihood of underreporting, mental health conditions are still listed as one of the most common causes for unfitness among aviation medical certificate holders, besides cardiovascular, neurological, and musculoskeletal conditions. In their review of 58 studies related to pilot mental health since 1980, Ackland et al. (2022) reported that the most common mental health conditions investigated were depression, anxiety, and suicide. Psychiatric causes for loss of medical certification among commercial pilots varied between 10% and 15% (Arva & Wagstaff, 2004; Evans & Radcliffe, 2012; Høva et al., 2017; Simons et al., 2021). Henssler et al. (2021) reported that in-flight incapacitation due to psychiatric conditions that subsequently resulted in suspension of privileges during a calendar year had occurred in six out of 16 (37.5%) cases when operating as a crew (including simulator or travelling as passenger), while nonspecific symptoms with psychiatric conditions likely to be contributory were reported in five other instances.

Adverse mental health outcomes are known to occur during quarantine and isolation, increasing the risks of depression, anxiety, and stress-related disorders (Henssler et al., 2021). There was an evident increase in the incidence of mental illnesses during the COVID-19 pandemic. Pilots operating humanitarian and repatriation flights during the pandemic were subjected to rigid quarantine and isolation requirements, which left them exposed and vulnerable to mental ill-health. Closures of national and state borders brought commercial flights to a near halt, resulting in countless numbers of pilots being grounded or laid off. Although the extent of psychiatric morbidity among pilots and other aviation professionals during the pandemic is not fully known, it has taken a significant toll on their mental health. A review of cabin crew by Görlich and Stadelmann (2020) during the pandemic revealed a significant deterioration in mental health as evident from symptoms of depression, anxiety, and stress. This was due to inability to work resulting from isolation and quarantine requirements as well as job insecurity.

Minor psychological disorders, unrecognized or undiagnosed, also have an impact on performance distinct from the potential to develop into severe disorders. Such minor psychological disorders were reported in a pre-pandemic anonymous survey to be prevalent among 6.7 % of Brazilian pilots (Feijó et al., 2012). Another pre-pandemic web-based anonymous survey among airline pilots across 50 countries by Wu et al. (2016) reported that 12.6 % met the criteria for depression with 4.1 % having suicidal thoughts. Among the respondents, 13.5 % reported using sleep-aid medication. Pasha and Stokes (2018) reported that the prevalence of depression among commercial pilots is between 1.9 % and 12.6 %. It can be reasonably assumed that the mental health rates identified in the aforementioned surveys would have readily increased during the pandemic (allowing, of course, for deliberate non-reporting behaviors based on how the survey was designed).

Even during normal times, there are prevailing work- and life-related stressors that may predispose a person to mental illness. They may present as symptoms of depression, anxiety, psychosomatic conditions, or inability to concentrate, poor decision-making, forgetfulness, irritability, fatigue, and sense of worthlessness. Such minor psychological conditions may remain unknown to the individual but have a bearing on performance and safety in aviation, and if left unaddressed, have direct bearing on long-term morbidity due to mental health conditions.

One of the major barriers in seeking treatment for mental illness is the effect of social avoidance on interpersonal relationships and mental health-care providers so as to deter a distressed individual from seeking treatment. The stigma associated with mental illness may not only delay seeking treatment due to social attitudes, it may also deny much-needed social support from family, friends, or colleagues and impact upon treatment outcomes due to poor compliance and adherence to treatment. In addition, stigmatizing attitudes of health-care workers toward mental illness may have adverse bearing on the professional relationship between practitioners and patients (Sickel et al., 2014).

Notwithstanding the aforementioned factors, the biggest barrier in seeking timely help for aviation professionals is the impact of a mental health diagnosis and treatment on their employability. A lack of peer support, including rumors or gossip, also contributes to such perceptions.

The World Health Organization (WHO) defines health as "a state of complete physical, mental and social well-being, and not merely the absence of disease" (WHO, 2010, p. 6). Specifically, mental health is a state of well-being in which individuals realize their own abilities, can cope with normal stresses of life, can work productively and are able to make a contribution to their community (WHO, 2013). Extending this to the workplace, the WHO defined a healthy workplace (WHO, 2010, p. 10) as:

> One in which workers and managers collaborate to use a continual improvement process to protect and promote the health, safety and well-being of all workers and the sustainability of the workplace by considering the following, based on identified needs:
> (a) health and safety concerns in the physical work environment;
> (b) health, safety and well-being concerns in the psychosocial work environment, including organization of work and workplace culture;
> (c) personal health resources in the workplace; and
> (d) ways of participating in the community to improve the health of workers, their families and other members of the community.

Use of salient words in the WHO definition, such as "promote," "well-being," "psychosocial," "personal health resources," and "community," assume a collaborative, participatory, and facilitative approach to health, including mental well-being, emphasizing an organizational safety culture with the focus on the worker. It also recognizes key concepts for a salutogenic approach.

However, the predominant current and historical approach to health care focuses upon a diagnosed disease requiring management (i.e., a pathogenic approach). The overt focus on disease – with the need to effect a cure and return to fitness and, in turn, social productivity and gainful employment – reflects such a pathogenic orientation to health. Implicit in that approach is the binary determination that one is either healthy or sick at any given time. Similarly, the medical certification of pilots and air traffic controllers under Chapter 6 of the International Civil Aviation Organization Annex 1 (ICAO, 2022) is premised upon the identification of diseases or medical conditions, which, in turn, may preclude medical certification. In other words, a binary determination of fitness or unfitness with limited scope for active management of medical conditions while maintaining aviation privileges.

Recognizing the potential loss of aviation professionals due to readily treatable conditions – since 1987 in Australia and subsequently in other jurisdictions including Canada, the United Kingdom, the United States, and New Zealand – pilots stable on acceptable treatment for depression can retain their flying privileges and many continue to do so.

Alternative to Current Pathogenic Approach – Salutogenesis

The term "salutogenesis" literally means "the origins of health" and is derived from the Latin word "salus" (meaning health) and the Greek word "genesis" (meaning origin or beginning). The term was coined by medical sociologist Aaron Antonovsky in a paper in 1979 and proposed an approach to studying how and why certain people stay healthy (Antonovsky, 1996).

While Bishop Desmond Tutu said, "There comes a point where we need to stop just pulling people out of the river. We need to go upstream and find out why they're falling in," Antonovsky considered the river to be a metaphor for life, with no one standing on the banks (to pull others out!; Vinje et al., 2022). We learn to swim as the river runs its course, where we float effortlessly most of the time until faced with treacherous currents, when we mostly strive to maneuver deftly even when sapped of our energies until entering calmer flow again.

This means that being in the river, each of us learns to swim, survive, and thrive, yet occasionally some may start to struggle, needing someone to assist them.

Antonovsky (1996) sought to understand the following: "What shapes one's ability to swim well?" This resulted in him propounding the salutogenic model of health where health/dis-ease is seen as a continuum, thus removing the dichotomy between health and ill-health. It also complements the predominant curative approach to health.

Briefly, a salutogenic approach to health promotion directs "efforts to encompass all persons, wherever they are on the continuum, and to focus on salutary factors" (Vinje et al., 2022, p. 43). Salutary factors are those factors that actively promote health. Antonovsky identified three traits - comprehensibility, manageability, and meaningfulness - which in combination are called the *sense of coherence* (SOC). More importantly, instead of a disease becoming the determining factor, the focus is on an individual's ability to withstand the stressors characterized by their SOC. Thus, according to Antonovsky (1996), determination of one's own well-being rests with the individual rather than being determined by a health practitioner. Unlike the view that coping and resilience are contextual and rigid in concept, salutogenesis reflects a dynamic and flexible approach toward problem-solving in life, with the individual's capacity and ability to manage health being of primary importance (Lindström & Eriksson, 2005). Considering health in this way as a resource helps a person live life meaningfully, including coping with stressors associated with daily life.

It is reiterated that the salutogenic approach helps focus on the person, rather than on the disease/ill-health. In a broader context, salutogenesis aims at tapping all available resources, both of the individual and the community, to improve health and well-being. Thus, the salutogenic model for managing health is an interactive and supportive system with application beyond merely the individual and extending to communities, organizations, and society as a whole (Lindström, 2018). Mittelmark and Bauer (2022, p. 16) summed this up as "processes wherein individuals' and communities' resources are engaged to further individual and collective health and well-being." Significantly, salutogenesis can be readily applied in an aviation context provided the aviation community understands the value of such a holistic approach.

Such an approach, especially in relation to mental well-being, has potential economic and cultural benefits, where healthier personnel means reduced absenteeism, ongoing employability, and optimal performance for safe aviation activities.

Salutogenesis in Practice

As noted earlier, a salutogenic orientation focuses on the origins of health rather than on the pathogenic. Antonovsky considered that humans inhabit a world where it is impossible to avoid stressors, hence the normal state of the human organism is one of *entropy* coping with stressors in life. This results in an ongoing state of heterostasis (disequilibrium), unlike the prevailing physiological concept of homeostasis (equilibrium). Therefore, salutogenesis differs from pathogenesis, where (a) each of us are on a health/dis-ease continuum without any dichotomy between health and disease; (b) the focus is on factors actively promoting health - the salutary factors - instead of risk factors causing disease; and (c) there is a need for health promotion for all, irrespective of where they are on the continuum, and going beyond the diagnosis-based curative approach for a disease (Antonovsky, 1996).

In a broader context, salutogenesis does not merely translate into absence of disease (i.e., any condition with symptoms or physical limitations affecting the quality of life and requiring medical intervention in terms of diagnosis and management). Instead, the focus is an individual's sense of well-being or fulfilment. The core construct of salutogenesis is SOC. This was explained by Antonovsky (Vinje et al., 2022, p. 35) as:

> A global orientation that expresses the extent to which one has a pervasive, enduring though dynamic feeling of confidence that (1) the stimuli deriving from one's internal and external environments in the course of living are structured, predictable, and explicable; (2) the resources are available to one to meet the demands posed by these stimuli; and (3) these demands are challenges, worthy of investment and engagement.

Effectively, and irrespective of state of health, it is the SOC that helps an individual with their *generalized resistance resources* (GRRs) cope with stressors in life. Temporary or permanent overwhelming of such resources, while coping with prevailing stressors, determines where one stands on the health/dis-ease continuum.

GRRs, coined by Antonovsky, are those resources that facilitate coping with stressors and help develop SOC. GRRs refer to the "phenomena that provide one with sets of life experiences characterized by consistency, participation in shaping outcomes and an underload-overload balance" (Idan et al., 2022, p. 93). This term broadly includes psychological and physiological resources, knowledge and intelligence, personality, personal, religious, and cultural beliefs, coping abilities, and financial resources. GRRs are part of a continuum state, which when inadequate or insufficient to cope, are called *generalized resistance deficits* (GRD). Thus, while GRRs help cope with stressors adequately to live meaningfully, GRDs result in inadequate, inappropriate, or failed coping and life experiences. Combined, the concept is *generalized resistance resources-resistance deficits* (GRR-RD) and helps toward the development of SOC, applying as much to an individual as to a community (Idan et al., 2022).

Mittelmark and Bauer (2022, p. 11) explain that:

> Salutogenesis refers to the salutogenic model of health, which posits that life experiences help shape one's sense of coherence—an orientation towards life as more or less comprehensible, manageable and meaningful. A strong sense of coherence helps one mobilise resources to cope with stressors and manage tension successfully. Through this mechanism, the sense of coherence helps determine one's movement on the health ease/dis-ease continuum.

As noted earlier, SOC is characterized by (a) comprehensibility - an understanding of the stressors and the challenges the person confronts; (b) meaningfulness - relating to coping and motivation; and (c) manageability - referring to the available resources to cope. Together, this combines the motivational, cognitive, and behavioral aspects of an individual. The GRRs help cope with stressors (or prevailing tensions) better by increasing predictability or consistency (comprehensibility) and creating a balance between the perceived load (manageability) about the prevailing circumstances, that is, environment, and making oneself as a stakeholder in decision-making (meaningfulness), together helping to strengthen the SOC. Determination of well-being rests with the individual rather than being determined by a diagnostician/clinician (Antonovsky, 1996). Unlike the view that coping and resilience are contextual and rigid in concept, salutogenesis reflects a dynamic and flexible approach toward problem-solving in life, with the individual's capacity and ability to manage health of primary importance (Lindström & Eriksson, 2005).

Enhancing SOC and Usefulness of Peer Support

The three components of the SOC – comprehensibility, manageability, and meaningfulness – and their effect on health can also be conceptualized as follows (Antonovsky, 1990, pp. 74, 77, 78):

- Stressor is defined as "a stimulus which poses a demand to which one has no ready-made, immediately available and adequate response."
  - An "organism confronting a stressor enters a state of tension."
    - "Tension, if readily and efficiently resolved, is not necessarily pathogenic."
    - "When, despite our best efforts, the tension remains, it is transformed into stress, which leads to disease."
- "Not the stressor load per se is pathogenic, but the inability to resolve tension and prevent its transformation into stress."
- "Thinking pathogenically, seeking to explain disease, we naturally think of risk factors" instead of focusing on salutary factors, which "have a direct positive effect on health status."
- GRRs are "a set of life experiences involving feedback, sending messages like: Here is the right track; you can handle things; you are of worth." In other words, such feedback "enables one to orient oneself in the world and cope successfully with stressors."
- SOC is "a way of viewing one's world (both inner and outer ...) as structured rather than as chaotic, and as posing problems which could be managed."

Antonovsky (1990, p. 79) specifically stated that "manageability was the sense that adequate resources to cope with the stressors were to be found either in one's own hands or in the hands of legitimate others." It is important to remember this to understand the value of peer support, which helps bring meaningfulness to an affected individual, for " ...seeing life in this way provides the motivational force which leads one to seek to order the world and to transform resources from potential to actuality" by enabling their "SOC as directly influencing health, in that it leads one to engage in behaviors (including the adoption of attitudes ...) which promote health" (Antonovsky, 1990, p. 79).

A salutogenic approach to strengthening GRR is by making available the resources for management of stressors while ensuring there is predictability, consistency, and active participation of the individual in defining the outcomes and setting achievable goals, thus ensuring the three components of SOC are met (Hochwälder, 2022).

Looking beyond the individual, there is also collective SOC, with individuals as part of their community, social group, or an organization, having the same three components of SOC as an individual: comprehensibility, meaningfulness, and manageability (Idan et al., 2022; Peled et al., 2013). At a collective level, comprehensibility is the predictability and security offered by an individual being a part of a community; manageability is the community's ability to render assistance whenever needed or sought; and meaningfulness is the ability of an individual to have a sense of belonging or interest in their community without any fear of adverse impact on their standing within the community (Idan et al., 2022). Social support, if available, is known to have a positive effect on SOC (Lindmark et al., 2010; Volanen et al., 2004; Wolff & Ratner, 1999). This helps explain the usefulness of peer support as a salutogenic approach to enhance individual SOC, besides enhancing the collective SOC as part of a community or an organization. Such a model is applied in varied social groups such as the workplace (Jenny et al., 2022), organizations (Bauer & Jenny, 2022), health care (Pelikan, 2022), including mental health care (Langeland & Vinje, 2022), and military settings (Antonovsky, 2022) with positive outcomes.

Strengthening an individual's SOC, particularly during stressful times when supported by trusted peers, helps the individual cope better. This is reinforced by empirical evidence of applying salutogenic principles in health promotion, with an observable correlation in terms of well-being and quality of life strongly reflecting the mental dimension of health, in addition to physical and social factors, brought about by an individual's SOC (Lindström, 2018). Helping individuals strengthen their SOC through peer support can have significant benefits beyond the individual by improving organizational productivity, economic outcomes, reduced sickness rates and absenteeism, and better motivated teams (Jenny et al., 2015).

Act-Belong-Commit is one of the earliest community-based, comprehensive mental health promotion campaigns. It originated in Western Australia with a focus on three major domains (Donovan & Anwar-McHenry, 2014):

- Act: Keep alert and engaged by keeping mentally, socially, spiritually, and physically active.
- Belong: Develop a strong sense of belonging by keeping up friendships, joining groups, and participating in community activities.
- Commit: Do things that provide meaning and purpose in life like taking up challenges, supporting causes, and helping others.

The Act-Belong-Commit campaign is consistent with the salutogenic approach focusing on mental well-being, irrespective of where one is on the health/dis-ease continuum (Koushede & Donovan, 2022).

Langeland et al. (2006) and Langeland and Vinje (2022) were the first to develop talk therapy based on the salutogenic approach for those with mental health problems encompassing "mental suffering, mental illness, mental disorders, mental problems, and psychosocial problem" (p. 434). They aimed to enhance the SOC of the participants and nurture mental well-being by increasing awareness of their potential – the aim being for them to actively cope with their responsibilities with fortitude and using mental health nurses as group leaders for empathetic listening. The success of this approach was evident in the ability of the participants to cope better with their mental health problems in a randomized controlled trial with increases in the manageability component of their SOC contributing the most improvement among the intervention group.

Peer support is becoming an integral part of mental health services to complement the care of those affected in the United Kingdom, the United States, Canada, Australia, and New Zealand (Gillard et al., 2015). A recent review by White et al. (2020) highlighted the safety and efficacy of peer support in mental health care and educational institutions. This review acknowledged that peer support is a synergistic resource to complement mental health outcomes alongside professional care. Further, it is beneficial as an adjunctive support, rather than as a substitute for normal mental health care practices. Analyzing the benefits of peer support from the available studies, this review summed up that peer support involves reciprocal relationships based on shared experiences and highlighted the importance of dedicated peer support training programs, ongoing supervision, and ready access to suitable peers to ensure that values-based peer support is delivered.

In a separate study, Gillard et al. (2021) developed a fidelity index to assess the setup and delivery of peer support in mental health services. Good inter-rater reliability was demonstrated across four domains: "sense of connection based on shared lived experience; relationships characterized by mutuality and reciprocity; peers' ability to exercise leadership, choice and control in the way peer support takes place; peer support focused on discovering individual strengths and making connections to community" (p. 1909).

In an aviation context, peer support programs are known to be a "safe initial point of contact to share experiences and receive support" using "the curative power of talking" and "empathic listening" to empower an individual (Santilhano et al., 2019, pp. 68, 73). However, because aviation professionals perform safety-critical tasks, the historical and orthodox approach to aviation medical certification has been to withdraw privileges or certification until the individual can demonstrate they meet the applicable medical standard. For this reason, it is well recognized that pilots especially may be reticent or unwilling to discuss any health concerns with others, including health professionals, due to the potential for that information being made available to the regulator and/or employer and the likelihood they will be "grounded."

Notwithstanding the above inhibitors, several well-established peer support programs in commercial aviation have been developed and successfully used to assist pilots since 1991 (UK Civil Aviation Authority, 2022). For example, the Airline Pilots Association – International (ALPA – I) has developed Pilot Peer Support (PPS) and New Zealand has the Peer Assistance Network New Zealand. Several leading airlines have their own peer support programs like the British Airways and Qantas Pilot Assistance Network (PAN), while various airlines in the United States are affiliate members of the International Pilot Peer Assist Coalition (IPPAC), with similar programs existing in Canada, Singapore, Hong Kong, South Africa, and the European Union. Such peer support programs assist pilots to help address mental health concerns, with many case studies demonstrating their usefulness in pilots being able to address their health issues and ultimately return to duties (Santilhano et al., 2019).

A unique peer support program in aviation with proven usefulness in the field of substance use is the Human Intervention Motivational Study (HIMS) program in the United States with funding from the Federal Aviation Administration (FAA; (HIMS, 2023; Porges, 2013; Steenbilk, 2007). Similar programs are now active in Canada, Germany, Mexico, and Australasia. They all provide for a triad of support – being the peer, the regulator, and the aviation medical examiner – to assist a recovering pilot return to the flight deck. This collaborative approach of dealing with one aspect of the human condition has facilitated well over 6,000 pilots in the United States alone returning to flying duties under supervision since its inception in 1974. The HIMS program also provides benefit by helping pilots return to work with formal commitment with the airline medical department for ongoing engagement with peer support besides other surveillance requirements. Aviation regulators, as in Australasia, generally support such arrangements upon being satisfied that any risks posed have been adequately mitigated.

Need for Salutogenic Approach to Mental Well-Being in Aviation

Changed circumstances, adverse situations, or stressors in any other form (including fear of uncertainty or the unknown) challenge a person's cognitive resources. Emotions also play a significant role, and different people cope differently depending on their ability for introspection/reflection. When coping mechanisms prove inadequate, there is a "breakdown" from a state of health toward feeling unwell and a potential slide across the health/dis-ease continuum toward disease, whether there is a diagnosable condition or not. For the individual, it can be difficult to know whether they need support or intervention. Yet, it is precisely in these instances that social and emotional support (founded on respect and shared responsibility) offered by another individual of equal standing and mutual agreement about what is helpful can make a significant difference. It also can be the difference between remaining productive in social and professional roles with peer support as opposed to being unable to do so. While reliance on peer support alone may not be appropriate for those with a psychiatric diagnosis and need for therapeutic and/or institutional intervention, it can improve the effectiveness of conventional mental health care in terms of recovery and a return to community (Solomon, 2004).

Individuals retain control of their mental well-being based on their GRR and ability to cope with stressors. In the health/dis-ease continuum there is a robust sense of mental well-being at one end and at the other end total psychological breakdown (Eriksson & Lindström, 2006). Adapting a stronger focus toward a salutogenic approach in aviation would result in an early engagement toward positive health promotion as an enabler to shift psychological dis-ease toward mental well-being. This is achievable by the use of conscious coping mechanisms by an individual (Vinje et al., 2022), assistance by trained peers, and facilitative coping resources, all in a timely and appropriate manner.

A salutogenic approach helps promote an individual's SOC using conversation as an analytical and, at times, cathartic tool. Comprehensibility of prevailing circumstances and stress-inducing events helps to understand and to judge reality as it is and to cope better. In effect, the individual is seen in the context of a person in their day-to-day life, rather than being identified by their diagnosis. It further helps explore meaningfulness relevant to an individual. This is an investment toward helping discover "inner feelings, immediate personal relationships, major activity, and existential issues" (Langeland & Vinje, 2022, p. 435).

Engagement with daily life with a balanced mindset and awareness of one's outlook, resources, and surrounding support structures of family and social groups helps actively manage circumstances and situations in life. Such manageability is not just coping through a stressful situation, but it promotes improved health through strengthening of the individual's SOC (Langeland & Vinje, 2022). Achieving such aims through peer support is based on the following principles (Gillard et al., 2017; Gillard et al., 2021):

1. Support the building of safe and trusting relationships based on shared lived experience as fundamental to peer support.
2. Ensure that the values of mutuality and reciprocity underpin peer support relationships.
3. Promote the validation and application of experiential knowledge in the provision of peer support.

4. Enable peers to exercise leadership, choice, and control over the way in which peer support is given and received.
5. Empower peers to discover and make use of their own strengths, and to build and strengthen connections to their peers and wider communities.

As observed by Antonovsky (1996, p. 14):

> The provider of care must indeed be highly empathetic and sensitive to withstand the pressure to forget the human being who has the disease. The health promoter, irrespective of her personal bent, is pressured to be concerned with the person.

Peer support is the first point of contact, indeed a circuit breaker, with trust as the foundation of such interaction to help recognize, utilize, or nurture an individual's resources and mental well-being. Peer support with an empathetic listening approach is to assist individuals believe, rediscover, and trust themselves vis-à-vis their prevailing situations or circumstances, which can seem challenging, adversarial, or insurmountable due to self-doubt or a lack of self-belief when facing stress, grief, or physical disease (but not mental illness). For example, based on a study of pilots in South Africa (Santilhano et al., 2019, p. 70), the role of a peer in aviation is premised upon trust and sensitivity where (a) the "peers can relate, holding a shared perspective and understanding, enabling them to identify with the person in their context"; and (b) "the essence of the role is to listen, support, and, when appropriate, refer to specialized assistance."

Peer support, applying a salutogenic approach, for mental health is arguably more important in the context of aviation, and it should be well established, dependable, and easily accessible to all aviation personnel. The aim should be to incorporate peer support as the foundation to support aviation personnel throughout their career, from early student-pilot days until retirement. It should also be available irrespective of an individual's position on the health/dis-ease continuum and be augmented by therapeutic and any other interventions whenever a slide toward the dis-ease end occurs. As an ongoing health promotion approach and in psychophysiological terms, it "places the brain (cognitions, emotions, information processing) at the crux of coping, and suggests mental processes — introspection, sensibility, and reflection — that can result in differential coping: changing one's situation, and/or changing one's perception of one's situation" (Mittelmark et al., 2017, pp. 54–55).

The proposed approach helps integrate salutogenesis into the practice of aviation neuropsychology by creating a holistic approach to promote well-being, besides optimizing performance within the aviation industry. This entails merging the principles of salutogenesis with the study and application of aviation neuropsychology. The connection between these two fields involves several key aspects: stress, coping, and resilience; SOC; promotion of healthy behavior; motivation; and positive psychology. Trained peer supporters are a positive influence on culture who can help promote salutogenic principles by enabling self-determination for their peers, thereby providing optimal cognitive performance that can help increase safety margins in aviation.

Salutogenic Approach and Aviation Regulations – Proposal for Inclusion in the Safety Management System

WHO suggests mental health promotion be aimed at three levels: individual, community, and societal (Lahtinen et al., 2005). Participatory engagement helps strengthen and empower the individual, whereas regulatory policies help plan and implement health programs at the organizational or community level. The intent of proposing a salutogenic approach to mental well-being in aviation is to achieve the same outcomes as in other areas, namely, to help individuals align their focus using their resources – strengths, resilience, and coping – through peer support.

One of the most significant recommendations as a result of the Germanwings investigation was that (Bureau d'Enquêtes et d'Analyses, 2016, p. 103):

> EASA ensure that European operators promote the implementation of peer support groups to provide a process for pilots, their families and peers to report and discuss personal and mental health issues, with the assurance that information will be kept in-confidence in a just-culture work environment, and that pilots will be supported as well as guided with the aim of providing them with help, ensuring flight safety and allowing them to return to flying duties, where applicable.

The ongoing usefulness of the PAN and HIMS programs shows an achievable path for approaching mental well-being by engaging all aviation stakeholders. However, unlike HIMS, where peer support is a postdiagnosis management resource during recovery, peer support as part of a salutogenic approach is advocated as an ongoing health promotion activity, including being a circuit-breaker or safe haven during stressful times.

Availability of peer support for the aviation community to support mental well-being would not only be beneficial to the individual but also foster the common aim to preserve aviation safety. However, for that to happen, there must be support by aviation employers and oversight by aviation regulators in developing and supporting such programs across the aviation industry. A lack of trust between employees and employers, a lack of consistency in handling health-related matters, and a perception that the regulator "just wants to pull the license off" at the slightest hint of change in mental health mean that there is a need for a paradigm shift at all levels – individual, unions, employers, and regulators. This is possible by building a bridge with active engagement of all stakeholders in planning, implementation, and ongoing reviews/audits to ensure the success of such an initiative. This will help create trust – the foundation stone of salutogenesis.

This proposal is consistent with the High-Level Conference on COVID-19 (ICAO, 2021) where ICAO advocated member states to make wellness programs, employee assistance programs, and peer support programs accessible to all aviation employees, with resources made available in conjunction with stakeholders, including aviation medical departments and industry.

One of the few positive outcomes from COVID-19 has been fast-tracking recognition of the need for such programs and resources as well as highlighting the need to encourage individual resilience and mental well-being. However, recognition and implementation are not the same, and the latter is still to be achieved. Except for a few airlines running peer support programs on their own initiative, smaller airlines, airlines without medical departments, and the general aviation sector largely do not have access to these types of programs and the perception is that such programs are aimed at individuals rather than operators and organizations. This strengthens the case for aviation regulators to intervene and mandate such programs to achieve widespread adoption across ICAO states and the aviation industry.

Australia has recently taken some early steps for inclusion of peer support for mental well-being of aviation medical certificate holders. This program – the Safe Haven – is a collaboration among certificate holders, their peers, and health experts including aviation medicine and mental health professionals, with the regulator largely staying in the background and intervening only if there is a threat to aviation safety (K. Manderson, personal communication, April 4, 2023). The potential benefits are that a certificate holder with a diagnosed mental illness (including substance use disorder), who remains engaged with the proposed Safe Haven program, may qualify for an earlier return to duties. The regulator remains responsible for approval and endorsement of peer support training programs.

Taking this further, Australia presented a paper entitled "Medical Certification and Mental Illness" (ICAO, 2022, p. 3) to address the mental health concerns during the 41st session of assembly of the ICAO, stating that:

> Mental health is not a binary sick/not sick status (pathogenic approach), rather it is a continuum of well/less well/illness ...Australia has developed a proposed model of medical certification for certificate-holders experiencing mental distress that is responsive to the individuals needs and status of the person, is supported through a peer network established by the Regulator, with oversight and governance of the system and processes by the Regulator.

This paper (ICAO, 2022, p. 4) concluded that:

> The support of ICAO through mechanisms such as expert panels, working groups and advisory bodies is imperative to supporting a consistent, global and safe approach for all. ICAO's endorsement of further development work on the salutogenic principle will enable each nation to review and implement their desired approach to medical certification in the presence of mental ill-health using evidence-based, safety-informed, internationally accepted principles.

A trust culture between stakeholders is required to create the environment for a salutogenic approach to mental health and well-being to thrive. With this understanding and as a pioneering step, Airservices Australia, the provider of air traffic management and ancillary services, and its stakeholder trade unions have, with the support of the regulator, signed a memorandum of understanding to establish a salutogenic working model within its existing peer support program and human resource policies. This peer support program, called Supportive Occupational Airservices Rehabilitation (SOAR) program, utilizes a multilayered approach incorporating both critical incident stress management (CISM) and substance use (HIMS).

The main caveat is that peer support is not espoused as the sole solution to mental well-being and does not deviate from the existing regulatory approach to medical certification. Instead, it is proposed that a salutogenic approach for mental well-being be recognized as one health promotion tool among others and that it be included as part of a stakeholder's SMS.

While Chapter 6 of Annex 1 to the Convention on International Civil Aviation sets out the requirement for uniform aviation medical standards and largely reflects a pathogenic approach for medical certification based on disease or disability, it is notable that Paragraph 1.2.4.3 in Chapter 1 of Annex 1 recommends that "the Licensing Authority shall implement appropriate aviation-related health promotion for license holders subject to a Medical Assessment to reduce future medical risks to flight safety" (International Civil Aviation Organization, 2022, p. 1–10).

Although the scope of the words "subject to a Medical Assessment" does not expressly include the utilization of peer support as an adjunctive and complementary tool to conventional health care, the promotion by ICAO of health outcomes mirrors a salutogenic approach and is sufficiently broad to include peer support and similar resources. The proposed approach is to help focus on the individual who copes with day-to-day stressors with their SOC, nurturing safety. This is further enhanced with enveloping peer support, duly supported by the aviation industry with appropriate regulatory oversight. It is up to individual states/aviation regulators to determine the nature and type of health promotion and whether such is mandated under domestic aviation laws. Peer support programs that are regulator mandated, aviation industry sponsored and supported, independent, and auditable would be the ideal outcome.

This proposed model could serve to provide a workable theory for collective action by all the stakeholders to revise a shift in medical assessment of aviation personnel at two levels: (a) from pathogenesis to salutogenesis and (b) from a wholly regulated assessment of disease/medical conditions to a more nurturing approach to mental well-being by making the individual the focus. This will help develop a support mechanism, based on the demonstrated success of the PAN and HIMS programs to bring peer support within the regulatory ambit and a commitment on the part of aviation industry to sponsor and support this commitment. Such peer support is a cornerstone for facilitating/nurturing the focus on mental well-being founded on structured and evidence-based practice to facilitate the aviation community, irrespective of roles and stages of career. This is also aligned with a recent review about pilot mental health unambiguously proposing a collaborative approach among the aviation industry stakeholders to help build trust among pilots with well-defined policies including reporting mental health concerns, treatment, and career opportunities (Ackland et al., 2022).

The proposal that a salutogenic model for mental well-being be incorporated into the SMS has already been supported by the Pilot Fitness Aviation Rulemaking Committee (ARC) of the FAA (2015), in the aftermath of the Malaysia Flight 370 and Germanwings investigations. Specifically, it was said that "a risk mitigation process built on Safety Management System (SMS) principles should be used by air carriers and pilot representative organizations to create an environment where early reporting, appropriate treatment, and rapid return to the flightdeck are the expectation" (FAA, 2015, p. 1). Such a realignment in approach to mental well-being emphasizes the connection among all stakeholders (including the general public and all air users) by building trust while retaining the focus on the individual for nurturing their SOC, with appropriate peer support, governed by employers under regulatory oversight. Undoubtedly, any shift toward the disease end in the health/dis-ease continuum would require medical intervention and, in turn, cessation of aviation duties at least on a temporary basis. This has been followed up by the Mental Health and Aviation Medical Clearances Aviation Rulemaking Committee of the FAA. The committee has made two vital recommendations to incorporate mental health into SMS (FAA, 2024), stating that "Mental health screening functions should be performance based upon and managed within an SMS framework" (pp. 46–47; and "The FAA should establish a recurrent evaluation process to assess whether its policies, aeromedical screening protocols, and mental health risk controls are evidence-based and consistent with SMS principles" (p. 48).

Interestingly, India has already initiated such an approach to mental health promotion of air crew and controllers by laying down guidelines to establish peer support as a "proactive and non-punitive programme ... applying the principles of 'just culture'" by all scheduled and non-scheduled operators, flying training organizations, and air traffic services (Directorate General of Civil Aviation, India, 2023, p. 4). Most significantly, the guidelines state that mental health promotion is to be embedded within the SMS of the organizations.

Conclusion

While peer support programs for the treatment of mental health, including substance use, have steadily become more accepted in the aviation industry, the level of support is by no means uniform. As the regulation of civil aviation is largely founded upon the accepted requirements of the Chicago Convention by member states, consistency of approach and conformance with convention obligations must be uppermost in considering improvements in these areas. As will be apparent, the Germanwings tragedy has drawn greater attention to these issues and the need for all stakeholders to be aware of the potential high risks posed by mental ill-health/disease. The COVID pandemic has also demonstrated the risks posed for all people by the uncertainties of life and matters outside of one's control. The aviation industry was one of the few essential services that could continue to operate (albeit at a much-reduced level) throughout the pandemic but with clearly adverse effects on aviation professionals.

The salutogenic approach propounded in this chapter provides a useful tool for individuals to try to make sense of the events and circumstances they are confronted with. In the current age of the individual where the predisposition is to look to blame others for adverse events, the ability to be introspective and to objectively frame one's position and situation provides a level of insight missing from currently prevailing purely subjective assessments. In a variation of the biblical admonition "physician heal thyself," the salutogenic approach invests the individual with the responsibility of developing their SOC with the aid of others and in the process emphasizing the need for collaboration and gaining insight. This move away from the pathogenic (and binary) mindset to a more nuanced notion of health as a continuum (with everyone at some time being in need of support), and the ability for health at times to fluctuate beyond the mean, provides opportunities to question the orthodox approach to the management of mental illness also.

In the context of aviation, the historical position has been that the presence of disease precludes aviation medical certification. Generally, only a full recovery would warrant the return of privileges. In the case of mental illness and the move to diagnostic criteria for assessment (e.g., the *Diagnostic and Statistical Manual of Mental Disorders*), assessing the level of recovery can be significantly more problematic and uncertain. While such approaches clearly place safety as the most important consideration, the downside is that it is also highly wasteful of human capital and of prior investment in the individual/stakeholders as well as being highly disruptive for the aviation professional's sense of self and worth. It is also questionable whether it can continue to be justified where aviation regulators are increasingly being held accountable for their decision-making, including by external review bodies.

Accordingly, it is the authors' contention that by shifting the focus to a salutogenic approach, better outcomes can be achieved across a range of measures and that the aviation professionals involved gain a better understanding of the issues and the solutions. While this chapter currently only propounds that further consideration be given to incorporating peer support tools based on a salutogenic approach into aviation operators' SMS, it is considered that an incremental step of this nature is both consistent with recommendations by aviation bodies internationally and most likely to result in education, engagement, and adoption of such methods for the benefit of all.

Without sounding aspirational, the authors exhort health practitioners supporting mental health and well-being among aviation personnel, including aviation neuropsychologists, to apply salutogenesis in their practice. This is possible by looking beyond a risk-averse accident-prevention kind of approach toward mental health, by focusing on SOC with "a sense of meaning and purpose in life, good social relations, and a feeling of contributing with and to something or someone" (Koushede & Donovan, 2022, p. 480).

Disclaimer

The views and opinions expressed in this chapter are solely those of the authors. This is not to be construed as opinion, policy, or guidelines of the organizations the authors are associated with.

References

Ackland, C.A., Molesworth, B.R.C., Grisham, J.R., & Lovibond, P.F. (2022). Pilot mental health, methodologies, and findings: A systematic review. *Aerospace Medicine and Human Performance, 93*(9), 696–708. https://doi.org/10.3357/AMHP.6043.2022

Antonovsky, A. (1990). A somewhat personal odyssey in studying the stress process. *Stress Medicine, 6,* 71–80. https://doi.org/10.1002/smi.2460060203

Antonovsky, A. (1996). The salutogenic model as a theory to guide health promotion. *Health Promotion International, 11,* 11–18. https://doi.org/10.1093/heapro/11.1.11

Antonovsky, A. (2022). Salutogenesis and mental health promotion in military settings. In M.B. Mittelmark, G.F. Bauer, L. Vaandrager, J.M. Pelikan, S. Sagy, M. Eriksson, B. Lindström & C.M. Magistretti (Eds.), *The handbook of salutogenesis* (2nd ed., pp. 337–348). Springer. https://doi.org/10.1007/978-3-030-79515-3_32

Arva, P., & Wagstaff, A.S. (2004). Medical disqualification of 275 commercial pilots: changing patterns over 20 years. *Aviation, Space, and Environmental Medicine, 75*(9), 791–794.

Bauer, G.F., & Jenny G.J. (2022). Applying salutogenesis in organisations. In M.B. Mittelmark, G.F. Bauer, L. Vaandrager, J.M. Pelikan, S. Sagy, M. Eriksson, B. Lindström & C.M. Magistretti (Eds.), *The handbook of salutogenesis* (2nd ed., pp. 283–295). Springer. https://doi.org/10.1007/978-3-030-79515-3_28

Bureau d'Enquêtes et d'Analyses. (2016). *Final report: Accident on 24 March 2015 at Prads-Haute-Bléone (Alpes-de-Haute-Provence, France) to the Airbus A320-211 registered D-AIPX operated by Germanwings.* https://bea.aero/uploads/tx_elyextendttnews/BEA2015-0125.en-LR_04.pdf

Cullen, S.A., Drysdale, H.C., & Mayes, R.W. (1997). Role of medical factors in 1000 fatal aviation accidents: Case note study. *BMJ, 314*(7094), Article 1592. https://doi.org/10.1136/bmj.314.7094.1592

Directorate General of Civil Aviation, India. (2023). *Medical circular: 01 of 2023 – Mental health promotion of flight crew and air traffic control officers (ATCOs).* https://www.dgca.gov.in/digigov-portal/Upload?flag=iframeAttachView&attachId=152077073

Donovan, R.J., & Anwar-McHenry, J. (2014). Act-Belong-Commit: Lifestyle medicine for keeping mentally healthy. *American Journal of Lifestyle Medicine, 10*(3), 193–199. https://doi.org/10.1177/1559827614536846

Evans, S., & Radcliffe, S.A. (2012). The annual incapacitation rate of commercial pilots. *Aviation, Space, and Environmental Medicine, 83*(1), 42–49. https://doi.org/10.3357/asem.3134.2012

Eriksson, M., & Lindström, B. (2006). Antonovsky's sense of coherence scale and the relation with health: A systematic review. *Journal of Epidemiology and Community Health, 60*(5), 376–381. https://doi.org/10.1136/jech.2005.041616

Federal Aviation Administration (FAA). (2015). *Pilot fitness aviation rulemaking committee report.* https://www.faa.gov/regulations_policies/rulemaking/committees/documents/media/Pilot%20Fitness%20ARC%20Report.11302015.pdf

Federal Aviation Administration (FAA). (2024). *Mental Health & Aviation Medical Clearances Aviation Rulemaking Committee recommendation report.* https://www.faa.gov/sites/faa.gov/files/Mental_Health_ARC_Final_Report_RELEASED.pdf

Feijó, D., Luiz, R.R., & Camara, V.M. (2012). Common mental disorders among civil aviation pilots. *Aviation, Space, and Environmental Medicine, 83*(5), 509–513. https://doi.org/10.3357/asem.3185.2012

Gillard, S., Banach, N., Barlow, E., Byrne, J., Foster, R., Goldsmith, L., Marks, J., McWilliam, C., Morshead, R., Stepanian, K., Turner, R., Verey, A., & White, S. (2021). Developing and testing a principle-based fidelity index for peer support in mental health services. *Social Psychiatry and Psychiatric Epidemiology, 56*(10), 1903–1911. https://doi.org/10.1007/s00127-021-02038-4

Gillard, S., Foster, R., Gibson, S., Goldsmith, L., Marks, J., & White, S. (2017). Describing a principles-based approach to developing and evaluating peer worker roles as peer support moves into mainstream mental health services. *Mental Health and Social Inclusion, 21*(3), 133–143. https://doi.org/10.1108/MHSI-03-2017-0016

Gillard, S., Holley, J., Gibson, S., Larsen, J., Lucock, M., Oborn, E., Rinaldi, M., & Stamou, E. (2015). Introducing new peer worker roles into mental health services in England: Comparative case study research across a range of organisational contexts. *Administration and Policy in Mental Health, 42*(6), 682–694. https://doi.org/10.1007/s10488-014-0603-z

Görlich, Y., & Stadelmann, D. (2020). Mental health of flying cabin crews: Depression, anxiety, and stress before and during the COVID-19 pandemic. *Frontiers in Psychology, 11*, Article 581496. https://doi.org/10.3389/fpsyg.2020.581496

Henssler, J., Stock, F., van Bohemen, J., Walter, H., Heinz, A., & Brandt, L. (2021). Mental health effects of infection containment strategies: Quarantine and isolation-a systematic review and meta-analysis. *European Archives of Psychiatry and Clinical Neuroscience, 271*(2), 223–234. https://doi.org/10.1007/s00406-020-01196-x

Hochwälder, J. (2022). Theoretical issues in the further development of the sense of coherence construct. In M.B. Mittelmark, G.F. Bauer, L. Vaandrager, J.M. Pelikan, S. Sagy, M. Eriksson, B. Lindström & C.M. Magistretti (Eds.), *The handbook of salutogenesis* (2nd ed., pp. 568–579). Springer. https://doi.org/10.1007/978-3-030-79515-3_53

Høva, J.K., Thorheim, L., & Wagstaff, A.S. (2017). Medical reasons for loss of license in Norwegian professional pilots. *Aerospace Medicine and Human Performance, 88*(2), 146–149. https://doi.org/10.3357/AMHP.4551.2017

Human Intervention Motivational Study. (2023). *About HIMS.* https://himsprogram.com/about-hims/

Idan, O., Erisksson, M., & Al-Yagon, M. (2022). Generalized resistance resources in the salutogenic model of health. In M.B. Mittelmark, G.F. Bauer, L. Vaandrager, J.M. Pelikan, S. Sagy, M. Eriksson, B. Lindström & C.M. Magistretti (Eds.), *The handbook of salutogenesis* (2nd ed., pp. 93–106). Springer. https://doi.org/10.1007/978-3-030-79515-3_12

International Civil Aviation Organization. (2022). *International standards and recommended practices – definitions and general rules concerning licences. Chapter in Annex 1 to the Convention on International Civil Aviation: Personnel licensing* (14th ed.) https://store.icao.int/en/annex-1-personnel-licensing

International Civil Aviation Organization. (2021). *High-level conference on COVID-19 (HLCC 2021). Draft report of the safety stream on agenda item 1* (HLCC2021-WP/241 SAF/153). https://www.icao.int/Meetings/HLCC2021/Documents/WP/EN/SAF/wp_241_en.pdf

International Civil Aviation Organization. (2022). *Working paper A41-WP/256 TE/98: Medical certification and mental illness.* https://www.icao.int/Meetings/a41/Documents/WP/wp_256_en.pdf

Jenny, G.J., Bauer, G.F., Vinje, H.F., Brauchli, R., Vogt, K., & Torp, S. (2022). Applying salutogenesis in the workplace. In M.B. Mittelmark, G.F. Bauer, L. Vaandrager, J.M. Pelikan, S. Sagy, M. Eriksson, B. Lindström & C.M. Magistretti (Eds.), *The handbook of salutogenesis* (2nd ed., pp. 321–336). Springer. https://doi.org/10.1007/978-3-030-79515-3_31

Jenny, G.J., Brauchli, R., Inauen, A., Füllemann, D., Fridrich, A., & Bauer, G.F. (2015). Process and outcome evaluation of an organizational-level stress management intervention in Switzerland. *Health Promotion International, 30*(3), 573–585. https://doi.org/10.1093/heapro/dat091

Koushede, V., & Donovan, R. (2022). Applying salutogenesis in community-wide mental health promotion. In M.B. Mittelmark, G.F. Bauer, L. Vaandrager, J.M. Pelikan, S. Sagy, M. Eriksson, B. Lindström & C.M. Magistretti (Eds.), *The handbook of salutogenesis* (2nd ed., pp. 478–490). Springer. https://doi.org/10.1007/978-3-030-79515-3_44

Lahtinen, E., Joubert, N., Raeburn, J., & Jenkins, R. (2005). Strategies for promoting the mental health of populations. In H. Herrman, S. Saxena, & R. Moodie (Eds.), *Promoting mental health: Concepts, emerging evidence, practice* (pp. 226–242). World Health Organization.

Langeland, E., Riise, T., Hanestad, B.R., Nortvedt, M.W., Kristoffersen, K., & Wahl, A.K. (2006). The effect of salutogenic treatment principles on coping with mental health problems: A randomised controlled trial. *Patient Education and Counseling, 62*(2), 212–219. https://doi.org/10.1016/j.pec.2005.07.004

Langeland, E., & Vinje, H.F. (2022). Applying salutogenesis in mental healthcare settings. In M.B. Mittelmark, G.F. Bauer, L. Vaandrager, J.M. Pelikan, S. Sagy, M. Eriksson, B. Lindström & C.M. Magistretti (Eds.), *The handbook of salutogenesis* (2nd ed., pp. 433–440). Springer. https://doi.org/10.1007/978-3-030-79515-3_39

Lindmark, U., Stenström, U., Gerdin, E.W., & Hugoson, A. (2010). The distribution of "sense of coherence" among Swedish adults: A quantitative cross-sectional population study. *Scandinavian Journal of Public Health, 38*(1), 1–8. https://doi.org/10.1177/1403494809351654

Lindström, B. (2018). Workshop salutogenesis and the future of health promotion and public health. *Scandinavian Journal of Public Health, 46*(20), 94–98. https://doi.org/10.1177/1403494817743902

Lindström, B., & Eriksson, M. (2005). Salutogenesis. *Journal of Epidemiology and Community Health, 59*(6), 440–442. https://doi.org/10.1136/jech.2005.034777

Mittelmark, M.B., & Bauer, G.F. (2022). Salutogenesis as a theory, as an orientation and as the sense of coherence. In M.B. Mittelmark, G.F. Bauer, L. Vaandrager, J.M. Pelikan, S. Sagy, M. Eriksson, B. Lindström & C.M. Magistretti (Eds.), *The handbook of salutogenesis* (2nd ed., pp. 11–17). Springer. https://doi.org/10.1007/978-3-030-79515-3_3

Mittelmark, M.B., Bauer, G.F., Vaandrager, L., Pelikan, J.M., Sagy, S., Eriksson, M., Lindström, B., & Magistretti, C.M. (Eds.). (2022). *The handbook of salutogenesis* (2nd ed.) Springer. https://doi.org/10.1007/978-3-030-79515-3

Mittelmark, M.B., Bull, T., & Bouwman, L. (2017). Emerging ideas relevant to the salutogenic model of health. In M.B. Mittelmark, G.F. Bauer, L. Vaandrager, J.M. Pelikan, S. Sagy, M. Eriksson, B. Lindström & C.M. Magistretti (Eds.), *The handbook of salutogenesis* (2nd ed., pp. 45–56). Springer. https://doi.org/10.1007/978-3-319-04600-6_6

Mulder, S., & de Rooy, D. (2018). Pilot mental health, negative life events, and improving safety with peer support and a just culture. *Aerospace Medicine and Human Performance, 89*(1), 41–51. https://doi.org/10.3357/AMHP.4903.2018

Pasha, T., & Stokes, P.R.A. (2018). Reflecting on the Germanwings disaster: A systematic review of depression and suicide in commercial airline pilots. *Frontiers in Psychiatry, 9*, Article 86. https://doi.org/10.3389/fpsyt.2018.00086

Peled, D., Sagy, S., & Braun-Lewensohn, O. (2013). Community perception as coping resource among adolescents living under rockets fire: A salutogenic approach. *Journal of Community Positive Practices, 4*, 681–702.

Pelikan, J.M. (2022). Applying salutogenesis in healthcare settings. In M.B. Mittelmark, G.F. Bauer, L. Vaandrager, J.M. Pelikan, S. Sagy, M. Eriksson, B. Lindström & C.M. Magistretti (Eds.), *The handbook of salutogenesis* (2nd ed., pp. 389–386). Springer. https://doi.org/10.1007/978-3-030-79515-3_36

Porges, C.R. (2013). Substance abuse in aviation: Clinical and practical implications. In C.H. Kennedy & G.G. Kay (Eds.), *Aeromedical psychology* (pp. 107–123). Taylor & Francis Group. https://www.taylorfrancis.com/chapters/edit/10.1201/9781315565811-5/substance-abuse-aviation-clinical-practical-implications-carlos-porges

Santilhano, W., Bor, R., & Hewitt, L. M. M. (2019). The role of peer support and its contribution as an effective response to addressing the emotional well-being of pilots: A qualitative study of South African stakeholders. *Aviation Psychology and Applied Human Factors, 9*(2), 67–76. https://doi.org/10.1027/2192-0923/a000163

Schwark, T., Severin, K., & Grellner, W. (2008). "I am flying to the stars" – suicide by aircraft in Germany. *Forensic Science International, 179*, e75–e78. https://doi.org/10.1016/j.forsciint.2008.06.004

Sickel, A. E., Seacat, J. D., & Nabors, N. A. (2014). Mental health stigma update: A review of consequences, *Advances in Mental Health, 12*(3), 202–215. https://doi.org/10.1080/18374905.2014.11081898S

Simons, R., Maire, R., Van Drongelen, A., & Valk, P. (2021). Grounding of pilots: Medical reasons and recommendations for prevention. *Aerospace Medicine and Human Performance, 92*(12), 950–955. https://doi.org/10.3357/AMHP.5985.2021

Solomon, P. (2004). Peer support/peer provided services underlying processes, benefits, and critical ingredients. *Psychiatric Rehabilitation Journal, 27*(4), 392–401. https://doi.org/10.2975/27.2004.392.401

Steenbilk, J. W. (2007). HIMS: The quiet success story. *Air Line Pilot, November–December, 76,* 25–29.

UK Civil Aviation Authority. (2022). *Pilot peer assistance and support programmes – is your airline ready?* https://caainternational.com/pilot-peer-assistance-and-support-programmes/

Vinje, H. F., Langeland, E., & Bull, T. (2022). Aaron Antonovsky's development of salutogenesis, 1979–1994. In M. B. Mittelmark, G. F. Bauer, L. Vaandrager, J. M. Pelikan, S. Sagy, M. Eriksson, B. Lindström & C. M. Magistretti (Eds.), *The handbook of salutogenesis* (2nd ed., pp. 29–45). Springer. https://doi.org/10.1007/978-3-030-79515-3_5

Volanen, S. M., Lahelma, E., Silventoinen, K., & Suominen, S. (2004). Factors contributing to sense of coherence among men and women. *European Journal of Public Health, 14*(3), 322–330. https://doi.org/10.1093/eurpub/14.3.322

Vuorio, A., Laukkala, T., Navathe, P., Budowle, B., Eyre, A., & Sajantila, A. (2014). Aircraft-assisted pilot suicides: Lessons to be learned. *Aviation, Space, and Environmental Medicine, 85*(8), 841–846. https://doi.org/10.3357/ASEM.4000.2014

White, S., Foster, R., Marks, J., Morshead, R., Goldsmith, L., Barlow, S., Sin, J., & Gillard, S. (2020). The effectiveness of one-to-one peer support in mental health services: A systematic review and meta-analysis. *BMC Psychiatry, 20*(1), 534. https://doi.org/10.1186/s12888-020-02923-3

Wolff, A. C., & Ratner, P. A. (1999). Stress, social support, and sense of coherence. *Western Journal of Nursing Research, 21*(2), 182–197. https://doi.org/10.1177/01939459922043820

World Health Organization. (2010). *Healthy workplaces: A model for action: for employers, workers, policymakers and practitioners.* https://www.who.int/publications/i/item/9789241599313

World Health Organization. (2013). *Mental health action plan 2013–2020.* https://www.who.int/publications/i/item/9789241506021

Wu, A. C., Donnelly-McLay, D., Weisskopf, M. G., McNeely, E., Betancourt, T. S., & Allen, J. G. (2016). Airplane pilot mental health and suicidal thoughts: A cross-sectional descriptive study via anonymous web-based survey. *Environmental Health: A Global Access Science Source, 15*(1), Article 121. https://doi.org/10.1186/s12940-016-0200-6

Chapter 9
Vulnerability and Protective Factors in Pilot Mental Health and Well-Being

Corrie Anna Ackland and Brett Robert Charles Molesworth

Introduction

This chapter provides a synopsis of the factors associated with pilot mental health from a neuropsychological perspective. In doing so, research both new and old is drawn upon to explore whether there are factors that may be protective against the development of mental health difficulties or rather create a vulnerability or predisposition toward developing mental health difficulties. Important theories are also discussed in order to contextualize these findings and suggest how they may be considered in managing pilots' mental health within the aviation industry.

Pilot mental health is a critical aspect of aviation safety. However, in terms of priorities for pilots, it is often not at the top of their list. Although the reasons for this may be varied and complex, there is likely an influence of the stigma associated with mental illness. This situation is not helped by aviation regulations in many countries, where the threat of loss of license (removal of medical certificate) remains real for reporting a mental illness. It remains a widely held belief with many regulatory agencies that various psychological conditions are incompatible with safe flying. Some agencies, and to their credit, have attempted to address this problem by promoting a policy where pilots are dealt with on a case-by-case basis. However, for many pilots this has had the reverse effect, as it adds to the uncertainty and fear a pilot may have about the consequences of reporting.

There may also be an assumption that pilots are less likely to experience mental illness thanks to extensive screening and selection procedures, thus leaving only individuals who possess exemplary psychological stability comprising the pilot cohort. However, due to many psychological disorders arising precipitated by the experience of a significant life stressor or being biological in nature, selection procedures at the outset of a pilot's career are unlikely to be sufficient in predicting such occurrences. Research in the area of pilot mental health has examined the instances of depression/depressive disorders, suicidality, and general anxiety symptoms, with varying results as to the extent to which pilots may experience these symptoms more or less than the general population. Recent research conducted during industry disruption due to the COVID-19 pandemic highlighted that pilots may experience symptoms of many psychological disorders similarly to the general population, including generalized anxiety disorder, specific phobias, social anxiety, adjustment disorder, attention-deficit/hyperactivity disorder (ADHD), major depressive disorder (MDD), dysthymia, and obsessive-compulsive disorder (OCD; Ackland et al., 2023). The neuropsychological symptoms of these disorders range from reduced capacity for sustained attentional functioning in MDD and ADHD to cognitive inflexibility and poor response inhibition in OCD and anxiety disorders; and they are possibly worse depending on the severity of the disorder. Additionally, when directly asked about the practical impairments caused by psychological symptoms in the study by Ackland et al. (2023), pilots primarily reported neuropsychological symptoms including poor concentration, distractibility, forgetfulness, increased mistakes, and "feeling less sharp" (p. 7).

Much of the symptomatology of the aforementioned disorders may go unnoticed or unmanaged due to a narrow focus on depressive symptoms, general anxiety symptoms, and suicidality; however, these conditions can be just as problematic to pilots as MDD and be more difficult to treat. The impact of unmanaged mental illness in pilots, due to underreporting or failure to detect, is potentially substantial, not least because without early intervention mild symptoms can worsen and increase the risk for a more impairing subsequent condition. Some symptoms of mental illness are known to directly affect cognitive ability (i.e., perception, memory, and decision-making), which for a pilot can impair their ability to fly effectively. Pilots carry the weight of the responsibility for the safety of passengers and other aircrew. Their role requires a calm-under-pressure approach, focus, clear and concise communication, effective decision-making, and a strict adherence to specific procedures and protocol. Presenteeism, the act of continuing to work when not fit to do so, adversely impacts cognitive abilities, increasing the risk of making critical mistakes and errors of judgment while flying and thus risking the safety of flight. The above highlights the importance of gaining a better understanding of pilot mental health; the link between mental health and cognitive performance; and, importantly, improving the approach to pilot mental health by encouraging early intervention and appropriate management.

Mental health issues do not exist in a vacuum. It is a common assumption that mental health issues develop as a response to significant stress. The diathesis–stress model of mental health asserts that, rather, mental health issues arise due to a combination of underlying vulnerability and precipitating stressor (Brannon & Feist, 2007). Extending upon the diathesis–stress model, the stress-buffering hypothesis outlines that protective factors may counteract the effect of the diathesis–stress combination, protecting the individual against a mental health issue that may otherwise have developed. These models highlight that in addition to trying to identify and reduce or manage stressors, mental health management should also attempt (a) to address specific vulnerability factors that serve to increase an individual's risk of mental health issues should they encounter a stressor as well as (b) to strengthen an individual's protective factors.

Research on aircraft-assisted suicide, although retrospective, has identified a number of risk factors that preceded the event of pilot suicide (Lewis et al., 2007; Politano & Walton, 2016). Such risk factors include pilot age, domestic stressors, workload, and state of physical health (Cooper & Sloan, 1985; Evans & Radcliffe, 2012; Lewis et al., 2007; Widyahening, 2007). These risk factors, or stressors, are known to directly impact cognitive processes and emotional states. Hudson and Herbert (2017) list several areas that would be important to include in routine enquiry, due to the effect these can have on pilot stress and well-being. These areas include family, job factors, finance, commuting, security, holidays, exercise and diet, medication, substance use, sleep, and hobbies. Taken together, these points emphasize how an assessment of the broader picture of a commercial pilot may allow for early intervention where there are identified risk factors, before any more serious problems develop. The following details the more prominent aspects of a pilot's life and how these may impact upon pilot mental health.

Occupational Factors

Workload and work type, and especially the changing nature of the role of the pilot, have been highlighted as sources of occupational stress for pilots. A study by Cooper and Sloan (1985) looked at pilot mental health with commercial pilots employed by British Airways, and importantly also looked at risk factors and coping strategies used by pilots to self-manage stressors. In their study of 442 commercial pilots, they identified that poor mental health was associated with fatigue, flying patterns, inability to relax, lack of autonomy at work, and lack of social support. Job satisfaction was largely affected by organizational factors such as career prospects, poor organization climate and morale, lack of work autonomy, and domestic stressors. Some of these factors, including fatigue, have been shown to have a direct link to pilot flight performance (Arsintescu et al., 2020).

It is worth noting, however, that the role of pilots has changed markedly since Cooper and Sloan's research in 1985. Bor et al. (2002) reported that the role of pilots had significantly changed in large part due to automation, and that a pilot's role now is more managerial than hands-on practical flying. They additionally hypothesized that there would be further implications to the occupational role of pilots post 9/11. In fact, Cooper and Sloan identified concerns such as "not enough time [manually] flying" and the impact of lack of flying as issues facing pilots in 1985, and it could be argued that pilots get even fewer hours flying in modern times. Additionally, Cooper and Sloan stated that there was a "mis-fit" between traditional flying roles and modern aviation. While "stick-and-rudder" skills deteriorate over time, the rate at which these skills deteriorate is significantly less than cognitive skills such as decision-making. For older pilots, it is conceivable that this effect is amplified due to aging. This was highlighted in performance assessments with older pilots, with the suggestion that stressors for this population could not be completely explained by uncertainty for their careers due to their life stage but rather that the role changes led to challenges such as flying less, anxiety about extensive checks (i.e., concerned about cognitive performance), and fatigue. The occupational circumstance for a pilot now includes heavy testing, monitoring, and supervision (Bor et al., 2017). Such factors are reported to contribute to *burnout* – the gradual depletion and loss of motivation (Freudenbergerm, 1974; Koutsimani et al., 2021; see "Fatigue and Burnout" section).

Bor et al. describe how a pilot's license becomes especially valued, in part due to the heavy commitment and sacrifices made to obtain it. As a result, medical assessments, along with recurrent training and testing, become a threat to a pilot, and are often accompanied by significant stress. While the threat of incapacitation is considered a marked stressor for pilots, the Aerospace Medical Association (AsMA; 2015) also identified that any period of actual incapacitation/impairment needs to be carefully managed. Events threatening incapacitation or impairment were also common in the recent histories of 10 of the 16 aircraft-assisted suicide case studies outlined by Lewis et al. (2007). These precipitating events included criminal issues ($n=8$) and health deterioration/diagnoses ($n=2$). Taken together, the above highlights that any transition phases for pilots, such as periods of testing, training, assessment, and incapacitation, present a risk factor that needs to be monitored and appropriately managed.

Other occupational challenges faced by pilots include the aircraft environment, air quality, noise, space; disrupted circadian rhythms, shift work, rostering issues and stressors; and disruption to regular social support as well as sleeping difficulties/fatigue (Bor et al., 2017). In the disputed facts surrounding Northwest Airlines Flight 188 in October 2009, which overflew its destination after the pilots were "unresponsive" to air traffic control for 77 min, the pilots cited distraction caused by discussion of "confusing" new airline procedures as the cause of their error (National Transportation Safety Board [NTSB], 2009). This example highlights the impact of increased cognitive load on attentional functioning, with attentional functioning demonstrated to deteriorate over sustained periods of time due to the accumulated cognitive load associated even with maintaining vigilance, let alone with additional demands (Head & Helton, 2014). It is increasingly important, as the industry and the role of pilots change, to understand the effect of occupational factors on pilots' mental health and the best way to address these risks with coping strategies.

Age

Evans and Radcliffe (2012) found that age was the biggest risk factor for pilot incapacitation, with the number of incapacitations significantly increased for pilots over 60 years of age and significantly decreased for younger pilots (younger than 40 years of age), presumably due to cognitive decline associated with age. Age-related cognitive decline has been shown to affect memory, spatial learning, working memory, and attention (Kausler, 1994). As noted earlier, Cooper and Sloane found that older pilots had greater concern with elements of modern aviation, such as fewer hours physically flying, extensive checks, and anxiety surrounding reviews. Evan and Radcliffe asserted that any increased risk posed by older age is likely offset by the benefit of their greater experience and, interestingly, reported all incapacitations attributed to psychiatric causes were found for pilots aged between 34 and 54 years.

Fatigue and Burnout

Fatigue and disrupted sleep patterns have been a noted risk factor to overall pilot physical and cognitive functioning and psychological well-being, as well as specifically increasing risk of mental illness. In February 2008, the captain and first officer of Go! Flight 1002 fell asleep and were "unresponsive" to air traffic control for 15 min. As this was during a midmorning flight, the report indicates the pilots were suffering from fatigue resulting from an accumulation of early flights in the preceding days (NTSB, 2009). O'Hagan et al. studied the relationship between pilot fatigue and experiences of depression and anxiety and found a number of pilots "microsleeping" on the flight deck as a manifestation of fatigue. The authors defined a microsleep as "falling asleep while on duty in the cockpit without prior agreement with the other pilot" (O'Hagan et al., 2016, p. 115). Even without resulting in drowsiness or microsleeps, fatigue can be impairing. The cognitive effects of fatigue can include slower processing speed, increased mistakes, and memory impairments, which may increase the risk of aviation errors and accidents (Bendak & Rashid, 2020). The effect of fatigue on work performance has been found to be quantitatively similar to the effect of alcohol (Roach et al., 2001). Moreover, a blood alcohol concentration of .05 was found to reduce performance by 10%, most notably in relation to coordination and gross motor control (Newman, 2004). As such, there are considerable regulations and procedures to address and manage fatigue concerns on the flight deck (Bor et al., 2017).

O'Hagan et al. (2016) found a positive correlation between pilot flight time/fatigue and increased rates of *perceived* anxiety and depression. Those that experienced fatigue even *rarely* (as opposed to *never*) reported a 2.3-fold increase in perceived anxiety and depression, and those who reported fatigue *often* were 5.3 times more likely to report perceived anxiety and depression. The relationship between fatigue and perceived anxiety and depression also eradicated differences related to fatigue and both work hours and age. The differences related to hours of work importantly indicate that there may be individual resilience characteristics that may be protective against the effects of fatigue. It was suggested that those working longer hours of 50+ per week were doing so on a voluntary basis and as such possibly self-identifying as being better equipped to tolerate these hours. This paper noted a number of confounding variables (demographics, job type, sleep disturbance) but failed to consider fatigue as a possible symptom of depressed mood, and thus the suggestion that reducing fatigue would reduce perceived mental health issue may be misleading.

In addition to physical fatigue associated with poor sleep and/or sustained physical output, mental or cognitive fatigue can occur from sustained cognitive output and result in impaired performance including recall of information, decision-making, response times, and learning. Cognitive fatigue could be considered to have a reciprocal relationship with burnout, where ongoing cognitive fatigue may lead to burnout while burnout may also increase cognitive fatigability (Gavelin et al., 2023). Burnout may also result from high job demands and, to a lesser extent, low job resources (Bakker & de Vries, 2021); and it has been associated with other cognitive impairments, including impact on working memory, processing speed, and attention (Gavelin et al., 2022). Burnout is also associated with poorer cognitive recovery (Gavelin et al., 2023), which may challenge standard fatigue management protocols.

Relationship Factors

Pilots' relationships have an acknowledged influence on performance and well-being. In a study looking at sources of pilot stress, Widyahening (2007) found a strong correlation for work stressors and a moderate correlation for home stressors. Known as the *spousal factor* (Bor et al., 2002), spousal support has been considered to either be protective against the stressors of the job or detrimental to performance. It should be noted that many of the papers on the spousal factor were dated in the 1980s and are likely less applicable to modern aviators for whom marital roles and home stressors may well be different. Nevertheless, significant relationship changes are widely recognized life stressors, represented in six items on the Holmes–Rahe Life Social Readjustment Stress Scale, five of which (death of a spouse, divorce, marital separation from a mate, marriage, marital reconciliation with mate) were listed among the 10 most stressful events (Holmes & Rahe, 1967). Such events are cognitively taxing and affect performance similar to other stressors. From a mental health perspective, they often manifest themselves in the form of depressed mood and/or anxiety. In a recent study by Zamorski et al. (2014) examining mental health problems in Canadian Armed Forces personnel screened after deployment between 2009 and 2012, relationship breakup or loss was identified as a risk factor with higher risk for mental health problems in personnel who were widowed, separated, or divorced.

Romantic relationship challenges aside, pilots also face unusual psychosocial challenges (Bor et al., 2017) including forming social relationships in the workplace and outside of work. By design, shift/rostering patterns means that crew are rarely working together over time to develop meaningful bonds. In addition to that, pilots are trained to critique the work of their colleagues and, hence, expect their colleagues on the flight deck to be critiquing (and possibly reporting on) their work, which could understandably create a barrier to social support. Outside of work, pilots' shifts are often at odds with the routines of non-aviation workers, and this can interfere with the maintenance of friendships (Bor et al., 2017; Cahill et al., 2019). Given that social support is a key protective factor for mental health, the disruption to this presents an additional risk factor for pilots.

Life Events

In addition to the possible occupational stressors and pilot risk factors, pilots of course share the risk factors common to all humans, such as exposure to negative life events, the development of physical health conditions and disorders, and organic mental health issues (Butcher, 2002). Mulder and de Rooy (2018) define negative life events as events that are accompanied by notable changes in a person's life. They list the most frequently occurring negative life events leading to suicide as "work problems, family discord, somatic illness, financial problems, unemployment, separation, and interpersonal loss" (p. 42). Politano and Walton (2016) analyzed the NTSB accident database to examine aircraft-assisted suicides and found that of 51 pilot suicides identified, 54.9% had an identifiable stressor categorized in the NTSB. Of these, 27.5% were relationship issues, 7.6% were legal problems, and 5.9% were related to a serious illness of either the pilot or someone close to the pilot. Although it was identified that most of these events were premeditated to some degree, they were nevertheless not likely predictable by prior psychological assessment and more likely in later life stages. This further highlights the limitation of psychological testing in the pilot recruitment process being insufficient in the long term due to the human occurrence of issues across the lifespan (Bor et al., 2017). Many psychological and physical issues have onset in later life, and one can be the victim of various unpredictable life events or be more prone to certain life events later in life such as divorce and the death of a loved one (i.e., bereavement). As such, this could also add a risk factor for mental health issues related to age.

The Holmes–Rahe Life Social Readjustment Stress Scale lists 43 life events to which they arbitrarily assign points to represent the weight of stress for each life event. Most notably, they highlight that stressful life events need not be negative events and include typically positive events such as getting married, having a baby, outstanding positive achievements, and vacation/holidays (Holmes & Rahe, 1967). Stressors outside of work, such as relationship, financial, or the myriad of personal stressors, impact everyone. However, the suggestion is that pilots should suspend their flying duties until "normal level of functioning is restored," due to the presumption that these events can result in neuropsychological impairments such as reduced concentration and lead to hesitation/decision delays on the flight deck (Bor et al., 2017), an environment which must have a zero tolerance to lapses of any kind (Jones et al., 2000).

Life event stressors have also been associated with psychological distress and the development of depressive episodes (Schotte et al., 2006). However, many individuals who experience life event stressors do not develop psychological issues. This points to the notion central to transactional stress theory that the life events themselves may not cause subsequent issues, but rather the subjective experience of the life event and/or the coping or protective factors that may be in play (Lazarus & Folkman, 1984). This view is in line with the diathesis–stress model of mental health.

The above notwithstanding, life events have the advantage of being objective as they are assessed by way of whether they have occurred or not, rather than gaining a subjective impression of their impact that is reliant on a self-report that is in turn reliant on self-awareness. Life event occurrences may also have the advantage of being less stigmatized in comparison with experiencing a mental illness. As such, Mulder and de Rooy (2018) suggest that the assessment of negative life events is a more valuable screening target for mental health risks in the pilot population, and assessing negative life events may circumvent the impression management of pilots during transparent self-report psychiatric screening assessment, which results in underreporting of mental health issues.

The limitation of assuming life stressors lead to psychological difficulty was highlighted in a recent study where pilots were found to have high life event and work stress scores and high numbers of stressors reported, although these scores failed to explain which pilots were experiencing psychological difficulties (Ackland et al., 2023). This finding reflects the assertion that the psychological impact of stressors and life events is highly dependent on the "individual's idiosyncratic interpretation of the events" (Schotte et al., 2006, p. 317), and is in line with the study by Loewenthal et al. (2000) of pilots, which found that it is not entirely the occurrence of a stressor that leads to psychological difficulties, but the extent of the emotional reaction or distress associated with the life event. Nevertheless, it is still important to understand the stressors pilot face and, at an organizational level, attempt to reduce these as much as possible.

While many significant life stressors may be difficult if not impossible to predict or prevent, they can serve as an objective cue to assess pilot mental health due to the recognition that they often precipitate the development of psychological difficulties. Further, having identified an occurrence of a life stressor, there is an opportunity to advocate for pilot coping strategies, especially for pilots who possess some vulnerability toward psychological difficulty (Ackland et al., 2022).

In exploration of these associated factors beyond stressors, the study by Ackland et al. (2023) identified specific vulnerability and protective factors associated with pilot mental health. Specifically, they identified that pilots' personality, obsessive passion, and lifestyle habits were associated with the incidence of psychological disorder in the context of pandemic stressors.

Personality Factors

The likely ability of a pilot to cope with the typical stressors of their occupation is generally assessed during recruitment. The right psychological fit of a pilot is somewhat dependent on the respective piloting role. For example, Bor et al. (2017) explain how different psychological factors are desired in the selection for "bush pilots" compared to commercial airline pilots. At recruitment, attempts are made to identify pilots who are "flexible and robust" to handle the noted physiological challenges of flying for an airline, indicating some level of recognition of stressors and risk factors of a pilot's job as well as the possible factors or qualities that may protect against the impact of these stressors.

Different rates of mental health issues in the pilot population could be attributed to the recruitment procedures pilots undertake, particularly in commercial aviation, and the personality factors common to pilots that are partly selected for in the industry. Mulder and de

Rooy (2018) posit that due to the pilot selection procedure, the pilot population is "incomparable to the general population." In explaining comparatively low rates of depressive illness in their study compared to the general US population, Lollis et al. (2009) argue that pilots have a different "mental makeup" compared to the general population, including intellectual (IQ 124 vs. 98), cognitive, and psychological factors, that protects them against psychiatric illness. Lollis et al. (2009) outline various other cognitive and psychological characteristics that distinguish pilots, such as good organization, planning, and analytic and decision-making abilities, and they summarize the protective factors that may be inherent in this by stating, "when attributes brought to the table by aviators are put in perspective, it is highly likely that they are a special population who, because of these attributes, are less prone to psychiatric illness, including MDD, than the general population" (p. 736).

Pilots are described as atypical (Lollis et al., 2009). Pilots generally process information quicker than the average person, are good at managing high physical workloads, and self-reflect a lot (Feijó et al., 2012). However, this self-reflection is likely regarding their performance, as other sources have indicated the pilot population typically has poor self-awareness (Lollis et al., 2009) and low emotional intelligence (Guo et al., 2017). Bowles et al. (2000) outline the stereotypical pilot personality, otherwise known as possessing "the right stuff," which includes being active, warm, confident, competitive, and preferring excellence and challenges. Further, pilot profiles in line with having the right stuff are also considered to have a positive effect on the crew, moderating the crew's response to stress as well. While there is not a single specific personality profile for the right stuff, due largely to the understanding that there are different personality attributes appropriate for different flying roles, as outlined above, there is one for "the wrong stuff." For example, Chappelle et al. (2010) outline that "highly anxious, hostile, depressed, isolative, or impulsive persons are considered incompatible" (p. 160) for military flying, and the same would be assumed for any flying role. Taken together, it is clear that there is an assumed overarching pilot personality that, although not a strict and prescribed profile to guide selection for all flying roles, is considered to be a positive attribute for the pilot with regard to both their performance and well-being.

Generally, personality is considered to be an enduring pattern of thoughts, feelings, and behavior (Allport, 1961), often conceptualized according to the Big Five personality factors of openness to experience, conscientiousness, extraversion, agreeableness, and neuroticism. The NEO (NEO-PI-R; Costa & McRae, 1994) is one measure of these factors and one that has a large research base in clinical and nonclinical populations, the latter including occupational and educational settings (Bleidorn et al., 2019). Clinical populations tend to be associated with a Big Five personality profile that is high in neuroticism, low in conscientiousness, low in agreeableness, and low in extraversion (Malouff et al., 2005). In commercial aviation, selection procedures to ensure good fit for a flying role might also serve to create a population that differs from the personality profile associated with clinical disorders outlined above. In a recent study (Ackland et al., 2023), pilots' overall Big Five personality profile (assessed with the NEO-PI-R) was different from population norm comparisons for neuroticism (lower), openness (higher), conscientiousness (higher), and agreeableness (lower). No differences were observed for extraversion. When examined in more detail, the pilot group could be distinguished into three groups, when referencing whether the pilots also met criteria for a diagnoseable mental health issue: the average pilot, the psychologically vulnerable pilot, and the resilient pilot. The above-described profile of the average pilot could be considered in line with possessing the right stuff, which has otherwise been characterized by high achievement motivation, social orientation, and low hostility (Musson, 2006).

Psychologically vulnerable pilots (those who also met criteria for a diagnoseable mental health issue) had higher neuroticism, lower conscientiousness, higher openness, and lower agreeableness than resilient pilots (those who did not meet criteria for a diagnosis). In the general population, high neuroticism, low conscientiousness, and low agreeableness are associated with greater psychological vulnerability (Malouff et al., 2005). As such, it may not seem surprising that those pilots with higher trait neuroticism, lower trait conscientiousness, and lower trait agreeableness have greater likelihood toward psychological disorder, as identified by Ackland et al. (2023). However, this is not an entirely accurate depiction of how the neuroticism and conscientiousness scores, in particular, differed between groups with respect to the general population. While vulnerable pilots did have higher neuroticism scores than resilient pilots, the scores were in line with the general population, meaning that their neuroticism scores were not higher than "normal." Rather, the resilient pilots had significantly *low* neuroticism scores compared with the general population. Similarly, while vulnerable pilots had lower conscientiousness scores compared with resilient pilots, these scores were also in line with the general population, and this difference was explained by the resilient pilots who had significantly *high* conscientiousness scores compared with the general population.

To explain this, it could be considered that pilots as a whole possess characteristically low neuroticism and high conscientiousness, and that the high neuroticism and low conscientiousness that are evidently associated with psychopathology effectively balance out for those who are both pilots and with psychological diagnoses. Importantly, the implication of this is that pilots with high neuroticism and low conscientiousness will not present this way with reference to the general population; they will only appear to differ in these ways with reference to other pilots. Additionally, the resilient pilots, being low in neuroticism and high in conscientiousness, possess two personality qualities that may explain their resilience against psychological symptoms. They have both low vulnerability toward the development of psychological issues, by nature of their low trait neuroticism, and high likelihood to establish good lifestyle habits, by nature of their high trait conscientiousness, such as habits that are protective against the development of stress-related symptoms.

Vulnerable pilots had lower agreeableness compared with both the resilient pilots and the general population. This finding is in line with personality research of pilots in the US Air Force (Callister et al., 1997; Chappelle et al., 2010). Low agreeableness (or disagreeableness) has also been associated with clinical disorders, particularly anxiety disorders (Malouff et al., 2005). The general implications of low agreeableness in the context of physical and psychological disorders includes poor help-seeking and treatment engagement and adherence, and is in line with other findings around health responsibility (Sykes et al., 2012) as well as the literature on pilots reverse malingering.

In summary, the research by Ackland et al. (2023) highlighted that, with respect to the general population, vulnerable pilots were less agreeable and more open than resilient pilots. Conversely, resilient pilots had low neuroticism and high conscientiousness when compared with vulnerable pilots and with respect to the general population.

Passion

As asserted in the previous section, pilots are unique, requiring a specific psychological make-up to perform a unique, stressful job. The path to becoming a pilot is lengthy and competitive and demands a dedication and passion toward the vocation to achieve success and then to maintain the position, amidst recurrent checks, ongoing training, and medical evaluations. Passion, defined as a strong inclination toward an activity that is self-defining, important, and meaningful (Vallerand et al., 2003), is often considered a positive and life-enriching experience. However, a dualistic model of passion has been proposed by Vallerand et al. (2003). In this model, passion may be "harmonious," that is, it is in harmony with one's life, adding value, and is associated with adaptive outcomes before, during, and after engagement as well as with overall psychological well-being. On the other hand, passion may be "obsessive," in which case there is an obligatory engagement in the activity, possibly at the cost of other life domains (and at an extreme can *oppress* other aspects of one's self; Houlfort et al. 2015), and which may be associated with poor outcomes before, during, or after engagement.

While both passions are associated with identity, passionate activities can become a central feature of one's identity, where an individual may self-identify as an actor of this activity foremost, as is the case with obsessive passion (Vallerand, 2012). The obsessive passion activity can also become the primary determinant of self-esteem (Mageau et al., 2011), making one's self-perceived value at the mercy of the passion activity and/or one's success in this activity. This may be a reason why people can experience an "identity crisis" at times where they lose the ability to undertake specific activities.

Pilots' passion for flying has been characterized in both a positive and potentially problematic light. The dedication and sacrifice to pursue the career are considered key to pilots' success, especially in commercial aviation where selection is competitive and sustaining the role is procedurally extensive. In the suggestion that a pilot's strong motivation to fly may influence reverse malingering or otherwise failing to report potentially grounding symptoms (Hudson & Herbert, 2017), there is a sense that this is not entirely a financial motivation, but also an emotional one. Further, pilots who have been unable to fly due to complicating or conflicting factors, or due to mandatory retirement, have been shown to struggle psychologically (Castelo-Branco et al., 1985; Lewis et al., 2007), and incapacitations have been highlighted as risk factors that require careful management (AsMA, 2015).

Passion has been studied in athletes who similarly strive to achieve success and struggle with disruption to their careers (Wylleman & Lavallee, 2004). To manage the difficulties athletes may experience when faced with exiting their sport, large organizations and sports psychologists encourage athletes to have fostered other educational and/or career interests to focus on during their time as an athlete (Aquilina, 2013; Wylleman & Lavallee, 2004).

In a recent study (Ackland et al., 2023), pilots overall scored highly in harmonious passion. However, pilots with mental health issues during the period of industry disruption associated with COVID-19 differed from those who did not develop mental health issues during this time with regard to obsessive passion, suggesting that obsessive passion toward flying was a risk factor for the development of mental health issues during periods of inability to fly. This finding is in line with the dualistic model of passion outlining obsessive passion as psychologically problematic and illustrates how pilots who position flying as a hallmark of their identity can suffer adverse psychological outcomes when their ability to fly is disrupted, as was the case during the study due to COVID-19.

In reference to previous research on pilots, obsessive passion for flying may explain the "reactive depression" identified in end-of-career pilots (Castelo-Branco et al., 1985). Obsessive passion for flying could also explain findings in previous research on aircraft-assisted suicide, which identified stressors that would prematurely sever a pilot's ability to fly (criminal charges, mental or physical health deterioration) as precipitants to pilot suicide (Lewis et al., 2007).

Overall, it is clear that passion can be advantageous and disadvantageous. Developing a passion activity can enhance psychological well-being. However, the risk in developing a passion activity, and by definition regularly engaging with it, is that it may become an activity of *obsessive* passion, which then may have the opposite effect on psychological well-being. By all accounts this seems to occur when one invests one's identity and attaches self-esteem contingencies in the engagement in the activity (Mageau et al., 2011). A suggestion might follow to temper one's emotional engagement in the passion activity and engage with other potential passion activities, too, to keep it from becoming obsessive and to foster a more balanced sense of self-worth and identity. In the case of flying, however, this might present a challenge to pilots, who must demonstrate a degree of dedication and determination toward their training and study in order to succeed. The commitment to a flying career would necessitate a level of passion, and due to the level of involvement required, may come at the sacrifice of being able to invest the time into developing other passion activities to facilitate a better balance and diffusion of sense of self. This would result in a higher likelihood that flying would quickly become a cornerstone of a pilot's identity and hence an obsessive passion.

This picture of passion for one's vocation is not unique to pilots. Athletes bear some similarity in relation to setting big career goals that require long-term dedication, commitment, and focus, and which often form an integral component of identity (Wylleman & Lavallee, 2004). Also similar to pilots, but perhaps to a greater extent, is the likelihood that an athlete's career goals might be jeopardized by medical incidences and end abruptly.

An athlete's career is expected to be shorter than the average pilot's; exiting their sport is considered a rather short- to medium-term inevitability, whereas pilots would reasonably expect both a longer and more predictable time in their flying career. As such, there is a greater rationale to prepare athletes for transitioning out of their sport, and in turn the athlete themselves may have greater preparation and acceptance of this eventuality, too. Nevertheless, future management of pilots could be informed by the athlete framework of fostering other interests and passions over the career, and in doing so may temper the maintenance of obsessive passion without dampening the harmonious passion for flying. In the present study (Ackland et al., 2023) this was illustrated by pilots' reports that having other interests (i.e., sailing, cycling) was helpful during the period of being unable to fly, by providing another opportunity for engagement and, in a few cases, employment opportunities. While promoting dual interests may well be difficult in the earliest phases of the career where the training and study demands on a pilot may be particularly overwhelming, support for this at a later point in the early career of a pilot may well improve pilot well-being and ease career transitions as well as periods of unexpected flying disruption.

Coping Strategies/Protective Factors

In line with the diathesis–stress model, Mulder and de Rooy (2018) highlight the interrelationship between negative life events and coping strategies in suggesting that coping difficulties may determine whether negative life events will lead to mental health issues or not. Specifically, they assert that while negative life events pose a risk factor, they should not be used to determine mental health issues. Rather, the pilot's coping strategies should be attended to in determining whether negative life events may pose a risk. Guo et al. (2017) found that proactive coping strategies were protective in "buffering" the effects of stress on pilots, moderating the development of depression and anxiety symptoms. They identified that emotional intelligence, in particular, could buffer the effects of stress; however, they noted that pilots tended to be low in emotional intelligence.

It has been suggested that pilots use specific styles of coping strategies, namely, active, practical, and problem-solving focused strategies, such as dealing directly with the stressor and, notably, using these rather than emotional strategies (Cuevas, 2003). Young (2008) describes a common strategy of compartmentalization, where a pilot may purposefully exclude emotions and personal thoughts and feelings from the cockpit in order to dedicate attention to performance. Generally, compartmentalization can be a useful strategy in this way but is cautioned against when it is used too rigidly to avoid emotions in the short term, most notably because such a technique may not always be effective and can lead to the problematic manifestations of internal symptoms (Young, 2008).

Lifestyle Factors

Common protective factors that buffer the effects of risk factors in the normal population include: sleep, diet, exercise, and social/family support (Cahill et al., 2019; Firth et al., 2020). Notably, a number of these are likely impacted by holding the job of a commercial pilot. The importance of sleep is widely understood, but establishing good sleep habits often requires a good overall routine, which is disrupted by the shift work of a pilot and additionally the extent to which these shifts cross time zones.

Healthy eating habits and exercise are also shown to be more achievable when imbedded in a normal daily routine. Feijó et al. (2012) specifically looked at workload as a risk factor and exercise as a protective factor. The results indicated that a combination of low workload and exercise was associated with lower common mental health disorders, which emphasizes that although the role of a pilot may have inherent risks, there are also opportunities to ameliorate these risks with coping strategies or protective factors, such as exercise. Despite the benefits of these lifestyle factors on physical and mental health, there appears to be few studies that have examined these factors alongside pilot mental health. From the studies that do, they generally conclude that sleep and exercise in particular are beneficial for pilot well-being and stress management (Cahill et al., 2019).

Coping strategies are advocated for as a way of managing and reducing the impact of stress as well as other psychological symptoms. Guo et al. (2017) found that, in particular, proactively applied coping strategies were effective at buffering depression and anxiety for pilots. In a recent study (Ackland et al., 2023), pilots showed a tendency to use task-orientated coping strategies. This trend contrasts with the coping profile previously found for people with MDD, which was increased for emotion-oriented and deflated for task-oriented (McWilliams et al., 2003) individuals, and may explain the resilience of pilots.

In addition to intentionally applied coping strategies, lifestyle factors can also be protective against the development of psychological difficulties and can enhance well-being (Lappalainen et al., 2014; Walsh, 2011). Lifestyle psychiatry emphasizes these benefits. Improvements in the areas of sleep, diet, exercise, and substances (i.e., tobacco) have been found to significantly improve symptoms of anxiety, ADHD, and depression (Firth et al, 2020) – three of the four most prevalent disorder types identified in a recent study on pilot mental health during the COVID-19 pandemic (Ackland et al., 2023). In previous studies of pilots, lifestyle factors have emerged as common coping mechanisms. For example, Feijó et al. (2012) found exercise was an effective strategy in managing specific work stress for pilots. Cahill et al. (2021) also identified an association between pilots reported use of sleep, diet, and physical activity as coping strategies and lower depression levels.

Pilots' scores on lifestyle factors are generally high (Ackland et al., 2023), in particular with regard to interpersonal relations, nutrition, and spiritual growth. Spiritual growth relates to achievement-striving and as such is not a surprising finding in the context of pilots. It is, however, perhaps a commonly overlooked lifestyle domain that can have positive psychological benefits (Boudreaux & Ozer, 2013; McGregor & Little,1998; Sheldon & Houser-Marko, 2001). In this regard, it could be likened to the human need for self-actualization (Maslow, 1943).

Interpersonal relations followed by nutrition were the most endorsed lifestyle factors for pilots in a recent study examining pilot mental health, although these were more endorsed by pilots who were not found to have mental health difficulties (Ackland et al., 2023). This identified that pilots without mental health difficulties engaged in more interpersonal activities and ate more healthily than pilots with mental health difficulties. This suggests that pilots' lifestyle habits do potentially protect against, or buffer the experience of, psychological symptoms. Although one could suggest that poor nutrition and low socializing may be causal in psychological difficulties or a corollary of experiencing psychological difficulties, it should be noted that both groups scored reasonably high on these subscales, although pilots without mental health difficulties scored highest. Nutrition emerged as the most beneficial lifestyle factor associated with not having a mental health issue, further highlighting the known relationship between mental health and diet.

The advantage of lifestyle factors being a key protective factor for mental health is that improvement of these factors is generally straightforward. This is not to say it is easy, and long-term adherence to healthy lifestyle practice is a common challenge. It is important to consider that a healthy lifestyle may be difficult to establish as a pilot, who is both a shift worker and often a remote worker (Bostock & Steptoe, 2012). In the case of long-haul, international pilots, establishing a healthy lifestyle routine may be incompatible with the nature of the job: eating and sleeping at odd hours, opportunistically, and fitting in other psychologically protective behaviors (exercise, socializing) around the roster when possible. This is in line with a study of cabin crew before and during the pandemic, which found that 7% of the sample felt their personal situation had improved during the pandemic, owing to relief from job-related stressors including "more time to rest, better sleep, more time for family, friends, pets, further professional training or reorientation, less stress, and healthier eating habits" (Görlich & Stadelmann, 2020, p. 4).

It has also been found that pilots score low on health responsibility, a scale measuring the extent to which pilots seek medical attention for their general health (Ackland et al., 2023).

This could be owing to pilots having generally better health and annual medical check-ups for their license requirements, and as such less need for interim medical attention. However, this is also in line with literature describing pilots' tendency to "reverse malinger" so as to not jeopardize their ability to continue flying, as well as previous research that showed pilots attending their GP far less than the general population (Sykes et al., 2012). Poor health- and help-seeking behavior is reported to be a risk factor for poorer health outcomes (Reavley et al., 2010). It has also been shown to be more prevalent among men than women, and this has been argued to be less attributable to gender and more so to occupational trends (Galdas et al., 2005). Taken together, this suggests an unsurprising result of pilots scoring low on health responsibility, but nevertheless an avenue to be further explored with the view of increasing pilots' comfort and willingness toward seeking appropriate supports for their overall health and well-being.

Conclusion

In summary, this chapter examined the factors associated with pilot mental health. When a pilot's mental health deteriorates, it can have a significant impact on their cognitive functioning and, hence, flying performance and aviation safety. In accordance with the diathesis–stress model of psychological health, while stressors may precipitate mental health difficulties for pilots, they are seldom the entire cause. Pilots who are disagreeable and less conscientious by nature, and who have obsessive passion for flying, have a vulnerability such that when flying is not possible (unavailable, or possibly jeopardized), they may begin to struggle psychologically. Further, they may be particularly reluctant to seek early intervention due to the complex and stigmatized mental health culture in aviation, which may worsen their circumstance. Conversely, pilots who are less neurotic and more conscientious by nature, and who are more nutrition conscious, tend to be more resilient against stressors including disruption to flying. These findings highlight the importance of a proactive approach to pilot mental health, which is often best achieved through a thorough and detailed neuropsychological assessment to assist with identifying protective and risk factors (i.e., encouraging pilots to have healthy lifestyles and other passions beyond flying). Given that the role of flying, particularly commercial long-haul flights, may be a large barrier to fostering both of these habits, adjustments may need to be made organizationally to facilitate this.

References

Ackland, C.A., Molesworth, B.R. C., Grisham, J.R., & Lovibond, P.F. (2022). Pilot mental health, methodologies and findings: A systematic review. *Aerospace Medicine and Human Performance, 93*(9), 1–13. https://doi.org/10.3357/AMHP.6043.2022

Ackland, C.A., Molesworth, B.R. C., & Grisham, J.R. (2023). Pilot mental health during the COVID-19 pandemic: Prevalence rates from semi-structured interviews, and associated vulnerability and protective factors. *Frontiers in Psychology, 14,* Article 1073857. https://doi.org/10.3389/fpsyg.2023.1073857

Aerospace Medical Association Working Group on Pilot Mental Health. (2015). Pilot mental health: Expert working group recommendations (revised 2015). *Aerospace Medicine and Human Performance, 87*(5), 505–507.

Allport, G.W. (1961). *Pattern and growth in personality.* Holt, Reinhart & Winston.

Aquilina, D. (2013). A study of the relationship between elite athletes' educational development and sporting performance. *The International Journal of the History of Sport, 30*, 374–392. https://doi.org/10.1080/09523367.2013.765723

Arsintescu, L., Chachad, R., Gregory, K. B., Mulligan, J. B., & Flynn-Evans, E. E. (2020). *The relationship between workload, performance and fatigue in a short-haul airline, Chronobiology International, 37*(9–10), 1492–1494. https://doi.org/10.1080/07420528.2020.1804924

Bakker, A. B., & de Vries, J. D. (2021). Job demands-resources theory and self-regulation: New explanations and remedies for job burnout. *Anxiety, Stress, & Coping, 34*(34), 1–21. https://doi.org/10.1080/10615806.2020.1797695

Bendak, S., & Rashid, H. S. J. (2020). Fatigue in aviation: A systematic review of the literature. *International Journal of Industrial Ergonomics, 76*, Article 102928. https://doi.org/10.1016/j.ergon.2020.102928

Bleidorn, W., Hill, P. L., Back, M. D., Denissen, J. J. A., Hennecke, M., Hopwood, C. J., Jokela, M., Kandler, C., Lucas, R. E., Luhmann, M., Orth, U., Wagner, J., Wrzus, C., Zimmermann, J., & Roberts, B. (2019). The policy relevance of personality traits. *American Psychologist, 74*(9), 1056–1067. https://doi.org/10.1037/amp0000503

Bor, R., Eriksen, C., Oakes, M., & Scragg, P. (2017). Pilot mental health in the modern era: Headlines and reality. In R. Bor, C. Eriksen, M. Oakes, & P. Scragg (Eds.), *Pilot mental health assessment and support* (pp. 1–20). Routledge.

Bor, R., Field, G., & Scragg, P. (2002). The mental health of pilots: An overview. *Counselling Psychology Quarterly, 15*, 239–256. https://doi.org/10.1080/09515070210143471

Bostock, S., & Steptoe, A. (2012). Influences of early shift work on the diurnal cortisol rhythm, mood and sleep: Within-subject variation in male airline pilots. *Psychneuroendocrinology, 38*, 533–541. https://doi.org/10.1016/j.psyneuen.2012.07.012

Boudreaux, M. J., & Ozer, D. J. (2013). Goal conflict, goal striving, and psychological well-being. *Motivation and Emotion, 37*, 433–443. https://doi.org/10.1007/s11031-012-9333-2

Bowles, S., Ursin, H., & Picano, J. (2000). Aircrew perceived stress: Examining crew performance, crew position and captains personality. *Aviation, Space, and Environmental Medicine, 71*, 1093–1097.

Brannon, L., & Feist, J. (2007). *Health psychology: An introduction to behaviour and health* (6th ed.). Thomson Higher Education.

Butcher, J. N. (2002). Assessing pilots with 'the wrong stuff'. *International Journal of Selection and Assessment, 10*, 168–184. https://doi.org/10.1111/1468-2389.00204

Cahill, J., Cullen, P., Anwer, S., Wilson, S., & Gaynor, K. (2021). Pilot work related stress (WRS), effects on wellbeing and mental health, and coping methods. *International Journal of Aerospace Psychology, 31*(2), 87–109. https://doi.org/10.1080/24721840.2020.1858714

Cahill, J., Cullen, P., & Gaynor, K. (2019). Interventions to support the management of work-related stress (WRS) and wellbeing/mental health issues for commercial pilots. *Cognition, Technology & Work, 22*, 517–547. https://doi.org/10.1007/s10111-019-00586-z

Callister, J. D., King, R. E., Retzlaff, P. D., & Marsh, R. W. (1997). *Using the NEO-PI-R to assess the personality of US Air Force pilots* [Interim technical report]. Armstrong Lab Brooks AFB TX Aerospace Medicine Directorate. https://doi.org/10.21236/ADA328908

Castelo-Branco, A., Cabral-Sa, A., & Coelho Borges, J. (1985). Comparative study of physical and mental incapacities among Portuguese airline pilots under and over age 60. *Aviation Space and Environmental Medicine, 56*, 752–57.

Chappelle, W. L., Novy, P. L., Sowin, T. W., & Thompson, W. T. (2010). NEO PI-R normative personality data that distinguish U.S. Air Force female pilots. *Military Psychology, 22*, 158–175. https://doi.org/10.1080/08995600903417308

Cooper, C., & Sloan, S. (1985). Occupational and psychosocial stress among commercial aviation pilots. *Journal of Occupational Medicine, 27*(8), 570–575.

Costa, P., & McCrae, R. (1994). *Revised NEO Personality Inventory (NEO PI-R) and NEO Five-Factor Inventory (NEO-FFI)*. Psychological Assessment Resources.

Cuevas, H. M. (2003). The pilot personality and individual differences in the stress response. *Proceedings of the Human Factors and Ergonomics Society 47th Meeting, 47*(9), P1092–1096.

Evans, S., & Radcliffe, S-A. (2012). The annual incapacitation rate of commercial pilots. *Aviation, Space, and Environmental Medicine, 83*(1), 42–49. https://doi.org/10.3357/ASEM.3134.2012

Feijó, D., Luiz, R., & Camara, V. (2012). Common mental disorders among civil aviation pilots. *Aviation, Space, and Environmental Medicine, 83*, 509–513. https://doi.org/10.3357/ASEM.3185.2012

Firth, J., Solmi, M., Wootton, R.E., Vancampfort, D., Schuch, F.B., Hoare, E., Gilbody, S., Torous, J., Teasdale, S.B., Jackson, S.E., Smith, L., Eaton, M., Jacka, F.N., Veronese, N., Marx, W., Ashdown-Franks, G., Siskind, D., Sarris, J., Rosenbaum, S., Carvalho, A.F., & Stubbs, B. (2020). A meta-review of "lifestyle psychiatry": The role of exercise, smoking, diet and sleep in the prevention and treatment of mental disorders. *World Psychiatry, 19*, 360–380. https://doi.org/10.1002/wps.20773

Freudenberger, H.J. (1974). Staff burn-out. *Journal of Social Issues, 30*(1), 159–165. https://doi.org/10.1111/josi.1974.30.issue-1

Galdas, P.M., Cheater, F., & Marshall, P. (2005). Men and health help-seeking behaviour: Literature review. *Journal of Advanced Nursing, 49*, 616–623. https://doi.org/10.1111/j.1365-2648.2004.03331.x

Gavelin, H.M., Domellof, M.E., AStrom, E., Nelson, A., Launder, N.H., Neely, A.S., & Lampit, A. (2022). Cognitive function in clinical burnout: A systematic review and meta-analysis. *Work and Stress, 36*(1), 86–104. https://doi.org/10.1080/02678373.2021.2002972

Gavelin, H.M., Stigsdotter Neely, A., Aronsson, I., Josefsson, M., & Andersson, L. (2023). Mental fatigue, cognitive performance and autonomic response following sustained mental activity in clinical burnout. *Biological Psychology, 183*, Article 108661. https://doi.org/10.1016/j.biopsycho.2023.108661

Görlich, Y., & Stadelmann, D. (2020). Mental health of flying cabin crews: Depression, anxiety, and stress before and during the COVID-19 pandemic. *Frontiers in Psychology, 11*, Article 581496. https://doi.org/10.3389/fpsyg.2020.581496

Guo, Y., Ji, M., & Huang, J. (2017). Protective effects of emotional intelligence and proactive coping on civil pilots' mental health. *Aerospace Medicine and Human Performance, 88*, 858–865. https://doi.org/10.3357/AMHP.4799.2017

Head, J., & Helton, W.S. (2014). Sustained attention failures are primarily due sustained cognitive load not task monotony. *Acta Psychologica, 153*, 87–94. https://doi.org/10.1016/j.actpsy.2014.09.007

Holmes, T.H., & Rahe, R.H. (1967). The Social Readjustment Rating Scale. *Journal of Psychosomatic Research, 11*, 213–218. https://doi.org/10.1016/0022-3999(67)90010-4

Houlfort, N., Fernet, C., Vallerand, R.J., Laframboise, A., Guay, F., & Koestner, R. (2015). The role of passion for work and need satisfaction in psychological adjustment to retire. *Journal of Vocational Behaviour, 88*, 84–94. https://doi.org/10.1016/j.jvb.2015.02.005

Hudson, M., & Herbert, K. (2017). The practicalities of fitting mental health screening into the time-limited annual medical check and the problems of confidentiality. In R. Bor, C. Eriksen, M. Oakes, & P. Scragg (Eds.), *Pilot mental health assessment and support* (pp. 208–225). Routledge.

Jones, D.R., Marsh, R.W., Patterson, J.C., Sowin, T.W., Drummond, F.E., Orme, D.R., & Callister, J.D. (2000). *Aviation neuropsychiatry*. USAF School of Aerospace Medicine.

Kausler, D.H. (1994). *Learning and memory*. Academic Press.

Koutsimani, P., Montgomery, A., Masoura, E., & Panagopoulou, E. (2021). Burnout and cognitive performance. *International Journal of Environmental Research and Public Health, 18*(4), Article 2145. https://doi.org/10.3390/ijerph18042145

Lappalainen, R., Sairanen, E., Järvelä, E., Rantala, S., Korpela, R., Puttonen, S., Kujala, U.M., Myllymaki, T., Peuhkuri, K., Mattila, E., Kaipainen, K., Ahtinen, A., Karhunen, L., Pihlajamaki, J., Jarnefelt, H., Laitinen, J., Kutinlahti, E., Saarelma, O., Ermes, M., & Kolehmainen, M. (2014). The effectiveness and applicability of different lifestyle interventions for enhancing wellbeing: The study design for a randomized controlled trial for persons with metabolic syndrome risk factors and psychological distress. *BMC Public Health, 14*, Article 310. https://doi.org/10.1186/1471-2458-14-310

Lazarus, R.S., & Folkman, S. (1984). *Stress, appraisal and coping*. Springer.

Lewis, R.J., Johnson, R.D., Whinnery, J.E., & Foster, E.M. (2007). Aircraft-assisted pilot suicides in the United States, 1993-2002. *Archives of Suicide Research, 11*, 149–161.

Loewenthal, K.M., Eysenck, M., Harris, D., Lubitsh, G., Gorton, T., & Bicknell, H. (2000). Stress, distress and air traffic incidents: job dysfunction and distress in airline pilots in relation to contextually-assessed stress. *Stress Medicine, 16*, 179–83. https://doi.org/10.1002/(SICI)1099-1700(200004)16:3<179::AID-SMI851>3.0.CO;2-4

Lollis, D.B., Marsh, R.M., Sowin, T.W., & Thompson, W.T. (2009). Major depressive disorder in military aviators: A retrospective study of prevalence. *Aviation, Space, and Environmental Medicine, 80*, 734–737. https://doi.org/10.3357/ASEM.2484.2009

Mageau, G.A., Carpentier, J., & Vallerand, R.J. (2011). The role of self-esteem contingencies in the distinction between obsessive and harmonious passion. *European Journal of Social Psychology, 41,* 720–729. https://doi.org/10.1002/ejsp.798

Malouff, J.M., Thorsteinsson, E.B., & Schutte, N.S. (2005). The relationship between the five-factor model of personality and symptoms of clinical disorders: A meta-analysis. *Journal of Psychopathology and Behavioral Assessment, 27*(2), 101–114. https://doi.org/10.1007/s10862-005-5384-y

Maslow, A.H. (1943). A theory of human motivation. *Psychological Review, 50*(4), 370–396. https://doi.org/10.1037/h0054346

McGregor, I., & Little, B.R. (1998). Personal projects, happiness, and meaning: On doing well and being yourself. *Journal of Personality and Social Psychology, 74*, 494–512. https://doi.org/10.1037//0022-3514.74.2.494

McWilliams, L.A., Cox, B.J., & Enns, M.W. (2003). Use of the Coping Inventory for Stressful Situations in a clinically depressed sample: Factor structure, personality correlates, and prediction of distress. *Journal of Clinical Psychology, 59,* 1371–1385. https://doi.org/10.1002/jclp.10228

Mulder, S., & de Rooy, D. (2018). Pilot mental health, negative life events, and improving safety with peer support and a just culture. *Aerospace Medicine and Human Performance, 89*, 41–51. https://doi.org/10.3357/AMHP.4903.2018

Musson, D.M. (2006). Psychological aspects of astronaut selection. In R. Bor & T. Hubbard (Eds.), *Aviation mental health. psychological implications for air transportation* (pp. 107–126). Ashgate Publishing Limited.

National Transportation Safety Board. (2009). *Report number SEA08IA080.* https://www.ntsb.gov/_layouts/ntsb.aviation/brief.aspx?ev_id=20080222X00229&key=1

Newman, D.G. (2004). *Alcohol and human performance from an aviation perspective* [Research report]. Australian Transport Safety Bureau. https://www.atsb.gov.au/media/36525/Alcohol_and_human_performance.pdf

O'Hagan, A.D., Issartel, J., Nevil, A., & Warrington, G. (2016). Flying into depression. Pilot's sleep and fatigue experiences can explain differences in perceived depression and anxiety associated with duty hours. *Workplace Health & Safety, 65*, 109–117. https://doi.org/10.1177/2165079916659506

Politano, P.M., & Walton, R.O. (2016). Analysis of NTSB aircraft-assisted pilot suicide: 1982-2014. *Suicide and Life-Threatening Behavior, 46*, 234–238.

Reavley, N.J., Cvetkovski, S., & Jorm, A.F. (2010). Help-seeking for substance use, anxiety and affective disorders among young people: Results from the 2007 Australian National Survey of Mental Health and Wellbeing. *Australian & New Zealand Journal of Psychiatry, 44*(8), 729–735. https://doi.org/10.3109/00048671003705458

Roach, G.D., Dorrian, J., Fletcher, A., & Dawson, D. (2001). Comparing the effects of fatigue and alcohol consumption on locomotive engineers' performance in a rail simulator. *Journal of Human Ergology, 30*, 1–2.

Schotte, C.K. W., Van Den Bossche, B., De Donker, D., Claes, S., & Cosyns, P. (2006). A biopsychosocial model as a guide for psychoeducation and treatment of depression. *Depression and Anxiety, 23,* 312–324. https://doi.org/10.1002/da.20177

Sheldon, K.M., & Houser-Marko, L. (2001). Self-concordance, goal-attainment, and the pursuit of happiness: Can there be an upward spiral? *Journal of Personality and Social Psychology, 80*, 152–165. https://doi.org/10.1037//0022-3514.80.1.152

Sykes, A.J., Larsen, P.D., Griffiths, R.F., & Aldington, S. (2012). A study of airline pilot morbidity. *Aviation Space and Environmental Medicine, 83*(10), 1001–1005. https://doi.org/10.3357/ASEM.3380.2012

Vallerand, R., Blanchard, C., Mageau, G.A., Koestner, R., Ratelle, C., Leonard, M., Gagne, M., & Marsolais, J. (2003). Les Passions de l'ame: On obsessive and harmonious passion. *Journal of Personality and Social Psychology, 85,* 756–767. https://doi.org/10.1037/0022-3514.85.4.756

Vallerand, R. J. (2012). The role of passion in sustainable psychological well-being. *Psychology of Well-Being: Theory, Research and Practice, 2*, Article 1. https://doi.org/10.1186/2211-1522-2-1

Walsh, R. (2011). Lifestyle and mental health. *American Psychologist, 66*(7), 579–592. https://doi.org/10.1037/a0021769

Widyahening, I. S. (2007). High level of work stressors increase the risk of mental-emotional disturbances among airline pilots. *Medical Journal Indonesia, 16*, 117–121. https://doi.org/10.13181/mji.v16i2.267

Wylleman, P., & Lavallee, D. (2004). A developmental perspective on transitions faced by athletes. In M. R. Weiss (Ed.), *Developmental sport and exercise psychology: A lifespan perspective* (pp. 503–523). Fitness Information Technology.

Young, J. A. (2008). *The effects of life-stress on pilot performance. Report number NASA/TM-2008-215375.* Ames Research Center.

Zamorski, M. A., Rusu, C., & Garber, B. G. (2014). Prevalence and correlates of mental health problems in Canadian forces personnel who deployed in support of the mission in Afghanistan: Findings from post-deployment screenings, 2009–2012. *Canadian Journal of Psychiatry, 59*, 319–326.

Chapter 10
The Clinical Utility of Structured Cognitive Training in Pilots

John Milanovich

Thousands of pilots are seen by neuropsychologists on an annual basis to help determine their eligibility to hold an airman medical certificate.[1] Until recently, those with identified neurocognitive deficiencies have had no means to reliably address the problems found, which leaves many pilots with negative, enduring life changes. Advances in computer-based technologies and electronics over the past 25 years have given pilots and others alike the opportunity to strengthen underlying weaknesses and potentially remediate detected impairments like never before, allowing neuropsychologists to finally begin moving from highly refined diagnostic methods to actual neurocognitive interventions.

Conditions that lead to neurocognitive concerns typical to pilots may be broadly divided into two categories: (1) acquired and (2) congenital. Of the first group, acquired neurocognitive deficits associated with pilots are similar to those seen in the general population, including cerebrovascular accident (CVA), traumatic brain injury (TBI), neurologically relevant infectious disease (i.e., human immunodeficiency virus [HIV], long-term COVID, encephalitis), mild cognitive impairment (MCI), and substance use disorders (SA), the latter of which tends to be associated with alcohol abuse or dependence.

Of the congenital conditions most frequently seen by the neuropsychologist, aspiring pilots with a history of ADHD are by far the most prevalent cases, followed by those with histories of an autistic spectrum disorder (ASD), learning disability (such as dyslexia), and/or cerebral palsy. Pilots or aspiring pilots who are currently using a non-disqualifying selective serotonin reuptake inhibitor (SSRI) as treatment for depression or anxiety are also commonly seen for FAA-based neuropsychological (NP) evaluation, although at a less frequent rate due to discontinuation of annual SSRI review requirements for special issuance renewal purposes (FAA, 2022).

Of the pilots evaluated each year for special issuance purposes by neuropsychologists familiar with FAA standards, most typically designated as Human Intervention Motivational Study (HIMS) neuropsychologists, an unknown but significant number are found to have some form of neurocognitive deficiency that is aeromedically significant (estimates of 18 % to roughly 30 % depending on the population examined; D. DaSilva, R. Elliot, & J. Guay, personal communications, July 28, 2023; S. Brown, personal communication, October 6,

1 While the Federal Aviation Administration (FAA) does not publish the number of pilots evaluated by neuropsychologists, at least 2,000 are screened in the United States on an annual basis (G. Kay, personal communication, July 31, 2023). Studies within the FAA that led to a recent change in assessment requirements for individuals with a history of attention-deficit/hyperactivity disorder (ADHD; FAA, 2023a) indicated more than 2,500 aspiring pilots are examined each year for that condition alone (R. Georgemiller, group communication, October 4, 2023)

2023); however, some estimates are even higher and may depend upon the pilot populations seen in one or another setting (Milanovich & Prosje, 2023). This suggests a significant number of pilots are likely to be found ineligible to hold an airman medical certificate following their NP evaluations.

Detected neurocognitive impairment is a substantial concern to the FAA due to the potential consequences of allowing an individual with known impairment to pilot aircraft (FAA, 2023b). Regardless of the underlying diagnostic picture or circumstances, including the number of logged flight hours or reports of normal functioning in the cockpit and daily life, neurocognitive deficiencies considered aeromedically significant will most likely ground an aviator until it is proven the deficiencies are no longer present. Of course, commercial pilots are highly motivated to return to duty, and for some being grounded may represent the greatest stressor ever experienced in their lifetime. While private pilots, personal aircraft owners, and aspiring pilots may have less at stake, private pilots required a great deal of dedication and personal resources to acquire their license and aspiring pilots often have organized much of their lives, and identity, around a potential career in aviation. To be eligible to hold an airman medical certificate following identification of neurocognitive impairment, a pilot must at some point in time demonstrate neurocognitive normalcy through follow-up neuropsychological re-testing, which in and of itself further taxes time and financial resources. Compounded by reasonable questions of what could be done to improve upon neurocognitive impairment and how a pilot or neuropsychologist will know when one is ready to re-test, a rather substantial gap between neurocognitive assessment and intervention has existed in the aviation environment, if not in neuropsychology as a whole. And although well-intentioned suggestions such as living a healthier lifestyle, staying active, establishing good sleep patterns, and playing online "brain games" have been the most informed guidelines available, more specific evidence-based practices have been sorely missed. It is within this context that efforts to more directly remediate neurocognitive deficiencies commonly seen in pilots began.

The Need: Interventions to Enhance *Abilities*, Not Skills

Neurocognitive assessment tends to primarily be concerned with one's abilities, not skills. Unlike the neuropsychologist's perspective, those in the aviation environment commonly view a pilot's abilities as being associated with the number of logged flight hours, ratings, hours on the job, a history of managing emergency situations, and a lack of accident history due to pilot-related error. If a pilot passes his or her simulator and line checks, all is often believed to be well. However, well-documented cases suggest a pilot's underlying neurocognitive functioning, even when everything else looks good "on paper," is critical to flight performance and safety, especially in unexpected or non-routine situations (e.g., Porges, 2013).

Neurocognitive abilities have been shown to be localized to one extent or another since Pierre Paul Broca's and Karl Wernicke's discoveries in the mid- to late 19th century (Heilman & Valenstein, 1993). Approximately 100 years later, Aleksandr Romanovich Luria made significant contributions to the way in which we understand relationships between these localized regions within the brain (Luria, 1960, 1973). In the latter half of the 20th century, through the present time, performance levels in various cognitive domains have been the basis of neuropsychological evaluations, which strive to measure constructs that include, but are not limited to, auditory/language capacities, visual-spatial analysis, processing speed, working memory (WM), long-term memory, problem-solving and reasoning, sensory-motor functioning, and of course executive functioning (Lezak, 1995). Although some overlap exists between constructs, through careful assessment the neuropsychologist is able to isolate otherwise "invisible" processes of impairment or weakness, thereby revealing the very factor(s) that could seriously disrupt a pilot's performance in the cockpit.

Over time, like other areas of biomedical development, neuropsychology has moved on from a focus on assessment procedures that identify problem areas to actual intervention efforts that attempt to remediate the specific neurocognitive deficiencies discovered upon examination. In this manner, strengthening a pilot's underlying abilities as related to piloting aircraft, rather than flying skills per se, has been far more plausible than what was possible in previous generations. As a result, those who have been deemed unfit to be pilot in command may now have the opportunity to remediate discovered deficiencies to the point of being able to manage unexpected events and unfamiliar situations at or above premorbid levels.

Forms of Neurocognitive Intervention in the General Population

Desires to enhance neurocognitive processing have most likely been present since time immemorial, at least from an unconscious standpoint. Adaptive functioning, something of which is found at the highest known level in *Homo sapiens*, is largely based upon interactions between an individual's innate capacities and transactions with the environment that lead to acquired skills (Greenspan, 1997). When either falls below a critical threshold, adaptation may no longer be accomplished, at least to the desired levels or standards. As noted in the previous section, a pilot's innate capacities (or, neurocognitive abilities) become a concern if certain thresholds critical to flight performance and safety are not met. In such situations, and others, enhancing underlying cognitive processes becomes a sought-after goal.

Unlike paper-pencil formats, as suggested above, recent developments in computer technology and electronics have afforded investigators the potential to "stress" and strengthen underlying neural functions with relatively great precision, thereby opening the doors to new pathways of intervention. Over the past 25 years, such avenues have been researched with vigor.

Cognitive rehabilitation (CR) methods have been developed over the past century, initially in response to war injuries and, eventually, as a response to deficiencies in language and other higher-order processes (Parente & Stapleton, 1997). While CR has mainly focused upon recovery to normal functioning, typically from acquired deficits, the science of neuroplasticity and mechanisms for neurocognitive enhancement that were eventually elucidated indicated neural enhancement was possible, even when physically damaged neural structures were present.[2] While CR has been indirectly quite valuable when considering neurocognitive impairment in pilots, the relatively remedial nature of CR interventions, and a focus upon more obvious rather than subtle areas of impairment as seen in pilots, has limited its role in the aviation environment.

As early as the 1960s it was found that individuals harbored some control over their brain waves and by the 1970s electroencephalographic (EEG) biofeedback showed some success in treating seizure disorder (Neurofeedback Alliance, n.d.). Over time, techniques evolved into what is known today as *neurofeedback* (NF), of which the US Food and Drug Administration (FDA) now regulates NF devices, if registered, with approval to promote relaxation. Although licensed practitioners may use such devices "off-label" to treat symptoms of various conditions, such as ADHD or anxiety, NF in and of itself is not considered a treatment for any specific mental health condition (About Neurofeedback, n.d.). In addition, while NF may have some merit in enhancing relaxation and treating select mental health conditions or symptoms, the potential of NF to enhance specific neurocognitive deficits identified upon neuropsychological inquiry has largely been unstudied, and the longevity of any potential benefits to processing speed (PS), WM, or other cognitive domains is unknown. Given these circumstances, along with the relatively high costs of NF to consumers (typical costs for a 10-session course of intervention range from $2,000 to $4,000; Dodge, 2022), the use of NF in pilots has been questionable and the motivation to pursue it as a viable intervention for pilots has been minimal to date.

In still more recent years, various brain stimulation methods have evolved from early electroconvulsive treatments as a means to provide potentially safer alternatives, either through refined electrical stimulation techniques (i.e., transcranial direct current stimulation, transdermal trigeminal or vagal nerve stimulation, and deep brain stimulation) or the use of magnetic fields (i.e., transcranial magnetic stimulation). In addition to the relatively aggressive nature of these noninvasive procedures, side effect profiles (National Institute of Mental Health, n.d.) would be of concern in the aviation environment and the capacity to choose specific neurocognitive capacities for enhancement is not well-established, unless disqualifying deep brain stimulation approaches are used.

Nevertheless, electrical stimulation techniques were found to enhance sustained attention and target detection in a program of studies conducted by researchers at Wright-Patterson Air Force Base in drone pilot operators (McKinley et al., 2019; Nelson et al., 2019). In the same set of studies, transcranial direct stimulation enhanced learning and memory in mice through identifiable neuronal pathways that were associated with synaptic plasticity (Hatcher-Solis, 2019). An external trigeminal nerve stimulation device (by Monarch) was fast-track approved for the treatment of ADHD in children (FDA, 2019), which has further

2 The potential for neural enhancement/neuroplasticity is most obvious in establishing new memories on a daily basis, of which one to two impressions may lead to long-term physiological changes. Learning a new skill may require many impressions or repetitions to be adept or "automatic" in its use (think of athletes, musicians, or thespians), with increasing repetitions and learning required as dependent on the complexity involved. While the line between skills and abilities may become blurred in some circumstances, the latter may be viewed as an underlying capacity that can be applied to various situations, including those that are novel (i.e., "far-transfer," generalized effects are present), by which skills are dependent. The neurophysiological mechanisms associated with any positive changes in neural functioning have been and continue to be studied and substantiated, including dendritic extension and myelin sheath growth, the latter of which is seen even in older adults (Lövdén et al., 2010b). Repetition in the right way (i.e., "perfect" practice) is often critical to such growth.

elucidated the potential use of brain stimulation approaches in the general population. The most common side effects for the Monarch device included drowsiness, trouble sleeping, and headache, which would likely be disqualifying for pilots.

Pharmacologic means, which are perhaps even more aggressive than the aforementioned interventions, have also been studied for the purposes of cognitive health and remediation, although results have not been as favorable as desired (J. Gibson, personal communication, December 11, 2021), with no FDA approvals to date and varying clinical practice guidelines that are at times contradictory (Chen et al., 2021). In addition, like many of the approaches discussed above, the study of pharmacologic agents has been primarily directed toward treating specific mental health conditions rather than select neurocognitive processes or abilities. Of course, the need to evaluate effective psychoactive agents for airspace safety would most likely require decades of study, making it an untenable approach at this time.

Overall, none of the aforementioned interventions appear to meet the demands of rather high-functioning pilots who require a reliable, long-lasting, generalizable intervention to strengthen specific underlying neurocognitive deficiencies, preferably through easily accessible and affordable means that are noninvasive and have a minimal to no side effect profile. Despite such hurdles, cognitive training (CTr) has shown high promise as an intervention for use by neuropsychologists and other practitioners in assisting pilots with identified impairment, while addressing many of the shortcomings found in other platforms.

Considerations for Cognitive Training in Pilots

CTr is defined as a set of computer-based, typically online, noninvasive exercises that tap into specific neurocognitive processes and is assembled into an intervention program by a knowledgeable practitioner for the purpose of enhancing specific areas of performance (Milanovich, 2019; Shah et al., 2017). A number of terms are often used interchangeably with CTr, including cognitive *retraining* and cognitive *remediation*. These should not be confused with more traditional forms of what is termed cognitive *rehabilitation*, which describes interventions typically employed for more acute conditions, such as TBI or CVA, with stimuli that are less complex and perhaps less specific than those used in CTr. Aeromedical examiners (AMEs) and others who are less familiar with various mental health interventions often need to know that CTr is not cognitive-behavioral therapy, neurofeedback, online brain games, or brain stimulation techniques; CTr is also not considered to include the use of commonly recommended mental activity "boosters," such as crossword or sudoku puzzles.

Still, CTr as defined earlier has been widely studied across continents for decades and, most recently, has won grants by the National Institute of Health in the United States of amounts in the tens of millions to potentially hundreds of millions of dollars as a means to help prevent Alzheimer's disease (ClinicalTrials.gov, 2022) or treat neurocognitive symptoms associated with long-haul COVID (National Institutes of Health, 2023; Doheny, 2023), just as two examples. Such awards, in conjunction with the studies upon which they are based, suggest the potential effectiveness of CTr has already been demonstrated to be exceptionally high. Nonetheless, many practicing neuropsychologists are unaware of the well-studied benefits from structured, computer-based CTr programming, perhaps in part as a result of assessment procedures being the primary focus in training programs, rather than more recent 21st century neurocognitive intervention efforts. Still, fortunately for pilots and patients alike, awareness of reliable CTr among neuropsychologists and other practitioners has grown rapidly and widely over the past 5 years, with pilots having used structured, coached CTr in nearly every state of the United States, select European countries, and Hong Kong to date (Milanovich & Prosje, 2023).

Research Studies in CTr Relevant to Pilots

Processing Speed

While a number of neurocognitive domains are important to flight performance and safety, none are more critical than PS and WM (Front, 2018), which leads to careful consideration in their remediation potential. The Advanced Cognitive Training for Independent and Vital Elderly (ACTIVE) study, which began in 2001 (Jobe et al., 2001), demonstrated compelling research relevant to pilots using a randomized, prospective, blinded, multicenter, NIH-funded, large-scale participant pool of older drivers. A subset of study participants who met stringent criteria as a means to create an especially controlled experimental design underwent either 5 weeks of PS CTr ($n=48$) or 5 weeks of driving simulator training ($n=22$), the latter of which makes this particular study especially appropriate to pilots. After training in either a PS CTr or simulator platform, a wide range of detailed driving behaviors were recorded by two to three evaluators specifically trained to the study demands, which used a varied 14-mile on-road driving course in the assessment. While those who trained in the simulator showed a significant improvement in left-turn signal usage, the CTr group had a very significant reduction in driver-related errors and accidents, which were maintained in the 18-month follow-up study (Roenker et al., 2003). No reduction in driver-related errors or accidents was seen in the simulator group (or a low-risk reference group with no intervention). It was concluded that the difference in findings was likely attributable to the CTr group's newfound capacity to manage *unexpected* events, something that pilots must contend with from time to time, of which increased PS assisted them in avoiding potential errors or accidents by adjusting their behavior before they could occur.

In the overall ACTIVE study, a review of state records in drivers who completed CTr who qualified for subsequent analysis ($n=908$) indicated they experienced 48 % fewer at-fault motor vehicle collisions over the course of the next 6 years post-CTr, indicating a long-term effect from the short-term (5 weeks, 20 hr) training involved (Ball et al., 2010; Ross et al., 2017). At 10 years post-CTr the drivers, most of whom were now in their 80s, had a 49 % greater chance of maintaining driver privileges, which rose to a 70 % chance when a 4-day per year booster CTr was present (Ross et al., 2017). These findings were also consistent with improved instrumental activities of daily living (IADLs) (Rebok et al., 2014) and a reduction in falls (Sprague et al., 2023) 10 years post-CTr in older adults. Finally, meta-analyses that examined PS CTr benefits found results with similar effect sizes: moderate to large (Ball et al., 2007; Edwards et al., 2018). In this manner, far-reaching, generalized effects and long-term processing speed benefits were clearly demonstrated through the use of CTr as defined in this chapter.

While such findings are quite compelling in and of themselves, yet another investigation within the ACTIVE series indicated PS CTr protected middle-age and older adults from age-related declines associated with processing speed by 3–4 years, of which gains when using computerized crossword puzzles of the same duration were not observed (Wolinsky et al., 2013). Preventing age-related neurocognitive declines, as well as associated conditions such as Alzheimer's disease (Edwards et al., 2017), is especially important when considering older pilot performance and related forced retirement considerations.

Working Memory

Advancing from pre-attentive processing involved in PS (Ball & Vance, 2008) to more complex WM processing, research in the second cognitive process considered most critical to flight performance and safety has also indicated favorable results. Sala et al. (2019) conducted a meta-analysis of WM CTr, of which first-order analyses indicated a moderate effect was present in near-transfer effects (i.e., results from neurocognitive tests in WM) while far-transfer effects were less robust, suggesting generalizability in WM was not well demonstrated in the Sala et al. study. Such a pattern was found in other meta-analyses that involved short-comings in design (e.g., Kable et al., 2017; Karbach & Verhaeghen, 2014; Schwaighofer et al., 2015; Soveri et al., 2017; Teixeira-Santos et al. 2019). However, studies with stronger designs that more closely followed guidelines especially important in WM CTr suggested effects are both generalizable (Bergman-Nutley & Klingberg, 2014; Holmes et al., 2009; Shinaver et al., 2014) and long-lasting (Shinaver et al., 2014; Spencer-Smith & Klingberg, 2015).

It is important to note that, compared with other mental activities utilized in an effort to enhance cognitive functioning, meta-analytic data from Sala et al. (2019) indicated WM CTr substantially outperformed playing video games, learning a musical instrument, playing chess, or engaging in physical exercise. Others found CTr to be significantly more effective in addressing a specific cognitive domain than, for example, crossword puzzles that use many aspects of cognition to solve problems (Fernandez et al., 2013). To this end, CTr practitioners and reviewers of extant research are encouraged to focus upon study outcomes that involve CTr exercises specific to a particular cognitive process (i.e., WM CTr for WM-related outcomes or PS CTr for PS-related outcomes), rather than highly heterogeneous diagnostic categories (Rebok et al., 2014) such as ADHD or TBI. While a greater number of more reasonably designed investigations into WM CTr would be useful, its use with pilots has remained quite compelling (Milanovich, 2019).

In comparison with PS CTr, as suggested above, studies in WM CTr vary widely in design quality and in ability to reliably address the hypotheses in question. Unfortunately, a number of, if not many, single and meta-analytic studies have examined the utility of CTr outside of recommended guidelines, such as using very few hours of training and therefore limited repetitions, or using exercises with little to no scientific basis, which will often not lead to the desired benefits (e.g., Kable et al., 2017; Teixeira-Santos et al. 2019). Unlike PS, CTr that is used to enhance WM abilities appears to require time for posttraining skill-building to actually enhance executive functioning in daily life, which few studies to date have considered (typically, benefits in students are observed 3–4 months posttraining; Cogmed, 2010). In addition, heterogeneous participant pools and the use of participants that cannot reasonably test the hypotheses in question are also frequently found. For example, one of the more highly cited, and otherwise very well-controlled, studies examined WM gains in children using a well-developed WM CTr program, although the authors examined children from 5 to 7 years of age (van Dongen-Boomsma et al., 2014). Young children in this age-band will not likely show benefits from WM CTr, as WM itself is largely undeveloped, and some may say WM per se is not reliably tested until a minimum of 8 years of age (Delis et al., 2001). Still, despite the obvious design flaw and teacher rating scales that revealed significant improvement in behaviors in children who showed significant WM CTr gains, the investigators conducting the study concluded that WM CTr simply does not work over placebo training. Yet another shortcoming in WM CTr study design includes, at times, the use of dependent variables that do not reflect the neurocognitive process being trained, such as examining the effects of WM CTr on nonverbal problem-solving or math calculation skills as a means to determine generalizability, which again limits the interpretation of results as the amount of WM variance in, say, nonverbal reasoning is rather low.

Perhaps most detrimental to solid scientific inquiry as related to CTr as a whole, it is common that review papers do not include well-designed landmark studies in their analyses (e.g., Gates et al., 2019; Moreau, 2022), and critiques can therefore be highly unbalanced. Nevertheless, while this author supports further research to better define the nature and scope of the real-world effects of WM CTr, well-constructed WM CTr studies clearly show significant near-transfer effects on a regular basis and suggest far-transfer (generalizable) effects are also present.

Other Supportive Research

In addition to long-lasting near- and far-transfer effects found in well-designed scientific studies of CTr, positive changes in important biological substrates have also been shown to be present. For example, a recent neurobiological study in PS CTr noted changes in functional magnetic resonance imaging (fMRI) functions associated with frontoparietal control network connectivity (Hardcastle et al., 2022). Miller et al. (2019) found improvement in EEG measures and a corresponding increase in work productivity for those with significant CTr input (30 hr) but not in those with minimal training (7 hr); other studies also suggest a dose-dependent response is associated with CTr (Ross et al., 2016) and additional benefits of "adaptive," rather than "static," training (Lövdén, et al., 2010a), the former of which includes exercises that adjust to the trainee's performance levels on a response-by-response basis. Findings in fMRI as related to increased connectivity between executive control and dorsal attention networks as a result of WM CTr (Thompson et al., 2016) have also been correlated with improved WM functioning.

As research progresses, other neurocognitive areas, such as auditory processing (AP), have also been shown to be significantly enhanced through use of AP CTr in well-controlled, randomized, blinded, multicenter, prospective, large-scale study (e.g., the Improvement in Memory with Plasticity-based Adaptive Cognitive Training [IMPACT] study, with 524 participants), again with both near- and far-transfer effects being demonstrated (Smith et al., 2009). While further study is required, anecdotal findings in clinical practice strongly suggest CTr has benefitted those with deficits in attention, visual-spatial, and/or executive control processes as well (Milanovich, 2019), in addition to the relatively well-established, research-based benefits of CTr seen in enhancing PS, WM, and AP domains. In all, CTr completed in a manner that is structured, coached, and research-based has been shown to be long-lasting and generalizable (both near- and far-reaching effects), while directly impacting expected underlying neurophysiological substrates.

Accessibility, Tunability, and Other Appealing Aspects of CTr

Computer-based CTr technologies have grown at a rapid pace over the past two decades. At this time, CTr is easily accessible via online platforms, of which exercise- and data-management companies store hundreds to thousands of data points for each individual trainee, which affords neuropsychologists a window into the daily life of trainees by allowing practitioners to understand both *input/effort* and *output/performance* training levels. Exercises are often adaptive, meaning they adjust to the trainee's current abilities on an ongoing basis, typically after each click of the mouse or keyboard. This greatly reduces training time, often from 300 hr in traditional programs to less than 40 hr in adaptive versions. Of course, this significantly reduces the amount of resources needed by the pilot, including financial. To date, adaptive CTr programs consider 10 hr or more for each cognitive domain to be adequate in creating lasting, generalizable improvement (Fernandez et al., 2013), although that would be considered a minimum and the time required to actualize significant gains could be longer. As an example, if WM, PS, and EC were to be addressed, the practitioner would assign a minimum of 30 hr of training. In addition to the number of hours that is typically helpful to reliably enhance one or another cognitive domain, understanding the duration of training and the intensity that appears most beneficial to an individual has grown substantially (Fernandez et al., 2013), especially as related to pilots (Milanovich, 2022). Furthermore, exercise parameters such as difficulty level or stopping points are now easily changed by the practitioner to meet the evolving needs of the pilot, and the types of exercises themselves can be changed to maintain training focus in one or another neurocognitive domain, all online and without the need for office visits. Of course, given the variables involved, it is important that trained personnel guide and coach trainees along the way, which can be reliably accomplished remotely and structured into a programmatic format, as found in this author's program. Efforts at credentialing practitioners, including neuropsychologists, are in their infancy but fortunately have begun (Milanovich & Prosje, 2023).

Further Considerations for the Use of CTr in Pilots

While uninformed CTr by a neuropsychologist can lead to the use of training exercises that appear similar to actual neuropsychological tests administered during evaluations, practitioners have the option to choose exercises that do not look like neuropsychological tests. This reduces indirect practice effects and reassures those reviewing neuropsychological test data that findings are the result of enhanced neurocognitive processing in one or another domain per se, rather than practice effects. This is an important ethical consideration when designing a CTr program, especially for pilots. It should also be noted that the development of CTr databases specific to pilots is relatively easy to accomplish and important to understanding the relationships between training data, neuropsychological test data, and flying itself. Development of one such CTr database has already been in progress to further understand a pilot's performance in the cockpit (Milanovich, 2022), which has generated multiple research studies to date and offers a number of exciting potentials in the scientific study of aviation neuropsychology.

The Scientific Study of CTr in Pilots

Use of a CTr program developed by the current author for pilots based upon the research, design, and guidelines discussed above has yielded compelling data that have given some reference to the clinical utility of CTr specific to the pilot population and allow for further, structured scientific inquiry.

Special Issuance Pilots

It is well known that a significant number of pilots are required to complete a neuropsychological evaluation for aeromedical purposes, and an unknown but not insignificant number of them are found with some form of neurocognitive deficiency. When a denial by the FAA is likely, a discussion between the neuropsychologist and pilot regarding the possible next steps is often valuable to a pilot's understanding of the situation as well as potential pathways forward, with the ultimate goal often involving being found to have normal results upon re-testing. Time and again, the question of "when to retest?" has been asked, although no clinical or data-driven guidance was available prior to 2019 (Milanovich, 2019; Milanovich & Prosje, 2023).

As a result, training data from pilots engaged in a structured CTr program from 2018 to 2019 were reviewed, with a cross-validation study of pilots in the same program seen from 2021 to 2022 (Milanovich, 2022). Of the first 70 pilots through 2019 who completed the program, all of whom were seeking special issuance with known neurocognitive deficits identified by a HIMS neuropsychologist, 30 provided feedback regarding their results from neurocognitive re-testing. Findings indicated 75% of those who reached target training levels (TTLs), using a cut-off score developed by the author, were successful in neurocognitive re-testing; chances of success fell to 40% for those who did not reach TTLs. When pilot presenting diagnoses were limited to the most common conditions seen for FAA NP evaluation purposes, including HIMS (alcohol only), ADHD, and SSRI use, 100% of those who reached the CTr program's TTLs were found to have normal results upon neurocognitive re-testing, while those who did not reach TTLs had a 33% chance of success. This initial study was the first to afford evidence-based guidance to neuropsychologists who were considering "when to re-test" a pilot who was found with neurocognitive deficiency, and it showed that CTr can be used to predict their neurocognitive performance levels with near-transfer tasks. It also demonstrated that some conditions might show less generalizability than others (i.e., ADHD vs. TBI, CVA, or ASD). Unexpectedly, initial studies gave important information regarding daily effort levels in pilots as well as one's capacity to overcome identified neurocognitive deficiencies.

A cross-validation study was subsequently conducted for pilots who completed the same CTr program from 2021 to 2022 (Milanovich, 2022). During that time, a pre- and post-raining online aviator cognitive assessment (OA Assess) tool based on the exercises used was developed by the author as a means to determine potential clinical utility. By this time, far more HIMS neuropsychologists were referring to the CTr program, and thus despite more pilots completing CTr over a 2-year period the number of pilots with full data, most especially as related to re-testing results, was somewhat lower than the initial study ($n=26$). As expected, less favorable results using the initial study's cut-off score were found in the cross-validation sample, with 92% of those who reached TTLs being found to have normal results compared with 64% of those who did not reach TTLs. As a result, use of the posttraining assessment score was employed to aid in better predicting whether or not a pilot would be successful with neurocognitive re-testing. The posttraining assessment score significantly enhanced the predictive power of success so that 100% of those who reached TTLs had normal results, compared with 40% who did not reach TTLs. Discriminating between pilots who are clearly ready for re-testing and those who are much less likely to be successful is no longer a hypothetical potential, but rather an actual evidence-based reality.

During the cross-validation study period, it was further discovered that the most amenable diagnoses to CTr were ADHD, alcohol abuse/dependence, and SSRI use, followed by TBI and CVA, the latter of which were very much on a case-by-case basis that appeared dependent on the site and severity of insult. Other conditions, such as ASD, below-average intellectual abilities, and/or drug abuse were less amenable to predicting outcomes, perhaps as a result of potentially poor generalizability in these conditions relative to the others.

Data from the above studies were combined to allow for more rigorous statistical procedures in the investigation of CTr in pilots seeking special issuance (Milanovich, 2024). Out of 192 pilots residing in various states across the United States who were found with neurocognitive impairment by a HIMS neuropsychologist and completed the fee-based CTr program, 74% of those who reported (n=77) posttraining neurocognitive re-testing results were found to no longer demonstrate impairment. Clinical utility of this online CTr program was further supported by one-way MANOVA analyses that indicated a pilot's training data (PTD) and OA Assess scores significantly predicted posttraining neurocognitive re-testing outcomes to a highly significant degree (p=.014) and classified whether or not a pilot would be found with neurocognitive impairment with 87% accuracy across all diagnoses. Those who reached the CTr program's research-based TTLs had an 88% chance of success, while those who did not reach the TTLs had a 33% chance of success (see Figure 10.1).

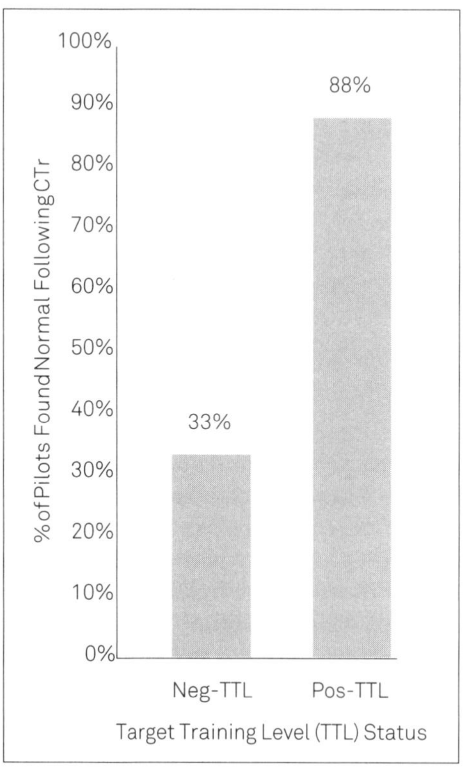

Figure 10.1. Percentage of initially impaired pilots who had normal test results after CTr with respect to TTLs. CTr = cognitive training. Initially impaired pilots with pre- and post-HIMS neuropsychological evaluation status data, of whom those who reached TTLs (Pos-TTL) within their CTr program were found to pass NP re-evaluations 88 % of the time while those who did not reach TTLs (Neg-TTL) had a 33 % chance of having normal results upon NP re-evaluation. TTLs were established based upon research by the current author.

The obvious benefits of having data as described in Figure 10.1 for clinicians and pilots alike allow those involved to work together in determining whether or not re-testing is appropriate or further training is recommended. For those who remain far from neurocognitive normalcy despite the use of appropriate CTr, the difficulties of accepting their new circumstances might be mitigated to one degree or another by the knowledge that they followed research-based guidelines and state-of-the-science methods to reach FAA standards, while gaining the understanding along the way that bona fide deficiencies might actually be present, whether observed by them in daily life or not (Milanovich & Prosje, 2023). Such research has helped change the neurocognitive intervention landscape to allow for informed, evidenced-based decision-making by the neuropsychologist while taking much of the guesswork out of re-testing decisions that was previously present when working with pilots.

Qualitative findings suggested pilots seeking special issuance were pleased with training itself, as it was structured and clear in scope with important weekly feedback from their CTr coach. Reports of benefits to daily life, including work life in those who were not professional pilots and improved in-cockpit experiences for those who were flying from a commercial standpoint, were quite frequent and overall hope and confidence appeared to increase (Milanovich, 2022; Nijveldt et al., 2021).

Student Pilots: Part 141 Programs – Kent State University and Ohio State University

Use of the same CTr program described in the previous section was also deployed with student pilots, first through a cornerstone study at Ohio State University (OSU) and then on a larger-scale study at Kent State University (KSU), both of which are Part 141 programs. Study conducted in a Part 141 environment is particularly appealing due to the structure and consistency across program requirements for those in the United States. The reason behind interest in CTr with student pilots is associated with the fact that pilot training is expensive and typically requires years to complete, with a number of pilots falling out of training at one stage or another. Brian Neff, Assistant Dean, College of Aeronautics and Engineering at KSU, indicated some pilots simply take significantly longer than others, while grades in school and college entrance examination scores do not always perform well at predicting success in the cockpit (B. Neff, personal communication, March 22, 2022). This negatively affects not only the student pilot, but also the aviation training program as a whole, due to having fewer available slots to offer pilots as the size of training fleets and available certified flight instructors (CFIs) have limitations (Nijveldt et al., 2021; Schaner et al., 2024). Thomas Schaner, Pilot Trainer at Flight Safety International, which by many is considered to be the premier professional aviation training organization in the world, indicated training to pilot aircraft safely is difficult and quite demanding on an individual's functional capacities, of which there are select points of heightened neurocognitive and executive functioning demands at certain stages of training (T. Schaner, personal communication, October 11, 2023). After graduation, certificated pilots transitioning from (often) CFI positions to professional work with the demands to add new type ratings may be found to struggle, of which the large investments in new pilots made by airlines are at risk. The fact that a newly hired pilot is certificated at required levels and liked by instructors does not always seem to discriminate between pilots who would complete training requirements efficiently and those who struggle (T. Schaner, personal communication, June 4, 2022). In this context, it became clear that CTr could be helpful for student pilots and new hires as a means to help reduce training time in the cockpit and more effectively transition to professional work life.

The focus on underlying abilities associated with flight performance and safety is different from a focus on academic learning potential, the latter of which IQ, grade point average (GPA), and American College Test (ACT)/Scholastic Aptitude Test (SAT) scores are considered traditional predictors. The initial OSU cornerstone study by students at the university indicated clear potential of CTr in training pilots, over and above traditional academic performance predictors (Nijveldt et al., 2021; Schaner et al., 2024). Although the ultimate number of students who had sufficient CTr data was small ($n=5$), findings indicated over a 21% increase in percentile points was observed in PS, WM, and AP as a result of training, which is consistent with the gains observed in many pilots seeking special issuance. More importantly, students themselves reported experiencing far-transfer effects and estimated CTr resulted in over a 10% reduction in cockpit time and associated costs, while throughput analyses conservatively suggested the OSU program could accept at least 10 more students per year. Qualitative findings were at least as impressive, with students attributing their ability to overcome long-standing obstacles to training with completion of structured CTr. For example, for some time one student reported struggling with air traffic control (ATC) communications while flying, although after 2 weeks of CTr indicated flying was much easier due to a capacity to better manage multitasking events during heightened-demand periods while in the cockpit. This allowed the student to move on to other aspects of flight training, which reduced training time and costs and ultimately opened up training slots in the cockpit for others. Another student indicated "maneuvers and landings seemed to get better due to better awareness" following CTr training, while still others believed CTr was overall helpful, as did their flight instructors (Nijveldt et al., 2021; Schaner et al., 2024).

Following the OSU study, KSU began a larger-scale research project using the same structured, coached CTr program described above, in which 32 aviation students registered. While relatively few students completed actual training in the program ($n=8$) during summer months, 17 completed the pretraining baseline CTr OA Assess. The CTr administrator (J. Milanovich, present author) was blind to the student performance levels within the cockpit, while the lead investigator from KSU (B. Neff) was blind to students' CTr performance. The investigation discovered that the OA Assess score, which is completed online and focuses directly upon neurocognitive processes critical to flight performance and safety, was significantly correlated with the time required to complete various stages of training/certification through the commercial rating, with a correlation of .85 between the OA Assess score and the total number of hours a student required to obtain his or her commercial rating (Neff et al., 2024). Perhaps not so surprisingly, the OA Assess showed significant correlations in six out of seven main comparisons, such as hours to complete various stages of training within the Part 141 program, while high school GPA, ACT/SAT scores; academic skill rankings in organization, reading, math, and writing; current college GPA; and years in college were poorly correlated with one's efficiency in learning to fly. More specifically to pilot selection, the average OA Assess score found in those who ultimately were within the top 50% of their class was 106, while the OA score for the bottom 50% was 11 (see Figure 10.2). Such discrimination in one CTr pre-assessment training tool, which was separated from in-cockpit hours by 2 years or more in some participants, underscores its predictive power as well as the various avenues CTr may explore in aviation neuropsychology. In all, use of this pretraining assessment tool that is cost-effective and requires less than 1 hr to complete within an online format appears useful in selecting pilot candidates who are most likely to be efficient in reaching their aviation goals. It also affords pilots who are likely

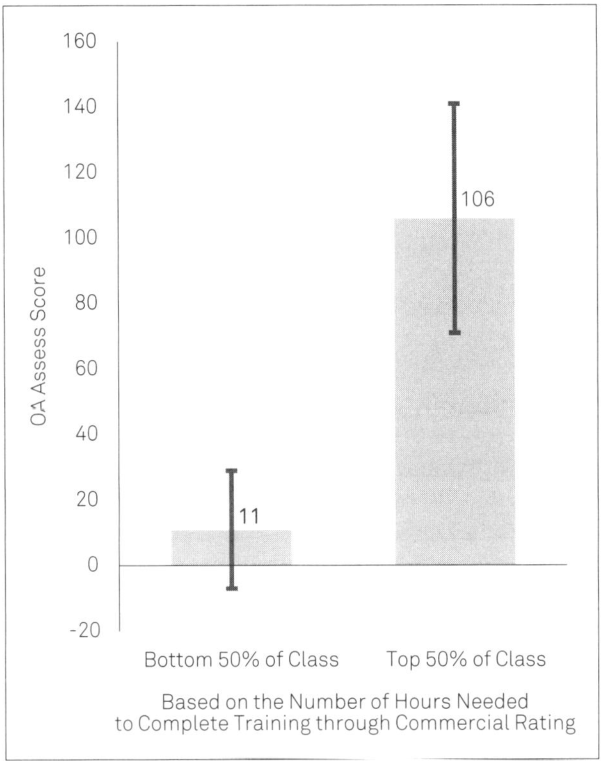

Figure 10.2. OA Assess scores (*M* ± *SE*) for the top and bottom 50 % of student pilots. Student pilots who required more hours to complete their training through the commercial rating (therefore, the bottom 50 % of their class) had an OA Assess score of 11 ± 18, while students who required the least amount of time in the cockpit (the top 50 %) to complete the same rating had an OA Assess score of 106 ± 35, thereby showing superior "aviator cognition" in the top 50 % of students.

to struggle the opportunity to complete specific neurocognitive training exercises that could ultimately enhance their efficiency in learning to fly or in making the transition to professional life.

Student pilot data support the hypothesis that pilot-specific neurocognitive processes are important to flight performance, and by extension, safety. It suggests that the neurocognitive abilities (what this author has termed "aviator cognition") associated with learning to fly, as well as flight performance and safety, can be further strengthened at any stage of pilot development to the benefit of the pilot. It also suggests that CTr has the potential to reduce in-cockpit training time, of which some students could more clearly benefit than others (i.e., when low pretraining CTr baseline assessment scores are found), which aids both pilot trainee and pilot training organization alike.

Features of a Research-Based CTr Program for Pilots

CTr is similar to physical therapy and personal training in that a condition or deficiency is identified, specific "muscles" are isolated for intervention, and an exercise program is developed and monitored (or "coached") along the way. A CTr program for pilots should use exercises that have undergone scientific scrutiny and do not look like tests used by neuropsychologists. Exercises should be selected by a trained practitioner to match a pilot's particular needs rather than training all neurocognitive areas, which would otherwise waste time and resources. A well-developed CTr program should have exercises in which parameters can be changed, both in intensity and kind, to match the evolving picture as seen in the pilot's training data. Demographic data, such as age, specific neurocognitive deficiencies, and presenting diagnoses could be helpful in the development of databases from which the scientific community may study, while other information such as aeromedical class or pilot level (i.e., student, private, commercia, special issuance; Schaner et al., 2024) may prove useful. Data are easily divided into both input and output categories that address a pilot's effort level or commitment and performance levels, all of which tend to be useful information. Providing regular feedback, usually weekly, to pilots appears critical to success, which greatly increases their input levels and thereby significantly enhances performance outputs (Milanovich, 2022). Such feedback (or coaching) is often completed in email form and can be a way to not only describe a pilot's performance, but also motivate and educate the pilot regarding personal brain health. It should be noted that social-emotional issues, such as anxiety, in the trainee may at times surface during such communications, which allows for education and, if needed, possible referrals to a professional. While past programs may have required 3 hr of training per day for 3 months or more, *adaptive* CTr tends to require less than 1 hr per day for less than 2 months to sufficiently enhance up to four cognitive domains in pilots, all without any office visits. Of course, not all pilots reach target training levels or FAA standards, but all who put in sufficient training time appear to make significant gains of one form, and degree, or another. More recent advancements in CTr, such as the aforementioned OA Assess, have led to pretraining and posttraining online testing that examine baseline starting points as well as current or final performance levels, which reflects the degree to which a pilot made progress within particular neurocognitive domains (Milanovich, 2022). Such information is vital in making decisions about a pilot's need for further training or readiness to re-test neurocognitive functioning.

Vignettes: Real-World CTr in Pilots

Special Issuance

Case 1

A 44-year-old HIMS airline pilot was referred for structured, coached CTr after 12 months' recovery and sobriety from a long-standing history of alcohol abuse, eventually discovered after unusual behavior during an evening layover. Her NP evaluation indicated deficiencies in long-term visual memory and processing speed in the context of a Full-Scale Intellectual Quotient from the Wechsler Adult Intelligence Scales-IV of 120 (91st percentile, WAIS-IV FSIQ); minor vulnerabilities in working memory were also present. Despite her superior IQ score, pretraining CTr assessment that was conducted online indicated this pilot's initial training performance was over one third of 1 *SD* (−0.43 *SD*) below the mean training level of most pilots seeking special issuance and over 1 SD below pretraining assessment levels in a sample of college-level commercial pilots (Milanovich, 2022). Her training data indicated effort levels were consistent and frequent over her 6 weeks of rigorous, intense training (approximately 1 hr per day, 6 days per week), with a primary focus on processing speed and visual working memory, the latter of which tends to assist pilots in long-term memory as well. After a course of online training, with weekly feedback via emails from her CTr coach, this pilot's posttraining CTr assessment was found to be 1.32 *SDs* above that of most pilots initially seeking special issuance, which technically did not meet the CTr program's

TTLs. An additional 3 weeks of training led to a posttraining CTr assessment that was 1.85 *SDs* above initial assessment findings and now within the TTLs of her training program. A full training report was sent to her HIMS neuropsychologist and retesting was reportedly successful in that she was subsequently found to have normal results on all neurocognitive tests administered.

Case 2

A 65-year-old private pilot who was 38 months post-CVA involving right hemispheric structures was found to have "near-normal" results after his first 2 months of occupational therapy and scored a 30/30 on the Montreal Cognitive Assessment (MoCA) 2 years later with no concerns by his neurologist, although upon NP evaluation he was found with significant deficiencies in visual-perceptual processing speed, visual-spatial analysis and visual-spatial memory, and multitasking capacities (with generally intact working memory). Coached CTr was used by the pilot over the course of 12 weeks, after poor initial gains during his first 6 weeks of training, using exercises consistent with his deficiencies. He never reached TTLs, with a posttraining CTr assessment of 1.01 *SDs* above initial findings from pilots seeking special issuance. He decided to train on his own another 12 weeks, with excessive input, but was not able to reach TTLs. Brief neurocognitive retesting indicated improvements in all areas but ultimately continued abnormality in visual-perceptual speed, visual-spatial analysis, and multitasking was present, leading to a determination that findings continued to be aeromedically significant. He decided to fly with friends in the right seat only, and as a passenger, while focusing more on other hobbies of interest during his retirement years.

Student Pilots

An 18-year-old aspiring pilot with a previous history of ADHD and poor academic effort was found to have neurocognitive deficits in processing speed and working memory upon completion of the initial ADHD NP battery. His mother set up his appointments and ensured he arrived on time, accompanying him on each occasion, while she presented as rather stressed that aviation has been the only career in which her son is motivated to succeed. Still, he seemed passive but not depressed or overly anxious, both in the office as well as in his daily life, all of which was ultimately reflected in his initial test results. Past psychoeducational test results as a child indicated his intellectual abilities were above average (WAIS-IV FSIQ=122) and he showed only behavioral problems at the time. He scored somewhat above most pilots in his initial pretraining assessment (0.24 *SD*), but data from his CTr program indicated his effort levels were very low throughout, despite weekly updates and encouragement. Ultimately, he was encouraged not to retest due to never reaching TTLs in two separate periods of training (1.18 *SD*), but he and his mother were determined, and a portion of the ADHD supplemental battery was eventually administered by his neuropsychologist. Making minimal gains in training due to lack of input, he continued to perform poorly in both processing speed and working memory, in the context of strong attentional capacities and above-average intellect. Upon seeing his failure to meet training minimums from the standpoint of input/effort levels, his parents ruled that he would have to pay for future aviation endeavors on his own.

Older Pilots

A 60-year-old commercial pilot without neurocognitive testing who always prided herself as a leader in the field indicated she would like to "stay sharp" as she, jokingly, approaches "adulthood." Like many commercial pilots, her pre-training CTr assessment (1.68 *SDs* above the mean of those seeking special issuance) was within the TTLs set for those likely to be found without neurocognitive deficiency, but processing speed was a relative weakness from a training perspective, most likely the result of normal age-related changes. She trained that area, as well as working memory and executive controls, visual-spatial awareness, and auditory processes, as a means to help spoken communications sound clearer when background noise is present. She trained above the recommended pace and intensity and in 6 weeks' time was found in posttraining CTr assessment data to be at 2.24 *SDs* above pilots who are initially seeking special issuance. She was told, per extant research, that the benefits she gained through her 6 weeks of training should last years rather than months or weeks, while she noted she could "clearly see the difference" in daily life and felt as "ahead of the plane" as when she was several years younger.

New Hires

A CFI starting her career in aviation with a large regional carrier that may lead to a major airline position took longer than most to complete her aviation program and ratings, but her perseverance and excellent work ethic led to ultimate success. A supervisor at her school recently learned about the potential of CTr in aiding students gain greater efficiency in the cockpit, and he suggested she complete a program. Her pretraining CTr assessment (OA Assess) was a score of 26, which was similar to students who tend to take longer than others to complete flight training (Neff et al., 2024). After completion of a structured, coached CTr program and a posttraining OA Assess score of 198, she reported "much clearer" experiences in the cockpit, while "feeling more comfortable" overall. She was more confident going into her new job training and after just 4 months as a new hire reported being "at the upper end" of her class in terms of learning a new flight management system and a new pursuing type rating, which also led her supervisors to see her as a well-equipped new hire.

Future of CTr in the Aerospace Environment

It is important for neuropsychologists, along with our allied health colleagues, to continue striving for the advancement of neurocognitive interventions, as the current potential is greater than ever before. While CTr has been determined by this author to be among the most judicious approaches to solving the problem of identified neurocognitive deficiency in pilots, other forms may prove beneficial as well, be they existing platforms or something that has not yet been invented. Still, CTr appears to have significant utility in the aerospace environment and solves many shortcomings of other approaches, while yielding data that guide neuropsychologists in making important decisions related to a pilot's particular case. Use of the information in this chapter, which has been carefully gleaned from decades of research as well as years of clinical experience, could aid in developing general guidelines, if not standards, for use in the aviation environment, including range of training duration, considerations in choosing exercises for specific areas of deficit, analysis of effort levels, analysis of training gains (or lack thereof), reporting, and platform accessibility, to name a few. Such considerations have been developed and studied in this examiner's program, and as noted previously, use of CTr is now found in pilots across the United States with important successes. Over time, credentialing efforts in CTr could advance the intervention aspect of neuropsychology, which from a neurocognitive perspective is relatively missing to date.

From a next-steps perspective in scientific inquiry, studying the associations between a pilot's CTr data, neurocognitive test results, and performance in the cockpit has the potential to yield a significant knowledge-base that allows the neuropsychologist to learn from pilots who test and train alike. Studies associated with pilot selection, aviation students, new hires, those transitioning to new aircraft, those seeking special issuance, aging pilots, astronauts in microgravity environments, or those seeking peak performance are open to curious investigators and will almost assuredly yield data that are as unexpected as they are useful.

References

About Neurofeedback. (n.d.). *Is neurofeedback experimental?* http://www.aboutneurofeedback.com/neurofeedback-info-center/faq/is-neurofeedback-experimental/#:~:text=EEG%20neurofeedback%20equipment%20is%20regulated%20by%20FDA.,providers.%20That%E2%80%99s%20a%20label%20required%20by%20the%20FDA

Ball, K., Edwards, J.D., & Ross, L.A. (2007). The impact of speed of processing training on cognitive and everyday functions. *The Journals of Gerontology: Series B, 62*(1), 19–31. https://doi.org/10.1093/geronb/62.special_issue_1.19

Ball, K., Edwards, J.D., Ross, L.A., & McGwin, G., Jr. (2010). Cognitive training decreases motor vehicle collision involvement of older drivers. *Journal of the American Geriatrics Society, 58*(11), 2107–2113. https://doi.org/10.1111/j.1532-5415.2010.03138.x

Ball, K.K., & Vance, D.E. (2008). Everyday life applications and rehabilitation of processing speed deficits: Aging as a model for clinical populations. In J. DeLuca & J.H. Kalmar (Eds.), *Information processing speed in clinical populations* (pp. 243–263). Taylor & Francis.

Bergman-Nutley, S., & Klingberg, T. (2014). Effect of working memory training on working memory, arithmetic and following instructions. *Psychological Research, 78*(6), 869–877. https://doi.org/10.1007/s00426-014-0614-0

Chen, Y.-X., Liang, N., Li, X.-L., Yang, S.-H., Wang, Y.-P., & Shi, N.-N. (2021). Diagnosis and treatment for mild cognitive impairment: A systematic review of clinical practice guidelines and consensus statements. *Frontiers in Neurology, 12*, Article 719849. https://doi.org/10.3389/fneur.2021.719849

ClinicalTrials.gov. (2022, November 22). *Preventing Alzheimer's with cognitive training (PACT)*. US Department of Health and Human Services, National Institutes of Health, National Library of Medicine, National Center for Biotechnology Information. https://clinicaltrials.gov/study/NCT03848312

Cogmed. (2010). *Cogmed working memory training manual*. Cogmed Publishing.

Delis, D.C., Kaplan, E., & Kramer, J.H. (2001). *D-KEFS technical manual*. The Psychological Corporation.

Dodge, D. (2022, January 12). What is neurofeedback therapy and can it help with mental health? *The New York Times*. https://www.nytimes.com/2022/01/12/well/mind/neurofeedback-therapy-mental-health.html

Doheny, K. (2023, July 31). *Long COVID treatment trials – finally – set to start*. WebMD. https://www.webmd.com/covid/news/20230731/long-covid-treatment-trials-finally-set-to-start

Edwards, J.D., Fausto, B.A., Tetlow, A.M., Corona, R.T., & Valdés, E.G. (2018). Systematic review and meta-analysis of useful field of view cognitive training. *Neuroscience and Biobehavioral Reviews, 84*, 72–91. https://doi.org/10.1016/j.neubiorev.2017.11.004

Edwards, J. D., Xu, H., Clark, D. O., Guey, L. T., Ross, L. A., & Unverzagt, F. W. (2017). Speed of processing training results in lower risk of dementia. *Alzheimer's & Dementia: Translational Research & Clinical Interventions, 3*(4), 603–611. https://doi.org/10.1016/j.trci.2017.09.002

Federal Aviation Administration (FAA). (2022, December 28). *FAA certification aid – SSRI recertification/follow up clearance.* US Department of Transportation. https://www.faa.gov/sites/faa.gov/files/SSRI_Recertification_Aid.pdf

Federal Aviation Administration (FAA). (2023a, August 30). *Fast track – FAA ADHD evaluation – general information.* US Department of Transportation. https://www.faa.gov/ame_guide/media/ADHD_fast_track_eval_general_info.pdf

Federal Aviation Administration (FAA). (2023b). *FAR/AIM 2024: Federal Aviation regulations/aeronautical information manual.* Aviation Supplies & Academics.

Fernandez, A., Goldberg, E., & Michelon, P. (with Pavel, M.). (2013). *The Sharpbrains guide to brain fitness: How to optimize brain health and performance at any age* (2nd ed.). Sharpbrains.

Front, C. M. (2018, September 22–23). *Aviation safety and the value of neuropsychological assessment of pilots* [Conference presentation]. 6th Annual Aerospace Psychology Seminar, Denver, Colorado, USA.

Gates, N. J., Vernooij, R. W. M., Di Nisio, M., Karim, S., March, E., Martínez, G., & Rutjes, A. W. S. (2019). Computerised cognitive training for preventing dementia in people with mild cognitive impairment. *Cochrane Database of Systematic Reviews, 3,* Article CD012279. https://doi.org/10.1002/14651858.CD012279.pub2

Greenspan, S. I. (1997). *Developmentally based psychotherapy.* International Universities Press.

Hardcastle, C., Hausman, H. K., Kraft, J. N., Albizu, A., O'Shea, A., Boutzoukas, E. M., Evangelista, N. D., Langer, K., Van Etten, E. J., Bharadwaj, P. K., Song, H., Smith, S. G., Proges, E., DeKosky, S. T., Hishaw, G. A., Wu, S. S., Marsiske, M., Cohen, R., Alexander, G. E., & Woods, A. J. (2022). Proximal improvement and higher-order resting state network change after multidomain cognitive training intervention in healthy older adults. *GeroScience, 44*(2), 1011–1027. https://doi.org/10.1007/s11357-022-00535-1

Hatcher-Solis, C. (2019). Transcranial direct current stimulation affects learning and memory associated synaptic proteins in rat hippocampus. *Aerospace Medicine and Human Performance, 90*(3), 240–241.

Heilman, K. M., & Valenstein, E. (Eds.). (1993). *Clinical neuropsychology* (3rd ed.). Oxford University Press. https://doi.org/10.1093/oso/9780195081237.001.0001

Holmes, J., Gathercole, S. E., & Dunning, D. L. (2009). Adaptive training leads to sustained enhancement of poor working memory in children. *Developmental Science, 12*(4), F9–F15. https://doi.org/10.1111/j.1467-7687.2009.00848.x

Jobe, J. B., Smith, D. M., Ball, K., Tennstedt, S. L., Marsiske, M., Willis, S. L., Rebok, G. W., Morris, J. N., Helmers, K. F., Leveck, M. D., & Kleinman, K. (2001). ACTIVE: A cognitive intervention trial to promote independence in older adults. *Controlled Clinical Trials, 22*(4), 453–479. https://doi.org/10.1016/S0197-2456(01)00139-8

Kable, J. W., Caulfield, M. K., Falcone, M., McConnell, M., Bernardo, L., Parthasarathi, T., Cooper, N., Ashare, R., Audrain-McGovern, J., Hornik, R., Diefenbach, P., Lee, F. J., & Lerman, C. (2017). No effect of commercial cognitive training on brain activity, choice behavior, or cognitive performance. *Journal of Neuroscience, 37*(31), 7390–7402. https://doi.org/10.1523/JNEUROSCI.2832-16.2017

Karbach, J., & Verhaeghen, P. (2014). Making working memory work: A meta-analysis of executive control and working memory training in younger and older adults. *Psychological Science, 25*(11), 2027–2037. https://doi.org/10.1177/0956797614548725

Lezak, M. D. (1995). *Neuropsychological assessment* (3rd ed.). Oxford University Press.

Lövdén, M., Bäckman, L., Lindenberger, U., Schaefer, S., & Schmiedek, F. (2010a). A theoretical framework for the study of adult cognitive plasticity. *Psychological Bulletin, 136*(4), 659–676. https://doi.org/10.1037/a0020080

Lövdén, M., Bodammer, N. C., Kühn, S., Kaufmann, J., Schütze, H., Tempelmann, C., Heinze, H.-J., Düzel, E., Schmiedek, F., & Lindenberger, U. (2010b). Experience-dependent plasticity of white-matter microstructure extends into old age. *Neupsychologia, 48*(13), 3878–3883. https://doi.org/10.1016/j.neuropsychologia.2010.08.026

Luria, A. R. (1960). *Higher cortical functions in man.* Springer.

Luria, A. R. (1973). *The working brain: An introduction to neuropsychology.* Basic Books.

McKinley, R., McIntire, L., Minnery, B., & Goodyear, C. (2019). Enhanced memory retention following image analyst training with transdermal vagal nerve stimulation (TVNS). *Aerospace Medicine and Human Performance, 90*(3), 239.

Milanovich, J. (2019, September 14). *Computer-based brain exercises: Do any work? If so, which ones?* [Conference presentation]. Aerospace Psychology Seminar, Washington, DC, USA.

Milanovich, J. (2022, October 21–23). *The use of online coached cognitive training (CTr) in pilots with "aeromedically significant" neurocognitive deficiencies: General and proprietary research data and outcomes in pilots seeking special issuance* [Conference presentation]. Aerospace Psychology Seminar, Crystal City, VA, USA.

Milanovich, J. (2024, May 5–9). *Aid to those in need: Online-based non-invasive neurocognitive intervention for pilots with aeromedically significant test results* [Conference presentation abstract]. Aerospace Medical Association Annual Scientific Meeting, Chicago, IL, USA.

Milanovich, J., & Prosje, M. (2023, November 3–5). *The clinical utility of cognitive training (CTr) in pilots: Recommendations for ways to reliably and judiciously walk with pilots after they receive bad news* [Conference presentation]. Aerospace Psychology Seminar, Crystal City, VA, USA.

Miller, S. L., Chelian, S., McBurnett, W., Tsou, W., & Kruse, A. A. (2019, July 23–27). *An investigation of computer-based brain training on the cognitive and EEG performance of employees* [Paper presentation]. International Conference of the IEEE Engineering in Medicine and Biology Society (EMBC), Berlin, Germany. https://doi.org/10.1109/EMBC.2019.8856758

Moreau, D. (2022). How malleable are cognitive abilities? A critical perspective on popular brief interventions. *American Psychologist, 77*(3), 409–423. https://doi.org/10.1037/amp0000872

National Institute of Mental Health. (n.d.). *What are brain stimulation therapies?* US Department of Health and Human Services, National Institutes of Health. https://www.nimh.nih.gov/health/topics/brain-stimulation-therapies/brain-stimulation-therapies

National Institutes of Health. (2023, July 31). *NIH launches long COVID clinical trials through RECOVER Initiative, opening enrollment* [Press release]. US Department of Health and Human Services. https://www.nih.gov/news-events/news-releases/nih-launches-long-covid-clinical-trials-through-recover-initiative-opening-enrollment

Neff, B., Schaner, T., & Milanovich, J. (2024, May 5–9). *A novel approach to selection: Online cognitive assessment outperforms traditional means in identifying the "Best of the best" and the "Least best"* [Conference presentation abstract]. Aerospace Medical Association Annual Scientific Meeting, Chicago, IL, USA.

Nelson, J., McKinley, R., McIntire, L., & Goodyear, C. (2019). Acceleration of image analyst training using transdermal trigeminal nerve stimulation (tTNS). *Aerospace Medicine and Human Performance, 90*(3), 239–240.

Neurofeedback Alliance. (n.d.). *NF history*. https://neurofeedbackalliance.org/nf-history/

Nijveldt, R., Mott, T., Sayer, N., Perez, M., & Gold, J. (2021). *Optimal aviation: Brain fitness training study* [Cornerstone project]. Center for Aviation Studies, College of Engineering, The Ohio State University.

Parente, R., & Stapleton, M. (1997). History and systems of cognitive rehabilitation. *NeuroRehabilitation, 8*(1), 3–11. https://doi.org/10.3233/NRE-1997-8102

Porges, C. R. (2013). Substance abuse in aviation: Clinical and practical implications. In C. H. Kennedy & G. G. Kay (Eds.), *Aeromedical Psychology* (pp. 107–123). CRC Press.

Rebok, G. W., Ball, K., Guey, L. T., Jones, R. N., Kim, H.-Y., King, J. W., Marsiske, M., Morris, J. N., Tennstedt, S. L., Unverzagt, F. W., & Willis, S. L. (2014). Ten-year effects of the advanced cognitive training for independent and vital elderly cognitive training trial on cognition and everyday functioning in older adults. *Journal of the American Geriatrics Society, 62*(1), 16–24. https://doi.org/10.1111/jgs.12607

Roenker, D. L., Cissell, G. M., Ball, K. K., Wadley, V. G., & Edwards, J. D. (2003). Speed-of-processing and driving simulator training result in improved driving performance. *Human Factors, 45*(2), 218–233. https://doi.org/10.1518/hfes.45.2.218.27241

Ross, L. A., Freed, S. A., Edwards, J. D., Phillips, C. B., & Ball, K. (2017). The impact of three cognitive training programs on driving cessation across 10 years: A randomized controlled trial. *The Gerontologist, 57*(5), 838–846. https://doi.org/10.1093/geront/gnw143

Ross, L. A., Sprague, B. N., Phillips, C. B., O'Connor, M. L., & Dodson, J. E. (2016). The impact of three cognitive training interventions on older adults' physical functioning across 5 years. *Journal of Aging and Health, 30*(3). https://doi.org/10.1177/08982643166829

Sala, G., Aksayli, N.D., Tatlidil, K.S., Tatsumi, T., Gondo, Y., & Gobet, F. (2019). Near and far transfer in cognitive training: A second-order meta-analysis. *Collabra: Psychology, 5*(1), Article 18. https://doi.org/10.1525/collabra.203

Schaner, T., Pruchnicki, S., & Milanovich, J. (2024, May 5–9). *Preliminary findings: Online cognitive training (CTr) enhances in-cockpit experiences in student pilots* [Conference presentation abstract]. Aerospace Medical Association Annual Scientific Meeting, Chicago, IL, USA.

Schwaighofer, M., Fischer, F., & Bühner, M. (2015). Does working memory training transfer? A meta-analysis including training conditions as moderators. *Educational Psychologist, 50*(2), 138–166. https://doi.org/10.1080/00461520.2015.1036274

Shah, T.M., Weinborn, M., Verdile, G., Sohrabi, H.R., & Martins, R.N. (2017). Enhancing cognitive functioning in healthly [sic] older adults: A systematic review of the clinical significance of commercially available computerized cognitive training in preventing cognitive decline. *Neuropsychology Review, 27*(1), 62–80. https://doi.org/10.1007/s11065-016-9338-9

Shinaver, C.S., III., Entwistle, P.C., & Söderqvist, S. (2014). Cogmed WM training: Reviewing the reviews. *Applied Neuropsychology: Child, 3*(3), 163–172. https://doi.org/10.1080/21622965.2013.875314

Smith, G.E., Housen, P., Yaffe, K., Ruff, R., Kennison, R.F., Mahncke, H.W., & Zelinski, E.M. (2009). A cognitive training program based on principles of brain plasticity: Results from the improvement in memory with plasticity-based adaptive cognitive training (IMPACT) study. *Journal of the American Geriatrics Society, 57*(4), 594–603. https://doi.org/10.1111/j.1532-5415.2008.02167.x

Soveri, A., Antfolk, J., Karlsson, L., Salo, B., & Laine, M. (2017). Working memory training revisited: A multilevel meta-analysis of n-back training studies. *Psychonomic Bulletin & Review, 24*(4), 1077–1096. https://doi.org/10.3758/s13423-016-1217-0

Spencer-Smith, M., & Klingberg, T. (2015). Benefits of a working memory training program for inattention in daily life: A systematic review and meta-analysis. *PLOS ONE, 10*(3), e0119522. https://doi.org/10.1371/journal.pone.0119522

Sprague, B.N., Ross, L.A., & Ball, K.K. (2023). Does cognitive training reduce falls across ten years?: Data from the ACTIVE trial. *International Journal of Environmental Research and Public Health, 20*(6), 4941. https://doi.org/10.3390/ijerph20064941

Teixeira-Santos, A.C., Moreira, C.S., Magalhães, R., Magalhães, C., Pereira, D.R., Leite, J., Carvalho, S., & Sampaio, A. (2019). Reviewing working memory training gains in healthy older adults: A meta-analytic review of transfer for cognitive outcomes. *Neuroscience & Biobehavioral Reviews, 103*, 163–177. https://doi.org/10.1016/j.neubiorev.2019.05.009

Thompson, T.W., Waskom, M.L., & Gabrieli, J.D. E. (2016). Intensive working memory training produces functional changes in large-scale frontoparietal networks. *Journal of Cognitive Neuroscience, 28*(4), 575–588. https://doi.org/10.1162/jocn_a_00916

US Food and Drug Administration (FDA). (2019, April 19). *FDA permits marketing of first medical device for treatment of ADHD* [Press release]. https://www.fda.gov/news-events/press-announcements/fda-permits-marketing-first-medical-device-treatment-adhd

van Dongen-Boomsma, M., Vollebregt, M.A., Buitelaar, J.K., & Slaats-Willemse, D. (2014). Working memory training in young children with ADHD: A randomized placebo-controlled trial. *Journal of Child Psychology and Psychiatry, 55*(8), 886–896. https://doi.org/10.1111/jcpp.12218

Wolinsky, F.D., Vander Weg, M.W., Howren, M.B., Jones, M.P., & Dotson, M.M. (2013). A randomized controlled trial of cognitive training using a visual speed of processing intervention in middle aged and older adults. *PLOS ONE, 8*(5), e61624. https://doi.org/10.1371/journal.pone.0061624

Chapter 11
Substance Use Disorders in Aviation

Quay Snyder

Introduction: Medical Certification of Aviation Professionals

Safety is a paramount concern in all aspects of aviation. Commercial aviation and business aviation have very high requirements for safe operations because of the responsibility of transporting the public. General aviation (private and personal flying) may involve nonprofessional pilots and maintenance personnel who are less well trained and experienced than professional operations. Military operations are extremely demanding because of mission requirements and aircraft capabilities. Air traffic control operations are usually conducted by career professionals with extensive training and resources.

For each of these operations, optimum cognitive functioning coupled with sound physical functioning is critical to maintaining the safety of aviation operations. Initial and periodic medical certification is required for all pilots, cockpit personnel, and air traffic control officers (ATCOs). Some regulatory agencies require medical certification for cabin crew. Military operations require regular medical examinations for all aircrew members.

Ironically, ground and maintenance personnel rarely have any medical certification requirements other than being subject to random substance use screening. This population (the so-called below-the-wing workers) often works in an environment with less automation, fewer redundant protections, limited recurrent training, and less direct oversight. Furthermore, this group frequently works during periods of circadian lows without regulatory protections on work-rest hours. This group of aviation safety-critical workers may be more susceptible to mental health challenges than those aviation professionals who work "above the wing" and are subject to periodic medical screening and certification (Brown et al., 2020). Medical certification requirements are set by the national regulatory authorities, meaning requirements may vary by profession.

Initial medical certification may have higher standards than recurrent medical certification examinations, particularly in the military. ATCO aspirants in some countries may also be subject to psychological testing as a "screen-in" or "screen-out" stage in the hiring process. The European Aviation Safety Agency (EASA) requires mental health evaluation for pilot applicants as well as drug testing for initial certification (EASA, n.d.). In most national jurisdictions, there may be additional testing requirements or more frequent examinations as certified personnel age. The International Civil Aviation Organization (ICAO) limits international commercial flying to pilots under the age of 65 years for aircraft with two or more pilots and age 60 for single pilots, but domestic flying is permitted for older pilots (ICAO, 2018).

Although psychological wellness and cognitive fitness are essential to optimize safe aviation operations, even those individuals who are periodically examined and medically certified rarely have formalized mental health evaluations. In most countries, pilots passing a simulator evaluation conducted by the employer are considered mentally fit to continue flying.

The use of alcohol and other drugs (AODs) may adversely impact cognition as well as mental and physical health. Each of these outcomes compromises aviation safety. However, most medical certification examinations do not assess whether evidence, either physical or biochemical, exists of excessive AOD use, abuse, or dependence. Some regulatory authorities require the applicant to estimate the amount of alcohol consumption and most ask if there is a history of substance abuse. Other regulatory authorities include blood testing that may include indirect biomarkers as proxies for possible excessive alcohol use.

The US Federal Aviation Administration (FAA) requires the applicant to report alcohol- or drug-related motor vehicle actions. FAA medical certificate holders are subject to verification of their response to substance-related motor vehicle actions against the National Driver's Registry with significant penalties for falsification (FAA, 2012). In 1987 the US Office of Inspector General found that 3.4% of pilots had a motor vehicle accident, and a 2005 study from Johns Hopkins University showed that pilots with a previous conviction of driving under the influence had a 43% increase in fatal aviation accidents (Li et al., 2005).

The Scope of Substance Use Disorders

The World Health Organization (WHO, 2023a) reports that there is a causal relationship between the harmful use of alcohol and a range of mental and behavioral disorders. The harmful use of alcohol causes 5.3% of global deaths annually and 13.5% of deaths in people aged 20–39 years. WHO also reports that 5.5% of the global population used psychoactive drugs in the previous year and 35 million people were affected by drug use disorders (WHO, 2023b).

The European Union states that alcohol use is responsible for 7% of all ill health and early deaths (European Commission, 2023). Australia reports 4.5% of the country's total burden of disease is due to alcohol (Australian Institute of Health and Welfare, 2023).

The US National Institute of Alcohol Abuse and Alcoholism estimates that 13.2% of American men and 9.5% of women aged 18 and over suffer from an alcohol use disorder (AUD). Only 8.2% of males with this disease have received treatment with lower percentages for women and minorities (NIAAA, 2024). The Centers for Disease Control and Prevention (CDC) indicate that 13.0% of Americans aged 12 and over have used illicit drugs in the past year (CDC, 2023). This figure does not include legally prescribed opioids, stimulants, and sedative hypnotic medications. The National Center for Drug Abuse Statistics reports that 21.4% of Americans age 12 and over have used illicit or illegally used prescription drugs in the last year (National Center for Drug Abuse Statistics, n.d.). The most common drugs used illicitly are cannabis, opioids, prescription pain medications, prescription sedatives, cocaine, stimulants, and methamphetamines. Approximately 5% of Americans have a drug use disorder.

Significant risk factors for having substance use disorders (SUDs) in adult life include early age at first use of a psychoactive substance, childhood trauma, a family history of substance abuse disorders, and coexisting mental health disorders (National Academies of Sciences, Engineering, and Medicine, 2023). Once the problem has progressed to a severe SUD – the point at which substance use becomes a chronic, relapsing condition — it is often referred to as *addiction*.

The Substance Abuse and Mental Services Administration (SAMHSA) publication "Key Substance Use and Mental Health Indicators in the United States: Results from the 2018 National Survey on Drug Use and Health" gives the following statistics on alcohol and use disorders (SAMSHA, 2018): The prevalence of *self-reported* alcohol use disorders was 10.1% of the population aged 18–25 and 5.1% of the population aged 26 years and older. For illicit drug use disorders, the corresponding figures are 7.6% and 2.2%, respectively. These figures do not include those who may be dependent on legally prescribed medications used by the individual for whom the medication was prescribed (Esser et al., 2022).

Pilots and other aviation safety personnel suffer from the adverse effects of AODs like any other person. The neurocognitive and mental health effects of these substances in those who abuse or are dependent on psychoactive substances compromises the safety of all aspects of aviation as well as personal health and well-being. Although there may be a "healthy worker effect" related to those who are required to maintain medical certification, many aviation personnel with unhealthy and harmful use of psychoactive substances still maintain medical certification. When a substance abuse disorder presents in the occupational environment, it has usually progressed to a severe level. Those aviation safety-sensitive personnel who do not require regular medical examination generally reflect the incidence and prevalence of disease in the general population.

The National Academy of Sciences (NAS, 2023, pp. 50–51) states: "There is also evidence that the occurrence of substance use among pilots involved in civil aviation accidents is similar to that found in the non-flying public (Botch & Johnson, 2009). Furthermore, findings from the National Transportation Safety Board (2020) suggest that misuse of licit and illicit substances among pilots is increasing." The Safety Study report found that 10% of pilots involved in fatal aviation accidents had postmortem positive test results for controlled substances and 5% tested positive for illicit drugs (see Figure 11.1). Alcohol was not tested for in this study (NTSB, 2020).

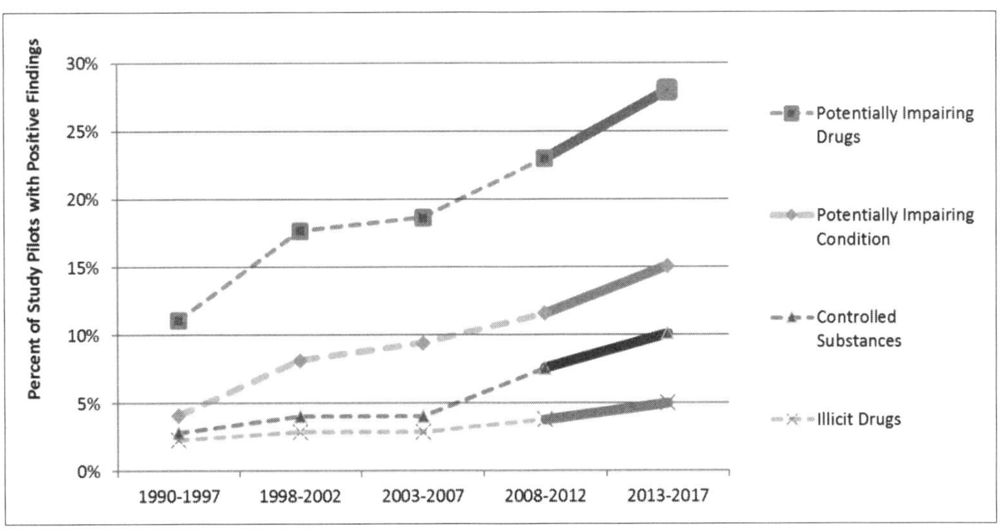

Figure 11.1. Percentage of study pilots with positive toxicology findings for potentially impairing drugs and conditions, controlled substances, and illicit drugs, 1990–2017. Reprinted with permission from National Transportation Safety Board, 2020, p. 11.

Furthermore, the NAS (2023) states:

> By the time a substance use problem presents within a work setting, the disease has typically progressed to a severe level. Professional identity can be paramount for safety-sensitive professionals, and they work hard to maintain their reputation for competence and control (DeHoff and Cusick, 2018), generally while masking even acceptable forms of struggle within our culture (e.g., raising children, work stressors, divorce). Commonly, professionals in these situations engage in positive impression management, attempting to control how they are perceived, highlighting their strengths, and downplaying any problems (Brown, 2015; Picard et al., 2023). (pp. 48f.)

Neuropsychological and Neurocognitive Effects of Substance Use Disorders

An SUD is a disease characterized by chronicity, progression, tendency toward relapse, and ultimate fatal outcomes if not effectively treated. SUDs are associated with many physical, mental, and cognitive comorbidities (McNeely & Adam, 2020). Many of the comorbidities as well as the primary disease are associated with negative effects on aviation safety. Those individuals with a history of mental illness are at increased risk for SUDs compared with the general population. Some of these individuals will not be able to obtain aviation medical certification, but, as stated above, many aviation professionals "below the wing" do not require medical certification and continue in safety-critical roles.

SUDs result from a disruption in the reward and pleasure pathways of the limbic system in the brain and ultimately the prefrontal and frontal cortex regions. Dopamine is the common neurotransmitter involved in addiction, although individual substances can affect other neurotransmitters (serotonin, noradrenaline, GABA, oxytocin). Addictive behavior is a cycle of three stages: the preoccupation/anticipation phase, the binging/intoxication phase, and the withdrawal/negative affect stage.

Dependence on a substance is characterized by tolerance and withdrawal. Tolerance is the need for increasing amounts of a substance to have the same effect as previously or the reduced physical or psychological effect produced by the same amount of the substance. Withdrawal is characterized by noxious physical and mental signs and symptoms when decreased amounts of the substance are present in the body. It is possible to be dependent on a substance such as a non-euphorigenic medication or caffeine and not have an SUD.

SUD "addictions" generally have adverse consequences associated with the use or restriction of the substance. Psychologically, craving for the substance initiates the preoccupation/intoxication/negative affect cycle described earlier that can lead to SUD.

Pilots tend to have personalities that are very adaptive for the psychologically demanding features of flying. Narcissistic and obsessive-compulsive traits help pilots consistently complete checklists, follow strict procedures, respond efficiently to emergencies, and have the confidence to transport an aluminum (or carbon fiber) tube across thousands of miles in bad weather, at night, trusting only instruments, and be confident that they can gently arrive on a narrow two-mile long runway. They are confident, independent problem-solvers. All of these valuable traits in the aviation environment make pilots reluctant to seek help for personal problems, particularly those that may be associated with public stigma or a lack of professional excellence.

Distinction Between Medical Diagnostic and Federal Regulatory Criteria

The *Diagnostic and Statistical Manual of Mental Disorders, Fifth Edition* (DSM-5-TR) characterizes SUD as mild (2–3), moderate (4–5), or severe (>5) depending on the number of criteria met within a total of four categories during the previous year (Hasin et al., 2018). There are four general categories of criteria including impaired control, social impairment, high risk use, and pharmacological evidence of tolerance or withdrawal. Each of the categories has 2–4 specific criteria within it.

The Federal Aviation Regulations (14 CFR Part 67.107/67.207/67.307; FAA, 2012) use much broader criteria for diagnosing substance "abuse" and substance "dependence," both of which are disqualifying for medical certification for all pilots. Importantly, meeting a single criterion of the four listed results in medical disqualification. As a result, pilots who may not meet DSM-5 criteria for an SUD may meet FAA criteria for substance dependence or abuse and may be disqualified from holding a medical certificate. Moreover, the lookback period for a certification determination may be as long as the pilot's lifetime rather than the previous year in the DSM-5 (TR) criteria.

The FAA regulatory criteria for substance dependence include any one of the following:

1. increased tolerance;
2. manifestation of withdrawal symptoms;
3. impaired control of use; or
4. continued use despite damage to physical health or impairment of social, personal, or occupational functioning.

According to the FAA criteria, substance abuse is defined as any one of the following findings in the preceding 2 years:

1. Use of a substance in a situation in which that use was physically hazardous, if there has been at any other time an instance of the use of a substance also in a situation in which that use was physically hazardous
2. A verified positive drug test result, an alcohol test result of 0.04 or greater alcohol concentration, or a refusal to submit to a drug or alcohol test required by the US Department of Transportation or an agency of the US Department of Transportation
3. Misuse of a substance that the Federal Air Surgeon, based on case history and appropriate, qualified medical judgment relating to the substance involved, finds
   a) makes the person unable to safely perform the duties or exercise the privileges of the airman certificate applied for or held; or
   b) may reasonably be expected, for the maximum duration of the airman medical certificate applied for or held, to make the person unable to perform those duties or exercise those privileges.

Professional pilots are required to hold a First Class FAA medical certificate and complete a medical application and undergo a physical examination by an FAA designated senior aviation medical examiner (AME) every 12 months if under age 40 or every 6 months at age 40 and beyond. Pilots who fly recreationally complete medical applications every 5 years for age 39 and below and every 2 years after reaching age 40. Pilots who fly powered aircraft (not gliders or noncommercial balloons) must maintain a current medical certificate to operate an aircraft.

Each time a pilot completes a medical application, the completion of the application authorizes the FAA to search the National Drivers Registry (NDR). Additionally, the pilot must declare any alcohol- or drug-related motor vehicle arrests, convictions, or administrative action such as education classes or license suspensions even if not convicted or if convicted of a lesser charge by the court. All aviator medical applications undergo a NDR search with serious potential administrative consequences for pilots not fully reporting substance-related motor vehicle incidents (cars, motorcycles, boats, snow machines, golf carts, and others) on the application. These consequences may include revocation of both the medical certificate and all pilot certificates and ratings earned in their lifetime. Without the required medical and pilot certificates, a pilot is frequently terminated by the employer and left without benefits for sick leave, disability, and medical care.

Two arrests (not necessarily convictions) related to alcohol/substance use and motor vehicle actions in a lifetime, a single breath/blood alcohol concentration of 0.15 mg/dl, or a refusal to submit to law enforcement directed testing each are criteria for the FAA to require a substance abuse evaluation by a psychiatrist or psychologist trained in the FAA Human Intervention Motivational Study (HIMS) program to determine whether the pilot meets FAA criteria for substance dependence or abuse. Pilots meeting the FAA dependence criteria must undergo treatment and demonstrate satisfactory recovery to the Federal Air Surgeon to regain medical certification through the special issuance process.

Neurocognitive functions that may be disturbed in aviation professionals afflicted with SUDs are numerous. Some include speed, accuracy, overall response efficiency (thruput) and quantitative features (process). Additionally, attention/concentration and executive functions, language functions, and memory can show decline. This is especially true in older aviators and those who have a long history of high substance consumption/use. Each of these can be aeromedically significant.

Additionally, SUDs may coexist with other mental disorders that can adversely affect safety such as anxiety disorders, affective disorders, and posttraumatic stress disorder. In many cases, the substance is used to self-medicate these mental health conditions because of fears of medical disqualification if a mental health diagnosis is made or treatment is sought (Hawn et al., 2020).

Why Not Seek Help for SUDS – Health Care Avoidance in Pilots

Professional pilots nearly universally equate their identity as that of a pilot over other traditional roles such as parent, hobbyist, civic participant, etc. Their passion is flying. Much of their life and early income are dedicated to the study and training for flying, obtaining pilot certificates and ratings, and the lifestyle/dress/prestige/public image associated with the positive image of professional aviation. Because of the requirement for medical certification to continue to fly and the requirement to report all encounters with medical professionals during the initial and periodic medical examinations, many pilots have not sought medical care for conditions, have sought information from nonprofessional sources (Internet, friends), or have concealed medical care when completing their medical examination.

An article in the *Journal of Occupational and Environmental Medicine* (Hoffman et al., 2022) Hoffman and Aden found that 56.1% of pilots reported avoiding health care for fear of being grounded. Several other studies have validated the pervasive nature of health-care avoidance in different populations of pilots including general aviation, military, female, and Canadian pilots (Hoffman et al., 2023; Patel et al., 2023).

Additionally, a strong societal stigma exists both among peers and the traveling public regarding SUDs in professional pilots. The stigma of being labeled as an "alcoholic" or "user" was much stronger in the late 20th century but persists today. Many individuals struggling with SUDs have suffered disruptions in family and marital relationships, loss of social connections, financial distress, legal consequences, and other health problems. The disease of addiction is associated with shame, guilt, remorse, and fear. For pilots, the occupational implications of this disease exacerbate these negative effects. Losing a flying career is losing a persona.

Aviation Lifestyle Risk Factors for Substance Use Disorders

In 1956, the American Medical Association classified alcoholism as a disease as opposed to a behavioral choice, character weakness, or a moral failing. However, prior to 1972, the FAA had not certified any pilots with a history of alcoholism, whether it was treated or the pilot was in long-term abstinence. Because of the career-ending implications of this diagnosis, pilots with "alcoholism," as it was termed then, would not come forward to ask for help or admit to having a problem. Other pilots actively participated in a conspiracy to cover up for their fellow pilots who may report for duty intoxicated (Buckingham, 2019).

The lifestyle of professional pilots and flight attendants in the airline industry allows for easy access and discrete use of alcohol and other drugs. Alcoholic beverages are stocked on aircraft for passenger consumption, which are readily available to crew members despite the possibility of a lifetime ban from any aviation career if use of alcohol or prohibited substance on duty is confirmed. Aircrew are exempt from security limitations for carrying fluids on board an aircraft. As a result, aircrew with SUDs may fill water bottles and thermoses with alcohol to have ready access after, and in some cases before and during, flight. Most airline crews have multiday trips with layovers in hotels with free or reduced priced "happy hours" where the crew meets for dinner and drinks. Some crew members will check into their hotel rooms, consume their own or mini-bar alcohol, and then join the other crew members for drinks and dinner to give the appearance of drinking only moderate amounts. They may also return to their rooms to consume more alcohol or drugs privately. This is termed "geographic drinking," where crew members may hide their use from family by just drinking on layovers. Pilots are generally "rule followers" who obey the FAA requirement to not consume alcohol within 8 hr of reporting for duty. However, the rare pilot who reports to work with a breath alcohol concentration (BAC) above the FAA 0.04 mg% limit consumed large quantities of alcohol in a binge fashion to give elevated residual BACs despite stopping drinking 8 hr prior to duty.

Obtaining illicit substances is easily done in a discrete manner at various cities without raising suspicion of frequent visits to a single location. Overseas layovers allow for access to substances legally obtained in the host country but not available or available only with a prescription in the United States. Opioid analogs and stimulants in some Asian countries and coca products in South America are common examples. Overseas flights are generally lengthy, and some require multiday layovers to meet crew rest requirements. This allows for prolonged substance use in isolated locations prior to reporting for duty for the return flight.

HIMS – A Program of Personal Recovery and Aviation Safety

In 1972, a survey by the National Institute of Alcoholism and Alcohol Abuse (NIAAA) Occupational Programs Branch found that few employee assistance programs had successfully implemented programs to assist those with alcohol abuse. Following that survey, Dr. Richard Masters, the Aeromedical Advisor to the Air Line Pilots Association (ALPA), proposed to the ALPA Board of Directors that they support an alcohol identification and treatment program within the airlines. The program required cooperation from the airlines, the pilot unions, medical professionals, and most importantly the FAA. Without the possibility of medical certification by the FAA and career preservation, the airlines and the pilots would not have the motivation to institute a program. From everyone's perspective, this program could enhance safety.

The NIAAA funded the study proposed by ALPA in 1974 under the moniker "Human Intervention and Motivation Study," which ran through 1982. At that time, over 800 pilots had been recertified by the FAA after recovery from alcoholism. Most but not all had successfully completed a treatment program. All were monitored for at least 2 years by the FAA, peer pilots, and airline employee assistance programs (EAP) and medical directors. These pilots had an 85% long-term sobriety rate and the airlines received a 9:1 return on investment. The safety objective had been met (Pakull, 1978, 1979). In the late 1980s, funding for the education of the HIMS program was intermittently provided by the airlines and pilot unions. Starting in the early 1990s, the US Congress funded the FAA to provide SUD education for pilots, airlines, and aviation medical professionals through semi-annual seminars. The funding for conducting the training has been awarded to the Air Line Pilots Association–International and been renewed annually since then.

First Aviation-Specific Peer Support Program

The HIMS program was the first aviation-specific program to involve peers in assisting fellow pilots who were facing a deterioration in their mental wellness. Because of the success attributed to the role of HIMS peers in removing barriers to entry and assisting in the recovery, other peer support programs modeled after the HIMS program have been created. These include Aeromedical (support for pilots with temporary or permanently disqualifying medical conditions), Critical Incident Response and Stress Management (proactive defusing and debriefing for those experiencing job related traumatic events), Professional Standards (resolving workplace disharmony in crew operations), and Mental Wellness Peer Support (those facing common challenges to mental wellness).

Key to the success of HIMS is the role of fellow pilots in recovery being a resource for those pilots voluntarily seeking assistance for substance misuse, those facing occupational disciplinary consequences related to substance use, those with legal or social problems related to misuse, and those with regulatory mandates to undergo evaluations for possible SUDs. Pilots who have previously faced these situations and have successfully returned to flying serve as peer models for those in earlier stages of evaluation and pretreatment. The peers serve in a "wingman" role and guide the peer through the daunting process of evaluation, treatment, recovery, recertification, and return to flying.

Peer pilots have taken a primary role in managing both the implementation of the elements of the HIMS program at their airline as well as providing the psychological support of pilots in earlier stages to recovery and sobriety. Cooperation and financial support from the airline employers are essential as the financial burdens for treatment and monitoring for medical certification are substantial. In most cases, this cooperative arrangement is done through collective bargaining agreements between the employer and the pilot union, letters of agreement, or memoranda of understanding completed in parallel to the collective bargaining agreement. Remarkably, even during times of labor strife, the airline HIMS programs have consistently remained fully operational. The benefits of the program to aviation safety and pilot well-being encourage cooperation between all parties involved in HIMS.

The American Society of Addition Medicine (ASAM) recognizes the unique treatment needs of safety-sensitive personnel based on several factors. The qualities of safety-sensitive professionals leading to important and distinct needs for assessment and treatment are as follows (ASAM, 2013):

1. People in safety-sensitive professions have a responsibility to the public. This responsibility is present both in the number of people safety-sensitive professionals interact with and the depth of impact their impairment can cause. Public trust is high for professionals in safety-sensitive occupations (e.g., law enforcement, health-care providers, pilots, flight attendants, and other transportation roles, attorneys) and challenges that disrupt this trust can significantly impact the perception of an entire profession.
2. People in safety-sensitive professions benefit most from cohort-specific treatment. This therapeutic environment helps facilitate self-disclosure while decreasing shame, guilt, and stigma. Peers in similar professions can normalize the impact substance misuse and addiction have on one professionally and how it puts others at risk, while maintaining public trust in the profession.
3. Many professionals in safety-sensitive occupations have direct access to substances that are addictive. This includes pilots and flight attendants who have access to alcohol served on the plane.
4. To heal from SUDs, people need to assume the role of patient. Professionals in safety-sensitive occupations, particularly those in positions of significant power like pilots and customer service like flight attendants, struggle to assume the patient role. They struggle to let go of their innate caretaking, their desire to be perceived as competent, and experience difficulty in relinquishing control. Accepting help and healing requires showing up authentically and vulnerably, letting others see their suffering, and accepting that they need help.

Elements of Aviation Substance Abuse Treatment Programs in Aviation

Evaluation

Denial is a common feature of those afflicted with SUDs. However, not all pilots who come to the attention of peers, management, or the regulator because of unprofessional behaviors or medical conditions (seizures, gastric bleeding, trauma, laboratory abnormalities, etc.) that may indicate an SUD will meet either diagnostic or regulatory criteria for a disqualifying medical condition. For pilots, approximately 30 % enter an SUD evaluation process from interventions with similar percentages entering by self-referral and also another 30 % by FAA-mandated evaluations following a substance-related motor vehicle event. Less than 10 % are referred for evaluation because of a Department of Transportation-required positive on-duty test for prohibited substances or suspicion by law enforcement and security personnel.

To determine whether a pilot or cabin crew member meets criteria for an SUD requiring treatment, an evaluation by a qualified addiction medicine professional is necessary. Because the regulatory standards for medical disqualification may be different from standard medical diagnostic criteria for SUDs, an addiction medicine professional familiar with that country's aviation regulatory standards is also essential.

As noted earlier, in the United States, the regulatory standards for substance dependence, abuse, and misuse are defined in the 14 Code of Federal Regulations Part 67 (Medical Standards). These differ from the criteria for an SUD listed in DSM-5 or the *International Classification of Diseases 10th Revision* (ICD-10). The regulatory criteria for abuse, misuse, and dependence are broader than those in standard medical taxonomy and definitions. As a result, pilots who may not meet criteria for an SUD, even mild or moderate, may be disqualified under the regulatory criteria. Cabin crew (flight attendants) do not have regulatory requirements for medical certification, as noted earlier, and generally undergo standard SUD evaluations using DSM-5 TR criteria.

The evaluation of a pilot for a possible disqualifying substance use problem is generally conducted by a psychiatrist or psychologist familiar with addiction medicine and the regulatory standards. Occasionally, an evaluation by both professionals is required. The evaluation includes obtaining information from several collateral resources, as pilots in particular are very skilled at presenting a strong positive image of self and minimizing the amount and consequences of their psychoactive substance use. The evaluations are augmented with biomarkers potentially in a variety of media (breath, oral fluid, urine, blood, hair, and nails).

The outcome of a *positive evaluation* has one of three usual results. One is that the pilot is persuaded that a problem exists, they accept the diagnosis, and voluntarily enter treatment. The more common one is that the evaluation is referred to the regulatory authority for determination of qualification to maintain medical certification, either with or without treatment. In some cases, even if a clear diagnosis of an SUD is made during the evaluation, the pilot will maintain denial and decline to enter treatment unless a definitive disqualifying determination is made by the regulatory authority. In these cases, an intervention by a peer pilot in the HIMS program is often persuasive in getting the pilot to enter treatment earlier because of the inevitability of the disqualifying regulatory decision and the earlier return to flying if treatment commences sooner.

If the regulator determines the pilot does *not* have a disqualifying condition or has a condition that requires monitoring but not treatment to maintain medical certification, several outcomes are possible:

1. The pilot may be given a warning that they are qualified to continue to hold a medical certificate, but a subsequent substance-related event may trigger a re-evaluation of their qualification.
2. A requirement may be made for a pilot to maintain abstinence from all mood-altering substances for a period of several years. The abstinence is monitored by a series of no-notice tests for metabolites and/or biomarkers of prohibited substances by the pilot's aviation medical examiner. This requirement is stated in a special issuance authorization for medical certification by the FAA.

For pilots unable to maintain abstinence during this period, they are medically disqualified by the regulator and required to enter treatment to regain medical certification. If there is no positive evidence of the use of psychoactive substances during that period, the pilot is medically certified without an abstinence requirement, but given the warning noted above that a further substance-related event will result in disqualification.

Flight attendants in the United States and many other countries do not require medical certification. Therefore, there is no requirement for an evaluation to determine whether a potentially disqualifying medical condition exists. Most US flight attendants enter the Flight Attendant Drug and Alcohol Program (FADAP) voluntarily or because of a duty-related event involving substance use. Flight attendants do undergo evaluations to determine the level of care appropriate for their disease state.

Treatment

Treatment for pilots with SUDs in North America usually involves a 4-week inpatient multimodality program. This removes the pilot from the environment conducive to sustaining the disorder. In many cases, the pilot may not meet ASAM criteria for an inpatient level of care. Medical certification determination by the regulators following inpatient treatment is felt to be faster and more likely to be favorable by the pilot groups. Some pilots have longer inpatient treatment stays, and a few will have partial hospitalization or intensive outpatient treatment experiences, but this is primarily only acceptable for general aviation pilots and not for professional pilots. Many airlines have agreements with treatment centers caring for pilot allowing 1-month inpatient care despite not meeting ASAM criteria for inpatient care. Flight attendants who do not have medical certification requirements often enter treatment programs that follow the ASAM treatment levels, as do some pilots in non-North American countries.

Initial intake evaluations include a substance-disorder-focused interview, a separate evaluation by a psychiatrist for psychiatric comorbidities, and a social worker to assess family and other needs following discharge. If medical problems are present, a physician will evaluate and treat those conditions. For those who have developed dependence and are experiencing physical withdrawal symptoms, they are managed in a setting with 24-hr medical observation and appropriate medication. This detoxification period from withdrawal is done prior to initiating any psychological interventions, as the uncomfortable and distracting manifestations of physical withdrawal preclude any ability to focus on the mental aspects of disease recovery.

Because neurocognitive testing is required for pilots in the United States for medical recertification after treatment for an SUD, most facilities treating pilots will do limited neurocognitive testing sometime during the treatment stay. If done near the time of admission, poor testing results may aid in breaking through a pilot's denial of the effects of their substance use early in the treatment experience. The testing also serves as an indicator of the need for neurocognitive rehabilitation or a longer period of abstinence from the substance before repeating neurocognitive testing to support recertification. Anecdotally, those pilots with longer use of substance(s), heavy consumption, more recent consumption, and older pilots perform more poorly on admission neurocognitive testing.

Treatment while an inpatient typically involves multiple group sessions with a trained counselor and individual sessions with a therapist and/or psychiatrist. The sessions focus on education about the disease, strategies for maintaining abstinence, achieving sobriety, and addressing treatment options for medical and psychological comorbidities (Krawczyk et al., 2017).

The ASAM endorses many levels of treatment according to their continuum of care including inpatient, residential, intensive outpatient, outpatient, and recovery residence. Many types of treatment including medication-assisted treatment (MAT). Using medications to substitute less euphorigenic effects for the addictive substance (methadone and buprenorphine for opioids), medications that can reduce cravings for the substance (naltrexone and acamprosate for opioids and alcohol), or medications causing aversive reactions when the substance is ingested (disulfiram for alcohol) are options for MAT. As of 2023, the FAA does not medically certify pilots who are using MAT as a basis for or adjunct to their long-term recovery, although MAT is acceptable in early phases of treatment for pilots prior to pursuing FAA medical certification. Possible reasons are aeromedically unacceptable side effects of the medications, and the reliance on using medications to maintain abstinence is not indicative of a good recovery that is compatible with certification.

Flight attendants may participate in any level of care appropriate for their SUD severity and may also use most forms of MAT when returning to duty. They frequently opt for outpatient-based treatments because of less financial resources than pilots and to limit time spent away from work.

Additional supportive therapies are common including mindfulness and meditation training, biofeedback sessions, journaling, group activities, diet and nutrition counseling, massage, and physical recreation. An important component for mutual support group (MSG)-focused facilities is introduction and early participation in MSGs, most commonly Alcoholics Anonymous (AA) or other similar MSG and "12-Step" programs. Pilots have a pilot-specific group within AA called "Birds of a Feather" or simply "Birds" and flight attendants participate in Wings of Sobriety groups to augment standard 12-Step meetings. Most treatment facilities for pilots will transport pilots to the local Birds meeting weekly during treatment or will host a Birds meeting in their facility. Pilots greatly value the opportunity to be in treatment with fellow pilots and to see those in Birds meetings with sustained recovery who have resumed flying and relate the positive changes in their lives since initiating their recovery.

The family is critical in a pilot's and flight attendant's recovery. SUDs are a family disease. Although the pilot is the one drinking/drugging, the family suffers. As a result of the unpredictable behavior of the person with an SUD, those around that person develop coping and protective strategies that are ingrained over years. Codependency is a survival reaction but is not helpful in supporting recovery. Therefore, the optimum support for a pilot following treatment must include the family. This can be accomplished by individual and family counseling and involvement in MSGs such as Al-Anon, Ala-Teen, and CoDA. The family issues should be addressed while the pilot is in treatment. Active family participation in the treatment program improves chances for a successful and prolonged recovery. Sometimes, relationships are so damaged by earlier behaviors that salvaging the relationships is not possible. It is beneficial to recognize this and have a strategy for addressing this situation following discharge.

Beginning Recovery

Discharge from a treatment center is the beginning of an individual's lifelong journey of recovery. Abstinence is a necessary but not sufficient element of the recovery process. Abstinence is the physical absence of an addictive substance or similar psychoactive substances in the person with a SUD. Recovery is a mental state of acceptance, serenity, and strategies to address inevitable challenges the pilot will face that previously would typically result in craving, binging, and intoxication with the substance of choice as a coping mechanism. Relapses are characterized by a compromise of the mental elements of recovery long before the physical intake of the substance (loss of abstinence) occurs.

Recommendations for the pilot leaving treatment focus on participation in mutual support groups such as Alcoholics Anonymous, Narcotics Anonymous , or alternative MSGs such as SMART Recovery, Women for Sobriety, Secular Organizations for Sobriety (SOS) programs, Refuge Recovery (mindfulness and Buddhist philosophy), and LifeRing Secular Recovery. Meaningful moderation is not abstinence based and therefore is not compatible with FAA certification. Pilots are expected to attend a minimum of 90 MSG meetings within the first 90 days of discharge.

The long-term benefits of support groups include:

- reduced rate of relapse;
- increased satisfaction with the overall treatment experience;
- increased treatment retention; and
- improved relationships with family, friends, and coworkers (Reif et al., 2014).

The Harvard Grant study found that the best predictor for long-term recovery is attendance at 12-Step meetings (Vaillant & Hiller-Sturmhöfel, 1996).

In addition to frequent regular attendance at MSG meetings, pilots and flight attendants are expected to initially obtain a temporary AA or other MSG sponsor and then a permanent sponsor and home group. The relationship with a sponsor is a long-term commitment of learning and "working" the steps together and sharing "strength, hope, and experience" to address threats to abstinence and sobriety. The pilot is also expected to establish a "home group," which is the primary place of meeting. AA has over 120,000 groups meeting in 181 countries with nearly 2 million members. Virtual meetings are available worldwide on a continuous basis for those who cannot attend an in-person meeting, with over 300 listed in North America (Alcoholics Anonymous, 2022).

The resources on the AA website (https://www.AA.org) include:

- The Big Book – Alcoholics Anonymous
- The 12 Steps and 12 Traditions
- The Meeting Guide Application
- The AA Grapevine Newsletter (not managed or controlled by the AA World organization)

For pilots, the subgroup of AA Birds of a Feather (https://www.boaf.org), as mentioned earlier, has meetings (termed "nests") across the globe and are open to all aviators, both professional and recreational. The electronic newsletter, the *BirdWord*, lists all meeting times, locations, and points of contact. This is particularly useful for airline pilots seeking meetings when they have resumed flying to many locations after medical certification.

Pilots are required to participate in weekly "aftercare" or "continuing care" group meetings led by a professional substance abuse counselor. This requirement was made mandatory by the FAA following an early HIMS study (Pakull, 1978) showing the abstinence rate in pilots who attended aftercare meetings was higher than those who did not. Individual and family counseling is also encouraged, but not required, by the FAA. Other nations' regulatory authorities may require individual counseling on a case-by-case basis.

Pilots employed by US airlines with a HIMS program are required to meet monthly with a peer pilot who is usually in recovery also and a management supervisor. The peer pilot is assessing the quality of the pilot's recovery from the perspective of someone very familiar with the disease and the occupational challenges the pilot may face. The management supervisor is also assessing the quality of the recovery while having input regarding crew interactions, operational efficiencies, sick leave usage, and training results, particularly after the pilot is recertified to return to flying. These reports are sent monthly to the AME as additional insights into the pilot's recovery.

An individual pilot's return to flying is coordinated through an AME with training in elements of substance abuse and regulatory requirements for certification through the HIMS educational seminars termed "HIMS AME." The AME reviews medical and treatment records of the pilot, meets with the pilot on a regular basis, and coordinates no-notice abstinence biomarker verification testing. The AME also receives monthly reports from the aftercare counselor on the pilot's progress in the recovery program. It is important that the pilot is not required to provide reports from the AA sponsor, as the relationship between a pilot and the AA sponsor is one of strict confidentiality so as not to inhibit full open and honest communications. With the mutual consent of the pilot and the sponsor, a report may be provided to the AME, but this is a relatively rare occurrence.

When the HIMS AME determines the pilot has made appropriate progress in recovery and is maintaining abstinence, the FAA requires neurocognitive testing and an addiction medicine psychiatric examination. The neuropsychologist and the psychiatrist review all medical and treatment records, aftercare and abstinence testing reports, the pilot's FAA medical file, and the referring AME's summary prior to conducting the evaluations. This usually occurs after at least 90 days after release from treatment. The observation period provides time for the toxicity of the substance to dissipate for improved cognitive functioning and for the commitment to and quality of recovery efforts to be determined. These combined assessments also determine whether any comorbidities are present and have been adequately treated.

Outside of the United States, neurocognitive assessments are not usually required and formal evaluations by an addiction medicine psychiatrist are not universally required. Possible reasons include availability of these resources, reliance on simulators as a primary means of assessing aeromedically relevant cognitive function, and philosophies that AMEs are best equipped to assess aviation safety implications for the recovering pilot.

Petition to Regulatory Authority for Reinstatement of Medical Certification

Upon receipt of favorable reports from all parties involved in the pilot's monitoring and treatment, the AME will then assemble a package containing all records and reports to the certifying regulatory agency. If evaluations raise questions about the pilot's recovery, the assembly of the package is usually postponed while potential high-risk areas for relapse are addressed.

The regulatory authority's review of all records and a current medical examination frequently results in a determination of the pilot's eligibility to have the medical certificate reinstated. This determination is based on absence of other conditions that are aeromedically significant and the quality of the pilot's recovery and perceived risk of relapse. A favorable determination usually results in medical certification with requirements for additional monitoring and status reports in addition to the standard medical certification protocols and limitations on the duration of medical certificate validity. The duration of the increased monitoring varies between regulatory authorities but is at least 2 years.

The FAA's initial monitoring period at the beginning of the HIMS program in the 1970s–1980s was 2 years and only recovery from alcohol was considered for certification. In the late 1990s, the minimum duration for monitoring was increased to 3 years for alcohol and a 5-year monitoring period was required for other psychoactive substances. In response to NTSB recommendations for continuous monitoring for a chronic disease similar to the FAA's monitoring of other chronic diseases, the FAA announced a "step-down" monitoring plan of reduced monitoring requirements for a minimum of the first 8 years after certification and a requirement to take a medical examination with a HIMS-trained AME for the duration of a pilot's medical certification (FAA, 2021; see Figure 11.2).

Pilots at increased risk for relapse but without evidence of resuming SUD behavior may have monitoring intensity and duration increased by the regulatory authority or on recommendation of the AME.

Relapses

Relapse of substance use is considered a natural part of the disease, although the relapse rate for pilots in the HIMS program is low compared to the general population who have gone through treatment or are participating in self-initiated abstinence recovery programs. Pilots and physicians in physician health programs (PHPs) have similar abstinence rates for those who are certified. The identity as a professional entrusted with public safety, the income associated with that profession, the rigorous monitoring, and the requirement for continued certification are contributors to these higher abstinence rates.

The data for pilots in the HIMS program only are maintained for those who gain medical certification, and thus estimates of long-term abstinence are skewed by those who do not participate in the HIMS certification process. Pilots with relapses are not precluded from subsequent medical certification, although the observation period prior to recertification is usually lengthened and the duration of more intense monitoring is increased. Pilots who

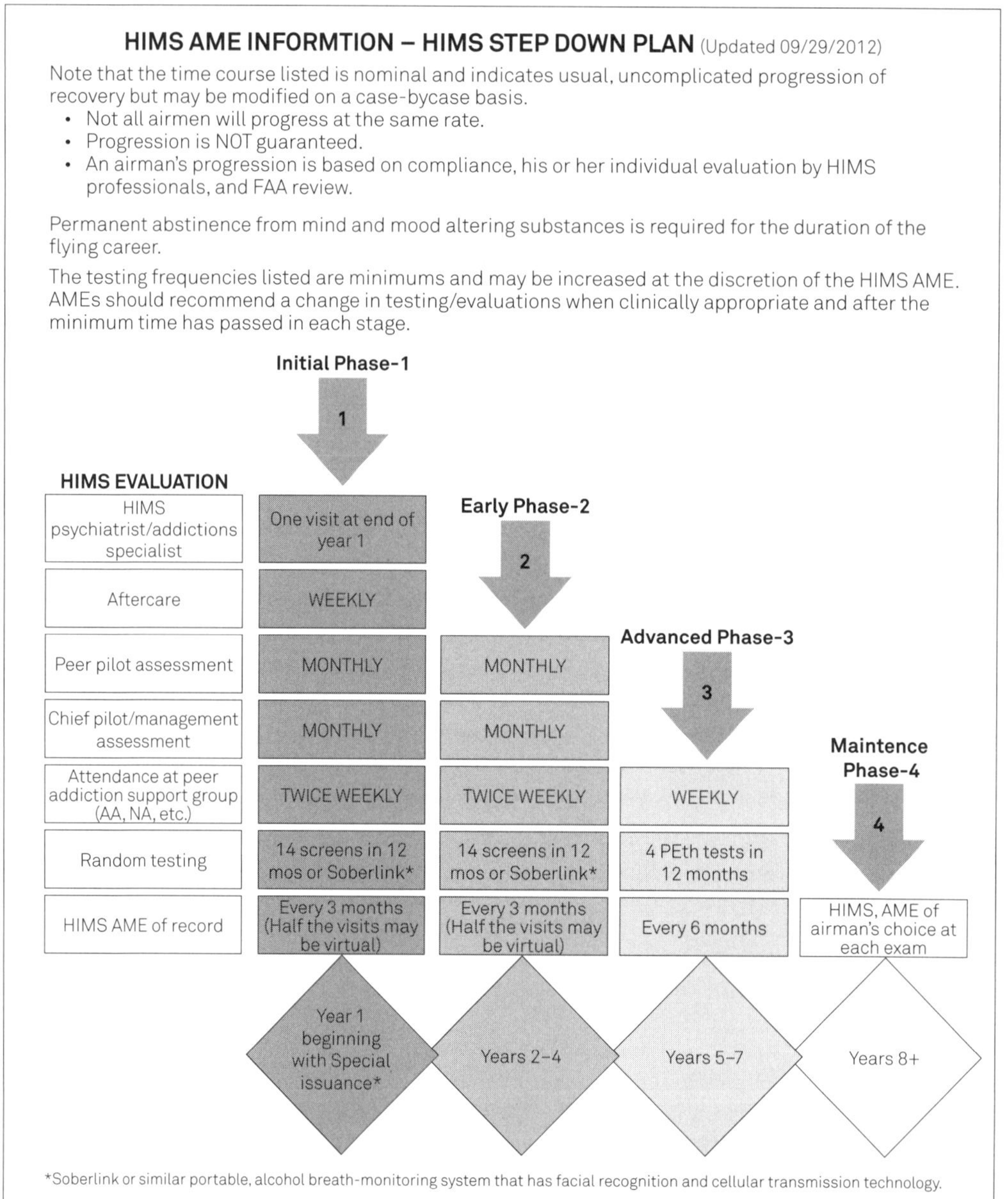

Figure 11.2. The Federal Aviation Administration step-down monitoring plan (FAA, 2021).

pursue certification after a relapse comprise 13.4 % of all pilots in the HIMS program (HIMS database accessed July 3, 2023, not publicly available). Pilots with opioid use disorders who were recertified after relapse have a 39.3 % relapse rate.

HIMS Database

The confidential database maintained by the HIMS program shows alcohol as the primary drug of choice in 92.9 % of pilots subsequently certified, with cocaine, cannabis, and opioids each representing less than 2 %. The age distribution of pilots certified with SUD mirrors that of the age distribution of pilots employed by the airlines. Pilots without any psychiatric comorbidities represented over 90 % of all pilots certified, although those with significant comorbid conditions may not have pursued certification.

Conclusion

Aviation professionals are afflicted by SUDs similar to the general population. Alcohol is the primary drug of choice. The use of psychoactive substances by safety-sensitive personnel has numerous deleterious effects on personal health, cognitive abilities, and efficiency of operations. Most importantly, use of these substances has the potential to compromise the safety of the travelling public.

Denial is a common component of SUDs, as is stigma from the public and fellow professionals. Evaluations by addiction medicine professionals familiar with aviation and regulatory requirements are essential prior to determining treatment decisions. Treatment for SUDs involves addressing psychiatric, medical, and cognitive consequences of the substances used. Sobriety, not simple abstinence, is the basis of a long-term recovery and reducing relapse risk. Regulatory authorities require total abstinence from mind- and mood-altering substances for the duration of medical certification following SUD treatment.

The success of the aviation substance use programs – HIMS for pilots and FADAP for flight attendants – is a result of several factors. Peer support and participation in mutual support groups are essential elements. For those aviation professionals requiring medical certification, extended comprehensive monitoring reinforces abstinence- and recovery-type behaviors. The cooperation and support of all involved – the employees' organizations/unions, the employer/airline, aviation-savvy addiction medicine professionals, and the regulatory authority – are critical to the ongoing success of these programs and to the safety of the traveling public.

References

14 CFR Part 67 Federal Aviation Regulations. (n.d.). *Medical standards.* https://www.ecfr.gov/current/title-14/chapter-I/subchapter-D/part-67

Alcoholics Anonymous. (2022). *Estimates of AA groups and members as of December 31, 2021.* https://www.aa.org/sites/default/files/literature/A.A.%20Around%20the%20Globe%20-%20SMF-165%20EN.pdf

American Society of Addiction Medicine (ASAM). (2013). *The ASAM criteria: Treatment criteria for addictive, substance-related, and co-occurring conditions. Safety-sensitive occupations.* https://www.asam.org/asam-criteria/about-the-asam-criteria

Australian Institute of Health and Welfare. (2023, June 21). *Alcohol factsheet.* https://www.aihw.gov.au/getmedia/8b07633c-2294-4025-bb22-23e78b96319e/PHE221-Factsheets-Alcohol-26042023.pdf.aspx

Botch, S.R., Johnson, R.D. (2009). Antiemetic and sedative levels found together in 26 civil aviation pilot fatalities, 2000–2006. *Aviation, Space, and Environmental Medicine, 79*(6), 607–610. https://doi.org/10.3357/asem.2274.2008

Brown, A.D. (2015). Identities and identity work. *International Journal of Management Reviews, 17*, 20–40. https://doi.org/10.1111/ijmr.12035

Brown, J.P., Martin, D., Nagaria, Z., Verceles, A.C., Jobe, S.L., & Wickwire, E.M. (2020). Mental health consequences of shift work: An updated review. *Current Psychiatry Reports, 22*, 1–7. https://doi.org/10.1007/s11920-020-1131-z

Buckingham, W. (2019). *Hope for challenged airline pilots.*

Centers for Disease Control and Prevention. (2023, June 20). *Illicit drug use.* https://www.cdc.gov/nchs/fastats/drug-use-illicit.htm

DeHoff, M.C., & Cusick, S.K. (2018). Mental health in commercial aviation – Depression & anxiety of pilots. *International Journal of Aviation, Aeronautics, and Aerospace, 5*(5), Article 5. https://doi.org/10.58940/2374-6793.1287

Esser, M.B., Sherk, A., Subbaraman, M.S., Martinez, P., Karriker-Jaffe, K.J., Sacks, J.J., & Naimi, T.S. (2022). Improving estimates of alcohol-attributable deaths in the United States: Impact of adjusting for the underreporting of alcohol consumption. *Journal of Studies on Alcohol and Drugs, 83*(1), 134–144. https://doi.org/10.15288/jsad.2022.83.134

European Aviation Safety Agency. (2023). *Easy access rules for aircrew: (Regulation (EU) No 1178/2011) Annex 4 23 August 2023.* https://www.easa.europa.eu/en/document-library/easy-access-rules/online-publications/easy-access-rules-aircrew-regulation-eu-no?page=54

European Commission. (2023, June 21). *Alcohol.* https://health.ec.europa.eu/alcohol/overview_en

Federal Aviation Administration (FAA). (2012). *Guide for aviation medical examiners: Application process for medical certification.* https://www.faa.gov/ame_guide/app_process/app_history/item20

Federal Aviation Administration (FAA). (2021). *HIMS AME Information – HIMS step down plan.* https://www.faa.gov/ame_guide/media/HIMSAMEStepDownPlan.pdf

Hasin, D.S., O'Brien, C.P., Auriacombe, M., Borges, G., Bucholz, K., Budney, A., Compton, W.M., Crowley, T., Ling, W., Petry, N.M., Schuckit, M., & Grant, B.F. (2018). DSM-5 criteria for substance use disorders: Recommendations and rationale. *American Journal of Psychiatry, 170*(8), 834–851. https://doi.org/10.1176/appi.ajp.2013.12060782

Hawn, S.E., Cusack, S.E., & Amstadter, A.B. (2020). A systematic review of the self-medication hypothesis in the context of posttraumatic stress disorder and comorbid problematic alcohol use. *Journal of Traumatic Stress, 33*(5), 699–708. https://doi.org/10.1002/jts.22521

Hoffman, W.R., Aden, J., Barbera, R.D., Mayes, R., Willis, A., Patel, P., & Tvaryanas, A. (2022). Healthcare avoidance in aircraft pilots due to concern for aeromedical certificate loss: A survey of 3765 pilots. *Journal of Occupational and Environmental Medicine, 64*(4), e245–e248. https://doi.org/10.1097/JOM.0000000000002519

Hoffman, W.R., Aden, J.K., Barbera, D., & Tvaryanas, A. (2023). Self-reported health care avoidance behavior in U.S. military pilots related to fear for loss of flying status. *Military Medicine, 188*(3-4), e446–e450. https://doi.org/10.1093/milmed/usac311

International Civil Aviation Organization. (2018). *International standards and recommended practices, annex 1, personnel licensing,* (12th ed.). https://www.icao.int/APAC/Meetings/2019%20COSCAP%20SEAE-ASA%20PEL/AN01_cons.2019_compressed.pdf

Krawczyk, N., Feder, K.A., Saloner, B., Crum, R.M., Kealhofer, M., & Mojtabai, R. (2017). The association of psychiatric comorbidity with treatment completion among clients admitted to substance use treatment programs in a US national sample. *Drug and Alcohol Dependence, 175*, 157–163. https://doi.org/10.1016/j.drugalcdep.2017.02.006

Li, G., Baker, S., Qiang, Y., Grabowski, J., McCarthy, M. (2005). Driving-while-intoxicated history as a risk marker for general aviation pilots. *Accident Analysis & Prevention*, *37*(1), 179–184. https://doi.org/10.1016/j.aap.2004.04.005

McNeely, J., & Adam, A. (2020). *Substance use screening and risk assessment in adults.* https://www.ncbi.nlm.nih.gov/books/NBK565474/table/nycgsubuse.tab9/

National Academies of Sciences, Engineering, and Medicine. (2023). *Substance misuse programs in commercial aviation: Safety first.* The National Academies Press. https://doi.org/10.17226/27025

National Center for Drug Abuse Statistics. (n.d.). *Alcohol abuse statistics.* https://drugabusestatistics.org/alcohol-abuse-statistics/

National Institute of Alcohol Abuse and Alcohollsm. (2024). *Alcohol's effects on health: Research-based information on drinking and its impact.* https://www.niaaa.nih.gov/alcohols-effects-health/alcohol-topics/alcohol-facts-and-statistics/alcohol-treatment-united-states#:~:text=Prevalence%20of%20Past%2DYear%20Alcohol%20Use%20Treatment&text=According%20to%20the%202022%20National,treatment%20in%20the%20past%20year

National Transportation Safety Board. (2020). *2013–2017 update on drug use trends in aviation.* https://www.ntsb.gov/safety/safety-studies/Documents/SS2001.pdf

Pakull, B. (1978, January). Alcoholism and aviation medical certification. *Alcoholism: Clinical and Experimental Research, 2*(1), 43–47. https://doi.org/10.1111/j.1530-0277.1978.tb04692.x

Pakull, B. (1979). The impact of alcohol and alcoholism on aviation safety. *Current Alcohol, 6*, 327–332.

Patel, P.K., Hoffman, W.R., Aden, J., & Acker, J.P. (2023). Health care avoidance among Canadian pilots due to fear of medical certificate loss: A national cross-sectional survey study. *Journal of Occupational and Environmental Medicine, 65*(6), e413–e417. https://doi.org/10.1097/JOM.0000000000002838

Picard, E., Aparccro, M., Nijdam-Joncs, A., & Roscnfcld, B. (2023). Idcntifying positivc imprcssion management using the MMPI-2 and the MMPI-2-RF: A meta-analysis. *The Clinical Neuropsychologist, 37*(3), 545–561. https://doi.org/10.1080/13854046.2022.2077237

Reif, S., Braude, L., Lyman, D.R., Dougherty, R.H., Daniels, A.S., Ghose, S.S., Salim, O., & Delphin-Rittmon, M.E. (2014). Peer recovery support for individuals with substance use disorders: Assessing the evidence. *Psychiatric Services, 65*(7), 853–861. https://doi.org/10.1176/appi.ps.201400047

Substance Abuse and Mental Health Services Administration. (2018). *National survey on drug use and health: National findings report 2018.* https://www.samhsa.gov/data/sites/default/files/cbhsq-reports/NSDUHNationalFindingsReport2018/NSDUHNationalFindingsReport2018.pdf

Vaillant, G.E., & Hiller-Sturmhöfel, S. (1996). The natural history of alcoholism. *Alcohol Health and Research World, 20*(3), 152–161.

World Health Organization. (2023a). *Alcohol.* https://www.who.int/news-room/fact-sheets/detail/alcohol

World Health Organization. (2023b). *Psychoactive drugs.* https://www.who.int/health-topics/drugs-psychoactive#tab=tab_2

Section III

Assessment

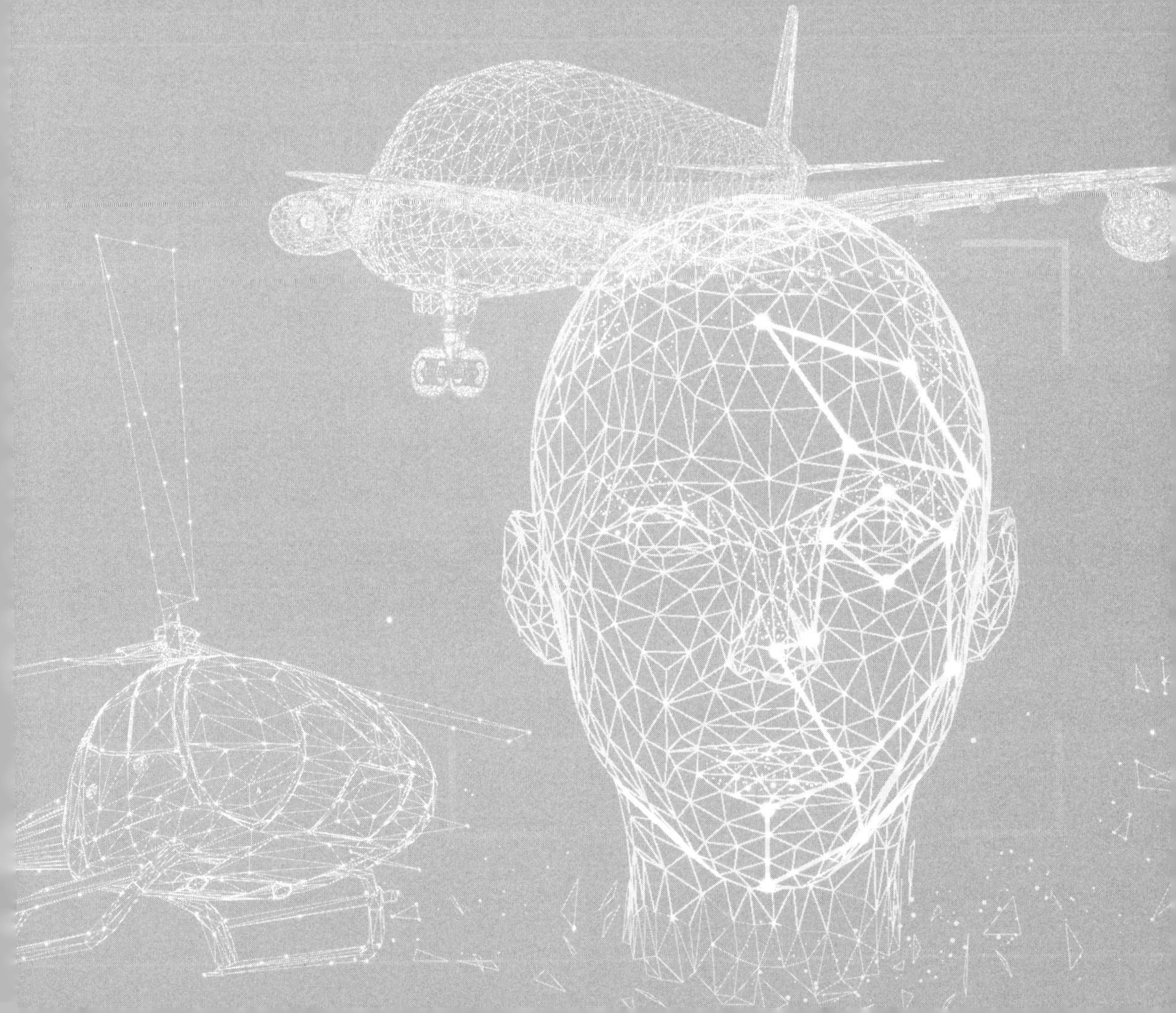

Chapter 12
The Role of Cognitive Screening for Pilot Medical Certification

Kelene A. Fercho

Introduction

Healthy cognitive functioning is critical to successfully piloting an aircraft and maintaining a safe aerospace system. Pilots operate in a cognitively demanding environment, making decisions under conditions of occupational stress not experienced by most workers. The outcome of a pilot's decisions has the potential to impact hundreds of lives; thus, it is critical that the pilot is operating at optimal cognitive capacity. This chapter focuses on the role of cognitive screening in pilot medical certification. The primary purpose of cognitive screening is to identify cognitive deficits that would make the pilot unsafe to perform their duties. The topics covered include a high-level overview of the cognitive skills required for piloting an aircraft, a discussion on computerized cognitive screening instruments, and the use of pilot normative data to interpret test results. The intent of this chapter is to provide an introductory guide for the practitioner who conducts neuropsychological evaluations of pilots for medical certification.

The Role of Cognitive Screening in Medical Certification

In the United States (US), the Federal Aviation Administration (FAA) is responsible for setting the requirements and guidance that prescribe the medical standards and medical certification procedures for civil aviation. These requirements are mandated by Title 14, Part 67 of the Code of Federal Regulations and articulated in the *Guide for Aviation Medical Examiners*. Outside of the United States, other civil aviation authorities (CAAs) set the minimum requirements for medical certification. This chapter takes the perspective of the US FAA requirements and policy, with the acknowledgment that other CAAs may have requirements and policy that are similar or different from those described here.

The FAA requires pilots to undergo a medical examination from a qualified aviation medical examiner (AME) at periodic intervals to ensure that they meet the medical standards for the class of medical certificate sought (i.e., FAA first-class, second-class, or third-class medical certificate). The FAA Flight Standards Service decides which class of medical certificate is required for certain types of flying. The FAA Office of Aerospace Medicine determines the medical requirements for each class of medical certificate. A pilot must have the appropriate class of medical certificate for the type of operation they wish to pursue. For example, pilots must hold an FAA first-class or second-class medical certificate to conduct commercial operations.

An AME is a medical doctor certified by the FAA to perform medical examinations, but they are not employed by the FAA. AMEs do not routinely screen pilots for cognitive impairment, and cognitive bedside assessments such as the Mini-Mental State Examination (MMSE; Folstein et al., 1975) may not be sensitive to detect aeromedically significant mild to moderate cognitive impairment. The AME is largely dependent on the pilot to disclose any concerns about their cognitive status during the clinical interview or through the FAA Form 8500-8 (i.e., the Application for Airman Medical Certificate or Airman Medical & Student Pilot Certificate).

Pilots are not administered a cognitive screening test as part of the physical exam process, and the FAA does not require baseline cognitive testing. An AME may refer pilots with known or suspected aeromedically significant cognitive impairment for further evaluation. In cases such as head trauma, stroke, encephalitis, multiple sclerosis, substance dependence or abuse, other suspected acquired or developmental conditions, and certain medications used for treatment, cognitive screening by a qualified psychologist or neuropsychologist with additional training in aviation-specific topics may be required by the FAA for medical certification. Examples of these aviation-specific topics include familiarity with important topics in the aviation psychology literature; occupational demands placed on pilots including those associated with various types of flight operations; and medical standards for an FAA first-class, second-class, and third-class medical certificate and the requirements to fly without a medical certificate. This book serves as a resource for many of these topics. The FAA also maintains an invitation-only Aerospace Neuropsychology website with resources for professionals with a subspecialty in aerospace neuropsychology and psychology, and there are several aviation psychology and aerospace medicine professional organizations which provide educational and professional opportunities. To learn more about aviation safety topics, the FAA Safety Team (FAASTeam) provides education and training through webinars, seminars, newsletters, and magazines that are freely available to the general public, with many of those resources available on their website.

Computer-administered cognitive screening tests are an important tool for the medical certification of pilots. These test batteries typically include several subtests to measure cognitive performance across different domains, such as memory, attention, and information processing speed. A cognitive screening test may be administered alone or as part of a battery of assessments, depending on the pilot's medical condition and the professional judgment of the psychologist or neuropsychologist. Follow-up assessment may sometimes be required either annually or bi-annually. Test results, based on user-selected normative data, are available soon after completion of the test. The virtues of such assessment methods for FAA medical certification are readily appreciable, particularly in the standardization of test administration, measurement accuracy, production of alternate forms, data management, availability on short notice, and the ability to automate scoring to determine the likelihood of impairment or change in scores across repeated testing sessions (Bauer et al., 2012). However, computer-administered cognitive screening tests are not in and of themselves diagnostic. While they may indicate the likelihood of cognitive impairment, they cannot replace a comprehensive assessment from a trained psychologist or neuropsychologist.

The results from a computer-administered cognitive screening test may indicate the risk of the pilot to fly. For example, higher scores may indicate low risk, or no greater risk than the average pilot. A borderline or impaired cognitive screening test score, along with self-report or supporting medical history, may indicate that the pilot requires a specialized assessment from a psychologist or neuropsychologist trained in aviation-specific topics. Whereas a paper-and-pencil mental status examination (e.g., MMSE) can reasonably be administered and scored in a few minutes and a computer-administered cognitive screening test may require approximately 1 hr or less, a comprehensive clinician-administered neuropsychological evaluation may take 1 day or more. This neuropsychological evaluation involves a consideration of the pilot's history, background, and present situation; qualitative observations; and quantitative scores from the administration of several assessments identified by the FAA as part of the initial or supplemental test batteries and customized for the pilot (Lezak et al., 2012). The FAA adheres to the recommendations of the American Academy of Clinical Neuropsychology on protecting neuropsychological and psychological test information, and does not publicly disclose the specific testing specifications (see Chapter 1 by Georgemiller for more discussion on this topic); this information is available on an invitation-only FAA Aerospace Neuropsychology website.

The success of a particular cognitive screening test depends on its sensitivity, specificity, and predictive value (Cullen et al., 2007). *Sensitivity* refers to the probability that a sign will be positive if the disorder is present. *Specificity* refers to the probability that a sign will be negative if the disorder is not present. *Predictive value* is the likelihood that the individual has a disorder given a positive sign. Additionally, a cognitive screening test may very well have predictive ability, but may not assess the level of cognitive functioning required to safely pilot an aircraft. For example, the MMSE is a widely administered screen for cognitive deficits, but it assesses cognition at a level far below that which is needed to safely pilot an aircraft, and thus would not be an effective instrument for FAA medical certification purposes. A cognitive screening test for medical certification should assess the perceptual, cognitive, and information processing abilities that are associated with the demanding task of piloting an aircraft. Additionally, the availability of normative data from a pilot population to interpret results is critical.

The FAA periodically reviews and updates its policy for cognitive screening to ensure that guidance is informed by the best current scientific knowledge. As one example, the FAA selective serotonin reuptake inhibitor (SSRI) program (2010) allowed pilots diagnosed with certain mental health conditions (e.g., depression) to fly while taking one of four approved SSRI medications. Pilots issued an FAA first-class or second-class medical certificate were required to take a computer-administered cognitive screening test annually; pilots issued an FAA third-class medical certificate were required to take a cognitive screening test every 2 years. A scientific review of 12 years of FAA SSRI data supported an update to the SSRI specifications. Starting in 2022, cognitive screening for SSRI renewal was eliminated except when clinically indicated on a case-by-case basis (see Chapter 22 by Norris et al. for more details on this research). Aerospace psychologists and neuropsychologists should regularly review the neuropsychology evaluation specifications provided by the FAA.

Occupational Stress Experienced by Aviation Pilots

Not only are the in-flight tasks associated with aviating cognitively demanding, pilots may experience additional psychological, physiological, and environmental stressors associated with job demands. For example, airline or corporate pilots may experience sleep or circadian rhythm disruption that accompanies multiple time-zone changes (Caldwell, 2005). Pilots flying multiple short-haul flights in a day may experience increased fatigue as the number of sectors flown increases (Powell et al., 2007). A recent large survey of commercial airline pilots suggested that 64 % of pilot respondents believed that occupational stress affects their performance, and the top four sources of work-related stress were (1) working irregular hours, (2) working antisocial hours, (3) divergence in values between pilots and management, and (4) working long duty hours (Cahill et al., 2021). The well-being issues suffered due to occupational stress included sleep difficulty, musculoskeletal symptoms, digestive symptoms, respiratory symptoms, cardiovascular symptoms, marital discord, loneliness, and psychological distress. Pilots flying other types of commercial aviation operations may also experience significant occupational stressors. For example, helicopter air ambulance and helicopter search and rescue pilots, in particular, operate in dynamic environments that require them to actively manage risks and make operational decisions *after* the flight has commenced. These pilots may be at an increased risk of encountering obstructions (e.g., physical structures such as towers or even moving vehicles) and stressors such as managing decision-making under a perceived need for urgency while considering patient outcomes (Nix et al., 2014). It is clear that across various commercial aviation operations, there are unique and serious occupational stressors with which the pilot must contend. Safe flight operations are dependent on the pilot's ability to anticipate, analyze, and mitigate risks during the flight – skills that require intact cognitive functioning.

Healthy cognitive functioning is important in general aviation (GA) as well, which includes all civil non-air carrier operations. Historically GA has had a lower safety record than commercial air carrier operations, with some estimates suggesting that GA accounts for more than 80 % of all civil aviation fatalities (Boyd & Stolzer, 2016). GA pilots are typically required to meet less stringent training requirements to operate an aircraft, and the aircraft that they operate may have fewer safety features (e.g., advanced alerting systems to assist the pilot with troubleshooting problems, real-time images of the weather). An analysis of 40,000 GA accidents and incidents suggested that GA pilots older than 60 were more likely to be involved in an accident caused by human error compared with GA pilots younger than 60 years of age; however, there were no differences between younger pilots and older pilots up to age 60 (Bazargan & Guzhva, 2011). Similar results have been observed in air carrier accident rates. For example, in an analysis of 558 air carrier accidents involving pilots aged 25–59 years, pilot error (e.g., inattentiveness, flawed decisions, mishandled aircraft kinetics, poor crew coordination) was identified as a factor in 35 % of accidents (Li et al., 2006). Again, the prevalence and pattern of these errors did not vary with pilot age. These findings suggest that pilot experience, training, and certification standards may offer some protection against age-related increases in human error, at least up to a certain age. Regardless, the average age of the GA pilot is slowly increasing (Boyd, 2018), and it is well accepted that the incidence of some neurological and medical conditions that may impair cognitive function increases with age (Hirtz et al., 2007). It is reasonable to assume that older pilots may require cognitive assessment, on average, more often than their younger counterparts. Unlike commercial air carrier operations that mandate a retirement age of 65 years, there is no such regulation for GA, suggesting that if this trend continues, the need for cognitive screening for GA pilots is likely to increase in the future.

Although the primary focus of this chapter is on cognitive screening for pilots, it is important to note that ATCSs also have an important role in maintaining the safety of the airspace system, and just like for pilots, the cost of human error may result in an accident and loss of life. ATCSs manage the flow of aircraft into and out of the airport airspace, guide pilots during takeoff and landing, and monitor aircraft as they travel through the skies while also promoting efficiency of air traffic flow. This is a demanding and stressful career, where most tasks are performed in a dynamic environment under time pressure. Like piloting an aircraft, managing airspace requires a variety of cognitive skills (e.g., working memory, attention), and working under pressure and stress may negatively affect cognitive performance.

Thus, it is critical that only ATCSs who are cognitively intact perform these duties. Like pilots, ATCSs with known or suspected aeromedically significant cognitive impairment may be referred for further evaluation to determine return to duty status.

Cognitive Skills Associated With Piloting an Aircraft

In an operational world, such as aviation, decision errors can be catastrophic. For example, the National Transportation Safety Board (NTSB) reviewed 37 major airline accidents where flight crew behavior was a causal factor, and found that approximately 67 % of accidents were associated with pilot decision error (NTSB, 1994). The aviation industry has implemented elaborate safeguards against errors, such as written standard operating procedures, checklists, requirements for the captain and first officer to cross-check each other's actions, complying with sterile flight deck rules, conducting stabilized approaches, and mandatory pilot training and skills checking. Regardless, decision errors can occur even during well-practiced procedures. This is especially true if the pilot is not operating at maximum cognitive capacity and if they are overloaded in a task-saturated environment. Take, for example, a single pilot in a light single-engine aircraft starting their descent to land at an unfamiliar airfield. The weather is rapidly deteriorating, and the pilot assesses that the aircraft does not have an adequate amount of fuel to safely divert to an alternate airport. The pressure to land is now increased, at a time when they are already overloaded from monitoring the changing weather conditions, tracking the aircraft's instruments along the flight path, and communicating on the radio with air traffic control. The pilot forgets to lower the landing gear, and only notices when the propeller and underside of the aircraft strike the runway during a belly landing. In this scenario, we see that the pilot forgot the critically important task of lowering the landing gear during a time when they were experiencing high workload due to operating at an unfamiliar airport in poor weather conditions, a diminishing supply of fuel, and the typical high task saturation associated with approach and landing. During high workload tasks, pilots are especially vulnerable to errors if they are distracted, experience a disruption, or multitasking breaks down.

Piloting a modern aircraft is a demanding task that requires a variety of cognitive skills to support safe flight operations. The pilot generally has four separate classes of tasks to perform, which include aviating, navigating, communicating (e.g., crew coordination and with air traffic control), and system management (e.g., managing fuel, cabin pressure, avionics; Wickens, 2002). Often, flight tasks are performed under time pressure and require the performance of critically timed, sequential operations. Workload varies during the flight and is highest during critical phases of flight such as taxi, take-off and initial climb, approach and landing; during emergency or non-normal operations; or in low visibility or bad weather. While perceptual-motor skills, such as making a millisecond-level response to avoid a mid-air collision, are important, the physical demands of flying a modern aircraft have decreased with advances in technology. Banich et al. (1989) identified six categories of cognitive skills that underlie flight abilities, including perceptual and motor abilities, spatial abilities, working memory, attentional performance, processing flexibility, and planning or sequencing abilities. Table 12.1 includes examples of piloting tasks and real-world scenarios for each of these cognitive skills as well as for short-term memory and long-term memory.

Table 12.1. Cognitive skills, piloting tasks, and real-world scenarios associated with piloting an aircraft

Cognitive skill	Piloting task examples	Real-world piloting scenario
Perceptual and motor abilities	• Two-hand coordination • Rudder or anti-torque pedal control • Manipulation of flight deck display controls and flight controls • Kinesthetic sensitivity • Proprioception • Sensorimotor performance • Perceiving auditory, visual, olfactory, or tactile stimuli • Accurate and timely reactions or responses to alerts, failures, emergencies, or non-normal conditions	Perceiving the red fire light on a flight deck display requires a checklist that may include, in specific order, steps such as turning off the autothrottle, reducing the affected thrust lever to idle, pulling the fire handle of the affected engine, discharging the first fire bottle, waiting 30 s, discharging the second fire bottle if the conditions persist, perceiving indications on the status of the fire light.
Spatial abilities	• Taxiing • Air navigation • Orienting to the runway of intended landing • Monitoring and controlling pitch, roll, yaw, altitude, lateral deviation from the flight path, and position along the flight path • Use of approach and airfield diagrams, airfield markings (e.g., hold short lines, taxi lines, approach lighting systems, taxi/runway inset lighting systems) • Using approach plate profile descriptions to create a mental model of the situation (e.g., to support steep approaches, offset final approaches, circling approaches) • Understanding ownship and traffic positions at non-towered airports that require self-integration into the airfield pattern	Maintaining spatial awareness of the aircraft's position throughout a low-visibility nighttime approach and landing to a non-towered airfield in a terrain challenged environment.
Working memory	• Listening to and immediately repeating back air traffic control clearances • Recovery from interruptions when completing a checklist • Mental math tasks such as calculating temperature conversions, crosswind components, time–speed–distance problems, reciprocal headings, and visual descent points • Remembering the approach speeds for the current aircraft weight, the approach fix altitudes, the minimum decision altitude/height, and the missed approach procedures	Air traffic control instruction: "November 1, descend and maintain 4,000'. Upon reaching 4,000' reduce speed to 200 knots." Pilot response: "Descend and maintain 4,000'. At 4,000', slow to 200 knots. November 1."

Table 12.1. continued

Cognitive skill	Piloting task examples	Real-world piloting scenario
Short-term memory	• Retaining information transmitted from air traffic control and acting on it after a short time delay of up to 30 s	Air traffic control instruction: "November 1, follow the Boeing 737, cross runway two seven-right at taxiway whiskey, hold short of runway two-seven left."
Long-term memory	• Memory for how aircraft systems work, including the effects of failures on other aircraft systems • Memory for appropriate procedures to follow, including emergency memory items • Meaning of display symbology	Understanding the meaning of the flight director and flight path vector symbology on a head-up display.
Attentional performance	• Directing visual attention toward the correct flight deck instrument at the correct time to obtain the required information • Maintaining focus on crucial information sources in the presence of distractions and noise • Dividing attention between communications with air traffic control and other piloting tasks • Making timely shifts of attention to aircraft alerts • Maintaining visibility and cloud clearance requirements while programming the avionics system	After a long period of flying the pilot has to stay awake, maintain focus on the tasks at hand (navigation, aircraft control, approach procedures; focused attention), do these tasks on extremely long flights (sustained attention) while not being distracted by irrelevant activities like reading non-flight documents, talking to the jumpseater, day dreaming, unnecessary discussions with flight attendants (selective attention), conducting instrument crosscheck especially during an approach (alternating attention), operating switches, controlling the aircraft with yoke and pedals, using the thrust levers at the same time (divided attention).
Processing flexibility	• Starting an approach to one runway, but because of shifting winds, air traffic control assigns a different runway • Air traffic control assigns a new departure procedure during taxi to the runway for departure • Changing route of flight during cruise due to airspace restrictions	In response to air traffic control advisement of a ground navigation aid failure, the pilot makes the decision to continue or to divert to an alternate airfield based on the remaining ground navigation aids.
Planning or sequencing abilities	• Actions required to transition from cruise to landing • Actions required to transition from taxi to cruise • Programming the flight management system for the cleared routing • Accomplishing checklists in a specified order at a specified time • Sequencing actions based on severity and systematic importance	Execution of instrument approach procedures requiring programming the avionics for the approach, accomplishing the checklists at specific times, maintaining altitudes and airspeeds at specific locations, making decisions to land at a specific location (e.g., decision altitude), properly configuring the aircraft for landing, landing and exiting the runway.

The results of task analyses, interviews with subject-matter experts, accident and incident investigations, and human-in-the-loop experiments have identified cognitive abilities critical to the task of piloting an aircraft. For example, one study that included a simulated flight task identified general cognitive speed and working memory efficiency as accounting for approximately 33 % of the variance of flight performance (Taylor et al., 2000). Others have found similar results. Causse et al. (2011) found that working memory, psychomotor reaction time, and reasoning were associated with skilled flight performance. Research from Van Benthem and Herdman (2016) identified cognitive speed, working memory, visual attention, and cognitive flexibility as the skills accounting for the most variance of flight performance in a simulated flight task. In sum, results from these flight simulator experiments suggest that there are several cognitive skills that underlie the task of piloting an aircraft. However, it is important to note that in real-world operations, flight performance may be affected by factors other than cognitive skills, including qualities of the aircraft itself, operational conditions, pilot training and expertise, and transient changes in the pilot's emotional state such as feelings of stress, fear, fatigue, arousal, motivation, anxiety, or boredom.

Other aviation psychology research has focused on "higher-level cognitive abilities," such as those related to complex decision-making, managing workload during critical phases of flight, or maintaining situation awareness, as a few examples. In particular, the ability to maintain situation awareness has been identified as a critical part of a pilot's responsibilities, and problems with situation awareness have been associated with the increased likelihood of human error and accidents. Endsley (1999) described situation awareness as a three-stage construct consisting of *perceiving* critical elements in the environment, *comprehending* what the elements mean when integrated together in relation to the pilot's goals, and *projecting* into the future to decide on the most favorable course of action with sufficient time to act – all the while keeping in mind that this is a dynamic, constantly changing environment. Thus, situation awareness can be considered a mental model of the flight environment, although others have provided alternative definitions. For example, situation awareness has been described as a higher-order attention management system (O'Hare, 1997) or used to refer to the ability to extract, integrate, assess, and act upon task-relevant information by coordinating multiple cognitive abilities (e.g., working memory, attention) central to complex dynamic tasks (Companion et al., 1990). In any case, there is some agreement on the cognitive processes and activities that underlie the attainment and maintenance of situation awareness. These cognitive skills include working memory, short-term memory, long-term memory, attention (divided and focused), perceptual speed, pattern-matching ability, cognitive flexibility (e.g., time-sharing between different cognitive processes), and mental simulation (Endsley, 1995; Goettl, 1997).

Maintaining situation awareness in a dynamic, rapidly evolving environment means that the pilot has rapid access to an accurate mental model of this changing environment that is more comprehensive and more durable than that which can be held within the limited capacity and duration of working memory. A pilot with good situation awareness will respond rapidly and appropriately to an unexpected event, because they maintain spatial awareness of the three-dimensional space and can rapidly access information from working memory, short-term memory, and long-term memory. In aviation psychology research, situation awareness is typically measured with a postexperiment subjective assessment or by periodically prompting the participant with probe questions during task completion (e.g., "How far are you from the destination airport?"). The Wondrous Original Method for Basic Awareness Testing (WOMBAT) test is a computer-based research instrument designed to assess situation awareness. It provides a multitasking environment consisting of a primary and ongoing psychomotor task (dual tracking), along with three secondary tasks, including a spatial processing task (three-dimensional rotation), skilled perception task (quadrant location), and a working memory task (two-back serial digit cancelling). The WOMBAT is not a test battery, but rather a program that attempts to create a complex operational environment that requires attention to be allocated to multiple sources of information and requires the user to select among multiple response options. Performance on the WOMBAT test has been shown to be predictive of some metrics of skilled pilot performance. For example, higher WOMBAT scores were associated with reduced time to solo flight, achieving flight licenses, and some early ratings of performance by flight instructors (Caponecchia et al., 2018). Other research has also demonstrated that the ability to time-share or to switch attention between multiple tasks or attention channels may be important for safe flight operations and is related to skilled flight performance (Damos, 1993; Endsley & Bolstad, 1994; O'Hare, 1997). In sum, in multitasking, the performance of two tasks simultaneously (dual-tasking) and repeatedly shifting attention between two tasks (task-switching) are both critical skills for maintaining situation awareness and piloting an aircraft.

Prospective memory is an emerging area of focus in aviation psychology, and failures in prospective memory have been identified as a contributing factor in aviation accident and incident reports (Dismukes & Nowinski, 2006). Failures in prospective memory include tasks such as forgetting to lower landing gear before landing, failing to set or reset the altimeter, or forgetting to monitor altitude for the appropriate moment to level-off, resulting in an altitude bust. Prospective memory refers to remembering to do something at a particular moment in the future or the timely execution of a previously formed intention (Brandimonte et al., 1996). Prospective memory appears to be related to the cognitive skills of attention and memory. Both prospective and retrospective memory involve retrieval from memory, although prospective memory requires retrieval at a specific point of time in the future when an action is to be performed. In aviation, errors in prospective memory may occur when the pilot is asked to perform a habitual task out of sequence, during emergency or non-normal conditions, or when asked to perform a task at a later time (e.g., to report to air traffic control passing through 10,000 ft when the aircraft is at 15,000 ft). An examination of aviation incidents in the NASA Aviation Safety Reporting System database suggested that 74 out of 75 reports associated with memory errors were prospective memory (as opposed to retrospective memory) failures (Nowinski et al., 2003). The authors suggested that retrospective memory errors were so low because pilots train and practice the same procedures to the point of overlearning, and flight deck design and documents are designed to support retrospective memory.

In sum, aeronautical decision-making depends on a variety of cognitive skills, many of which fall under the label of executive functions. Executive functions are considered a multidimensional construct comprising a number of distinct processes, including inhibitory control or response inhibition, working memory, cognitive flexibility (i.e., multitasking, task switching, or dual-task performance), planning, and attention (Baggetta & Alexander, 2016). Executive function is often measured through test batteries (i.e., Delis–Kaplan Executive Function System; Delis et al., 2001), or through individual tasks such as the Stroop task, digit span task, go/no-go task, trail making test, and n-back tasks. Together, this suggests that there are a variety of cognitive skills that underlie piloting tasks, and that an effective instrument for aerospace medicine should target a variety of those skills.

Selection of a Cognitive Screening Test Battery

The FAA provides specified neuropsychology test batteries to use when an evaluation is requested for medical certification for pilot applicants who report a history of attention-deficit/hyperactivity disorder (ADHD), human immunodeficiency virus (HIV), SSRI use, Human Intervention Motivational Study (HIMS) substance use and dependence, neuropsychological disorder, or potential neurocognitive impairment. Each of these testing specifications requires the administration of a cognitive screening test battery. Because of the demanding requirements of piloting an aircraft, cognitive screening test batteries should be both relevant to the level of difficulty of the tasks performed by pilots and sensitive to detect aeromedically significant cognitive impairment. Piloting an aircraft demands a high level of performance across a variety of cognitive skills, and a cognitive screening test should be comprehensive and assess a range of cognitive abilities. It is important to remember that the validity of a test is not due to its resemblance to the task of piloting an aircraft, but rather because the test taps into an ability that underlies those skills required by pilots.

An important criterion for a cognitive screening test is the breadth of cognitive domains covered. A cognitive test battery needs to cover a wide range of cognitive domains but should also meet additional requirements such as availability of pilot normative data for test interpretation. Ideally, human factors considerations and usability factors related to test administration should be a consideration, as these factors may impact test results. Factors that should be considered include the adequacy of test administrator training, intuitiveness of the user interface including the on-screen test instructions, availability of a test manual and other technical support documents, and software compatibility with different operating systems. Factors that contribute to hardware usability may include the mode of test administration, such as handheld device, tablet, or computer; and the peripheral devices used to input responses, such as a keyboard, mouse, stylus pen, or touchscreen. Tests administered on a tablet or handheld device may affect the consistency of test administration, as it is more difficult to standardize the testing environment across pilots. In general, a computer setup with the participant sitting at a desk or table often results in more accurate and reliable measurements. User interfaces that accept touch may initially appear as an attractive, intuitive option for a computer-naïve user. However, touchscreens may introduce undesirable variability for tests that record reaction or response times, due to the added amount of time it takes to move the entire hand to the screen. There is also the risk that the touchscreen may fail to register the user's response on the first touch, requiring another control input. This added variability could have an undesirable effect on the interpretation of any tests with a response time component, and a simple wired mouse may provide more accurate and reliable measurements. Other factors that should be considered include the length of test administration (preferably less than one hour); millisecond precision timing accuracy; repeatability of testing; and demonstrated psychometric foundations. The format of the test report may also contribute to the consistency and accuracy of interpreting the test results.

The FAA sponsored the development of a cognitive screening test battery, CogScreen–Aeromedical Edition (AE), for medical certification in the early 1990s (Kay, 1995). This test was developed in response to a need for an instrument that could detect subtle changes in cognitive function that could affect aviation safety; it assesses a wide range of cognitive skills such as visual scanning and sequencing, attribute identification, visual perception and spatial processing, motor coordination, reaction time, working memory, tracking, and calculation skills. CogScreen-AE also has a large set of pilot normative data to support test interpretation. Since the early 1990s, there has been a proliferation of computerized cognitive screening test batteries, many of which include subtests that assess cognitive domains relevant to piloting an aircraft. The FAA Office of Aerospace Medicine Policy Division maintains a list of neuropsychology testing specifications and may be consulted for information on computerized cognitive screening tests with available pilot normative data.

Normative Data for Interpretation of Test Results

After a test has been administered and scored, the scores are interpreted in reference to another source of data. This other source of data is typically either an individual's baseline or earlier test score, or a normative dataset. Normative data represent the range of performance on each subtest of a cognitive screening test battery for a neuropsychologically intact population. These data provide an empirical context for evaluating the functional strengths and weaknesses of the individual taking the test, and thus careful consideration should be given to the normative data used for interpreting the test results (Lezak et al., 2012). There are unique considerations for normative data when used for the cognitive screening of pilots for medical certification. Potential consumers of normative data should consider how closely matched the normative sample is to the pilot being tested. The normative data referenced should be limited to use with individuals whose demographic and cultural characteristics are similar to those in the normative data sample. Cultural background factors may include the timeframe when the normative data were collected, the country of origin of the population, the language, and the familiarity with the technology used for data collection, as a few examples (Casaletto & Heaton, 2017; Mitrushina et al., 2005). The larger the discrepancy between the individual being assessed and the population from which the normative data were derived, the greater the possibility that the test results will not reflect the construct it was intended to measure. Pilot medical certification (i.e., FAA first-class, second-class, or third-class medical certificate) should also be considered.

The size of the normative data is another factor that should be considered. A sample size of 50 cases is generally considered desirable (Crawford & Howell, 1998). A sample that is too small may be positively skewed, which may undermine the accuracy of the test results. A larger sample size is not necessarily better if the data are outdated or not representative of the target population. In general, more recently collected data are preferred to older sets of data. Normative data are most valid when the norms are created, and validity decreases over time due to changes in the culture of the population of interest and advancements in technology that could affect the accuracy or precision of any response-timing metrics. Details of the normative data should be readily available to the consumer, and at a minimum should include the methodology used to obtain the data; participant inclusion and exclusion criteria; a description of the hardware and software to include the software version; demographic information of the participant sample including information on medical certificate class, pilot certificates, and ratings; the methodology used for identifying and excluding outliers; and information on research ethics oversight (i.e., Institutional Review Board approval or exemption).

Conclusion

This chapter has provided a high-level overview of the role of cognitive screening for pilot medical certification, including the cognitive skills required for piloting an aircraft, and important factors to consider when selecting cognitive screening test batteries and the normative data used to support the interpretation of test results. Cognitive screening tests that tap into the skills that underlie piloting tasks may help to identify individuals who may pose a significant safety risk to the aerospace system. Cognitive screening may reveal subtle, yet aeromedically significant cognitive issues that are not readily detectible from other clinical assessments such as neuroimaging or neurological examinations. A neuropsychological assessment from a clinical psychologist or neuropsychologist with training in aviation psychology is an effective method of determining aeromedically significant cognitive deficits and different capabilities are assessed than those that can be observed during a check in a flight simulator. Cognitive screening may also enable many pilots to return to flight status as quickly as possible by providing a means for the pilot to objectively demonstrate their current level of cognitive function relative to representative pilot normative data. In sum, aerospace psychologists and neuropsychologist play an important role in pilot medical certification and in promoting a safe aerospace system.

Acknowledgments

The author would like to thank Bryan L. Watson for valuable discussions regarding cognitive skills and piloting tasks, and Dr. Judith Frazier for helpful feedback on the chapter.

References

Baggetta, P., & Alexander, P.A. (2016). Conceptualization and operationalization of executive function. *Mind, Brain, and Education, 10*(1), 10–33. https://doi.org/10.1111/mbe.12100

Banich, M.T., Stokes, A., & Elledge, V. (1989). Neuropsychological screening of aviators: A review. *Aviation, Space, and Environmental Medicine, 60*(4), 361–366.

Bazargan, M., & Guzhva, V.S. (2011). Impact of gender, age and experience of pilots on general aviation accidents. *Accident Analysis & Prevention, 43*(3), 962–970. https://doi.org/10.1016/j.aap.2010.11.023

Bauer, R.M., Iverson, G.L., Cernich, A.N., Binder, L.M., Ruff, R.M., & Naugle, R.I. (2012). Computerized neuropsychological assessment devices: Joint position paper of the American Academy of Clinical Neuropsychology and the National Academy of Neuropsychology. *Archives of Clinical Neuropsychology, 27*(3), 362–373. https://doi.org/10.1093/arclin/acs027

Boyd, D.D. (2018). General aviation accidents involving octogenarian airmen: Implications for medical evaluation. *Aerospace Medicine and Human Performance, 89*(8), 687–692. https://doi.org/10.3357/AMHP.5107.2018

Boyd, D.D., & Stolzer, A. (2016). Accident-precipitating factors for crashes in turbine-powered general aviation aircraft. *Accident Analysis & Prevention, 86*, 209–216. https://doi.org/10.1016/j.aap.2015.10.024

Brandimonte, M.A., Einstein, G.O., & McDaniel, M.A. (1996). *Prospective memory: Theory and applications.* Erlbaum.

Cahill, J., Cullen, P., Anwer, S., Wilson, S., & Gaynor, K. (2021). Pilot work related stress (WRS), effects on wellbeing and mental health, and coping methods. *The International Journal of Aerospace Psychology, 31*(2), 87–109. https://doi.org/10.1080/24721840.2020.1858714

Caldwell, J.A. (2005). Fatigue in aviation. *Travel Medicine and Infectious Disease, 3*(2), 85–96. https://doi.org/10.1016/j.tmaid.2004.07.008

Caponecchia, C., Zheng, W.Y., & Regan, M.A. (2018). Selecting trainee pilots: Predictive validity of the WOMBAT situational awareness pilot selection test. *Applied Ergonomics, 73*, 100–107. https://doi.org/10.1016/j.apergo.2018.06.004

Casaletto, K.B., & Heaton, R.K. (2017). Neuropsychological assessment: Past and future. *Journal of the International Neuropsychological Society, 23*(9–10), 778. https://doi.org/10.1017/S1355617717001060

Causse, M., Dehais, F., & Pastor, J. (2011). Executive functions and pilot characteristics predict flight simulator performance in general aviation pilots. *The International Journal of Aviation Psychology, 21*(3), 217–234. https://doi.org/10.1080/10508414.2011.582441

Companion, M.A., Corso, G.M., Kass, S.J., & Herschler, D.A. (1990). *Situational awareness: An analysis and preliminary model of the cognitive process (IST-TR-89-5)*. University of Central Florida, Institute for Simulation and Training.

Crawford, J.R., & Howell, D.C. (1998). Comparing an individual's test score against norms derived from small samples. *The Clinical Neuropsychologist, 12*(4), 482–486. https://doi.org/10.1076/clin.12.4.482.7241

Cullen, B., O'Neill, B., Evans, J.J., Coen, R.F., & Lawlor, B.A. (2007). A review of screening tests for cognitive impairment. *Journal of Neurology, Neurosurgery & Psychiatry, 78*(8), 790–799. https://doi.org/10.1136/jnnp.2006.095414

Damos, D.L. (1993). Using meta-analysis to compare the predictive validity of single-and multiple-task measures to flight performance. *Human Factors, 35*(4), 615–628. https://doi.org/10.1177/001872089303500403

Delis, D.C., Kaplan, E., & Kramer, J.H. (2001). *Delis-Kaplan executive function system (D-KEFS)*. Psychological Corporation.

Dismukes, K., & Nowinski, J. (2006). Prospective memory, concurrent task management, and pilot error. In A. Kramer, D. Wiegmann, & A. Kirlik (Eds.), *Attention: From theory to practice* (pp. 225–236). Oxford University Press. https://doi.org/10.1093/acprof:oso/9780195305722.003.0016

Endsley, M.R. (1995). Toward a theory of situation awareness in dynamic systems. *Human Factors, 37*(1), 32–64. https://doi.org/10.1518/001872095779049499

Endsley, M.R. (1999). Situation awareness in aviation systems. In D.J. Garland, J.A. Wise, & V.D. Hopkins (Eds.). *Handbook of aviation human factors* (pp. 257–276). Lawrence Erlbaum Associates.

Endsley, M.R., & Bolstad, C.A. (1994). Individual differences in pilot situation awareness. *The International Journal of Aviation Psychology, 4*(3), 241–264. https://doi.org/10.1207/s15327108ijap0403_3

Folstein, M.F., Folstein, S.E., & McHugh, P.R. (1975). "Mini-mental state": A practical method for grading the cognitive state of patients for the clinician. *Journal of Psychiatric Research, 12*(3), 189–198. https://doi.org/10.1016/0022-3956(75)90026-6

Goettl, B.P. (1997). Situation awareness and executive control processes: Quot homines, tot sententiae. *Proceedings of the Human Factors and Ergonomics Society, 1*, 61. https://doi.org/10.1177/107118139704100115

Hirtz, D., Thurman, D.J., Gwinn-Hardy, K., Mohamed, M., Chaudhuri, A.R., & Zalutsky, R. (2007). How common are the "common" neurologic disorders? *Neurology, 68*(5), 326–337. https://doi.org/10.1212/01.wnl.0000252807.38124.a3

Kay, G.G. (1995). *CogScreen Aeromedical edition professional manual.* Psychological Assessment Resources.

Lezak, M.D., Howieson, D.B., Bigler, E.D., & Tranel, D. (2012). *Neuropsychological assessment*. Oxford University Press.

Li, G., Grabowski, J.G., Baker, S.P., & Rebok, G.W. (2006). Pilot error in air carrier accidents: Does age matter? *Aviation, Space, and Environmental Medicine, 77*(7), 737–741.

Mitrushina, M., Boone, K.B., Razani, J., & D'Elia, L.F. (2005). *Handbook of normative data for neuropsychological assessment*. Oxford University Press.

National Transportation Safety Board. (1994). *A review of flightcrew-involved, major accidents of US air carriers, 1978 through 1990. Safety Study Report No. PB94-97001.*

Nix, S., Buckner, S., & Cercone, R. (2014). A review of risk analysis and helicopter air ambulance accidents. *Air Medical Journal, 33*(5), 218–221. https://doi.org/10.1016/j.amj.2014.06.011

Nowinski, J.L., Holbrook, J.B., & Dismukes, R.K. (2003). Human memory and cockpit operations: An ASRS study. *Proceedings of the 12th International Symposium on Aviation Psychology*, 888–893.

O'Hare, D. (1997). Cognitive ability determinants of elite pilot performance. *Human Factors, 39*(4), 540–552. https://doi.org/10.1518/001872097778668004

Powell, D., Spencer, M.B., Holland, D., Broadbent, E., & Petrie, K.J. (2007). Pilot fatigue in short-haul operations: Effects of number of sectors, duty length, and time of day. *Aviation, Space, and Environmental Medicine, 78*(7), 698–701.

Taylor, J.L., O'Hara, R., Mumenthaler, M.S., & Yesavage, J.A. (2000). Relationship of CogScreen-AE to flight simulator performance and pilot age. *Aviation Space and Environmental Medicine, 71*(4), 373–80.

Van Benthem, K., & Herdman, C.M. (2016). Cognitive factors mediate the relation between age and flight path maintenance in general aviation. *Aviation Psychology and Applied Human Factors, 6*(2), 81–90. https://doi.org/10.1027/2192-0923/a000102

Wickens, C.D. (2002). Situation awareness and workload in aviation. *Current Directions in Psychological Science, 11*(4), 128–133. https://doi.org/10.1111/1467-8721.00184

Chapter 13
The Cognitive Challenges of Aviation

Exploring the Demands on Pilots and Air Traffic Controllers

Nadine Belser and Viktor Oubald

Introduction

Safety in aviation is more than a theoretical concept. It is a fundamental characteristic of the entire industry, encompassing the preservation of people's lives and the safe and efficient operation of this vital transport sector. Psychology plays a pivotal role in maintaining and increasing safety and economy. The rationale behind this lies in recognizing that people have to collaborate with one another and operate machines alone or together in order to minimize errors that could lead to grave consequences.

The importance of psychological assessments is also reflected in their increased consideration on the regulatory side. With EASA Regulation CAT.GEN.MPA.175(b) (European Union Aviation Safety Agency [EASA], 2023), for the first time a mandatory rule came into force in 2021 requiring the psychological assessment of cognitive and noncognitive characteristics and abilities in pilots before they take up their duties in an airline. It identifies the following areas:

- Cognitive abilities
- Personality traits
- Operational and professional competencies
- Social competences in accordance with crew resource management principles

The difficulty lies in the implementation of regulations and compliance with professional psychological standards. The new regulation reflects the pivotal role of cognitive abilities in aviation.

Purpose and Scope of the Chapter

Psychological fitness and medical fitness ensure that only those people work in this industry who can withstand the requirements permanently. The chapter addresses two essential roles in aviation: pilots and air traffic controllers (ATCOs). The majority of the work of these professions comprises cognition (Broach, 2013; Goeters et al., 2004; Martins, 2016; Terelak & Pinska, 2010), and cognition determines to a huge extent the performance in the human-machine interaction in these roles. Accordingly, this chapter places special focus on the area of mental performance. First, we elaborate on what cognitive abilities are and how the cognitive requirements of pilots and ATCOs can be assessed. Then, these specific requirements are outlined separately for pilots and ATCOs. Additionally, noncognitive factors that can affect cognitive performance in the context of aviation are discussed.

Understanding Cognitive Abilities in Aviation

In this chapter, we use a definition of abilities based on Carroll (1993), as a quality of individuals that varies between individuals and describes the liminal level of task difficulty under which a person can successfully perform the task given perfect conditions. Furthermore, even though ability can be influenced by experience and predisposition, it is an inherent quality.

Accordingly, cognitive abilities are innate mental processes or mental functions a person possesses, and these can be shaped by education and experiences. Mental functions allow a person to perform mental tasks, such as perceiving, processing, and storing information. Cognitive abilities contribute to everyday functioning, like recalling items from the grocery shopping list left behind, but also to more complex functions like job-related tasks. Examples of mental functions are attention, memory, decision-making, reasoning, and problem-solving (e.g., Deary et al., 2010).

When talking about specific cognitive abilities, it is important to use the appropriate terms. In the field of cognitive psychology, the terms used in the Cattell–Horn–Carroll (CHC) model are widely accepted and frequently used (McGrew, 2005; Mouratille et al., 2022). However, in the field of aviation psychology the terms used to describe cognitive abilities are usually more diverse (Mouratille et al., 2022), and at times they differ from the taxonomy of the CHC model. For the purpose of this chapter, we will use terms that are widely used in aviation psychology.

There are numerous cognitive abilities, but only a specific subset is relevant for the job demands of operative aviation personnel. However, how does one determine which specific cognitive dimensions are required by pilots and ATCOs? Typical methods include job requirement and task requirement analyses (e.g., Goeters et al., 2004; Seamster et al., 1993; Wium & Eaglestone, 2022) and validation studies (King et al., 2013; Mouratille et al., 2022; Pecena et al., 2013).

Firstly, job and task requirement analyses examine which cognitive dimensions are considered essential for job performance. Then, this information is used to design personnel selection procedures accordingly; that is, it is ensured that the procedures measure the relevant cognitive abilities. Later on, validation studies evaluate whether the cognitive abilities assessed actually contribute to performance in training and on the job. Beyond job requirement analyses and validation studies, there are other methods for examining which cognitive abilities are associated with a specific job or job-related task. Some examples are studies that compare differences in cognitive ability between aviation experts and novices (Bruder & Hasse, 2019; Rantanen & Nunes, 2005), studies that compare differences in cognition between aviation experts with and without error history (e.g., Hedayati et al., 2021), or studies that analyze the cognitive causes of errors in aviation (Pape & Wiegman, 2001; Shorrock, 2005, 2007).

In the following, we outline the cognitive abilities found essential for pilots or ATCOs by experts in the field. Additionally, we describe noncognitive factors that can affect cognitive performance in the context of aviation.

Cognitive Abilities That Predict Pilot Performance

The job of commercial aviation pilots is teamwork in a demanding environment. To meet the requirements, a distinctive cognitive performance is necessary, which must be provided as part of a team (Oubaid et al., 2012). Several studies have been carried out to identify the pilot's characteristics for civil (e.g., Maschke & Goeters, 1999) and military aviation (Gnan et al., 1995). A common problem with job requirements analysis is the small number of participants. For example, a minimum size of eight participants is usually set or recommended in relevant procedures, but this size is far too low. Another weak point of most job requirement analyses is their low representativeness because, for example, only certain professionals are surveyed. Most of the surveys use questionnaire methods with weak psychometric qualities.

For this reason, a large, representative study was carried out in 2012, with pilots of various aircraft types (Oubaid & Graefe zu Baringdorf, 2014). In that study, 230 pilots of a large age distribution (covering the full age distribution of airline instructors in the captain's position, ranging from 30 to 64 years, $M = 46{,}85$ and $SD = 7.50$ years) were surveyed with an extended version of the Fleishman Job Analysis Survey (Fleishman & Reilly, 1992), from different aircraft on short-haul or long-haul flights. In order to further secure the results, only training pilots with a higher level of knowledge about the necessary requirements, compared with regular airline pilots, were asked to participate. The results showed that cognitive abilities are of considerable importance from the experts' point of view: Six out of the 10 characteristics in the top-10 ranking are attributable to mental performance including psychomotor control (see Table 13.1).

Table 13.1. Top-10 ranked means and standard deviations from a job requirement analysis with 230 pilots on various aircraft

Requirements	Cognitive ability	*M*	*SD*
Self-control		6.33	.761
Spatial orientation	X	5.78	.819
Time sharing	X	5.77	.926
Dependability		5.74	.836
Perseverance		5.73	.874
Rate control	X	5.69	.854
Operational monitoring	X	5.65	.916
Resistance to premature judgment		5.49	.929
Auditory attention	X	5.42	.747
Speed of closure	X	5.41	.910

Note. Scale: 1 = required on a minimum level to 7 = required on a maximum level; mental abilities marked with "X."

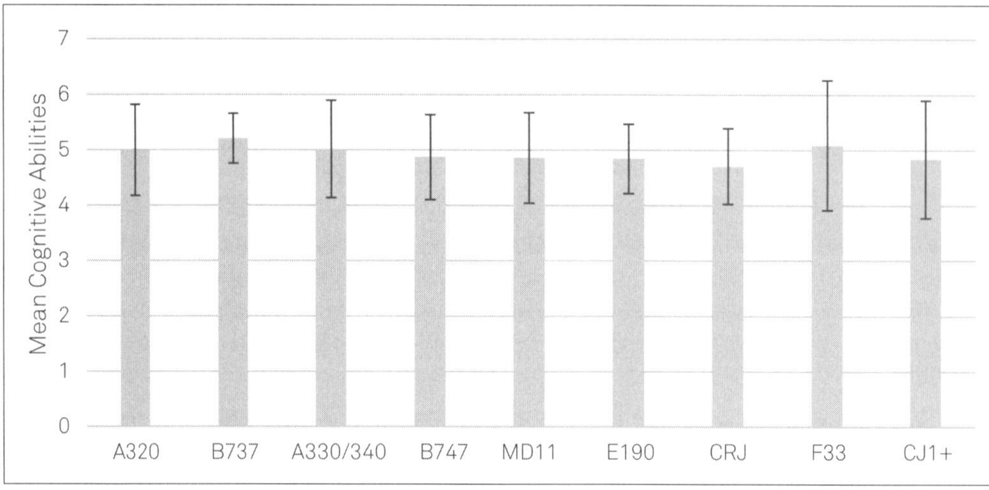

Figure 13.1. Means and standard deviations for different types of aircraft; total $N = 230$ pilots. Scale: 1 = required on a minimum level to 7 = required on a maximum level.

Furthermore, the results of this study indicated that there are some clear differences in terms of aircraft type and affiliation to a flight operation (see Figure 13.1). A one-way ANOVA revealed a nearly significant difference between B737 versus all other aircraft types, $F(9, 220) = 2.578$; $p = .008$; (see Figure 13.1 for the mean scores for all aircraft types).

The important role of mental performance also becomes clear when validation studies are conducted, with success or failure in training as a criterion. Zierke (2014) conducted a study to examine the predictive validity of cognitive and knowledge tests for flight training assessments. The predictive validity (multiple correlation) for cognitive tests was $R = .47$ (corrected) for seven cognitive tests. The entire test battery (cognitive tests and knowledge tests) showed an even higher validity of $R = .55$ (corrected). These results are consistent with the findings of Martinussen (1996), who analyzed the predictive validity of different measures on pilot performance in a meta-analysis study. According to Martinussen, the combination of cognitive and psychomotor tests had the highest predictive validity ($R = .37$) for pilot performance.

The previous sections highlighted the importance of cognitive abilities for pilots by illustrating results from job requirement analyses, validation studies, and meta-analyses.

Cognitive Abilities and ATCO Performance

When discussing the cognitive demands of the ATCO job, the concept of situational awareness arises frequently (Broach, 2013; Durso et al., 1998; Eißfeldt, 2000; Gronlund et al., 1998; Wium & Eaglestone, 2022). Endsley (1988) has described situational awareness as "the perception of the elements in the environment within a volume of time and space, the comprehension of their meaning, and the projection of their status in the near future " (p. 97) or as others described it as having "the picture" (Durso et al., 1998; p. 2). Applied to the tasks of ATCOs, this translates to perceiving all the information on aircraft and the respective airspace sector from a multitude of resources (e.g., radar, radio, flight strips, briefings) at a given time, understanding their relation to one another, and imagining the status of the respective aircraft in the near future so as to maintain safety and efficiency.

In order to gain situational awareness, ATCOs need several specific cognitive abilities, or in other words situational awareness is a product of several distinct cognitive abilities. For instance, in order to perceive the information, ATCOs need the abilities of precise and fast visual and acoustical perception as well as (sustained) attention. To understand the relation of the information and project future outcomes, working memory and visuospatial processing are needed. In order to react quickly and adapt to sometimes rapidly changing information (e.g., weather conditions or emergencies), processing speed is required. Moreover, many tasks often need to be time-shared, as ATCOs usually need to monitor and separate several aircraft at the same time. Accordingly, being able to process different kinds of information at the same time (e.g., information on the radar and over the radio) and act concurrently, that is, being able to multitask, is also an important quality for ATCOs.

Exactly these cognitive abilities have been found essential for ATCOs (Broach, 2013; Eißfeldt & Heil, 2002; Hedayati et al., 2021). Accordingly, they are assessed in ATCO selection procedures (Bleckley et al., 2009; Eurocontrol, 2023; King et al., 2007; Mouratille et al., 2022; Pecena et al., 2013; Zhong et al., 2022). In the following section, these cognitive abilities and their relation to ATCO performance are outlined.

Attention comprises orientation toward sensory information and perceiving important information, detecting relevant stimuli for further in-depth processing, and allocating attention for a sustained time (Petersen & Posner, 2012; Posner & Petersen, 1990; van Schie et al., 2021). ATCOs need to be able to turn toward sensory-relevant events (e.g., aircraft on the radar), detect relevant stimuli while ignoring irrelevant information (e.g., ignoring background noise while in contact with a pilot on the radio), and hold focus and react to relevant stimuli even if they occur infrequently during a prolonged period (e.g., during night shifts). They also need to shift attention rapidly, for example, from focusing on a specific aircraft back to monitoring the entire screen. It has been shown that attentional capabilities predict air traffic control (ATC) training performance (Pecena et al., 2019). Hedayati et al. (2021) showed shat ATCOs without error history outperformed those with error history in a test of sustained attention, indicating that the ability of sustained attention is important for preventing errors. Shorrock (2007) argues that the most dominant type of ATC errors, namely, hear-back errors, are impacted by limited attentional resources. In sum, adequate attentional abilities are crucial for ATCOs both for training and on-the-job performance and for error prevention.

The cognitive ability to perceive and process information quickly and accurately is called *perceptual speed* and *processing speed* (e.g., Ackerman, 2004; Rantanen & Nunes, 2005). Sometimes, both terms are used synonymously (Mouratille et al., 2022). Being able to perceive and process information quickly and accurately is a crucial ability for ATCOs (Broach & Brecht-Clark, 1993). Most of the information in the context of ATC is either visual (e.g., radar, flight strips) or acoustic (e.g., radio, calls), and responses based on this information need to be fast and accurate. Mouratille et al. (2022) found processing speed to be a large predictor of ATCO training success. Also, Pecena et al. (2013) found processing speed to be a predictor of ATCO training performance and success. Heil (1998) argued that processing speed is among the most relevant abilities for the ATCO job and reported results indicating an age-related decline in tests assessing abilities related to processing speed. The results imply that processing speed is important for ATCO training outcomes. As processing speed seems to decline with age, adequate countermeasures are needed.

Memory is essential for situational awareness and ATCO tasks (Gronlund et al., 1998; Hedayati et al., 2021; Shorrock, 2005; Tremblay et al., 2012). When talking about memory, it is important to specify and differentiate between different kinds of memory (Baddeley, 1988), such as long-term storage and retrieval and working memory. Another differentiation is that between retrospective and prospective memory, that is, recalling information memorized in the past versus memorizing information you need to act at a certain time in the future and then recalling it at the right time (Shorrock, 2005). Long-term memory is important for ATCOs for retrieving previously learned information such as specific airspace regulations. Working memory, on the other hand, is required in the short term to maintain information on "the mental board" in order to manipulate it (Adams et al., 2018; Shorrock, 2005). An ATCO needs working memory, for example, to further elaborate information they received on the radio. Prospective memory is needed in a situation where an ATCO might not be able to act immediately. For example, giving an instruction might be delayed in order to get further information, because workload is too high or because another task is more pressing at the time. In such a situation, an ATCO needs to remember their intention to act at the right time. For all these reasons, memory performance is usually assessed during selection procedures. Furthermore, in validation studies, working memory was related positively to ATCO training performance and success (Mouratille et al., 2022; Pecena et al., 2019). Impairment of memory capacity for spatial and verbal sequential information, on the other hand, can impact ATCO performance (Tremblay et al., 2012). Also, impairment of memory, working memory, and prospective memory is related to errors in ATC (Pape & Wiegman, 2001; Shorrock, 2005).

Visuospatial processing abilities are required by ATCOs to form a mental picture of the aircraft in airspace, their trajectory, and their relation to one another in order to maintain separation and safety (D'Oliveira, 2003). In the literature regarding spatial abilities, there is great variance regarding the definition of visuospatial processing abilities, the number of different spatial abilities, and their respective label (Colom et al., 2003; D'Oliveira, 2003, 2004; Zhong et al., 2022). However, most of these views share the differentiation between visuospatial processing of static versus dynamic spatial information. In general, visuospatial processing involves forming mental pictures of visuospatial information and then manipulating this mental image, for example, by mentally rotating it. An example for static visuospatial processing might involve rotating a mental image of a figure (e.g., dice). Dynamic spatial performance on the other hand reflects mental imagery and manipulation of moving spatial information (e.g., forming a mental trajectory of moving objects). ATCOs need to translate spoken or written (e.g., information from flight strips) and two-dimensional spatial information (e.g., radar) into a mental three-dimensional model. Furthermore, this mental image of the airspace situation also needs to include dynamic information like flight speed or rate of climb/descent. Accordingly, ATCOs need good visuospatial processing abilities in order to cope with these job demands. Mouratille et al. (2022) found visuospatial processing to be a predictor of ATCO training (see also Pecena et al., 2013). Zhong et al. (2022) gave an overview of the literature regarding a positive association of spatial abilities and ATCO performance. Furthermore, they reported results indicating that spatial orientation ability was associated with conflict detection in a low-fidelity ATC tasks among young adults eligible for ATCO training. In contrast to the aforementioned studies, Brown et al. (2019) found no association between spatial abilities and ATCO training success. However, one reason might lie in the lack of common demands between the task and ATCO training (Brown et al., 2019; Zhong et al., 2022).

We have illustrated the cognitive demands ATCOs face in their job. Overall, ATCOs need appropriate cognitive abilities in attention, processing speed, memory, and visuospatial processing. Each of these cognitive abilities comprise several lower-level cognitive abilities that have been depicted briefly in light of their relevance for ATCO training and job performance.

Noncognitive Factors Relevant for Cognitive Performance in Aviation

Beyond cognitive abilities affecting ATCO and pilot job performance, there are other factors that can influence whether a person can utilize their cognitive abilities in a situation (Bongo & Seva, 2022). Accordingly, noncognitive factors can affect the training and job performance of ATCOs and pilots. Among these factors are personality traits, the impact of fatigue, the demands of workload, and the challenges of stress. This section provides a concise overview of these influential factors, examining their implications for aviation professionals. Although the scope of this chapter is pilots and ATCOs, challenges like fatigue, workload, and stress also affect other aviation professions.

Personality is defined as a person's long-lasting pattern of thoughts, feelings, and behavior, which is shaped by predisposition and environment (e.g., Bergner, 2020; Mouratille et al., 2022). The most commonly used personality model is the Big Five (McCrae & Costa, 1999) or OCEAN model, comprising five factors of personality: openness (to new experiences), conscientiousness, extraversion, agreeableness, and neuroticism. Assessment of personality is a common part of pilot and ATCO selection procedures (Chaparro et al., 2020; Dehn & Damitz, 2022; Goeters et al., 2004; Hörmann & Maschke, 1996; Mouratille et al., 2022; Pecena et al., 2013). Personality factors and performance in aviation seem related (Dehn & Damitz, 2022; Oakes et al., 2001). For example, Oakes et al. (2001) reported a link between personality and skill acquisition during ATCO training. Chaparro et al. (2020) conducted a meta-analysis on the comparison of personality profiles between pilots and the general population, between different types of pilots (commercial, military, in-training), and between male and female pilots. Among others, they reported a distinct difference in neuroticism between pilots and the general population, indicating that pilots have a comparably higher tendency toward emotional stability and calmness under stress, which is an important characteristic for pilots. They argue that these insights could be used to make selection procedures more efficient. By contrast, Mouratille et al. (2022) reported only small to nonexistent associations of personality and ATCO training outcomes in their meta-analysis. Furthermore, Dehn and Damitz (2022) implied that associations of personality and aviation training outcomes might be rather curvilinear or quadratic than linear (see, also, Oakes et al., 2001). Accordingly, the overall relationship between personality and training or on-the-job performance of ATCOs and pilots seems to be more complex. One reason for this is the self-report character of personality assessment, which might be skewed for various reasons like social desirability or a lack of introspection. The findings imply that aviation selection decisions should not be based solely on personality assessments. However, personality assessment still offers valuable insights and can be used for further exploration in psychological selection interviews (e.g., Dehn & Damitz, 2022).

The job of both pilots and ATCOs comprises a dynamic environment, challenging and time-sensitive tasks, immense responsibility, multitasking, and 24/7 work schedules. Accordingly, mental workload, stress, and fatigue play crucial roles in the performance of these core aviation professions (Avers & Johnson, 2011; Friedrich et al., 2018; Martins, 2016). The rest of this section provides a brief outline of these factors and their impact on cognition in aviation.

Fatigue can be defined as a state of reduced mental, emotional, and physical capabilities as well as reduced efficiency due to sleep deprivation, disruption of the circadian rhythm, maladaptation to shiftwork, prolonged wakefulness, and workload (Avers & Johnson, 2011; Bendak & Rashid, 2020; Caldwell et al., 2009; Johnson et al., 2017). Fatigue can have a detrimental impact on cognitive performance, including increased reaction time, decreased sustained attention, and impaired memory (Avers & Johnson, 2011; Bendak & Rashid, 2020; Caldwell et al., 2009; Fan & Smith, 2020; Krueger, 1989). Accordingly, fatigue increases the risk of errors and represents a great risk for safety in aviation. Mental workload is tied to the limited cognitive processing resources needed for tasks. States of high mental workload indicate depleted cognitive processing resources, and states of low mental workload reflect unused or free processing resources (Friedrich et al., 2018; Young et al., 2015). As indicated in the definition of high workload, cognitive processing resources in situations of task load are scarce, leading to a heightened risk for cognitive errors (Friedrich et al., 2018; Young et al., 2015). Furthermore, even low workload can increase the risk of errors in situations where relevant stimuli occur infrequently (Martins, 2016). Thus, both too high and too low levels of workload can increase the risk of safety, stressing the importance of examining what defines the optimal level of workload.

When a person's subjective capabilities and possibilities for action are lower than the objective demand in a given situation, this can lead to a physical and psychological state defined as *stress* (Bongo & Seva, 2022; Dismukes et al., 2015; Rodrigues et al., 2018). This definition of stress comprises a person's subjective perception of not being able to cope with the situation and demands at hand. Stress can impair attention, working memory, and decision-making (Dismukes et al., 2015; Martins, 2016). Research suggests an interconnection of workload, stress, and fatigue (Bongo & Seva, 2022; Friedrich et al., 2018; Martins, 2016); for example, trying to cope with a high workload situation can result in fatigue and stress (Martins, 2016).

Adequate countermeasures are needed to support the human actors in circumstances of high workload, stress, or fatigue. Various measures have been examined and introduced over the years, for example, regulations, interface and automation designs, technological support like fatigue detection, crew resource management training, schedule adjustments, and in-flight countermeasures like naps or activity breaks (Avers & Johnson, 2011; Bendak & Rashid, 2020; Caldwell et al., 2009; Martins, 2016).

Here, we have highlighted the relationship of cognitive performance with noncognitive factors such as personality, fatigue, workload, and stress and underlined the importance of considering these noncognitive factors when it comes to cognitive performance in aviation.

Conclusion

This chapter examined the role of cognitive abilities of two core aviation professions: pilots and ATCOs. The job performance in these roles is hugely impacted by cognitive abilities. Accordingly, considering cognitive abilities during selection and training of ATCOs and pilots is crucial in maintaining safety and efficiency in aviation. Regular job and task requirement analyses can ensure that the current and future demands of these professions are considered during selection and training.

The cognitive abilities important for pilots and ATCOs were outlined separately. While memory, spatial orientation, perception, and attention play a pronounced role in both professions, psychomotor skills are of significantly greater importance in the pilot profession than in ATCOs. Pilots have to permanently manipulate the flight attitude (altitude, heading, speed, bank), which involves complex eye-hand coordination. This difference is also evident in the design of the workplace: The sidestick, rudder, thrust lever, and the controls of the autopilot require permanent monitoring and input, depending on the flight condition. On the other hand, the job of ATCOs requires an even higher level of abstraction skills than that of pilots.

Additionally, noncognitive factors that can impact cognitive performance in the field of aviation were outlined. These comprise personality factors linked to training and on-the-job performance of ATCOs and pilots, fatigue, stress, and workload. The importance of considering the interplay of these noncognitive internal and external factors with cognitive performance was highlighted to provide a comprehensive perspective on human cognition in aviation.

Accordingly, beyond selecting optimally suited candidates for these core aviation professions, it is important to design technology to aid human performance, provide training to overcome challenges, adjust regulations, and offer adequate support systems to aid human cognition in order to maintain safety and efficiency in aviation.

References

Ackerman, P.L. (2004). *New Approaches to assessment and evaluation of perceptual speed abilities.* Georgia Institute of Technology. https://doi.org/10.21236/ada419862

Adams, E.J., Nguyen, A.T., & Cowan, N. (2018). Theories of working memory: Differences in definition, degree of modularity, role of attention, and purpose. *Language, Speech, and Hearing Services in Schools, 49*, 340–355. https://doi.org/10.1044/2018_LSHSS-17-0114

Avers, K., & Johnson, W.B. (2011). A review of federal aviation administration fatigue research: Transitioning scientific results to the aviation industry. *Aviation Psychology and Applied Human Factors, 1*(2), 87–98. https://doi.org/10.1027/2192-0923/a000016

Baddeley, A. (1988). Cognitive psychology and human memory. *Trends in Neuroscience, 11*(4), 176–181. https://doi.org/10.1016/0166-2236(88)90145-2

Bendak, S., & Rashid, H.S. (2020). Fatigue in aviation: A systematic review of the literature. *International Journal of Industrial Ergonomics, 76*, Article 102928. https://doi.org/10.1016/j.ergon.2020.102928

Bergner, R.M. (2020). What is personality? Two myths and a definition. *New Ideas in Psychology, 57*, Article 100759. https://doi.org/10.1016/j.newideapsych.2019.100759

Bleckley, M.K., Crutchfield, J., King, R.E., Manning, C.A., & Carretta, T.R. (2009). Selection for aviation related careers: Air traffic control in the Air Force and the FAA. In *2009 International Symposium on Aviation Psychology* (pp. 69–75). Wright State University.

Bongo, M., & Seva, S. (2022). Effect of fatigue in air traffic controllers' workload, situation awareness, and control strategy. *The International Journal of Aerospace Psychology, 32*(1), 1–23. https://doi.org/10.1080/24721840.2021.1896951

Broach, D. (2013). *Selection of the next generation of air traffic control specialists: aptitude requirements for the air traffic control tower cab in 2018* (DOT/FAA/AM-13/5). Office of Aerospace Medicine.

Broach, D., & Brecht-Clark, J. (1993). Validation of the Federal Aviation Administration Air traffic control specialist pre-training screen. *Air Traffic Control Quarterly, 1*(2), 115–133. https://doi.org/10.2514/atcq.1.2.115

Brown, N.L., Foroughi, C.K., Coyne, J.T., Sibley, C., Olson, T., & Myrick, S. (2019). Predicting attrition and performance in Navy and Marine Corps Air Traffic Control School. *Proceedings of the Human Factors and Ergonomics Annual Meeting, 63*(1), 863–867. https://doi.org/10.1177/1071181319631460

Bruder, C., & Hasse, C. (2019). Differences between experts and novices in the monitoring of automated systems. *International Journal of Industrial Ergonomics, 72*, 1–11. https://doi.org/10.1016/j.ergon.2019.03.007

Caldwell, J.A., Mallis, M.M., Caldwell, J.L., Paul, M.A., Miller, J.C., & Neri, D.F. (2009). Fatigue countermeasures in aviation. *Aviation, Space, and Environmental Medicine, 80*(1), 29–59. https://doi.org/10.3357/ASEM.2435.2009

Carroll, J.B. (1993). *Human cognitive abilities: A survey of factor-analytic studies*. Cambridge University Press. https://doi.org/10.1017/CBO9780511571312

Chaparro, M., Carroll, M., & Malmquist, S. (2020). Personality trends in the pilot population. *Collegiate Aviation Review International (CARI), 38*(2), 1–24. https://doi.org/10.22488/okstate.20.100219

Colom, R., Contreras, M.J., Shih, P.C., & Santacreu, J. (2003). The assessment of spatial ability with a single computerized test. *European Journal of Psychological Assessment, 19*(2), 92–100. https://doi.org/10.1027//1015-5759.19.2.92

Deary, I.J., Penke, L., & Johnson, W. (2010). The neuroscience of human intelligence differences. *Nature Reviews Neuroscience, 11*, 201–211. https://doi.org/10.1038/nrn2793

Dehn, D.M., & Damitz, M. (2022). Do personality traits predict training performance? *Aviation Psychology and Applied Human Factors, 12*(2), 72–83. https://doi.org/10.1027/2192-0923/a000222

Dismukes, R.K., Goldsmith, T.E., & Kochan, J.A. (2015). *Effects of acute stress on aircrew performance: Literature review and analysis of operational aspects* (NASA/TM – 2015-218930). National Aeronautics and Space Administration (NASA).

D'Oliveira, T.C. (2003). Dynamic spatial ability & ability to coordinate information: Predictive contributions of dynamic spatial ability and the ability to coordinate information for air traffic controller and pilot selection. *International Journal of Applied Aviation Studies, 3*(2), 227–241.

D'Oliveira, T.C. (2004). Dynamic spatial ability: An exploratory analysis and a confirmatory study. *The International Journal of Aviation Psychology, 14*(1), 1–38. https://doi.org/10.1207/s15327108ijap1401_2

Durso, F.T., Hackworth, C.A., Truitt, T.R., Crutchfield, J., Nikolic, D., & Manning, C.A. (1998). Situation awareness as predictor of performance for en route air traffic controllers. *Air Traffic Control Quarterly, 6*(1), 1–20. https://doi.org/10.2514/atcq.6.1.1

Eißfeldt, H. (2000, September 4–8). *Ability requirements for air traffic controllers – review and integration* [Paper presentation]. 24th EAAP Conference, Crieff Hydro, Scotland.

Eißfeldt, H., & Heil, M.C. (Eds.). (2002). *Staffing the ATM system – the selection of air traffic controllers*. Routledge. https://doi.org/10.4324/9781315242538

Endsley, M.R. (1988). Situation awareness global assessment technique (SAGAT). *Proceedings of the IEEE 1988 National Aerospace and Electronics Conference, 3*, 789–795. https://doi.org/10.1109/NAECON.1988.195097

Eurocontrol. (2023). *FEAST first European air traffic controller selection test tool*. https://feast-info.eurocontrol.int/docs/FEAST-Factsheet-Jan2023.pdf

European Union Aviation Safety Agency. (2023). *Easy access rules for air operations*. https://www.easa.europa.eu/en/document-library/easy-access-rules/online-publications/easy-access-rules-air-operations?page=1%20%20%20Revision

Fan, J., & Smith, A.P. (2020). Effects of occupational fatigue on cognitive performance of staff from a train operating company: A field study. *Frontiers in Psychology, 11*, 558520. https://doi.org/10.3389/fpsyg.2020.558520

Fleishman, E.A., & Reilly, M.E. (1992). *Handbook of human abilities: Definitions, measurements, and job task requirements*. Consulting Psychologists Press.

Friedrich, M., Biermann, M., Gontar, P., Biella, M., & Bengler, K. (2018). The influence of task load on situation awareness and control strategy in the ATC tower environment. *Cognition, Technology & Work, 20*(2), 205–217. https://doi.org/10.1007/s10111-018-0464-4

Gnan, M., Flynn, C.F., & King, R.E. (1995). *Psychological Pilot Selection in the U.S. Air Force, the Luftwaffe, and the German Aerospace Research Establishment.* https://doi.org/10.1037/e622592007-001

Goeters, K.M., Maschke, P., & Eißfeldt, H. (2004). Ability requirements in core aviation professions: Job analysis of airline pilots and air traffic controllers. In K.M. Goeters (Ed.), *Aviation psychology: Practice research* (pp. 99–119). Ashgate.

Gronlund, S.D., Ohrt, D.D., Dougherty, M.R.P., Perry, J.L., & Manning, C.A. (1998). Role of memory in air traffic control. *Journal of Experimental Psychology: Applied, 4*(3), 263–280. https://doi.org/10.1037/1076-898X.4.3.263

Hedayati, S., Sadeghi-Firoozabadi, V., Bagheri, M., Heidari, M., & Sze, N.N. (2021). Evaluating differences in cognitive functions and personality traits among air traffic controllers with and without error history. *Safety Science, 139*, 105208. https://doi.org/10.1016/j.ssci.2021.105208

Heil, M.C. (1998). *Air traffic control specialist age and cognitive test performance* (DOT/FAA/AM-98/23). Federal Aviation Administration. https://rosap.ntl.bts.gov/view/dot/40471

Hörmann, H.J., & Maschke, P. (1996). On the relation between personality and job performance of airline pilots. *The International Journal of Aviation Psychology, 6*(2), 171–178. https://doi.org/10.1207/s15327108ijap0602_4

Johnson, J.F., Barron, L.G., Carretta, T.R., & Rose, M.R. (2017). Predictive validity of spatial ability and perceptual speed tests for aviator training. *The International Journal of Aerospace Psychology, 27*(3-4), 109–120. https://doi.org/10.1080/24721840.2018.1442222

King, R.E., Manning, C.A., & Herndon, G. (2013). *Operational use of the air traffic selection and training battery* (DOT/FAA/AM-07/14). Office of Aerospace Medicine. https://www.tc.faa.gov/its/worldpac/techrpt/am07-14.pdf

King, R.E., Manning, C.A., Schroeder, D.J., Carretta, T.R., & Rathje, H. (2007). A worldwide review of selection for air traffic control personnel. *International Symposium on Aviation Psychology, 2007*, 328–332. https://corescholar.libraries.wright.edu/isap_2007/79

Krueger, G.P. (1989). Sustained work, fatigue, sleep loss and performance: A review of the issues. *Work & Stress, 3*(2), 129–141. https://doi.org/10.1080/02678378908256939

Martins, A.P.G. (2016). A review of important cognitive concepts in aviation. *Aviation Psychology and Applied Human Factors, 20*(2), 65–84. https://doi.org/10.3846/16487788.2016.1196559

Martinussen, M. (1996). Psychological measures as predictors of pilot performance: A meta-analysis. *The International Journal of Aviation Psychology, 6*(1), 1–20. https://doi.org/10.1207/s15327108ijap0601_1

Maschke, P., & Goeters, K.-M. (1999). *Anforderungen an Flugschüler in der Ab-Initio-Ausbildung im Vergleich zu aktiven Linienflugzeugführern: 14 Tabellen (Als Ms. gedr). Forschungsbericht/Deutsches Zentrum für Luft- und Raumfahrt: Vol. 1999, 16* [Requirements for student pilots in ab initio training compared to active airline pilots: 14 tables (printed as Ms.)] [Research report]. DLR, Bibliotheks- und Informationswesen.

McCrae, R.R., & Costa, P.T. (1999). A five-factor theory of personality. In L.A. Pervin & O.P. John (Eds.), *Handbook of personality: Theory and research* (2nd ed., pp. 139–153). Guilford Press.

McGrew, K.S. (2005). The Cattell-Horn-Carroll theory of cognitive abilities: Past, present, and future. In D.P. Flanagan & P.L. Harrison (Eds.), *Contemporary intellectual assessment: theories, tests, and issues* (pp. 136–181). The Guilford Press.

Mouratille, D., Amadieu, F., & Matton, N. (2022). A meta-analysis on air traffic controllers selection: cognitive and non-cognitive predictors. *Journal of Vocational Behavior, 38*, 103769. https://doi.org/10.1016/j.jvb.2022.103769

Oakes, D.W., Ferris, G.R., Martocchio, J.J., Buckley, M.R., & Broach, D. (2001). Cognitive ability and personality predictors of training program skill acquisition and job performance. *Journal of Business and Psychology, 15*(4), 523–548. https://doi.org/10.1023/A:1007805132107

Oubaid, V., Zinn, F. & Gundert, D. (2012). GAP: assessment of performance in teams - a new attempt to increase validity. In A. De Voogt & T.C. D'Oliveira (Eds.), *Mechanisms in the chain of safety: Research and operational experiences in aviation psychology* (pp. 7–17). Aldershot.

Oubaid, V. & Graefe zu Baringdorf, J. (2014). Job requirements of instructor pilots. In *Proceedings of the 31rd Conference of the European Association for Aviation Psychology* (pp. 159–164). EAAP.

Pape, A.M., & Wiegman, D.A. (2001). *Air traffic control (ATC) related accidents and incidents: A human factor analysis.* https://www.researchgate.net/publication/254002198_AIR_TRAFFIC_CONTROL_ATC_RELATED_ACCIDENTS_AND_INCIDENTS_A_HUMAN_FACTORS_ANALYSIS

Pecena, Y., Gayraud, K., & Eißfeldt, H. (2019). Aiming high: maximizing predictive validity of selection processes for air traffic controller candidates. In R. Bor, C. Eriksen, T.P. Hubbard, & R. King (Eds.), *Pilot selection: Psychological principles and practice* (pp. 355–368). Taylor & Francis Group, CRC Press. https://doi.org/10.4324/9780429492105

Pecena, Y., Keye, D., Conzelmann, K., Grasshoff, D., Maschke, P., Heintz, A., & Eißfeldt, H. (2013). Predictive validity of a selection procedure for air traffic controller trainees. *Aviation Psychology and Applied Human Factors, 3*(1), 19–27. https://doi.org/10.1027/2192-0923/a000039

Petersen, S.E., & Posner, M.I. (2012). The attention system of the human brain: 20 years after. *The Annual Review of Neuroscience, 35*, 73–89. https://doi.org/10.1146/annurev-neuro-062111-150525

Posner, M.I., & Petersen, S.E. (1990). The attention system of the human brain. *The Annual Review of Neuroscience, 13*, 25–42. https://doi.org/10.1146/annurev.ne.13.030190.000325

Rantanen, E.M., & Nunes, A. (2005). Hierarchical conflict detection in air traffic control. *The International Journal of Aviation Psychology, 15*(4), 339–362. https://doi.org/10.1207/s15327108ijap1504_3

Rodrigues, S., Paiva, J.S., Dias, D., Aleixo, M., Filipe, R.M., & Cunha, J.P.S. (2018). Cognitive impact and psychophysiological effects of stress using a biomonitoring platform. *International Journal of Environmental Research and Public Health, 15*(6), 1080. https://doi.org/10.3390/ijerph15061080

Seamster, T.L., Redding, R.E., Cannon, J.R., Ryder, J.M., & Purcell, J.A. (1993). Cognitive task analysis of expertise in air traffic control. *The International Journal of Aviation Psychology, 3*(4), 257–283. https://doi.org/10.1207/s15327108ijap0304_2

Shorrock, S.T. (2005). Errors of memory in air traffic control. *Safety Science, 43*, 571–588. https://doi.org/10.1016/j.ssci.2005.04.001

Shorrock, S.T. (2007). Errors of perception in air traffic control. *Safety Science, 45*, 890–904. https://doi.org/10.1016/j.ssci.2006.08.018

Terelak, J., & Pinska, E. (2010). Influence of the new way of pilot-controller communication "DATA LINK" for air traffic controller performance in Europe. *Journal for Perspectives of Economic Political and Social Integration: Journal for Mental Changes, 16*(1), 57–94. https://doi.org/10.2478/v10241-012-0003-9

Tremblay, S., Parmentier, F.B.R., Hodgetts, H.M., Hughes, R.W., & Jones, D.M. (2012). Disruption of verbal-spatial serial memory by extraneous air-traffic speech. *Journal of Applied Research in Memory and Cognition, 1*(2), 73–79. https://doi.org/10.1016/j.jarmac.2012.04.004

van Schie, M.K.M., Lammers, G.J., Fronczek, R., Middelkoop, H.A.M., & van Dijk, J.G. (2021). Vigilance: Discussion of related concepts and proposal for a definition. *Sleep Medicine, 83*, 175–181. https://doi.org/10.1016/j.sleep.2021.04.038

Wium, J., & Eaglestone, J. (2022). Job analysis for air traffic control: A review of the literature from 1949 to 2020. *Aviation Psychology and Applied Human Factors, 12*(1), 31–49. https://doi.org/10.1027/2192-0923/a000218

Young, M.S., Brookhuis, K.A., Wickens, C.D., & Hancock, P.A. (2015). State of science: mental workload in ergonomics. *Ergonomics, 58*(1), 1–17. https://doi.org/10.1080/00140139.2014.956151

Zhong, J.Y., Goh, S.K., Woo, C.J., & Alam, S. (2022). Impact of spatial orientation ability on air traffic conflict detection in a simulated free route airspace environment. *Frontiers in Human Neuroscience, 16*, 739866. https://doi.org/10.3389/fnhum.2022.739866

Zierke, O. (2014). Predictive validity of knowledge tests for pilot training outcome. *Aviation Psychology and Applied Human Factors, 4*(2), 98–105. https://doi.org/10.1027/2192-0923/a000190

Chapter 14
The Challenges of Defining the Aeromedical Significance of Neuropsychological Test Results

Robert L. Kane, Kelene A. Fercho, Jerry Crutchfield, Carlos Porges, and Thomas A. Van Dillen

Introduction and Background

The Federal Aviation Administration (FAA) oversees the safety and regulation of civil aviation in the United States, encompassing diverse areas such as safety regulation, air traffic management, aircraft certification, and more. Human factors play a crucial role in aviation safety. The percentage of accidents in general aviation attributed to human error can vary and be influenced by other factors such as changes in technology, training, and regulations. The National Transportation Safety Board (NTSB) publishes an online interactive dashboard that presents data from completed investigations of general aviation accidents that occurred between 2012 and 2021 (https://www.ntsb.gov/safety/data/Pages/GeneralAviationDashboard.aspx). For any accident, more than one factor can be assessed as having contributed to the incident. Of the 11,739 accidents that occurred over this 10-year period with completed investigations, 7,335 involved task performance, 3,339 were influenced by actions and decisions, and 1,263 were assessed as involving psychological factors. The NTSB interactive dashboard parses the information into categories, subcategories, sections, and subsections. The reader is referred to the dashboard subsection analysis for an appreciation of the ways in which judgment, cognition, and behavioral factors potentially contributed to adverse aviation outcomes. The top two subsection factors noted contributing to aviation accidents were issues controlling the aircraft and problems related to decision making and judgment. Underlying cognitive factors presumptively include skills needed to maintain situational awareness, to process and keep track of incoming information, to coordinate responses, and to appropriately implement existing knowledge.

Aviation necessitates individuals in safety-sensitive roles to undergo medical certification, evaluating both physical and cognitive health. Neuropsychologists play a crucial role in this process, assessing applicants' cognitive status to determine whether any compromising conditions raise safety concerns. Defining the aeromedical significance of test scores presents challenges especially when an individual's scores vary on measures putatively evaluating a specific cognitive domain. This chapter aims to explore the concept of aeromedical significance, discussing challenges in relating test scores to risk and performance, and proposing research recommendations to enhance decision-making processes.

What Can Be Learned From the Study of Aviation Accidents?

Data from accidents and adverse events can help inform models for understanding what constitutes aeromedically relevant cognitive skills. The Pilot Institute posted an online analysis of aviation accidents (Pilot Institute, 2023). In their report they note that commercial aviation is significantly safer than general aviation. The report references the fact that commercial aviation is highly regulated and monitored to ensure strict adherence to safety standards. When looking at fatal accidents between 2002 and 2021, 78 % occurred in the context of general aviation. Various factors contribute to accidents with the largest contributor being a loss of control in flight. Weather is a contributing factor and within this context; going from visual flight rules (VFR) into instrument meteorological conditions (IMC) accounts for 60 % of weather-related accidents (Aircraft Owners and Pilots Association [AOPA] Air Safety Institute, 2023a). Loss of aircraft control when flying from VFR to IMC conditions can occur in under 3 min. According to the aforementioned Pilot Institute report, 69.1% of general aviation accidents involving fixed-wing aircraft were related to pilot error. The authors of this report concluded that many of the reviewed accidents could have been prevented if pilots had exercised better judgment, had better knowledge of aircraft systems, and had a better understanding of weather patterns and general aircraft procedures. The authors also noted issues such as fatigue, stress, and distractions contributed to pilot error. The report indicated that fuel management was an important factor ranking fourth on the list of pilot-related accidents. Aircraft Owners and Pilots Association (AOPA) educational materials address multiple aspects of flight operations including understanding weather, fuel management, collision avoidance, and understanding density altitude. While proficiency, judgment, and adherence to procedures are critical components for flight safety, at its core, aviation is a cognitive task. The challenge for psychologists in aviation, including neuropsychologists, is to define the cognitive skills needed to engage in flight operations and to develop aviation-related standards of performance. Accident reporting is often general and not focused on underlying cognitive skills. Nevertheless, analyses of accidents and adverse events can provide relevant information for developing models of cognitive capabilities related to aviation safety. Cognitive skills related to information processing efficiency, working memory, mental flexibility, and problem solving seem critical.

How Flight Instructors Think About Flight Demands and Safety

Several focus groups were recently held at the FAA Civil Aerospace Medical Institute (CAMI) in Oklahoma City, where certified flight instructors (CFIs) were asked about training scenarios and challenges in rating student performance. The goal was to obtain information to design a flight simulator scenario to be used in a particular project. Some student characteristics such as having a "mechanical mindset," inquisitiveness, preparation, attention to detail, and planning were seen as advantageous. Personality factors were deemed important and concerns were expressed about risk-takers and individuals failing to follow procedures and attend to detail. Communication skills and cultural factors were seen as playing a role in performance (see Chapter 17 by Irani et al. for additional information about cultural and language factors). From a cognitive perspective, the ability to problem solve, having the mental flexibility and bandwidth to adapt to changing circumstances and manage task saturation, situational awareness, and having in memory critical information about the plane being flown were viewed as important.

Cognitive Skills and Flight Performance: Data From Published Studies

Piloting an aircraft is a complex cognitive task. The reader is referred to Chapter 12 in this volume by Fercho on the role of cognitive screening for medical certification for additional discussion. Examples of studies focused on cognitive skills in civil aviation are reviewed here.

Flight simulator studies have examined the relationship between cognitive skill assessments and flight performance. In recent studies, pilot research participants are typically administered computerized cognitive tests and also fly a prescribed scenario in a flight simulator. Cognitive test batteries include measures that assess various cognitive domains, such as working memory, attention, spatial ability, cognitive flexibility, and cognitive speed. In some cases, the intent of the research was to establish the operational validity of the cognitive assessment based on how well it could predict flight performance. If there was a strong relationship between cognitive performance and flight performance, it was inferred that the cognitive assessment measured constructs that underlie piloting tasks. Often, this research has examined the relationship between pilot age and flight simulator performance as well as the mediating role that individual cognitive skills play in this relationship. (See Chapter 31 by Causse et al. for additional discussion about age and aviator performance.)

Van Benthem and Herdman (2016) examined the relationship between pilot age, expertise, and cognitive function as measured by CogScreen-Aeromedical Edition™ (CogScreen-AE). A total of 54 general aviation (GA) pilots (21–79 years of age) flew a pattern circuit around a runway in a GA flight simulator. As expected, older and less experienced pilots showed larger flight path deviations. Older pilots tended to have lower scores on measures of working memory, cognitive speed, and visual attention. Each of these cognitive skills was correlated with flight performance. The relationship between age and skilled flight performance was mediated by scores on cognitive measures. The study findings suggested that the relationship between pilot age and flight performance may be mediated by age-related declines in specific cognitive skills that underlie skilled flight. These cognitive skills included working memory, cognitive speed, and visual attention.

In another flight simulator study, 100 older pilots (50–69 years of age) completed CogScreen-AE™ and performed simulated flight tasks, such as take-off, landing, maneuvering, avoiding traffic, scanning flight deck instruments, and air traffic control communication (Taylor et al., 2000). Overall, performance on the cognitive skills assessment decreased with pilot age for visual scanning/sequencing, attribute identification, visual perceptual/spatial processing, choice visual reaction time, visual associative memory, working memory, and numerical operations; only motor coordination and tracking task performance did not decline with age. Examining cognitive factors related to skilled flight performance indicated that general cognitive speed and working memory efficiency accounted for approximately 33% of the variance in flight performance. Visual associative memory, tracking, and motor coordination were also positively correlated with flight performance.

Causse et al. (2011) examined the relationship between the multidimensional construct of executive functions, general cognitive ability, and pilot age on skilled flight performance. GA pilots (22–78 years of age) completed a series of individual computerized cognitive tests and performed a simulated take-off, navigation, and landing flight simulator scenario. Performance on all of the measured cognitive skills, with the exception of general reasoning, decreased with age. Cognitive skills related to skilled flight performance were cognitive speed, working memory, and reasoning. These cognitive capabilities offered a stronger account of pilot performance than pilot age, again suggesting that cognitive ability may serve as a mediating variable between age and skilled flight performance.

In another study designed to examine the relationship between pilot age and performance, 40 experienced pilots, (aged 41–71 years; minimum of 5,000 hr total flight time) flew low-, medium-, and high-workload simulator scenarios (Hyland et al., 1994). Pilots also completed three computerized test batteries — CogScreen-AE™, WOMBAT, and Flightscript. WOMBAT was originally designed for pilot selection and presents a multitasking scenario that requires users to simultaneously perform several tasks. Flightscript requires the user to listen to an air traffic control communication sequence and either recall the sequence or select the correct description from a set of alternatives. Performance on WOMBAT and CogScreen-AE™ was correlated, suggesting that they measure similar cognitive abilities. Neither WOMBAT nor CogScreen-AE were correlated with Flightscript scores. Notably, none of the three test batteries correlated with objective flight performance metrics. Pilot age was correlated with performance on the three task batteries; however, pilot age was not correlated with flight simulator performance. On CogScreen-AE™, older pilots demonstrated slower reaction times and lower levels of accuracy.

In sum, cognitive skills identified as related to skilled flight performance in these flight simulator studies included working memory, cognitive speed, visual attention, tracking performance, motor coordination, reasoning, and psychomotor reaction time. The strength of the relationship between cognitive capabilities and flight simulator task performance varied. Taylor et al. (2000) were able to account for 33% of simulator task performance variance, whereas in the Hyland et al. (1994) study computerized cognitive measures failed to correlate appreciably with simulator task performance. Study differences may have been attributable to differences in the flight simulator tasks and scenarios. However, the discrepancy in study results underscores the need for enhanced modeling of cognitive assessments in relation to pilot performance.

Cognitive Skills Needed by Air Traffic Cottrol Specialists: Data From Published Studies

Air traffic control specialists (ATCSs) manage complex environments to ensure the safe and efficient flow of air traffic. Monitoring airspace, radio frequencies, and pilot compliance, they stay vigilant for up to 2 hr, performing demanding tasks such as predicting flight paths and anticipating conflicts with terrain, weather, or other aircraft. When conflicts arise, they implement resolutions. Whether working alone or in a team, ATCSs handle handoffs for aircraft entering or leaving their airspace, ensuring seamless communication and coordination. Their role is crucial in maintaining order and safety in the dynamic and challenging aviation environment. The ATCS keeps in mind information about flight plans, headings, altitudes, and speeds, in order to project flight paths in four dimensions.

Research is conducted within the industry to identify and characterize the skills ATCSs need to successfully carry out air traffic control tasks. Although no longer in use, the Air Traffic Selection and Training (AT-SAT) test battery, was validated with data from 1,000 incumbent ATCSs (Ramos et al., 2001b). This measure included seven cognitive tests and an experiential questionnaire. The cognitive tests included tasks that involved scanning to detect and to interpret readings, solving math problems and verbal and nonverbal analogies, judgment of the angle of intersecting lines, and two tasks that required the application of multiple cognitive abilities combined. Two subtests, Letter Factory and the Air Traffic Scenarios Test, were dynamic and interactive tasks that tapped categorization, working memory, decision-making, and prioritization (Ramos et al., 2001a). A meta-analysis of ATCS selection tests, published in 2022 (Mouratille et al., 2022), implicated similar cognitive abilities as the AT-SAT validation. The meta-analysis identified six measures with the largest predictive validity. These predictors were tests of math, processing speed, working memory, and visuospatial processing.

Error analysis has also been used to evaluate cognitive factors related to successful ATC performance. Factors that have led to performance errors included workload, memory, and situational awareness in relation to decision-making. It is generally accepted that the use of working memory is a fundamental part of air traffic control, playing a role in most if not all tasks (Stein & Garland, 1993). When controlling air traffic, ATCSs are often called upon to switch their attention quickly between several aircraft, sources of information both visual and auditory, or between control tasks. In addition to working memory, studies have linked vulnerabilities in prospective memory to the occurrence of errors (Loft, 2014).

Some challenges exist in studying cognitive skills related to ATCS performance. Collecting live operations data would provide a high level of validity; however, the data needed to derive these measures are often not available, and the safety-critical aspect of tasks prevent the collection of invasive or distracting measures. Also, the privacy of the ATCSs must be maintained. Data collection employing high-fidelity simulation and scripted scenarios helps to control many of the extraneous variables, but also has drawbacks related to the sample sizes needed for statistical power in relation to the limited number of ATCSs familiar with a particular airspace.

Ecological Validity

The term "ecological validity," introduced by Brunswik (1955), refers to how data from clinical or laboratory assessments align with real-world tasks. Franzen and Wilhelm (1996) delineated two facets: veridicality, assessing the predictive capability of test data for real-world performance, and verisimilitude, assessing how closely an assessment measure mirrors a real-world task. In aviation psychology, prioritizing the correlation between test results and actual performance (veridicality) is paramount.

Neurocognitive assessment in aviation aims to evaluate an applicant's cognitive status, emphasizing capabilities crucial for safe flight operations. However, establishing the ecological validity of cognitive assessments in aviation presents challenges akin to those of traditional clinical assessments. The task is to use data derived from test instruments designed to evaluate putative cognitive domains to make inferences about how well an individual can perform a real-world task.

Positive data supporting ecological validity (veridicality) exist in the clinical realm, with Marcotte et al. (2022) concluding that tests assessing basic cognitive abilities generally exhibit a moderate correlation with real-world task performance. On the basis of a meta-analysis, these authors noted that cognitive test data typically account for 21 %–27 % of variance in everyday functioning. They also noted a review article by Sternberg et al. (2001), who concluded that cognition accounted for between 4 % and 30 % of the variance when measured against job performance. Challenges arise when translating laboratory or clinical test scores into decision-making contexts, such as medical certification. Establishing cut points distinguishing nominal (no aeromedical concerns) from off-nominal (aeromedically deficient) performance is crucial. Predication is also complicated by the fact that aviation work environments are dynamic, requiring adaptation to changing conditions and varied workloads. Aviators and ATCSs face challenges related to personality, environmental factors, and stressors impacting task performance. These challenges underscore the complexity of translating cognitive test scores into meaningful decisions in aviation contexts.

Overview of Cognitive Assessments for Medical Certification

The FAA employs protocols for assessing cognitive status in medical certificate applicants, with general information available online through the *Guide for Aviation Medical Examiners*. Specific cognitive test protocols are confidential in order to maintain test security and examination validity. The evaluation, conducted by board-certified and board-eligible neuropsychologists, focuses on neurocognitive domains relevant for aviation. Periodic reviews and updates of test protocols occur as needed. Assessments consider aeromedically significant neurocognitive difficulties based on history and test performance. FAA neuropsychologists or consultants may further evaluate reports, with final decisions made by the Office of the Federal Air Surgeon.

There are no predefined decision rules used to classify an individual's test performance as nominal or off-nominal. An additional challenge of distinguishing nominal from off-nominal test performance is that the medical certification decision process is one of "selecting out" and not "selecting in." The goal is not to find the strongest applicants. Rather, the issue is to determine whether an individual meets basic medical standards needed to safely fly an airplane or manage air traffic. While guided by the literature and experience, defining aeromedically significant cognitive difficulties is an evolving science, explored further in subsequent sections on decision-making and risk assessment in this chapter.

The Positive and Negative Predictive Value of Test Measures

An approach for assessing the capability of a test to identify a specific condition involves determining its sensitivity and specificity (Hannay & Lezak, 2004). Sensitivity gauges accuracy in detecting the condition, while specificity measures accuracy in identifying those without it. These metrics, along with the prevalence of the condition, determine positive and negative predictive values (Der & Everitt, 2012). In aviation safety evaluations, challenges arise in applying these metrics due to limited data on real-world flight proficiency, especially in GA. Using base rate data for rare events, like aviation accidents, poses limitations. For instance, AOPA data (AOPA, 2023b) indicate, on average, a 5 % GA accident rate annually per 100,000 flight hours from 2012 to 2020. Even if a test has a high level of sensitivity and specificity, the low prior probability yields an extremely low positive predictive value, limiting practical utility. While valuable in specific studies, evaluating predictive values faces challenges in assessing risks related to rare events (Smith et al., 2000). Its utility depends on the ability to measure relevant outcome variables, the frequency of adverse events, and the consistency and frequency of off-nominal test scores.

Population-Based Approach to Risk Assessment

Accident or adverse event prediction is difficult when evaluating individuals. An individual's performance of a specific task can vary at different time points. Environmental, situational, and personal factors as well as stressors can all effect operator performance. In establishing performance parameters, population-based metrics are often used to derive parameters for safe performance. A classic example of this approach is the use of population-based statistics to set values for legal intoxication when driving a motor vehicle. Transportation safety studies have been conducted to assess the effects of different substances. For the purposes of this chapter and to focus on the broader topic of risk assessment, data are provided related to the effects of alcohol. Studies fall into two broad categories: One type of study assesses the effects of different alcohol doses on task performance, the other relates alcohol levels to accident frequency. For the latter type of study, data reviewed in an NTSB report show accident risk increasing with blood alcohol level (NTSB, 2022). At a blood alcohol concentration (BAC) of .08, the relative risk was 2.5 times greater than for alcohol-free drivers. At a BAC of 1.0, the relative risk was close to 5 times higher. The approach of assessing factors that increase risk is different from the positive and negative predictive value analysis noted earlier. A BAC level that would raise safety concerns for increasing the probability of an adverse event would likely have a low positive predictive value for an individual having an accident at a particular time considering the frequency of accidents occurring in the population.

Also relevant for risk assessment are studies assessing off-nominal changes in performance related to levels of alcohol. This category of study makes use of controlled environments and controlled doses of alcohol. Outcome measures include dependent variables such as visual acuity, performance on tasks requiring divided attention, lane violations, response times when reacting to situations or events, and speed variability (NTSB, 2022). In the aforementioned literature review, studies focused on the relationship of cognitive domains to aviation-relevant task performance. Studies of BAC and driving performance use an induced impairment model to evaluate performance changes. The goal of these studies is to assess the effects of a drug or stressor on performance. Induced impairment studies can elucidate operator performance decrements related to safety. The traffic safety model assesses accident frequency rates related to specific levels of a risk factor bolstered by studies of the effects of alcohol on objective measures of performance. This model partially translates into aviation in that, as noted in the aforementioned studies, cognitive capabilities correlate with pilot and ATCS task performance. However, in aviation, it is difficult to correlate cognitive skill measures of an individual with accident frequency.

Impairment Ratings and the Assessment of Cognitive Domains

The focus of the neuropsychological evaluation in informing the medical certification process is to evaluate whether a candidate has cognitive difficulties that would be considered aeromedically significant. If an applicant performs poorly on tests evaluating neurocognitive domains deemed important for aviation safety, then problems noted on testing are determined to be aeromedically relevant. As noted in the sections of this chapter pertaining to cognitive factors related to aviation, cognition accounts for relevant variance in task performance. Nevertheless, the challenge remains of how best to assess test data and to establish decision rules for classifying an individual's test performance as off-nominal and indicative of cognitive difficulties that present an enhanced safety risk. In areas outside of aviation, the relationship between laboratory-based cognitive assessment and everyday task performance has been modest, underscoring challenges relating test performance to risk assessment.

Historically in neuropsychology, impairment ratings have been used as a metric of an individual's general cognitive status (Boll, 1981; Heaton et al. 2004; Russell et al., 1970). Global impairment scores reflect an individual's general cognitive status and do not elucidate performance in relation to specific cognitive domains. However, in their review of ecological validity in traditional clinical settings, Marcotte et al. (2022, p. 13) stated: "We have the most confidence in the very general statement that global cognitive impairment is associated with worse performance on everyday functioning measures."

CogScreen™ generates various scores including the logistic regression probability value (LRPV) score, which captures the extent to which a test-taker's performance resembles that of individuals with known cognitive impairment (Kay, 1995). Additionally, CogScreen™ provides base rate scores allowing for a more refined evaluation of off-nominal test scores by considering the frequency of low scores produced by healthy pilots. Base rates provide a more refined method of assessing the number of off-nominal tests scores obtained during an examination by accounting for the frequency of low scores that occur in healthy individuals taking a specified number of tests. As demonstrated by Schretlen et al., (2007), the number of test scores produced by healthy individuals deemed abnormal increases as a function of the number of tests given. Abnormal scores decrease with more stringent cut points and they vary with the correlation among tests. The frequency of abnormal scores obtained by healthy individuals also varies with age and demographic variables. Hence, base rate scores based on the performance of healthy pilots in different age ranges and from different sectors of aviation enhance the interpretation of an individual's general performance on CogScreen™. FAA test protocols also incorporate conventional measures for assessing cognitive risk factors, providing clinicians with an impression of global impairment. However, no summary metric accompanies an individual's performance on these conventional test measures.

While global impairment may be the most robust predictor of performance problems in everyday life (Marcotte et al., 2022), the assessment of cognition in aviation places emphasis on specific areas of performance and relevant cognitive domains. Marcotte et al. (2022) also stated that with respect to specific cognitive domains, executive functioning measures have the strongest and most consistent relationships with everyday functioning. In addition to global summary scores, CogScreen™ produces factor scores for aviation-relevant cognitive domains, and additional data are obtained from evaluating individual subtest performance.

As noted, conventional test measures focus on specific aspects of cognitive functioning, examined test by test. Conventional measures are not combined to produce an index score within a specific neurocognitive domain.

Examiners must develop decision rules for interpreting patterns and weights of inconsistent test scores within the same cognitive domain. Similarly, when CogScreen™ and conventional test data present inconsistencies regarding domain-specific performance, examiners must devise decision rules to reconcile the information.

A model for combining test data organized into relevant domains along with rules for assessing impairment within a domain, and then evaluating overall impairment, was developed by the National Football League (NFL, 2022) as part of the concussion compensation settlement with the players association. The specifics of their decision logic are not pertinent here, and the way in which tests and scores were combined is open to discussion. This approach is mentioned since it is a method for addressing the issue of consistency in test interpretation across providers as would be required in a legal settlement. The model is an impairment rating model within domains and across various domains for tests in a prescribed test battery.

Developing Decision Rules

The current FAA neuropsychological assessment approach involves employing standardized protocols for evaluating cognitive deficits related to specific medical or behavioral health issues. The interpreting clinicians assess for the presence of aeromedically relevant cognitive difficulties, and results are sent to the FAA for final certification decisions, with potential input from FAA neuropsychologists or consultants. The FAA provides training via the yearly Aerospace Psychology Seminar, and individuals experienced in providing FAA neuropsychological evaluations offer consultation to examining neuropsychologists to help with challenging cases. While there is substantial commitment to improving and refining processes, to date there has not been an effort to standardized test interpretation. The prevailing view has been that individuals present with complex histories and they can vary in their neuropsychological test performance. These varied presentations require careful clinical assessment and judgment in reaching a decision about risk and aeromedical significance. As noted earlier, predicting that a person may be involved in an adverse aviation event at some point in the future is difficult at best. Thus, the neuropsychological evaluation is part of risk assessment with the implication that off-nominal test performance in certain areas is aeromedically significant due to the relationship between cognitive capabilities and safe operator performance.

While this approach has served well the goal of maintaining the safety of the federal air space, there are issues to consider moving forward. The idea that there is no algorithm is problematic. Thoughtful clinicians explicitly or implicitly employ decision rules. They evaluate test data and when some scores assessing an area of cognitive functioning are nominal and other scores evaluating this same area are off-nominal, they employ a decision-making strategy. The clinician may assign greater weight to some tests when making their evaluation. They may be influenced by the fact that some test scores in a domain are low and indicative of a potential problem independent of the fact that scores on other measures in that domain are in a normal range. However the examiner approaches the data, there are decision rules in play. Saying there is no algorithm implies that in actuality there are various algorithms that can differ across examiners, that are not always explicitly stated, and that are not empirically evaluated. While challenging to develop considering the multiple factors that affect human performance and that result in adverse aviation events, explicit algorithms are essential for refining decision rules and conducting studies to enhance consistency and accuracy in defining the aeromedical significance of test findings. Establishing clear, empirically evaluated algorithms would contribute to a more systematic and informed approach to neuropsychological assessments in the context of aviation safety.

Developing algorithms may benefit from exploring different performance models as well as from advanced data analytic methods. There has been a push in medicine for translation research. The common phrase is from "bench to bedside" and the concept is to facilitate and conduct research in a manner that expedites clinical implementation. There is a need for programmatic research to define patterns of neurocognitive test scores related to safe operator performance that can directly inform the development of decision rules for separating nominal and off-nominal test performances. Considering the complexity of the process, implementing various computational and data analytic models should be explored for performance classification related to aviation safety.

Caveats and Human Factors Not Measured in the Laboratory

This chapter addresses the challenges of connecting test scores to aviation safety. Nevertheless, many adverse aviation incidents related to human performance, judgment, and decision-making are not directly related to capabilities measured in a clinical setting or laboratory. In addition, factors such as anxiety can affect test performance. While exploring these factors exceeds this chapter's scope, acknowledging them is crucial when linking cognition to safety.

A notable portion of aircraft accidents results from critical information gaps among stakeholders, often due to communication issues or a failure to grasp data significance. In commercial aviation, crew resource management (CRM) and threat and error management (TEM) enhance pilot problem-solving, incorporating personality and cognition. Although cognitive test performance correlates with CRM proficiency (Hoffman et al., 1998), assessing the various variables involved in CRM skills can be a challenge in a clinical laboratory setting.

GA accidents involve diverse factors such as taking shortcuts in following procedures and safety recommendations, insufficient instruction when transitioning to a new airplane, failing to stay current on changing weather conditions, and fuel management and flight planning errors. Judgment errors that an aviator might make at a given point in time are not readily assessed during the course of psychological or neuropsychological evaluations. Some aspects of behavior and character can be assessed through personality testing and a review of an individual's medical, behavioral health, educational, and adjustment history (see Chapter 9 for a discussion on aviator character traits). However, more programmatic research is needed to enhance assessment models.

Pilots and ATCSs can have varied educational and cultural backgrounds. Nonimpaired individuals bring different backgrounds to the examination process. While having core cognitive abilities is necessary for safety-sensitive activities in aviation, examiners should focus on those skills most pertinent to aviation and not overweight low test scores in areas less associated with task performance.

In commercial aviation, the examining neuropsychologist should appreciate airline culture, airline-specific work rules, and the different missions the wider airline pilot group performs. For example, if the examining neuropsychologist does not understand how the seniority system works, he or she will not fully understand what is at stake for a pilot submitting for an examination and the resultant test anxiety.

Conclusion

In this chapter we attempted to review the complexities involved in assessing neurocognitive test performance when making determinations about aeromedical relevance. Accidents and adverse occurrences in aviation are all too frequent rare events. They are challenging to predict due to their statistically low frequency and the complex interplay of factors leading to the adverse event. Cognitive assessment strategies can involve those typically employed clinically as well as those associated with a human factors approach. Depending on the case, both clinical validity and ecological validity (veridicality) can be of relevance. Applying standard clinical metrics to real world performance can be difficult due to the multiple factors that are associated with successfully managing various tasks. Human error is a significant contributor to aviation accidents. However, not all errors can be attributed to cognitive skills assessed in clinical or laboratory settings and not all poor decisions are due to cognitive compromise. While more studies are needed relating cognitive skills to aviation, in general the amount of variance in real-world performance explained by cognitive test findings tends to be modest. Nevertheless, cognitive capabilities are essential elements of safe operator performance and test interpretation models are based on risk reduction similar to population-based highway safety approaches. The lack of explicit and testable interpretation algorithms introduces a subjective element into neuropsychological evaluations, despite clinicians making well-reasoned conclusions. Consistency like reliability does not guarantee accuracy, but clearly stated decision rules can be evaluated and refined. To achieve refinement, a programmatic research approach is necessary, specifically targeting decision-making and incorporating various computational and data analytic models.

References

Aircraft Owners and Pilots Association Air Safety Institute. (2023a). *Accident analysis*. https://www.aopa.org/training-and-safety/air-safety-institute/accident-analysis

Aircraft Owners and Pilots Association Air Safety Institute. (2023b). *Joseph T. Nall 32nd AOPA Air Safety Institute accident report*. https://www.aopa.org/training-and-safety/air-safety-institute/accident-analysis/joseph-t-nall-report/nall-report-figure-view?category=all&year=2020&condition=all&report=true

Boll, T. (1981). The Halstead–Reitan neuropsychology battery. In S. B. Filskov & T. J. Boll (Eds.), *Handbook of clinical neuropsychology* (pp. 577–607). Wiley.

Brunswik, E. (1955). Representative design and probabilistic theory in a functional psychology. *Psychological Review, 62*(3), 193–217. https://doi.org/10.1037/h0047470

Causse, M., Dehais, F., & Pastor, J. (2011). Executive functions and pilot characteristics predict flight simulator performance in general aviation pilots. *The International Journal of Aviation Psychology, 21*(3), 217–234. https://doi.org/10.1080/10508414.2011.582441

Der, G., & Everitt, B.S. (2012). *Applied medical statistics using SAS.* CRC Press. https://doi.org/10.1201/b12738

Franzen, M.D., & Wilhelm, K.L. (1996). Conceptual foundations of ecological validity in neuropsychological assessment. In R.J. Sbordone & C.J. Long (Eds.), *Ecological validity of neuropsychological testing* (pp. 91–112). GR Press/St. Lucie Press.

Hannay, H.J., & Lezak, M.D. (2004). The neuropsychological examination: Interpretation. In M.D. Lezak, D.B. Howieson, & D.W. Loring (Eds.), *Neuropsychological Assessment* (4th ed., pp. 133–156). Oxford University Press.

Heaton, R.K., Miller, S.W., Taylor, M.J., & Grant, I. (2004). *Revised comprehensive norms for an expanded Halstead-Reitan battery: Demographically adjusted neuropsychological norms for African American and Caucasian Adults.* Psychological Assessment Resources.

Hoffman, C.C., Hoffman, K.P., & Kay, G.G. (1998, October 5–9). *The role that cognitive ability plays in CRM* [Paper presentation]. NATO Symposium, Human Factors & Medicine Panel on Collaborative Crew Performance in Complex Operational Systems, Edinburgh, Scotland.

Hyland, D.T., Kay, E.J., & Deimler, J.D. (1994). *Age 60 study, part IV: Experimental evaluation of pilot performance* (No. DOT/FAA/AM-94/23). Federal Aviation Administration.

Kay, G.G. (1995). *CogScreen™ Aeromedical Addition.* Psychological Assessment Resources.

Loft, S. (2014). Applying psychological science to examine prospective memory in simulated air traffic control. *Current Directions in Psychological Science, 23*(5), 326–331. https://doi.org/10.1177/0963721414545214

Marcotte, T.D., Schmitter-Edgecombe, M., Scott, J.C., Kamat, R., & Heaton, R.K. (2022). Neuropsychology and the prediction of everyday functioning. In T.D. Marcotte, M. Schmitter-Edgecombe, & I. Grant (Eds.), *Neuropsychology of everyday functioning* (pp. 5–38). The Guilford Press.

Mouratille, D., Amadieu, F., & Matton, N. (2022). A meta-analysis on air traffic controllers selection: Cognitive and non-cognitive predictors. *Journal of Vocational Behavior, 138*(4), 103769. https://doi.org/10.1016/j.jvb.2022.103769

National Football League. (2022). *Neuropsychologist handbook: The clinician's interpretation guide* (Version 6.0).

National Transportation and Safety Board. (2022). *Alcohol, other drug, and multiple drug use among drivers.* NTSB SRR-22-02 Safety Research Report.

Pilot Institute. (2023). *Why do aircraft crash – aviation accident statistics revealed.* https://pilotinstitute.com/aviation-accident-causes/

Ramos, R.A., Heil, M.C., & Manning, C.A. (2001a). *Documentation of validity for the AT-SAT computerized test battery, Vol. I.* (DOT/FAA/AM-01/5). Federal Aviation Administration Office of Aerospace Medicine. https://doi.org/10.1037/e412202004-001

Ramos, R.A., Heil, M.C., & Manning, C.A. (2001b). *Documentation of validity for the AT-SAT computerized test battery, Vol. II.* (DOT/FAA/AM-01/6). Federal Aviation Administration Office of Aerospace Medicine. https://doi.org/10.1037/e446082004-001

Russell, E.W., Neuringer, C., & Goldstein, G. (1970). *Assessment of brain damage: A neurpsychological key approach.* Wiley-Interscience.

Schretlen, D.J., Mesta, M., Winicki, J.M., Pearlson, G.D., & Gordon, B. (2007). Frequency and bases of abnormal performance by healthy adults on neuropsychological testing. *Journal of the International Neuropsychological Society, 14*, 436–445.

Smith, J.E., Winkler, R.L., & Fryback, D.G. (2000). The first positive: computing positive predictive value at the extremes. *Annals of Internal Medicine, 132*(10), 804–809. https://doi.org/10.7326/0003-4819-132-10-200005160-00008

Stein, E.S., & Garland, D. (1993). *Air traffic controller working memory: Considerations in air traffic control tactical operations.* (DOT/FAA/CT-TN93/37). Federal Aviation Administration.

Sternberg, R.J., Grigorenko, E.L., & Bundy, D.A. (2001). The predictive value of IQ. *Merrill-Palmer Quarterly, 47*(1), 1–41. https://doi.org/10.1353/mpq.2001.0005

Taylor, J.L., O'Hara, R., Mumenthaler, M.S., & Yesavage, J.A. (2000). Relationship of CogScreen-AE to flight simulator performance and pilot age. *Aviation Space and Environmental Medicine, 71*(4), 373–380.

Van Benthem, K., & Herdman, C. M. (2016). Cognitive factors mediate the relation between age and flight path maintenance in general aviation. *Aviation Psychology and Applied Human Factors, 6*(2), 81–90. https://doi.org/10.1027/2192-0923/a000102

Chapter 15
Assessing Cognition for Aviation

Findings From a Systematic Review of Neuropsychological Tests Used to Assess Pilots

Eilis Boudreau and Annette M. Totten

Introduction

Optimal neuropsychological and cognitive functioning is critical for safely piloting an aircraft, which is why recruits and trainees are evaluated and assessed before they are granted licenses. As the age and length of flight careers for recreational and commercial pilots have increased due to changes in both population demographics and mandatory retirement ages, the likelihood experienced pilots will face chronic medical problems, injuries, or a temporary or permanent neurological impairment increases (Simons et al., 2021) The result is a growing number of requests for medical certification of pilots after head injury, stroke, tumor, and episodes of temporary incapacitation of known and unknown etiology. The task of re-evaluating a pilot for return-to-flight duties is complicated by the patchwork of international and regional approaches and regulations for continuing medical certification.

Neuropsychological assessment of individuals who want to re-engage in aviation activities is a complex endeavor that includes testing, clinical assessment, and judgment. The gold standard is evaluation by a neuropsychologist with aerospace expertise. Comprehensive evaluation and assessment require an understanding of the key cognitive domains critical to aviation activities and the regulatory environment in which the pilot operates. Although the need for neuropsychological fitness in real-world aircraft operations is universally accepted, methods of assessment vary and there remain differences of opinions across experts and advocates about the ideal approach.

This chapter is based on a systematic review undertaken to identify, summarize, and analyze the research evidence that evaluated the tests used in the neuropsychological assessments of pilots. The objective of the review was to inform future research about assessing cognition in pilots, which could help move toward more consistent policies and thereby increase confidence in pilot assessments.

The goals of this chapter, which run parallel to the goals of the review, are to (1) specify the cognitive domains identified as important for aviation through the lens of test development for the assessment of pilots; (2) describe the tests that have been used or suggested for use for each domain; (3) highlight what outcome measures have been used when evaluating the performance of these tests in pilots in the available evidence; (4) highlight the role and need for aviation neuropsychology and neuropsychologist involvement in this critical process; and (5) outline areas for future research.

Method

The systematic review that is the basis for this chapter was conducted by Pacific Northwest Evidence-based Practice Center (EPC) at Oregon Health and Science University. The EPC adapts the standards established by the Agency for Healthcare Research and Quality (Agency for Healthcare Research and Quality, 2023) and Medicine Division of the National Academies of Sciences, Engineering and Medicine (formerly known as the Institute of Medicine; (Eden et al., 2011) to the topic and scope of each project. The protocol for this review was registered in the PROSPERO international database of systematic reviews (registration number CRD42018113045) and the full report and methods are available from the corresponding author or at https://www.ohsu.edu/evidence-based-practice-center/epc-reports #section-319666 (see Totten et al., 2019).

The goal of the systematic review was to answer two questions: (1) What neuropsychological tests have been studied in active pilots to determine fitness to fly?; (2) What is known about the psychometric properties of these tests including how well these tests or test batteries predict pilot performance and discriminate between impaired and nonimpaired pilots?

To identify published studies, we conducted a systematic search of Ovid MEDLINE®, PsycINFO, and Scopus from 1980 through March 15, 2019. We also searched OpenGrey, Google Scholar, FAA Aerospace Medicine Technical Reports, and the National Technical Reports Library to identify other available data. Studies that directly addressed the review questions and were published in English were included regardless of their design. However, we excluded descriptive studies that provided no data on how the test or assessment performed and we excluded studies of groups other than pilots or astronauts, such as other transportation workers and candidates for pilot training.

All abstracts and the full text of the selected articles were independently reviewed by two members of the research team who were blinded to each other's initial decisions. Any disagreements about inclusion or exclusion were resolved by consensus. For each included study we extracted the data provided on the subjects (e.g., type of pilot, age), the test (e.g., domains, intended use), and the results of the evaluation of the test (e.g., ability to predict performance or discriminate different types of subjects or correlation with an outcome measure).

Literature Search and Identified Studies

After reviewing the 1,976 potentially relevant citations identified by our search and excluding 1,751, we reviewed the full text of 225 articles. Overall, 39 articles that reported the results of 28 studies met our inclusion criteria. Common reasons for exclusion were that studies only described, rather than evaluated, the test or that the test was not evaluated in pilots.

The included studies evaluated several different neuropsychological tests. Some studies evaluated discrete tests, designed to assess one domain of cognitive function. Other studies evaluated all or parts of test batteries containing multiple tests that targeted several functions or tasks requiring capacity across cognitive domains. Most of the identified studies were reports of analyses generated when the tests and assessments were developed. These focused on linking aviation tasks to cognitive domains and then to specific tests. A subset of studies assessed test performance and used this information to refine the tests. Fewer studies explored the reliability of the cognitive tests after they were in general use or measured performance across different pilot groups or over time.

Most of the included articles were published in the 1990s. This reflects the attention to related topics such as age limits for pilots at the time and the publication of research funded by the FAA, including the work leading up to the development of the CogScreen-Aeromedical Edition, which has been a core assessment tool in US aviation. This is also likely why almost three quarters of the studies were conducted in the United States studying US pilots. Military pilots were the subject of 36% of the studies, although 21% of the studies did not provide information on the type of pilot. While 64% of the studies analyzed samples of 51 or more people, 36% would be considered small with sample sizes of 50 or fewer participants and these studies were more likely to be underpowered, limiting possible analyses and confidence in the conclusions. When studies included multiple analyses containing data on different numbers of people, we classified the study based on the largest sample size.

Assessment of Pilots: Cognitive Domains Identified in Studies Evaluating Tests

Once the research studies on tests and assessment of pilots were identified, we extracted information about what cognitive domains the test developers identified as important and attempted to assess. We reviewed this list and compared it with common practice and foundational textbooks, and reviewed the studies with experts who were part of an advisory panel for our research. Based on this, we identified seven key domains: *attention*, *reasoning*, *perception*, *memory* (both short and long-term), *motor performance*, *executive function*, and *situational awareness*.

For the systematic review, for each test or battery of tests we determined how many studies had evaluated how the test performed in assessing pilots. Then we assessed the quality of the individual studies and considered the overall strength of evidence supporting (or not supporting) the use of the test. Given the focus for this chapter, we have abstracted and reorganized information from this review. In the following sections, we provide a list of the tests we identified for each cognitive domain. In a table for each domain, we list each test and provide a brief description. We also provide the outcome measures used when evaluating the test for the assessment of pilots and the citations for the studies. As the inclusion of the actual study results is beyond the scope of the chapter, the reader is referred to the full systematic review for this information (Totten et al., 2019).

The outcome measure used in assessing a test is important for several reasons. It needs to be relevant to the population and task of interest. The outcome used to evaluate a test for assessing pilots might be different from the outcome used to evaluate the same test for use with surgeons. What is essential is that the outcome used to evaluate a test for use with pilots represents how the cognitive domain has to be employed in tasks by pilots. Additionally, it is important to consider whether the outcome measure is valid and reliable and whether potential users of the test are confident that this outcome is relevant and can be measured. The outcome measure may be what the test is intended to predict (e.g., errors in flight), detect (e.g., deficit or disability), or measure in a way that is easier, faster, more consistent, more efficient, or more feasible.

The purpose of the tables is to document the diversity of tests and outcome measures and provide citations to the studies for those who might want to delve into study results or explore a particular domain or topic further. The last section of this chapter outlines several needs for future research; these studies may provide inspiration or a foundation for future work.

A couple of characteristics of the data and process are important to note.

- We mapped the tests to the cognitive domains based on a combination of what the study authors stated and input from experts among our advisors. Some tests could be under multiple domains, and we realize this mapping is not perfect.
- The same tests were often evaluated in several studies, a study may evaluate multiple tests at once, and a single study may be the subject of multiple publications. As a result, the numbers of tests, studies, and publications are not the same.
- Furthermore, the number of tests identified does not directly correspond to the importance of the domain. It could be that more tests were available to be tried with pilots or it could reflect lack of consensus in the field around measurement.

Tests That Have Been Evaluated for Use in Assessing Pilots by Cognitive Domains

Attention

Attention was the most frequently evaluated neuropsychological domain. We divided it into simpler tests presented in Table 15.1 and more complex attention tests in Table 15.2. Simple attention was almost always measured by more than one task. The outcome measures for tests of simple attention were simulator performance in several studies. Other outcomes used included the ability to classify study subjects and situational awareness. The two studies that considered the relationship to brain injury outcomes were very different: One examined brain images and test performance and found no significant relationship (McGuire et al., 2014), while the other found that test scores were significantly correlated with the duration of posttraumatic amnesia (Moore & Kay, 1995). However, each of these approaches has limitations – imaging modality and resolution for the former, and accuracy of recall and reporting on the duration of amnesia for the latter.

Tests of complex attention included tests where the examinee was expected to complete two tasks simultaneously, such as a simulated flight and math problems, or where attention is needed to recognize patterns. The idea is to test the abilities that may be needed in routine or emergency aircraft operation. The results for these types of tests are included in Table 15.2. In some cases the results suggested that a complex attention task can more accurately categorize someone who is impaired than a simpler test can (e.g., Zhang et al., 1997). While the results are varied, most of the identified studies suggested there is a relationship between complex attention abilities and performance. The studies that did not report this relationship were designed to assess other factors such as age or expertise but were included as they provided data on the assessment (Taylor et al., 2005; Taylor et al., 2007; Yesavage et al., 2011) and how it performs across groups who are expected to have different abilities.

Table 15.1. Simple attention

Test	Test description	Outcome measure	Reference
Timers 1 & 2	The reaction time domain on MicroCog. Examinees must press the Enter key to respond successively to five aural tones, five on-screen images, and then five images proceeded briefly by a tone.	Brain injury indicators (imaging)	McGuire et al., 2014
CogScreen subtests	Several tests included in the CogScreen Battery	Brain injury indicators (duration of posttraumatic amnesia)	Moore & Kay, 1995
Auditory sequence comparison	Comparison of two series of tone sequences.	Group comparison or classification	Kay, 1995; Kay et al., 1991
Backward digit span	Sequential visual presentation of three to six digits. The task is to reproduce the sequence in reverse order.		
Matching to sample	Following a brief presentation of a four-by-four pattern of colored squares, the examinee identifies the matching pattern from two choices.		
Visual sequence comparison	Comparison of two simultaneously presented series of letters and numbers.		
Auditory sequence comparison	See row above	Group comparison or classification	Kay, 1995
Matching to sample			
Visual sequence comparison			
Divided Attention Test	Examinee monitors the vertical movements of a bar within a circle and returns the bar to the center position when the deviation from center exceeds an upper or lower boundary. The monitoring task is presented alone and in combination with the visual sequence comparison task.		

Table 15.1. continued

Test	Test description	Outcome measure	Reference
Color–Word Test (modified Stroop)	Requires the examinee to name the color in which a word is written even though the word may be the name of that color or of a different color.	Group comparison or classification	O'Donnell et al., 1992
Dynamic memory test	Requires the examinee to note the bottom number of a fraction. When a new fraction appears, the examinee must respond by saying whether the top number is the same as the previous bottom number. However, the new bottom number must first be noted because as soon as a response is given the original fraction is replaced by a new one.		
Spatial processing	A four-bar histogram is presented. After 3 s it is removed and replaced (after a delay) with another histogram rotated either 90° or 270°. The examinee must decide whether the second histogram is the same as the first.		
Visual monitoring	Requires the examinee to monitor four dials (similar to aircraft dials) to detect a randomly occurring bias in one of them.		
Backward digit span Matching to sample	See Row 3 in this table	Performance	Kay, 1995; Yakimovich et al., 1994
Processing speed composite	Letter comparison and pattern comparison tasks. Scored as a mean processing speed score of both tasks.	Performance	Morrow, 2003
Sentence-span test	Contains a listening and reading component measuring "the ability to simultaneously store and manipulate information in memory." Scored as mean span score of listening and reading components.		
Single condition (as part of dichotic listening)	A series of letter/digit string sets presented to examinees aurally over binaural headphones via two voice synthesizers. Examinees were told which ear to attend to for each trial. Part I was a series of 16 pairs of letters and/or numbers; Part II was a series of six more pairs. Examinees were to indicate the digits (0–9) presented to the designated ear in the order of their occurrence. Examinees responded with their left hand using a separate keypad placed immediately in front and slightly left of center.	Performance	Griffin et al., 1987

Table 15.1. continued

Test	Test description	Outcome measure	Reference
2-Back Test	Examinee views continuous stream of stimuli and determines if object matched the shape of the stimulus 2-back in the sequence. Scored as percentage of correct responses.	Simulator performance	Causse et al., 2010; Causse, Dehais, & Pastor, 2011
Spatial Stroop	Meaning of the word and location on the screen may or may not match. Examinee asked to respond based on meaning or location.		
Matching to sample	See Row 3 in this table	Simulator performance	Tolton, 2014
Visual sequence comparison			
Auditory letter span test	Letters in series of varying length are read at a speed of one per second. Examinees write down the letters in the exact order in which they were called out after the series has been completed. Scored as number of series correct.	Situational awareness (SAGAT)	Sulistyawati et al., , 2011
Number comparison test	Inspects pairs of multi-digit numbers and indicates whether the two numbers in each pair are the same or different.		
Visual number span test (modified)	Similar to auditory letter span, but numbers are flipped over on cards or presented in other way.		
Continuous opposites	Participants are required to remember the last three words (or their opposites) in a list presented one word at a time. If a word appears in the color red, the participant is required to remember its opposite.	Situational awareness	Carretta et al., 1996
XYZ assignment	Must combine or delete simple line figures assigned to three letters (X, Y, and Z). Two figures are assigned to each letter in the form of an addition or subtraction equation. Participants must mentally combine or delete the lines of these figures and then memorize the combination. Information about one figure is sometimes needed to solve the equation for one of the other figures.		

Table 15.1. continued

Test	Test description	Outcome measure	Reference
Internal timing	Participants view three labeled points (A, B, and C) placed in a straight line on a computer screen. When they depress the space bar on the keyboard, a target begins moving from A at a constant velocity and is blanked from the screen as it passes B. The participant's task is to determine when in time the target would reach C and to press the space bar at that time in response.	Situational awareness	Endsley & Bolstad, 1994
Perceptual vigilance	Participants are shown a computer screen with 25 rows of 80 red dots on a black background. They are instructed to scan the screen thoroughly for a change in one of the dots from red to magenta that is just above visual threshold. The participant signals when they notice the change by pressing any key on the keyboard.		

Note. SAGAT = Situation Awareness Global Assessment Technique.

Table 15.2. Complex attention

Test	Test description	Outcome measure	Reference
Attention/mental control	Several subtests Numbers forward and numbers backward from the MicroCog, Alphabet, and Wordlist 1 requires that examinees press the Enter key whenever a word appears that belongs to a category specified in each of four trials. Two categories are phonemic, the other two semantic. Wordlist 2 uses the typical word list recognition format and presents the 16 words from Wordlist 1 imbedded with 20 others. Examinees respond whenever one of the words from the first list appears on the screen.	Brain injury indicators (imaging)	McGuire et al., 2014
Difference score: visual sequence comparison and Divided Attention Test	Comparison of two simultaneously presented series of letters and numbers. (see below for Divided Attention Test)	Group comparison or classification	Kay, 1995; Kay et al., 1991
Symbol digit coding	Substitution of digits for symbols using a key followed by testing of immediate and delayed recall of symbol–digit pairs.		
Divided Attention Test	Examinee monitors the vertical movements of a bar within a circle and returns the bar to the center position when its deviation from center exceeds an upper or lower boundary. The monitoring task is presented alone and in combination with the visual sequence comparison task.		
Divided Attention Test Dual-task test (dual condition)	Examinee monitors the vertical movements of a bar within a circle and returns the bar to the center position when its deviation from center exceeds an upper or lower boundary. The monitoring task in combination with the visual sequence comparison task.	Group comparison or classification	Kay, 1995
Dual task: flight simulator and math (dual and single conditions)	Task performed without flight (baseline) or during flight (as secondary task). Examinee presented with arithmetic problems of 3-digit addition and subtraction then must respond by indicating whether the obtained sum was greater or less than a prespecified value of 5 using two button keys on the throttle by the left hand. The arithmetic problems were randomly generated using only the numbers 1–9. The problem changed either after examinee responded or after a 4-s time limit. Scores include reaction time, error, lost rate (no response in time limit), and information processing speed	Group comparison or classification	Zhang et al., 1997

Table 15.2. continued

Test	Test description	Outcome measure	Reference
Symbol digit substitution test	Requires the participant to substitute numbers for geometric symbols.	Group comparison or classification	O'Donnell et al., 1992
Trail Making Test	A: Twenty five numbered circles are to be joined in sequence. B: Twenty five numbered circles are numbered 1 to 13 and A to L and are to be joined in alternating sequence.		
Dichotic listening task: multitask	Participants perform combinations of a psychomotor task involving manipulating a joystick and rudder pedals and the listening task simultaneously. The listening task requires indicating what digits are presented in the designated ear in order by either entering them in a key pad with the left hand or voicing them in the condition when both hands are operating joysticks.	Performance	Griffin et al., 1987
Divided Attention Test	Participant monitors the vertical movements of a bar within a circle and returns the bar to the center position when its deviation from center exceeds an upper or lower boundary. The monitoring task is presented alone and in combination with the visual sequence comparison task.	Performance	Kay, 1995; Yakimovich et al., 1994
Dual-task test (single and dual condition)	Consists of two tasks, each of which is performed alone and then together as a simultaneous task. One task is a visual-motor tracking test. The second task is a continuous memory task, involving recall of the previously presented number.		
Dual-task test (single and dual conditions)	See row above	Simulator performance	Van Benthem & Herdman, 2016
Dual-task test (dual condition)	See row above	Simulator performance	Taylor et al., 2007; Tolton, 2014
Dual-task test (single and dual conditions)	See row above	Simulator performance	Yesavage et al., 2011
Symbol digit coding	Substitution of digits for symbols using a key followed by testing of immediate and delayed recall of symbol–digit pairs.		

Table 15.2. continued

Test	Test description	Outcome measure	Reference
Working memory span composite	Comprised of 5 tests: computational span, sentence span, forward digit span (from WAIS-R), backward digit span (from WAIS-R), and visual backward digit span accuracy (from CogScreen).	Simulator performance	Taylor et al., 2005
Attention sharing	Two-dimensional tracking task coupled with a digit cancellation task. A tracking task is presented during all three subtests based on a random-order, sinusoidal, rose-petal forcing function. To keep the tracking task at the same level of perceived difficulty for all participants across the testing period, the program automatically increased or decreased tracking difficulty to keep tracking errors at a constant prescribed level. In the digit cancellation task, a digit appeared at a random interval of between 5 and 15 s. If participants did not respond to the digit within 4 s of its presentation, the tracking circle disappeared, forcing the participants to cancel the digit in order to resume tracking.	Situational awareness	Endsley & Bolstad, 1994
Scheduling 2	Five horizontal logarithmic scales can be presented. A line beneath each scale increases at a unique, constant rate. Each line and scale appear on a separate screen that may be viewed by entering the scale number on the response keypad. Participants score points equal to the current value of the line displayed on the scale by pressing the ENABLE key. When the ENABLE key is pressed, the participant's total score is incremented by the value of the line, which is then reset to 0, where it will start increasing again. If the value of a line reaches the upper limit of the scale and the participant has not responded by pressing the ENABLE key, the value of the line will reset to 0 without the participant receiving any points.	Situational awareness	Carretta et al., 1996
Time sharing 2	Part 1, compensatory tracking: "participants maneuver the right-hand control stick to keep a 'gunsight' centered on an airplane"; Part 2, attention: "Numbers appear one at a time in sequence at the lower part of the screen. Occasionally, a number will be missing from the sequence. Participants are required to type the missing number on the keypad." Part 3 combined: "during the final part of this test, participants simultaneously perform tracking and attention tasks."		

Table 15.2. continued

Test	Test description	Outcome measure	Reference
Working memory capacity	Participants view a series of altitude indicator displays positioned in different flight orientations. Upon presentation, they are asked to say aloud whether the aircraft was pitched up or down. Participants are asked to remember the orientation of the horizon line displayed on the altitude indicator and the number below the altitude indicator.	Situational awareness	Doane, 2003

Reasoning

Table 15.3 lists the 17 tests of reasoning we identified. The results for reasoning are more consistent, with most studies reporting a relationship between scores on a reasoning test and the selected outcome measure. The studies were nearly equally split between those that assessed the test in terms of ability to classify examinees as healthy or impaired, or compared mean scores across groups, and studies that compared test scores with simulator performance.

Perception

Six studies included evaluations of 15 different tests of perception. These are presented in Table 15.4. Most studies reported correlations with situational awareness scores or levels. One study provided some information on the relationship between perception and flight performance, but this was in a study designed to compare pilots of manned and remotely operated aircraft (Barron et al., 2016). The one study that used simulator performance scores reported that perception was not significant once age and expertise were added to the model, suggesting they explain more of the variance in performance than perception scores do (Taylor et al., 2007).

Memory

Table 15.5 provides information on the tests used in six studies that evaluated different assessments of memory. Most of these examined the relationship between memory and situational awareness. One study compared memory scores with imaging results that documented pathophysiological changes in brain tissue (McGuire et al., 2014). One study by O'Donnell was part of the development of a battery called "Neuropsychological Test Battery" (NTB). The proposed battery included a memory retrieval task. While this study was well designed, it is difficult to draw a definitive conclusion about the memory task as the results differed for the memory test when it was included in different versions of the battery that were evaluated over time, since the battery was revised as part of the development process.

Table 15.3. Reasoning

Test	Test description	Outcome measure	References
Reasoning/calculation domain	Domain of the MicroCog. Subtests: Analogies, Object Match A & B, Math calculation.	Brain injury indicators (imaging)	McGuire et al., 2014
Logical reasoning test nonsense syllogisms	Participant is presented with a series of syllogisms and must decide in each case whether the conclusion is valid or invalid.	Group comparison or classification	O'Donnell et al., 1992
Arithmetic test	Provides a measure of the ability to understand arithmetic relations expressed as word problems.	Group comparison or classification	O'Donnell et al., 1992
Math test	Traditional math word problems with multiple-choice answers.	Group comparison or classification	Kay, 1995; Kay et al., 1991
		Simulator performance	Tolton, 2014
Pathfinder	Adapted from trail making test. After viewing a number or letter displayed in the center of the screen, the task is to select 1 of 4 quadrants containing the next character in a previously specified sequence. Three sequencing rules using numbers, letters, or alternating series of numbers and letters are used. Performance measured in terms of speed, response accuracy, thruput (number of correct responses per minute); and coordination.	Group comparison or classification	Kay et al., 1991 Kay, 1995; Kay et al., 1991
		Simulator performance	Tolton, 2014 Yesavage et al., 2011 Kennedy et al., 2013; Kennedy et al., 2015
Verbal thinking test	The participant has to classify two letters of the alphabet by each of two rules. One rule involves physical identity alone (whether both are the same letter in the same case). The other involves a semantic rule (whether they both are vowels or consonants).	Group comparison or classification	O'Donnell et al., 1992
Verbal analogies	Measures the ability to reason and determine relationships between words.	Performance	Barron et al., 2016
Deductive reasoning test	The goal of the task is to solve syllogisms by choosing from among three suggested solutions, the one that follows logically.	Simulator performance	Causse et al., 2010; Causse, Dehais, & Pastor, 2011
Reasoning test	Same as deductive reasoning test above.	Simulator performance	Causse, Dehais, Arexis, et al., 2011

Table 15.3. continued

Test	Test description	Outcome measure	References
Wisconsin Card Sorting test	Computerized sorting cards according to three different unknown categories (color, shape, number) with audio feedback as yes/no for correct response; target category automatically changed when participant successfully categorized 10 cards; task ended when six categories achieved (color, shape, number, color, shape, number) or deck of 128 cards used. Scored as total number of perseverative errors (≥2 unsuccessful sorting on the same category).	Simulator performance	Causse et al., 2010 Causse, Dehais, & Pastor, 2011
Analytic test	Designed to measure a participant's ability to understand a given structure of arbitrary relations among the presented items and to deduce new information from the relations given. For each question, there are five choices from which to select the correct response. Scored as number of correct responses. Subtest of the Graduate Record Examination; 25 questions with a time limit of 30 min.	Situational awareness	Endsley & Bolstad, 1994
Figure classification	Each item presents two or three groups each containing three geometrical figures that are alike in accordance with some rule. The second row of each item contains eight test figures. The task is to discover the rules and assign each test figure to one of the groups. Scored as number identified correctly minus a fraction of those incorrect.	Situational awareness	Sulistyawati et al., 2011
Following direction	Task is to determine the point in a matrix of letters that would be reached by following a complex set of directions. Scored as number of letters marked correctly minus a fraction of those incorrect.	Situational awareness	Sulistyawati et al., 2011
Math aptitude test	Five-choice word problems requiring arithmetic or very simple algebraic concepts only. Scored as number correct minus a fraction of incorrect	Situational awareness	Sulistyawati et al., 2011
Logical reasoning test	A series of symbols are presented, along with a verbal description of the logical relationships between them. The participant must determine whether the logical relations described are true or not with respect to the presented symbols.	Situational awareness	Stokes et al., 1992

Table 15.3. continued

Test	Test description	Outcome measure	References
Rapid serial classification 4-square	Participants are shown a 4-square (2×2) display in which a letter pattern can be drawn (C, X, or Z) between points. Participants must determine which letter is being drawn by following the pattern of dots as they are sequentially illuminated and extinguished.	Situational Awareness	Carretta et al., 1996
Raven's Advanced Progressive Matrices	Participants are shown a pattern with a piece missing and instructed to select the missing piece from eight choices; 12 familiarization problems followed by 36 problems arranged in increasing order of difficulty. Scored as number of correct responses.	Situational awareness	Endsley & Bolstad, 1994

Table 15.4. Perception

Test, $N = 15$	Test description	Outcome measure	Reference
Aerial Orientation Test	The participant's task was to select from five aircraft outlines presented at various rotations the one that showed the same side as a presented aircraft. The test consists of 30 items. Time to complete the test and accuracy were recorded.	Situational awareness	Endsley & Bolstad, 1994
Block counting	Assesses spatial ability through the analysis of three-dimensional representations of a set of blocks	Performance	Barron et al., 2016
Block design test	Test in the WAIS-R to measure spatial ability. Described as "a commonly used measure of visualization that accounts for age differences in performance of spatial memory and problem-solving tasks."	Performance	Morrow, 2003
Cube comparison test	Participants presented with 21 drawings of pairs of cubes (similar to children's blocks) that had a unique letter or number on each face of the cube. The task is to determine if the two drawings could represent the same block by mentally rotating the blocks so that they would have the same orientation.	Situational awareness	Endsley & Bolstad, 1994 Sulistyawati et al., 2011
Dot estimation	Participants are shown two equal-sized square boxes on a computer screen with a number of white dots. The task is to indicate as quickly as possible which box contains more dots, using designated keys on the keyboard. Accuracy and response time are recorded for each trial.	Situational awareness	Endsley & Bolstad, 1994
Encoding speed	Participants were presented with two pairs of letters and had to decide whether the pairs of letters were the same or different. The pairs remained on the computer screen until the participants responded. Each subtest used a different rule for similarity: physical identity, letters in both pairs must be identical in letter and in case (AA and AA); name identity, both pairs of letters must be composed of the same letter regardless of case (AA and Aa); or categorical identity, and letter pairs need to be either all vowels or all consonants (Ai and Ea). Accuracy and response time are recorded.	Situational awareness	Endsley & Bolstad, 1994

Table 15.4. continued

Test, $N = 15$	Test description	Outcome measure	Reference
Form board test	Each items presents five shaded drawings of pieces, some or all of which can be put together to form a figure presented in outline form. The task is to indicate which of the pieces, when fitted together, would form the outline. Scored as number correct minus number incorrect.	Situational awareness	Sulistyawati et al., 2011
Group Embedded Figures Test	Each problem in the test consists of a complex geometric pattern that contains one of eight simple geometric figures that are presented to the participant. Participants were required to trace with a pencil the simple geometric figure that is embedded in each complex pattern; 3 min is provided for a practice section with seven problems, and 5 min for each of two test sections with eight problems. Accuracy and time to complete each section are recorded.	Situational awareness	Endsley & Bolstad, 1994
Hidden figure test	The task is to decide which of five geometrical figures is embedded in a complex pattern. Scored as number marked correctly minus a fraction of the number marked incorrectly.	Situational awareness	Sulistyawati et al., 2011
Hidden patterns recognition	Participants must detect an abstract line drawing embedded within a more complex pattern of lines.	Situational awareness	Stokes et al., 1992
Manikin	Participant identifies the hand in which a rotated human figure is holding a flag.	Simulator performance	Taylor et al., 2007
		Group comparison or classification	Kay, 1995; Kay et al., 1991
Mental rotation ability	Not described in publication; appears to be the same as Rotated Hidden Patterns.	Situational awareness	Stokes et al., 1992
Perceptual speed	A three- to seven-digit number was presented on the computer screen for the prescribed stimulus time. After a 500-ms delay, a second number was presented. Participants had to decide as quickly as possible whether the two numbers were the same or different (due to transposed digits) by pressing designated keys on the keyboard in response. Scored for accuracy and reaction time.	Situational awareness	Endsley & Bolstad, 1994

Table 15.4. continued

Test, $N = 15$	Test description	Outcome measure	Reference
Revised Minnesota Form Board Test	The test consists of 64 two-dimensional diagrams, each comprised of a collection of pieces analogous to an unassembled jigsaw puzzle. For each diagram, the examinee is to select from five possible answers the one that correctly represents the pieces put together as a whole figure. Scored as number of correct responses in 20 min.	Situational awareness	Endsley & Bolstad, 1994
Rotated hidden patterns	Participants must detect an abstract line drawing embedded within a more complex pattern of lines, and the target figure may be rotated. Mirror images are considered non-targets.	Situational awareness	Stokes et al., 1992

Table 15.5. Memory

Test	Test description	Outcome measure	Reference
Memory on MicroCog	Participants to simply read and remember a fictional name and address, then later asked multiple-choice questions about it. Presented with two short stories separated by several other subtests with multiple-choice questions immediately and again after a delay.	Brain injury indicators (imaging)	McGuire et al., 2014
Sternberg memory retrieval	Ask if a "probe" letter of the alphabet is a member of a previously memorized target set.	Group comparison or classification	O'Donnell et al., 1992
Immediate/ delayed memory	One-digit numbers are flashed on a computer screen for .05 s, with 2 s between for half of each subtest (immediate) and 5 s for the remainder (delayed). Participants were asked what number that appeared immediately prior and then two numbers prior to the number on the screen.	Situational awareness	Endsley & Bolstad, 1994
Long-term working memory	Two cockpits are displayed for 40 s. Then the participant counts from a given number backwards aloud by threes for 30 s. Then the computer asks for situation specific values displayed in either cockpit. In six trials the cockpits are related. In three, they are unrelated cockpits.	Situational awareness	Doane, 2003
Building memory	Asked to indicate the location of a number of buildings (12 items) seen on a previously studied map; provided after 4 min for memorizing.	Situational awareness	Sulistyawati et al., 2011
ATC Situation Recognition task	Asked to build a mental picture of a situation from air traffic control calls and selecting appropriate diagrams of the scenario.	Situational awareness	Stokes et al., 1992
Spatial memory test	Participant views a set of nonsense figures. About 20 min minutes after initial presentation Participant views 40 figures and decides for each one whether or not it had been a member of the previously viewed set.	Situational awareness	Stokes et al., 1992

Motor Performance

Table 15.6 contains the results reported on assessments of motor performance or response. This was one of the least common domains represented in the included studies and the only significant findings were correlations in two studies; one with simulator performance and one with situational awareness.

Executive Function

Assessments of executive function use tests that required judgments about how and when to shift attention or that required completing a complex task such as a maze. We identified three tests that were used in a total of 11 studies (reported in 14 articles). These are summarized in Table 15.7. The outcomes that test scores were expected to indicate or be associated with included brain injury indications, classification, and situational awareness, but the majority (seven of 11) used flight or simulator performance. Most of the studies reported a significant relationship between the test and the outcome, either statistically significant correlations with function (e.g., duration of posttraumatic amnesia) or differences in scores across subject groups defined by patient status (e.g., healthy or not).

Situational Awareness

While situational awareness was used as an outcome in some studies, four studies evaluated situational awareness in terms of its correlations with simulator performance. These are summarized in Table 15.8.

Batteries and Subsets of Batteries

Batteries

Table 15.9 provides an overview of the six studies that evaluated full test batteries. Studies that included only subsets of items from batteries are included in Table 15.10. These studies included assessment of the CogScreen, a battery created specifically to evaluate pilots, as well as other studies of shorter mini-mental tests created for general screening. Most of these publications (by Kay, 1995, by O'Donnell et al., 1992, and by Stokes et al., 1991) reported evaluations conducted as part of the development of what were new or proposed batteries at the time of the study. The studies by Kay (1995) were part of the development of the CogScreen, while O'Donnell et al. (1992) developed The Neuropsychological Test Battery. Both of these evaluated the set of tests in terms of their ability to discriminate or sort people into healthy or impaired. Stokes et al. (1991) took a similar approach but also evaluated two common mental status tests to allow comparisons of tests designed to be used for standard screening and diagnosis in the general population to ones designed for pilots.

Table 15.6. Motor performance

Test	Test description	Outcome measure	Reference
Interval production test	Required to tap at a regular rate two to three times per second for 3 min.	Group comparison or classification	O'Donnell et al., 1992
Unstable tracking test	Must keep a computer generated "target" centered with a tracking knob or a joystick while the computer generates offsets for the target.	Group comparison or classification	O'Donnell et al., 1992
Psycho-motor task: single- and multitask	Required participants to maintain first one, then two, and finally three, randomly displaced cursors on fixed targets on the CRT by manipulating joysticks and foot pedals.	Performance	Griffin et al., 1987
Target hitting test	Instructed to click as fast as possible on each target. Test of basic psychomotor reaction time, measured by velocity index.	Simulator performance	Causse et al., 2010; Causse, Dehais, & Pastor, 2011
			Causse, Dehais, Arexis, et al., 2011
Laser aiming task 2	Instructed to imagine they are shooting from an aircraft at the bottom of the screen; must match the apparent altitude (size) of the target and the laser to get the laser beam on target.	Situational awareness	Carretta et al., 1996

Table 15.7. Executive function

Test	Test description	Outcome measure	Reference
Shifting attention	Three rules are set for selecting a response about an arrow that is displayed and the respondent applies them. Then the respondent is told what rule to apply for next set of questions. Then, the respondent is not told the rule in effect, only if the answer is correct or not. The respondent needs to determine what rule is in effect.	Brain injury indicators	Moore & Kay, 1995; Kay, 1995
		Performance	Kay, 1995; Yakimovich et al., 1994
		Simulator performance	Kennedy et al., 2013; Kennedy et al., 2015
		Simulator performance	Taylor et al., 2005; Taylor et al., 2007; Tolton, 2014; Van Benthem & Herdman, 2016; Yesavage et al., 2011
Maze task	Comprises 4 three-dimensional mazes. Total time to reach the endpoint after a practice maze.	Situational awareness	Endsley & Bolstad, 1994
Maze tracking test	Line mazes of increasing complexity are traced as rapidly as possible to decide if there is an unbroken path from beginning to end.	Situational awareness	Stokes et al., 1992

Table 15.8. Situational awareness

Tests	Test description	Outcome	References
Situation awareness	Subjective ratings from pilot, flight lead and trained observer during simulation. Ratings based on planned and executed tactics, response to situations and awareness of ongoing events.	Simulator performance	Venturino et al., 1989
Situation Awareness Global Assessment Technique	Includes queries about all awareness requirements: Level 1 (perception of data), Level 2 (comprehension of meaning), and Level 3 (projection of the near future) components. This approach minimizes the possible bias of attention, as participants cannot prepare for the queries in advance.	Simulator performance	Sulistyawati et al., 2011; Venturino et al., 1989
Situation Awareness Rating Scale	Respondents rate themselves or their subordinates on 31 items	Simulator performance	Bell & Waag, 1997

Table 15.9. Batteries

Test	Test description	Outcome measure	Reference
MicroCog	Computer-administered test battery containing 18 subtests that contribute to summary scores for nine interrelated cognitive areas (domains): attention/mental control, memory, spatial processing, reasoning/calculation, reaction time, information processing accuracy, information processing speed, cognitive functioning, and cognitive proficiency.	Brain injury indicators	McGuire et al., 2014
Multidimensional Aptitude Battery–II	Broad-based test of intellectual and cognitive ability. The test yields a full-scale intelligence quotient (IQ) score, a verbal IQ score, and a performance IQ score. Verbal components are tapped by the information, comprehension, arithmetic, similarities, and vocabulary subtests. Performance measures include the digit symbol coding, picture completion, spatial, picture arrangement, and object assembly subtests.	Brain injury indicators	McGuire et al., 2014
CogScreen	Computer-administered and scored designed to rapidly assess deficits or changes in attention, immediate- and short-term memory, visual–perceptual functions, sequencing functions, logical problem-solving, calculation skills, reaction time, simultaneous information processing abilities, and executive functions. The battery consists of 13 subtests, each of which may be scored in multiple ways such as speed, accuracy, and thruput (number of correct responses per minute), depending on the individual subtest.	Group comparison or classification Simulator performance	Kay, 1995 Kay, 1995; Kay et al., 1991 DeVoll, 2013 Hyland & Kay, 1994
Neuropsychological Test Battery	Test battery using step approach to testing (3 steps); revised battery (second-generation) Level 1 tests: Trails A; Trails B; symbol digit; tracking. Level 2 tests: logical reasoning (% correct); dynamic memory; arithmetic (attempts). Level 3 tests: memory (slope); Zung depression; manifest anxiety; dynamic memory (reaction time)	Group comparison or classification	O'Donnell et al., 1992
Illinois Screening Test	Assesses skills for performance in complex dynamic environments such as flying; two neuropsychological tests for each of six skills in each battery (Version 1 or 2), skills are: perceptual-motor ability, spatial ability, working memory capacity, attentional performance (visual scanning), processing flexibility, and planning/sequence ability.	Group comparison or classification	Stokes et al., 1991)

Table 15.9. continued

Test	Test description	Outcome measure	Reference
FFM mini-mental test	Assesses five areas of cognitive functioning: orientation in time and space, "registration" (naming three objects), attention and calculation (decrementing a value by sevens aloud), language skills (following spoken instructions, repeating and generating sentences), and recall (of three objects).	Group comparison or classification	Stokes et al., 1991
AMA mini-mental test	Shortened version of FFM mini-mental test; includes registration, recall, attention, and calculation, plus two short-term memory tasks involving recall of digits and a spatial figure.	Group comparison or classification	Stokes et al., 1991
SPARTANS	Designed to assess individual differences in pilots; nine subtasks: dual task tracking, risk taking task, Sternberg task, maze tracing, hidden figures, visual scanning, schedule task, dual task decrement, visual number span.	Group comparison or classification	Stokes et al., 1991
Flitescript (situational knowledge in long-term memory)	Index pilots' representations of situational knowledge in long-term memory. Two versions: a recall version and a recognition version. The recall version of the test involves reconstructing both randomized and coherent air traffic control (ATC) radio call sequences from memory. The recognition version requires listening to an ATC communication sequence and selecting the correct graphic depiction of the situation represented by the ATC communications from a set of alternatives.	Simulator performance	Hyland & Kay, 1994
WOMBAT	Requires that the test participant judge the relative worth of a particular action at each moment and dynamically reorder task priorities. Requires that the test participant develop a strategy for dealing with constantly changing priorities. Provides a rigorous test of the pilot's ability to attend to varying sources of information and to shift priorities appropriately.	Simulator performance	Hyland & Kay, 1994

Subsets of Batteries

Eight studies evaluated subsets of test batteries. Some of these results are from studies that also evaluated the entire battery (Kay, 1995; McGuire et al., 2014). In these cases the goal was often to determine whether a subset was driving the results when they were significant, or whether a subset performed well but was "hidden" in overall scores when the analysis provided inconclusive or insignificant findings. These subset analyses used the same outcomes – brain injury indicators and accuracy of classification – as they did for the analysis of the complete battery. Other studies used subsets either to reduce burden on study participants (it may be feasible to do a 1-hr assessment with more people than a 6-hr assessment) or because the subset corresponds to the underlying construct they wanted to test. Most of these studies assessed the battery subsets in terms of their correlations with actual flight evaluations (Barron et al., 2016) or simulator flight performance (Kennedy et al., 2013; Taylor et al., 2000; Tolton, 2014).

Table 15.10. Subsets from test batteries and outcomes used in their evaluation

Test	Outcome measure	Reference
Air Force Officer Qualifying Test: subset	Performance	Barron et al., 2016
MicroCog: subset	Brain injury indicators (imaging)	McGuire et al., 2014
CogScreen: subset	Brain injury indicators	Moore & Kay, 1995
CogScreen: subset	Group comparison or classification	Kay, 1995; Kay et al., 1991
CogScreen: subset	Group comparison or classification	DeVoll, 2013
CogScreen: subset	Simulator performance	Kennedy et al., 2010
CogScreen: subset	Simulator performance	Kennedy et al., 2013
CogScreen: subset	Simulator performance	Kennedy et al., 2015
CogScreen: subset	Simulator performance	Taylor et al., 2000
CogScreen: subset	Simulator performance	Tolton, 2014
CogScreen: subset	Simulator performance	Tolton, 2014
CogScreen: subset	Simulator performance	Van Benthem & Herdman, 2016

Summary of Test Evaluation Results From the Systematic Review

While inclusion of the results from each study discussed in the systematic review was beyond the scope of this chapter, several major themes were summarized in the systematic review and are outlined here. In general, test batteries such as the CogScreen (Kay, 1995) and The Neuropsychological Test battery (O'Donnell et al., 1992) had moderate to good ability to discriminate between healthy and impaired participants in the development of the test. After tests are developed, there is typically further study using these tests on a larger set of the population of interest. There were several studies that evaluated subsets of batteries, generally the CogScreen (Kay, 1995), in order to determine whether the subtest performance was a driver of overall battery results. Furthermore, there was an attempt to correlate these results with flight evaluations and flight simulator data, which may make the data more relevant to real-life pilot operations. However, a limitation of the current literature is that because of the variability in study design and analytic methods, it is not possible to combine data across studies. This, combined with the fact that some of the strongest published data were from test development stages, meant that there were very limited data available on the replicability of any one given finding.

Many of the issues noted above with the test batteries and subbatteries were also seen in the studies that focused on individual cognitive domains. Variability in study design and analytic methods prevented quantitative or qualitative summaries across studies. One example that illustrated this challenge is that when a well-designed memory test was used from one of the test batteries, the results varied from substudy to substudy when the test was part of different versions of the overall test battery (O'Donnell et al., 1992).

Studies evaluating tests of attention, especially complex attention, and those evaluating tests of reasoning produced the most consistent results, showing a relationship between the test and the chosen outcome measure across the variety of study designs and analysis approaches used.

Application of Findings to Neuropsychologists

Neurological issues are a common cause of pilot grounding. As part of the evaluation for returning aviators to flight duties, neuropsychological and cognitive testing is often ordered. While instruments that are widely used and standardized for the general population are sometimes chosen for pilot evaluations, the unique skills required to safely pilot an aircraft often require the use of tests or test batteries specifically designed to identify subtle but operationally significant problems. Some of these tests have been formally evaluated, and these results were part of the systematic review that was the basis for this chapter. It is important that the neuropsychologist evaluating the pilot is familiar with the specialized environment in which aviators operate and understands the various instruments available, including the data available (or not available) to support the use of the tool specifically with pilots. This would help ensure that tests are appropriately used and interpreted and that appropriate recommendations are made.

Future Directions for Advancing the Field

Reviewing the literature on studies of tests used in the neuropsychological evaluation of pilots underscores that there are many opportunities to improve our understanding of how to return pilots to flight activities in a safe and time-efficient manner.

An overarching recommendation is that there should be support for the development of a research agenda in aerospace neuropsychology that includes clinical experts in the field, but also individuals with broad expertise in neuropsychological testing, and representatives from all key groups such as regulators, pilots, and individuals working in other safety-sensitive fields.

Additional specific recommendations include:

1. Identify key tests, including those that are aerospace-specific and those used in the general population, which are most frequently used in the clinical evaluation of active pilots.
2. Identify (a) appropriate populations and minimum numbers needed for normative data collection for the measures most frequently used in the clinical evaluation of active pilots and (b) the frequency with which normative data should be updated that is consistent with current best practices in the broader field of neuropsychology.
3. Consensus should be developed regarding the most appropriate study designs (including comparators, outcomes, and statistical approaches) needed to assure that future studies are rigorous and directly address key operational questions. This will increase the likelihood that data can be compared and combined across studies and is especially important given the expense involved in conducting research studies and the relatively select population being studied.
4. Consensus development should involve all stake-holder groups including physicians most likely to request neuropsychological testing, regulators, and pilots. This should include ongoing collection of operational data.
5. Identify other safety-sensitive fields in which neuropsychological testing may be important and include representatives from these fields in the development of the research agenda. Given the long history of work in this area within aviation, it is likely that aviation-specific neuropsychology work may have relevance to other fields. Identifying opportunities to contribute to neuropsychological evaluation of individuals working in other safety-sensitive areas will increase the impact of future work and increase potential funding opportunities.
6. Identify existing unpublished data that could provide an important starting place for future research. Data are currently collected by airlines, airline pilot unions, and regulatory agencies. A set of guidelines based on what has been done in other fields would need to be developed that outline how such data could be protected, deidentified, and used in a fashion to strengthen the knowledge base for aviation neuropsychological testing without compromising safeguards for pilot privacy and airline business models.
7. Increase opportunities for the mentorship of junior neuropsychologists and researchers to encourage the development of research programs that sequentially build on prior studies and support the practice of the neuropsychological evaluation in safety-sensitive professions such as aviation. Pathways for doing this are well established in other fields.

Conclusion

This chapter highlights the complexity inherent in understanding the state of the science of assessing a pilot for return-to-flight duties after illness, injury, or when a performance issue potentially related to neurocognitive issues arises. While the starting point for these evaluations is rooted in general expertise with neuropsychological evaluation, a large number of possible tests that could be used require additional experience and knowledge of the aircraft and aviation environment in which the pilot will be operating. This highlights the need for pathways to train and mentor junior neuropsychologists interested in working in this field. Lastly, specific and actionable recommendations for further research are provided so that we are able to safely return more pilots to flight activities after injury and illness.

Acknowledgments

We would like to thank our colleagues at the Pacific Northwest Evidence Based Practice Center at Oregon Health & Science University for their assistance. Tamara P. Cheney, MD, and Cynthia Davis-O'Reilly, BS, were coauthors of the original review, and Elaine Graham, MLS (retired), and Tracy Dana, MLS, were essential in producing the literature searches and report. We would also like to thank Pam Day from the Aerospace Medical Association for helping us locate conference presentations.

In designing the study questions and methodology at the outset and during the preparation of this report, the Pacific Northwest Evidence-based Practice Center (EPC) consulted an Advisory Panel. Advisory Panel members were not involved in the analysis of the evidence or the writing of the report or this chapter. After the report was drafted, it was sent to experts for review and comment (see final report for further details).

We would like to acknowledge the important professional contributions made by Drs. Jack Hastings (d. 2021) and Muriel Lezak (d. 2021) as well as their personal support for this project and friendship. We are saddened by their deaths, although still buoyed by our memories and in awe of their dedication and accomplishments.

Funding

The systematic review was funded in part by contributions from the Allied Pilots Association, the Aerospace Medicine Association, and private donors; funds were administered through the OHSU Foundation. No additional funding was received for this chapter.

Disclaimer

The authors of this chapter are responsible for its content. Suggestions and comments of advisors, reviewers, and funders were considered, but ultimately the research team decided on the final content of this report and the author are responsible for the chapter. The study questions, design, methodological approaches, and/or conclusions do not necessarily represent the views of individual Advisory Panel members, Reviewers, or Funders. Statements in the report or this chapter do not necessarily represent the official views of or imply endorsement by the funders.

References

Agency for Healthcare Research and Quality. (2023). *Methods guide for effectiveness and comparative effectiveness reviews*. Effective Health Care Program, Agency for Healthcare Research and Quality, Rockville, MD. https://effectivehealthcare.ahrq.gov/products/collections/cer-methods-guide

Barron, L.G., Carretta, T.R., & Rose, M.R. (2016). Aptitude and trait predictors of manned and unmanned aircraft pilot job performance. *Military Psychology, 28*(2), 65–77. https://doi.org/10.1037/mil0000109

Bell, H.H., & Waag, W.L. (1997). *Using observer ratings to assess situational awareness in tactical air environments* (AL/HR-TP-1996-0050). Armstrong Laboratory.

Carretta, T.R., Perry, D.C., Jr., & Ree, M.J. (1996). Prediction of situational awareness in F-15 pilots. *International Journal of Aviation Psychology, 6*(1), 21–41. https://doi.org/10.1207/s15327108ijap0601_2

Causse, M., Dehais, F., Arexis, M., & Pastor, J. (2011). Cognitive aging and flight performances in general aviation pilots. *Aging, Neuropsychology, and Cognition, 18*(5), 544–561. https://doi.org/10.1080/13825585.2011.586018

Causse, M., Dehais, F., & Pastor, J. (2010, June 3). *Flight experience and executive functions predict flight simulator performance in general aviation pilots* [Paper presentation]. 4th International Conference on Research in Air Transportation (ICRAT), Budapest, Hungary.

Causse, M., Dehais, F., & Pastor, J. (2011). Executive functions and pilot characteristics predict flight simulator performance in general aviation pilots. *The International Journal of Aviation Psychology, 21*(3), 217–234. https://doi.org/10.1080/10508414.2011.582441

Doane, S. (2003). *New measures of complex cognitive abilities: Relating memory processes to aviation flight situation awareness abilities*. https://doi.org/10.21236/ADA416315

DeVoll, J. (2013, March). FAA experience with neuropsychological testing for airmen with Depression on SSRI medications. *Aviation Space & Environmental Medicine, Abstract 448*, 409.

Eden, J., Levit, L., Berg, A., & Morton, S. (Eds.) (2011). *Finding what works in healthcare: Standards for systematic reviews*. National Academic Press.

Endsley, M.R., & Bolstad, C.A. (1994). Individual differences in pilot situation awareness. *The International Journal of Aviation Psychology, 4*(3), 241–264. https://doi.org/10.1207/s15327108ijap0403_3

Griffin, G.R., Morrison, T.R., Amerson, T.L., & Hamilton, P.V. (1987). *Predicting air combat maneuvering (ACM) performance: Fleet fighter ACM readiness program grades as performance criteria*. (NAMRL-1333). Naval Aerospace Medical Research Laboratory.

Hyland, D., & Kay, E. (1994). *Age 60 study, Part IV: Experimental evaluation of pilot performance* [report]. Civil Aerospace Medical Institute. https://rosap.ntl.bts.gov/view/dot/21421

Kay, G., Horst, R., Pakull, B., & Hordinsky, J. (1991, May 5–9). *Automated cognitive function assessment of civilian pilots* [Paper presentation]. 62nd Annual Scientific Meeting of the Aerospace Medical Association, Cincinnati, Ohio, United States.

Kay, G.G. (1995). *CogScreen-Aeromedical Edition professional manual*. Psychological Assessment Resources. https://cogscreen.com/

Kennedy, Q., Taylor, J., Heraldez, D., Noda, A., Lazzeroni, L.C., & Yesavage, J. (2013). Intraindividual variability in basic reaction time predicts middle-aged and older pilots' flight simulator performance. *Journals of Gerontology Series B-Psychological Sciences & Social Sciences, 68*(4), 487–494. https://doi.org/10.1093/geronb/gbs090

Kennedy, Q., Taylor, J., Noda, A., Yesavage, J., & Lazzeroni, L.C. (2015). The STEP model: Characterizing simultaneous time effects on practice for flight simulator performance among middle-aged and older pilots. *Psychology and Aging, 30*(3), 699–711. https://doi.org/10.1037/pag0000043

Kennedy, Q., Taylor, J.L., Reade, G., & Yesavage, J.A. (2010). Age and expertise effects in aviation decision making and flight control in a flight simulator. *Aviation Space & Environmental Medicine, 81*, 489–497. https://doi.org/10.3357/ASEM.2684.2010

McGuire, S.A., Tate, D.F., Wood, J., Sladky, J.H., McDonald, K., Sherman, P.M., Kawano, E.S., Rowland, L.M., Patel, B., Wright, S.N., Hong, E., Rasmussen, J., Willis, A.M., & Kochunov, P.V. (2014). Lower neurocognitive function in U-2 pilots: Relationship to white matter hyper intensities. *Neurology, 83*(7), 638–645. https://doi.org/10.1212/WNL.0000000000000694

Moore, J.L., & Kay, G.G. (1995, May 7–11). *Cog-Screen-Aeromedical Edition in the assessment of the head injured military aviator* [Paper presentation]. Aerospace Medical Association, Cologne, Germany.

Morrow, D. (2003). Expertise, Cognitive ability, and age effects on pilot communication. *International Journal of Aviation Psychology, 13*(4), 345–371. https://doi.org/10.1207/S15327108IJAP1304_02

O'Donnell, R.D., Hordinsky, J.R., Madakasira, S., Moise, S., & Warner, D. (1992). *A candidate automated test battery for neuropsychological screening of airmen: Design and preliminary validation.* Civil Aeromedical Institute. https://www.govinfo.gov/content/pkg/GOVPUB-TD4-PURL-LPS84027/pdf/GOVPUB-TD4-PURL-LPS84027.pdf

Simons, R., Maire, R., Van Drongelen, A., & Valk, P. (2021). Grounding of pilots: Medical reasons and recommendations for prevention. *Aerospace Medicine and Human Performance, 92*(12), 950–955. https://doi.org/10.3357/AMHP.5985.2021

Stokes, A.F., Belger, A., Banich, M.T., & Taylor, H. (1991). Effects of acute aspartame and acute alcohol ingestion upon the cognitive performance of pilots. *Aviation, Space, and Environmental Medicine, 62*(7), 648–653.

Stokes, A., Kemper, K., & March, R. (1992). *Time-stressed flight decision making: A study of expert and novice aviators.* Idaho National Engineering Laboratory.

Sulistyawati, K., Wickens, C.D., & Chui, Y.P. (2011). Prediction in situation awareness: Confidence bias and underlying cognitive abilities. *The International Journal of Aviation Psychology, 21*(2), 153–174. https://doi.org/10.1080/10508414.2011.556492

Taylor, J.L., Kennedy, Q., Noda, A., & Yesavage, J.A. (2007). Pilot age and expertise predict flight simulator performance: A 3-year longitudinal study. *Neurology, 68*(9), 648–654. https://doi.org/10.1212/01.wnl.0000255943.10045.c0

Taylor, J.L., O'Hara, R., Mumenthaler, M.S., Rosen, A.C., & Yesavage, J.A. (2005). Cognitive ability, expertise, and age differences in following air-traffic control instructions. *Psychology & Aging, 20*(1), 117–133. https://doi.org/10.1037/0882-7974.20.1.117

Taylor, J.L., O'Hara, R., Mumenthaler, M.S., & Yesavage, J.A. (2000). Relationship of CogScreen-AE to flight simulator performance and pilot age. *Aviation Space & Environmental Medicine, 71*(4), 373–380.

Tolton, R.G. (2014). *Relationship of individual pilot factors to simulated flight performance* [Master's thesis]. University of Otago, New Zealand.

Totten, A.M., Boudreau, E., Cheney, T.P., & Davis-O'Reilly, C. (2019). *A systematic review of neuropsychological tests used to assess pilots for fitness to fly* [report]. Pacific Northwest Evidence-based Practice Center. https://www.ohsu.edu/sites/default/files/2024-07/Neuro%20Tests%20Pilots%20Report%20Revised%20Final.pdf

Van Benthem, K., & Herdman, C.M. (2016). Cognitive factors mediate the relation between age and flight path maintenance in general aviation. *Aviation Psychology and Applied Human Factors, 6*(2), 81–90. https://doi.org/10.1027/2192-0923/a000102

Venturino, M., Hamilton, W.L., & Dvorchak, S. (1989, October 2–6). *Performance-based measures of merit for tactical situation awareness* [Paper presentation]. Aerospace Medical Panel Symposium: Situational Awareness in Aerospace Operations, Copenhagen, Denmark.

Yakimovich, N.V., Strogin, G.L., Govorushenko, D., Schroeder, D., & Kay, G.G. (1994, May 8–12). *Flight performance and CogScreen test battery in Russian pilots* [Paper presentation]. Aerospace Medical Association, San Antonio, TX.

Yesavage, J.A., Jo, B., Adamson, M.M., Kennedy, Q., Noda, A., Hernandez, B., Zeitzer, J.M., Friedman, L.F., Fairchild, K., Scanlon, B.K., Murphy, G.M., & Taylor, J.L. (2011). Initial cognitive performance predicts longitudinal aviator performance. *The Journals of Gerontology: Series B: Psychological Sciences and Social Sciences, 66*(4), 444–453. https://doi.org/10.1093/geronb/gbr031

Zhang, L.M., Yu, L.S., Wang, K.N., Jing, B.S., & Fang, C. (1997). The psychophysiological assessment method for pilot's professional reliability. *Aviation Space & Environmental Medicine, 68*(5), 368–372.

Chapter 16
Toward a Systematized Interpretation for the Pilot Neuropsychological Examination

Michael Chafetz

Introduction

The Federal Aviation Administration (FAA) is tasked with regulating the safety of the airways in the United States and its territories, which is done at least in part by having strict requirements for a medical certificate (US Department of Transportation, 2025). As part of this regulatory effort, neuropsychological evaluations are scheduled for pilots and applicants who have any history of potential brain dysfunction, including (but not limited to) attention deficits, seizure disorders, traumatic brain injury, substance abuse, HIV infection, stroke, or use of psychoactive medications.

If the pilot is found to have "aeromedically significant" impairments, a medical certificate will not be issued, and the pilot will not be able to fly. If no significant neurocognitive impairments are found (and there are no impairing psychological problems), there is an increased likelihood that the pilot will be issued a medical certificate and be permitted to fly.

The determination by a neuropsychologist as to whether there is significant impairment involves a decision that should ideally be optimized to avoid errors. In particular, the neuropsychologist wants to make as few false-positive and false-negative errors as possible. If the neuropsychologist makes a false-positive error about impairment, saying there is impairment when there is truly not impairment, then a healthy intact pilot may not be able to fly. If a false-negative error is made, an impaired pilot may be granted a medical certificate and be allowed to fly. Arguably, for the safety of the airways, the minimization of false-negative errors would be more important than the minimization of false-positive errors, especially given the tradeoff between sensitivity and specificity. Figure 16.1 illustrates these decision errors.

Similar reasoning about decision rules can be found in TSA residue screening and in cancer detection, where a false-negative error (missing the bomb residue or the nascent cancer) would be far more serious than a false-positive error, which involves a little embarrassment or fear until it is shown from later investigation that there is no bomb residue or cancer. For pilots, a false-positive error can be handled through an appeal, which certainly involves greater expenditure on the part of the pilot. On the other end of the spectrum, performance validity tests are designed to have low false-positive error so as not to mislabel an honest claimant.

	Pilot Impaired	Pilot Not Impaired
Examiner Says Impaired	*Good Impairment Decision*	**False-Positive for Impairment**
Examiner Says Not Impaired	**False-Negative for Impairment**	*Good No Impairment Decision*

Figure 16.1. Matrix of decision errors by neuropsychologists in pilot evaluations.

As neuropsychologists, we are trained to gather evidence from relevant records and thorough interviews, combining and analyzing that evidence with regard to the test findings. However, our decisions about impairment tend to vary according to the biases of our training mentors and our own biases and values, along with clinical experience from the types of cases we have mostly seen. Some of us tend toward more sensitivity, choosing normative cutoffs that lean toward finding impairment, while others might lean toward specificity, trying to be more certain about particular pathology. This is not to mention the error that is introduced by mixing different normative systems that contain different comparative reference groups (e.g., age vs. age-and-education vs. age-and-education-and-race-and-gender).

In pilot evaluations, we neuropsychologists have essentially the same mission as that of the FAA: the safety of the airways. This mission practically demands that we attempt to minimize false-negative errors for impairment, not missing an important impairment that would be aeromedically significant; that is, it is important to find those impairments most relevant to the safety of the airways.

To be sure, the aviation neuropsychology community, under the watchfulness of the FAA Chief Neuropsychologist, has developed firm standards and specifications for the tests to be used in various types of neuropsychology evaluations. For example, the evaluation for a history of attention-deficit/hyperactivity disorder (ADHD)/attention-deficit disorder (ADD) utilizes a tiered approach, with a fuller set of neurocognitive tests if the first level of testing signals the need to do so. However, for a substance evaluation, a full set of neuropsychological testing is demanded from the start.

Moreover, we have a set of strong guidelines for the use of the main aviation cognitive screener: CogScreen-Aeromedical Edition-2 (AE2; Kay, 2022), which has recently supplanted the first aeromedical edition. In particular, base-rate analysis uses a double cutoff approach: a more sensitive cutoff at the 15th percentile and a more specific cutoff at the 5th percentile. This allows neuropsychologists to analyze the greater number of test findings necessary to show impairment at the 15th percentile and/or the fewer test findings to show impairment at the 5th percentile. An evaluator is also obliged to use the logistic regression probability value (LRPV), using age-normed calculations for general aviation (GA) pilots, to determine the relative probability of brain dysfunction. Additionally, the factor scores allow neuropsychologists to determine impairment relative to relevant constructs of flight performance.

Rationale for Impairment Decision Rules

We have firm standards and specification rules for the tests we are supposed to use in pilot neuropsychological evaluations but no firm impairment decision rules for these tests. In particular, we have strong guidance for CogScreen-AE2, but no firm guidance for the decisions about neuropsychological findings.

Standardization and systematizing decision rules lead to safety by providing a research heuristic for better classification of correct and incorrect decisions about impairment.

Firm impairment decision rules can ultimately help resolve challenges/disputes over neuropsychological findings by providing evidence in terms of probabilities of impairment. This evidence will ultimately be derived from the research heuristic.

Firm impairment decision rules do not eliminate neuropsychological judgment but strengthen it, as they provide clarity about impairment rather than merely a statistical level (e.g., 1 *SD*), and they obviate the practice of pattern-matching that is fraught with individual variability.

Underlying Principles for Decision Rules

FAA medical certification evaluations are designed to determine whether there are medically disqualifying conditions that prevent the pilot from exercising the responsibilities granted by the medical certificate for the time period for which the certificate is valid. According to the Code of Federal Regulation (CFR, Title 14, Chapter I, Subchapter D, Part 67), these are conditions that: (a) make the person unable to safely perform the duties or exercise the privileges of the airman certificate applied for or held; or (b) may reasonably be expected, for the maximum duration of the airman medical certificate applied for or held, to make the person unable to perform those duties or exercise those privileges. As the client of the evaluator is not the employer (e.g., airline company), these are not fitness-for-duty (FFD) evaluations, but the thinking on the part of the evaluator is similar. In particular, the evaluation is about the underlying capacity for safe operation of aircraft. The pilot must not have impairment that would have an impact on the routine tasks necessary for safe operation but also must not be impaired for rare novel tasks that suddenly arise outside of the normal routine.

Basic routine operation requires intact auditory and visual vigilance/attention, good inhibition of distractions, intact auditory and visual memory, and ability to process flexibly and correctly based on feedback from air traffic control operations and other environmental information.

Operation under novel and/or surprising conditions requires good concept formation based on feedback from the environment and/or air traffic control, good inhibition of distractions, selection of the most important information on which to focus, intact auditory and visual memory, and a psychological steadiness and emotional stability.

Sensitivity focus: Considering air traffic safety, we have to ask, how many false-negative errors are acceptable? The answer to this question must keep in mind the *dormancy* of false-negative errors. In particular, most of the flight (over all flights) will be uneventful, and the operation of aircraft under these conditions requires only smooth over-learned performance. It is in novel or surprising conditions that the dormant false-negative errors become critical to the safe handling of the aircraft.

Burden of proof: Disability or litigation claimants must “prove” impairment to the criteria required for compensation. In disability evaluations, the claimant must meet criteria for inability or limitations from work. In litigation, the criteria are not contractually based, but the claimant must still prove impairment. Arguably, given this burden of proof, interpretation of impairment should be more focused on specificity so as to avoid false-positive errors for impairment. In an FAA evaluation, the burden is on the applicant/pilot to prove capacity/competence/fitness for the operation of aircraft (both routine and novel). Given this burden of proof, interpretation of impairment should be more focused on sensitivity so as to avoid the false-negative errors for impairment.

Duty/mission: The mission of the evaluator is the same as that of the FAA: the safety of the airways. The examiner owes the examinee respect for their dignity and person, but the examiner's duty is to the ultimate principle/value of air traffic safety. To be sure, this author is very friendly toward examinees, and I tell them that I always root for the success of the pilots that I see. However, by my informed consent rules, I make it clear that there will be no doctor-patient relationship and that the findings may advance the pilot's case but that they may also work against the pilot's interests. This is clear from the first phone call as well as on the informed consent that must be signed.

Aeromedical significance: Domains of assessment and tests within neurocognitive domains are chosen for aeromedical significance, not just because certain tests are usually included in certain domains.

Limits of assessment: We must keep in mind that random statistical failures are the norm when multiple neurocognitive tests are administered; for example, in intact healthy individuals, there are many test findings at the cutoff of 1 *SD* for impairment and even some at more restrictive cutoffs (Binder et al., 2009). Thus, it is important not to over-interpret (as impairment) a few scattered diverse findings that are below cutoff. This same principle was adopted in CogScreen-AE2, in which it takes several findings within a domain (e.g., speed, accuracy, thruput) for a base-rate cutoff at the 15th percentile to produce a low enough *T* score that indicates impairment, but fewer findings at the 5th percentile cutoff for a *T* score at an impairment level.

Impairment is the referral question: For civil litigation, a typical question is whether the claimant is impaired by a traumatic brain injury (TBI) from the motor vehicle accident (MVA). In criminal cases, the question might be whether a defendant is too impaired (incompetent) to proceed to trial. In pilot evaluations, the neuropsychologist must determine if there is aeromedically significant impairment that would render the pilot unfit for a medical certificate. Moreover, aeromedically significant impairment is occupationally referenced for pilots (Kay & Atkins, 2016).

Measurement of the construct of impairment: As indicated by Chafetz (2020), neuropsychology does not have a gold standard test for the measurement of neuropsychological constructs (e.g., memory). The reasoning behind this is that it takes more than one test finding to measure "impairment" within a neuropsychological domain (e.g., memory) that is itself an abstraction (see Evans et al., 1984).

Cognitive reserve may be a factor in the differences in symptoms and performance following an acquired brain injury in individuals who have similar pathology (Satz, 1993). In particular, the cognitive status of those who are further away from (higher than) impairment cutoffs may have less risk of aeromedically significant impairment than those who are lower functioning and already closer to impairment cutoffs. Lower cognitive reserve can also come about from a history of alcohol or drug abuse, psychiatric illness, and/or previous neurologic insult, which would be a factor when there is a new acquired brain injury (Ropacki & Elias, 2003). It will thus be important in pilot evaluations to gather evidence of premorbid functioning (e.g., from the use of the Test of Premorbid Functioning [TOPF]; Holdnack et al., 2013), along with a careful history of previous brain insult. At this point, we do not expect to change cutoffs based on higher cognitive reserve (e.g., raising cutoffs due to high education or premorbid IQ estimation), as the aeromedically significant impairment standard is not related to a comparison with oneself but with other pilots within the age group.

Rational choices of impairment cutoffs are necessary in the absence of the guidance of known base rates (as in CogScreen-AE2). The starting suggestion would be to use a firm impairment cutoff at the lower 5% (similar to Cogscreen-AE2) and a more sensitive (at-risk) cutoff at the lower 10% level (as in forensic work). In the absence of base rates, the more sensitive cutoff is more restrictive than CogScreen-AE2 but requires only two findings at this level to be significant. Within a neurocognitive domain, the measurement of impairment would require two impairment findings at the 5th percentile level or one finding at the 5th percentile and two findings at the 10th percentile level or three to four findings at the 10th percentile alone (three for smaller domains and four for larger domains).

Uniform score labeling (Guilmette et al., 2020), while helpful for communication, is not the focus in a pilot evaluation report. This is because score labels, which reflect ranges of test scores, do not provide a specific rationale for impairment decisions.

Interpretation requires valid data. It is exceedingly rare for any FFD examinee, including pilots, to fail performance validity tests (PVTs). In particular, there were no PVT failures (no positive findings) in a preliminary assessment of validity data from 38 pilots. Thus, if this actually happened, something would be seriously wrong, and the examination would be invalid. Our PVTs included the Medical Symptom Validity Test (MSVT; Green, 2004), the A-Test within a mental/cognitive status examination (Chafetz, 2012), and a reliable digit span (RDS; Greiffenstein et al., 1994) as well as the recognition memory trials from the WMS-4 (see *Advanced Clinical Solutions* [ACS] guidelines; Holdnack & Drozdick, 2009). (While there were a few RDS findings at the ACS 25% cutoff, these did not occur with any other positive PVT finding and were thus not considered positive.) More typically, the pilot examinee would be at greater risk for "faking good" on the Minnesota Multiphasic Personality Inventory-2 (MMPI-2), which may require a retest with an adjustment of the test instructions (Front's version of Butcher's retest instructions; Front, 2018).

Impairment decisions are ultimately based on Bayesian reasoning in contrast to the frequentist reasoning under which we were trained (e.g., deviation from a mean). In Bayesian reasoning, the probability of impairment changes with each new positive finding. At this early stage, the Bayesian probabilities are not known, but the method will ultimately differ from the Rohling Interpretive Method (RIM; Miller & Rohling, 2001) and its use in the Meyers Neuropsychological Battery (https://meyersneuropsychological.com/mnb/). The essential nature of the proposed method for pilots is modeled after the techniques of the neuropsychological evaluation for the NFL Baseline Assessment Program (BAP), but the cutoffs are different to reflect that pilot evaluations are similar to the FFD rubric, while BAP evaluations are within the disability framework.

Occupational norms: The development of neuropsychological evaluations for pilots has exemplified leadership in the use of occupational norms (Kay & Atkins, 2016). Historically, pilot norms have been extended to certain tests (e.g., Coding, PASAT, Trails), but otherwise the Heaton norms (Heaton et al., 2004) have been used for neuropsychological testing. The neuropsychological tests included with Pearson-based norms (WAIS-IV; WMS-IV) do not have the same demographic corrections as the Heaton norms. Thus, currently, apart from the racial incongruities introduced by the Heaton norms, impairment decisions are being made from findings based on considerable variability of normative corrections (e.g., sometimes only age; sometimes with age and education; sometimes with age, education, sex, and race; and sometimes with pilot norms that are age-based but typically with a college-level education). Uniformity of decision-making about impairment would best be achieved by a more uniform normative set, ideally with age–education corrections (but not race-based corrections). For the uniform impairment decision rules proposed here, it is suggested that the age–education corrections from ACS (Holdnack & Drozdick, 2009) be used for the Pearson tests (WAIS-IV; WMS-IV; except for Coding), and the Mitrushina Meta Norms (Mitrushina et al., 2005) be used for the other neurocognitive tests. General Aviation (GA) pilot norms should still be used where applicable. (Note that while there is no education requirement for GA pilots, the average education for GA pilots is a college education (16 years). Thus, arguably, the education level should be set to 16 years for all parts of the neurocognitive evaluation, but this is a developmental evaluation issue that is still too early to decide.)

Rules of Interpretation in A Single Case

CogScreen-AE2 is interpreted according to the usual rules.

For the neuropsychological examination, five domains of neurocognitive impairment are used for assessment, each containing multiple tests within the domain: (1) complex attention-processing speed, (2) learning and memory, (3) visual–perceptual, (4) language, and (5) executive functioning. These domains correspond to the DSM-5 categories for neurocognitive disorders, with minor modifications (e.g., absence of social cognition measures, which are not as well developed). Moreover, a test of receptive language is added (apart from the specifications) to reflect the aeromedical significance of language understanding and processing.

In pilot evaluation for a medical certificate, the burden is on the pilot to prove fitness. Due to the greater risks inherent in false-negative errors (e.g., missing the impairment that causes a crash) than in false-positive errors, it is incumbent on the examiner to have a stance of greater sensitivity than specificity for impairment.

Where applicable, the pilot's findings are compared with those of other similar GA pilots.

Typically, the CogScreen-AE2 findings are compared with those of the relevant pilot group (e.g., GA pilots in the age group). Where applicable, neurocognitive findings are compared with GA pilot norms (P); otherwise, demographically adjusted norms were used (D; clearly marked in Table 16.2 and Table 16.4). It is considered that a finding in the lower 10% (≤ 37T) relative to appropriate norms (e.g., similarly aged pilots) places the pilot in an at-risk category. (The lower 10% level, instead of the lower 15% level used on CogScreen, was chosen for the neuropsychological portion of the examination, as it will be more specific in the absence of base rates that are established on CogScreen). An ability level in the lower 5% (≤ 33T) is considered impaired for a pilot (compared to other pilots). Any score finding above the at-risk level is considered within defined limits (WDL). However, as with CogScreen, multiple scores (at least three) in the at-risk range would signal impairment within a neurocognitive domain. A combination of one impairment finding plus two to three at-risk findings within a domain would lead to an impairment rating. One impairment finding plus one at-risk finding would lead to an at-risk rating. Any score finding above the at-risk level is considered WDL.

Because individuals without brain pathology can have a few very low scores when many tests are given, it takes at least two at-risk scores in a neurocognitive domain to consider that the pilot is at-risk for those neurocognitive problems or at least two scores below the impairment cutoff to consider impairment within that domain. If the domain does not have at least two at-risk levels, it is considered WDL. For overall neurocognitive impairment diagnosis, at least two domains have to be affected. However, given the concerns for safety and the sensitivity stance of the examiner, even one affected domain may be disqualifying. (These principles address only neurocognitive issues; psychological problems can be independently disqualifying.) Interpretation requires valid findings.

Two Cases With Systematized Interpretation of the Pilot Neuropsychological Evaluation

The cases presented here have been sanitized, with altered background information that did not change the essentials of the case. Table 16.1 (for Case 1) and Table 16.3 (for Case 2) show the continuous performance testing results for each case.

Case 1: Mr. (Ted) Bean

- A 55-year-old state agency pilot, 10,000 flying hours
- Had stroke about 2 years before the pilot evaluation
- Small left thalamic infarct; right-sided weakness/numbness
- Hypothyroidism, hypertension, obesity, high lipids
- "Full recovery from stroke," without seizures
- Denial of medical certificate for stroke; needed neuropsychological examination
- My examination: denied symptoms/problems, except occasional tingling in right arm
- Mental/cognitive status: intact, except for mistakes in RH on 3-step movements
- Valid examination
- But had to retest on MMPI-2 with instructions for high L
- Then valid MMPI-2 and valid Paulhus Deception Scales
- Average estimated premorbid functioning

CogScreen-AE Findings

- LRPV = 0.9975 but GA pilot norms for age —> 41T; 19th percentile > 15th percentile
- Taylor factors: 3 of 5 average or above
- Taylor factors: speed (40T; 16th percentile); deductive (41T; 19th percentile); both > 15th percentile
- Speed/WM factor correlates most with overall flight simulator performance: $r = 0.57$*
- Base rates (main issue): 6 speed measures ≤ 5th percentile! (overall < 2.5 percentile)
- Re-calculate using GA pilot norms —> 3 speed scores ≤ 5th percentile
- Combined base-rate rank for 3 speed scores ≤ 5th percentile is 37T (10th percentile)
- Auditory sequence comparison, divided attention: visual alone, manikin: ≤ 5th percentile
- Manikin: visuospatial reasoning —> in NP examination did well on visuospatial tasks
- Overall: at-risk findings on CogScreen-AE

Table 16.1. Case 1: IVA-2 – Continuous Performance Test (Sanford & Turner, 2004)

IVA-2 Scale	ss	T	Percentile	Score Level
Full Scale Response Control	102S	51T	54th	Average
Auditory Response Control	99S	49T	46th	Average
Visual Response Control	104S	53T	62nd	Average
Full Scale Attention	93S	45T	31st	Average
Auditory Attention Quotient	87S	41T	18th	Low average
Visual Attention Quotient	99S	49T	46th	Average

Note. No IVA-2 finding below 16th percentile.

The systematized neuropsychological findings for this case are shown in Table 16.2. In a transparent manner, the table lays out the tests in each neurocognitive domain, the cutoffs for impairment and at-risk findings (IMP ≤ 33T, 5th percentile; AR≤37T, 10th percentile), or whether the finding is WDL. Where applicable, the unadjusted age-scaled scores are provided, and then the adjusted T scores are given (based on either age–education demographic adjustments [D] or adjustments based on pilot norms [P].

Table 16.2. Case 1: Results of neuropsychological testing

Domain	Ability	Raw	ss	T	Percentile	P/D	WDL/ AR/IMP
Complex Attention/ Processing Speed	**IMP ≤ 33T; AR ≤ 37T**						**WDL**
	Attention & Working Mem	28	11	50	50	D	WDL
	Mental Arithmetic	13	9	41	18	D	WDL
	Complex Attention Working Mem	20	10	48	42	D	WDL
	Attention & Working Memory	48	–	59	83	P	WDL
	Attention & Working Memory	31	–	43	25	P	WDL
	Visual-Process/Clerical Speed	45	7	36	8	P	AR
	Visual-Scan/Process Speed	23	8	41	18	D	WDL
	Visual Sequence Speed	27	10	51	54	P	WDL
Learning and Memory	**IMP ≤ 33T; AR ≤ 37T**						**WDL**
	Immediate Memory Stories	32	13	59	82	D	WDL
	Delayed Memory Stories	25	12	56	73	D	WDL
	Immediate Memory Word Pairs	26	9	46	35	D	WDL
	Delayed Memory Word Pairs	7	8	43	24	D	WDL
	Immediate Memory Designs	40	13	57	76	D	WDL
	Delayed Memory Designs	40	16	67	96	D	WDL

Table 16.2. continued

Domain	Ability	Raw	ss	T	Per-centile	P/D	WDL/ AR/IMP
Visual-Perceptual	**IMP ≤ 33T; AR ≤ 37T**						**WDL**
	Spatial Skills/Problem-Solving	44	12	53	62	D	WDL
	Visual Perceptual Reasoning	15	12	52	58	D	WDL
	Visual Perceptual Reasoning	18	12	54	66	D	WDL
Language	**IMP ≤ 33T; AR ≤ 37T**						**WDL**
	Language Comprehension	8	3	15	<1	D	IMP
	Confrontation Naming	60	16	71	98	D	WDL
	Semantic Fluency	23	12	58	79	D	WDL
	Word Knowledge	51	14	61	86	D	WDL
Executive Functioning	**IMP ≤ 33T; AR ≤ 37T**						**WDL**
	Verbal Reasoning	28	11	50	50	D	WDL
	Complex Sequencing	65	10	47	39	P	WDL
	Word Fluency/Initiation	35	9	45	32	D	WDL
	Conceptual Reasoning	65	7	41	18	D	WDL
	Focus/Impulse Control	40	–	45	32	D	WDL

Note. AR = At risk; IMP = Impairment; P/D = pilot/demographic norms; WDL = within defined limits

The findings in Case 1 showed no domain-level impairment in any of the five neurocognitive domains. In fact, there was only one test finding at the IMP level and one at the AR level. The impairment-level finding on a test of language comprehension was interpreted under the *To Err Is Human* (Binder et al., 2009) rubric, particularly as he scored in the high average range on the Immediate Logical Memory test. The one at-risk finding was on the Coding subtest (pilot norms), although his age-scaled score was low average. Although this most likely represented some slight residual motor slowing from his stroke, it was considered not a problem as he scored WDL on all other timed tasks, including the Trailmaking Test, Forms A and B. He scored in the high average range with both hands on the finger-tapping test.

Thus, the at-risk screening findings (CogScreen-AE) were not upheld in the neuropsychological examination, and Mr. (Ted) Bean was thought not to have aeromedically significant impairment, even though he had had a stroke about 2 years before this examination.

Case 2: Mr. (Blue) Bean

- A 25-year-old firefighter, 150 flying hours
- History of taking Adderall for ADHD/ADD

- Prescribed in college but no formal diagnosis at that time
- Previously assessed with obstructive sleep apnea but AME said not at risk
- In 2021, diagnosed with ADHD and put on Adderall (25 mg/day)
- Adderall helped him with focus and attention —> Cs to As
- Stopped using Adderall in late 2021 —> "Doing fine off medication"!
- Stopped because of FAA rules —> He would not be allowed to fly
- Able to stay focused, listened well, got reports done: "No symptoms or problems now"
- Valid examination (no failed validity; valid MMPI-2)
- Average estimated premorbid functioning.

CogScreen-AE Findings

- LRPV = 0.9998 but GA pilot norms for age 25 —> 31T; 3rd percentile < 5th percentile
- Higher probability of brain dysfunction than similarly aged pilots!
- Taylor factors: 3 of 5 average or above
- Taylor factors: speed (35T; 7th percentile); deductive (19T; < 1st percentile)
- Speed/WM factor correlates most with overall flight simulator performance: $r = 0.57^*$
- Base rates: 8 speed measures ≤ 5th percentile! (overall < 2.5 percentile)
- Re-calculate using GA pilot norms —> Worse! Now 10 speed measures ≤ 5th percentile
- Combined base-rate rank for 10 speed scores ≤ 5th percentile is < 2.5th percentile)
- Overall: did NOT pass CogScreen-AE; now NP findings (supplemental battery added)

Table 16.3. Case 2: IVA-2 – Continuous Performance Test (Sanford & Turner, 2004)

IVA-2 Scale	SS	T	Percentile	Score Level
Full Scale Response Control	98S	48T	46th	Average
Auditory Response Control	110S	57T	76th	High Average
Visual Response Control	86S	41T	18th	Low Average
Full Scale Attention	98S	48T	46th	Average
Auditory Attention Quotient	91S	44T	27th	Average
Visual Attention Quotient	107S	54T	69th	Average

Note. No IVA-2 finding below 16th percentile.

The systematized neuropsychological findings for this case are shown in Table 16.4. The findings in Case 2 showed impairment in the visual-perceptual domain (two of three findings below impairment cutoffs) and at-risk (for impairment) performance in the complex attention-processing speed domain. In particular, he showed impairment in his constructional skills (Block Design) and visual-perceptual reasoning (Matrix Reasoning), giving overall impairment in the domain. He also showed impairment in visual sequencing speed (Trails A) and an at-risk (for impairment) level of performance on a mental arithmetic task, meeting at-risk criteria for the complex attention-processing speed domain. Given the corroboration of the CogScreen impairment with the impairment in the neuropsychological examination, he was considered to have aeromedically significant impairment for the operation of aircraft. The recommendations were for maturity and improvement of processing speed.

Table 16.4. Case 2: Results of neuropsychological testing

Domain	Ability	Raw	ss	T	Per-centile	P/D	WDL/ AR/ IMP
Complex Attention/ Processing Speed	**IMP ≤ 33T; AR ≤ 37T**						**AR**
	Attention & Working Mem	30	11	46	35	D	WDL
	Mental Arithmetic	12	9	37	10	D	AR
	Complex Attention Working Mem	22	11	51	54	D	WDL
	Attention & Working Mem	36	–	46	37	P	WDL
	Attention & Working Mem	31	–	40	16	P	WDL
	Visual-Process/Clerical Speed	70	9	42	21	P	WDL
	Visual-Scan/Process Speed	36	11	49	46	D	WDL
	Visual Sequence Speed	32	9	27	1	P	IMP
Learning and Memory	**IMP ≤ 33T; AR ≤ 37T**						**WDL**
	Immediate Memory Stories	31	12	54	66	D	WDL
	Delayed Memory Stories	30	13	59	82	D	WDL
	Word pair association immediate	34	9	44	27	D	WDL
	Word pair association delayed	12	11	50	50	D	WDL
	Immediate Memory Designs	42	13	57	76	D	WDL
	Delayed Memory Designs	30	10	47	38	D	WDL
Visual-Perceptual	**IMP ≤ 33T; AR ≤ 37T**						**IMP**
	Spatial Skills/Problem-Solving	32	7	32	4	D	IMP
	Visual Perceptual Reasoning	12	8	38	12	D	WDL
	Visual Perceptual Reasoning	13	7	33	5	D	IMP
Language	**IMP ≤ 33T; AR ≤ 37T**						**WDL**
	Verbal Reasoning	29	12	49	46	D	WDL
	Semantic Fluency	24	12	47	38	D	WDL
	Word Knowledge	23	7	25	< 1	D	IMP
Executive Functioning	**IMP≤ 33T; AR ≤ 37T**						**WDL**
	Focus/Inhibition competing tendency	47	–	52	58	Age	WDL
	Complex Sequencing	63	11	41	18	P	WDL
	Word Fluency/Initiation	54	14	57	76	D	WDL
	Conceptual Reasoning	14	–	49	47	D	WDL

Note. AR – At risk; IMP – Impairment; P/D – pilot/demographic norms; WDL – within defined limits

Conclusion

The systematized method of neurocognitive testing interpretation within the neuropsychological examination for pilots aids the examiner in the determination of impairment by (1) having a systematic way of interpreting test findings so that one's habits from training and experience do not yield (biased) over-interpretation or under-interpretation of test findings, (2) permitting a heuristic for the determination of classification accuracy of impairment findings (as well as cutoffs), and (3) allowing for the establishment of a standardized research base for the FAA going forward. Research is underway in my laboratory to provide an initial determination of classification accuracy by comparing CogScreen results with the neuropsychological examination results. The two cases shown here displayed the methods of determining impairment along with a systematic comparison of CogScreen and neurocognitive findings.

Acknowledgments

I started thinking these issues through around the Aerospace Psychology Seminar (APS) of 2018, currently an FAA-sponsored educational event. I appreciated encouragement and advice from Keith Atkins, Jason King, Kevin O'Brien, Dan DaSilva, Bob Elliott, Heather Pedersen, Gary Kay, and Joseph Snow. Later, for the presentation of these ideas at APS 2022, I appreciated encouragement and advice from Randy Georgemiller and Hope Wright. Feedback from the participants of that workshop was very helpful. More recently, for this chapter I benefited from the advice and encouragement of Randy Georgemiller, Joseph Snow, and Keith Atkins. I also thank Paige Haley and Magda Ospina for more recent help with data and editing of this chapter.

Publication Ethics

The two cases presented here have been sanitized, with altered background information that did not change the essentials of the cases. Moreover, both individuals signed informed consent for anonymized research.

References

Binder, L.M., Iverson, G.L., & Brooks, B.L. (2009). to err is human: "Abnormal" neuropsychological scores and variability are common in healthy adults. *Archives of Clinical Neuropsychology, 24*, 31–46. https://doi.org/10.1093/arclin/acn001

Chafetz, M.D. (2012). The A-Test: A symptom validity indicator embedded within a mental status examination for social security disability. *Applied Neuropsychology, 19*, 121–126. https://doi.org/10.1080/09084282.2011.643953

Chafetz, M.D. (2020). Deception is different: Negative validity test findings do not provide "evidence" for "good effort. *The Clinical Neuropsychologist, 36*, 1244–1264. https://doi.org/10.1080/13854046.2020.1840633

Evans, S., Gage, F.H., & Chafetz, M.D. (1984). Taxonomic abstractions in psychobiology. *The Journal of General Psychology, 111*, 12–18. https://doi.org/10.1080/00221309.1984.9921111

Front, C.M. (2018). *Personality assessment in FAA evaluations: Airmen and air traffic control specialists (ATCSs).* 6th Annual Aerospace Psychology Seminar, Denver, CO.

Green, P. (2004). *Medical Symptom Validity Test.* Green's Publishing.

Greiffenstein, M.F., Baker, W.J., & Gola, T. (1994). Validation of malingered amnesia measures with a large clinical sample. *Psychological Assessment, 6,* 218–224. https://doi.org/10.1037/1040-3590.6.3.218

Guilmette, T.J., Sweet, J.J., Hebben, N., Koltai, D., Mahone, E.M., Spiegler, B.J., Stucky, K., Westerveld, M., & conference participants. (2020). American Academy of Clinical Neuropsychology consensus conference statement on uniform labeling of performance test scores. *The Clinical Neuropsychologist, 34,* 437–453. https://doi.org/10.1080/13854046.2020.1722244

Heaton, R.K., Miller, S.W., Taylor, M.J., & Grant, I. (2004). *Revised comprehensive norms for an expanded Halstead-Reitan battery: Demographically adjusted neuropsychological norms for African American and Caucasian adults. Professional manual.* Psychological Assessment Resources.

Holdnack, J.A., & Drozdick, L.W. (2009). *Advanced Clinical Solutions for WAIS-IV and WMS-IV: Clinical and interpretive manual.* Pearson Clinical.

Holdnack, J.A., Schoenberg, M.R., Lange, R.T., & Iverson, G.L. (2013). Predicting premorbid ability for WAIS-IV, WMS-IV and WASI-II. In J.A. Holdnack, L.W. Drozdick, L.G. Weiss, & G.L. Iverson (Eds.), *WAIS-IV, WMS-IV, and ACS: Advanced clinical interpretation* (pp. 217–278). Elsevier Academic Press. https://doi.org/10.1016/B978-0-12-386934-0.00005-5

Kay, G.G. (2022, October 21). *Advanced CogScreen-AE2 Interpretation Workshop, Crystal City, VA.*

Kay, G. & Atkins, K. (2016, September 18). *Which norms should I be using?* Workshop at 4th Annual Aerospace Psychology Seminar, Denver, CO.

Miller, L.S. & Rohling, M.L. (2001). A statistical interpretive method for neuropsychological test data. *Neuropsychology Review, 11,* 143–169. https://doi.org/10.1023/A:1016602708066

Mitrushina, M., Boone, K.B., Razani, J., & D'Elia, L.F. (2005). *Handbook of normative data for neuropsychological assessment* (2nd ed.). Oxford University Press.

Ropacki, M.T., & Elias, J.W. (2003). Preliminary examination of cognitive reserve theory in closed head injury. *Archives of Clinical Neuropsychology, 18,* 643–654. https://doi.org/10.1093/arclin/18.6.643

Sanford, J.A., & Turner, A. (2004). *IVA+plus: Integrated visual and auditory continuous performance test, administration manual.* BrainTrain, Inc.

Satz, P. (1993). Brain reserve capacity on symptom onset after brain injury: A formulation and review of evidence for threshold theory. *Neuropsychology, 7,* 273–295. https://doi.org/10.1037/0894-4105.7.3.273

US Department of Transportation. (2023). *Federal Aviation Regulations/Aeronautical Information Manual [FAR/AIM]. Rules and procedures for aviators, from titles 14 and 19 of the Code of Federal Regulations.* Federal Aviation Administration.

Chapter 17
Language and Cultural Considerations in Neuropsychological Evaluations With Aviators

Farzin Irani, Lauren Drag, Mi-Yeoung Jo, and Delia Silva

Introduction

It has been estimated that 50%–90% of all aviation accidents are related to human factors (Diehl, 1991). Despite increasing reliance on automation and technology, human error is still the biggest threat to flight safety. A comprehensive understanding of human behaviors and causes of human error cannot be achieved without first understanding culture. Humans are a product of our cultural surroundings, which have a significant impact on aviation safety. One might erroneously assume that aviation is immune to cultural influences given that, in theory, all pilots should operate the same aircraft in the same ways regardless of culture. However, as will be outlined in this chapter, there is a strong influence of cultural and linguistic factors on aerospace safety. These influences extend to aeromedical neuropsychological and psychological evaluations.

Aviation neuropsychologists are tasked with understanding regulatory standards and identifying the presence of a condition that could pose a hazard to safety in performance of flight or air traffic control (ATC) duties. Thus, they need to have the knowledge, awareness, and skills to appropriately assess culturally and linguistically diverse aviators. This includes understanding that culture permeates all aspects of the neuropsychological assessment process, from the identification and definition of relevant constructs, the development and construction of tests, the ability to adequately build rapport during the clinical interview, accurately interpret behavioral observations, and throughout the process of test administration and interpretation of data (Fernandez & Abe, 2018). The American Psychological Association (APA) Ethics Code entitles all people to equal access to and benefit from the contributions of psychology, with awareness and respect for cultural differences (APA, 2002). Thus, culturally and linguistically diverse examinees deserve a fair and just neuropsychological evaluation that accurately distinguishes genuine aeromedically significant neurocognitive and psychological deficits from those that are artifacts of culturally uninformed diagnostic errors that have no impact on flight safety.

In this chapter, we first aim to increase understanding of why it is important to consider cultural influences on aerospace safety in the United States. It is worth noting that our worldview regarding aviation neuropsychology originates from the United States since that is where the authors practice. While the intersectionality of several demographic and cultural variables can impact neuropsychological outcomes, this chapter focuses on two variables that are more relevant for aviation neuropsychology, that is, language and culture. We begin by reviewing global and national aviation-specific changes in demographics. We then turn to aviation safety and review historical deadly flight errors that were influenced by language and cultural misunderstandings. Next, we provide practical suggestions for aviation neuropsychologists to ensure a linguistically and culturally appropriate evaluation. This includes considerations that can enhance rapport and trust to allow gathering of accurate biopsychosociocultural histories, evaluate the impact of language and culture on cognitive and personality test data, make appropriate normative test data selections, and identify future needs for the field. Ultimately, increasing understanding of the role of these linguistic and cultural influences on neuropsychological evaluations can increase the precision of diagnostic impressions that guide decisions about aeromedical safety.

Global and National Aviation-Specific Demographic Trends

The demographics of the world and those who secure the skies are changing. According to the United Nations world population prospects (United Nations Department of Economic and Social Affairs, 2022), in the next three decades, regions of the world will experience different growth rates of their populations. The regional distribution of the population in 2050 will significantly differ from that of today. Central and Southern Asia are expected to become the most populous regions in the world by 2037, and between 2022 and 2050, the population of sub-Saharan Africa is expected to almost double, and will account for more than half of the growth of the world's population. Europe and Northern America are projected to reach their peak population size and experience population decline in the late 2030s due to sustained low levels of fertility and high emigration rates in some countries.

According to the most recent US Census Bureau population reports, the non-Hispanic White population in the United States is projected to shrink over coming decades due to falling birth rates and rising deaths with aging (Vespa et al., 2020). The population of people who are two or more races is projected to be the fastest growing racial or ethnic group over the next several decades, followed by Asians and Hispanics/Latinx, whose populations are predicted to double. The nation's foreign-born population is projected to rise, and beginning in 2030, net international migration from Asian and Latin American countries is expected to overtake natural increase as the driver of population growth. An increasing ethnoracially pluralistic society has also changed the languages spoken in US homes. According to a 2019 US Census Bureau (Dietrich & Hernandez, 2022) report on language use in the United States, while English remains the most common language spoken at home for 78 % of the US population, over time there has been a significant increase in those who speak a language other than English at home (Dietrich & Hernandez, 2022). Spanish is the most frequent non-English language spoken in US homes, followed by Chinese, Tagalog, Vietnamese, and Arabic, while several Indigenous languages are becoming endangered (Cranney, 2019; Dietrich & Hernandez, 2022). Thus, it is increasingly likely that aviation neuropsychologists will interface with linguistically and culturally diverse aviators.

The field of aviation has slowly been recognizing these demographic shifts. On its website, the Federal Aviation Administration (FAA) states: "The mission of the FAA involves securing the skies of a diverse nation. It only makes sense that the workforce responsible for that mission reflects the nation that it serves" (FAA, 2022). This is a much-needed but not yet fulfilled aspiration; 2022 data from the US Bureau of Labor Statistics (2023) indicated that 96% of pilots and flight engineers were White, and 91% of pilots and flight engineers were male. This is notably less diverse than the demographics for all management and professional occupations, in which 52% of workers were male and 78% were White. A review of US Civil Airmen Statistics from 2022 also suggests similar homogeneity in gender (FAA, 2023). Of 166,738 pilot certificate holders, 9.5% were women, an increase from 6.6% in 2013. A total of 4.9% of all airline transport pilots were women (slightly up from 4.1% in 2013) and 8% of all flight instructors were women.

Formal efforts have been made to address this need for increasing representation. The European Union Aviation Safety Agency held a workshop on inclusion and diversity in 2022 to develop a position paper to ensure a diverse talent pipeline. Also in 2022, the European Civil Aviation Conference created a network on diversity and inclusion in civil aviation. Another initiative through the International Air Transport Association, 25by2025, was founded to raise awareness of the need to improve female representation in the aviation industry. There have also been many other important milestones achieved towards this goal of increased diversity. In the United States, in 2021 Dr. Susan Northrop was appointed as the Federal Air Surgeon of the FAA, the first woman to serve in this position. Also in 2021, United Airlines announced a goal for women and people of color to comprise 50% of the 5,000 pilots trained in the next decade as part of their Aviate flight school.

The field of neuropsychology has also increasingly recognized the need to increase representation of the workforce to serve an increasingly diverse national and global population. As one example, the American Academy of Clinical Neuropsychology Relevance 2050 Initiative recognized that by the year 2050, a full 60% of the American population will be "un-testable" with our current toolkit of largely monolingual, monocultural neuropsychological assessment strategies. This lack of access to neuropsychological services by non-primarily English-speaking, non-European Americans has been viewed as both a social justice concern as well as a market share issue that could make the profession increasingly irrelevant in the health-care marketplace. Additional efforts are also ongoing in various national and international contexts that underscore the importance of considering sociodemographic influences on aeromedical decisions.

Culture and Aviation Safety

There have been multiple deadly airplane crashes that revealed the significant impact of culture on flight crew behaviors such as communication, leadership styles, and decision-making. In 1990, Avianca Flight 052 from Colombia to New York crashed after Colombian pilots were directed into a holding pattern by American ATCs while the aircraft was running out of fuel. Before discussing the specifics of the culturally based miscommunications involved in this accident, it is worth understanding Hofstede's (1983) commonly used framework for studying the influences of national culture on aviation safety in pilots (see Merritt, 2000; Soeters & Boer, 2000). Hofstede (1983) has proposed four separate dimensions of work-related cultural values:

1. *Power–distance (PD):* This dimension reflects how superiors and subordinates view the distribution of power in their relationship. In cultures with high PD, subordinates are afraid to disagree with their superiors, and superiors make decisions in an autocratic and directive style. Inequality between the superior and subordinate is to be expected and

subordinates may be reluctant to speak up if there is a concern. By contrast, in low-PD cultures, superiors adopt a more consultative and cooperative decision-making style. To some extent, high levels of PD are inherent to cockpits. There are predetermined hierarchies for the captain and first officer in the cockpit, with each pilot having clearly defined duties and a distribution of power based on their position in the cockpit. The captain automatically assumes the command role. Since pilots are constantly sharing the cockpit with other pilots they have never flown with before, this minimizes any ambiguity in new pilot pairings, as the delineation of duties is based on the role rather than the person. However, there is also an implicit assumption of low PD in cockpit communications. Safe operation of the aircraft depends on two pilots who are cross-monitoring each other's actions; this is predicated on the belief that crew members will freely alert each other to irregularities and errors.
2. *Uncertainty avoidance (UA):* This dimension addresses tolerance for rule compliance, anxiety/nervousness, and uncertainty. In cultures with high UA, there is a preference for avoiding situations that can bring uncertainty; value is placed on predictability and clearly defined risks. Individuals in high-UA cultures are less willing to take risks and place emphasis on written rules and regulations. Unfamiliar situations bring on anxiety and stress, which are avoided when possible. In a high-UA cockpit, there is a focus on following orders, following the flight plan with minimum deviations from standard operating procedure, and discouraging questions that could raise uncertainty. By contrast, individuals from cultures with low UA tend to solve problems independently, improvise, and act outside the bounds of rules if needed. By nature, aviation is high in UA, as there is a high reliance on checklists, manuals, and standard and emergency operating procedures. However, there are still significant differences across cultures in UA.
3. *Individualism (IND) versus collectivism:* This dimension focuses on the prioritization of individual initiative and individual achievements (high IND) compared to those of the group. In highly individualist cultures, importance is placed on autonomy, individual rights, personal rewards, leisure time, freedom, and self-reliance. Highly collectivist cultures place emphasis on belonging to an organization, improving working relationships, and building a career within an organization.
4. *Masculinity (MAS) versus femininity:* This cultural dimension describes the extent to which emphasis is placed on ambitiousness versus interpersonal harmony. Cultures with high MAS emphasize assertiveness, ambition, and competitiveness. Priority is placed on performance and the recognition of one's own achievements. Cultures with low MAS prioritize cooperation, job security, service, and a good relationship with management.

Given the nature of flying, many pilots with innately high UA, PD, IND, and MAS traits most likely self-select into aviation. Nevertheless, there are still differences to be found across cultures. For example, pilots' endorsement of the statement, "Written procedures are required for all in-flight situations" can vary significantly by country (Helmreich et al., 2001). A higher risk of aviation accidents has been associated with cultures higher in collectivism, UA, and PD (Soeters & Boer, 2000). In particular, high PD has been associated with a higher number of operational errors (Mjøs, 2004) and has been implicated in some accidents in which crew resource management was identified as a factor (Harris & Li, 2008).

In the 1990 Avianca Flight 052 crash, the Colombian first officer informed New York ATCs, "I think we need priority" but never formally declared a fuel emergency despite being asked to do so by the captain. This crash ultimately resulted in 73 fatalities, and investigations identified cultural factors as notable contributors to the crash (see Cookson, 2015; Helmreich, 1994, for review).

The collectivist mindset of the Colombian pilots may have contributed to a reluctance to take actions that could disrupt the group (e.g., jumping the queue and requesting priority over other planes waiting to land). Additionally, the high-PD culture in the cockpit may have led to a reluctance for the first and second officers to question the actions and decisions of the captain. The flight engineer was reportedly aware of the fuel situation (at one point making a throat-cutting gesture to a flight attendant) but did not verbally communicate his concerns to the other officers. Cultural values most likely influenced the pilots' failure to advocate for alternative courses of action. In addition, high levels of UA may have led to adherence to one course of action, avoiding discussions of alternatives and alternative decision-making. Finally, cultural influences on communication in the cockpit were also at play. A culture of high PD most likely resulted in the first officer approaching both his captain and the American ATCs with high levels of deference. This resulted in indirect communications that did not adequately convey the urgency of the situation to the low-PD ATCs. The first officer may have also been reluctant to question the directions of the ATCs. For example, the ATCs ordered the aircraft to go-around after a missed approach and asked the pilots if that would work. Despite their fuel emergency, the first officer responded, "I guess so, thank you very much." Even when the situation became dire, communications were more tentative than urgent: "We just, ah, lost two engines and we need priority please." The ATCs, being from a low-PD culture, may not have understood the seriousness of the situation, as they would have been accustomed to and expected more direct communication.

While there were likely multiple points of failure that ultimately resulted in the crash of Avianca Flight 052, culturally based factors probably played a significant role. Thus, even the operation of a highly technologically advanced aircraft is heavily dependent on the culture of those flying the equipment. While culture is not a direct cause of operational failures, its influences on essential factors such as crew resource management, communication, and decision-making can generate conditions that, in combination with other factors, can make aviation failures more probable (Mjøs, 2004).

Language Considerations in Aviation Neuropsychology

Other high-profile airline crashes have specifically highlighted the impact of language barriers in the cockpit. Given the high communication demands of aeromedical operations, these have become unfortunate but valuable historical lessons for neuropsychologists to be aware of. The aviation industry has traditionally considered English to be its primary language, but for many years the standards for English proficiency varied from country to country. This led to miscommunication and contributed to accidents. For example, in 1996, there was a mid-air collision over the Indian village of Charkhi Dadri between two passenger jets from Kazakhstan and Saudi Arabia. A total of 349 passengers and crew members were killed. It was determined that the cause of this accident was the Kazakh pilot's failure to respond to ATC commands and warnings, most likely due to the pilot's lack of English proficiency.

Following that event, the International Civil Aviation Organization (ICAO) passed Assembly Resolution (A32-16) in 1998 to require that all pilots, ATC personnel, and flight crews involved in international flight operations meet an operational level of proficiency to conduct and comprehend radiotelephonic communications in the English language. The ICAO developed a proficiency rating scale for "Aviation English"' ranging from Level 1 (pre-elementary) up to Level 6 (expert). Aviators must meet a minimum standard of Level 4 (operational). The ICAO Aviation English Test assesses six areas of proficiency: vocabulary, structure, pronunciation, fluency, comprehension, and interactions. The final rating is based on the lowest score obtained in either of these six domains. Level 4 operational proficiency ensures that the aviator possesses the necessary work-related vocabulary or be able to paraphrase in unusual circumstances to communicate effectively. Comprehension for common and concrete topics needs to be mostly accurate. The aviator must also be able to effectively deal with apparent misunderstandings by checking, confirming, or clarifying.

While aviation neuropsychologists are not tasked with determining English language proficiency of FAA medical certificate candidates, it is worth noting that the ICAO Level 4 (operational English) does not require speaking English as a native language. As a result, aviators who present for neuropsychological evaluations may speak English as a second language (ESL) and not be at expert levels in English proficiency for "aviation English." These non-native English speakers could be balanced bilinguals who speak their native language and English equally well, or they could have limited English language proficiency and primary dominance in their native language. Aviation neuropsychologists therefore need to be prepared to understand and appropriately evaluate linguistically diverse aviators.

Ensuring a Linguistically Appropriate Evaluation

Neuropsychological evaluations provide a reliable means of predicting piloting and decision-making performance through reliable identification of subtle but aeromedically significant neurocognitive deficits (Causse et al, 2011). Specific tools such as the CogScreen-Aeromedical Edition have been empirically demonstrated to have good criterion/ecological validity with flight performance, and various validated and reliable testing specifications have been developed to assess the presence or absence of disqualifying conditions based on regulatory standards. Yet, historically there has been little attention paid to identifying and addressing relevant influences of linguistic diversity on the validity and accuracy of measured neurocognitive skills that are considered essential for skilled aviation performance.

According to the APA *Guidelines for Providers of Psychological Services to Ethnic, Linguistic, and Culturally Diverse Populations* (APA, 1993), evaluations should be in the language requested by the examinee, and, if this is not feasible, psychologists need to make an appropriate referral to a qualified provider who speaks the examinee's best language and has knowledge of relevant cultural factors. Refusing services can be unjust, but psychologists also do not practice outside the boundaries of competence without obtaining necessary training, experience, consultation, or supervision to have expertise with the population served (Ethics Code Standard 2.01, Multicultural Guidelines). Yet, it is unclear how many bilingual neuropsychologists are available to conduct aviation examinations. If representation parallels that of practice surveys published more broadly in the field of neuropsychology (Sweet et al., 2021), then there is likely a dearth of bilingual aviation neuropsychologists who are available to conduct examinations. This raises concern about ethical responsibilities to avoid harm caused by an invalid evaluation.

Alternatively, best practices suggest that an interpreter-mediated evaluation would be the next best option if a linguistically matched provider is not available. While data on the use of interpreters in an aviation specific context do not appear to have been published yet, there are general guidelines for use of interpreters in clinical neuropsychology evaluations (e.g., Fujii et al., 2022; Sanchez & Judd, 2022). For instance, use of family members or clinic staff who speak the same language as the examinee should be avoided due to issues around bias, competency, and confidentiality, among others (Fujii, 2018). Professional interpreters or those who have extensive experience with interpretation and translation should be used, although there can be barriers to access to appropriate interpreters. Interpreters should also speak the dialect or variant of the target language and be familiar with the regional culture of the examinee (Paltzer & Jo, 2022). Spending time beforehand preparing the interpreter about specific test administration procedures, informing them about the importance of standardized administration, and requesting input from the interpreter about how best to convey certain neuropsychological concepts in a culturally relevant manner are also important to minimize measurement error that can occur with the use of an interpreter (Romero et al., 2009). Well-trained interpreters allow the involved parties to know precisely what each speaker has said, maintain trust and confidentiality between the parties involved, eliminate the effect of interpreter bias or preference, facilitate communication across cultural differences, and strive to prevent harm to parties involved, among others (National Council on Interpreting in Health Care, 2005).

In addition, when proceeding with either an interpreter-mediated or neuropsychological evaluation with a bilingual neuropsychologist, the importance of determining a non-native English speaker's English language proficiency cannot be understated. When an aviator does not have operational fluency in English, administering a standard battery of tests in English and misinterpreting the test data could result in false-positive errors that are confounded by English language proficiency rather than capturing true neurocognitive abilities. This could rob an already underrepresented workforce from the expertise of a capable aviator. Assessment of English language proficiency can also help determine whether translated/adapted tests are needed in the native language, decide on which normative data set is most appropriate to use, and guide appropriate interpretation of test performance.

Fluency for bilinguals runs on a continuum and thus there needs to be a distinction made between basic interpersonal fluency skills in English and cognitive academic language proficiency to ensure fairness in test taking (Artiola i Fortuny, 2008). Fujii (2018) acknowledges that establishing English proficiency is complex and recommends the use of multiple sources such as self-report, demographics (e.g., generation in the United States, age of immigration, years educated in the United States, years living in the United States, education level, proficiency of native language), formal assessment of skills in English and the native language, and careful consideration of neuropsychological tests that are known to be correlated with English proficiency (e.g., verbal fluency, naming).

Influences of Language on Cognitive Test Performance

Once a linguistically appropriate evaluation has been administered, it is important to avoid misinterpreting standardized tests that have been developed and normed for monolingual populations for the assessment of bilinguals (Gasquoine & Gonzalez, 2012). There is a robust literature highlighting the influence of bilingualism on cognitive test performance. Speaking more than one language offers several cognitive and functional advantages. For instance, bilingualism has been shown to enhance cognitive flexibility, provide higher cognitive reserve with aging, delay the onset of dementia, enhance literacy development, benefit employability and academic achievement, and positively impact the development of cross-cultural awareness and communicative competence (Bialystok, 2011; Fox et al., 2019). Similarly, bilinguals across the lifespan have shown advantages over monolinguals on some executive functioning tasks involving switching, conflict, and interference (Bialystok et al., 2004; Bialystok et al., 2012; Coderre et al., 2013; Mindt et al., 2008; Prior & MacWhinney, 2010;) and a small advantage for working memory capacity that is moderated by language used (Monnier et al, 2022). Cognitive disadvantages in relation to bilingualism have included reduced vocabulary knowledge, verbal fluency, poorer naming performance, and retrieval failures (Gollan & Brown, 2006; Portocarrero et al., 2007; Roberts et al., 2002). Other key variables such as language proficiency, age of acquisition, immigrant status, and language of test administration appear to influence the degree of advantage or disadvantage experienced during test performance, along with cross-linguistic differences in demands on lexical access and executive control (Celik et al., 2022).

In aviation neuropsychology, Kay (1995) has found that on the CogScreen–Aeromedical Edition (AE), ESL status impacted performance on the Math, Pathfinder (Letter & Combined), Shifting Attention (Instruction), and Visual Sequence Comparison subtests. In addition, the CogScreen-AE requires an eighth-grade reading level in English (Kay, 1995), which highlights the need to accurately assess English language reading comprehension if proceeding in English. This may be less of a factor for the most recent edition of CogScreen-AE version 2 (AE2), which provides video (or optional text) instructions designed to facilitate translation to alternative languages. The CogScreen has been professionally translated into multiple languages using certified translators and procedures for back-translations to assure comparable instructions and use in regulatory clinical trials (Gary Kay, personal communication, August 15, 2021). Available versions include Spanish, French, Dutch, Russian, Hindi, and Hebrew, but there are many other languages that remain unavailable.

A related concern in evaluating linguistically diverse aviators is that current FAA specifications for neuropsychological test administration for various protocols are not linguistically specific. Thus, when testing bilingual populations who have operational fluency in English, but may not be necessarily matched to the standardization samples, the onus is on the aviation neuropsychologist to ensure that they are conducting a linguistically appropriate evaluation with awareness of the existing literature and the limitations of the available tools. Consultation with a cultural broker and carefully considering the pros and cons of the language of test administration and sensitivity of measures used are necessary.

Normative Data Considerations Related to Linguistic Diversity

A primary goal of an aviation neuropsychological evaluation is to determine whether test performance indicates the presence of aeromedically significant cognitive deficits. When comparing test performance with available normative standards, the challenge is often whether available normative data adequately represent the person being evaluated. There are a myriad of considerations related to demographic adjustments for test data that have yet to be resolved by the field, but when evaluating linguistically diverse aviators in high-stakes evaluations, it is worth noting that some normative data and appropriately translated/adapted tests do exist for several linguistically diverse groups. The majority of available resources are for Spanish speakers (e.g., Arango-Lasprilla, 2015; Cherner et al, 2021), although resources across Asian, Latin American and Caribbean, sub-Saharan African, Arab, Israeli, Persian, Russian, European, and North American regions have also been collated (see Appendix in Irani, 2022). While available language- or country-specific normative data in the general population are by no means comprehensive and inclusive of the larger variety of tests available, it is useful to know that these options are available.

Currently available aviation norms have not considered language-based influences. Aviation norms are also more stringent compared to general population norms. Thus, neuropsychological profiles may reflect "normal" cognitive profiles that are not clinically significant when compared with general population normative samples, yet when compared with other aviators, these scores may fall in "impaired" ranges. In the absence of aviation normative data that have specifically stratified groups based on ESL status, language-based confounds may further reduce scores and magnify concerns about the aeromedical significance of test data. Aviation neuropsychologists will need to continue to consider these limitations and any impact of potentially erroneously false-positive errors in their diagnostic impressions and related decision-making about the aeromedical significance of cognitive performance.

It is also worth noting that there have been insufficient published reports of demographic characteristics in available aviation-specific normative samples. At the time of this writing (2023), there are three sets of aviation norms used for aeromedical neuropsychological evaluations: (1) CogScreen-AE norms, (2) Class 3 general aviation norms, and (3) Class 1 pilot norms. The information available related to known demographic characteristics of each of these normative data sets is described next.

CogScreen-AE Norms

The CogScreen-AE major carrier sample of 584 was collected from 1991 to 1993. Table 17.1 describes the basic demographic makeup of the sample as published by Kay (1995). The average level of education was a bachelor's degree, and 92.6% of the sample were men. The CogScreen manual indicates that there was low variance between genders, thus the test publishers decided not to separate norms by gender. The CogScreen manual does not include a breakdown of English language proficiency or racial/ethnic group. Verbal correspondence with the test's developer, Dr. Gary Kay, indicated that the sample was comprised of 97% White, 1% African American, 1.5% Hispanic, 0.5% Asian, and 0.3% as "Other." Regarding education, 28% of the sample had 11–12 years of education, 15% had some college education, and 25% had graduate education. Overall, 93% of the sample was male and 7% was female.

The CogScreen-AE2 uses the same subtests as the prior version, with equivalence of AE and AE2 tested extensively by demonstration of identical timing, stimulus/item characteristics, and performance (Gary Kay, personal communication, August 15, 2021). The test author indicates that normative data collected with AE can be used with AE2, with two additional normative data sets now available in AE2. Specifically, there are now new air transport pilot norms (n=1,447), which includes airline pilots qualified for regional, cargo, and airlines. These data were collected between 2008 and 2020 for samples that ranged in age from 23 to 80 (mean age=45.2, mode=44), had a sex distribution of 92.7% male and 7.3% female, and mean education of 16.1 years (range=12–22 years). Regarding the education distribution, 5.6% had 12–13 years of education, 16.8% had 1–15 years of education, 46% had 16 years of education, 29.2% had 16.5–18 years, and 2.6% had more than 18 years of education. Racial/ethnic data and language proficiency data were not collected. According to the test author, additional normative comparison groups for AE2 will soon include Colom-

Table 17.1. Demographic characteristics of CogScreen-AE normative data

Variable	Airline			
	Large ($n = 403$)	Medium ($n = 120$)	Small ($n = 61$)	Total ($N = 584$)
Gender (%)				
Male	92.6	97.3	95.1	93.8
Female	7.4	2.7	4.9	6.2
Mean age (in years)	44.6	43	42.1	42.8
Mean years of education	16.1	16	16	16.1
Estimated full-scale IQ	118	120	110	118
Medical certificate (%)				
Class I license	90	98	98	92
Class II license	10	2	2	8

Note. Adapted from Kay, 1995, p. 34.

bian norms, Indian norms, and Swedish norms. Most of these will be available to the organization that provided the data unless the organization chooses to make their data available for clinicians. For example, there are now US Air Force normative data available for use by Air Force psychologists that include norms for enlisted individuals from diverse racial and ethnic groups and a higher percentage of females.

There may be some differences in CogScreen subtest performance across linguistically diverse groups. Early CogScreen AE studies presented at the Annual Meeting of the Aerospace Medical Association (Kay et al, 1993; Yakimovich et al., 1994) in the early 1990s showed general comparability between Russian and English versions of CogScreen AE in a population of White male Aeroflot pilots. Yet, the Russians outperformed US pilots on the Math, but did not perform as well as the US pilots on the Pathfinder Letter/Combined subtests, possibly because there is no alphabet song in Russian. Performance was correlated with flight performance. Similarly, more recently, some CogScreen-AE normative data have been collected in India and show significant differences for Indian aviators on subtests such as Math, Divided Attention, and Auditory Sequencing (cited with permission of Dr. Sowgandhi Chaturvedula based on Irani et al., 2021). Efforts have also been underway in Colombia to develop CogScreen-AE norms for aviators (cited with permission of Dr. Claudio de la Rosa, based on Irani et al., 2021). Preliminary findings indicate that the Colombian aviation population has cognitive profiles that are very similar to those of the US and general international aviation population, especially for younger pilots and aviation personnel. According to Dr. de la Rosa, there are, however, elevated CogScreen logistic regression probability values (LRPVs), lower Math and Manikin subtest scores, and slower speeds compared with greater accuracy in the Colombian general population. Since the CogScreen-AE2 provides two LRPV scores, one with and one without the contribution of Math, it will be interesting to see the extent to which LRPV differences are eliminated based on the LRPV-M score. The other linguistically sensitive measure in LRPV is SAT Instruction, which may also provide valuable insights into the influence of language. Additional preliminary findings from these Colombia studies suggest an increased predictive value of CogScreen for the early detection of neurological conditions and good predictions for future development of dementia, cognitive decline, and other neurological conditions. Overall, there is scope to continue to increase our understanding of linguistic and cultural factors on CogScreen performance.

General Aviation and Pilots Norms

The general aviation (GA) norms provide mean scores for pilots and ATCs for various commonly used neuropsychological tests. These norms were collected at the EAA AirVenture OshKosh and Sun N Fun events in 2013. The sample is comprised of 207 pilots and ATCs, with a mean age of 58.2 years (*SD*=14.8), mean education level of 16.4 years (*SD*=2.3), and a mean estimated IQ of 117 (*SD*=7.2). A racial or ethnic breakdown of this sample group was not available, and neither was English language proficiency status (Gary Kay, personal communication, August 15, 2021). Additional data were collected from 132 pilots for the pilot norms used on other commonly used neuropsychological tests (Kay, 2002). These additional data include published normative data on conventional neuropsychological tests administered during the validation of CogScreen-AE. While the racial and ethnic background of that sample was not recorded, it is helpful to know that all of these normative data are now incorporated in the CogScreen-AE2 program.

Normative Needs for the Future

Neuropsychologists must be aware that while this may be changing, aviation norms have typically reflected a largely homogeneous demographic group consisting of college-educated White men who are likely monolingual English speakers. Therefore, when evaluating an aviator who does not match this group, how do you determine if "impaired" scores are in fact aeromedically significant? This challenges our future ability to serve the rapidly changing national and aviation-specific demographic landscape, and underscores the need for the aviation industry to invest in expanding our toolkit of more linguistically and culturally appropriate tools and comparative groups.

Cultural Influences in Aviation Neuropsychology

The *Guidelines for Multicultural Education, Training, Research, Practice, and Organizational Change for Psychologists* (APA, 2003) state that "*All* individuals are cultural beings who possess a cultural, racial, and ethnic heritage." In neuropsychology, culture has been defined as (Rivera-Mindt et al., 2010, p. 430):

> The quintessence of a worldview born of learned and transmitted belief systems and value orientations that influence customs, norms, practices, and social institutions, including psychological processes (cognition, behavior, etc.) and organizations [aerospace] and that is transmitted from one generation to the next.

Neuropsychologists tasked with gathering accurate bio-psycho-socio-cultural histories to adequately inform diagnostic impressions and decisions about aerospace safety need to be aware of cultural influences on history gathering, testing, and data interpretation.

Building Rapport for Accurate History Gathering

Pilots and ATCs applying for medical certificates can be psychologically defensive and present themselves in the best possible light given the high stakes of hiring and flying decisions (Front, 2014). As a result, complete information may not be volunteered during history gathering, and even less so if there is not adequate trust or rapport with the examiner. Rapport is important and there are many things that can help build rapport with culturally diverse aviators.

Increasing rapport through cultural understanding necessitates having knowledge of various surface- and deep-level aspects of cultural backgrounds that can impact the accuracy of the clinical information and test data collected. For example, this could include inquiring about preferred terminology for cultural identification, ethnocultural history, immigration/relocation background, language history, communication style, education quality and quantity, literacy levels, socioeconomic influences, values and customs, gender- and sexuality-based influences, spirituality- and religion-based influences, acculturation and systemic barriers, mental health views, and approaches to neuropsychological assessment (Irani, 2022). While it is beyond the scope of this chapter to highlight all the cultural competencies needed to work with diverse examinees, it is important for aviation neuropsychologists to seek out the relevant knowledge, self- and other awareness, skills, and action orientation needed to appreciate various cultural influences that impact clinical presentations and neuropsychological test data (Díaz-Santos et al, 2022; Fujii, 2016, 2018; Hamilton et al., 2022; Sanchez & Judd, 2022; Sandeen et al., 2018).

A clinical interview is the first opportunity to build rapport and trust with an aviator whose cultural outlook may be different or similar to the examiner. The *Diagnostic and Statistical Manual of Mental Disorders, Fifth Edition* (DSM-5) Cultural Formulation Interview (CFI) can be one helpful tool to support eliciting culturally relevant perspectives on their condition or symptoms (accessible online at https://www.psychiatry.org/File Library/Psychiatrists/Practice/DSM/APA_DSM5_Cultural-Formulation-Interview.pdf). However, beyond the style of the clinical interview, a neuropsychologist's communication style has the potential to impact how much and what kind of information is shared by the examinee (Tannen, 1984). For example, an examiner who speaks too quickly or too slowly, or talks too much or too little, may be seen as rude, insensitive, or incompetent depending on cultural expectations. In addition, there may be unfamiliarity with psychological evaluations for some aviators, and thus it becomes important to ensure that aviators understand the purpose of the interview and why certain questions are asked. While it is possible that refusals or avoidance about answering certain questions reflect defensiveness or avoidance observed in many pilot or ATC applicants, in someone who comes from a culturally diverse background, cultural viewpoints could also guide what is considered appropriate or not to disclose to a stranger (Fujii, 2018).

Examiners also need to be aware that many, if not most, examinees from ethnoracially or linguistically diverse backgrounds have been subjected to assumptions, stereotyping, and other microaggressions. Intrinsic variables such as perceived discrimination and stereotype threat have been reliably shown to negatively impact performance on neuropsychological tests (Thames et al., 2013; Whaley, 2021). Perceived ethnoracial discrimination also has a significantly greater impact on mental health outcomes than on physical health outcomes (Paradies et al., 2015). Acculturation is a related complex and multidimensional moderator that describes the process by which one adapts to, modifies, replaces, and/or rejects elements or customs of the dominant or mainstream culture (Berry, 1997; Fedi et al., 2019; Schwartz et al., 2010; Tan et al., 2021). The level of acculturation can impact how much personal information an examinee is willing to disclose and overall engage in the assessment process, including willingness to say "I don't know" or ask clarifying questions (Fujii, 2018; Kim & Zabelina, 2015).

Considering Influences of Culture on Cognitive Test Data

After gathering accurate history, the next step is to ensure cultural fairness in the testing process as exemplified by American Education Research Association standards (AERA, 2014). This includes ensuring that test-takers feel comfortable with the examiner and the testing situation, tests are free of biases, test-takers do not experience disadvantages in processing and responding to test items, and valid interpretations for the intended use of a specific test can be drawn from the test-taker's score (Fujii, 2018).

While there is limited information regarding the influence of cultural variables on cognitive test performance specifically in aviators, the neuropsychological literature has clearly identified the effect of cultural variables on neuropsychological test performance (e.g., Agranovich & Puente, 2007; Ardila, 2005, 2007a; Fujii 2016, 2018; Loewenstein et al., 1994; Weiss & Saklofske, 2020). Since cognitive measures administered in aviation evaluations have been developed in Western, English-speaking countries, it is important for aviation neuropsychologists to be aware that cultural variables can exert a greater impact on test performance in individuals who do not match the mainstream culture (Fujii, 2016; Wong, 2000). While some aspects of this literature are briefly discussed below, the onus of increasing knowledge and understanding of the specific cultural influences on an aviator's neuropsychological test performance lies with the examining neuropsychologist. After all, the *Guidelines for Providers of Psychological Services to Ethnic, Linguistic, and Culturally Diverse Populations* (https://www.apa.org/pi/oema/resources/policy/provider-guidelines) clearly indicate that psychologists are responsible for obtaining the necessary knowledge and training to maintain competence in working with individuals of diverse backgrounds (Standard 1.08, Human Differences).

Several cultural variables have been found to influence performance on neuropsychological tests. Speed and timed tasks have been especially found to be affected by social customs. For example, being cautious and careful are more highly valued in many African societies than quickness, whereas in many Western cultures, speed is seen to be synonymous with intelligence (Ardila, 2007a; Rosselli & Ardila, 2003). Familiarity with American cultural products also impacts performance on popular naming, list learning, story memory, and math tests. Native English speakers who are born in the United States but are from an ethnocultural group score lower on tests like the Boston Naming Test, indicating cultural differences in test performance that go beyond language (Ardila, 2007b; Boone et al., 2007). Cultural experiences and values also play a role in the development of executive functioning skills, such as inhibition and cognitive flexibility (Cho et al., 2021; Sabbagh et al., 2006). Additionally, nonverbal tests, traditionally thought to be "culture free," are also impacted by cultural variables. Skills such as drawing, nonverbal reasoning, and nonverbal memory are influenced by the physical environment, schooling, and daily cultural practices. Some studies have observed even larger group differences in performance-based and other nonverbal tests than in verbal tests (Rosselli & Ardila, 2003). Test wiseness, or familiarity with the particulars of a testing situation (e.g., working quickly, social facility with a stranger), also influences test performance (Ardila, 2007a). The level of acculturation impacts performance on specific neuropsychological tasks, both verbal and nonverbal (Tan et al., 2021), and accounts for 11 %–14 % of the variance in overall neuropsychological functions (Arentoft et al, 2012).

These cultural differences in cognitive test performances have cognitive neuroscientific underpinnings. Experience leads to functional organizational changes in the brain (Cagigas, 2009; Draganski et al., 2004; Maguire et al., 2000; Park & Huang, 2010). Theories and findings in cultural neuroscience have identified environmental influences on brain development and organization, and highlighted the role of intersectionality principles in access and validity of neuropsychological findings (Fujii, 2023). Various studies have demonstrated that culture impacts how the brain processes information, how it pays attention, how it categorizes information, and how it affects one's thinking about the world (Boroditsky, 2001; Nisbett et al., 2001; Nisbett & Masuda, 2003; Senzaki et al., 2014). Thus, it is important to consider that the performance of culturally diverse aviators on neuropsychological tests may be mitigated by an interaction of various linguistic and cultural variables that do not necessarily reflect a direct relationship between cognition and test performance.

Selection of Appropriate Normative Data

The diagnostic utility of neuropsychological tests is subject to the influence of the demographic (e.g., education level, gender, disability status) and sociocultural (e.g., English language status, socioeconomic status, acculturation, neighborhood deprivation) composition of the normative reference sample (Byrd & Rivera-Mindt, 2022). While the Human Genome Project has taught us that human beings are 99.9 % similar at the DNA level, with the remaining 0.1 % not varying according to sociopolitically defined categories (Possin et al., 2021), it is also clear that neuropsychological test performance is influenced by several proxy variables that have not yet been routinely incorporated into clinical practice. Diagnostic precision can be increased by comparing individual test performance with appropriate normative reference groups. Towards that goal, various demographically adjusted normative data sets have been generated to provide adjustments based on race, age, education, gender, socioeconomic status, or literacy in more representative standardization samples (e.g., Dotson et al., 2008; Heaton et al., 2004; Lucas et al., 2005; Norman et al., 2000, Verney et al, 2019). Alternative approaches have focused on the development, validation, and standardization of more widely applicable cross-cultural tests (e.g., Franzen et al., 2021). Others have emphasized that future norming efforts need to consider variables involving nativity and acculturation, language, education, literacy, psychosocial stress, occupation, economic and financial status, and residential characteristics (Possin et al, 2021).

In aviation neuropsychology practice, beyond age and occupational carrier-specific demographic adjustments, the influence of these other demographic or sociocultural influences has been explored. The industry needs to pay greater attention to the generation of larger, more heterogeneous standardization samples that represent diverse populations with detailed sociocultural characterization to facilitate more nuanced norms that incorporate evidence-based sociocultural factors that are known to affect test performance. In the meantime, neuropsychologists will need to continue to be vigilant in considering false-positive diagnostic errors and test specificity in overall impressions, while also acknowledging the limitations of available tools and measures.

Considerations of Culture in Mood and Personality Data

Cultural influences related to aviation safety extend to the mood and personality testing that are routine components of several specifications for aviation psychological or neuropsychological evaluations. Inadequate consideration of cultural influences on personality test data can result in cultural misunderstandings, misinterpretations, and a culturally invalid evaluation. Cultural outlook and practices often influence concepts assessed by personality tests (e.g., extroversion–introversion, dominance–submission, expression–suppression; Butcher, 1996). Cultural influences also color idioms of distress, which can affect symptom development, symptom expression, and symptom attribution. One example is that of an aviator from an ethnocultural background who appears depressed but is reporting more physically oriented symptoms such as pain, headaches, and fatigue. This may be a more culturally acceptable way to convey symptoms; therefore, taking extra time to obtain a thorough history can help understand relevant cultural influences on test data.

English-language-based personality measures being translated for use with examinees from a different cultural group should not only go through the appropriate rigors of being translated and validated for cross-cultural use, but appropriate cultural norms should also be ideally available. Use of "on the spot" or sight translations of English personality tests scored with US norms can be highly problematic and is not recommended as it may lead to grossly inaccurate conclusions about mood symptoms, personality traits, and symptom validity. Instead, officially translated versions of different personality measures are available. As an example, translations of the various MMPI versions are available in 26 languages (available at https://www.upress.umn.edu/test-division/translations-permissions/available-translations). Studies have shown that US norms can be used with certain translated MMPI versions (e.g., Hebrew, Hmong, Philippines), but not others (e.g., Korean; Butcher et al., 2003; Butcher & Gur, 1974).

Conclusion

Culture impacts all aspects of a neuropsychological evaluation including decisions regarding aeromedical significance of cognitive and emotional test data. Aviation neuropsychologists are ethically responsible for obtaining the necessary cultural knowledge, awareness, and skills to conduct a fair and just evaluation with culturally and linguistically diverse aviators. The costs of inadequately attending to linguistic and cultural factors in aviation can lead to deadly miscommunications that have historically resulted in high-profile airline crashes. An inability to meet the demands of rapidly changing global and national demographics also limits the ability to provide accurate and valid predictions about safety and increases the likelihood of false-positive errors in decision-making.

Best practices related to ensuring a linguistically and culturally appropriate evaluation may include ensuring that aviators are evaluated in their preferred language either by a bilingual neuropsychologist or with the support of an interpreter in the hands of a culturally competent neuropsychologist. Assessment of English language proficiency through a culturally competent lens is crucial since it can help determine whether translated/adapted tests are needed in the native language, as well as increase understanding of the effects of bilingualism on test performance, and guide decisions regarding the most appropriate normative data to use with aviators who may have minimal operational fluency in English. This highlights several areas of necessary attention in aviation neuropsychology that include greater reporting of demographic characteristics of aviator samples, greater representation in normative samples, and more attention to international findings that are preliminarily showing culturally mediated neurocognitive differences on certain tests.

Beyond linguistic considerations, a culturally competent evaluation also requires adequate history gathering that can be supported by building rapport and seeking out relevant surface- and deep-level cultural knowledge, having self- and other awareness, acquiring cultural competence skills, and having the necessary action orientation to understand the impact of various cultural influences on clinical presentations and cognitive test data. Cultural fairness in the testing process also demands careful consideration of the influence of several linguistic and cultural variables that have been reliably linked to neuroscientific underpinning of brain-behavior relationships and that do not necessarily reflect a direct relationship between cognition and test performance. There is a pressing need for expanding the aviation toolkit to better serve diverse populations and incorporate evidence-based sociocultural factors that are known to affect neuropsychological and psychological evaluation processes. In high-stakes evaluations such as those involved in the aviation industry, it becomes imperative to develop appropriate tools that have sensitivity and specificity to detect potential cognitive impairment while reducing the risk of false-positive errors that would rob the workforce of a capable aviator.

Cory (2021) challenged neuropsychologists with reflection questions such as: "When I shop for tests, I can readily select measures that are widely available, standardized, and validated for individuals of my own linguistic, cultural, and racial background" and "I do not need to purchase or be linguistically competent in the administration of tests in non-English languages." He argued that responses to these statements reflect privileges that English-speaking, White neuropsychologists carry in their invisible knapsacks. If by the year 2050, when global and national societies are predicted to be even more ethnoracially and linguistically pluralistic, the answer to these questions remains the same for aviation neuropsychologists, then we have not been successful in adequately supporting efforts to secure the skies of a diverse nation and world.

References

Agranovich, A.V., & Puente, A.E. (2007). Do Russian and American normal adults perform similarly on neuropsychological tests? Preliminary findings on the relationship between culture and test performance. *Archives of Clinical Neuropsychology, 22*(3), 273–282. https://doi.org/10.1016/j.acn.2007.01.003

American Education Research Association, American Psychological Association, & the National Council on Measurement in Education. (2014). *Standards for educational and psychological testing* (2nd ed.). American Education Research Association.

American Psychological Association (APA), Office of Ethnic Minority Affairs. (1993). Guidelines for providers of psychological services to ethnic, linguistic, and culturally diverse populations. *American Psychologist, 48*(1), 45–48. https://doi.org/10.1037/0003-066X.48.1.45

American Psychological Association (APA). (2002). Ethical principles of psychologists and code of conduct. *American Psychologist, 57*(12), 1060–1073. https://doi.org/10.1037/0003-066X.57.12.1060

American Psychological Association (APA). (2003). Guidelines on multicultural education, training, research, practice, and organizational change for psychologists. *American Psychologist, 58*, 377–402. https://doi.org/10.1037/0003-066X.58.5.377

Arango-Lasprilla, J.C. (2015). Commonly used neuropsychological tests for Spanish speakers: Normative data from Latin America [Editorial]. *NeuroRehabilitation, 37*(4), 489–491. https://doi.org/10.3233/NRE-151276

Ardila, A. (2005). Cultural values underlying psychometric cognitive testing. *Neuropsychology Review, 15*(4), 185–195. https://doi.org/10.1007/s11065-005-9180-y

Ardila, A. (2007a). The impact of culture on neuropsychological test performance. In B. Uzzell, M. Pontón, & A. Ardila (Eds.), *International handbook of cross-cultural neuropsychology* (pp. 23–44). Routledge.

Ardila, A. (2007b). Toward the development of a cross-linguistic naming test. *Archives of Clinical Neuropsychology, 22*(3), 297–307. https://doi.org/10.1016/j.acn.2007.01.016

Arentoft, A., Byrd, D., Robbins, R.N., Monzones, J., Miranda, C., Rosario, A., Coulehan, K., Fuentes, A., Germano, K.K., D'Aquila, E., Sheynin, J., Fraser, F., Morgello, S., & Rivera Mindt, M. (2012). Multidimensional effects of acculturation on English-language neuropsychological test performance among HIV+ Caribbean Latinas/os. *Journal of Clinical and Experimental Neuropsychology, 34*, 814–825. https://doi.org/10.1080/13803395.2012.683856

Artiola i Fortuny, L. (2008). Research and practice: Ethical issues with immigrant adults and children. In J. Morgan & J. Ricker (Eds.), *Textbook of clinical neuropsychology* (pp. 960–982). Psychology Press.

Berry, J.W. (1997). Immigration, acculturation, and adaptation. *Applied Psychology, 46*(1), 5–34. https://doi.org/10.1111/j.1464-0597.1997.tb01087.x

Bialystok, E. (2011). Reshaping the mind: The benefits of bilingualism. *Canadian Journal of Experimental Psychology/Revue canadienne de psychologie expérimentale, 65*(4), 229–235. https://doi.org/10.1037/a0025406

Bialystok, E., Craik, F.I., Klein, R., & Viswanathan, M. (2004). Bilingualism, aging, and cognitive control: Evidence from the Simon task. *Psychology and Aging, 19*(2), 290–303. https://doi.org/10.1037/0882-7974.19.2.290

Bialystok, E., Craik, F.I., & Luk, G. (2012). Bilingualism: Consequences for mind and brain. *Trends in Cognitive Sciences, 16*(4), 240–250. https://doi.org/10.1016/j.tics.2012.03.001

Boone, K.B., Victor, T.L., Wen, J., Razani, J., & Ponton, M. (2007). The association between neuropsychological scores and ethnicity, language, and acculturation variables in a large patient population. *Archives of Clinical Neuropsychology, 22*, 355365. https://doi.org/10.1016/j.acn.2007.01.010

Boroditsky, L. (2001). Does language shape thought? Mandarin and English speakers; conceptions of time. *Cognitive Psychology, 43*(1), 1–22. https://doi.org/10.1006/cogp.2001.0748

Butcher, J.N. (1996). (Ed.). *Understanding abnormal behavior across cultures: The use of objective personality assessment methods, in international adaptations of the MMPI-2.* University of Minnesota Press.

Butcher, J.N., Cheung, F.M., & Lim, J. (2003). Use of the MMPI-2 with Asian populations. *Psychological Assessment, 15*(3), 248–256. https://doi.org/10.1037/1040-3590.15.3.248

Butcher, J.N., & Gur, R. (1974). A Hebrew translation of the MMPI: An assessment of translation adequacy and preliminary validation. *Journal of Cross-Cultural Psychology, 5*(2), 220–227. https://doi.org/10.1177/002202217400500207

Byrd, D.A., & Rivera-Mindt, M.G. (2022). Neuropsychology's race problem does not begin or end with demographically adjusted norms. *Nature Review Neurology, 18*, 125–126. https://doi.org/10.1038/s41582-021-00607-4

Cagigas, X.E. (2009). Cultural neuropsychology: A recapitulation of Vygotsky's crisis in psychology. *The California Psychologist, July/August,* 16–19.

Causse, M., Dehais, F., Arexis, M., & Pastor, J. (2011). Cognitive aging and flight performance in general aviation pilots. *Aging, Neuropsychology & Cognition, 18*(5), 544–561. https://doi.org/10.1080/13825585.2011.586018

Celik, S., Kokje, E., Meyer, P., Frölich, L., & Teichmann, B. (2022). Does bilingualism influence neuropsychological test performance in older adults? A systematic review. *Applied Neuropsychology: Adult, 29*(4), 855–873. https://doi.org/10.1080/23279095.2020.1788032

Cherner, M., Marquine, M., Umlauf, A., Morlett Paredes, A., Rivera Mindt, M., Suárez, P., Yassai-Gonzalez, D., Kamalyan, L., Scott, T., Heaton, A., Diaz-Santos, M., Gooding, A., Artiola i Fortuny, L., & Heaton, R. (2021). Neuropsychological norms for the U.S.-Mexico border region in Spanish (NP-NUMBRS) Project: Methodology and sample characteristics. *The Clinical Neuropsychologist, 35*(2), 253–268. https://doi.org/10.1080/13854046.2019.1709661

Cho, I., Park, J., Song, H.J., & Morton, J.B. (2021). Disentangling language status and country-of-origin explanations of the bilingual advantage in preschoolers. *Journal of Experimental Child Psychology, 212,* Article 105235. https://doi.org/10.1016/j.jecp.2021.105235
Coderre, E.L., Van Heuven, W.J., & Conklin, K. (2013). The timing and magnitude of Stroop interference and facilitation in monolinguals and bilinguals. *Bilingualism: Language and Cognition, 16*(2), 420–441. https://doi.org/10.1017/S1366728912000405
Cookson, S. (2015). "We need priority please". Mitigated speech in the crash of Avianca Flight 052. *18th International Symposium on Aviation Psychology* (pp. 578–583). https://corescholar.libraries.wright.edu/isap_2015/9
Cory, J.M. (2021). White privilege in neuropsychology: An "invisible knapsack" in need of unpacking? *The Clinical Neuropsychologist, 35*(2), 206–218. https://doi.org/10.1080/13854046.2020.1801845
Cranney, S. (2019). *Which American languages are dying? Quantifying the demographic vulnerability of indigenous languages in the United States. Working Paper Number SESHD-WP2019-08.* United States Census. https://www.census.gov/content/dam/Census/library/working-papers/2019/demo/sehsd-wp2019-08.pdf
Díaz-Santos, M., Anderson, K., Miranda, M., Wong, C., Yañez, J. & Irani, F. (2022). Stepping into action: The role of neuropsychologists in social justice advocacy. In F. Irani (Ed.), *Cultural diversity in neuropsychological assessment: Developing understanding through global case studies* (pp. 63–78). Routledge. https://doi.org/10.4324/9781003051862-10
Diehl, A. (1991). The effectiveness of training programs for preventing aircrew error. In R.S. Jensen (Ed.), *Proceedings of the Sixth International Symposium on Aviation Psychology* (pp. 640–655). Ohio State University.
Dietrich, S., & Hernandez, E. (2022). *Language use in the United States: 2019 American Community Survey Reports.* United States Census Bureau. https://www.census.gov/content/dam/Census/library/publications/2022/acs/acs-50.pdf
Dotson, V.M., Kitner-Triolo, M., Evans, M.K., & Zonderman, A.B. (2008). Literacy-based normative data for low socioeconomic status African Americans. *The Clinical Neuropsychologist, 22*(6), 989–1017. https://doi.org/10.1080/13854040701679017
Draganski, B., Gaser, C., Busch, V., Schuierer, G., Bogdahn, U., & May, A. (2004). Neuroplasticity: Changes in grey matter induced by training. *Nature, 427,* 311–312. https://doi.org/10.1038/427311a
Fedi, A., Brodsky, A., Buckingham, S., Mannarini, T., Rochira, A., Emergy, L., Godsay, S., & Scheibler, J. (2019). Acculturation in the discourse of immigrants and receiving community members: Results from a cross-national qualitative study. *American Journal of Orthopsychiatry, 89*(1), 1–15. https://doi.org/10.1037/ort0000325
Federal Aviation Administration. (2022, March 23). *Diversity and inclusion.* https://www.faa.gov/jobs/diversity_inclusion
Federal Aviation Administration. (2023, January 19). *U.S. civil airmen statistics.* https://www.faa.gov/data_research/aviation_data_statistics/civil_airmen_statistics
Fernandez, A., & Abe, J. (2018). Bias in cross-cultural neuropsychological testing: problems and possible solutions. *Culture & Brain, 6,* 1–35. https://doi.org/10.1007/s40167-017-0050-2
Franzen, S., European Consortium on Cross-Cultural Neuropsychology (ECCroN), Watermeyer, T.J., Pomati, S., Papma, J.M., Nielsen, T.R., Narme, P., Mukadam, N., Lozano-Ruiz, Á., Ibanez-Casas, I., Goudsmit, M., Fasfous, A., Daugherty, J.C., Canevelli, M., Calia, C., van den Berg, E., & Bekkhus-Wetterberg, P. (2021). Cross-cultural neuropsychological assessment in Europe: Position statement of the European Consortium on Cross-Cultural Neuropsychology (ECCroN). *The Clinical Neuropsychologist, 36*(3), 546–557. https://doi.org/10.1080/13854046.2021.1981456
Front, C.M. (2014). Commentary on the article by King: Good to go or disqualified? Interrelated but distinct tasks, challenges, and tools in pilot selection. *The International Journal of Aviation Psychology, 24*(1), 74–77. https://doi.org/10.1080/10508414.2014.860841
Fox, R., Corretjer, O., Webb, K. (2019). Benefits of foreign language learning and bilingualism: An analysis of published empirical research 2012–2019. *Foreign Language Annals, 52,* 699–726. https://doi.org/10.1111/flan.12424
Fujii, D. (2016). *Conducting a culturally-informed neuropsychological evaluation.* American Psychological Association Press.

Fujii, D. (2018). Developing a cultural context for conducting a neuropsychological evaluation with a culturally diverse client: The ECLECTIC framework. *The Clinical Neuropsychologist, 32*(8), 1356–1392. https://doi.org/10.1080/13854046.2018.1435826
Fujii, D.. (2023). Incorporating intersectionality in neuropsychology: Moving the discipline forward. *Archives of Clinical Neuropsychology, 38*(1), 154–167. https://doi.org/10.1093/arclin/acac075
Fujii, D., Santos, O., & Della Malva, L. (2022). *Interpreter-assisted neuropsychological assessment: clinical considerations* (pp. 135–147). Routledge. https://doi.org/10.4324/9781003051497-14
Gasquoine, P.G., & Gonzalez, C.D. (2012). Using monolingual neuropsychological test norms with bilingual Hispanic Americans: Application of an individual comparison standard. *Archives of Clinical Neuropsychology, 27*(3), 268–276. https://doi.org/10.1093/arclin/acs004
Gollan, T.H., & Brown, A.S. (2006). From tip-of-the-tongue (TOT) data to theoretical implications in two steps: When more TOTs means better retrieval. *Journal of Experimental Psychology: General, 135*(3), 462–483. https://doi.org/10.1037/0096-3445.135.3.462
Hamilton, A., Brown, S., Johnson, V., & Lad, S. (2022). Liberating the narratives of BIPOC neuropsychologists: Unpacking microaggressions through lived experiences. In F. Irani (Ed.), *Cultural diversity in neuropsychological assessment: Developing understanding through global case studies* (pp. 50–61). Routledge.
Harris, D., & Li, W. (2008). Cockpit design and cross-cultural issues underlying failures in crew resource management. *Aviation, Space, and Environmental Medicine, 79*(5), 537–538. https://doi.org/10.3357/ASEM.2271.2008
Heaton, R.K., Miller, S.W., Taylor, M.J., & Grant, I. (2004). *Revised comprehensive norms for an expanded Halstead-Reitan Battery: Demographically adjusted neuropsychological norms for African American and Caucasian adults*. Lutz.
Helmreich, R.L. (1994). Anatomy of a system accident: The crash of Avianca Flight 052. *The International Journal of Aviation Psychology, 4*(3), 265–284. https://doi.org/10.1207/s15327108ijap0403_4
Helmreich, R.L., Wilhelm, J.A., Klinect, J.R., & Merritt, A. (2001). Culture, error, and crew resource management. In E. Salas, C.A. Bowers, & E. Edens (Eds.), *Improving teamwork in organizations: Applications of resource management training* (pp. 305–331). Erlbaum.
Hofstede, G. (1983). National cultures in four dimensions: A research-based theory of cultural differences among nations. *International Studies of Management & Organization, 13*(1/2), 46–74. https://doi.org/10.1177/106939718301800403
Irani, F. (2022). *Cultural diversity in neuropsychological assessment: developing understanding through global case studies*. Routledge. https://doi.org/10.4324/9781003051862
Irani, F., Drag, L., Jo, M., & Silva, D. (2021, October). *Cultural diversity considerations in neuropsychological evaluations with aviators* [Webinar]. Aerospace Psychology Seminar, Federal Aviation Administration.
Kay, G.G. (1995). *CogScreen aeromedical edition professional manual*. Psychological Assessment Resources.
Kay, G.G. (2002). Guidelines for the psychological evaluation of air crew personnel. *Occupational Medicine, 17*(2), 227–245.
Kay, G.G., Strongin, G., Hordinsky, J., & Pakull, B. (1993, May). *Georgetown/Russian collaborative project: Development of aviator norms for CogScreen* [Paper presentation]. 64th Annual Scientific Meeting of the Aerospace Medical Association, Toronto, Canada.
Kim, K.H., & Zabelina, D. (2015). Cultural bias in assessment: Can creativity assessment help? *International Journal of Critical Pedagogy, 6*(2), 129–147.
Loewenstein, D.A., Argüelles, T., Argüelles, S., & Linn-Fuentes, P. (1994). Potential cultural bias in the neuropsychological assessment of the older adult. *Journal of Clinical and Experimental Neuropsychology, 16*(4), 623–629. https://doi.org/10.1080/01688639408402673
Lucas, J.A., Ivnik, R.J., Willis, F.B., Ferman, T.J., Smith, G.E., Parfitt, F.C., Petersen, R.C., & Graff-Radford, N.R. (2005). Mayo's older African Americans normative studies: Normative data for commonly used clinical neuropsychological measures. *The Clinical Neuropsychologist, 19*, 162–183. https://doi.org/10.1080/13854040590945265
Maguire, E.A., Gadian, D.G., Johnsrude, I.S., Good, C.D., Ashburner, J., Frackowiak, R.S., & Frith, C.D. (2000). Navigation-related structural change in the hippocampi of taxi drivers. *Proceedings of the National Academy of Sciences, 97*, 4398–4403. https://doi.org/10.1073/pnas.070039597

Merritt, A. (2000). Culture in the cockpit: Do Hofstede's dimensions replicate? *Journal of Cross-Cultural Psychology, 31*(3), 283–301. https://doi.org/10.1177/0022022100031003001

Mindt, M. R., Arentoft, A., Kubo Germano, K., D'Aquila, E., Scheiner, D., Pizzirusso, M., Sandoval, T. C., & Gollan, T. H. (2008). Neuropsychological, cognitive, and theoretical considerations for evaluation of bilingual individuals. *Neuropsychology Review, 18*(3), 255–268. https://doi.org/10.1007/s11065-008-9069-7

Mjøs, K. (2004). Basic cultural elements affecting the team function on the flight deck. *International Journal of Aviation Psychology, 14*(2), 151–169. https://doi.org/10.1207/s15327108ijap1402_3

Monnier, C., Boiché, J., Armandon, P., Baudoin, S., & Bellocchi, S. (2022). Is bilingualism associated with better working memory capacity? A meta-analysis. *International Journal of Bilingual Education and Bilingualism, 25*(6), 2229–2255. https://doi.org/10.1080/13670050.2021.1908220

National Council on Interpreting in Health Care. (2005). *National standards of practice for interpreters in health care*. https://www.ncihc.org

Nisbett, R. E., & Masuda, T. (2003). Culture and point of view. *Psychological and Cognitive Sciences, 100*(19), 11163–11170. https://doi.org/10.1073/pnas.1934527100

Nisbett, R. E., Peng, K., Choi, I., & Norenzayan, A. (2001). Culture and systems of thoughts: Holistic versus analytic cognition. *Psychological Review, 108,* 291–310. https://doi.org/10.1037/0033-295X.108.2.291

Norman, M., Evans, J. D., Miller, W., & Heaton, R. K. (2000). Demographically corrected norms for the California Verbal Learning Test. *Journal of Clinical and Experimental Neuropsychology, 22*(1), 80–94. https://doi.org/10.1076/1380-3395(200002)22:1;1-8;FT080

Paltzer, J. Y., & Jo, M. (2022). Cultural considerations in geriatric neuropsychology. In S. S. Bush & B. P. Yochim (Eds.), *A handbook of geriatric neuropsychology: Practice essentials* (2nd ed.). Routledge.

Paradies, Y., Ben, J., Denson, N., Elias, A., Priest, N., Pieterse, A., Gupta, A., Kelaher, M., & Gee, G. (2015). Racism as a determinant of health: a systematic review and meta-analysis. *PLoS One, 10*(9), Article e0138511. https://doi.org/10.1371/journal.pone.0138511

Park, D. C., & Huang, C. M. (2010). Culture wires the brain: A cognitive neuroscience perspective. *Perspectives on Psychological Science, 5*(4), 391–400. https://doi.org/10.1177/1745691610374591

Portocarrero, J. S., Burright, R. G., & Donovick, P. J. (2007). Vocabulary and verbal fluency of bilingual and monolingual college students. *Archives of Clinical Neuropsychology, 22*(3), 415–422. https://doi.org/10.1016/j.acn.2007.01.015

Possin, K. L., Tsoy, E., & Windon, C. C. (2021). Perils of race-based norms in cognitive testing: The case of former NFL players. *JAMA Neurology, 78*(4), 377–378. https://doi.org/10.1001/jamaneurol.2020.4763

Prior, A., & MacWhinney, B. (2010). A bilingual advantage in task switching. *Bilingualism: Language and Cognition, 13*(2), 253–262. https://doi.org/10.1017/S1366728909990526

Rivera-Mindt, M., Byrd, D., Saez, P., & Manly, J. (2010). Increasing culturally competent neuropsychological services for ethnic minority populations: A call to action. *The Clinical Neuropsychologist, 24*(3), 429–453. https://doi.org/10.1080/13854040903058960

Roberts, P. M., Garcia, L. J., Desrochers, A., & Hernandez, D. (2002). English performance of proficient bilingual adults on the Boston Naming Test. *Aphasiology, 16*(4–6), 635–645. https://doi.org/10.1080/02687030244000220

Romero, H. R., Lageman, S. K., Kamath, V., Irani, F., Sim, A., Suarez, P., Manly, J. J., Attix, D. K., & the Summit Participants. (2009). Challenges in the neuropsychological assessment of ethnic minorities: Summit proceedings. *The Clinical Neuropsychologist, 23*(5), 761–779. https://doi.org/10.1080/13854040902881958

Rosselli, M., & Ardila, A. (2003). The impact of culture and education on non-verbal neuropsychological measurements: A critical review. *Brain and Cognition, 52*(3), 326–333. https://doi.org/10.1016/S0278-2626(03)00170-2

Sabbagh, M. A., Xu, F., Carlson, S. M., Moses, L. J., & Lee, K. (2006). The development of executive functioning and theory of mind. A comparison of Chinese and U. S. preschoolers. *Psychological Science, 17*(1), 74–81. https://doi.org/10.1111/j.1467-9280.2005.01667.x

Sanchez, O., & Judd, T. (2022). Multicultural education and training in neuropsychology: Let's talk about skill acquisition. In F. Irani (Ed.), *Cultural diversity in neuropsychological assessment: Developing understanding through global case studies* (pp. 18–33). Routledge.

Sandeen, E., Moore, K., & Swanda, R. (2018). Reflective local practice: A pragmatic framework for improving culturally competent practice in psychology. *Profession Psychology: Research and Practice, 49*, 142–150. https://doi.org/10.1037/pro0000183

Schwartz, S.J., Unger, J.B., Zamboanga, B.L., & Szapocznik, J. (2010). Rethinking the concept of acculturation: Implications for theory and research. *American Psychologist, 65*(4), 237–251. https://doi.org/10.1037/a0019330

Senzaki, S., Masuda, T., & Ishii, K. (2014). When is perception top-down and when is it not? Culture, narrative, and attention. *Cognitive Science, 38*, 1–14. https://doi.org/10.1111/cogs.12118

Soeters, J.L., & Boer, P.C. (2000). Culture and flight safety in military aviation. *The International Journal of Aviation Psychology, 10*(2), 111–133. https://doi.org/10.1207/S15327108IJAP1002_1

Sweet, J., J. Klipfel, K.M., Nelson, N.W., & Moberg, P.J. (2021). Professional practices, beliefs, and incomes of U.S. neuropsychologists: The AACN, NAN, SCN 2020 practice and "salary survey". *The Clinical Neuropsychologist, 35*(1), 7–80. https://doi.org/10.1080/13854046.2020.1849803

Tan, Y.W., Burgess, G.H., & Green, R.J. (2021). The effects of acculturation on neuropsychological test performance: A systematic literature review. *The Clinical Neuropsychologist, 35*(3), 541–571. https://doi.org/10.1080/13854046.2020.1714740

Tannen, D. (1984). The pragmatics of cross-cultural communication. *Applied Linguistics, 5*, 189–195. https://doi.org/10.1093/applin/5.3.189

Thames, A.D., Hinkin, C.H., Byrd, D.A., Bilder, R.M., Duff, K.J., Mindt, M.R., Arentoft, A., & Streiff, V. (2013). Effects of stereotype threat, perceived discrimination, and examiner race on neuropsychological performance: Simple as black and white? *Journal of the International Neuropsychological Society, 19*(5), 583–593. https://doi.org/10.1017/S1355617713000076

United Nations Department of Economic and Social Affairs, Population Division. (2022). *World population prospects 2022: Summary of results. UN DESA/POP/2022/TR/NO.* https://www.un.org/development/desa/pd/sites/www.un.org.development.desa.pd/files/wpp2022_summary_of_results.pdf

US Bureau of Labor Statistics. (2023, January 25). *Labor force statistics from the current population survey.* https://www.bls.gov/cps/cpsaat11.htm

Verney, S.P., Suchy-Dicey, A.M., Cholerton, B., Calhoun, D., Nelson, L., Montine, T.J., Ali, T., Longstreth, W.T., & Buchwald, D. (2019). The associations among sociocultural factors and neuropsychological functioning in older American Indians: The Strong Heart Study. *Neuropsychology, 33*, 1078–1088. https://doi.org/10.1037/neu0000574

Vespa, J., Medina, L., & Armstrong, D.M. (2020). Demographic turning points for the United States: Population projections for 2020 to 2060. *Current Population Reports, P25-1144*, U.S. Census Bureau. https://www.census.gov/library/publications/2020/demo/p25-1144.html

Weiss, L.G., & Saklofske, D.H. (2020). Mediators of IQ test score differences across racial and ethnic groups: The case for environmental and social justice. *Personality and Individual Differences, 161*, 109962. https://doi.org/10.1016/j.paid.2020.109962

Whaley, A.L. (2021). Stereotype threat and neuropsychological test performance in the US African American population. *Archives of Clinical Neuropsychology, 36*(7), 1361–1366. https://doi.org/10.1093/arclin/acab020

Wong, T.M. (2000). Neuropsychological assessment and intervention with Asian Americans. In E. Fletcher-Janzen, T.L. Strickland, & C.R. Reynolds (Eds.), *Handbook of cross-cultural neuropsychology* (pp. 43–53). Springer. https://doi.org/10.1007/978-1-4615-4219-3_4

Yakimovich, N.V., Strongin, G.L., Govorushenko, V.V., Schroeder, D.J., & Kay, G.G. (1994, May 9). *Cogscreen as a predictor of flight performance in Russian pilots* [Presentation]. Annual Meeting of the Aerospace Medical Association, San Antonio, TX.

Chapter 18 The Development and Deployment of Future Integrated Neuropsychological Support for Operations

The Case for and Definition of Real-Time Computational Human Performance

Lea Sophie Vink

An fMRI in the Cockpit and an EEG for Every Air Traffic Controller!

In 2021, a curious and subtle shift in the governance of human operators took place at the International Civil Aviation Organization (ICAO). *The Human Factors Guidelines for Safety Audits Manual* (Document 9806) was superseded by a new document called the *Manual on Human Performance for Regulators* (Doc 10151). The keen observer will note here the subtle yet crucial change in terminology in the title. Human factors, one of the key bedrocks of training and skills for pilots and air traffic controllers, has given way to the concept of *human performance* (HP). This was a deliberate choice by ICAO and mirrors a major shift in aviation psychology and engineering towards the understanding that people achieve and perform their tasks in a myriad of ways that cannot always be broken down into individual factors (ICAO, 2021). The ICAO definition also includes a nod toward the idea of a socio-technical system and notes that HP represents the human contribution to system performance.

Whereas human factors (HF) is about the application of the knowledge of human beings, their abilities, characteristics, and limitations and the design of the equipment and environments in which we function and conduct our jobs (ICAO, 2021), HP is the total coming together of all of these factors to produce or "perform" the required contribution to a system. This is a vital step forward not only for safety and efficient delivery of aviation operations but also in the field of being able to conceptualize and visualize the performance of different kinds of operators (Vink & Walzl, 2024).

Traditionally, HP is often conceived of as an abstract construct. Indeed, everyone usually has a notion of what it means, but pinpointing what it is at a given moment and what is needed to achieve a set of tasks is an almost impossible job (Shorrock, 2019). Generally, it is accepted that for any system – such as in aviation – a certain amount of HP needs to be achieved to sustain the requirements of the system. If you increase the amount of HP output, then, theoretically, the system should produce higher results. However, utilizing neuropsychological approaches in live operations is often too expensive, too time consuming, and too impractical. But perhaps there is another way to not only capture HP in real time, but to control it like the throttle of an aircraft (Vink & Walzl, 2024).

This chapter outlines a pathway to deploying real-time neuropsychological tools into the existing framework and infrastructure of operating systems (cockpits sand operations room/towers) that could allow us to achieve an integrated support system that can capture HP, manage human error and fatigue, and also dive deeper into patterns of cognitive performance that can be useful in postoperational analysis, in individual development, and in training and ultimately to sustain HP in the face of changing technologies such as more automation and less human operators in the system.

Conceptual Foundations

The Brain as Black Hole

On April 10, 2019, the world's first digital picture of a black hole was announced. What can its production tell us about imaging the mind and what does a black hole have to do with the mind anyway?

Professor Katie Bouman of the Event Horizon Telescope project said in a lecture at Caltec: "How do we take a picture of something [that] is by definition unseeable?" She was speaking of the almost unbelievably remarkable success that the project had achieved in rendering the world's first picture of a black hole (Bouman, 2016). The digital image captures a black hole 54 million light years away in the galaxy known as M87. Unlike all previous illustrations of black holes, this was a digital image of the same kind that your phone or camera might produce, only achieved on a truly industrial digital data scale. Bouman described the challenge of photographing something the size of a grain of sand lying in New York from the other side of the United States as almost mathematically impossible in the conventional sense. To capture something this far away should require a telescope the size of a planet. The project did not obviously have this size of telescope and so the project has effectively created a "virtual telescope" by computer algorithm. The image that they generated is the result of a week's data captured by eight radio telescopes located around the world. All the data were transported back to the project headquarters where four different teams worked on producing the image using two distinct approaches. The four teams worked independently to cross-validate each other's work and reduce the possibility that human biases might distort thc imagc (Bouman, 2016).

The result is truly a remarkable feat of human ingenuity on par with other recent breakthroughs such as the unlocking of the human genome in 2001 or the discovery of the Higgs boson in 2012. But what is more interesting from a neuropsychological perspective was the method of rendering the image. Effectively, a few scraps of light and data that have been traveling across the universe for 54 million light years was all that was needed to be put together by a computer that filled in the gaps of the missing information using modeling and prediction. In effect, the big data approach to rendering this image provides not only the ability to advance astrophysics but also a template for approaching other topics that might be hidden from the directly observable, such as a brain or mind (Ziakkas & Vink, 2023).

In fact, this is not entirely new. Neuroscientists and cognitive psychologists have for the past 20 years been attempting to piece together vast quantities of data and map, model, image, create, and view the brain (Burkeman, 2015). But most of these approaches are created to continue to try and see what is inside the black hole that is our mind instead of looking at the small number of data that we give off when we interact with the world.

In his book *The Brain From Inside Out* , the Hungarian neuroscientist György Buzsaki describes the glaringly obvious problem with rendering the mind to a simple set of computational cognitions. He points out that unlike computer code, which is linear and systematic, the brain is capable of almost unlimited simultaneous thoughts and actions (Buzsaki, 2019). The brain in fact undertakes an active search of thousands of alternative possibilities and tests various options. Daniel Kahneman has suggested that unconsciously, in fact, our brains perform the type of probability weighting computation that computers might do by comparing previous experiences with their relative emotional or outcome states and deciding based on the best outcome but, crucially, all at the same time (Kahneman, 2011). In fact, the past 10 years has seen a sizable shift in the way we think of the brain interacting with the world. Previously, almost all psychology rested on the idea of *reacting* to the world and processing the right response to it. But, if this was true, our species would have been wiped out long ago by larger and faster predators (Vink, 2022). Instead, the brain is more likely to be a *predicting* machine capable of *filling in the gaps* of things we do not perceive in order to actively prepare the body to respond before an event even occurs (Rao & Ballard, 1999). In the words of Buzsaki, the brain does not represent information that it perceives, rather *it constructs it* (Buzsaki, 2019)

Returning to the black hole analogy, if we start with the premise of "how do we take a picture of that we cannot see," as suggested by Bouman, let us also start with an assumption that the brain as black hole cannot be fully and wholly understood at this point. In fact, if we just ignore the inner workings of the brain for now and look at what we can observe, we quickly arrive at the concept of how we interact with the world. In other words, we – as human beings – interact every second of every day with the world in observable and measurable ways (Ziakkas & Vink, 2023).

Knowledge of what the brain does and why it does it might be shut off to us and we cannot know what happens inside. But does this necessarily matter? Let us say you are an employee of any company. Does it matter to the company how your mind gets things done? No, it does not, not at a business or social level. The business is concerned with your HP output relative to the output of another mind. Your performance affects this business output. If you do not perform, you could be replaced by someone else who performs better. Sports teams do this all the time, we call it "on form" when, for example, a football player is at the top of their game.

But how do we in fact measure HP? We first need to define what the performance of our system looks like. Consider our football player. The performance of a goal-kicker is measured at the simplest level, usually in terms of the number of goals scored over a season. Is this performance, however, the same as the goalkeeper's? Of course not. While goalkeepers scoring goals at the other end are impressive, this is usually extremely rare, and a goalkeeper is more likely to be measured on the number of goals saved during a season. So, do we necessarily need to know how the mind is working to figure out the performance? The answer is *not necessarily* (Breedlove & Watson, 2017).

But what if the very performance itself could shine a halo around our black hole? Physicists looking for black holes look for light features and radio waves that indicate the locations because they cannot see what is unseeable. They are also able to work out the sizes, densities, masses, and relative strengths of black holes. Machine learning is improving the way physicists can do this with remarkable effectiveness (Ziakkas & Vink, 2023). As we have seen, the world's first picture of a black hole was published after an algorithm compiled data from multiple telescopes around the world. And this is exactly the approach that industries are beginning to do with performance data. This chapter attempts to illustrate how the "event horizon" or "halo" of interaction data shines a light on our brain and allows businesses and industries to create finely tuned systems. I believe this is important because much of pop psychology and most media articles focus on the inside of the black hole, and as we have stated, when it comes to everyday work and living, this might not be so important. The method proposed here is ambivalent to individuals and assumes that computational HP will never be able to achieve the validity needed to reveal the same level of individuality as other medical neuroimaging devices such as functional magnetic resonance imaging (fMRI) or electroencephalographic (EEG) devices (Van Horn & Toga, 2014), but it can reveal greater patterns and information about how humans in general perform cognitions.

So, what does this have to do with HP? The basic premise so far is this: that a human being performing in a system gives clues into how the brain is working by signaling interactions with the physical world around them. Consider now an air traffic controller (ATCO). He or she is interacting with computers and radios constantly. So constantly in fact that the machine data can tell us remarkably accurate stories about what the human being is doing. Collect enough data and these data, like the picture of the black hole, can reveal in minute detail what the brain might be doing in real time.

Making Use of What Already Exists: The ATCO and Their Systems

Air traffic management (ATM) is a complex sociotechnical system the relies heavily upon human ATCOs and pilots to successfully monitor, decide, and act to achieve safety and efficiency (Shorrock & Williams, 2016). For ATCOs this means ensuring that air traffic is directed and de-conflicted safely while attempting to give pilots their desired routing (enhancing efficiency and reducing emissions). To achieve this, several sources of data such as navigational, communication, and radar surveillance data are condensed and integrated by the ATCO in a continuous process (Friedrich et al., 2018). The central source therefore of acute ATCO stress comes from the management of an increasing number of aircraft movements, the associated time pressure, managing different tasks, and the serious consequences of errors (Kontogiannis & Malakis, 2011). In this context, two key risks can arise: the risk of a controller overloading and being unable to perform their tasks and the gradual buildup of fatigue leading to exhaustion. One traditional way to predict the amount of stress an ATCO may face is to count and control the number of aircraft moving through a sector of airspace (Friedrich et al., 2018). From this, rules for sectors are usually derived that specify the maximum number of aircraft one controller can handle. However, this is not always the most optimum way of understanding a controller's workload. For example, many aircraft might all be moving in the same direction in an orderly fashion and pose little risk if all the minimum separation distances are maintained and they do not interact with each other. By contrast, intersections of traffic routes, geographical pinch-points, or frequent descents or ascents such as in and out of busy airports are more likely to significantly increase the risk of

ATCO stress (Boag et al., 2006; Wang et al., 2018). As suggested by Vink (2022) and Ohneiser et al. (2017), when these aircraft movements are included, the dynamic traffic density can provide better information about the workload of ATCOs. Wang et al. (2018) provide a useful proposal to understand these factors by calculating the different components of airspace by different weightings. Three specific components – the volume of traffic in the airspace (known as *traffic complexity*), the environmental components (*environmental complexity*), and the physical characteristics of airspace, such as tricky geographical areas or known pinch-points (known as *airspace complexity*) – can be used. The total airspace complexity (hereafter Cx) can therefore be calculated by adding these variables together to create a Cx index. Knowing Cx can allow for many useful operational solutions and as such it led the Austrian air navigation service provider (ANSP) Austro Control to develop a tool that can be used to calculate Cx based on the conditions of the airspace sectors as well as data from the ATM operating system. This tool was validated internally by the company in 2021 and showed strong results.

The Cx tool was not designed to capture psychological constructs; however, it was theorized due to the subjective nature of rating airspace by controllers and the relationships between taskload and number of aircraft that there must be links to several psychological constructs (Ziakkas & Vink, 2023). Accordingly, the following key research question was proposed:

> What is the relationship between airspace complexity and the mental workload, exhaustion, and fatigue of ATCOs?

Both excessive workload and insufficient workload, as well as fatigue, pose significant risks to safe air traffic control service in modern aviation. As Li et al. (2020) noted, exhaustion can have a significant negative impact on the work performance of ATCOs. Other work has found that exhaustion can have similar effects on the human body to alcoholization (Dawson et al., 2021; Dawson & Reid, 1997). Among other things, this decreased cognitive performance can increase reaction time, lead to reduced attention and decreased alertness, and result in losses in concentration (Zadehgholam et al., 2015). The problem with mental workload and fatigue is that both are subjective constructs. Therefore, it is often difficult to directly ask affected individuals how they are feeling, especially in situations where distractions from current tasks can pose a significant safety risk (Young et al., 2014).

There has also been a steady rise in automation in the ATM domain. Supervisors and controllers now have at their disposal far more tools to enhance decision-making than they have ever had (Ziakkas & Vink, 2023). These tools have been essential in delivering the year-on-year traffic growth that has occurred globally. However, these tools still do not have built into them any kind of usable, real-time HP metrics. Any kind of breakthrough for day-to-day operations would be a revelation for supervisors and could enhance safety and efficiency.

With all of this in mind, the potential of a noninvasive, objective, and real-time tool to measure HP and psychological constructs is high. The goal of this work is therefore to determine whether the airspace complexity calculated by the tool can objectively measure and predict the mental workload, fatigue, and potentially other constructs of ATCOs.

Relevant Theoretical Background

The role of ATCOs is extensively covered by Eurocontrol (Eurocontrol et al., n.d.). The model proposed here was built focused on the area control environment in Austria. Area control or en-route control includes all flight movements outside of approach and departure zones. The main task for these controllers is to manage air traffic and to detect and resolve conflicts such as crossing flight paths or conflicts during climb and descent. To do this, an ATCO must constantly monitor all aircraft in the sector for potential conflicts, deviations from the flight plan, or complex situations such as an approaching thunderstorm. If a conflict occurs, planning must be done on how to resolve it, such as diverting an aircraft to a different direction or different altitude. Finally, this plan must be communicated to the pilot in question. This so-called scan–plan–execute loop is repeated permanently until an aircraft has left the respective sector and has been handed over to the next sector (Eurocontrol et al., n.d.; Wang et al., 2018).

Task Complexity From Air Space Complexity

As noted above, traffic density is a common measure used to determine the workload of an ATCO (Friedrich et al., 2018). However, the sheer number of aircraft often cannot represent the true complexity of an airspace. Unlike land vehicles, traffic movements in the air take place in a three-dimensional space, which may lead to more complex interactions between aircraft. Therefore, there may be a high workload for a controller even with a small number of aircraft in a sector (Wang et al., 2018). This complexity of an airspace depends on structural factors and traffic flow. The structural factors of a sector are static and do not change. These include, for example, elevations such as mountains and hills, the number of flight paths, airway intersections, and navigation points. The characteristics of traffic flow change over time and depend on, for example, the number of aircraft, the weather, the distances between aircraft, and their speeds (Sridhar et al., 1998). These considerations result in a dynamic traffic density or dynamic density. This is calculated based on the weighting of various factors. These include the physical aspects of an airspace (airspace complexity), the characteristics of traffic flow (traffic complexity), and operational constraints imposed by the environment such as weather phenomena (environmental complexity). On the basis of these foundations, Wang et al. (2018) created a model for calculating the complexity of a sector in their article, which includes the structural conditions and the relationships between different aircraft, the relationships between aircraft and waypoints, and the flight routes. These formulas of these calculations were used by Austro Control as a basis for the development of a tool that can calculate the complexity of all sectors in Austrian airspace at different flight altitudes in real time (Steinheimer et al., 2016). In addition, a function was added to the calculation that adds the influence of weather to the overall complexity. Thus, for example, the influence of a thunderstorm in a sector on the overall complexity can be calculated. The influence of weather phenomena such as a thunderstorm on the complexity of a sector stems from safety concerns. Thunderstorms can cause severe turbulence and therefore should be flown around as large an area as possible (Lane et al., 2012). These changes and deviations from the planned flight path due to weather conditions or to avoid conflicts must be planned, executed, and communicated by ATCOs.

Contributing Neuropsychological Theory

Can system or air traffic complexity be linked to *task complexity* in psychological terms? In defining the concept of task complexity, Wood described three key elements: products, (required) acts, and information cues (Wood, 1986). Using component complexity, coordinative complexity, and dynamic complexity can therefore give a total task complexity and the formulas provided by Wood served as a starting point for identifying whether the Austro Control complexity algorithm could de deconstructed to indicate the psychological indicators.

Wood's theory facilitates the understanding of the knowledge and skills required to perform a task. But the indications that are given off by operators achieving these tasks need to be correlated. Several contributing theories have gone into the identification of these indicators and of the proposed neural network that follows. Wickens (2008) in his multiple resource theory proposes that humans have multiple cognitive resources that can be allocated to different tasks. Each resource has limited capacity, and when resources are overtaxed, performance decrements and errors can occur. This indicates that there is an effort-burning process over time that results in the deletion of HP relative to task complexity. Similarly, the cognitive activation theory of stress (Hockey, 1997) proposes that stress leads to changes in cognitive and physiological processes that can impact performance. When individuals are exposed to stressors such as high workload or fatigue, their cognitive and physiological systems are activated to cope with the stress. However, if stressors persist or become too great, performance decrements and errors can occur. Kaplan (1995) argued for the attention restoration theory, which augments the concepts of Wickens and suggests key cumulating factor that might be relevant in an HP model. Specifically, he referred to the need of restorative stimuli to replenish depleted attentional resources. The dynamic model of situational awareness of Endsley (1995) also contributed to the underlying theoretical framework. This model proposes that situational awareness is a dynamic process that involves the continuous gathering and integration of information from the environment. Situational awareness can be impacted by factors such as workload, fatigue, and attentional demands. All these models begin with the idea of *load*, *input*, or *stressor*, which is understood in this context to be represented by task complexity (Wood, 1986).

Two key modern steps are involved in calculating HP. Firstly, the bottom-up predictive coding theory of Rao and Ballard (1999) – which I have argued provides a missing link to the understanding of human error and HP in terms of the utilization of predicted versions of "normal" and "abnormal" in the mind (Vink, 2022) – is combined with the early workload network model by Vidulich and Tsang (2012). The workload model provides a much more in-depth theoretical framework that suggest a larger number of perceptual, cognitive, and motor sub-networks. The model proposed by Vidulich and Tsang (2012) needs to be simplified primarily because the main predictive algorithm of complexity itself does not have enough subelements to be able to accurately calculate the 26 subelements proposed in that model, although one day in the future with enough validation data, this may be achieved.

These underlying concepts all suggested that if enough data could be collected from live traffic data, then they could be compiled and compared with observable psychological data. Several studies were carried out in 2022 collecting various elements of this specifically to see whether complexity, if calculated more deeply, could reveal more than just workload.

Computational Human Performance and Neuropsychological Indicators

The validation studies were conducted at Austro Control in 2022 and these showed fundamentally that the complexity algorithm was a valid predictor of not only task load but also workload (Ziakkas & Vink, 2023). To complete the validation studies, the main methodology involved ATCOs being followed for 12-hr shifts by psychologists, who conducted a battery of psychological measures throughout their day. The measures included the Instantaneous Self-Assessment (ISA; Tattersall & Foord, 1996) shown every 5 min on the workstation to collect workload, and the NASA Task Load Index (NASA TLX; Hart & Staveland, 1988) conducted at the end of each run to measure workload. To measure fatigue, a shortened version of the Visual Analogue Scale–Fatigue (VAS-F; Lee et al., 1991) was used at the beginning and end of each day and consisted of two "energy domains," that is, drive and commitment, and six items from the fatigue subscales (tired, sleepy, exhausted, drained, debilitated, and concentration). Additionally, the Karolinska Sleepiness Scale (KSS; Åkerstedt & Gillberg, 1990) was administered every 30 min throughout the day. To observe objective and acute fatigue, the Psychomotor Vigilance Test (PVT; Wilkinson & Houghton, 1982) was administered at the beginning of the day and the end of duty.

The correlations show enough predictive validity to indicate that air traffic complexity as measured by this algorithm is a close enough approximation for task complexity (Wood, 1986) and subsequent workload that further computation could be achieved. Early evidence suggested that relationships existed with the other fatigue measures, but these would require deeper analysis. This led to a dynamic structural equational modeling approach (after McNeish & Hamaker, 2020), which reveals a lag time effect of fatigue as well as strong correlations with reduced reaction times throughout the day and enough evidence to suggest that complexity can predict fatigue build up. Crucially, "time in position" appears to be a key mediating factor in the controller's ability to sustain performance.

From these results, a theoretical neural network has begun to emerge consisting of five steps: contributing factors; the measurement of complexity in real time; the resultant workload and situational awareness as well as measurement of time-in-position; the cumulating factors including mediators such as boredom, vigilance, and mental effort; and finally, the outputs of the model including a calculated HP index, human error, and other psychological factors such as satisfaction. The proposed neural network prediction model is shown in Figure 18.1.

Figure 18.1 shows how complexity can be used to calculate psychological outcomes and generate an HP index. Raw source data (shown in green) is fed into the model, which is built using data collected during the studies (shown in orange). HP is calculated by looking at the number of flights moved during a time period combined with the basic human error rates. These error rates were collected by counting the number of times ATCOs miss-typed or clicked data into a system and miss-spoke on radio and needed to correct themselves. These error rates correlated also with time-in-position ranging between 3% and 11%. Performance is indexed against the tasks achieved (i.e., aircraft moved) and the error rates. Further studies are planned to increase the validity and calibration of the model.

As can be seen from the model, it is acknowledged that each individual brings in contributing factors to their watch. These would be balanced out with the aggregation of data over many years. As stated previously, the idea is not to calculate individual personal HP, but

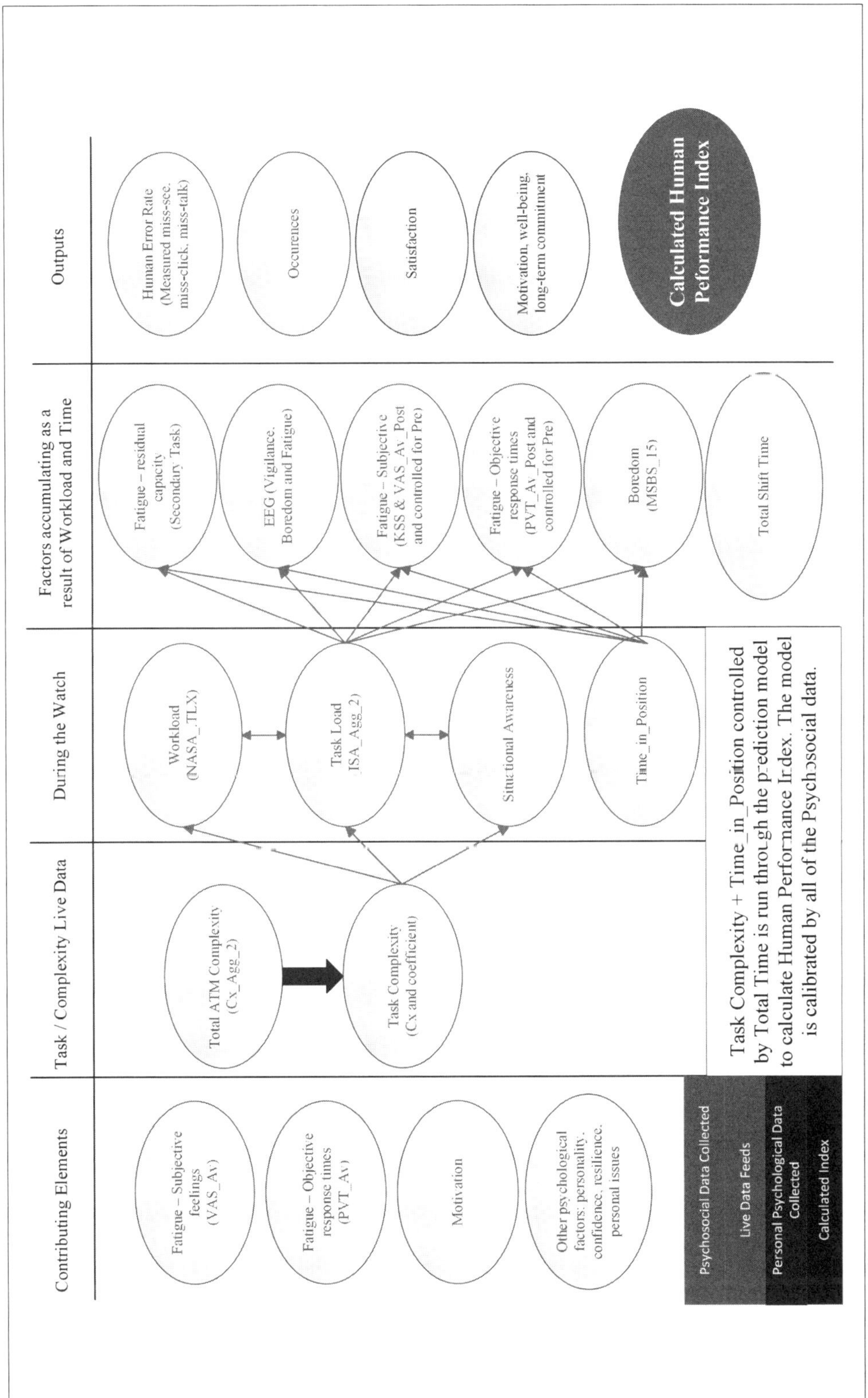

Figure 18.1. Computational human performance model.

rather a highly precise aggregate of HP index in relation to a given complexity and time. Computational HP is generated using a predictive model. As argued by Wickens (2002) and Kaplan (1995), the key determinant of sustained HP must be a factor of how long an operator is sitting in position performing the tasks. Therefore, our model hinges on the amount of complexity that a controller must deal with over the period of time in position. This must also be controlled for by the total time working that day.

Validating the Models

The computational HP index model was created in RStudio (RStudio, 2020) and has now been integrated into the complexity software at Austro Control. The prediction model needs to be queried in a standalone way now and is visualized using spider diagrams, which show the complexity, workload, cognitive fatigue, situational awareness, HP index, and vigilance rates at any given time (see Ziakkas & Vink, 2023). The tool has been tested through the busy summer months of 2023, and each new safety incident (occurrence) that is recorded by the complexity picture is also analyzed using computation HP data and then compared with subjective investigation evidence. For example, a new study has reported that ATCO overloads (a dangerous situation where controllers freeze and can no longer manage traffic; Eurocontrol, n.d.) have shown some key consistent patterns, for example, that 90% of overloads occurred when the controller had been in position longer than 65 min and the HP index rate dropped below 40.

Eventually, it is planned that the HP index will be calculated alongside the parameters of complexity and time in position to reveal a continuous picture of operational performance. This may be incorporated into other software for use in decision-making by supervisors in the operations room.

Implications for Aviation Performance

For the time being, complexity and HP are not used for operational decision-making but are shadowed in the operation. The ability to query the predicted complexity and HP is undergoing development to test different ways of displaying the outputs.

The next steps will be to engage in machine learning from complexity data over a year to create a better prediction model. As mentioned earlier, ongoing validation studies will continue to provide validation evidence to further enhance the coefficients used to calculate each HP element. It is theorized that EEG data will provide a far greater depth of calculation particularly for fatigue, which is based mainly on reaction time data currently, and studies with wearable EEG headsets are planned to further refine the models, particularly for vigilance and cognitive fatigue.

MAHCO Analysis

In 2022, I published an academic article introducing a new approach to human error analysis which I dubbed "MAHCO" or a "method of analyzing human contribution to occurrences" (Vink, 2022). In this method, I argued that investigators need a new way to understand the human element and that they could do this by using increasingly focused comparisons of occurrence events with "normal events." To achieve this, they can use tools that create pictures of what normal looks like – a given sector, regular traffic flow, normal weather conditions etc. – and then compare occurrence events or non-normal with what the computer says is normal. Human error occurs subconsciously in over 80% of occasions and when this is balanced against experience and qualifications, even conscious decisions can be understood as being simply "less than optimal choices" or as they are more often called "knowledge-based mistakes" (Rasmussen, 1988, p. 23). MAHCO provides a bottom-up approach to help us weed out all of the human factors issues and uncover the truly risky and adverse behaviors that might trigger just culture proceedings. Crucially, MAHCO is designed with a future in mind where complex machine learning algorithms are able to calculate all of these optimums based on real-time system data (Vink, 2022)

For a MAHCO analysis, the normal sector values can be calculated by aggregating performance over time. During a safety incident, smaller aggregates of the HP (e.g., 30 min) can be taken and compared. The difference between abnormal sector performance and normal can be analyzed to understand the patterns of HP that might exist during certain types of incidents. The use of spider diagrams like this can help to reconstruct occurrences objectively, which will lead to more just and objectively based occurrence investigations.

Enhanced Rostering and Staff Usage

The use of calculated HP can also be combined with increasingly sophisticated rostering tools. Ziakkas and Vink (2023) have shown that by feeding complexity as a parameter alongside time-in-position data to a rostering tool, real-time analytics can be captured showing how controllers are utilized during their shifts and the impact of performance on various wider factors such as when to open and close sectors, send controllers on breaks, bring them back to assist in high-workload situations, and better utilize their performances over the shifts. Longer-term simulation of optimal staff usage versus predicted traffic and weather complexities can be used to simulate different models of how future staffing needs may be accommodated by available staff or to reveal shortfalls in the amount of manpower available (Shneiderman, 2020).

Postoperational Safety Intelligence

The computational HP index outlined here represents a concept known as "bottom-up data analysis" showing local-level decision-making and staff usage to deal with geographical small areas of the air traffic management system. When these data are used to calibrate larger top-down big data with massive amounts of ADS-B data, then a highly precise safety intelligence picture can emerge (Ziakkas & Vink, 2023). Eurocontrol is now experimenting with being able to show stories of entire network performance that can describe a story like, "this week, we moved this much traffic under these complexity conditions and we needed this much HP to achieve it. The resultant cost in terms of manpower, fatigue risk mitigation, and delay to the network was so much."

Being able to model normal-sector HP values as well as complexity will allow for better airspace design because the number of flights over a year with varying complexity and HP factors can be simulated using machine learning. This means that real safety assurance can be given by using real objective data collected over years and not one or two validation studies (Shneiderman, 2020).

Just Culture Implications

At the heart of finding the optimum balance between holding people to account and open, learning, and transparent cultures is the idea of *trust*. After any occurrence, the operator must trust that the investigation is conducted in a professional, transparent, and fair manner. But trust is not a feature that is won lightly.

The core of MAHCO and using artificial intelligence (AI) and machine-learning-based tools is an idea of building greater trust between the operator and the investigator. The basic theory is that investigators and operators have flawed memories and can introduce their own biases. Studies such as those by Wells (2006) and Kovera and Aronson (2023) show that eye witness evidence can be highly inaccurate because our memories begin to breakdown or are even influenced by suggestions from the investigators themselves. Tools that use real-time data and machine learning can easily overcome these pitfalls and show exactly what happens and when, but they must always be built with operators, for operators to maintain trust.

Adaptions for Cockpits

Finally, there is the adaption to cockpits. The model shown in Figure 18.1 is built using a task complexity algorithm for air traffic management, but similar task complexity algorithms already exist for cockpits. There is no reason why integrated eye-tracking combined with task complexity cannot monitor pilot workload, fatigue, and vigilance in real time. In this way, the flight management system could assist by taking tasks away from the pilot in high-stress situations, and in underloading situations where pilots are in more monotonous stages of flight the flight management system could give tasks back to the pilot to keep them stimulated and engaged in the aircraft performance (Ziakkas & Vink, 2023).

Conclusion

As stated at the outset, this is one pathway toward using big data analysis to reveal the black hole of the operational brain in real time. This approach utilizes available data from the system and has created a prediction model based on observed psychological data. The models are currently limited by the number of variation data and the inherent issues with the subjective measures of workload, fatigue, and vigilance discussed in Chapter 2 of this book. Furthermore, as the data are from live traffic, gathering fluctuations in complexity are difficult especially in quieter months. However, on-going and future studies are aiming to fill out the prediction model with far more data. This is then combined with machine learning data from complexity over the coming years. A final step is to adapt the complexity algorithm to other environments such as terminal maneuvering areas or towers and to other countries. Other complexity algorithms have been developed around the world. However, the issues with almost all other complexity algorithms in development are that they have not been built with the idea of task complexity in mind (Wood, 1986) and therefore do not reveal the depth of psychological insight that this algorithm can provide. The pathway outlined in this chapter could be expanded in other complexity algorithms to make the most of raw system data.

Finally, it must be repeated that the measures are not of individual performance, but rather aggregations of "normal" versus "abnormal" sector performance. This is because the model cannot possibly account for or collect all the individual nuances that contribute to daily HP. But, as argued, to get to real-time data monitoring, sometimes all we need is to know where the black hole is and what it is doing, and not necessarily what is going on inside it.

We believe that computational HP will provide a method of getting inside the available data and revealing the collective decision-making, fatigue impacts, and usages of staff to deliver different demands. In neuropsychological terms, this takes us truly up to the event horizon of operational support in real time. With machine learning to refine modes, this may be all that is needed to introduce the adaptive automation solutions that will take us toward fully automated systems safely (Scerbo, 2018). It may also allow us to monitor well-being, motivation, and satisfaction at work in the years ahead as the roles of ATCO and other aviation operator change.

References

Åkerstedt, T., & Gillberg, M. (1990). Subjective and objective sleepiness in the active individual. *International Journal of Neuroscience, 52*(1–2), 29–37. https://doi.org/10.3109/00207459008994241

Boag, C., Neal, A., Loft, S., & Halford, G.S. (2006). An analysis of relational complexity in an air traffic control conflict detection task. *Ergonomics, 49*(14), 1508–1526. https://doi.org/10.1080/00140130600779744

Bouman, K. (2016, November). *How to take a picture of a black hole* [TED conference]. https://www.ted.com/talks/katie_bouman_how_to_take_a_picture_of_a_black_hole

Breedlove, S.M., & Watson, N.V. (2017). *Behavioral neuroscience* (8th ed.). Oxford University Press.

Burkeman, O. (2015, January). Why can't the world's greatest minds solve the mystery of consciousness? *The Guardian*. https://www.theguardian.com/science/2015/jan/21/-sp-why-cant-worlds-greatest-minds-solve-mystery-consciousness

Buzsáki, G. (2019). *The brain from inside out*. Oxford University Press. https://doi.org/10.1093/oso/9780190905385.001.0001

Dawson, D., & Reid, K. (1997). Fatigue, alcohol and performance impairment. *Nature, 388*(6639), 235–235.

Dawson, D.M., Sprajcer, M., & Thomas, M. (2021). How much sleep do you need? A comprehensive review of fatigue related impairment and the capacity to work or drive safely. *Accident Analysis & Prevention, 151*, 105955. https://doi.org/10.1016/j.aap.2020.105955

Endsley, M.R. (1995). Measurement of situation awareness in dynamic systems. *Human Factors, 37*(1), 65–84. https://doi.org/10.1518/001872095779049499

Eurocontrol, ICAO, & Flight Safety Foundation. (n.d.). *The area controller. SKYbrary Aviation Safety*. https://skybrary.aero/articles/area-controller

Eurocontrol. (n.d.). *ATM sector management. SKYbrary Aviation Safety*. https://skybrary.aero/articles/atm-sector-management

Friedrich, M., Biermann, M., Gontar, P., Biella, M., & Bengler, K. (2018). The influence of task load on situation awareness and control strategy in the ATC tower environment. *Cognition, Technology & Work, 20*, 205–217. https://doi.org/10.1007/s10111-018-0464-4

Hart, S.G., & Staveland, L.E. (1988). Development of NASA-TLX (Task Load Index): Results of empirical and theoretical research. In P.A. Hancock & N. Meshkati (Eds.), *Advances in psychology* (Vol. 52, pp. 139–183). Elsevier.

Hockey, G.R.J. (1997). Compensatory control in the regulation of human performance under stress and high workload: A cognitive-energetical framework. *Biological Psychology, 45*(1–3), 73–93. https://doi.org/10.1016/S0301-0511(96)05223-4

International Civil Aviation Organization. (2021). *Human performance manual for regulators. ICAO Doc 10151.*

Kahneman, D. (2011). *Thinking, fast and slow*. Macmillan.

Kaplan, S. (1995). The restorative benefits of nature: Toward an integrative framework. *Journal of Environmental Psychology, 15*, 169–182. https://doi.org/10.1016/0272-4944(95)90001-2

Kontogiannis, T., & Malakis, S. (2011). Strategies in controlling, coordinating and adapting performance in air traffic control: modelling 'loss of control' events. *Cognition, Technology & Work, 15*(2), 153–169. https://doi.org/10.1007/s10111-011-0209-0

Kovera, M.B., & Aronson, E. (2023). *Eyewitness identification. Routledge handbook of evidence-based criminal justice practices.* Routledge. https://doi.org/10.4324/9781003219286-33

Lane, T.P., Sharman, R.D., Trier, S.B., Fovell, R.G., & Williams, J.K. (2012). Recent advances in the understanding of near-cloud turbulence. *Bulletin of the American Meteorological Society, 93*(4), 499–515. https://doi.org/10.1175/BAMS-D-11-00062.1

Lee, K.A., Hicks, G., & Nino-Murcia, G. (1991). Validity and reliability of a scale to assess fatigue. *Psychiatry Research, 36*(3), 291–298. https://doi.org/10.1016/0165-1781(91)90027-M

Li, W., Kearney, P., Zhang, J., Hsu, Y., & Braithwaite, G. (2020). The analysis of occurrences associated with air traffic volume and Air Traffic Controllers' alertness for fatigue risk management. *Risk Analysis, 41*(6), 1004–1018. https://doi.org/10.1111/risa.13594

McNeish, D., & Hamaker, E.L. (2020). A primer on two-level dynamic structural equation models for intensive longitudinal data in Mplus. *Psychological Methods, 25*(5), 610. https://doi.org/10.1037/met0000250

Ohneiser, O., Vink, L., Helmke, H., Ferrer Herrer, D., Marin, G., Boyero, M., & Bromwich, T. (2017). *PJ16.04 Controller human performance metrics conceptual framework.* SESAR, Eurocontrol.

Rao, R.P., & Ballard, D.H. (1999). Predictive coding in the visual cortex: a functional interpretation of some extra-classical receptive-field effects. *Nature Neuroscience, 2*(1), 79–87. https://doi.org/10.1038/4580

Rasmussen, J. (1988). Approaches to the control of the effects of human error on chemical plant safety. *Professional Safety, 33*(12), 23. https://doi.org/10.1016/0003-6870(88)90099-3

RStudio Team. (2020). *RStudio: Integrated development for R.* RStudio, PBC, Boston, MA. http://www.rstudio.com/

Scerbo, M.W. (2018). Theoretical perspectives on adaptive automation. In M. Mouloua & J. Koonce (Eds.), *Automation and human performance* (pp. 37–63). CRC Press.

Shneiderman, B. (2020). Human-centered artificial intelligence: Reliable, safe & trustworthy. *International Journal of Human-Computer Interaction, 36*(6), 495–504. https://doi.org/10.1080/10447318.2020.1741118

Shorrock, S. (2019). "Human factors" and "human performance": What is the difference? *Humanistic Systems.* https://humanisticsystems.com/2019/04/24/human-factors-and-human-performance-whats-the-difference/

Shorrock, S.T., & Williams, C.A. (2016). Human factors and ergonomics methods in practice: Three fundamental constraints. *Theoretical Issues in Ergonomics Science, 17*(5–6), 468–482. https://doi.org/10.1080/1463922X.2016.1155240

Sridhar, B., Sheth, K., & Grabbe, S. (1998). *Airspace complexity and its application in ATM.* 2nd USA/Europe Air Traffic Management R&D Seminar, Federal Aviation Administration. https://stuff.mit.edu/afs/athena/course/16/16.459/OldFiles/www/sridhar.pdf

Steinheimer, M., Gonzaga-Lopez, C., Kern, C., Kerschbaum, M., Strauss, L., Eschbacher, K., & Rokitansky, C.H. (2016, November). *Air traffic management and weather: The potential of an integrated approach.* Proceedings of the International Conference on Air Transport, University of Zilina, Air Transport Department, Zilina, Slovakia.

Tattersall, A.J., & Foord, P.S. (1996). An experimental evaluation of instantaneous self-assessment as a measure of workload. *Ergonomics, 39*(5), 740–748. https://doi.org/10.1080/00140139608964495

Vidulich, M. A., & Tsang, P. S. (2012). Mental workload and situation awareness. In G. Salvendy (Ed.), *Handbook of human factors and ergonomics* (pp. 243–273). Wiley.
Vink, L.-S. (2022). A new methodology for assessing human contributions to occurrences (MAHCO) in air traffic management utilising a Bayesian hierarchical predictive coding approach to the brain, and the benefits for just culture. *Transportation Research Procedia, 66*, 201–213. https://doi.org/10.1016/j.trpro.2022.12.021
Vink, L.-S., & Walzl, B. (2024). A framework to redefine human performance in complex socio-technical systems. *Journal of Aviation Psychology and Applied Human Factors*. Manuscript submitted for publication.
Van Horn, J. D., & Toga, A. W. (2014). Human neuroimaging as a "Big Data" science. *Brain Imaging and Behavior, 8*, 323–331. https://doi.org/10.1007/s11682-013-9255-y
Wang, H., Song, Z., & Wen, R. (2018). Modeling air traffic situation complexity with a dynamic weighted network approach. *Journal of Advanced Transportation*, Article 5254289. https://doi.org/10.1155/2018/5254289
Wells, G. L. (2006). Eyewitness identification: Systemic reforms. *Wisconsin Law Review, 2006*, 615–643.
Wickens, C. D. (2002). Multiple resources and performance prediction. *Theoretical Issues in Ergonomics Science, 3*(2), 159–177. https://doi.org/10.1080/14639220210123806
Wickens, C. D. (2008). Multiple resources and mental workload. *Human Factors, 50*(3), 449–455. https://doi.org/10.1518/001872008X288394
Wilkinson, R. T., & Houghton, D. (1982). Field test of arousal: A portable reaction timer with data storage. *Human Factors, 24*(4), 487–493. https://doi.org/10.1177/001872088202400409
Wood, R. E. (1986). Task complexity: Definition of the construct. *Organizational Behavior and Human Decision Processes, 37*(1), 60–82. https://doi.org/10.1016/0749-5978(86)90044-0
Young, M. S., Brookhuis, K. A., Wickens, C. D., & Hancock, P. A. (2014). State of science: mental workload in ergonomics. *Ergonomics, 58*(1), 1–17. https://doi.org/10.1080/00140139.2014.956151
Zadehgholam, Z., Kiani, F., Hashjin, H., & Khodabakhsh, M. R. (2015). The role of fatigue and work overload in predicting work situation awareness among workers. *International Journal of Occupational Hygiene, 7*(1), 38–44.
Ziakkas, D., & Vink, L.-S. (Eds.). (2023). *Implementation guide for Artificial Intelligence in Aviation: A human-centric guide for practitioners and organisations*. EATO & Independent.

Chapter 19
Cognitive Assessment of Astronauts

Mathias Basner, Gary Strangman, and Ruben C. Gur

Spaceflight Environmental, Operational and Psychological Stressors

Astronauts face various operational and environmental challenges, including, among others, microgravity, radiation, non-24-hr light-dark cycles, and increased carbon dioxide levels (Afshinnekoo et al., 2020; Flynn-Evans et al., 2016; Scully et al., 2019). Additionally, they experience psychological stress due to prolonged periods of living in an isolated, confined, and extreme (ICE) environment. Studies indicate that reduced sensory stimulation and monotony contribute to sleep disturbances, cognitive impairment, negative emotions, and interpersonal conflicts (Choukér & Stahn, 2020). While each of these factors can be considered a significant stressor on its own, their interactions may synergistically worsen an astronaut's stress response (Tu et al., 2022).

Research has demonstrated structural and functional changes in the brains of astronauts returning from 6-month International Space Station (ISS) missions, with some measures not fully returning to preflight levels even months after returning to Earth (see next section; Seidler et al., 2022). Consequently, it is not surprising that adverse cognitive and behavioral conditions, along with psychiatric disorders, present significant risks in space exploration (Slack et al., 2009). Maintaining consistently high levels of cognitive performance is crucial for astronauts, as even minor errors can have catastrophic consequences leading to mission failure. Despite the rigorous training and selection process for astronauts, they share with the general population a relative inability to self-assess performance, particularly in chronic exposure situations (Van Dongen et al., 2003). This underscores the importance of regular objective cognitive performance testing for ensuring mission success (Seidler et al., 2022).

Structural Brain Changes Induced by Spaceflight

Magnetic resonance imaging (MRI) of the brain post-flight has revealed structural changes relative to preflight baseline measurements. Some of these differences may be directly related to the development of spaceflight-associated neuro-ocular Syndrome (SANS), characterized by swelling of the optic disc, posterior ocular globe flattening, optic nerve sheath distension, choroidal folds, peripapillary choroid thickening, cotton wool spots, and hyperopic refractive error shifts (Laurie et al., 2019; Macias et al., 2020; Marshall-Goebel et al., 2019; Roberts et al., 2019). Correspondingly, structural brain changes include an upward shift of the brain (Lee et al., 2019; Roberts et al., 2017; Roberts et al., 2019), changes in gray matter volume (Koppelmans et al., 2016), cerebrospinal fluid (CSF) volume increases in the third and lateral ventricles (Van Ombergen et al., 2019), a narrowing of CSF spaces at the vertex (Roberts et al., 2017), periventricular white matter hyperintensities (Alperin et al., 2017), and deformations of the pituitary gland (Kramer et al., 2020). Potential mechanisms implicated in the increased CSF volume include a rotation of the cerebral aqueduct with increased CSF outflow resistance (Roberts et al., 2017) as well as a compression of the superior sagittal sinus and Pachioni's granulations, two important sites for CSF resorption (Marshall-Goebel et al., 2021; Roberts et al., 2017; Sakka et al., 2011; Van Ombergen et al., 2019; Wostyn et al., 2022).

Most MRI studies of astronauts were retrospective in nature with limited follow-up periods. To our knowledge, few studies investigated the recovery of spaceflight-induced changes in brain structure longer than 1 month postflight (Sakka et al., 2011; Van Ombergen et al., 2018; Van Ombergen et al., 2019). One study of seven cosmonauts on 6-month ISS missions found CSF volume increases in the third and lateral ventricles and reductions in both gray and white matter volume immediately postflight that did not fully return to preflight levels ~7 months postflight (Van Ombergen et al., 2018; Van Ombergen et al., 2019). Another study of 11 astronauts on 6-month ISS missions found an expansion of the sum of brain and total CSF volume immediately postflight that remained elevated until 1-year postflight (Kramer et al., 2020). A study of 18 astronauts who underwent a mean of 173.4 days in spaceflight, reported greater increase in periventricular volume per year than the control (Roberts et al., 2021). Another study evaluated 15 astronauts who underwent six T1-weighted 3-T MRI scans, twice prior to launch and four times following their return to Earth after ~6-month missions to the ISS. They reported that "novice" astronauts showed an increase in the volume of total periventricular spaces from pre- to postflight, whereas experienced crewmembers did not, suggesting that experienced astronauts may exhibit holdover effects from prior spaceflights (Hupfeld et al., 2022). Barisano et al. (2022) evaluated 24 NASA astronauts and a "small" (unspecified) number of European Space Agency astronauts after a 6-month spaceflight on the ISS. They reported an increased volume of the basal ganglia and white matter periventricular space and ventricular enlargement associated with spaceflight. Another study (Koppelmans et al., 2022) examined structural and diffusion MRI scans from 14 astronauts collected before launch and motor measures collected preflight and postflight. Paracentral and precentral gyri thickness significantly predicted recovery from fall postflight. The thickness of vestibular and sensorimotor regions, including the posterior insula and the superior temporal gyrus, predicted balance performance postflight and pre- to postflight decrements. Together, these findings suggest that changes in brain structure induced by 6-month ISS missions do not revert to preflight levels up to 1 year postflight. Thus, a longer follow-up period is required to assess whether the changes in brain structure are fully reversible, and if so, when. Also, as several studies found a dose–response relationship between mission duration and the magnitude of the observed structural changes (Alperin et al., 2017; Koppelmans et al., 2016; Lee et al., 2019; Roberts et al., 2019), and as NASA's design reference mission to Mars lasts ~1,000 days, it is imperative that future studies include astronauts on missions exceeding the typical 6-month ISS mission.

Despite the obvious links between brain structure and function, few studies assessed the relationship between spaceflight-induced changes in brain structure and cognitive performance. One study used NASA's WinSCAT battery with 12 astronauts on 6-month ISS missions (Roberts et al., 2019). The study found correlations between changes in ventricular volume and white matter with performance on two subtests of the WinSCAT battery, but there was no long-term follow-up in either cognitive testing or neuroimaging. A study that examined specifically the link between regional brain activation and connectivity following prolonged spaceflight investigated whether any brain changes correlated with changes in spatial working memory performance from pre- to postflight (Salazar et al., 2022). Brain activity was measured using functional MRI while astronauts ($n=15$) performed a spatial working memory task. No significant effects on performance or brain activity were found due to spaceflight, but pre- to postflight changes in brain connectivity were evident. The superior occipital gyrus showed pre- to postflight reductions in task-based connectivity with the rest of the brain. There was also decreased connectivity between the left middle occipital gyrus and the left parahippocampal gyrus, left cerebellum, and left lateral occipital cortex during performance. Further, increased visual and visuomotor connectivity was correlated with improved performance from pre- to postflight. These results corroborate the link between spaceflight-induced changes in brain structure and function, and they further highlight the need for long-term follow-up studies. Finally, larger sample sizes are needed to establish regional effects of prolonged spaceflight both on functional and on structural measures.

Domains of Cognitive Performance

When evaluating effects of spaceflight on cognitive performance it is helpful to consider the broader context of measuring individual differences in performance and conditions that affect performance within individuals. Multiple measures have been developed by psychologists to assess performance on a wide range of domains, and selecting which to implement within time constraints of any specific project can be daunting. Traditional tests depend heavily on general intellectual abilities ("g factor") as reflected in the intelligence quotient (IQ), and those targeting specific abilities that could be affected by spaceflight require large investment of time and instrumentation (Deary & Batty, 2007). Traditional psychometric theory has generally divided cognitive abilities into language-mediated or *verbal* intelligence and visual-spatial *performance* abilities. Verbal measures examine abilities such as vocabulary, analogical reasoning, comprehension, arithmetic, and knowledge of the sociocultural environment. Spatial performance tests examine the ability to assemble objects, construct configurations, derive meaning from pictorial sequences, and speed of object matching. Several psychological batteries have been developed to estimate verbal and performance IQ, with some ability to measure effects of psychiatric disorders and environmental stressors. These batteries excel in predicting academic performance but are of more limited use for either screening or examining the effects of spaceflight. A high-IQ dental student can prove to be a total failure at dentistry when tasked with handling a tooth, and we do not expect stressors such as involved in spaceflight to affect someone's vocabulary.

The advent of behavioral neuroscience has helped hone our understanding of how behavioral domains relate to the integrity of specific brain systems, and these advances have created the field of neuropsychology and behavioral neuroscience, markedly impacting cognitive testing. Neuropsychological batteries were constructed to examine behavioral consequences of brain damage, and therefore they assess performance on behavioral domains related to specific brain systems. Thus, frontal lobe functions are assessed with tests of the *executive* domain (abstraction and mental flexibility, attention, impulsivity, *working memory*), temporolimbic functioning with tests of episodic memory (such as recognition or recall of words, faces, or shapes), left temporoparietal functioning with measures of verbal comprehension, and so forth (Lezak, 1994). Since the effects of spaceflight on performance are mediated through the effects on brain function, such a testing framework has better potential for identifying a mechanistic chain linking stressor effect on brain function to a behavioral performance domain. Elucidating such a chain would yield strategies for prevention and remediation.

The applicability of the first wave of neuropsychological batteries to spaceflight was limited by several factors. The batteries were based on effects of brain lesions and hence were susceptible to disease-specific effects that may not generalize to normal brain functioning and the distribution of brain systems. Furthermore, these tests were typically paper-and-pencil and required advanced training for administration and scoring. Special tests had to be designed for spaceflight, and the success of computerized tests such the Psychomotor Vigilance Test (PVT; Dinges & Powell, 1985) and computerized batteries such the WinSCAT (Kane et al., 2005) demonstrated the utility of targeted behavioral measures and underscored the limitations of traditional neuropsychological tests.

The advent of functional neuroimaging has rapidly enhanced our understanding of how behavioral domains relate to specific brain systems by enabling a more precise application of narrowly defined tests designed to activate specific brain systems, and charting the distributed neural network recruited for performance (Gur et al., 1992). These paradigms have produced a new generation of tests that are computerized, targeted to specific brain systems, and sensitive both to individual differences and to environmental stress effects. The computerized format importantly permits accurate measurement of performance speed, which affords documentation of subtle effects and of compensatory strategies (e.g., Gur et al., 2019; Gur et al., 2010; T.M. Moore et al., 2019). The tests cover a wide range of domains, and their computerized format allowed for the development of adaptive testing procedures (Moore et al., 2023) that vastly reduce the time needed to obtain valid performance measures, an important consideration for assessing performance in spaceflight. Notably, the battery (termed "Cognition" by NASA) has been adapted for spaceflight (Basner et al., 2015; Moore et al., 2017; see next section) and deployed in long duration ISS missions (Garrett-Bakelman et al., 2019).

The new computerized neurocognitive batteries vary in length and coverage of behavioral domains, but current conceptualizations are in agreement that several major facets of behavior can be reliably linked to brain systems. In addition to the aforementioned executive, episodic memory, and verbal comprehension domains, tests of spatial processing are included, as they have been linked to right parietal functioning and tests of nonverbal reasoning to functioning of a bilateral frontoparietal system. Sensorimotor tests evaluate the functioning of the precentral and postcentral cortex and its connectivity to the cerebellum. More recently, tests have been designed to measure aspects of social cognition, which relates to a corticolimbic system, and tests based on neuroeconomics to assess domains such as risk and reward valuation, related to striatal functioning (Sharma et al., 2017). Not all these domains are relevant to spaceflight, but an investigator can now tailor tests that were validated with functional neuroimaging to examine general and specific effects of stressors in a way that will allow for mechanistically based prevention and intervention.

Cognitive Testing in Space

While spaceflight is becoming more and more routine, it remains inherently dangerous. Incidents of fire, toxin exposure, sleep deprivation, radiation bursts, CO_2 spikes, and dehydration have been documented as have episodes of depression and serious crew conflict (Slack et al., 2009). Such events, among others, can adversely affect the brain and cognitive performance. However, even when such extreme events do not occur, anecdotal reports from spacefarers have described cognitive deficits during flight. Such cognitive concerns have been reported with sufficient frequency to earn the name “space fog” (Welch et al., 2009). The most frequently mentioned symptoms include difficulty paying attention or concentrating, memory impairments, and generalized mental slowing (Schroeder & Tuttle, 1991).

Three reviews of the spaceflight cognitive performance literature have been conducted to date (Casler & Cook, 1999; Christensen & Talbot, 1986; Strangman et al., 2014). The most recent found 32 studies that address at least one aspect of cognitive performance during spaceflight. Typically, flight studies are classified as short duration (0–21 days) or long duration (22+ days). In light of potential missions to asteroids or Mars that could last up to 2.5 years, studies of 90+ days in duration have been given a classification of very long duration. A breakdown of the published spaceflight studies by mission duration appears in Table 19.1. Table 19.2 shows these same studies categorized according to specific cognitive domains or types of experimental tests. As only seven individuals have spent more than 1 year consecutively in space, our knowledge on the long-term cognitive effects of spaceflight is very limited, stressing the importance of research in space analog environments (e.g., Antarctic stations) for exploration-type missions.

Table 19.1. Distribution of spaceflight study durations and astronauts

Duration	Number of studies	Number of astronauts	Astronauts/study
Very long: 90+ days	7	31	4.4
Long: 22–89 days	4	11	2.7
Short: 0–21 days	21	68	3.2
Total	**32**	**110**	**3.4**

Table 19.2. Distribution of spaceflight studies across cognitive domains

Category	Number of studies	Number of astronauts
Perception	24	62
Motor	22	53
Memory	12	42
Attention	7	37
Spatial transformation	8	28
“Complex”/operational	7	11
Executive function	5	11
Emotional processing	1	2
Social processing	0	0

Most experiments have been conducted during short-duration missions, largely due to the high volume of ~14-day Space Shuttle flights during the construction of the ISS. During the first few days or weeks of spaceflight, astronauts are commonly affected by space adaptation syndrome (SAS, or space motion sickness), resulting in significant sensitivity to head motion, queasiness, and general malaise. Cognitive performance deficits during this period include reductions in motor speed and accuracy, some perceptual deficits, impairments in attention-switching, and emotional interference in cognitive decision-making (Reschke et al., 1998; Strangman et al., 2014).

Longer-duration studies are less common, but have identified some impacts that endure beyond the first few weeks. Reduced motor speed, increased motor variability, and time period overestimation observed during short-duration flights continue well beyond the first month, although the time course remains to be thoroughly characterized. Sustained impairments in dual-task performance (motor tracking plus working memory) have been reported to last for at least 5–6 months in flight. That said, performance on a battery of cognitive tests run 29 times over 1.2 years with a single individual (Dr. Vasily Polyakov) showed no substantial declines, except briefly following acute gravitational transitions (Manzey et al., 1998). Operationally speaking, one study also showed progressively increasing throughput during an 84-day mission (Kubis et al., 1977).

There are key caveats with regard to spaceflight cognitive findings. According to Table 19.1, essentially all spaceflight studies have insufficient numbers of participants – for cognitive studies, the typical "bend in the curve" for power analysis occurs around $N=16$. While certainly a challenge, low N can be partially overcome with strong experimental controls. Unfortunately, 75 % of the studies summarized here also failed to include control groups, and an additional 10 % had inadequate controls or did not report control data. Thus, in 85 % of the studies, any observed performance changes related to time (e.g., task fatigue or boredom), task repetition (e.g., learning effects), and the spaceflight environment itself (e.g., microgravity exposure duration, chronic stress, radiation exposure, etc.) are confounded. This confounding needs to be considered carefully when drawing conclusions regarding spaceflight cognitive performance.

Another limitation is variability regarding which cognitive tests were used. This makes generalization difficult and, combined with rare reporting of effect sizes, has even led to substantial limitations on the use of meta-analysis. The tests used were also rarely modified for the high-performing astronaut population, leading to potential ceiling and boredom effects. The standardized Cognition test battery is a step in the right direction.

What has been most consistently observed is high inter-individual and within-individual variability in cognitive performance during spaceflight. This effect is seen both over time in a given individual, as well as between individuals. Such variability may reflect a dynamic mix of time-varying stressors and/or differences in individual sensitivities to the spaceflight environment (or the associated stressors). For example, different perceptions of chronic stress, differential vulnerabilities to sleep restriction, prior spaceflight experience, genetic makeup, or other factors may all play a role. The observation of variable performance across astronauts may also correspond with variability in self-reports of attention, memory, or other cognitive concerns in flight. These topics remain to be investigated further, both in flight and in analog environments on Earth.

NASA's Cognition Test Battery

NASA's standard operational cognitive test battery WinSCAT is heavily focused on working memory and is likely not broad enough to fully assess cognitive performance in astronauts. Therefore, the National Space Biomedical Research Institute (NSBRI) funded the development of a brief, comprehensive, and sensitive computerized neurocognitive test battery for spaceflight called "Cognition" (Basner et al., 2015). Cognition passed NASA's Operations Readiness Review in 2017. It is part of both ISS and Behavioral Health and Performance (BHP) Standard Measures whose goal is to ensure that a minimal set of measures is consistently captured in both astronauts and analog crews on the ground.

Cognition consists of 10 brief neurocognitive tests administered on an MS Windows laptop or an Apple iPad and was specifically designed to repeatedly assess astronaut cognitive performance on long-duration missions. It has the following unique features: (1) The 10 Cognition tests assess a range of cognitive domains relevant for spaceflight success and were chosen to represent largely orthogonal concepts (see Table 19.3). Eight out of the 10 Cognition tests are based on the Computerized Neurocognitive Battery (CNB) developed at the University of Pennsylvania and validated with functional neuroimaging and in multiple normative, military, and clinical populations (Gur et al., 2010). Cognition provides feedback (including from previous administrations) after each test. (2) The 10 tests were tailored for high-performing astronauts to avoid boredom and ceiling effects. (3) Cognition was found to be acceptable to astronaut and astronaut surrogate populations (Casario et al., 2021). Feedback received during early development was overwhelmingly positive, with users reporting

Table 19.3. Overview of the 10 cognition tests

Test	Cognitive domains assessed	Principal brain regions recruited
Motor praxis (MP)	Sensory-motor speed	Sensorimotor cortex
Visual object learning (VOLT)	Spatial learning and memory	Medial temporal cortex, hippocampus
Fractal 2-back (F-2B)	Working memory	Prefrontal cortex, hippocampus
Abstract matching (AM)	Abstraction, concept formation	Prefrontal cortex
Line orientation (LOT)	Spatial orientation	Temporo-parietal cortex, visual cortex
Emotion recognition (ERT)	Emotion identification	Amygdala, hippocampus
Matrix reasoning (MRT)	Abstract reasoning	Prefrontal cortex, parietal cortex, temporal cortex
Digit symbol substitution (DSST)	Visual search, paired associate learning, working memory	Temporal cortex, motor cortex, prefrontal cortex
Balloon analog risk (BART)	Risk decision making	Orbital frontal cortex, amygdala, anterior cingulate cortex, ventral striatum
Psychomotor vigilance (PVT)	Attention	Prefrontal cortex, motor cortex, inferior parietal cortex

the software was easy to use. Negative feedback was addressed in a revision prior to delivery to NASA. (4) Cognition consists of 15 unique versions that allow for repeated assessments without repeating stimuli. Importantly, correction factors for both practice and stimulus set difficulty effects have been established (Basner, Hermosillo, et al., 2020). More recently, further correction factors have been developed to translate performance across platforms (i.e., laptop and iPad). (5) Each of the 10 tests was shortened in a data-driven manner to minimize administration time. After familiarization, it typically takes less than 20 min to administer the full Cognition battery. ISS astronauts needed on average only 16 min to complete the full battery. (6) Cognition can be installed, administered, and updated both offline and online. In the latter scenario, Cognition automatically encrypts and syncs data collected on the client laptop or iPad with a central database in real time. The data can then be viewed and downloaded from any web browser. All Cognition systems are calibrated for timing accuracy to minimize bias (Basner, Moore, et al., 2021). (7) German, French, Italian, and Russian translations of Cognition facilitate administration in international crews. (8) A version of Cognition that can be administered in MRI scanners for functional neuroimaging (fCog) was used to establish links for each of the 10 Cognition tests to cerebral networks. (9) The sensitivity of Cognition to a number of common spaceflight stressors has been established. These include elevated CO_2 (Basner et al., 2017; Basner, Stahn, et al., 2021; Scully et al., 2019), hypoxia (Sönksen et al., 2022), head-ward fluid shift (Basner, Dinges, et al., 2021; Basner et al., 2017; Basner, Stahn, et al., 2021), sleep deprivation (Nasrini et al., 2020; Smith et al., 2021), and long-term isolation in ICE and ICC environments (Garrett-Bakelman et al., 2019). (10) Links between Cognition and operational performance have also been established. Three Cognition outcomes were able to predict 30 % of the variance (cross-validated and adjusted for age and sex) in complex 6df ISS docking performance (Basner, Moore, et al., 2020).

Performance on neuropsychological tests that assesses individual cognitive domains is only one tool in an arsenal of tools that try to understand and predict complex operational performance (Tu et al., 2022). However, Cognition is uniquely positioned to elucidate the brain network origin and thus neural basis of performance changes induced by spaceflight. Also, performance on neuropsychological tests will likely always play a critical role in the development, understanding, and validation of different approaches to assess complex operational performance.

Assessment of Operational Performance in Spaceflight

Despite decades of experience in spaceflight for durations of hours to over 1 year, operational performance is rarely recorded and hence very limited research has been conducted on operational tasks in space. Various types of simulators have flown in space for proficiency maintenance, in particular the Portable In-flight Landing Operations Trainer (PILOT) system for Shuttle landing, the Robotic On-Board Trainer (ROBoT) system for use of the Canadarm, and the 6df system (based on PILOT) for docking maneuvers. For most of their existence, however, these simulators also did not record performance data, and therefore rigorous behavioral performance studies were not possible there either.

To date, two published in-flight studies looking at performance on multiple operational tasks have been identified. Garriott and Doerre examined crew operational efficiency when performing 120 spaceflight tasks during the 84-day Spacelab 4 mission (Garriott & Doerre, 1977). In this study, operational efficiency was defined as the number of tasks accomplished divided by total man-hours available to accomplish them. Steady improvements in efficiency were observed during the flight, findings that were attributed to the waning of initial motor and physiological adaptation processes. Such improvements could additionally (or alternatively) be explained by task-specific learning and improvements due to practice in microgravity. The second spaceflight study involved two astronauts from each of three Spacelab flights (Kubis et al., 1977). This highly detailed study quantitatively examined 31,000 ft of preflight video to 10,000 ft of in-flight video to measure the time required to perform specific operational tasks. Performance was defined as time on task, and this improved as the mission progressed. Notably, the first in-flight performance took longer than the last performance prior to launch, suggesting task-related interference by early adaptation to microgravity.

Beyond in-flight operational studies, numerous studies have been conducted pre- and postflight with astronauts on operationally relevant tasks. In particular, these include the Functional Mobility Test (FMT; Mulavara et al., 2010) and the Functional Task Test (FTT; Spiering et al., 2011). The Joint Russia–USA Field Test (Reschke et al., 2020) is derived from the FTT, designed for use in the field including up to 24 hr postlanding. The Field Test includes tasks such as ladder climbing, hatch opening, jump down, manual manipulation of objects and tool use, seat egress and obstacle avoidance, recovery from a fall, and object translation tasks. While these tests require gravity and hence cannot be conducted in flight, testing on R+1 day postlanding from 6-month missions revealed degraded performance specifically when body coordination and postural stability control were needed (e.g., seat egress and walk, recovery from fall/stand, object translation, jump down, and ladder climb). These functional changes were paralleled by reductions in postural and dynamic gait control (Mulavara et al., 2018). As a second example, S. T. Moore et al. (2019) investigated two full-motion driving simulations (car and Mars Rover) and one flight simulation (T38 Talon landing), also preflight as well as on R+0, R+4, and R+8 days postlanding (i.e., not in flight). Astronauts were dramatically and significantly impaired on driving postlanding, including more crossings into the wrong lane, delays in correction, and spending more time in the wrong lane. T38 control and rover dockings showed increased performance variability. These effects generally recovered by R+4 (S. T. Moore et al., 2019). Finally, Tays et al. (2021) used the FMT to operationally assess ambulation and dynamic posturography via the sensory organization test (SOT-5/5M). These tests were also performed pre-/postflight since they cannot be performed without gravity. Significant declines in mobility and balance were identified on R+4 postflight (their first time point), which were normalized by the next time point (R+30). Various other studies involving operationally relevant tasks in astronauts, including in-flight tasks, are underway as of this writing, but a considerable amount remains unknown about subtle (or not-so-subtle) changes in operationally relevant performance in and immediately postflight.

Conclusion

This chapter highlights the importance of high levels of astronaut cognitive performance for space mission success. Due to small sample sizes, lack of adequate controls, and inconsistent use of different cognitive assessment tools, our knowledge on how the spaceflight environment affects astronaut cognitive performance is still somewhat limited. NASA's Cognition test battery was specifically designed for high-performing astronauts, covers a range of cognitive domains, allows for repeated assessments, and is currently consistently used in both ground and spaceflight studies to mitigate some of the problems discussed here. Likewise, the Robotic On-Board Trainer (ROBoT) system is consistently used to assess complex operational performance. Together, these tools will hopefully shed more light onto the effects of spaceflight on cognitive and complex operational performance in astronauts.

Acknowledgments

Some of the content in this chapter (specifically the sections "Domains of Cognitive Performance" and "Cognitive Testing in Space") is reproduced from "Cognitive Performance in Space" by G.E. Strangman, R.C. Gur, and M. Basner, 2021, In "Handbook of Bioastronautics" (Editors: L.R. Young and J.P. Sutton), pp. 399–405, Springer Nature Switzerland, 2021, with permission from Springer Nature.

Conflict of Interest

The authors declare no conflict of interest related to the work presented here.

References

Afshinnekoo, E., Scott, R.T., MacKay, M.J., Pariset, E., Cekanaviciute, E., Barker, R., Gilroy, S., Hassane, D., Smith, S.M., Zwart, S.R., Nelman-Gonzalez, M., Crucian, B.E., Ponomarev, S.A., Orlov, O.I., Shiba, D., Muratani, M., Yamamoto, M., Richards, S.E., Vaishampayan, P.A., ... Beheshti, A. (2020). Fundamental biological features of spaceflight: Advancing the field to enable deep-space exploration. *Cell, 183*(5), 1162–1184. https://doi.org/10.1016/j.cell.2020.10.050

Alperin, N., Bagci, A.M., & Lee, S.H. (2017). Spaceflight-induced changes in white matter hyperintensity burden in astronauts. *Neurology, 89*(21), 2187–2191. https://doi.org/10.1212/WNL.0000000000004475

Barisano, G., Sepehrband, F., Collins, H.R., Jillings, S., Jeurissen, B., Taylor, J.A., Schoenmaekers, C., De Laet, C., Rukavishnikov, I., Nosikova, I., Litvinova, L., Rumshiskaya, A., Annen, J., Sijbers, J., Laureys, S., Van Ombergen, A., Petrovichev, V., Sinitsyn, V., Pechenkova, E., ... Wuyts, F.L. (2022). The effect of prolonged spaceflight on cerebrospinal fluid and perivascular spaces of astronauts and cosmonauts. *Proceedings of the National Academy of Sciences of the United States of America, 119*(17), Article e2120439119. https://doi.org/10.1073/pnas.2120439119

Basner, M., Dinges, D.F., Howard, K., Moore, T.M., Gur, R.C., Muhl, C., & Stahn, A.C. (2021). Continuous and intermittent artificial gravity as a countermeasure to the cognitive effects of 60 days of head-down tilt bed rest. *Frontiers in Physiology, 12*, Article 643854. https://doi.org/10.3389/fphys.2021.643854

Basner, M., Hermosillo, E., Nasrini, J., Saxena, S., Dinges, D.F., Moore, T.M., & Gur, R.C. (2020). Cognition test battery: Adjusting for practice and stimulus set effects for varying administration intervals in high performing individuals. *Journal of Clinical and Experimental Neuropsychology, 42*(5), 516–529. https://doi.org/10.1080/13803395.2020.1773765

Basner, M., Moore, T.M., Hermosillo, E., Nasrini, J., Dinges, D.F., Gur, R.C., & Johannes, B. (2020). Cognition test battery performance is associated with simulated 6df spacecraft docking performance. *Aerospace Medicine and Human Performance, 91*(11), 861–867. https://doi.org/10.3357/AMHP.5602.2020

Basner, M., Moore, T.M., Nasrini, J., Gur, R.C., & Dinges, D.F. (2021). Response speed measurements on the psychomotor vigilance test: How precise is precise enough? *Sleep, 44*(1), Article zsaa121. https://doi.org/10.1093/sleep/zsaa121

Basner, M., Nasrini, J., Hermosillo, E., McGuire, S., Dinges, D.F., Moore, T.M., Gur, R.C., Rittweger, J., Mulder, E., Wittkowski, M., Donoviel, D., Stevens, B., & Bershad, E.M. (2017). Effects of -12° head-down tilt with and without elevated levels of CO2 on cognitive performance: The SPACECOT study. *Journal of Applied Physiology, 124*(3), 750–760. https://doi.org/10.1152/japplphysiol.00855.2017

Basner, M., Savitt, A., Moore, T.M., Port, A.M., McGuire, S., Ecker, A.J., Nasrini, J., Mollicone, D.J., Mott, C.G., McCann, T., Dinges, D.F., & Gur, R.C. (2015). *Development and validation of the Cognition test battery Aerospace Medicine and Human Performance, 86*(11), 942–952. https://doi.org/10.1037/t62872-000

Basner, M., Stahn, A.C., Nasrini, J., Dinges, D.F., Moore, T.M., Gur, R.C., Muhl, C., Macias, B.R., & Laurie, S.S. (2021). Effects of head-down tilt bed rest plus elevated CO2 on cognitive performance. *Journal of Applied Physiology, 130*(4), 1235–1246. https://doi.org/10.1152/japplphysiol.00865.2020

Casario, K., Howard, K., Cordoza, M., Hermosillo, E., Ibrahim, L., Larson, O., Nasrini, J., & Basner, M. (2021). Acceptability of the Cognition Test Battery in astronaut and astronaut-surrogate populations. *Acta Astronautica, 190*, 14–23. https://doi.org/10.1016/j.actaastro.2021.09.035

Casler, J.G., & Cook, J.R. (1999). Cognitive performance in space and analogous environments. *International Journal of Cognitive Ergonomics, 3*(4), 351–372. https://doi.org/10.1207/s15327566ijce0304_5

Choukér, A., & Stahn, A.C. (2020). COVID-19 – the largest isolation study in history: the value of shared learnings from spaceflight analogs. *npj Microgravity, 6*(1), Article 32. https://doi.org/10.1038/s41526-020-00122-8

Christensen, J.M., & Talbot, J.M. (1986). A review of the psychological aspects of space flight. *Aviation Space and Environmental Medicine, 57*(3), 203–212. https://www.ncbi.nlm.nih.gov/pubmed/3516133

Deary, I.J., & Batty, G.D. (2007). Cognitive epidemiology. *Journal of Epidemiology and Community Health, 61*(5), 378–384. https://doi.org/10.1136/jech.2005.039206

Dinges, D.F., & Powell, J.W. (1985). Microcomputer analysis of performance on a portable, simple visual RT task during sustained operations. *Behavior Research Methods, Instruments &Computers, 6*(17), 652–655. https://doi.org/10.3758/BF03200977

Flynn-Evans, E.E., Barger, L.K., Kubey, A.A., Sullivan, J.P., & Czeisler, C.A. (2016). Circadian misalignment affects sleep and medication use before and during spaceflight. *npj Microgravity, 2*, Article 15019. https://doi.org/10.1038/npjmgrav.2015.19

Garrett-Bakelman, F.E., Darshi, M., Green, S.J., Gur, R.C., Lin, L., Macias, B.R., McKenna, M.J., Meydan, C., Mishra, T., Nasrini, J., Piening, B.D., Rizzardi, L.F., Sharma, K., Siamwala, J.H., Taylor, L., Vitaterna, M.H., Afkarian, M., Afshinnekoo, E., Ahadi, S., ... Turek, F.W. (2019). The NASA Twins Study: A multidimensional analysis of a year-long human spaceflight. *Science, 364*(6436), Article eaau8650. https://doi.org/10.1126/science.aau8650

Garriott, O.K., & Doerre, G.L. (1977). *Crew efficiency on first exposure to zero-gravity. Biomedical results from Skylab*. NASA Lyndon B. Johnson Space Center.

Gur, R.C., Erwin, R.J., Gur, R.E., Zwil, A.S., Heimberg, C., & Kraemer, H.C. (1992). Facial emotion discrimination: II. Behavioral findings in depression. *Psychiatry Research, 42*(3), 241–251. https://doi.org/10.1016/0165-1781(92)90116-k

Gur, R.C., Richard, J., Hughett, P., Calkins, M.E., Macy, L., Bilker, W.B., Brensinger, C., & Gur, R.E. (2010). A cognitive neuroscience-based computerized battery for efficient measurement of individual differences: standardization and initial construct validation [Research support, NIH, Extramural]. *Journal of Neuroscience Methods, 187*(2), 254–262. https://doi.org/10.1016/j.jneumeth.2009.11.017

Gur, R.E., Moore, T.M., Rosen, A.F.G., Barzilay, R., Roalf, D.R., Calkins, M.E., Ruparel, K., Scott, J.C., Almasy, L., Satterthwaite, T.D., Shinohara, R.T., & Gur, R.C. (2019). Burden of environmental adversity associated with psychopathology, maturation, and brain behavior parameters in youths. *JAMA Psychiatry, 76*(9), 966–975. https://doi.org/10.1001/jamapsychiatry.2019.0943

Hupfeld, K.E., Richmond, S.B., McGregor, H.R., Schwartz, D.L., Luther, M.N., Beltran, N.E., Kofman, I.S., De Dios, Y.E., Riascos, R.F., Wood, S.J., Bloomberg, J.J., Mulavara, A.P., Silbert, L.C., Iliff, J.J., Seidler, R.D., & Piantino, J. (2022). Longitudinal MRI-visible perivascular space (PVS) changes with long-duration spaceflight. *Scientific Reports, 12*(1), Article 7238. https://doi.org/10.1038/s41598-022-11593-y

Kane, R.L., Short, P., Sipes, W., & Flynn, C.F. (2005). Development and validation of the spaceflight cognitive assessment tool for windows (WinSCAT) [Validation studies]. *Aviation Space and Environmental Medicine, 76*(6 Suppl.), B183–191.

Koppelmans, V., Bloomberg, J.J., Mulavara, A.P., & Seidler, R.D. (2016). Brain structural plasticity with spaceflight. *npj Microgravity, 2*(1), Article 2. https://doi.org/10.1038/s41526-016-0001-9

Koppelmans, V., Mulavara, A.P., Seidler, R.D., De Dios, Y.E., Bloomberg, J.J., & Wood, S.J. (2022). Cortical thickness of primary motor and vestibular brain regions predicts recovery from fall and balance directly after spaceflight. *Brain Structure & Function, 227*, 2073–2086. https://doi.org/10.1007/s00429-022-02492-z

Kramer, L.A., Hasan, K.M., Stenger, M.B., Sargsyan, A., Laurie, S.S., Otto, C., Ploutz-Snyder, R.J., Marshall-Goebel, K., Riascos, R.F., & Macias, B.R. (2020). Intracranial effects of microgravity: A prospective longitudinal MRI study. *Radiology, 295*(3), 640–648. https://doi.org/10.1148/radiol.2020191413

Kubis, J.F., McLaughlin, J.M., Jackson, J.M., Rusnak, R., McBride, G.H., & Saxon, S.V. (1977). Task and work performance on Skylab Missions 2, 3 and 4: Time and motion study – experiment M151. In R.S. Johnston & L.F. Dietlein (Eds.), *Biomedical results from Skylab* (pp. 136–154). NASA Lyndon B. Johnson Space Center.

Laurie, S.S., Lee, S.M.C., Macias, B.R., Patel, N., Stern, C., Young, M., & Stenger, M.B. (2019). Optic disc edema and choroidal engorgement in astronauts during spaceflight and individuals exposed to bed rest. *JAMA Ophthalmology, 138*(2), 165–172. https://doi.org/10.1001/jamaophthalmol.2019.5261

Lee, J.K., Koppelmans, V., Riascos, R.F., Hasan, K.M., Pasternak, O., Mulavara, A.P., Bloomberg, J.J., & Seidler, R.D. (2019). Spaceflight-associated brain white matter microstructural changes and intracranial fluid redistribution. *JAMA Neurology, 76*(4), 412–419. https://doi.org/10.1001/jamaneurol.2018.4882

Lezak, M.D. (1994). Domains of behavior from a neuropsychological perspective: The whole story. *Nebraska Symposium on Motivation, 41*, 23–55. https://www.ncbi.nlm.nih.gov/pubmed/7739748

Macias, B.R., Patel, N.B., Gibson, C.R., Samuels, B.C., Laurie, S.S., Otto, C., Ferguson, C.R., Lee, S.M.C., Ploutz-Snyder, R., Kramer, L.A., Mader, T.H., Brunstetter, T., & Stenger, M.B. (2020). Association of long-duration spaceflight with anterior and posterior ocular structure changes in astronauts and their recovery. *JAMA Ophthalmology, 138*(5), 553–559. https://doi.org/10.1001/jamaophthalmol.2020.0673

Manzey, D., Lorenz, B., & Poljakov, V. (1998). Mental performance in extreme environments: results from a performance monitoring study during a 438-day spaceflight. *Ergonomics, 41*(4), 537–559. https://doi.org/10.1080/001401398186991

Marshall-Goebel, K., Damani, R., & Bershad, E.M. (2019). Brain physiological response and adaptation during spaceflight. *Neurosurgery, 85*(5), E815–821. https://doi.org/10.1093/neuros/nyz203

Marshall-Goebel, K., Macias, B.R., Kramer, L.A., Hasan, K.M., Ferguson, C., Patel, N., Ploutz-Snyder, R.J., Lee, S.M.C., Ebert, D., Sargsyan, A., Dulchavsky, S., Hargens, A.R., Stenger, M.B., & Laurie, S. (2021). Association of structural changes in the brain and retina after long-duration spaceflight. *JAMA Ophthalmology, 139*(7), 781–784. https://doi.org/10.1001/jamaophthalmol.2021.1400

Moore, S.T., Dilda, V., Morris, T.R., Yungher, D.A., MacDougall, H.G., & Wood, S.J. (2019). Long-duration spaceflight adversely affects post-landing operator proficiency. *Scientific Reports, 9*(1), Article 2677. https://doi.org/10.1038/s41598-019-39058-9

Moore, T.M., Basner, M., Nasrini, J., Hermosillo, E., Kabadi, S., Roalf, D.R., McGuire, S., Ecker, A.J., Ruparel, K., Port, A.M., Jackson, C.T., Dinges, D.F., & Gur, R.C. (2017). Validation of the cognition test battery for spaceflight in a sample of highly educated adults. *Aerospace Medicine and Human Performance, 88*(10), 937–946. https://doi.org/10.3357/AMHP.4801.2017

Moore, T.M., Di Sandro, A., Scott, J.C., Lopez, K.C., Ruparel, K., Njokweni, L.J., Santra, S., Conway, D.S., Port, A.M., D'Errico, L., Rush, S., Wolf, D.H., Calkins, M.E., Gur, R.E., & Gur, R.C. (2023). Construction of a computerized adaptive test (CAT-CCNB) for efficient neurocognitive and clinical psychopathology assessment. *Journal of Neuroscience Methods, 386*, Article 109795. https://doi.org/10.1016/j.jneumeth.2023.109795

Moore, T.M., Gur, R.C., Thomas, M.L., Brown, G.G., Nock, M.K., Savitt, A.P., Keilp, J.G., Heeringa, S., Ursano, R.J., Stein, M.B., & Army, S.C. (2019). Development, administration, and structural validity of a brief, computerized neurocognitive battery: Results from the army study to assess risk and resilience in servicemembers. *Assessment, 26*(1), 125–143. https://doi.org/10.1177/1073191116689820

Mulavara, A.P., Feiveson, A.H., Fiedler, J., Cohen, H., Peters, B.T., Miller, C., Brady, R., & Bloomberg, J.J. (2010). Locomotor function after long-duration space flight: Effects and motor learning during recovery. *Experimental Brain Research, 202*(3), 649–659. https://doi.org/10.1007/s00221-010-2171-0

Mulavara, A.P., Peters, B.T., Miller, C.A., Kofman, I.S., Reschke, M.F., Taylor, L.C., Lawrence, E.L., Wood, S.J., Laurie, S.S., Lee, S.M.C., Buxton, R.E., May-Phillips, T.R., Stenger, M.B., Ploutz-Snyder, L.L.,

Ryder, J.W., Feiveson, A.H., & Bloomberg, J.J. (2018). Physiological and functional alterations after spaceflight and bed rest. *Medicine and Science in Sports and Exercise, 50*(9), 1961–1980. https://doi.org/10.1249/MSS.0000000000001615

Nasrini, J., Hermosillo, E., Dinges, D.F., Moore, T.M., Gur, R.C., & Basner, M. (2020). Cognitive performance during confinement and sleep restriction in NASA's Human Exploration Research Analog (HERA). *Frontiers in Physiology, 11,* Article 394. https://doi.org/10.3389/fphys.2020.00394

Reschke, M.F., Bloomberg, J.J., Harm, D.L., Paloski, W.H., Layne, C., & McDonald, V. (1998). Posture, locomotion, spatial orientation, and motion sickness as a function of space flight. *Brain Research: Brain Research Reviews, 28*(1–2), 102–117. https://doi.org/10.1016/s0165-0173(98)00031-9

Reschke, M.F., Koslovskaya, I.B., Lysova, N., Kitov, V., Rukavishnikov, I., Kogman, I.S., Tomilovskaya, E.S., Rosenberg, M.J., Osetsky, N., Fomina, E., Grishin, A., & Wood, S.J. (2020). Joint Russia-USA field test: Implications for deconditioned crew following long duration spaceflight. *Aerospace and Ecological Medicine, 54*(6), 94–100. https://doi.org/10.21687/0233-528x-2020-54-6-94-100

Roberts, D.R., Albrecht, M.H., Collins, H.R., Asemani, D., Chatterjee, A.R., Spampinato, M.V., Zhu, X., Chimowitz, M.I., & Antonucci, M.U. (2017). Effects of spaceflight on astronaut brain structure as indicated on MRI. *New England Journal of Medicine, 377*(18), 1746–1753. https://doi.org/10.1056/NEJMoa1705129

Roberts, D.R., Brown, T.R., Nietert, P.J., Eckert, M.A., Inglesby, D.C., Bloomberg, J.J., George, M.S., & Asemani, D. (2019). Prolonged microgravity affects human brain structure and function. *American Journal of Neuroradiology, 40*(11), 1878–1885. https://doi.org/10.3174/ajnr.A6249

Roberts, D.R., Inglesby, D.C., Brown, T.R., Collins, H.R., Eckert, M.A., & Asemani, D. (2021). Longitudinal change in ventricular volume is accelerated in astronauts undergoing long-duration spaceflight. *Aging Brain, 1,* Article 100017. https://doi.org/10.1016/j.nbas.2021.100017

Sakka, L., Coll, G., & Chazal, J. (2011). Anatomy and physiology of cerebrospinal fluid. *European Annals of Otorhinolaryngology, Head and Neck Diseases, 128*(6), 309–316. https://doi.org/10.1016/j.anorl.2011.03.002

Salazar, A.P., McGregor, H.R., Hupfeld, K.E., Beltran, N.E., Kofman, I.S., De Dios, Y.E., Riascos, R.F., Reuter-Lorenz, P.A., Bloomberg, J.J., Mulavara, A.P., Wood, S.J., & Seidler, R. (2022). Changes in working memory brain activity and task-based connectivity after long-duration spaceflight. *Cerebral Cortex, 33*(6), 2641–2654. https://doi.org/10.1093/cercor/bhac232

Schroeder, J.E., & Tuttle, M.L. (1991). *Investigation of possible causes for human-performance degradation during microgravity flight* (SwRI Project No. 12-4075).

Scully, R.R., Basner, M., Nasrini, J., Lam, C.-w., Hermosillo, E., Gur, R.C., Moore, T., Alexander, D.J., Satish, U., & Ryder, V.E. (2019). Effects of acute exposures to carbon dioxide on decision making and cognition in astronaut-like subjects. *npj Microgravity, 5*(1), Article 17. https://doi.org/10.1038/s41526-019-0071-6

Seidler, R.D., Stern, C., Basner, M., Stahn, A.C., Wuyts, F.L., & Zu Eulenburg, P. (2022). Future research directions to identify risks and mitigation strategies for neurostructural, ocular, and behavioral changes induced by human spaceflight: A NASA-ESA expert group consensus report. *Frontiers in Neural Circuits, 16*, Article 876789. https://doi.org/10.3389/fncir.2022.876789

Sharma, A., Wolf, D.H., Ciric, R., Kable, J.W., Moore, T.M., Vandekar, S.N., Katchmar, N., Daldal, A., Ruparel, K., Davatzikos, C., Elliott, M.A., Calkins, M.E., Shinohara, R.T., Bassett, D.S., & Satterthwaite, T.D. (2017). Common dimensional reward deficits across mood and psychotic disorders: A connectome-wide association study. *American Journal of Psychiatry, 174*(7), 657–666. https://doi.org/10.1176/appi.ajp.2016.16070774

Slack, K.J., Shea, C., Leveton, L.B., Whitmire, A.M., & Schmidt, L.L. (2009). *Risk of behavioral and psychiatric conditions: NASA evidence-based review.* NASA Lyndon B. Johnson Space Center.

Smith, M.G., Wusk, G.C., Nasrini, J., Baskin, P., Dinges, D.F., Roma, P.G., & Basner, M. (2021). Effects of six weeks of chronic sleep restriction with weekend recovery on cognitive performance and wellbeing in high-performing adults. *Sleep, 44*(8), Article zsab051. https://doi.org/10.1093/sleep/zsab051

Sönksen, S.E., Kühn, S., Basner, M., Gerlach, D., Hoffmann, F., Mühl, C., Tank, J., Noblé, H.J., Akgün, K., Ziemssen, T., Jordan, J., & Limper, U. (2022). Brain structure and neurocognitive function in two professional mountaineers during 35 days of severe normobaric hypoxia. *European Journal of Neurology, 29*(10), 3112–3116. https://doi.org/10.1111/ene.15470

Spiering, B.A., Lee, S.M., Mulavara, A.P., Bentley, J.R., Buxton, R.E., Lawrence, E.L., Sinka, J., Guilliams, M.E., Ploutz-Snyder, L.L., & Bloomberg, J.J. (2011). Test battery designed to quickly and safely assess diverse indices of neuromuscular function after unweighting. *Journal of Strength and Conditioning Research, 25*(2), 545–555. https://doi.org/10.1519/JSC.0b013e3181f56780

Strangman, G.E., Sipes, W., & Beven, G. (2014). Human cognitive performance in spaceflight and analogue environments. *Aviation Space and Environmental Medicine, 85*(10), 1033–1048. https://doi.org/10.3357/ASEM.3961.2014

Tays, G.D., Hupfeld, K.E., McGregor, H.R., Salazar, A.P., De Dios, Y.E., Beltran, N.E., Reuter-Lorenz, P.A., Kofman, I.S., Wood, S.J., Bloomberg, J.J., Mulavara, A.P., & Seidler, R.D. (2021). The effects of long duration spaceflight on sensorimotor control and cognition. *Frontiers in Neural Circuits, 15,* Article 723504. https://doi.org/10.3389/fncir.2021.723504

Tu, D., Basner, M., Smith, M.G., Williams, E.S., Ryder, V.E., Romoser, A.A., Ecker, A., Aeschbach, D., Stahn, A.C., Jones, C.W., Howard, K., Kaizi-Lutu, M., Dinges, D.F., & Shou, H. (2022). Dynamic ensemble prediction of cognitive performance in spaceflight. *Scientific Reports, 12*(1), Article 11032. https://doi.org/10.1038/s41598-022-14456-8

Van Dongen, H.P., Maislin, G., Mullington, J.M., & Dinges, D.F. (2003). The cumulative cost of additional wakefulness: Dose-response effects on neurobehavioral functions and sleep physiology from chronic sleep restriction and total sleep deprivation. *Sleep, 26*(2), 117–126. https://doi.org/10.1093/sleep/26.2.117

Van Ombergen, A., Jillings, S., Jeurissen, B., Tomilovskaya, E., Ruhl, R.M., Rumshiskaya, A., Nosikova, I., Litvinova, L., Annen, J., Pechenkova, E.V., Kozlovskaya, I.B., Sunaert, S., Parizel, P.M., Sinitsyn, V., Laureys, S., Sijbers, J., Zu Eulenburg, P., & Wuyts, F.L. (2018). Brain tissue-volume changes in cosmonauts. *New England Journal of Medicine, 379*(17), 1678–1680. https://doi.org/10.1056/NEJMc1809011

Van Ombergen, A., Jillings, S., Jeurissen, B., Tomilovskaya, E., Rumshiskaya, A., Litvinova, L., Nosikova, I., Pechenkova, E., Rukavishnikov, I., Manko, O., Danylichev, S., Rühl, R.M., Kozlovskaya, I.B., Sunaert, S., Parizel, P.M., Sinitsyn, V., Laureys, S., Sijbers, J., zu Eulenburg, P., & Wuyts, F.L. (2019). Brain ventricular volume changes induced by long-duration spaceflight. *Proceedings of the National Academy of Sciences, 116*(21), 10531–10536. https://doi.org/10.1073/pnas.1820354116

Welch, R.B., Hoover, M., & Southward, E.F. (2009). Cognitive performance during prismatic displacement as a partial analogue of "space fog". *Aviation Space and Environmental Medicine, 80*(9), 771–780. https://doi.org/10.3357/asem.2415.2009

Wostyn, P., Mader, T.H., Gibson, C.R., & Nedergaard, M. (2022). Does long-duration exposure to microgravity lead to dysregulation of the brain and ocular glymphatic systems? *Eye Brain, 14*, 49–58. https://doi.org/10.2147/EB.S354710

Section IV

Investigation

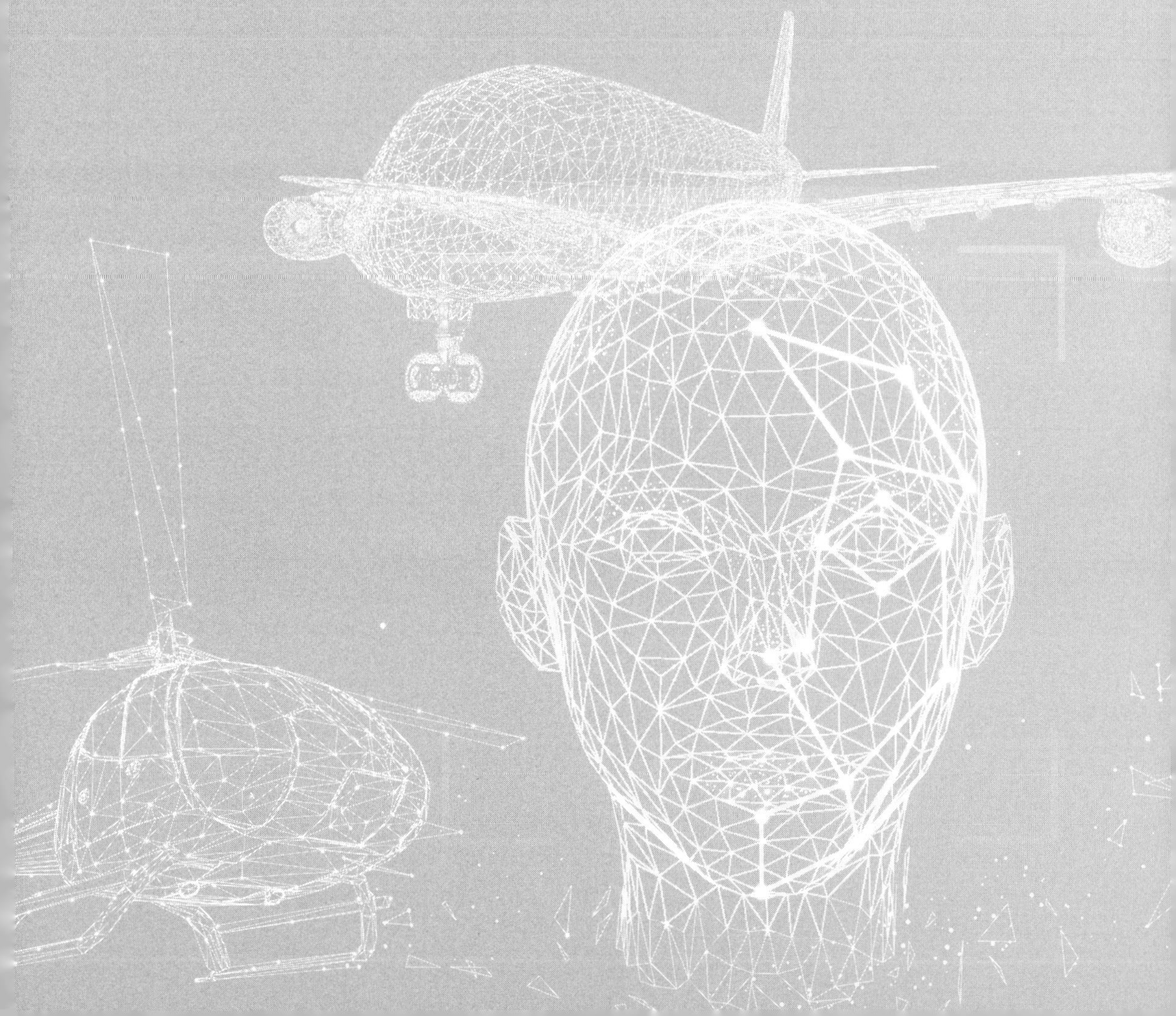

Chapter 20
Air Accident Investigation With a Focus on Relevant Neuropsychological Factors

Robert Bor, Carina Eriksen, and Alpo Vuorio

Introduction

The exceptional safety record of the airline industry is well documented and, among many complex and interrelated factors, an outstanding testament to our understanding of human factors in safety-critical work environments. It is an accepted fact, however, that from time to time incidents and accidents will occur. Some accidents may be, in part, attributable to "the human factor" and specifically the cognitive performance – and limitations – of key operators including pilots, air traffic controllers, and ground-based maintenance engineers and associated personnel. It is difficult to predict or anticipate a mishap or accident occurring due to human error, but it is always important to understand the sequence of events leading up to these in safety-critical environments and identify possible ways to prevent future occurrences, when they sadly do occur. The focus in this chapter is on how in the aftermath of an air accident, investigators, pathologists, lawyers, aircraft manufacturers, crew, managers, aviation regulators, engineers, aeromedical examiners, clinical aviation psychologists, and neuropsychologists go about exploring the relevance of human factors, generally, and cognitive performance, specifically, to the accident.

Human Performance and Limitations

Genetic, environmental, and lifestyle factors are all thought to influence cognitive health and human performance. Some of these factors may contribute toward a decline in thinking skills as well as in the ability to perform both everyday routine tasks and more complex ones in unexpected situations in which several decisions must be made simultaneously. Workers in safety-critical roles are subjected to a wide and sometimes varied range of cognitive challenges when in role. For some, the need for mental acuity or preparedness for this may extend to periods of rest where they must maintain a state of alertness and vigilance, as is frequently the case among military personnel, air ambulance operators, and commercial and private jet operators. Pilots – and to a comparable although not entirely identical extent, air traffic controllers – require a high level of sustained cognitive performance to cope with several environmental, motoric, physiological, psychological, and social challenges and stressors (Longo et al., 2022). Brain-based skills are needed when performing tasks related to perception, learning, memory, understanding, awareness, reasoning, judgment, intuition, and language, as has been highlighted elsewhere in this book. Some examples of cognition include paying attention to something in the environment, dealing with novel situations, solving problems, and higher-level decision-making processes. Psychological and physiological limitations in these skills in the complex aviation system often play an important role in the original sequence of events leading to aircraft accidents, or they are cofactors in the genesis of a series of compounding and related errors, with potentially devastating outcomes (Reason, 2016). There are also language and cultural factors shown to play an important role in either causing or contributing to aircraft accidents (see Chapter 17 by Irani et al. for further details).

During their regular and normal routine work, pilots may be exposed to numerous cognitive and health challenges including sleep disturbance, fatigue, circadian desynchronization, dehydration, phases of intense activity followed by lengthy periods of inactivity, multiple sensory inputs, and unexpected or unwelcome occurrences (e.g., severe weather, mechanical defects, cases of serious illness on board, among many others). They will be repeatedly exposed to many predictable – and occasionally unusual or abnormal – events or occurrences that can affect, and be impacted by, perceptions, motoric functioning, memory, attention, visuospatial functioning, sensory functioning, emotional processing, and, of course, executive functioning, among others. When things go awry for a pilot or air traffic controller, their cognitive functions may be central to the cause of the incident or accident. Additionally, human reactions to common, rare, or complex situations may trigger unusual or unhelpful behaviors, which either lead to unfavorable outcomes or exacerbate situations in which jeopardy is present. An example of this is recovery from a high-altitude stall where the pilot is startled and immobilized (they fail to react) or responds incorrectly to the challenge by misreading or misinterpreting data. It is important to gain insight into the relevant effects of cognitive functioning in these situations to learn why the accident happened and, where possible, to prevent similar outcomes in the future.

Human factors may include fatigue, distraction, communication difficulties between the pilots or between the pilots and air traffic control, information processing limitations or errors, sensory problems, becoming immobilized or over-reacting to a situation, misjudgment, under-developed handling skills among pilots for handling specific conditions, and cultural or language issues, among others. Each of these alone or combined could result in, for example, a runway incursion, landing on the wrong runway, shutting down the wrong engine during a technical mishap, or flying into terrain as well as other potentially devastating outcomes. Unlike sudden and incapacitating medical problems, such as acute myocardial infarction or stroke, human factors associated with aircraft handling may be more difficult to attribute in the case of incidents or accidents. The same caveat applies to subtle incapacitation – such as the incipient, early stages of progressive neurological disorders such as Huntington's and Parkinson's disease – where determining the precise cause of an incident or accident may be clinically and forensically problematic. The mild symptoms may be difficult to detect in routine medical assessments but may be pertinent in high stress or novel aviation challenges.

Human error typically occurs in the complex aviation system when two effects of human factors combine. On the one hand, the operator may have reduced competence or have inadequate knowledge or experience of what they are required to do. Errors and accidents are often related to situations when an individual or team experiences stress, is under pressure, or is up against environmental challenges and faces both complexity and uncertainty. It is under these conditions that either or both effects combine, and the frailty and limitations of cognitive processing may lead to undesired outcomes (Scott, 2009).

Accidents are typically caused by a range of common factors including fatigue, poor training, stress, and distraction. Aging can also be a relevant factor (Causse et al., 2011). Human error is broadly categorized into two main types: (a) slips and lapses and (b) mistakes. Slips and lapses are closely related and can be caused by a lack of attention or loss of concentration as well as momentary memory loss. They are not generally considered to be related to motivation, training, or experience. A slip is a failure to properly execute a task or follow correct actions. A slip is an action typically taken at the wrong time (too early or too late) within a working procedure.

A mistake is deemed to occur when an individual believes they are carrying out the correct action, but it turns out that they have acted incorrectly. It is therefore an error of judgment. A mistake may occur when an individual remembers the rule that needs to be followed but applies this incorrectly. This is regarded as a rule-based mistake. Knowledge-based mistakes may occur when rules are misunderstood and when frequently executed methods are used inappropriately. Not all deviations from standard procedures are considered to significantly degrade safety. Amalberti et al. (2008) asserted that some deviations are part of normal human behavior and may enhance safety by showing that the operators are indeed in fact attentive and demonstrate high levels of concentration and therefore do not necessarily impede safety. They regard some deviations and violations of operating procedures to be inconsequential to safety and related outcomes.

Focus on Error Versus Focus on Competence

The primary objective of aviation management and aviation regulators historically has been to ensure no harm comes to passengers and crew and the third party, which are, for example, people on the ground. Definitions of safety are predominately centered around as few things as possible going wrong rather than focusing on learning from what goes right. Accidents are thought to be caused by failures and malfunctions, and the purpose of an investigation is to identify the causes and contributing factors. This approach is generally referred to as "Safety-I" and continues to serve an invaluable process in aviation safety. In more recent years, the aviation industry is also moving toward a second approach, Safety-II, to be used in conjunction with Safety-I. Safety-II is more concerned with seeking to understand how things usually go right as a basis for explaining how things occasionally go wrong.

This is often thought of as a more optimistic and positive approach widely used in the healthcare sector and other safety-related professions. This model seeks to understand the conditions where performance variability can become difficult to monitor and how we can strengthen or modify such conditions (MacKinnon et al., 2021).

The Role of Illness or Disease in Human Behavior

There are certain physical and psychological health conditions that can come to affect a pilot's health status and medical certification. Being diagnosed with a condition is not necessarily disqualifying, and therefore the condition needs to be referred to an aviation medical examiner and an aviation regulator in order to consider whether any limitations are placed to mitigate potential incapacitation on the pilot who has any of these conditions. In the aftermath of an air accident, investigators will seek to understand whether any of the following were relevant to or implicated in the incident or crash:

1. Was the crash directly due to of a medical condition that could affect flight safety? A further question will be whether the pilot had had this investigated and whether any limitation was placed on them as a result of them being aware of their diagnosis.
2. Are there related medical cofactors that may have reduced the capacity of the crew member, and could this be related to the incident or accident? This point is distinguished from the one above where the causal relationship is clear, unequivocal, and firmly established. In this second scenario, there is deemed to be a relationship between the medical condition and the accident, but the extent of the causation cannot be clearly quantified or defined. Has, for example, the medical condition caused partial or gradual incapacitation?
3. Is the accident due to medication or drug treatment for the condition and, therefore, an unwelcome effect of the treatment? Investigators will also need to understand whether the treatment was legally prescribed and accepted in aviation, whether this was appropriate for the individual, and whether the dosage and monitoring of the medication were adequate. They will also seek to understand whether the pilot has self-medicated for the condition and whether this may have any bearing in understanding the cause of the accident.
4. There may be an undiagnosed or a nondetectable medical condition that could affect human performance leading to the crash. Investigators will pursue enquiries relating to undiagnosed conditions through gathering information from the pilot, if they survived, and through health records and pathology analyses; in the case of fatalities, this will be via autopsy.

Clinically established baseline assessments of levels of neurocognitive performance of safety-critical workers within the airline industry are not routinely undertaken. In initial pilot selection, there are typically some forms of psychological testing undertaken; however, this differs from neuropsychological assessment (Studwick et al., 2023). Neurocognitive assessments may be implied or aspects of them may be "embedded" within simulator assessments and checks or during initial and subsequent training. This raises questions as to whether a pilot's baseline – and therefore comparable neurocognitive performance – is accessible or available where an incident or accident occurs in aviation, as simulator training or line operations performance may not be directly comparable with the wide and complex set of parameters confronting the pilot involved in an accident.

Illness or medical conditions attributable to a pilot are rarely the sole cause of an air crash (Schuite, 2019). In this regard, undiagnosed or non-reported neurological or psychiatric conditions are infrequently the single cause of an accident, although it is generally considered necessary to rule out neurological or psychiatric illness in pilots and air traffic controllers, as well as in others who may have been involved in the flight, as a cause of the accident. Pilots may, however, be affected by minor, subclinical, or transient neurocognitive changes or limitations, and these are more commonly contributing factors in air crashes and incidents (Bor et al., 2017; Flynn et al., 2022).

Where detected either during routine medical checks or between these, medical problems can lead to at least the temporary grounding of pilots by their aviation medical examiner. The protocols and checks in place for monitoring and assessing pilot health are generally considered to be robust and effective. Air crashes may, of course, be attributable to other causes including mechanical failures, meteorological conditions, and cargo overload or displacement, but human factors are generally considered an important and relevant cause of air crashes or a cofactor in the sequence of events leading to the crash. It should be noted that behind mechanical failure can be human factors in maintenance personnel when performing related tasks.

An important factor that can affect cognitive abilities is stress. Stress can be related to aviation work or to personal challenges. People with elevated stress levels are more likely to experience a decline in cognitive functioning affecting their capacity to concentrate, remember, and learn new things. Stress is an emotional and physical reaction to adverse events and circumstances. A certain level of stress can be helpful, allowing us to perform and rise to challenges. However, prolonged or repeated exposure to stressful conditions can have a detrimental effect on our cognitive functioning leading to a reduced ability to concentrate, remember information, and plan (Soares et al., 2012). This could have a devastating impact on air safety, especially if prolonged underlying stress has gone undetected or not declared due to fear of loss of license or loss of a job. Airline pilots, ground-based engineers, military personnel, and air traffic controllers are first and foremost humans and, as such, are subject to a whole host of stressors including job security, financial worry, relationship difficulties, family bereavement, work–life challenges, and health concerns, to name a few.

When the cognitive system overloads, attentional resources in the brain that are used for memory and executive functioning get redirected to parts of the brain that are compromised (Girotti et al., 2018). An example may be a pilot who is suffering from stress where the attentional focus gets routed to the amygdala, the emotional center of the brain, instead of the information processes required for situational awareness and higher-level decision-making. It could also lead to routine tasks being performed inaccurately or even missed. A second situation may be an air traffic controller being preoccupied by worry and therefore having less attentional capacity to process information pertaining to monitoring air space activity, resulting in missing, for example, a radio call.

One of the most difficult challenges in aviation medicine is the identification and diagnosis of pilots' and air traffic controllers' specific psychiatric disorders and cognitive impairments that may adversely affect performance. These are (a) psychiatric disorders, (b) psychiatric disorders with neurocognitive problems, and (c) neurocognitive problems without psychiatric disorder. Timely assessment of behavioral difficulties, neurocognitive impairments, and neurological and psychiatric problems as well as reactive and transient mental well-being challenges is important for flight safety (Douglas & Porter, 2009). Significant findings in such assessments may lead to referral for more detailed and complex investigations, temporary or permanent grounding or removal from flight duty, or exclusion from working in the airline industry altogether. This may be life changing and arguably unwelcome for an individual who is affected, but safety must take precedence. While certain conditions that may affect neurocognitive performance may be "screened out" in the initial assessment before or during pilot selection, the full range of medical and specifically neurocognitive impediments due to physical health conditions may develop gradually or present with sudden onset and are therefore an insidious threat to safety due to the degradation of performance in attention that may later contribute to an incident or accident (Studwick et al., 2023).

Pilots may be unwilling to report to their medical examiner mental health or well-being concerns or symptoms for fear of the deleterious impact they may perceive this will have on their career if their medical certification is withdrawn and this prevents them from working. The pilot suicide crash on March 24, 2015 involving Germanwings Flight 9525 while flying over the French Alps emphasizes the importance of medical assessments among pilots and the relevance of the mental health check during this assessment and between periodical examinations. The focus should be on the well-being of those who suffer from known mental health problems and on communicating concerns about the pilot to their aviation medical examiner and employer, where relevant, to ensure support is forthcoming and safety is not compromised (Bor et al., 2017).

Psychiatric disorders among student pilots as well as licensed pilots are among the top three reasons for loss of medical license. There are several challenges for assessing and diagnosing mental health problems among pilots. While studies have shown that many pilots recognize the stresses and challenges of their job and the impact on their well-being and performance, some would be unaware of the specific mental health and neurocognitive exclusions and arguably a proportion would be unaware that they are suffering from an excluding serious mental health problem. It is common knowledge among aviation medical examiners and aviation regulators that social stigma and a fear of losing one's livelihood through the loss of one's medical certification speak against openness about medical and mental health problems among pilots when being assessed by the aeromedical examiner (Hoffman et al., 2023). While mild to moderate depression after treatment typically allows for continued flying, mental health conditions such as bipolar disorder (Vuorio et al., 2017) or significant alcohol misuse, among others, can lead to nondisclosure due to a lack of insight and self-awareness.

Attention-Deficit/Hyperactivity Disorder

Attention-deficit/hyperactivity disorder (ADHD) is a neurodevelopmental disorder. Hyperactive/impulse symptoms are characteristic of this disorder. Neurocognitive defects touch a wide range of neurocognitive domains including working memory, response inhibition, and planning/organization. Very typical for this disorder is that the brain has difficulty in switching from the rest mode to an active mode. In aviation, ADHD is associated with an increased risk of accidents and is therefore not acceptable for pilots (Laukkala et al., 2017). In very rare cases, ADHD may be acceptable for some pilots after comprehensive neurocognitive evaluation.

Posttraumatic Stress Disorder

Posttraumatic stress disorder may arise after suffering a traumatic life event. This trauma-induced exposure may lead to neurocognitive changes in specific parts of the brain including the amygdala, prefrontal cortex, and hippocampus. As an example, as a result of neurocognitive changes following exposure to trauma, intrusion errors may present leading to the incorrect recall of words. Unfortunately, the majority of medical guidance issued by aviation authorities does not stipulate whether or how neuropsychological assessment should be carried out in PTSD cases among pilots (Laukkala et al., 2018).

Recreational Drug Usage

Impairment derived from alcohol or recreational drug use that affects flight safety is arguably a greater problem than addiction to these substances, which is generally rarer. The use of cannabis, including any cannabidiol (CBD) derivatives, can lead to side effects such as, but not limited to, addiction, chronic pain, insomnia, sedation, and anxiety and is not compatible with medical certification. Some who may use cannabis and CBD derivatives do so in order to manage common and unwelcome sensations or symptoms, such as chronic pain and anxiety, and therefore their use and effects can be intricately connected. Air accident investigators will seek to establish whether the individual pilot or crew members have any of these substances in their system and for what reasons the individual was using them, whether for medicinal or recreational purposes. Irrespective of the reasons for their use, these substances currently lead to a permanent "medically unfit" assessment in all jurisdictions, as exposure to these substances can impair psychomotor performance.

The use of CBD products has been associated with accidents in road traffic (Preuss et al., 2021), although studies of the relationship between usage and accidents are not without their limitations. Aviation regulators are universally unambiguous in placing limitations on crew who have used cannabis or CBD products in the previous 28 days, as is the case in Canada. The results of a recent meta-analysis (see above) point to a sevenfold estimated risk of being involved in a fatal accident following cannabis use, a threefold estimated risk of a fatal accident following opiate use, and a twofold estimated risk of a fatal accident after benzodiazepine use. There are reported to be endurable and measurable deficits in decision-making, concept formation, and planning 3 weeks after abstinence (Crean et al., 2011). Accordingly, the case for testing for a range of substances and referral for toxicological assessments after an air incident or accident is compelling.

Investigating an Incident and Accident

In the aftermath of an aircraft incident, accident, or crash, a wide range of human factors will be considered and examined. This is time consuming and needs to be based on several sources. Air accident investigation is a required undertaking and the Chicago Convention covers the procedures that should be followed (see Article 26, Annex 13 of the Chicago Convention; International Civil Aviation Organization [ICAO], 2016). The actions of pilots, air traffic controllers, cabin crew, maintenance engineers, and others in the safety-critical team will typically be scrutinized, with the aim of establishing what happened, how this may have occurred, and how similar outcomes can be prevented in the future (Strauch, 2017). The relative place of and extent to which cognitive performance has contributed to the occurrence will form part of a systemic understanding of why the accident occurred. The purpose of an investigation after an incident or accident is, therefore, threefold:

1. To investigate the course of events, causes, and consequences as well as the rescue operations performed
2. To help to understand why the accident happened
3. To prevent future accidents and incidents without apportioning blame or liability

It is internationally recommended by the ICAO that aircraft accident investigators will be appointed by and within the jurisdiction in which the accident occurs to undertake and possibly lead the investigation and subsequent reporting. Other specialists and interested parties often join the investigation who typically come from foreign agencies or organizations, including representatives of the aircraft manufacturer, engine manufacturer, registered state of the aircraft, the country of the primary demographic of the passenger list (if appropriate), meteorological experts, and other specialists. Air accident investigators are drawn from several different backgrounds, and those with a psychological, neuropsychological, and human factors background are often part of the team that carries out the investigation. The report and findings will most likely be circulated internationally well beyond the country or jurisdiction in which the accident took place, as the lessons typically have implications for the industry at large.

A surviving or injured crew member is both a witness casualty to the accident and is also potentially implicated in the event or events leading to the accident. Assuming that there are survivors, accident investigators will want to gain insights by interviewing them and seeking an understanding of their version of events and likely causes. This is itself a highly sensitive enquiry and endeavor. It is possible that there has been damage to equipment or property as well as injury or loss of life to others, including crew, passengers, and people on the ground. Crew members may be shocked, in an emotionally distressed state, fearful of the implications of their sharing information, and mindful that their career and insurances as well as their well-being may be at stake. There needs to be careful consideration exercised by the investigators between the crucial interests of establishing the facts with a view to improving flight safety and the well-being of surviving crew. There are also potential medical confidentiality considerations and these may vary between countries (Schuite, 2019).

Turning to the operating crew members and performance (as opposed to external to the individual, equipment and technical problems, weather-related factors, air traffic control challenges etc.), there will be interest in exploring and establishing the extent of involvement in the accident of the following:

1. Directly affected human factors including handling and operating skills, omissions, or errors will be examined.
2. Contributing human factors -which can also be primary factors - that may have impaired performance, including, but not restricted to, fatigue and circadian anomalies and challenges, crew rostering issues, communication problems or ambiguities, crew/team relationships, a background of industrial action in the airline, and operational pressures, among many others. Alcohol, recreational drug, and prescribed medications use will be considered.
3. Whether the accident may be linked to the operating crew members' acute or chronic medical conditions, and if so whether this may be due to a gradual degradation of medical fitness or a sudden and acute medical event.
4. Of special interest to the psychologist will be whether the pilot was challenged by a degenerative and/or subclinical but insidious neurocognitive condition that may have affected their ability to safely handle the aircraft, such as undiagnosed motor neuron disease, attentional problems, neurodiversity, or autism spectrum disorders, among others, or whether it may have been caused by a sudden but severely impairing event such as an aneurysm or acute vestibular problem, among others.
5. Also of special interest to the psychologists involved in the investigation will be the psychological state and well-being of the crew member, including the impact of recent life

events, the state of their social and intimate relationships, stress, dysregulated mood, use of psychotropic or medications (especially for mood, anxiety, and sleep), financial challenges, and the possible cumulative effect of two or more of these.

The Psychological "Autopsy"

Aircraft incidents and accidents present their own unique challenges. Where there is a fatal outcome, particularly if the pilot is among the deceased, determining why the accident happened may be difficult due to a reduction in the amount of information that can be gleaned about the incident because of the absence of crucial witness evidence.

The investigator undertaking a postincident or postaccident review will seek to place this event in context and, importantly, also to systematically gather information around the event that may shed light on the personal background and circumstances of the individual being assessed. This is a very time-consuming phase. Some or many details may be neither accessible nor available to the assessor. This may be due to the lack of absence of documented history and evidence; legal restraints on the sharing of personal information, which vary from country to country; and gaps in information due to the absence of evidence having been gathered in the first place. Typically, a range of different aspects of the individual's whole life as well as a more detailed investigation of their recent health and performance will be the focus of the assessment. This will be in addition to any formal neurocognitive assessments that have been carried out, where this is rarely the case. In most cases there will be anecdotal and collateral information available to the investigating team derived from performance and employment records, selection performance and reports, colleague accounts, and corroborating information from the individual's personal health and social records, including from their family doctor, friends and family, school, and previous employers.

The main subject areas of enquiry include:

1. The context, events, and timeline leading to the incident or crash will be scrutinized.
2. The personal life story and background history of the individual including developmental milestones, education, career and training, relocation etc. as well as notable life events, trauma, and challenging life events will be examined.
3. Their recent and lifetime health and mental health history will be analyzed. This will include family doctor medical records, aviation medical examiner records, occupational health records, mental health and well-being records including previous or current counseling, psychological therapy and related assessments, suicide risk assessment, chronology of health issues and challenges including significant life events, personal loss, and lifetime medical investigations and assessments as well as prescribed medications. There will be specific enquiry into past experiences of physical and/or psychological trauma and any neurodevelopmental challenges or neuropsychological assessments. Investigators will seek relevant medical records particularly relating to neurology, central nervous system functioning, and medication usage and whether substances such as alcohol and recreational drugs are detected in toxicology assessments. They will be interested in possible cognitive and performance limitations, sensory deficits or problems (visual, auditory, cutaneous, olfactory, vestibular, somatosensory), and perceptual difficulties (visual perception, attention error, memory failure, decision errors).

4. Relationship history and circumstances as well as any noteworthy changes of these over time will be explored; possible additional relationships outside of a primary relationship will also be taken into account. Where relevant, a psychosexual history may be sought.
5. Information stored on the flight data recorder (FDR) and cockpit voice recorder (CVR) as well as air traffic control and communications records will be sought and studied, as these may provide useful insights into the actions of the pilots and controllers and offer clues as to their neurocognitive performance preceding the accident.
6. A work and performance history will be sought, and any challenges and limitations will be noted. This will include documented training records in flight school, workplace history with a detailed chronology, performance records, number of hours of experience operating the aircraft or being an air traffic controller, current roster, fatigue records, crew relationships, simulator performance records and experience, history of job progression and promotion(demotion), instances of performance management, disputes and cautions, and suspensions by their employer.
7. Legally obtained personal communications may be an important part of the investigation and typically include scrutiny of emails, notes, letters, access to websites, flight simulators, and telephone history etc., as far as these shed light on the individual's behavior.
8. Assuming the pilots have survived, they would typically be interviewed and assessed in order to gain insight into their actions and reasoning into the circumstances of what occurred.
9. Family and relatives may be interviewed if there is a suggestion that they can offer useful and relevant insights into the psychological state of the related crew member, their behavior prior to leaving home for work, and more enduring behavioral characteristics or possible indicators. Airport staff such as security personnel, the flight dispatcher, and others who may have come into contact with the crew member may also be interviewed.

The investigating human factors expert, clinical psychologist, neuropsychologist, or aeromedical specialist must be mindful of methodological challenges, bias, or error that can affect interpretation of events and facts and therefore conclusions. These include the following:

Hindsight Bias: People have an inherent tendency to view events as being more predictable than they may be, especially in hindsight. This may affect the interpretation of results of assessments and conclusions drawn from these.

Measurement Error: There may be some bias or error in the use of tests and their interpretation. There may be different levels of sensitivity and specificity around the use of different tests, and different people undertaking assessment may produce different results.

The expertise and proficiency of the assessor may affect the findings. Furthermore, some assessment tools may have limitations when used with different individuals from a demographic perspective (age, culture, language proficiency etc.).

Inconsistent Assessment Results: Different tests and subtests may yield varying and at times contradictory results. They may also be missing pieces of information that degrade or hamper the clinician's ability to provide definitive and unequivocal results.

Attribution Bias: There may be a tendency to blame an individual or machine (aircraft) without an extensive and deep investigation into the relevant factors. In situations of some complexity, those investigating an incident or accident may seek to simplify the circumstances and cause of the accident or become overly fixated with one aspect of this to the detriment of seeing a wider picture.

Access to Subjects or Witnesses: In the highly sensitive context in which there has been serious injury or death, the forensic examiners may not have access to key witnesses or protagonists in the situation, as the event may have sadly led to their incapacity or death. There is therefore a reduced number of data they can access pertinent to the investigation concerning that individual.

Post Hoc Analysis: Almost every incident or accident relies on post hoc assessment methods. It is thus an assessment of an individual after an incident or accident, and, therefore, a best estimation of what may have happened. Furthermore, the individual may have experienced or suffered psychological trauma as well as other related or unrelated life experiences since the incident or accident and this may affect, distort, or bias the results, as the physical and psychological state and condition of the individual may have shifted after the incident.

Limitations of Data and Observation: There may be limitations or gaps in the available data after an incident or accident. This could be due to technology (such as loss of the FDR) as well as limitations of witnesses (if there are any) and their own ability to objectively recall events and facts.

The Individual's Own Intended or Unintended Bias: An individual being subjected to an assessment may have reason to misrepresent their own account of what they experienced or suffered, or indeed emphasize certain parts of their account or story over others. Some of this may be due to intended or unintended bias.

Legal Considerations: There may be a degree of bias or distortion among witnesses or subjects where important legal consequences could follow as a result of the investigation. If, for example, a pilot feels that they will be blamed for an incident or accident, they may understate or exaggerate their own account of what had happened or how they had interacted with aircraft systems.

Baseline and Comparison Limitations: There may be minimal or no baseline measures of an individual before the incident or accident, and therefore it may be more challenging to link the outcome of the incident or accident to causal factors relating to their behavior. It is uncommon and unusual in aviation, for example, for pilots worldwide to undergo extensive neuropsychological assessments at different points in their career. Therefore, individual or group comparisons may be difficult, if not impossible, to make. There are few neurocognitive assessment tools that have pilot or air traffic controller norms. This is not necessarily problematic beyond it being a limitation insofar as it is important for the assessor to clarify with whom they are comparing the individual.

Variance in Human Behavior: It is well understood that people react differently in similar situations. For example, the consumption of one unit of alcohol may have different effects on individuals when measured within a defined period after the ingestion of alcohol. All behaviors can be predictable.

Critical Incident Support

Passengers and crew who have been exposed to critical incidents are likely to feel stressed and perhaps even traumatized. It is important to offer basic support for their well-being (e.g., food, fresh clothing, toiletries, access to telephones, lodging etc.). Taking care of the basic needs of survivors, relatives, and crew members cannot be overemphasized after an accident. This can help victims recover from trauma. After basic support, psychoeducation should be offered in the form of a debrief that is both compassionate and promotes resilience. This should ideally take place no more than 24–48 hr after the incident took place. Mitchell and Everly (2000) suggest a seven-stage debriefing process to help emergency services and other professional work through their response to a highly stressful event. In aviation this could be an emergency landing, aircraft collision on the runway, or any other aviation mishaps or near-misses. The goal of this process is to provide peer and professional support immediately after the event. This is considered to reduce the risk of developing trauma symptoms, posttraumatic stress disorder, or other mental health problems in the aftermath of a critical incident.

Although the process of critical incident debriefing can be flexible, tailored to suit the specific context or group of people involved, it typically involves one or more facilitator(s) and will usually cover seven stages. These do not have to be linear but often a facilitator may start by noting factual details to try to understand what has happened. This allows the intervention to be tailored to the specific needs of the group. It then moves to the fact phase where group members are encouraged to share the facts from their perspective. This phase typically focuses on facts rather than on emotional reactions. The third phase encourages those affected to share their emotions and thoughts in a supportive environment.

Sometimes it may be necessary to explore what potential difficulties everyone may experience in the aftermath of the critical incident and how to best manage these. The facilitator can offer guidance on further support if needed such as seeing a counsellor; speaking to a manager, a friend, or a partner; or visiting their general practitioner. Psychoeducation on stress and trauma may also be helpful. The final phase tends to focus on a summary of what everyone who has been affected has learned and how to best move forward in their life. Only a small minority of individuals will require more specialist and intensive trauma-related psychological therapy, as natural healing in the fullness of time is the norm.

Conclusion

A persistent challenge in neuropsychology and aeromedical practice is to be able to specify and determine the most likely cognitive challenges that shed light on incidents and accidents in order to determine, with the highest level of probability, the relationship between human behavior and its consequences. When someone's career may be on the line – or when an aviation incident or accident report may have far-reaching implications for operating procedures, operating costs, litigation, medical assessments, as well as future career aspirations, among others – it is essential that the investigators act with the highest levels of probity and draw on the latest evidence-based data and practices within aviation clinical psychology, neuropsychological assessments, and aviation medicine. In the most sensitive of these scenarios, and where there has been loss of life, the investigating clinician is duty-bound to adopt a "fair and just culture" perspective. Tentative, although growing, interest in "pilotless" civil aircraft in the future will not eliminate the relevance of understanding and determining the role of human factors in flight safety and related accidents, but it will most likely shift the main focus in accident investigations to systems designers and remote operators.

References

Amalberti, R., Vincent, C., Auroy, Y., & de Saint Maurice, G. (2008). Violations and migrations in health care: A framework for understanding and management. *BMJ Quality and Safety, 15*, 66–71. https://doi.org/10.1136/qshc.2005.015982

Bor, R., Eriksen, C., Oakes, M., & Scragg, P. (Eds.). (2017). *Pilot mental health assessment and support*. Taylor & Francis.

Causse, M., Dehais, F., Arexis, M., & Pastor, J. (2011). Cognitive aging and flight performances in general aviation pilots. *Neuropsychology and Cognition, 18*(5), 544–561. https://doi.org/10.1080/13825585.2011.586018

Crean, R., Crane, N., & Mason, B. (2011). An evidence-based review of acute and long-term effects of cannabis use on executive cognitive functions. *Journal of Addiction Medicine, 5*(1), 1–8. https://doi.org/10.1097/ADM.0b013e31820c23fa

Douglas, K., & Porter, R. (2009). Longitudinal assessment of neuropsychological function in major depression. *Australian and New Zealand Journal of Psychiatry, 43*, 1105–1117. https://doi.org/10.3109/00048670903279887

Flynn, C., King, R., Bor, R., & Tvaryanas, A. (2022). Mental health implications for aviators from COVID-19. *Reviews in Human Space Exploration, 27–28*, Article 100050. https://doi.org/10.1016/j.reach.2022.100050

Girotti, M., Adler, S.M., Bulin, S.E., Fucich, E.A., Paredes, D., & Morilak, D.A. (2018). Prefrontal cortex executive processes affected by stress in health and disease. *Progress in Neuro-Psychopharmacology and Biological Psychiatry, 85*, 161–179. https://doi.org/10.1016/j.pnpbp.2017.07.004

Hoffman, W.R., Patel, P.K., Aden, J., Willis, A., Acker, J.P., Bjerke, E., Miranda, E., Luster, J., & Tvaryanas, A. (2023). Multinational comparison study of aircraft pilot healthcare avoidance behaviour. *Occupational Medicine, 73*(7), 434–438. https://doi.org/10.1093/occmed/kqad091

International Civil Aviation Organization. (2016). *Convention on international civil aviation, Annex 13. Aircraft accident and incident investigation* (11th ed). http://ffac.ch/wp-content/uploads/2020/10/ICAO-Annex-13-Aircraft-Accident-and-Incident-Investigation.pdf

Laukkala, T., Bor, R., Budowle, B., Pooshan Navathe, P., Sajantila, A., Sainio, M., & Vuorio, A. (2018). Pilot's posttraumatic stress disorder and fatal aviation accidents: A descriptive study. *Aviation Psychology and Applied Human Factors, 8*(2), 93–99. https://doi.org/10.1027/2192-0923/a000144

Laukkala, T., Bor, R., Budowle, B., Sajantila, A., Navathe, P., Sainio, M., & Vuorio, A. (2017). Attention-deficit/hyperactivity disorder and fatal accidents in aviation medicine. *Aerospace Medicine and Human Performance, 88*(9), 871–875. https://doi.org/10.3357/AMHP.4919.2017

Longo, L., Wickens, C., Hancock, G., & Hancock, P. (2022). Human mental workload: A survey and a novel inclusive definition. *Frontiers of Psychology, 13*, Article 883321. https://doi.org/10.3389/fpsyg.2022.883321

MacKinnon, R., Pukk-Härenstam, K., Kennedy, C., Hollnagel, R., & Slated, D. (2021). A novel approach to explore Safety-I and Safety-II perspectives in in situ simulations – the structured what if functional resonance analysis methodology. *Advances in Simulation, 6*, Article 21. https://doi.org/10.1186/s41077-021-00166-0

Mitchell, J., & Everly, G. (2000). Critical incident stress management and critical incident stress debriefings: Evolutions, effects and outcomes. In B. Raphael & J.P. Wilson (Eds.), *Psychological debriefing: Theory, practice and evidence* (pp. 71–90). Cambridge University Press. https://doi.org/10.1017/CBO9780511570148.006

Preuss, U., Huestis, M., Schneider, M., Hermann, D., Lutz, B., Hasan, A., Kambeitz, J., Wong, J., & Hoch, E. (2021). Cannabis use and car crashes: A review. *Frontiers of Psychiatry, 12*, Article 643315. https://doi.org/10.3389/fpsyt.2021.643315

Reason, J. (2016). *Organizational accidents revisited*. CRC Press. https://doi.org/10.4324/9781315562841

Schuite, J. (2019). Aviation safety vs. medical confidentiality: Disclosure of health information for accident prevention and investigation. *Aerospace Medicine and Human Performance, 90*(10), 872–881.

Scott, I. (2009). Errors in clinical reasoning: Causes and remedial strategies. *British Medical Journal, 339*, 22–25. https://doi.org/10.1136/bmj.b1860

Soares, J., Sampaio, A., Ferreira, L., Santos, N., Marques, F., Palha, J., Cerqueira, J., & Sousa, N. (2012). Stress-induced changes in human decision-making are reversible. *Translational Psychiatry, 2*(7), Article e131. https://doi.org/10.1038/tp.2012.59

Strauch, B. (2017). *Investigating human error: Accidents and complex systems*. Routledge. https://doi.org/10.4324/9781315251851

Studwick, J., Gayed, A., Deady, M., Haffar, S., Mobbs, S., Malik, A., Akhtar, A., Braund, T., Bryant, R., & Harvey, S. (2023). Workplace mental health screening; a systematic review and meta-analysis. *Occupational and Environmental Medicine, 80*, 469–484. https://doi.org/10.1136/oemed-2022-108608

Vuorio, A., Laukkala, T., Navathe, P., Budowle, B., Bor, R., & Sajantila, A. (2017). Bipolar disorder in aviation medicine. *Aerospace Medicine and Human Performance, 88*(1), 42–47. https://doi.org/10.3357/AMHP.4620.2017

Chapter 21
Cognitive Functioning and Piloting in the Context of Incidents and Trauma

Mark W. Wiggins and Monique Crane

Introduction

Among organizations that function in high-consequence environments, operators are expected to work at an optimal level to ensure that unsafe acts and associated system failures are minimized. This requires both an awareness of those latent conditions that are likely to impact performance together with an ongoing process of evaluation to ensure that changes in the capabilities of operators are identified at the earliest opportunity. In combination, this capacity for awareness and evaluation enables the implementation of evidence-based interventions that can assist operators to return to optimal performance.

For aircraft pilots, effective and efficient cognitive functioning is critical to ensure that potential hazards and threats are identified quickly and accurately, that they possess a repertoire of strategies to manage these threats, and that they have the capability and resources necessary to implement remedial strategies efficiently and effectively. However, cognitive functioning varies according to intrinsic and extrinsic demands, with increases in demands impeding the capacity to function effectively (Morris & Leung, 2006). The aim of this chapter is to discuss the potential impact of exposure to trauma on pilots' cognitive functioning and to consider systemic approaches to the management of trauma-related symptoms, including resilience strengthening and assessments of cue utilization.

Features of Cognitive Functioning

Cognition is the science of the mind. Models of human cognition typically refer to a three-stage process of perception, processing, and response (O'Hare et al., 1994). Information must be perceived and interpreted, its meaning understood through a processing stage, and then a response initiated. However, this process is predicated on the availability of cognitive resources, including attention and short-term and long-term memory (Vidulich et al., 2010).

Short-term memory is a feature of cognitive functioning that enables information to be processed consciously (Jonides et al., 2008). However, the capacity to process information is also constrained to a limited number of items, and the information tends to be transient if it is not transferred to the larger-capacity long-term memory (Baddeley, 2007). It is typically referred to as the "bottle-neck" in processing where information beyond that capable of being processed is disregarded (Lambez et al., 2020). The potential consequence is a lapse where task-related information is overlooked.

Allied to short-term memory is attention that directs cognitive resources toward features of interest. Attention acts as a filter that enables the prioritization of information processing, either through intentional, selective or unintentional, focused mechanisms (Pashler, 1998). Where focused attention occurs in the absence of conscious deliberation, selective attention typically involves an active process whereby attentional resources are directed toward stimuli that embody a degree of perceived importance or priority (Wickens, 2021).

The distinction between selective and focused attention presumably enables rapid responses, particularly in engaging with threats. In the context of selective attention, cognitive resources are directed toward sensemaking where there is a degree of uncertainty or complexity that needs to be resolved and meaning derived (McDowd, 2007). This process is akin to novices engaging in an unfamiliar situation and drawing on declarative knowledge from long-term memory to make sense of a situation (Chauvel et al., 2013).

Drawing on declarative knowledge imposes demands on short-term memory, increasing mental workload and potentially impeding the capacity to process information (Stevens et al., 2022). This relationship is evident in an aircraft accident involving a Beechcraft Baron (Callsign ZK-SUN) that was approaching Napier Airport in New Zealand on a private flight in 1989. The pilot had only recently received his endorsement to operate twin-engined aircraft. Importantly, he achieved his endorsement flying a Beechcraft Duchess, an aircraft with a significantly slower airspeed than the Beechcraft Baron, and an aircraft that he had not flown previously, other than a 45-min training flight with an instructor (Transport Accident Investigation Commission, 1989).

On approach to Napier, the pilot prepared for an instrument approach for Runway 16. However, he was subsequently re-cleared by the air traffic controller to Runway 34 due to the immediate arrival of a commercial flight. The change in the clearance would have required the pilot to revise his planned approach while operating the aircraft safely. This increase in cognitive demands, together with his lack of familiarity with both the aircraft and the approach, most likely resulted in a situation where the demands of the task exceeded his cognitive capacity, leading to load-shedding and increasing the likelihood of a lapse. In the event, it appeared that the pilot failed to maintain sufficient control of the aircraft, descending below the minimum altitude, possibly misreading the altimeter, and colliding with terrain.

During the approach to Napier, the air traffic controller noted that, in successive readbacks, the pilot referred to the incorrect title of the approach and read back an incorrect callsign. It suggests that, at this point in the flight, the pilot did not have the capacity to interpret the information accurately and was reverting to previously acquired associations in memory. This is a common response under extreme cognitive demands and is similar to the effects of trauma on performance.

Extreme cognitive demands, such as those experienced by the pilot of ZK-SUN, are typically associated with extreme levels of anxiety. One of the characteristics of anxiety is a reduced capacity to retain and process information in short-term memory (Lapointe et al., 2013). In practice, responses may include prioritizing engagement with task-related stimuli, drawing on previously acquired associations in long-term memory, constraining attention to selected stimuli, persevering with a strategy or goal-directed behavior in the absence of inquiry, or, in some cases, physical and/or cognitive rigidity (Bor et al., 2002).

The Problem of Anxiety

Anxiety is a normal part of human function. It constitutes a critical cue for survival, typically initiating behavior that is associated with avoiding threatening stimuli. It is usually a feeling of discomfort, largely due to the activation of the sympathetic nervous system, resulting in an increase in heart rate and perspiration, together with dizziness, nausea, and stomach churn (Green et al., 2019). For individuals with chronic anxiety, the activation of the sympathetic nervous system can further exacerbate the intensity of the response, leading to temporary paralysis in extreme situations (Martin et al., 2015).

At a psychological level, increases in anxiety can be associated with negative thoughts leading to fear and a perceived lack of control. These negative thoughts occupy short-term memory, reducing the cognitive resources available to process new information, explaining temporary physical and cognitive paralysis as there is an inability to acquire, integrate, and/or respond to changes in the system state (Allsop & Gray, 2014). Alternatively, the lack of cognitive resources may lead to rapid responses, either to engage with the challenge or to withdraw from a perceived threat.

Anxiety presents as a disorder when it impairs social and/or occupational functioning (Morse & Bor, 2016). This is especially evident in avoidance behavior, and/or in other coping strategies such as the excessive use of alcohol and/or in the ingestion of other drugs. In general, these coping strategies moderate the symptoms of anxiety but do not provide a long-term solution and may increase the severity of the symptoms, creating a spiral of dysfunction.

Among adults, generalized anxiety disorder (GAD) tends to be most prevalent. It is characterized by excessive anxiety targeted toward a range of stimuli on frequent occasions over a period of 6 months (DeMartini et al., 2019). It is differentiated from anxiety disorders that are the focus of specific fears such as phobias. The most commonly experienced phobias include arachnophobia (fear of spiders), ophidiophobia (fear of snakes), acrophobia (fear of heights), and aerophobia (fear of flying; Eaton et al., 2018).

GAD is frequently associated with posttraumatic stress disorder (PTSD), a condition that emerges in response to potentially traumatic events (Grant et al., 2008). Posttraumatic reactions manifest across various areas of functioning. These encompass re-experiencing the trauma through flashbacks, nightmares, and intrusive memories. Other signs involve heightened vigilance, concentration difficulties, depression, sleep issues, self-devaluation, avoiding trauma reminders, emotional detachment, and withdrawing from meaningful aspects of life (Benight & Bandura, 2004; Friedman et al., 2011). These recurrent reactions can impair occupational functioning (Van der Kolk et al., 1996). It is a particularly debilitating condition that reportedly affects approximately 3.9 % of the general population (Koenen et al., 2017).

PTSD is categorized as a disorder of memory and is associated with various impairments in cognitive functioning, including a reduction in the capacity for sustained attention (Esterman et al., 2019). There is less clear evidence concerning the impact on learning, but it appears to be associated most explicitly with general attentional deficits (Qureshi et al., 2011). Importantly, conclusions have yet to be drawn concerning the impact of PTSD on executive function in the context of high-risk, high-consequence operational settings such as aircraft piloting.

The etiology of PTSD generally involves exposure to a potentially traumatic event or experiences. However, not all potentially traumatic experiences are associated with the onset of

PTSD and neither do individuals exposed to the same traumatic events necessarily develop the disorder. While PTSD tends to be more common among military personnel and first responders, members of the general population who are exposed to a traumatic event, such as a motor vehicle accident, may develop symptoms that are associated with PTSD (Norris & Sloane, 2007). Similarly, in the aviation context, a near-miss or a particularly difficult approach may, depending on the propensity of the individual, result in symptoms that align with PTSD.

While the impact of preexisting, diagnosed PTSD on aircraft accident involvement is difficult to establish conclusively, post-analyses of reports in the United States suggest a level of involvement in a minimum 0.16 % of fatal aircraft accidents (Laukkala et al., 2018). These accidents may be due to unsafe acts associated with generalized cognitive impairment, unintended flashbacks or intrusive thoughts that impede the capacity to process information, the impact of coping strategies including self-medication, and/or the corresponding effects of PTSD including fatigue due to sleep disruption. The aviation system is vulnerable to deteriorations in cognitive function especially when there is an increase in cognitive demands, as occurs during emergencies or during higher-risk or non-standard maneuvers.

Managing increases in cognitive demands successfully depends on the efficiency with which information is processed. For example, in the absence of experience, novices need to invest significant short-term memory resources to interpret and reason through options that might be available in response to a deteriorating situation (Tolvanen et al., 2022). This is due to the need to draw related information from long-term memory to make sense of the information available. The consequence is a slow, effortful, and often error-prone process, as evident in the outcomes associated with ZK-SUN.

By contrast, intermediate and expert processing tends to be recognition-driven, enabling rapid sensemaking in response to changes in the operational environment (Bitan et al., 2023). Encounters with environmental cues trigger preexisting associations in long-term memory, patterns of which enable the interpretation of complex scenes quickly and accurately. The activation of preexisting associations from long-term memory obviates the requirement to process large volumes of information in short-term memory, thereby reducing the likelihood that excessive demands will result in critical information being overlooked or discarded (Wiggins, 2021).

In addition to the demands on short-term memory, the challenge associated with both anxiety disorders and PTSD are the demands that are imposed on attentional resources. Depending on the severity of the symptoms, they can distract operators from critical cues. At a theoretical level, anxiety and the preoccupation that arises from the symptoms tend to consume short-term memory to a point where operators reach overload and new information, however relevant, is no longer identified nor processed (Driskell et al., 2022).

As in other high-performance occupations, higher levels of anxiety can result in lower attentional control that impedes cognitive function and the capacity for situational awareness (Allsop & Gray, 2014). Situational awareness is a process that involves the identification of changes in the system state, the comprehension of any changes, and the projection of the future state of the system (Endsley, 2020). This enables an operator to effect inputs that ensure the management of the system within safe boundaries. For example, a pilot on an approach to landing might identify changes in the wind direction and speed as a portent of windshear, thereby executing a go-around or maintaining a readiness to execute an immediate response, should the aircraft experience a loss of performance.

A lack of situational awareness, likely due to extreme anxiety, was evident in the loss of US-Bangla Airlines Flight 211 at Kathmandu, Nepal, on March 12, 2018. The aircraft was undertaking a scheduled flight between Dhaka, Bangladesh, and Kathmandu, and the pilots were expecting to enter a holding pattern as was typical at Kathmandu due to the single-runway operations and the limitations that this imposed on the frequency of departures and arrivals (Accident Investigation Commission, 2019).

As the aircraft was approaching the holding point, the flight was cleared for an approach to Runway 02. However, the flight management system had been configured for a holding pattern consistent with the pilots' expectations. As the aircraft reached the holding point, the aircraft turned to the left to enter the holding pattern. The captain recognized that the aircraft was turning off course and turned the heading selector to intercept the approach path. This disengaged the flight management system, and the aircraft was under manual control.

Manual control of the approach imposed a higher-than-normal cognitive load on the pilots, and the captain became distracted as he tried to negotiate the approach to Runway 02. A number of audible alerts became activated, warning of an excessive sink rate and the proximity to terrain. Unbeknown to the pilots, the aircraft had, by this time, passed the runway and the air traffic controller clarified whether the pilots intended to land on the reciprocal Runway 20.

With the aircraft flying in a northeasterly direction, the first officer spotted the threshold of Runway 20, reporting the observation to the captain, who made a sharp right-turn, presumably attempting to reposition the aircraft for an approach. The result was an erratic overflight of the runway and terminal area at approximately 450 ft, after which the aircraft touched down approximately 5,600 ft along the runway at an angle of 190°, skidding off the runway and crashing through a fence. A total of 51 passengers and crew perished in the crash (Accident Investigation Commission, 2019).

The analysis of the cockpit voice recorder revealed that the captain was experiencing extreme levels of anxiety over an extended period that had impacted his sleep the night before the flight. Further, much of the conversation during the final stages of the flight was dominated by the captain, who recounted a distressing interaction with a trainee colleague and rumors concerning their relationship. The level of anxiety was so extreme that the captain was heard to become emotional during the flight, acting as a distracting stimulus that led to a lack of preparation for the approach, together with an apparent unwillingness to execute a missed approach and return to the initial approach point. The combination of extreme anxiety and the unexpected change in the nature of the approach most likely impeded the captain's cognitive functioning to a point where he became fixated on achieving the outcome of landing the aircraft.

Trauma-Induced Depression

For pilots and other aviation personnel, involvement in aircraft accidents and incidents may also be associated with the onset of depressive episodes. Often occurring alongside anxiety, depression is considered a clinical condition when a person experiences persistent feelings of sadness or hopelessness, a loss of interest in everyday activities, feelings of worthlessness, and recurrent thoughts of death (Maurer et al., 2018). In extreme cases, clinical depression may be evident in suicidal thoughts or attempted suicide.

In response to incidents and accidents, depression may be associated with guilt in having survived while others perished, or self-blame in either failing to recover from a deteriorating situation and/or committing an unsafe act that was associated with a system failure (DeHoff & Cusick, 2018). In the operational context, it may be associated with unexplained absences from duty or an apparent lack of engagement while on duty (Johnston et al., 2019). These demands can impose constraints on the operational system, reducing the margin of error and increasing the likelihood of system failures.

During depressive episodes, deteriorations in cognitive functioning tend to be most evident in episodic memory, processing speed, and executive function (McDermott & Ebmeier, 2009). In the aviation context, this is likely to be evident in relatively slower responses to changes that may occur in the operational environment, leading to errors in timing, consistent with what might be evident when pilots are fatigued. Importantly, depression appears not to be associated with deteriorations in semantic or visuospatial memory, suggesting that memory associated with systems and system operation, together with the interpretation of previously acquired patterns of features, may remain unaffected, particularly among more experienced pilots (McDermott & Ebmeier, 2009).

Of greatest concern for pilots experiencing depression is the incidence of suicidal thoughts and the associated actions that might lead to suicide. Approximately 13.5 % of airlines pilots meet the threshold for a diagnosis of a depressive disorder, of whom approximately 4 % report suicidal thoughts (Wu et al., 2016). However, among pilots, there is generally a reluctance to engage with mental health professionals or to report declines in mental health. This appears to be due to both the perceived negative impact on current and future employment, and an implicit culture that advocates perseverance in response to adversity (Bor et al., 2002).

For people who experience PTSD, approximately 50 % will also be diagnosed with a depressive disorder (Flory & Yehuda, 2022). Although this rate of comorbidity has yet to be established among pilots involved in aircraft incidents or accidents, comorbidity is evident among passengers, with 47 % of survivors of a Boeing 737 crash near Amsterdam reporting symptoms of PTSD and 35 % reporting symptoms of depression up to 9 months following the event (Gouweloos et al., 2016).

Comorbid PTSD and depression tend to be associated with greater impairment than either disorder in isolation and are less amenable to treatment (Rapaport, 2001). Therefore, the potential impact on aviation operations is likely to be significant, with support likely to be required over an extended period. On a pilot's return to duty, system defenses may need to be reconsidered, including the requirement for additional oversight, particularly during episodes that have the potential to trigger flashbacks.

While suicidal risk among pilots is a critical concern associated with undiagnosed or untreated depressive disorders, it also has an insidious impact on pilot performance. For example, an agricultural pilot in New Zealand who witnessed his colleague collide with terrain following a wire strike during an agricultural operation reported feeling "alone and lost ... useless and unneeded" in the months following the accident (Blake, 2021/2022). After a series of significant in-flight events, he experienced a panic attack during flight and an overwhelming emotional response that provided the catalyst to withdraw from flying operations and seek support from a psychologist.

In addition to the direct impact of depression, performance can be impacted by efforts to self-medicate, including the consumption of alcohol and illegal drugs. While alcohol addiction is often a precursor to the incidence of depression in adults, the consumption of alcohol may increase following a traumatic event in an effort to cope with the symptoms (Boden

& Fergusson, 2011). However, the use of alcohol and other drugs, including benzodiazepines (e.g., Valium), as a coping mechanism is problematic over the longer term since it can strengthen the association with depressive symptoms (Sullivan et al., 2005), leading to secondary issues, including addiction.

Among a sample of working pilots, approximately 16.2 % who consumed more than one alcoholic drink per day met the threshold for depression (Wu et al., 2016). While it is difficult to infer causality, this suggests that, in addition to the depressive symptoms that may arise following a traumatic incident or accident, pilots and their employers need to be cognizant of the potential impact of self-medication as a coping strategy. This includes the consumption of alcohol that may mask symptoms but nevertheless, impact cognitive functioning.

Evidence-based options that are available for the treatment of depression include antidepressant medication such as selective serotonin reuptake inhibitors (SSRIs; e.g., Sertraline and Citalopram). While individual differences are evident in the effectiveness of these medications, they tend to be most effective when administered in combination with psychological treatments such as cognitive behavior therapy (CBT; Pigott et al., 2010).

In the context of cognitive functioning, antidepressants do not appear to be associated with significant deficits in pilot performance. For example, in a case-controlled comparison among pilots who had been prescribed antidepressants in Australia, there were no significant differences in accident involvement over a 10-year period (Ross et al., 2007). Similarly, the administration of the antidepressant Medifoxamine to pilots over a 3-day period did not impact psychomotor performance, including response latency (Poirier & Vieillefond, 1986).

Managing the Impact of Accident/Incident Involvement on Cognitive Function

Despite the aviation industry leading improvements in industrial safety and reliability, incidents and accidents occur from time to time. Therefore, there is a need to anticipate the possibility of occurrences and develop and implement strategies that enable the successful management of psychological outcomes for pilots and others who might be involved in traumatic events. This combination of strategies can be implemented proactively and/or in response to an occurrence to prevent and/or remediate deteriorations in cognitive functioning.

Proactively, pilots need to be prepared psychologically for situations where they may be involved in traumatic occurrences. These may range from the death of a passenger and passenger aggression to unstabilized approaches and collisions on the tarmac or with terrain. Developing the resilience necessary to cope effectively with these occurrences is necessary to optimize cognitive functioning.

Resilience as an outcome is defined as the maintenance or quick recovery of mental health during and/or after exposure to stressors (Kalisch et al., 2017). While measures of emotional distress and mental ill-health post-trauma are most frequently used to determine resilience, other indicators of resilience, such as job performance and cognitive functioning, are also important (e.g., Gucciardi et al., 2018), particularly in the occupational setting. The transactional model of stress and coping (Lazarus & Folkman, 1987) highlights the importance of the primary and secondary event appraisal processes in influencing the initial stress response.

During the initial stage of appraisal, individuals evaluate the significance of the situation or event as either irrelevant, positive, or threatening with the potential for harm or loss. The secondary appraisal process occurs if the event is evaluated as threatening and, in this stage, the individual evaluates whether one has the resources available to satisfy or exceed the demands imposed by that situation or task. However, where resources are perceived as sufficient to cope with the demands, the stressor is more likely to be viewed as manageable. If perceived coping resources are lacking, the stressor may be viewed as overwhelming, prompting the individual to experience distress (Folkman et al., 1986).

In advance of a task, appraisals of situations depend on perceptions of individual capability against the anticipated demands. These appraisals are often associated with performance even among operators with similar levels of experience and objective assessments of capability. For example, pilots who perceive demanding simulated scenarios as threatening tend to underperform when compared with pilots who perceive the same scenario as a challenge (Vine et al., 2014). This appears to be partly attributable to self-efficacy. In novices learning to land a flight simulator, greater general self-efficacy is associated with greater skill acquisition during high-demand training scenarios, but not during low-demand scenarios (Crane, Brabazon et al., 2017).

Where a pilot experiences a loss of self-efficacy due to a traumatic occurrence, increases in cognitive demand during subsequent aircraft operations are likely to be associated with distress. Previous work highlights the loss of perceived coping efficacy as a consequence of traumatic events and its role as a mediator in the relationship between the experience of a potentially traumatic event and posttraumatic recovery (Benight & Bandura, 2004). Given that the conditions of potentially traumatic events can often overwhelm coping capabilities, there is the potential for such events to erode an individual's belief in their ability to exercise agency and control the stressors in their environment. Longitudinal research with Israeli soldiers demonstrates that those experiencing battlefield trauma had a significantly diminished sense of efficacy to manage combat situations (Solomon et al., 1991). Thus, deteriorations in efficacy may relate to coping efficacy and to occupational-based efficacy (e.g., combat efficacy) with specific effects on occupational functioning.

This sense of lowered self-efficacy whether specific to coping or a work-based task may create distress as one evaluates situations to be beyond one's coping capacity. During a task, distress draws attentional resources and thereby impedes cognitive functioning, including short-term memory (Eysenck et al., 2007). By contrast, positive affect appears to be associated with improvements in cognitive functioning during problem-solving (Crane, Brouwers et al., 2017). Therefore, developing the psychological resources of pilots in advance of an occurrence is likely to provide a buffer against deteriorations in cognitive functioning, should a traumatic occurrence occur.

Ahead of potentially traumatic events, some organizations have focused on the development of coping mechanisms and psychological resources among employees. Resilience training interventions have served as a method to reduce psychological vulnerabilities and promote the well-being of personnel. Earlier research illustrates that implementing resilience training can enhance results among first responders, including police and military personnel (e.g., Adler et al., 2015; Arnetz et al., 2013). Such training methods typically involve the direct training of cognitive and behavioral coping skills, sometimes in simulated stressor scenarios, to support the broadening of coping strategies.

More recent resilience programs focus on encouraging two mechanisms thought to underpin the development of resilience across the life course: *coping self-reflection* and *coping self-*

insight. Self-reflective training strategies use the everyday workplace stressors as a means to encourage reflection and self-insight. Referred to as a metacognitive skill, Crane, Boga, et al. (2019) consider the development of these capacities as key to the refinement and broadening of one's capacities for resilience (e.g., coping strategies, coping resources, resilient self-belief) in a way that is personalized and contextualized.

Through the use of coping self-reflection, participants develop greater self-insight into several aspects of their coping process including triggers for stress, the effects of stress on performance and decision-making, and coping strategies that can be applied (Crane & Searle, 2016). Importantly, this process provides the foundation for development through a self-reflective assessment of more and less successful responses that can be employed to change behavior and strengthen responses to future events.

Self-reflective approaches to resilience training are based on the systematic self-reflection model of resilience strengthening (Crane, Searle et al., 2019). It is founded on the principle that exposure to moderate, everyday stressors provides the opportunity to enhance capacities for resilience, such as coping strategies and coping self-efficacy. However, stressors alone do not necessarily lead to improvements in the capacity for resilience. Rather, stressor experiences need to be scaffolded in reflective practices that unpack the coping processes to draw out coping self-insights (Falon et al., 2022). In organizations such as airlines, this process can occur through guided self-reflection where exposure to ambient or simulated stressors provides an opportunity for reflection on one's coping process to enhance the refinement and broadening of one's capacities for resilience, ensuring that the impact of downstream exposure to traumatic occurrences is minimized to the greatest extent possible.

In addition to the development of capacities for resilience, pilots need to ensure that they maintain a level of skilled performance that maximizes the residual resources available to respond effectively to changes in cognitive demands that occur during aircraft operations. Where pilots have been involved in potential traumatic events, it must account for the possibility that intrusive thoughts and distress may impact cognitive functioning, possibly during high-demand operational tasks. This requires a considered and comprehensive approach involving systematic assessment and, where necessary, appropriate remediation.

For pilots who are operating advanced technology aircraft, the critical cognitive challenge lies in making sense of the information derived from the aircraft. Under normal conditions, this process of sensemaking or situational assessment is relatively routine. However, in non-normal, unexpected situations, information may be drawn from a range of sources, none of which explicitly describes the problematic event (Rankin et al., 2016). In this case, the pattern of features needs to be interpreted accurately and often within a short period of time to enable an appropriate and timely response.

For operators of advanced technology systems, the capacity for situational assessment is not immediately evident. Advanced technology is both increasingly capable and reliable, rendering aspects of human cognitive function unnecessary, other than to oversee and assess the accuracy of automated responses. However, the challenge in relying too heavily on advanced technology is the concomitant deterioration in skilled performance among human operators. Unless monitored, this deterioration in capability compounds as a potential latent condition that is only evident in those situations where rapid and accurate situational assessment is necessary to resolve a situation.

Skilled situation assessment draws on patterns in memory that constituted cues (Wiggins, 2017). Cues are relationships that have been established between environmental features and events or objects. For example, a pattern of green lights on an aircraft cockpit panel (feature) might be associated with, and therefore signify, the safe extension of the aircraft undercarriage (event). Over frequent associations, this relationship is strengthened, and the pattern of green lights acquires status as a cue that activates the association automatically from long-term memory.

A large and precise repertoire of cue-based associations in memory is characteristic of expertise and facilitates rapid and accurate responses to otherwise demanding tasks (Loveday et al., 2014). Importantly, it reduces the demands on short-term memory, maximizing the residual resources available. The availability of residual resources is critical should pilots experience intrusive, distressful thoughts and/or where unanticipated changes in the system state trigger a startle response (Martin et al., 2015).

The challenge in assessing the capacity for situational assessment lies in the idiosyncratic nature of the cue-based associations on which the capability depends. Differences in both cognitive processing and exposure to task-related experiences lead to the differences in the types of associations that are acquired and retained in memory. However, despite these differences, performance among skilled operators remains remarkably similar (Morrison et al., 2013).

Using performance outcomes as a marker, it is possible to infer the application of cues (McCormack et al., 2014). For example, the application of a cue-based association might be inferred where a response to a task-related hazard is both rapid and accurate, relevant cues are distinguished from less relevant cues in problem-solving, relevant cues are prioritized in problem orientation, and differences in the strength of association between features and events are quickly established. These capabilities comprise the R-A-P-I-D approach to the assessment of cue utilization (Wiggins, 2021).

Assessments of cue utilization based on the RAPID approach have differentiated performance across a wide range of domains, including pathology (Carrigan et al., 2022), electricity control (Sturman et al., 2020), software engineering (Loveday et al., 2014), and general aviation (Wiggins et al., 2014). Improvements in cue utilization following task-related exposure are evident in audiology (Watkinson et al., 2018) and in the operation of remote-piloted vehicles (RPV; Renshaw & Wiggins, 2020). In combination, the results suggest that the approach demonstrates validity and reliability across domains where situational assessment is a critical determinant of operational performance.

Within an operational context, the assessment of cue utilization should occur regularly to identify changes in performance. The direction and rate of change provides a marker for further investigation and the impetus for remediation as necessary. However, in ensuring the capacity for timely and accurate situational assessment, the demands on short-term memory are minimized, enabling the allocation of residual resources as necessary. For pilots who have been exposed to traumatic occurrences and where symptoms continue to present a risk, maximizing the residual resources available improves the capacity to maintain task performance.

Although the combination of resilience strengthening and assessments of cue utilization offers a proactive approach in the event of exposure to traumatic occurrences, it also provides a framework in responding to situations where pilots may have been exposed to trauma. For example, a strong tenant of critical incident stress debriefing (CISD) involves a teaching phase where reactions and responses to trauma can be reframed as a basis for the development of coping strategies (Tuckey & Scott, 2014). This teaching phase succeeds a process that begins with an initial orientation to psychological debriefing, a description of the event and significant thoughts concerning the event, and an exploration of the reactions and symptoms that have emerged following the event (Chung, 2016). These techniques are intended to prevent deteriorations in mental health that might be associated with involvement in a traumatic occurrence (Mitchell & Leonhardt, 2010).

Despite the prevalence of CISD in response to trauma, the effectiveness in preventing symptoms of PTSD has been subject to debate (Tamrakar et al., 2019). While there is an amelioration of symptoms amongst some individuals (e.g., Tuckey & Scott, 2014), meta-analyses suggests that psychological debriefing following trauma fails to prevent the symptoms of PTSD and may, in some cases, exacerbate symptoms (Kenardy, 2000; Rose et al., 2003). However, this approach to CISD tends to overlook the role of workplace culture and organizational processes that might be engaged as part of a broader response to the management of critical incidents.

There is an increasing body of research suggesting that, rather than debriefing in isolation, a broader response is necessary that assists with the management of critical incidents at an organizational level and over the longer term. For example, Mitchell (2016) advocates a strategic response to the management of critical incidents involving a range of support services that are provided in addition to psychological debriefing. Referred to as critical incident stress management (CISM), services include family support, referrals, peer support, and postincident education.

Once any posttraumatic symptoms are managed successfully, it may be necessary to reevaluate the cognitive functioning of pilots prior to their return to line operations. In cases where pilots may have taken time away from work, assessments of cue utilization can provide a preliminary assessment of performance prior to simulator checks. The outcomes can be used to target areas of concern, ensuring that pilots have the opportunity to practice and thereby re-establish the cue-based associations that may have deteriorated.

Conclusion

Exposure to potentially traumatic events is a risk among pilots given the nature of the environment within which they operate. Psychological responses to traumatic events may include anxiety disorders, PTSD, and/or depression. Each has the potential to impact cognitive functioning through intrusive thoughts, distress, fixation, and/or disengagement. From an operational perspective, the outcomes include delayed or inappropriate responses to changes in the system state.

At a cognitive level, emotional responses directly impact short-term memory and the capacity to process information. This is particularly challenging during unanticipated changes to the system state that impose demands on cognitive resources. The consumption of resources in managing emotional responses associated with traumatic events reduces the residual resources available to manage operational demands, increasing the probability of a system failure.

Preempting exposure to traumatic events requires a systematic approach as occurs in the management of system safety. This includes resilience strengthening where pilots learn to appraise stressors as challenges, identify triggers, and manage emotional responses, reducing the demands on cognitive resources. It also includes periodic assessments of cue utilization to ensure that the operational performance is optimal, maximizing the residual cognitive resources available should changes in the system state impose demands on cognitive processing.

In the event of exposure to a traumatic experience, responses need to be flexible and meet the needs of individual pilots. These responses should include opportunities for debriefing, peer support, and education that encourages the development of coping strategies and the reappraisal of traumatic experiences. Re-engaging with line operations should involve an assessment of cue utilization to identify any areas for development that can be remediated through simulator training, ensuring that the demands on cognitive resources are minimized should symptoms of anxiety and posttraumatic stress emerge during flight operations.

References

Accident Investigation Commission. (2019). *The accident investigation of US Bangla Airlines Bombardier (UBG-211) DHC-8-402 S2-AGU at Tribhuvan International Airport, Kathmandu, Nepal on 12 March, 2018.* https://asn.flightsafety.org/reports/2018/20180312_DH8D_S2-AGU.pdf

Adler, A.B., Bliese, P.D., Pickering, M.A., Hammermeister, J., Williams, J., Harada, C., Csoka, L., Holiday, B., & Ohlson, C. (2015). Mental skills training with basic combat training soldiers: A group randomized trial. *Journal of Applied Psychology, 100,* 1752–1764. https://doi.org/10.1037/apl0000021

Allsop, J., & Gray, R. (2014). Flying under pressure: Effects of anxiety on attention and gaze behavior in aviation. *Journal of Applied Research in Memory and Cognition, 3*(2), 63–71. https://doi.org/10.1016/j.jarmac.2014.04.010

Arnetz, B.B., Arble, E., Backman, L., Lynch, A., & Lublin, A. (2013). Assessment of a prevention program for work-related stress among urban police officers. *International Archives of Occupational and Environmental Health, 86*(1), 79–88. https://doi.org/10.1007/s00420-012-0748-6

Baddeley, A. (2007). *Working memory, thought, and action.* Oxford University Press. https://doi.org/10.1093/acprof:oso/9780198528012.001.0001

Benight, C.C., & Bandura, A. (2004). Social cognitive theory of posttraumatic recovery: The role of perceived self-efficacy. *Behaviour Research and Therapy, 42*(10), 1129–1148. https://doi.org/10.1016/j.brat.2003.08.008

Bitan, Y., Lilach-Gueta, S., & Parush, A. (2023). Unmasking expert decisions: Clinicians decision making during a pandemic outbreak. *International Journal of Healthcare Management, 16*(2), 268–276. https://doi.org/10.1080/20479700.2022.2097763

Blake, P. (2021/2022, Summer). To hell and back. *Vector,* 13–16.

Boden, J.M., & Fergusson, D.M. (2011). Alcohol and depression. *Addiction, 106*(5), 906–914. https://doi.org/10.1111/j.1360-0443.2010.03351.x

Bor, R., Field, G., & Scragg, P. (2002). The mental health of pilots: An overview. *Counselling Psychology Quarterly, 15*(3), 239–256. https://doi.org/10.1080/09515070210143471

Carrigan, A.J., Charlton, A., Foucar, E., Wiggins, M.W., Georgiou, A., Palmeri, T.J., & Curby, K.M. (2022). The role of cue-based strategies in skilled diagnosis among pathologists. *Human Factors, 64*(7), 1154–1167. https://doi.org/10.1177/0018720821990160

Chauvel, G., Maquestiaux, F., Ruthruff, E., Didierjean, A., & Hartley, A.A. (2013). Novice motor performance: Better not to verbalize. *Psychonomic Bulletin & Review, 20,* 177–183. https://doi.org/10.3758/s13423-012-0331-x

Chung, M.C. (2016). Posttraumatic stress reactions following aircraft disasters. In R. Bor & T. Hubbard (Eds.), *Aviation Mental Health* (pp. 83–104). Routledge.

Crane, M.F., Boga, D., Karin, E., Gucciardi, D.F., Rapport, F., Callen, J., & Sinclair, L. (2019). Strengthening resilience in military officer cadets: A group-randomized controlled trial of coping and emotion regulatory self-reflection training. *Journal of Consulting and Clinical Psychology, 87*(2), 125–140. https://doi.org/10.1037/ccp0000356

Crane, M.F., Brabazon, G., Gucciardi, D.F., Loveday, T., & Wiggins, M. (2017). General self-efficacy and psychological resilience promote skill acquisition rate under psychological pressure. *The Australasian Journal of Organisational Psychology, 10*, Article e3. https://doi.org/10.1017/orp.2017.3

Crane, M.F., Brouwers, S., Forrest, K., Tan, S., Loveday, T., Wiggins, M.W., Munday, C., & David, L. (2017). Positive affect is associated with reduced fixation in a realistic medical simulation. *Human Factors, 59*, 821–832. https://doi.org/10.1177/0018720817695191

Crane, M.F., & Searle, B.J. (2016). Building resilience through exposure to stressors: The effects of challenges versus hindrances. *Journal of Occupational Health Psychology, 21*(4), 468–479. https://doi.org/10.1037/a0040064

Crane, M.F., Searle, B.J., Kangas, M., & Nwiran, Y. (2019). How resilience is strengthened by exposure to stressors: The systematic self-reflection model of resilience strengthening. *Anxiety, Stress, & Coping, 32*, 1–17. https://doi.org/10.1080/10615806.2018.1506640

DeHoff, M.C., & Cusick, S.K. (2018). Mental health in commercial aviation-depression & anxiety of pilots. *International Journal of Aviation, Aeronautics, and Aerospace, 5*(5), Article 5. https://doi.org/10.58940/2374-6793.1287

DeMartini, J., Patel, G., & Fancher, T.L. (2019). Generalized anxiety disorder. *Annals of Internal Medicine, 170*(7), ITC49–ITC64. https://doi.org/10.7326/AITC201904020

Driskell, T., Salas, E., Burke, C.S., & Driskell, J.E. (2022). A lexical approach to assessing stress: Development and proof-of-concept. *Human Factors, 65*(6), 1105–1129. https://doi.org/10.1177/00187208211045167

Eaton, W.W., Bienvenu, O.J., & Miloyan, B. (2018). Specific phobias. *The Lancet Psychiatry, 5*(8), 678–686. https://doi.org/10.1016/S2215-0366(18)30169-X

Endsley, M.R. (2020). The divergence of objective and subjective situation awareness: A meta-analysis. *Journal of Cognitive Engineering and Decision Making, 14*(1), 34–53. https://doi.org/10.1177/1555343419874248

Esterman, M., Fortenbaugh, F.C., Pierce, M.E., Fonda, J.R., DeGutis, J., Milberg, W., & McGlinchey, R. (2019). Trauma-related psychiatric and behavioral conditions are uniquely associated with sustained attention dysfunction. *Neuropsychology, 33*(5), 711–724. https://doi.org/10.1037/neu0000525

Eysenck, M.W., Derakshan, N., Santos, R., & Calvo, M.G. (2007). Anxiety and cognitive performance: Attentional control theory. *Emotion, 7*, 336–353. https://doi.org/10.1037/1528-3542.7.2.336

Falon, S.L., Hoare, S., Kangas, M., & Crane, M.F. (2022). The coping insights evident through self-reflection on stressful military training events: Qualitative evidence from self-reflection journals. *Stress and Health, 38*(5), 902–918. https://doi.org/10.1002/smi.3141

Flory, J.D., & Yehuda, R. (2022). Comorbidity between post-traumatic stress disorder and major depressive disorder: Alternative explanations and treatment considerations. *Dialogues in Clinical Neuroscience, 17*(2), 141–150. https://doi.org/10.31887/DCNS.2015.17.2/jflory

Folkman, S., Lazarus, R.S., Gruen, R.J., & DeLongis, A. (1986). Appraisal, coping, health status, and psychological symptoms. *Journal of Personality and Social Psychology, 50*, 571–579. https://doi.org/10.1037/0022-3514.50.3.571

Friedman, M.J., Resick, P.A., Bryant, R.A., & Brewin, C.R. (2011). Considering PTSD for DSM-5. *Depression and Anxiety, 28*, 750–769. https://doi.org/10.1002/da.20767

Gouweloos, J., Postma, I.L., Te Brake, H., Sijbrandij, M., Kleber, R.J., & Goslings, J.C. (2016). The risk of PTSD and depression after an airplane crash and its potential association with physical injury: A longitudinal study. *Injury, 47*(1), 250–256. https://doi.org/10.1016/j.injury.2015.07.005

Grant, D.M., Beck, J.G., Marques, L., Palyo, S.A., & Clapp, J.D. (2008). The structure of distress following trauma: posttraumatic stress disorder, major depressive disorder, and generalized anxiety disorder. *Journal of Abnormal Psychology, 117*(3), 662–672. https://doi.org/10.1037/a0012591

Green, N., Gaydos, S., Ewan, H., & Nicol, E. (2019). Aviation psychiatry. In N. Green, S. Gaydos, E. Hutchison, & E. Nicol, (Eds.), *Handbook of aviation and space medicine* (pp. 377–382). CRC Press. https://doi.org/10.1201/9780429021657-64

Gucciardi, D., Crane, M., Ntoumanis, N., Parker, S., Thogersen-Ntoumani, C., Ducker, K. Peeling, P., Chapman, M.T., Quested, E., & Temby, P. (2018). The emergence of team resilience: A multilevel conceptual model of facilitating factors. *Journal of Occupational and Organizational Psychology, 91,* 729–768. https://doi.org/10.1111/joop.12237

Johnston, D.A., Harvey, S.B., Glozier, N., Calvo, R.A., Christensen, H., & Deady, M. (2019). The relationship between depression symptoms, absenteeism and presenteeism. *Journal of Affective Disorders, 256,* 536–540. https://doi.org/10.1016/j.jad.2019.06.041

Jonides, J., Lewis, R.L., Nee, D.E., Lustig, C.A., Berman, M.G., & Moore, K.S. (2008). The mind and brain of short-term memory. *Annual Review of Psychology, 59,* 193–224. https://doi.org/10.1146/annurev.psych.59.103006.093615

Kalisch, R., Baker, D., Basten, U., Boks, M., Bonanno, G., Brummelman, E., Chmitorz, A., Fernandez, G., Fiebach, C.J., Galatzer-Levy, I., Geuze, E., Groppa, S., Helmreich, I., Hendler, T., Hermans, E.J., Jovanovic, T., Kubiak, T., Lieb, K., ... Kleim, B. (2017). The resilience framework as a strategy to combat stress-related disorders. *Nature Human Behavior, 1*(11), 784–790.

Kenardy, J. (2000). The current status of psychological debriefing. *BMJ, 321*(7268), 1032–1033.

Koenen, K.C., Ratanatharathorn, A., Ng, L., McLaughlin, K.A., Bromet, E.J., Stein, D.J., Karam, E.G., Ruscio, A.M., Benjet, C., Scott, K., Atwoli, L., Petukhova, M., Lim, C.C.W., Aguilar-Gaxiola, S., Al-Hamzawi, A., Alonso, J., Bunting, B., Ciutan, M., de Girolamo, G., Degenhardt, L., Gureje, O., Haro, J.M., Huang, Y., Kawakami, N., Lee, S., Navarro-Mateu, F., Pennell, B-E., Piazza, M., Sampson, N., ten Have, M., Torres, Y., Viana, M.C., Williams, D., Xavier, M., & Kessler, R.C., & Kessler, R. (2017). Posttraumatic stress disorder in the world mental health surveys. *Psychological Medicine, 47*(13), 2260–2274.

Lambez, B., Agmon, G., Har-Shai Yahav, P., Rassovsky, Y., & Zion Golumbic, E. (2020). Paying attention to speech: The role of working memory capacity and professional experience. *Attention, Perception, & Psychophysics, 82,* 3594–3605. https://doi.org/10.3758/s13414-020-02091-2

Laukkala, T., Bor, R., Budowle, B., Navathe, P., Sajantila, A., Sainio, M., & Vuorio, A. (2018). Pilot posttraumatic stress disorder and fatal aviation accidents. *Aviation Psychology and Applied Human Factors, 8*(2), 93–99. https://doi.org/10.1027/2192-0923/a000144

Lapointe, M.L.B., Blanchette, I., Duclos, M., Langlois, F., Provencher, M.D., & Tremblay, S. (2013). Attentional bias, distractibility and short-term memory in anxiety. *Anxiety, Stress & Coping, 26*(3), 293–313. https://doi.org/10.1080/10615806.2012.687722

Lazarus, R.S., & Folkman, S. (1987). Transactional theory and research on emotions and coping. *European Journal of Personality, 1,* 141–169. https://doi.org/10.1002/per.2410010304

Loveday, T., Wiggins, M.W., & Searle, B.J. (2014). Cue utilization and broad indicators of workplace expertise. *Journal of Cognitive Engineering and Decision Making, 8*(1), 98–113. https://doi.org/10.1177/1555343413497019

Martin, W.L., Murray, P.S., Bates, P.R., & Lee, P.S. (2015). Fear-potentiated startle: A review from an aviation perspective. *The International Journal of Aviation Psychology, 25*(2), 97–107. https://doi.org/10.1080/10508414.2015.1128293

Maurer, D.M., Raymond, T.J., & Davis, B.N. (2018). Depression: Screening and diagnosis. *American Family Physician, 98*(8), 508–515.

McCormack, C., Wiggins, M.W., Loveday, T., & Festa, M. (2014). Expert and competent non-expert visual cues during simulated diagnosis in intensive care. *Frontiers in Psychology, 5,* Article 949. https://doi.org/10.3389/fpsyg.2014.00949

McDermott, L.M., & Ebmeier, K.P. (2009). A meta-analysis of depression severity and cognitive function. *Journal of Affective Disorders, 119*(1–3), 1–8. https://doi.org/10.1016/j.jad.2009.04.022

McDowd, J.M. (2007). An overview of attention: Behavior and brain. *Journal of Neurologic Physical Therapy, 31*(3), 98–103. https://doi.org/10.1097/NPT.0b013e31814d7874

Mitchell, J.T. (2016). Critical incident stress management in aviation: A strategic approach. In J. Leonhardt & J. Vogt (Eds.), *Critical incident stress management in aviation* (pp. 13–42). Routledge.

Mitchell, J., & Leonhardt, J. (2010). Critical incident stress management (CISM): An effective peer support program for aviation industries. *International Journal of Applied Aviation Studies, 10*(1), 97–116.

Morris, C.H., & Leung, Y.K. (2006). Pilot mental workload: How well do pilots really perform? *Ergonomics, 49*(15), 1581–1596. https://doi.org/10.1080/00140130600857987

Morrison, B.W., Wiggins, M.W., Bond, N.W., & Tyler, M.D. (2013). Measuring relative cue strength as a means of validating an inventory of expert offender profiling cues. *Journal of Cognitive Engineering and Decision Making, 7*(2), 211–226. https://doi.org/10.1177/1555343412459192
Morse, J.S., & Bor, R. (2016). Psychiatric disorders and syndromes among pilots. In R. Bor & T. Hubbard (Eds.), *Aviation mental health* (pp. 107–125). Routledge.
Norris, F.H., & Sloane, L.B. (2007). The epidemiology of trauma and PTSD. In M.J. Friedman, P.P. Schnurr, & T.M. Keane (Eds.), *Handbook of PTSD: Science and practice* (pp. 78–98). Guildford Press.
O'Hare, D., Wiggins, M., Batt, R., & Morrison, D. (1994). Cognitive failure analysis for aircraft accident investigation. *Ergonomics, 37*(11), 1855–1869. https://doi.org/10.1080/00140139408964954
Pashler, H.E. (1998). *The psychology of attention.* MIT Press.
Pigott, H.E., Leventhal, A.M., Alter, G.S., & Boren, J.J. (2010). Efficacy and effectiveness of antidepressants: Current status of research. *Psychotherapy and Psychosomatics, 79*(5), 267–279. https://doi.org/10.1159/000318293
Poirier, J.L., & Vieillefond, H. (1986). Etude des effets de Clédial® sur la performance psychomotrice [Study of the effects of Clédial® on psychomotor performance]. *Psychologie Médicale, 18*, 1925–1930.
Qureshi, S.U., Long, M.E., Bradshaw, M.R., Pyne, J.M., Magruder, K.M., Kimbrell, T., Hydson, T.J., Jawaid, A., Schulz, P.E., & Kunik, M.E. (2011). Does PTSD impair cognition beyond the effect of trauma? *The Journal of Neuropsychiatry and Clinical Neurosciences, 23*(1), 16–28. https://doi.org/10.1176/appi.neuropsych.23.1.16
Rankin, A., Woltjer, R., & Field, J. (2016). Sensemaking following surprise in the cockpit – a re-framing problem. *Cognition, Technology & Work, 18*, 623–642. https://doi.org/10.1007/s10111-016-0390-2
Rapaport, M.H. (2001). Prevalence, recognition, and treatment of comorbid depression and anxiety. *Journal of Clinical Psychiatry, 62*(24), 6–10.
Renshaw, P.F., & Wiggins, M.W. (2020). The sensitivity of Cue utilization when learning to operate a visual line of sight multi-rotor remotely piloted aircraft. *International Journal of Industrial Ergonomics, 77*, Article 102953. https://doi.org/10.1016/j.ergon.2020.102953
Rose, S., Bisson, J., & Wessely, S. (2003). A systematic review of single-session psychological interventions ('debriefing') following trauma. *Psychotherapy and Psychosomatics, 72*(4), 176–184. https://doi.org/10.1159/000070781
Ross, J., Griffiths, K., Dear, K., Emonson, D., & Lambeth, L. (2007). Antidepressant use and safety in civil aviation: A case-control study of 10 years of Australian data. *Aviation, Space, and Environmental Medicine, 78*(8), 749–755.
Solomon, Z., Benbenishty, R., & Mikulincer, M. (1991). The contribution of wartime, pre-war, and post-war factors to self-efficacy: A longitudinal study of combat stress reaction. *Journal of Traumatic Stress, 4*(3), 345–361.
Stevens, C.A., Morris, M.B., Fisher, C.R., & Myers, C.W. (2022). Profiling cognitive workload in an unmanned vehicle control task with cognitive models and physiological metrics. *Military Psychology, 35*(6), 507–520. https://doi.org/10.1080/08995605.2022.2130673
Sturman, D., Wiggins, M.W., Auton, J.C., & Helton, W.S. (2020). Cue utilisation predicts control room operators' performance in a sustained visual search task. *Ergonomics, 63*(1), 48–60. https://doi.org/10.1080/00140139.2019.1680873
Sullivan, L.E., Fiellin, D.A., & O'Connor, P.G. (2005). The prevalence and impact of alcohol problems in major depression: A systematic review. *The American Journal of Medicine, 118*(4), 330–341. https://doi.org/10.1016/j.amjmed.2005.01.007
Tamrakar, T., Murphy, J., & Elklit, A. (2019). Was psychological debriefing dismissed too quickly? *Crisis, Stress, and Human Resilience, 1*(3), 146–155.
Tolvanen, O., Elomaa, A.P., Itkonen, M., Vrzakova, H., Bednarik, R., & Huotarinen, A. (2022). Eye-tracking indicators of workload in surgery: A systematic review. *Journal of Investigative Surgery, 35*(6), 1340–1349. https://doi.org/10.1080/08941939.2021.2025282
Transport Accident Investigation Commission. (1989). *Aircraft accident report: Beechcraft 95-A55 Baron ZK-SUN. 16 May 1989.*

Tuckey, M.R., & Scott, J.E. (2014). Group critical incident stress debriefing with emergency services personnel: A randomized controlled trial. *Anxiety, Stress & Coping*, *27*(1), 38–54.
Van der Kolk, B.A., McFarlane, A.C., & Weisaeth, L. (Eds.). (1996). *Traumatic stress: The effects of overwhelming experience on mind, body, and society*. Guilford Press.
Vidulich, M.A., Wickens, C.D., Tsang, P.S., & Flach, J.M. (2010). Information processing in aviation. In E. Salas & D. Maurino (Eds.), *Human factors in aviation* (pp. 175–215). Academic Press. https://doi.org/10.1016/B978-0-12-374518-7.00007-9
Vine, S.J., Uiga, L., Lavric, A., Moore, L.J., Tsaneva-Atanasova, K., & Wilson, M.R. (2014). Individual reactions to stress predict performance during a critical aviation incident. *Anxiety, Stress, and Coping, 28*, 467–477. https://doi.org/10.1080/10615806.2014.986722
Watkinson, J., Bristow, G., Auton, J., McMahon, C.M., & Wiggins, M.W. (2018). Postgraduate training in audiology improves clinicians' audiology-related cue utilisation. *International Journal of Audiology, 57*(9), 681–687. https://doi.org/10.1080/14992027.2018.1476782
Wickens, C. (2021). Attention: Theory, principles, models and applications. *International Journal of Human-Computer Interaction*, *37*, 403–417.
Wiggins, M.W., Azar, D., Hawken, J., Loveday, T., & Newman, D. (2014). Cue-utilisation typologies and pilots' pre-flight and in-flight weather decision-making. *Safety Science*, *65*, 118–124.
Wiggins, M.W. (2017). Cues in diagnostic reasoning. In M.W. Wiggins & T. Loveday (Eds.), *Diagnostic expertise in organizational environments* (pp. 15–26). CRC Press. https://doi.org/10.1201/9781315576947
Wiggins, M.W. (2021). A behaviour-based approach to the assessment of cue utilisation: Implications for situation assessment and performance. *Theoretical Issues in Ergonomics Science, 22*(1), 46–62. https://doi.org/10.1080/1463922X.2020.1758828
Wu, A.C., Donnelly-McLay, D., Weisskopf, M.G., McNeely, E., Betancourt, T.S., & Allen, J.G. (2016). Airplane pilot mental health and suicidal thoughts: A cross-sectional descriptive study via anonymous web-based survey. *Environmental Health, 15*(1), 1–12. https://doi.org/10.1186/s12940-016-0200-6

Chapter 22
Advancing Aerospace Medicine

Integrating Data-Driven Approaches for Flight Safety and Pilot Well-Being

Ann Norris, Valerie Skaggs, and Thomas Chidester

Introduction: Importance of Data-Driven Policy-Making in Aerospace Medicine

The purpose of aerospace medicine is the prevention or mitigation of suddenly (i.e., loss of consciousness, death) or subtly (i.e., reduced cognitive function) incapacitating events in flight and the mitigation of any condition producing disability that could impact pilot performance. Aerospace medicine works to ensure adequate capacity for extraordinary demands in flight, such as complex problem-solving or physical demands in the cockpit. In a perfect world, clinical and operational practice would follow an understanding of the incidence and prevalence of medical conditions and their consequent symptoms or events, sequela, and disability. We would know, for a given condition, the probability and time course of spontaneous incapacitation, accumulation of sequela, and development of disability and we would have a continuum of safety criteria for the range of flight operations in which a pilot proposes to engage.

Thus, for example, to understand the population probability of an extreme incapacitation such as cardiac arrest, we would assess a pilot's relative risk using predictors and measures of cardiac disease, and given the onset of a cardiovascular condition, the pilot's likelihood within a given time of an incapacitating incident. We would follow the pilot's accumulation of disease burden, and we would have probabilistic criteria to decide when the risks have grown too high for different types of flight operations.

Former Federal Air Surgeon Michael Berry (2017) argued that aerospace medicine has had a profound impact on flight safety – medical causes of accidents have declined from the most frequent to extremely rare causal factors. However, he also identified that while aerospace safety standards are often based on expert opinion, many policy decisions have been shaped by legislative definitions, including age limitations, the creation of classes that do and do not require medical certificates, the definition of specific disqualifying conditions, and the authorization of special issuances provided in legislation, and often individual case events ultimately have driven policy decisions. We are now in an era of standards rooted in best practices, constrained by legislative, executive, and judicial mediation of competing interests, but also responsive to population statistics. We have the tools needed to start analyzing unmitigated medical risk that was previously impossible due to a lack of data required to predict individual variability in physiological responses to flight conditions.

In that environment, how do we approach a more perfect aerospace medicine world? What is the acceptable level of safety for each type of flight operation for which a pilot would seek certification? What conditions produce aeromedical risks? What are the probabilities of incapacitation and disability over time after diagnosis?

Believing "perfection" develops from continuous improvement and that solutions will develop iteratively, we propose a method for moving forward by:

- selecting conditions aerospace medical certification organizations find challenging to certify and mitigate;
- conducting a literature review to understand the state of clinical practice;
- examining certification datasets for conformance to state of practice and population statistics;
- recommending standards and practices and examining their impact on the certificated population; and
- reporting to policy makers.

We present four conditions with neuropsychological implications where the US Federal Aviation Administration (FAA) Office of Aerospace Medicine has applied this approach to advance policy:

- Use of selective serotonin reuptake inhibitors (SSRIs)
- Multiple sclerosis (MS)
- Parkinson's disease (PD)
- Human immunodeficiency virus (HIV) infection

The purpose of this chapter is to explore the role of data in supporting policy decisions for these specific conditions.

Understanding Challenges of Cognitive Research in Aerospace Medicine

The Office of Aerospace Medicine (AAM) houses a medical certification database that is used to process and issue all medical certifications for US civilian pilots. Although it is used for operational purposes, it is not designed for research. This limitation, combined with the challenge of collecting ongoing surveillance data, has led to a lack of research on pilots with certain conditions, for example, pilots taking SSRIs or undergoing cognitive testing.

An aviation medical examiner (AME) is an FAA-designated physician who conducts medical examinations for pilots to issue FAA medical certificates. These certificates are categorized into three classes, each with slightly different requirements (Medical Standards and Certification, 1996). The certificate's validity duration varies based on the class and the pilot's age. The length of certificate validity is also impacted by aviators who do not meet the standards required under 14 CFR 67. Instead, they are cleared to fly for a specified period where the pilot's duties, determined by the federal air surgeon (FAS), can be performed without endangering public safety during the enforcement period (Special Issuance of Medical Certificates, 1996). This type of temporary authorization is defined as a *special issuance* (SI).

To keep the AAM policies in line with current medical care standards and assess policy effectiveness, we reviewed four conditions that all require a special issuance to fly: mental health conditions requiring SSRIs, multiple sclerosis (MS), Parkinson's disease (PD), and

HIV infection. For these conditions, AAM uses cognitive testing as a way to gauge a pilot's cognitive health over time. CogScreen testing (LRPV score = logistic regression probability value), developed by Kay (2013a), is highly sensitive to subtle cognitive changes. It focuses on attention, concentration, information processing, immediate memory span, and working memory. The test produces a probability of brain dysfunction score ranging from 0 to 1. A higher LRPV score indicates a higher likelihood of brain dysfunction. CogScreen – Aeromedical Edition (CogScreen-AE), tailored for pilots, is available with norms and samples of each of the cognitive domains of pilot concern (Kay, 2013a). AAM has made adjustments and explored specific thresholds and score changes between tests that trigger the need for comprehensive neuropsychological assessments. However, these thresholds have not been uniformly applied across all conditions in the past.

The following three sections focus on methodology and results we established to enhance current AAM policy on these four areas in the pilot population.

Data-Driven Policy-Making: SSRI Use in Pilots

FAA allows pilots diagnosed with certain mental health conditions, including depression, to fly while using SSRIs. This policy was based on expert opinion and literature review and became effective in 2010 (DeVoll, 2013). After 13 years of experience, the question arose if the requirements for pilots to remain on an SSRI could be reduced. The main questions to answer included: (1) Is there an apparent association between use of SSRIs and cognitive decline in pilots?; and (2) Is there an optimal testing interval to lessen the frequency of when a neurocognitive evaluation would be required of a pilot? Using a specific population of pilots on SSRIs in the Aerospace Medicine dataset, the goal of this analysis (Norris et al., 2022) was to collect data and analyze neurocognitive testing to answer these two questions.

Method

This research involved medically certificated pilots who had a psychiatric diagnosis and were previously certified on an allowable SSRI medication. They applied for a new medical certificate between October 2019 and January 2022 (Norris et al., 2022). Our main focus was to check for any cognitive decline in pilots, and thus we looked for suspicious cases based on abnormal values on a pilot's CogScreen. We defined an abnormal case as (1) having an LRPV score higher than 0.8 on any CogScreen; (2) having total base and Taylor T scores of <40 on three or more categories; or (3) a combination of the two on any CogScreen test, which could indicate potential cognitive deficiency. Also, we considered age as a factor that could influence the likelihood of higher LRPV scores and covariates, and therefore we categorized participants as ≥35 years and <35 years in the logistic regression models. Lastly, we included baseline medical certificate class status as a covariate in the model.

Results

We looked at 425 pilots for our study. In Table 22.1, we see that the average time a pilot was taking an SSRI was 9.4 years. The mean time in the AAM actual SSRI surveillance program (meaning they maintained a valid medical certificate) was 4.8 years. The mean number of

CogScreen tests during the program was similar to the time pilots were actively monitored, with the majority dropping out after only three or four CogScreen tests. Lastly, the average age was 42.9 years.

Table 22.1. Mean, median, and range for variables of interest

Variable	*N*	*M*	*Mdn*	*SD*	Min.	Max.
Years on SSRI	425	9.4	8.3	6.0	0.6	36.6
Time on SSRI program	425	4.8	4.0	3.1	0	13.2
Number of CogScreens	425	4.4	4.0	2.7	1	13
Baseline age	425	42.9	45.6	12.8	16.	72.5

Note. M = mean; *Mdn* = median; *SD* = standard deviation; SSRI = selective serotonin reuptake inhibitor.

CogScreen Outcome Assessment

To assess our hypotheses about cognitive deficiency, we looked at the results of the pilots' individual CogScreens. We examined the average LRPV scores and the total base and Taylor T scores <40 in three or more categories, dividing the participants into those under 35 and those 35 and older. For those over 35, the average initial LRPV score was 0.4, compared with 0.17 for those under 35 ($p<.001$). The average initial low T scores of 3 or more for those over 35 were 1.61, significantly higher than the 1.13 for those younger than 35 ($p=.0246$). This trend held true for both variables across all the CogScreen time points. Mean LRPV and low T scores of 3 or greater were highest at the initial CogScreen and decreased significantly during the second CogScreen, regardless of age.

Our main goals were twofold: to determine whether AAM was over-testing for this specific diagnosis and treatment combination, and to find evidence of cognitive decline in the pilots on the SSRI program. We looked at categories of abnormal cases. Since there is limited research on the sensitivity and specificity of CogScreen in measuring cognitive function changes reliably, we used high LRPV values and unusually high numbers of low T scores as outcome measures while considering age. We performed multivariate logistic regression to identify any variables significantly associated with having an abnormal LRPV score and/or base and Taylor T scores <40.

We did not find any significant factors that indicated trends in cognitive decline, except for age, which was expected, and baseline medical class issued. The highest LRPV values and abnormal T scores were mostly seen during the initial CogScreen testing. After the first test, the average scores improved significantly, suggesting that repetition of the test could benefit pilots. However, we did identify some significant associations between certain variables and the length of time pilots stayed in the program, although these did not seem to affect the cognitive deficiency detected by the CogScreen testing.

The second question was whether AAM is over-testing pilots for cognitive decline, and whether there is a better testing interval to reduce this frequency. Although no specific trend was established due to many pilots leaving the system early, a few noteworthy findings emerged. Only seven out of the 425 pilots were identified by any of the three outcome definitions as not being issued a certificate again after their last flagged abnormal value. Among the seven abnormal cases, only one came after the first and second cognitive screenings. Moreover, even when pilots were "flagged," most of the time, AAM issued medical certificates regardless.

Discussion and Practical Implications for Pilots

This study group contained pilots who had been granted an SI for SSRI use at least once before. Therefore, studying only this group did invite some survivorship selection bias, since they were more likely to be consistent and stable enough to provide the required information. However, these results generated a lot of thought and discussion from AAM leadership. While it is important for AMEs and AAM to ensure pilots are fit to fly at the time of each AME exam and for the entire duration of the pilot's medical certificate, mental health disorders like anxiety and depression can impair a pilot's ability to maintain control of an aircraft in subtle, and sometimes not-so-subtle, ways. These results were encouraging because they validate that pilots who made it through the initial evaluation were not identified on any follow-up testing to have enough cognitive decline to withdraw their special issuance medical certificate.

Based on our analyses of these 425 pilots in the SSRI program, in late 2022, the FAS determined that the neuropsychologist evaluation and routine CogScreen-AE administration are no longer necessary for renewal of an SSRI special issuance, except when clinically indicated or when specified on the authorization letter (FAA, 2022). However, future research will need to address how other cognitive screening in pilots as an alternative to CogScreen-AE may detect more subtle changes in cognition, and whether AAM management needs to revise this policy in the future.

Data-Driven Policy-Making for Pilots With Multiple Sclerosis and Parkinson's Disease

In 2017, we examined the current MS and PD certification standards and compared them with best practices in the general population. An extensive literature review identified several tests and metrics used in clinical practice that might be useful for aeromedical decision-making. The following summaries document our recommendations based on literature review and subsequent analysis of the certificated pilot population with MS (Skaggs et al., 2021a) and PD (Skaggs et al., 2021b).

Pilots With Multiple Sclerosis

Based on the AAM MS literature review (Skaggs et al., 2021a), these are the key factors that would have implications for aeromedical certification:

1. Given the emphasis on preventing sudden and subtle incapacitation of a pilot during the period of certification, we assume only clinically isolated syndromes (CIS), radiologi-

cally isolated syndromes (RIS), and relapsing-remitting MS (RRMS) are amenable to certification. Evidence of good functioning will be necessary for clearance (Olek, 2024).
2. Application for pilot certification with MS should include diagnosis based on the 2017 McDonald criteria and supporting magnetic resonance imaging (MRI), other testing, and narrative. Current clinical guidance might support up to 24 months between MRI examinations under an SI for pilots without relapse and minimal impairment (Thompson et al., 2018).
3. Pilot applicant prognosis should be considered at initial SI and renewal. Persons presenting with less severe and infrequent relapses and low lesion burden of disease may be symptom free for longer time periods. Mental health consequences or comorbidities may require assessment (Korostil & Feinstein, 2007; Marrie et al., 2015).
4. Screening and evaluation processes for cognitive impairment are necessary to certification. Ongoing monitoring will be required. Use of CogScreen-AE for screening and neuropsychological batteries for comprehensive evaluation may be appropriate. It also appears that in pilots with MS, the effect of aging on cognition is more prominent on those who are older than 60 (Kay, 2013b; G. G. Kay, personal communication, June 30, 2018).
5. Certification criteria could reasonably include language emphasizing "disease quiescence," "stable disease," or "no evidence of disease activity (NEDA)," meaning up to absence of disability progression, active inflammation/new lesion on MRI, and relapses.
6. Of 12 FDA-approved disease-modifying therapies (DMTs), only seven have been cleared for flight by the FAS, along with one longstanding off-label immunosuppressant. The remainder should be reviewed for efficacy and side effect profile for potential approval. The dearth of effective treatments for progressive forms of the disease means further caution to certification of pilots diagnosed with secondary or primary progressive MS (SPMS or PPMS; Olek, 2024; McGinley et al., 2017).

Method

On the basis of these factors, we reviewed a random sample of pilots with MS to assess whether the current standards identified in the literature review would modify certification outcomes of pilots cleared over the past decade (Skaggs et al., 2021a). To do this, we randomly sampled 50 cases from the total of 315 pilots who had examinations from January 2007 to December 2017 and had a designation of MS. Of the 50 cases selected for review, five were excluded due to insufficient data.

Results

The mean age at MS diagnosis was 39.6 ($SD = 11.1$). Table 22.2 displays the demographic and MS characteristic variables of the sample.

The type of MS was undocumented in nearly half of the cases reviewed (46.7 %) and 35.6 % had been in our medical surveillance system for at least 11 years. The four that never had an MRI and were issued a certificate were all issued a third-class medical certificate. Of the four that had a CogScreen, one was denied for issues not related to CogScreen; one had a result that was abnormal and the test was repeated, the result of which was normal and the pilot was issued a certificate; one had a normal result and the certificate was issued; and one had an abnormal test result (LRPV = 0.9576) but the certificate was issued regardles.

Table 22.2. Demographic and MS characteristics

Characteristics		Frequency (%)
Gender	Male	35 (77.8)
	Female	10 (22.2)
Type of MS	RRMS	24 (53.3)
	Unknown	21 (46.7)
Years in AAM system with MS	< 1 year	6 (13.3)
	1–5 years	14 (31.1)
	6–10 years	9 (20.0)
	11–15 years	9 (20.0)
	≥ 16 years	7 (15.6)
McDonald criteria ever	Yes	8 (17.8)
	No	37 (82.2)
Issued but no MRI ever	Yes	4 (8.9)
	No	41 (91.1)
Issued with new lesions present on MRI	Yes	11 (24.4)
	No	34 (75.6)
Ever had a CogScreen	Yes	4 (8.9)
	No	41 (91.1)

Note. RRMS = relapsing-remitting multiple sclerosis; MS = multiple sclerosis; MRI = magnetic resonance imaging; *SD* = standard deviation.

Discussion and Practical Implications for Pilots

In general, we discovered that the information in our surveillance system did not align with the current clinical practice recommendations. As mentioned earlier, nearly half of the reviewed records did not specify the type of MS the pilots had, around one quarter showed new lesions on MRI scans, only 17.6 % had documentation following the McDonald criteria, CogScreen tests were not consistently requested or used, and symptoms were not consistently recorded. Our suggestion was that regardless of whether MS certification policies became more or less strict, it was important for AMEs to review current standards through training, and for AAM to be more consistent in enforcing the certification review policy. After our recommendations were assessed by AAM management, they included cognitive testing and MRI brain and spinal scans as mandatory for pilots with MS in the certification protocol (FAA, 2023a).

Pilots With Parkinson's Disease

Based on the AAM PD literature review (Skaggs et al., 2021b), these were the key factors that would have implications for aeromedical certification:

1. PD is likely to be diagnosed among older pilots. This same group has elevated vulnerability to other pathologies, illustrating the challenging nature of certification with PD. A

worldwide prevalence of 0.35% (McPherson & Cummings, 2009) would predict 1,960 cases among the pilot population. This is substantially higher than what we have observed in our pilot population, with only 89 pilots having a valid medical certificate in 2016, or 0.016%.
2. PD is a complex disorder, and both the motor and non-motor manifestations are aeromedically significant. Motor features can affect dexterity, coordination, accuracy, and the speed of actions critical for flying. In addition, patients may develop soft, less distinct, monotonous speech, which may become slurred or poorly articulated, potentially affecting cockpit communications. Cognitive impairment is common, may precede other symptoms, and may be a sign of prodromal PD (Darweesh et al., 2017; Jagathesan & O'Brien, 2015).
3. PD is a debilitating and progressive disease impacting multiple dimensions critical to pilot performance. Time from diagnosis to loss of certificate is finite, even with treatment. But understanding of the disease is evolving rapidly, and those minimally impaired should be able to function effectively. Ensuring health maintenance and recognizing when the burden of impairment becomes incompatible with flight are the core challenges (Clem et al., 2016).
4. Cognitive impairment is likely in PD, even among those early in the disease process with minimal motor impairment. Impairment is likely to proceed to dementia. Executive and visuospatial functions are most likely to be impaired. Screening for impairment and broad neuropsychological testing when screening is failed are sound approaches to certification decisions (Carretta et al., 1999; G. G. Kay, personal communication, June 30, 2018).
5. Certification decisions will require a diagnosis using the Movement Disorder Society (MDS) criteria and severity of impairment assessment using the MDS-UPDRS, or an alternative acceptable to the FAS, similarly yielding norms amenable to certification decisions (Hoehn & Yahr, 1967; Martinez-Martin et al., 2015). Because the disease progresses over time, repeated assessments will be necessary, presumably limiting the length of SI. We assume that clinically probable and clinically confirmed PD with mild severity ratings in all MDS-UPDRS parts are compatible with certification for flight (assuming stable response to acceptable medications), while severe ratings in any part are incompatible. Expert consultation may be required to set policy for pilots with moderate ratings in any part. Expert consultation may be required to set policy for pilots with related differential diagnoses; some may be acceptable with individualized assessment while others may be incompatible with certification for flight.
6. Most PD patients can expect a 5- to 10-year window of good functioning with treatment using levodopa. The FAS has approved its use for a number of years. So long as a pilot has no aeromedically significant side effects and maintains no more than mild levels of impairment, certification may be be appropriate. Challenges appear for pilots who do not respond well to levodopa treatment, who prefer to delay their use of levodopa through alternative medications, or who pursue device-assisted therapies as their disease advances (Liang, 2024). Pharmacological expertise is required to assess or reassess compatibility of flight for each of the alternative medications. Sound criteria for motor function and cognitive impairment must be applied to individual assessment.

On the basis of these factors, the purpose of the research was to perform a case review of a random sample of pilots with PD to determine the consistency of certification by AAM and to explore whether updated policy based on the current literature was needed.

Method

There were 325 pilots who had PD between 2007 and 2017 (Skaggs et al., 2021b). In total, 89 pilots held a valid medical certificate as of December 2016, and we randomly sampled 50 cases. Records were reviewed from the date of PD diagnosis through July 2019. Of the 50 cases selected for review, four were excluded due to insufficient data.

Results

The average age at PD diagnosis was 62 (*SD*=8.8) and all pilots were male. The average age on their last medical examination was 65.8 (*SD*=8.1). Table 22.3 shows the demographic and PD characteristic variables of the sample.

Table 22.3. Characteristics of pilots with PD

Characteristics		Frequency (%)
Years in AAM system with PD diagnosis	0	3 (6.5)
	<1	1 (2.2)
	1–1.99	5 (10.9)
	2–2.99	11 (23.9)
	3–3.99	8 (17.4)
	4–4.99	7 (15.2)
	5–5.99	4 (8.7)
	6–6.99	3 (6.5)
	≥7	4 (8.7)
PD diagnosis using International Parkinson Disease and Movement Disorder Society diagnostic criteria	Yes	11 (23.9)
	No	35 (76.1)
Ever had a flight test	Yes	4 (8.7)
	No	42 (91.3)
Ever used device-assisted therapies or DBS and levodopa-carbidopa intestinal gel infusion	Yes	3 (6.5)
	No	43 (93.5)
Ever denied	Yes	4 (8.7)
	No	42 (91.3)

Note. DBS = deep brain stimulation; PD = Parkinson's disease.

The average time from symptoms to PD diagnosis was 1.4 years (*SD*=2.2). The average duration in AAM surveillance with PD was 3.9 years (*SD*=3.1), with 58.7% surveilled for less than 4 years. We also reviewed medications, and 43 (93.5%) reported currently taking Sinemet (carbidopa-levodopa) or Sinemet CR (continuous release). Regardless of medication use, only 25% of the pilots were in our medical surveillance system for more than 5 years.

Among the four pilots who were denied a medical certificate, each had a different reason for the denial (cognitive issues, disease progression, non-FAA-approved medication, and failure to provide information). In these cases, once the pilots were denied a certificate, they did not undergo any further medical examinations.

We also assessed at each examination whether the pilot's disease progression was medically stable. There were six instances where a pilot was initially seen as unstable, and in five of these cases, additional information was provided by the pilot, leading to them being ultimately deemed stable and issued a certificate at a later time. In the sixth case, the pilot was denied a certificate.

Furthermore, we examined the various neuropsychological testing that was being reported. Table 22.4 displays the frequency of testing. Three pilots had LRPV values higher than 0.6. One pilot had two high scores, and after the second high score had a full battery performed. All Montreal Cognitive Assessment (MoCA) scores were 26 or greater. On the MDS-Unified Parkinson's Disease Rating Scale (UPDRS), there were no Part I or Part IV scores recorded, a few Part II scores, and the remaining scores were Part III. Of the Part III scores, there were no pilots who had scores greater than 33.

Table 22.4. Neuropsychological testing

Test	Yes Frequency (%)	No Frequency (%)
CogScreen ever	7 (15.2)	39 (84.8)
MoCA ever	17 (37)	29 (63)
MDS-UPDRS ever	21 (45.7)	25 (54.3)
Full battery of tests ever	8 (17.4)	38 (82.6)

Note. MoCA = Montreal Cognitive Assessment; MDS-UPDRS = Movement Disorder Society Unified Parkinson's Disease Rating Scale.

Discussion and Practical Implications for Pilots

Pilots with third-class certificates were older on average at their PD diagnosis compared with those who had first-/second-class certificates (56 vs. 68 years old, $p < .0001$). When we looked at the time spent in the AAM system after being diagnosed with PD, the median duration was notably longer for the combined first-/second-class group compared with the third-class group (3.8 vs. 2, $p = .0087$). Generally, the average time in the AAM system after diagnosis was 3.9 years.

The current practice standard according to the literature called for diagnosis by MDS diagnostic criteria, disability assessment by MDS-UPDRS, cognitive testing and a neurological workup, and a comprehensive ophthalmologic report. If these standards were applied to pilots in our study, the following percentages would not have been compliant: 76.6% did not report that they met the criteria for PD diagnosis using the MDS diagnostic criteria; 54.3% never reported an MDS-UPDRS assessment; 34.8% never reported any type of neuro/psychological testing performed during any of their examinations, with 84.8% specifically not having had a CogScreen; and 2.2% failed to report information about an ophthalmologic examination.

Overall, this group of pilots and the AMEs certificating them were more compliant about following certification policy guidelines than the group of pilots with MS we reviewed. However, based on the literature, we recommended a change in policy for all pilots to routinely undergo cognitive screening. After AAM management reviewed our recommendations, they added cognitive testing and MRI requirements to the mandatory certification protocol for pilots with PD. In addition, they added the requirement of a unified Parkinson's UPDRS-III motor rating scale as part of the neurologic evaluation for these pilots (FAA, 2023b).

Data-Driven Policy-Making for Pilots With HIV

Today, someone diagnosed with HIV can maintain good health through proper antiretroviral therapy (ART) selection and consistent viral suppression (Bonacci & Holtgrave, 2017). However, a concern for HIV-positive pilots is the possibility of developing HIV-associated neurocognitive disorders (HAND) as the disease progresses. HAND refers to changes in memory, concentration, attention, and motor skills that cannot be attributed to a cause other than HIV infection. For this reason, it is recommended that HIV patients should be regularly screened for possible neurocognitive issues (Eggers et al., 2017).

Factors that increase the risk of HAND include disease-related aspects like lower CD4 cell counts, older age when HIV was contracted, how long the person has had HIV, and the presence of a prior AIDS-defining illness. Aging appears to be a factor in HAND, particularly in patients over age 50. As individuals with HIV get older, HAND could lead to significant morbidity and mortality and ultimately accelerate the aging process (Watkins & Treisman, 2015).

Comorbidities and potentially genetic factors might also contribute to HAND risk. Comorbidities that can raise the likelihood of HAND include mental health issues like depression (which can be seen in about 50 % of cases), anxiety disorders (seen in around 38 % of cases), bipolar disorder, and increased risky behavior (Woods et al., 2009).

Testing, for example, CogScreen, and checking CD4 cell count as well as viral load are all important ways to gauge how the disease is progressing. With treatment improvements over several decades, people living with HIV who actively monitor and manage the disease can now expect similar lifespans to those without HIV (Passaes & Saez-Cirion, 2014). Keeping the immune system strong and suppressing the virus could potentially delay or even prevent cognitive issues. Considering these improvements in quality of life and overall health outcomes for those with HIV, medical certification should adapt to reflect these changes, especially since better therapies are also reducing the risk of cognitive problems.

When we started our study, HIV-positive pilots were required to undergo cognitive impairment screening when applying for an SI, renewing annually for first- or second-class certificates, and renewing biennially for a third-class certificate (FAA, 2021).

Between 2016 and 2018, we conducted an initial study looking into the impact of changing the cognitive screening from yearly to once every 5 years among 298 HIV-positive pilots with typical CD4 counts and viral suppression (Skaggs et al., 2018). During our analysis, we found that with this new approach, about 4.5 % of cases where pilots did not pass their cognitive screening test would have been missed. However, only two of these cases (1 %) would have affected the final certification outcome. While discussing using this new approach in policy changes, new research from the general population emerged, indicating that neurocognitive issues caused by HIV worsen over time with infection and could affect as many as 20%–50% of HIV cases (Molsberry et al., 2018; Tierney et al., 2017).

Additionally, considering the rate of people leaving the surveillance system and the potential development of cognitive issues in this group under our current conditions, it did not seem reasonable to reduce the frequency of cognitive screening to every 5 years. However, we could not firmly conclude the reasons behind the dropout rate, given the archival nature of the study, the lack of a control group, and the lack of comparison with drop-out rates for other aeromedically significant conditions.

In addition, Levine (2021) reviewed research regarding both cross-sectional and longitudinal studies assessing prediction of cognitive impairment among men with HIV and those without (Oliveira et al., 2021; Wang et al., 2019). The findings from the cross-sectional analysis failed to demonstrate statistical significance that HIV status was associated with cognitive impairment (Wang et al., 2019). In fact, when examining comparisons between those cognitively impaired and those who were not, the only ways the two groups statistically differed were by age, ethnicity, education, and current alcohol use. The cognitively impaired and unimpaired groups did not differ according to HIV status or CD4 cell counts (Wang et al., 2019).

These cross-sectional findings were then followed up with a 5-year longitudinal study that modeled individual risk of cognitive impairment (Oliveira et al., 2021). The results from the longitudinal study indicated that while a diagnosis of AIDS was a critical factor in neurocognitive impairment, HIV infection did not convey additional risk. Hepatitis B and hepatitis C were also independently associated with increased risk of cognitive impairment as well (Oliveira et al., 2021). Levine concluded that the inconsistent results from research regarding cognitive impairment in those with HIV may be due to past studies containing methodological limitations that result in selection and information biases. Thus, Levine suggested it may be comorbidities, which might occur more often in people with HIV, that are in fact the primary driver of cognitive dysfunction rather than the virus itself (Levine, 2021).

AAM must balance our data with published findings from the general population. It is necessary to evaluate for cognitive impairment in HIV-infected pilots that might result in incident or accident. This prompted us to carry out a more recent study to bring the information in our original report up to date. Because new data were available, we expanded our analysis to incorporate more recent cognitive evaluations and introduced additional details to explore how these updated factors were connected to cognitive issues observed in pilots (Norris et al., 2023).

Method

In our 2022 study, all pilots who were identified as having HIV or AIDS and had at least one medical examination between January 1, 2007 and December 31, 2020 were reviewed for inclusion (Norris et al., 2023). To be included in the study, the pilot must have had at least one CogScreen score or other FAA-approved neuropsychological test result reported, have a diagnosis of HIV or AIDS, and apply for a pilot medical certificate during the specified time period.

Results

Out of the initial 727 cases we identified, 451 fit these criteria after reviewing the records. These pilots were reviewed over time, and we followed their cognitive assessments, neuropsychological evaluations, viral loads, and CD4 cell counts. Besides the original 298 pilots we studied from 2007 to 2016, we added 153 pilots from January 1, 2017 through 2020, making a total of 451 pilots for this analysis. Among these, 165 (36.6 %) had just one cognitive assessment, and an additional 75 (16.6 %) had only two cognitive assessments available. Overall, 350 (77.6 %) of the 451 pilots had six or fewer cognitive assessments. Out of the 451 pilots who underwent cognitive testing as part of their application, 369 (81.8 %) were granted an SI for HIV.

Among these 369 pilots who were issued an SI at least once, the retention rate in our surveillance system was 37.7 % at 5 years, 17.6 % at 10 years, and 6.2 % at 15 years. This 5-year retention rate was lower compared with all pilots holding a valid medical certificate around the time the study began in 2007 (the overall pilot population had a 5-year retention rate of 55 %). When we compared further, the 5-year retention rate for pilots with HIV around a similar time frame was better than among active pilots with conditions like atrial fibrillation, myocardial infarction, diabetes, or cranial and peripheral nerve disorders. However, retention for pilots with HIV was worse compared to active pilots with other arrhythmias, vascular conditions, hypertension, valvular heart disease, brain disorders, spinal cord disorders, and no reported conditions.

New research published after our initial 2018 report has highlighted that the severity of the disease and the presence of other health issues, especially neurodegenerative and cerebrovascular diseases, might play a significant role in causing cognitive problems among individuals with HIV. Additionally, those with HIV who do not already have cognitive issues or a history of HAND tend to maintain stable cognitive performance after undergoing suppressive therapy (Chan & Valcour, 2022). Another study showed that participants experiencing declining cognitive functions were generally older, had poorer initial cognitive performance, and had been living with HIV for a longer period. Despite the AAM internal medical pathology codes making it challenging to study specific medical conditions, we included the count of medications and additional health conditions alongside the HIV diagnosis in our updated analysis. This way, we aimed to mirror the recent findings regarding these associations within our group of pilots.

Our analysis was somewhat surprising, given that baseline age, HIV comorbidities, and counts of medications and medical conditions did not have an apparent association with odds of having a subsequent abnormal cognitive examination result.

While recent scientific literature remains mixed about whether virally suppressed pilots with HIV experience faster cognitive decline compared with other groups, it is well documented that certain medical conditions and the aging process can accelerate cognitive decline in the general population (Kay, 2013a; Taylor et al., 2000; Watkins & Treisman, 2015). Thus, assuming the AAM cognitive assessments are able to detect changes in cognitive function, we expected to find associations with abnormal cognitive assessments and aging and/or increased medical conditions. However, examining all medical count and age cutoff points, we did not find any associations with cognitive function and these variables in follow-up cognitive tests. We did, however, find associations between follow-up abnormal cognitive assessments and initial abnormal assessment results, ever having abnormal CD4 counts and/or viral loads, and HIV duration. Thus, our assessment differs from the analysis of the cross-sectional study mentioned earlier that found no association with abnormal CD4 counts and cognitive impairment (Wang et al., 2019). Our assessment was similar to the CHARTER cohort study cited in the recent Chan and Valcour (2022) publication with our significant associations between follow-up cognitive tests and baseline assessments and HIV duration.

Discussion and Practical Implications for Pilots

Unlike other populations we have examined, most pilots with HIV fail to come back to get an SI after they have been denied. While this may be for a number of reasons, one major reason that pilots who fail their cognitive tests may not come back into our program is likely due to cognitive changes, as demonstrated by the significant association between baseline score and subsequent scores. With the recent 2021 change (FAA, 2021) in the AAM protocol to administer the comprehensive battery of cognitive tests upon initial application of each pilot with HIV, this should enhance the future ability of AAM to identify more subtle cognitive issues at baseline and thus gather more detailed information to base decisions on for future applications. Therefore, the updated study supported the current new guidelines and continued active cognitive assessments in this pilot population.

Conclusion

To summarize, this chapter highlights the significance of data-driven policy-making in the field of aerospace medicine. It emphasizes the need to move away from relying solely on expert opinion and reacting to prominent cases but additionally to integrate empirical evidence to ensure flight safety. The presented findings shed light on specific areas of interest, including cognitive testing and policy decisions surrounding usage of SSRIs and pilots with MS, PD, and HIV. The studies conducted provide insights into the association between SSRIs and cognitive stability, the certification standards for pilots with MS and PD, and the risk of HIV-associated neurocognitive disorders. These findings have led to recommendations for improving certification protocols, enhancing consistency in decision-making, and implementing comprehensive cognitive assessments. By incorporating data-driven standards, policymakers and stakeholders can make informed decisions that prioritize the well-being and safety of pilots while maintaining the highest standards in aerospace medicine.

References

Berry, M. A. (2017, May 2). *Have flight surgeons and aerospace medicine improved aviation safety?* [Conference presentation]. Aerospace Medical Association 2017 Annual Scientific Meeting, Denver, CO. https://asma.org/asma/media/AsMA/home-page-rotator/Annual Meeting/4th-Reinartz-Lecture.mp4

Bonacci, R. A., & Holtgrave, D. R. (2017). U.S. HIV incidence and transmission goals, 2020 and 2025. *American Journal of Preventive Medicine, 53*(3), 275–281. https://doi.org/10.1016/j.amepre.2017.03.012

Carretta, T., Ree, M., & Callister, J. (1999). *Factor structure of the CogScreen-AE test battery.* Wright-Patterson Air Force Base, Air Force Research Laboratory.

Chan, P., & Valcour, V. (2022). Neurocognition and the aging brain in people with HIV: Implications for screening. *Topics in Antiviral Medicine, 29*(5), 423–429. https://pubmed.ncbi.nlm.nih.gov/35191658

Clem, P., Navathe, P., & Drane, M. (2016). Identifying pilots with Parkinson's disease. *Aerospace Medicine and Human Performance, 87*(6), 545–549. https://doi.org/10.3357/AMHP.4428.2016

Darweesh, S., Wolters, F., & Postuma, R. (2017). Association between poor cognitive functioning and risk of incident Parkinsonism: The Rotterdam Study. *JAMA Neurology, 74*(12), 1431–1438. https://doi.org/10.1001/jamaneurol.2017.2248

DeVoll, J.R. (2013, May 16). *FAA experience with neuropsychological testing for airmen with depression on SSRI medications* [Conference presentation]. Aerospace Medical Association 2013 Annual Scientific Meeting, Chicago, IL.

Eggers, C., Arendt, G., Hahn, K., Husstedt, I.W., Maschke, M., Neuen-Jacob, E., Obermann, M., Rosenkranz, T., Schielke, E., & Straube, E. (2017). HIV-1-associated neurocognitive disorder: epidemiology, pathogenesis, diagnosis, and treatment. *Journal of Neurology, 264*(8), 1715–1727. https://doi.org/10.1007/s00415-017-8503-2

Federal Aviation Administration (FAA). (2021, June 30). *Guide for aviation medical examiners – human immunodeficiency virus (HIV) specification.* Federal Aviation Administration Office of Medicine. https://www.faa.gov/ame_guide/media/HIV-Spec-Sheet-Initial.pdf

Federal Aviation Administration (FAA). (2022, December 28). *Guide for aviation medical examiners – SSRI recertification/follow-up clearance.* Federal Aviation Administration Office of Medicine. https://www.faa.gov/ame_guide/media/HIMS_AME_Checklist_SSRI_Recertification.pdf

Federal Aviation Administration (FAA). (2023a, January 25). *Guide for aviation medical examiners – Multiple sclerosis.* Federal Aviation Administration Office of Medicine. https://www.faa.gov/ame_guide/media/Multiple-Sclerosis.pdf

Federal Aviation Administration (FAA). (2023b, January 25). *Guide for aviation medical examiners – Parkinson's disease and Parkinsonism (secondary).* Federal Aviation Administration Office of Medicine. https://www.faa.gov/ame_guide/media/Parkinsons_Disease.pdf

Hoehn, M., & Yahr, M. (1967). Parkinsonism: Onset, progression and mortality. *Neurology, 17*(5), 427–442. https://doi.org/10.1212/wnl.17.5.427

Jagathesan, T., & O'Brien, M. (2015). The aeromedical implications of Parkinson's disease. *Aerospace Medicine and Human Performance, 86*(12), 1046–1051. https://doi.org/10.3357/AMHP.4251.2015

Kay, G.G. (2013a). Aviation neuropsychology. In C.H. Kennedy & G.G. Kay (Eds.), *Aeromedical psychology* (pp. 239–268). CRC Press Taylor and Francis Group. https://doi.org/10.1201/9781315565811-10

Kay, G.G. (2013b). *CogScreen overview.* https://www.cogscreen.com/Default.aspx

Korostil, M., & Feinstein, A. (2007). Anxiety disorders and their clinical correlates in multiple sclerosis patients. *Multiple Sclerosis, 13*(1), 67–72. https://doi.org/10.1177/1352458506071161

Levine, A. (2021, May). *Questioning the prevalence of HIV-associated neurocognitive disorders* [Conference presentation]. Aerospace Medical Association 2021 Annual Scientific Meeting, Denver, CO.

Liang, T.W. (2024). *Medical management of motor fluctuations and dyskinesia in Parkinson disease.* https://www.uptodate.com/contents/medical-management-of-motor-fluctuations-and-dyskinesia-in-parkinson-disease

Marrie, R.A., Reingold, S., Cohen, J., Stuve, O., Trojano, M., Sorensen, P.S., Cutter, G., & Reider, N. (2015). The incidence and prevalence of psychiatric disorders in multiple sclerosis: A systematic review. *Multiple Sclerosis, 21*(3), 305–317. https://doi.org/10.1177/1352458514564487

Martinez-Martin, P., Rodriguez-Blazquez, C., Alvarez, M., Arakaki, T., Arillo, V., Chana, P., Fernandez, W., Garretto, N., Martinez-Castrillo, J.C., Rodriguez-Violante, M., Serrano-Duenas, M., Ballesteros, D., Rojo-Abuin, J.M., Chaudhuri, K.R., & Merello, M. (2015). Parkinson's disease severity levels and MDS-Unified Parkinson's Disease Rating Scale. *Parkinsonism & Related Disorders, 21*(1), 50–54. https://doi.org/10.1016/j.parkreldis.2014.10.026

McGinley, M.P., Moss, B.P., & Cohen, J.A. (2017). Safety of monoclonal antibodies for the treatment of multiple sclerosis. *Expert Opinion on Drug Safety, 16*(1), 89–100. https://doi.org/10.1080/14740338.2017.1250881

McPherson, S., & Cummings, J. (2009). Neuropsychological aspects of Parkinson's disease and Parkinsonism. In I. Grant & K. Adams (Eds.), *Neuropsychological assessment of neuropsychiatric disorders* (pp. 199–222). Oxford University Press.

Medical Standards and Certification, 14 C.F.R. § 67 (1996). https://www.govinfo.gov/content/pkg/FR-1996-03-19/html/96-6358.htm

Molsberry, S., Cheng, Y., Kingsley, L., Jacobson, L., Levine, A., Martin, E., Miller, N., Munro, C., Ragin, A., Sacktor, N., & Becker, J. (2018). Neuropsychological phenotypes among men with and without HIV disease in the multicenter AIDS cohort study. *AIDS, 32*, 1679–1688. https://doi.org/10.1097/QAD.0000000000001865

Norris, A., Skaggs, V., & Chidester, T. (2023). *Assessing potential risk factors of abnormal cognitive function among HIV-positive airmen – an updated analysis* [Unpublished internal AAM report].

Norris, A., Skaggs, V., Flynn, C., Georgemiller, R., Harper-Tam, J., & Guay-Terry, P. (2022). *Review of SSRI cases to assess potential for cognitive decline* [Unpublished internal AAM report].

Olek, M.J. (2024). *Evaluation and diagnosis of multiple sclerosis in adults.* https://www.uptodate.com/contents/evaluation-and-diagnosis-of-multiple-sclerosis-in-adults

Oliveira, N.L., Kennedy, E.H., Tibshirani, R.J., Levine, A.J., Martin, E., Munro, C.A., Ragin, A.B., Rubin, L.H., Sacktor, N., Seaberg, E.C., Weinstein, A.M., & Becker, J.T. (2021). Longitudinal 5-year prediction of cognitive impairment among men with HIV disease. *AIDS, 35*(6), 889–898. https://doi.org/10.1097/qad.0000000000002827

Passaes, C.P., & Saez-Cirion, A. (2014). HIV cure research: advances and prospects. *Virology, 454–455*, 340–352. https://doi.org/10.1016/j.virol.2014.02.021

Skaggs, V., Norris, A., Chidester, T., Silberman, W., Ricaurte, E., & Pardo, G. (2021a). *Certification issues for airmen diagnosed with multiple sclerosis: Literature review analysis population comparisons and recommendations* [Unpublished internal AAM report].

Skaggs, V., Norris, A., Chidester, T., Silberman, W., Ricaurte, E., & Boudreau, E. (2021b). *Certification issues for airmen diagnosed with Parkinson's disease: Literature review, analysis, population comparisons, and recommendations* [Unpublished internal AAM report].

Skaggs, V., Norris, A., Ricaurte, E., & Chidester, T. (2018). *Assessing cognitive function among HIV-positive airmen over a 10-year period* [Unpublished internal AAM report].

Special Issuance of Medical Certificates, 14 C.F.R. § 67.401 (1996). https://www.govinfo.gov/content/pkg/FR-1996-03-19/html/96-6358.htm

Taylor, J., O'Hara, R., Mumenthaler, M., & Yesavage, J. (2000). Relationship of CogScreen-AE to flight simulator performance and pilot age. *Aviation, Space and Environmental Medicine, 71*(4), 373–380.

Thompson, A.J., Banwell, B.L., Barkhof, F., Carroll, W.M., Coetzee, T., Comi, G., Correale, J., Fazekas, F., Filippi, M., Freedman, M.S., Fujihara, K., Galetta, S.L., Hartung, H.P., Kappos, L., Lublin, F.D., Marrie, R.A., Miller, A.E., Miller, D.H., Montalban, X., ... Cohen, J.A. (2018). Diagnosis of multiple sclerosis: 2017 revisions of the McDonald criteria. *Lancet Neurology, 17*(2), 162–173. https://doi.org/10.1016/s1474-4422(17)30470-2

Tierney, S., Sheppard, D., Kordovski, V., Faytell, M., Avci, G., & Woods, S. (2017). A comparison of the sensitivity, stability, and reliability of three diagnostic schemes for HIV-associated neurocognitive disorders. *Journal of NeuroVirology, 23*(3), 404–421. https://doi.org/10.1007/s13365-016-0510-z

Wang, Z., Molsberry, S., Cheng, Y., Kingsley, L., Levine, A.J., Martin, E., Munro, C.A., Ragin, A.B., Rubin, L.H., Sacktor, N., Seaberg, E.C., & Becker, J.T. (2019). Cross-sectional analysis of cognitive function using multivariate normative comparisons in men with HIV disease. *AIDS, 33*(14), 2115–2124. https://doi.org/10.1097/qad.0000000000002312

Watkins, C.C., & Treisman, G.J. (2015). Cognitive impairment in patients with AIDS – prevalence and severity. *HIV AIDS (Auckl), 7*, 35–47. https://doi.org/10.2147/hiv.s39665

Woods, S.P., Moore, D.J., Weber, E., & Grant, I. (2009). Cognitive neuropsychology of HIV-associated neurocognitive disorders. *Neuropsychology Review, 19*(2), 152–168. https://doi.org/10.1007/s11065-009-9102-5

Chapter 23
Toxic Fumes in Airplane Cabins

A Health and Flight Safety Risk?

Sarah Mackenzie Ross

Introduction

Air travel is reported to be the safest form of transport, and numerous regulatory bodies and processes exist to maintain safety standards (UK Civil Aviation Authority [CAA], 2024a; International Air Transport Association [IATA], 2023). Commercial airline pilots are responsible for transporting thousands of people a day to a variety of different destinations, and safety is their highest priority. They are extensively trained to acquire the skills and knowledge to do their job, and they are monitored and reviewed regularly to ensure they are physically and mentally fit to fly. However, their psychological well-being (emotional and cognitive) does not receive the same level of scrutiny as their physical health and maintenance of flying skills (Ackland et al., 2022).

Commercial airline pilots are an occupational group where intact cognitive function is essential because human error in the cockpit can have catastrophic consequences. Cognitive function can become compromised at any time during service by a number of factors such as the working environment (cabin pressure, humidity, temperature, hypoxia, ozone, poor air quality); job characteristics (jet lag, sleep disruption, fatigue, stress); and because the incidence of various medical and neurological conditions that impair cognitive function increases with age (Hirtz et al., 2007). Therefore, it is important that appropriate and sensitive procedures are in place to identify pilots whose mental state may be deteriorating.

In the United Kingdom, cognitive function is not routinely assessed following initial personnel selection, the assumption being that any cognitive problems that develop during a pilot's career will be disclosed by the pilot during regular health checks and/or detected during line and simulator checks. In a previous publication, I reviewed the validity of this assumption and suggested regular health and simulator checks may not be sensitive enough to detect mild to moderate cognitive impairment or the early stages of neurological illness (Mackenzie Ross, 2017). In this chapter, I introduce the reader to a controversial topic in aviation: Do toxic fumes in airplane cabins adversely affect health and cognitive functioning?

Symptom Reporting: Acute and Chronic Health Effects

Over the past two to three decades, there have been increasing reports from aircrew of short- and long-term neurological, neuropsychological, respiratory, cardiological, and various other symptoms thought to be a consequence of breathing contaminated cabin air (Cox & Michaelis, 2002; Hageman et al., 2020; Harper, 2005; Mackenzie-Ross, 2008; Mackenzie-Ross et al., 2011; Michaelis, 2003, 2011; Michaelis et al., 2017; Montgomery et al., 1977; Murawski & Supplee, 2008; Somers, 2005; Winder & Balouet, 2000). Of interest is the fact that this increase in reporting occurred shortly after inflight smoking was banned on commercial aircraft (mainly during the late 1990s), suggesting that up until then, contaminated cabin air was masked by cigarette smoke.

Acute symptoms that are frequently reported to start at the time of exposure include eye irritation, respiratory problems headache, skin problems, nausea, dizziness, fatigue, and cognitive impairment. These symptoms are often reported to recede following cessation of exposure but may become persistent after repeated exposures over time.

Symptoms of chronic ill health include fatigue, gastrointestinal problems, respiratory difficulties, palpitations, muscle pain/weakness, immunosuppression, and neurological problems such as headache, paresthesia, and cognitive impairment.

The term "aerotoxic syndrome" was coined by two toxicologists in 2000 to refer to this constellation of symptoms (Winder & Balouet, 2000). This is not a recognized diagnostic category as far as the medical profession is concerned, nor is the term accepted by the aviation industry because it implies causation, which is disputed. Considerable disagreement and debate are ongoing between important stakeholders regarding aerotoxic syndrome. The aviation industry recognizes that cabin air can become contaminated by engine oil fumes and hydraulic fluids and combusted or pyrolyzed materials. They acknowledge that some people may experience acute symptoms following exposure with transient discomfort; but they consider long-term ill health due to any toxic effects in cabin air is unlikely, although such a link cannot be ruled out (CAA, 2024b).

Toxic Fumes in Cabin Air

In the United Kingdom, the CAA has a duty of care to protect the health of all people on board aircraft, aircrew and passengers alike. According to their website, the CAA spends a considerable amount of time inspecting operations in order to identify potential causes of accidents and reduce their likelihood so that safety standards can be continuously improved (CAA, 2024a). Cabin safety is a vital part of any safety management system, and cabin crew play a vital role in identifying hazards and informing flight crew of abnormal situations in the cabin such as pressurization problems, smoke, fumes, or fire.

Regarding the latter, cabin air on commercial aircraft can become contaminated by synthetic jet engine oil, hydraulic fluids, and combusted or pyrolyzed materials. This problem was first described in military aircraft in the 1950s (Anderson, 2021) and is acknowledged by the aviation industry, to be an ongoing issue on commercial aircraft to this day.

The process by which cabin air can become contaminated is as follows. Most commercial aircraft (except for the Boeing 787) draw air from outside, which is circulated around the engine where it is heated and pressurized to a breathable level. Contamination can occur in two ways: (1) chronic repeated low-level exposure due to jet aircraft design that allows continuous leaking of oil past wet-oil seals for lubrication purposes and may occur without a detectable fume event occurring; (2) acute high-level exposure associated with odors and sometimes a visible haze (fume event), caused by engine power and/or air supply configuration changes and less frequently general system failures such as seal bearing failure, worn seals, and overfilling of oil and hydraulic reservoirs (Burdon et al., 2023; Howard et al., 2017; Shehadi et al., 2016).

These oils contain a large number of chemicals, some of which are irritating and sensitizing (e.g., phenyl-naphthylamine) resulting in ear, nose, and throat irritation; respiratory difficulties; and skin lesions; and some of which are neurotoxic with the potential to cause cognitive impairment (e.g., toluene, benzene, xylenes, and organophosphates). Pyrolyzed products such as carbon monoxide, volatile and semi-volatile organic compounds are also potentially neurotoxic, and ultrafine particles are generated when oils are exposed to high temperature. These particles carry droplets of other toxic substances (e.g., organophosphates) deep into the respiratory system, into the bloodstream, and across the blood/brain barrier (Burdon et al., 2023; Howard et al., 2018; Michaelis et al., 2021; Winder & Balouet, 2002).

Nevertheless, the general consensus among aviation regulatory bodies and manufacturers is that contaminant levels are low and within health and safety standards for ground-based environments, thus cabin air is safe to breathe (Boeing, 2016; CAA, 2024b; European Aviation Safety Agency [EASA], 2017; Federal Aviation Administration, 2020;). This view has been challenged by a number of advocacy groups, trade unions, scientists, and law firms.

The first government inquiry regarding contaminated cabin air took place in Canberra, Australia, in 1999 (Australian Senate Inquiry into air safety and cabin air quality in the BAe 146 aircraft type) and concluded that oil fumes are a health and safety risk (Parliament of the Commonwealth of Australia, 2000).

In 2006 a UK government scientific advisory committee (Committee on Toxicity of Chemicals in Food, Consumer Products and the Environment [COT]) was asked to review data provided by the British Airline Pilots' Association regarding the link between contaminated air and ill health. The author was asked to give evidence to this committee. COT concluded in 2007 that the evidence available at that time was not of sufficient quantity or quality to determine whether a causal relationship exists between cabin air exposures and ill health among flight crew. They recommended air quality studies and further epidemiological studies be undertaken, and they also stated the available evidence "supported further investigation of neuropsychological impairment in commercial pilots," but did not indicate any other specific health outcome should be studied (COT, 2007, p. 26, paragraph 94).

The House of Lords Science and Technology Committee undertook a much broader review of air travel and health in 2007, which was not restricted to the contaminated air issue. They, too, invited the author to give evidence to the committee. They made a number of recommendations regarding different aspects of health, most of which are beyond the remit of this chapter, but also recommended real-time monitoring of air quality and other aspects of the cabin environment and exploration of the ways in which different aspects of the aircraft cabin environment might impact individuals of less-than-average health (House of Lords, 2007).

In 2013 COT reviewed findings from four air quality studies undertaken since their 2007 review and concluded that cabin air was contaminated by components and/or combustion products of engine oils and that episodes of acute illness, sometime incapacitating, had occurred in temporal relation to contamination. They thought acute illness might reflect the toxic effect of one or more chemicals, but that it could also have occurred through nocebo effects. More generally they concluded that a toxic mechanism was unlikely but could not be ruled out. Further research was recommended again (COT, 2013).

Outside of the research domain, several lawsuits have been brought against the airline industry by employees who attribute their ill health to occupational exposure to pyrolyzed engine oil, for example, *Turner v. East West Airlines vs. Turner* (Gold, 2011) and *Terry Williams v. Boeing* (High Court of Australia, 2010). In both cases it was accepted that the claimant's health had been adversely affected by exposure to engine oil fumes (Lambert-James & Williams, 2014). Many other cases have settled out of court with nondisclosure agreements. In the United Kingdom, the Unite union reported in 2019 that legal notice had been served in 51 cases against five of the largest airlines operating out of the United Kingdom.

Air Quality Studies

Commercial aircraft do not have air quality monitoring systems on board, and thus the presence and full spectrum of contaminants and levels in cabin air are poorly understood.

A number of industry- and government-funded cabin air quality studies have been undertaken over the past two decades in response to recommendations from government inquiries and scientific committees (Chen et al., 2021; Crump et al., 2011; de Ree et al., 2014; Guan et al., 2014; Houtzager et al., 2013; Schindler et al., 2013; Schuchardt et al., 2019; Shehadi et al., 2015; Solbu et al., 2011; Wang, Yang, Guan, & Gao, et al., 2014; Wang, Yang, Guan, & Gao, 2014; Wolkoff et al., 2016). These studies primarily focused on levels of organophosphate compounds (OPs) in cabin air, but a few other chemicals have also been measured including volatile organic compounds (VOCS), carbon dioxide, carbon monoxide, and ozone.

Results indicate that low levels of contaminants enter the air supply on a continuous basis during routine flight, but at levels that seldom exceed exposure levels permitted in ground-based environments such as offices and buildings (Chen et al., 2021). Airlines and regulatory authorities have concluded from these findings that the health risk of exposure to chemical contaminants in cabin air is negligible and that other factors are to blame for 'aerotoxic syndrome such as hyperventilation, the nocebo effect, or some other aspect of flying (COT, 2007; EASA, 2017).

As mentioned previously, unions representing aircrew and several scientists disagree and argue that firm conclusions cannot be drawn from air quality studies undertaken to date because all are flawed by methodological and procedural issues such as:

- Failure to measure the full spectrum of contaminants that may be found on aircraft (OPs make up only a small proportion of what an individual may be exposed to onboard aircraft).
- Sampling a small number of aircraft and flights.
- Failure to capture a fume event of sufficient severity to trigger formal reporting procedures and concluding cabin air is safe to breathe from a small number of flights during routine conditions. This is irresponsible and akin to concluding that as none of the planes crashed during the study, airplanes never crash.
- Inadequate sample volumes, collection times, sampling methods, and analytical techniques.
- Inappropriate use of exposure standards founded on ground-based workplaces that may not be applicable to the aircraft environment (Howard, 2020).
- Failure to consider synergistic effects of chemical mixtures that can be additive, synergistic, antagonistic, or completely novel in their neurotoxic effect (Hartman, 1995); and failure to consider the synergistic impact of hypoxia and altitude.

- Individual differences in rate or ability to metabolize certain compounds were not taken into consideration. This means the health risks may be higher than assessed hitherto.
- Failure to consider the impact of chronic low-level cumulative exposure over a prolonged period of time as opposed to acute high-level exposure events (Howard, 2020).

Recent systematic reviews of the literature regarding cabin air quality and risk to human health identify these gaps in knowledge and highlight the need for further research (Chen et al., 2021; de Boer et al., 2015; Hayes et al., 2021).

An interesting new avenue of research concerns the possibility that exposure to ultrafine particles (UFPs) is responsible for adverse health effects reported by aircrew (Bendtsen et al., 2021; Michaelis et al., 2021). Jet engine emissions contain large amounts of nano-sized particles that can reach lower airways via inhalation and increase the risk of disease. Unburned jet engine oil is a major component of emissions from aircraft (Fushimi et al., 2019), which means UFP measurements may be a useful surrogate for oil contamination in aircraft cabin air. Michaelis et al. (2021) found UFP levels vary dramatically according to the phase of flight or engine/auxiliary power unit (APU) power or air supply settings (lowest levels being recorded during the cruise phase of flight); and peak levels were higher in aircraft than other ground-based environments, for example, a busy London street. Howard et al. (2017) suggest VOCs and OPs may bind with nanoparticles, which are then transported across the blood/brain barrier.

Clearly, the controversy surrounding aerotoxic syndrome continues, and this chapter is unable to resolve this debate. However, assessment and monitoring of cognitive function in pilots are essential for safety reasons, and it is important that those involved in evaluating pilots, such as medical examiners and clinical psychologists, are aware of the contaminated air issue. This is because at some point in their career, they are likely to encounter aircrew who report ill health and cognitive impairment following exposure to contaminated cabin air. When they do, they will find the evidence base to support their work is woefully insufficient to guide practice.

This chapter documents the experience and learning of the author and her research team, who have examined over 100 aircrew over the past 18 years, in order to illustrate more clearly to clinicians the range of symptoms reported and neuropsychological difficulties identified, and how these impact upon a pilot's ability to perform his/her duties. Some of the diagnostic challenges and clinical issues encountered as well as flight safety concerns are also discussed in the rest of the chapter.

Case Study 1

A Single Fume Event (Acute Exposure): Oil Leak Confirmed by Aircraft Engineers

In 2006 the author assessed a commercial airline pilot who had been involved in a very serious incident on a short-haul domestic flight in 1999. He had flown the same aircraft on two inter-city domestic flights that day and several crew members complained of feeling increasingly unwell during these flights. On the third and final flight, as the plane took off, both the pilot and copilot noticed a horrible sulfurous smell, which then dissipated.

Immediately prior to descent, the pilot began to feel dizzy and his copilot suddenly announced that he felt sick and was about to vomit, so he put on his oxygen mask. Shortly afterwards the pilot decided to do the same as he began to feel nauseous and thought he might lose consciousness. He feared for his life as he could not lift his arm or talk and was unable to fulfil his duties. Fortunately, the copilot recovered quickly after breathing oxygen and was able to land the plane on his own. Gradually, the pilot recovered too. On landing, cabin crew reported that a number of passengers were asleep and impossible to rouse. While on the ground, engineers boarded the aircraft and commented on how ill the pilot looked and the strong smell of fumes. There was no medical follow-up of the pilots or passengers. An official air accident investigation concluded there had been a minor oil leak and that the pilots were temporarily affected by polluted cabin air.

The pilot informed the author that he had fully recovered from this incident and had been told he was fit to fly. Neuropsychological assessment was limited in scope because the pilot's first language was not English. Testing did not find evidence of cognitive impairment, beyond slightly weak performance on tests of processing speed (low average to average range) in comparison with visual reasoning tests (superior range). The pilot passed a test of effort.

However, the pilot met criteria for a diagnosis of posttraumatic stress disorder and had not resumed flying since the incident for fear of triggering traumatic memories. The pilot did not have a significant medical or psychiatric history or a history of substance abuse prior to the cabin air incident. He has since appeared in a number of film documentaries to raise awareness of the contaminated cabin air issue (BBC Panorama, 2008).

Case Study 2

Cumulative Exposure to Fumes Over Time (Acute on Chronic Exposure): Evidence of Exposure Not Available

The author previously described the case of a middle-aged commercial airline pilot who reported a gradual deterioration in health over an 11-year period of flying (Mackenzie Ross et al., 2006). The pilot often smelled oily fumes while flying, which caused a sore throat on occasion, but he thought this was a normal aspect of flying the type of aircraft he had been assigned.

Within a year, he developed gastrointestinal problems and skin ulcerations on the parts of his body exposed to air vents and he reported a gradual deterioration in cognitive function. Medical investigations undertaken by his general practitioner and two specialists failed to identify a cause for his symptoms.

The pilot suffered a marked deterioration in cognitive function after experiencing a more serious fume event that provoked symptoms of dizziness as well as eye and throat irritation in both the pilot and copilot, and they filed a flight safety report on landing. The pilot resumed flying within a few days but developed insomnia, fatigue, coordination problems, joint weakness, excessive sweating, and poor memory and concentration. He was signed off work and referred to neurology and neuropsychology.

Neurological examination found evidence of coordination problems and positive Romberg sign, mild sensory neuropathy, autonomic dysfunction, and increased autoantibodies against nervous system proteins suggesting neuronal injury had occurred. As with Case 1, neuropsychological assessment did not find evidence of global intellectual decline, but the pilot's performance on tests of processing speed, auditory working memory, verbal learning, and mental flexibility (below average to average range) appeared weak relative to his overall level of intellectual functioning (high average range). The pilot passed a test of effort. Objective measurement of mood state did not find evidence of mood disorder, somatic symptoms, or related disorders. The pilot did not have a significant medical or psychiatric history or a history of substance abuse.

The aviation authority did not accept his symptoms had been caused by contaminated air and withdrew his license to fly on psychiatric grounds, despite the fact he was not suffering from any mood disorder and had not been examined by a psychiatrist.

Case Study 3

Cumulative Exposure to Fumes Over Time (Chronic Exposure): Toxic Fumes Identified by Air Quality Analysis

The author previously described the case of a middle-aged pilot who flew private jets and whose health suddenly deteriorated over a 3-year period after he began flying a particular aircraft type (Mackenzie Ross, 2023). The pilot had been in good health for the first 10 years of his career when he worked as a commercial airline pilot. He then took a job that involved flying a business man to meetings around the world on private jets, and he remained in good health for the next few years.

Four years into his new job, the pilot was assigned a new aircraft that was being monitored because the APU was showing signs of depreciation and was not functioning properly. Aircrew on this aircraft repeatedly complained of oily smells. The pilot developed a sudden-onset chesty cough, fatigue, and change of taste shortly after he began flying this aircraft, but his symptoms resolved within a matter of days.

One year later he developed pins and needles in his hands and feet and stabbing pain in his right foot and groin. He was referred for nerve conduction studies, which did not identify any abnormalities. One month later he developed fever, sweating, headache, diarrhea, fatigue, and shortness of breath, which persisted for weeks, and he was referred to specialists in tropical diseases. An infectious process could not be identified and the specialist asked whether the pilot had been exposed to toxic chemicals. The pilot eventually responded to antibiotic treatment but suffered further bouts of bronchitis over the next year. He felt progressively more tired during this time, his eyesight deteriorated, and he continued to suffer intermittent paresthesias in his limbs and groin.

The pilot's employer and five cabin crew who worked on the aircraft also developed ill health, with various symptoms being reported such as paresthesias, cognitive impairment, headaches, visual difficulties, nausea and balance problems, coughs, and severe mood swings.

Gradually a link was suspected between the strange smells on the aircraft and the deteriorating health of those who flew on it, and therefore air quality analysis was commissioned. This found high concentrations of VOCs (mainly solvents found in fuels) and the APU was replaced.

The pilot took a period of leave and returned to work after the APU had been replaced, but he continued to feel fatigued and cognitively impaired and suffered intermittent episodes of paresthesias. He subsequently lost his license to fly. Routine medical investigations failed to identify a cause for his symptoms. One day the pilot was contacted by a colleague who told him about aerotoxic syndrome and suggested he pay for specialist tests including neuropsychological assessment.

The author assessed him in 2015. Premorbid IQ was estimated to be in the high average range. Neuropsychological assessment did not find evidence of global intellectual decline but did reveal subtle under-functioning on tests of processing speed (low average to average range), auditory memory (average), and executive tasks (low average range). The pilot passed tests of effort. He did not have a significant medical or psychiatric history prior to flying the aircraft with a faulty APU. He did not report significant levels of depression or anxiety or other psychiatric symptoms on questionnaire measures or on a personality test.

With no income or a formal diagnosis that might have enabled him to claim insurance, the pilot was forced to sell his home and investments. These financial difficulties had a great impact on the pilot, his partner, and their children.

The author re-interviewed the pilot 6 years after assessing him and found his symptoms had improved and he no longer complained of cognitive impairment, only fatigue. He had been re-assessed by a neuropsychologist, who did not identify any abnormalities, for example, performance on processing speed tests was in the very superior range, performance on executive tests was in the high average to very superior range, and performance on auditory memory tests was above average.

Fortunately, the pilot was able to obtain his Class 1 medical certificate and resume flying. He took a job on a regional airline, but struggled to cope with the workload because of fatigue; he developed tingling in his lips, which he suspected was caused by exposure to fumes, so he stopped flying within a couple of months. Fatigue continues to limit what he can do and he feels he has no choice but to accept a "lesser" job than the one he had before. He also feels frustrated and upset by the way he was treated by some healthcare professionals, who dismissed his complaints or charged him large sums of money for tests that were not useful to him in the end, and for the financial losses he sustained and the impact of this on his partner and children.

Case Series Analyses

Series 1

In 2006, the author was asked to collate data from all of the airline pilots who had been assessed in her department up until that date and present the findings to the Department of Transport and the COT. This work was described and published in a scientific paper (Mackenzie Ross, 2008).

Overall, 27 pilots had undergone neuropsychological and adult mental health assessment undertaken by 12 examiners instructed to search for alternative explanations for their symptoms other than exposure to toxic fumes. To reduce the risk of false-positive findings, nine pilots were excluded from further analysis because they had a medical or psychiatric condition that might otherwise explain their difficulties, leaving a final sample size of 18 pilots. The average number of years spent flying was 22 years (range=5–40 years).

Of these pilots, 13 reported acute symptoms that started immediately after exposure to contaminated air such as eye, ear, nose, throat irritation; breathing difficulties; headache; nausea; gastrointestinal problems; dizziness; fatigue; and cognitive impairment. The impact on the pilots' ability to perform their duties was alarming and included being unable to retain information or confusing numerical information from air traffic control, completing tasks in the wrong sequence, feeling unable to problem-solve, feeling intoxicated, losing track of conversations, becoming easily distracted, and memory difficulties. Several pilots reported being unaware of the extent of impairment until it was pointed out by colleagues. Others found it necessary to ask for assistance from colleagues.

Acute symptoms were reported to resolve initially on cessation of exposure (or donning of oxygen masks). However, 17 pilots reported development of more persistent symptoms after repeated exposures over time, which included fatigue, insomnia, fluctuating gastrointestinal problems, numbness and tingling in fingers and toes, and memory and word-finding difficulties. Two pilots reported being so fatigued they had micro-sleeps while flying the aircraft. Nine pilots were still working. The remainder were on sick leave or had retired on ill health grounds or for personal reasons.

Neuropsychological assessment found language, perceptual skills, and general intellectual ability were preserved (mean full-scale IQ 119), but performance on tests of psychomotor speed, attention, and executive functioning was below expected levels. None of the pilots was suffering from mood or anxiety disorder and none failed effort testing. Statistical analyses confirmed the cognitive deficits were not due to mood disorder or malingering. A number of significant correlations were observed between indices of exposure (e.g., hours flying and duration of flying), verbal memory, information processing speed, and executive function, but some of these correlations became nonsignificant when the potentially confounding effect of age was controlled for. Firm conclusions could not be drawn regarding a causal link with contaminated air because the cohort of pilots was small, self-selected, and only crude indices of exposure were available (i.e., self-report); therefore, further research was recommended.

Series 2

In 2008 two doctoral students undertook further research, under the supervision of the author. They randomly selected 29 pilots from a union database and invited them to undergo neuropsychological assessment. The average number of years spent flying was 21 years. A total of 21 pilots had experienced at least one contaminated air event.

Performance on neuropsychological tests was compared with normative comparison standards. Overall IQ was higher than the UK standardization sample (mean FSIQ=136). Just over one third of pilots performed significantly lower than expected on a test of psychomotor speed, and 18.2% performed lower than expected on tests of auditory working memory span, visual sequencing, and verbal reasoning. This was consistent with subjective complaints of attentional problems and mental slowing. Performance was compared with two other cohorts: Case Series 1 and a cohort of farmers who had been exposed to pesticides containing organophosphate compounds. Although the three groups differed in terms of overall level of intellectual functioning, their neuropsychological profiles mirrored each other with pronounced dips on tests of attention, psychomotor speed, and visual sequencing.

Discussion

At some point in their career, during their clinical practice aviation neuropsychologists are likely to encounter aircrew who report ill health and cognitive impairment following exposure to contaminated cabin air. They will find the evidence base to support their work insufficient to guide practice due to ongoing scientific debate and disagreement between important stakeholders regarding aerotoxic syndrome. The purpose of this chapter was to document the experience and learning of the author and her team in the hope of improving recognition, care, and management of these cases and to stimulate interest and further research.

A great deal of neuropsychological knowledge has emerged from the study of single cases and this chapter has documented the neuropsychological profiles observed, the clinical issues encountered, and the flight safety concerns and challenges of working with aircrew who believe their health and cognitive function have been compromised by exposure to neurotoxic substances.

The neuropsychological profiles observed in pilots reporting a history of exposure to contaminated cabin air were remarkably similar. Overall intellectual functioning was relatively intact, but pilots showed evidence of subtle under-functioning on tests of processing speed, working memory, and executive function.

Deficits were subtle and unlikely to be picked up by cognitive screening tools or simulator checks, and a pilot may be reluctant to disclose these difficulties to aviation medical examiners for fear of losing their license. Indeed, around half of the pilots we examined in Case Series 1 were still flying, while the remainder were on sick leave or had retired on ill health grounds. All were concerned about their ability to fly aircraft safely.

Furthermore, although neuropsychological assessment identified subtle deficits, the impact on the pilot's ability to fly aircraft was alarming, with some pilots becoming completely incapacitated at the controls. Others confused information form air traffic control, and one pilot reporting the need to sleep during flight. Several pilots were unaware of their difficulties until it was pointed out to them by colleagues.

Consistency of Findings With Other Research

A small number of neuropsychological studies have been undertaken in different countries over the past two decades, exploring the nature and severity of cognitive complaints reported by aircrew following exposure to fumes on board aircraft.

In 2002, Coxon published findings from a case series of eight Australian aircrew who reported mental confusion, concentration difficulties, and memory problems following alleged exposure to oil emissions on BAe 146 aircraft. All were female, their ages ranged from 24 to 56 years, and they had worked on this aircraft type for between 2 and 12 years. Psychometric assessment revealed evidence of reduced choice and sequential reaction time, psychomotor speed, grip strength, and auditory verbal memory compared with normative data, in all but one member; reduced auditory working, memory span, concentration, and recall of visual information in four aircrew; and five aircrew showed impairment on a sequencing task. Although this was a case series in which no control group was available for comparison and no statistical analyses were undertaken, Coxon concluded that there were sufficient grounds to warrant further investigation. She recommended a wider study of BAe 146 aircrew be undertaken.

In 2005, Heuser et al. reported findings from an evaluation of 26 North American flight attendants with complaints after probable exposure to cabin fumes on one or multiple occasions. In most cases, fume events resulted in flight interruption, emergency room visits, or sick leave. All underwent a neurological examination and neuropsychological assessment and 12 underwent positron emission tomography (PET) brain imaging. Unfortunately, the authors did not specify the psychometric tests used or test scores, but they reported that all flight attendants exhibited neuropsychological deficits (particularly memory impairment); neurological examination results were abnormal in nine and mildly abnormal in six flight attendants; and PET imaging showed decreased activity in frontal regions and increased activity in occipital and limbic areas. The authors recommend further research and that a protocol be created, outlining the evaluations flight personnel should undergo following exposure to cabin fumes.

In 2014, Coxon described three case studies involving pilots repeatedly exposed to fume events over very long careers (17–30 years). They reported a variety of physical symptoms (fatigue, skin rashes, eye irritation, headaches, sinusitis) and a gradual decline in cognitive function. Neuropsychological assessment found evidence of impaired processing speed, executive functioning, and new learning/memory. All three pilots eventually ceased flying due to ill health. They had complained of ill health and cognitive problems many times beforehand, but their symptoms were dismissed as "temporary problems." These cases highlight how neurotoxic effects can take time to fully evolve. Coxon recommended that every worker exposed to neurotoxic chemicals, who complains of cognitive impairment, is thoroughly investigated and has follow-up evaluations at regular intervals, because slowed processing speed and executive dysfunction would impair a pilot's ability to handle aircraft in an emergency situation.

In 2016, Reneman et al. published findings from a case series of 12 aircrew who complained of cognitive impairment, who underwent neuropsychological assessment and magnetic resonance imaging (MRI) brain imaging including diffuse tensor imaging, spectroscopy, and functional MRI. Results were compared with those obtained from 11 healthy volunteers, matched for gender, age, and IQ. Aircrew performed more poorly than controls on a working memory task and two reaction time tests. On MRI, white matter macrostructure did not differ between the groups, but small differences were noted in microstructure in specific brain regions in the corpus callosum. Higher cerebral blood flow was noted in the left occipital cortex and hypoactivation in the right prefrontal cortex when performing an executive task. The extent of cognitive impairment correlated with subjective reports and white matter integrity, but none of these variables correlated with flight hours. No significant differences in brain metabolites or volume were observed between the groups. Given the obvious aviation safety implications, the authors concluded further research was warranted in which alternative explanations should be considered such as irregular work schedules and dysregulation of biological clocks.

Neuropsychological studies have consistently documented cognitive deficits in aircrew who report exposure to toxic fumes on aircraft, which involve reduced processing speed, executive, and memory difficulties. However, every study has methodological weaknesses such as recruitment of very small, self-selected samples, lack of comparison groups, and objective indices of exposure, making it difficult to establish causation. Nevertheless, these initial findings highlight the need for further research because any form of central nervous system dysfunction is dangerous in a safety-critical environment and constitutes a flight safety risk. Unfortunately, industry, regulatory authorities, and government departments appear reluctant to fund or commission large-scale epidemiological studies, despite being advised to do so by scientific advisory committees and government inquiries.

Clinical Issues

Some of the clinical issues encountered by the author when assessing pilots were distressing, challenging, and difficult to respond to due to ongoing controversy in the industry and insufficient evidence to guide practice. For example:

- Many pilots asked if they should continue or return to flying, a question that was difficult to answer with any degree of confidence for a host of different reasons. Neuropsychological tests used in routine clinical practice were not designed to predict flying ability. They measure cognitive skills assumed to be important for the job, but the decision as to whether a pilot is fit to fly needs to be taken by aviation specialists. As far as the author can ascertain, there is no research that specifically addresses the link between cognitive difficulties reported by aircrew who believe they are suffering from aerotoxic syndrome and a pilot's ability to safely operate an aircraft. Successful treatment of chemical poisoning requires early diagnosis and cessation of exposure. If there is a link between exposure to toxic fumes in cabin air and ill health (a topic that continues to be debated), then returning a pilot to flying puts them at risk of further exposure and further cognitive deterioration and is a potential flight safety risk for everyone else on board.
- Pilots often asked what the prognosis is for aerotoxic syndrome and what treatment is available because they all loved their jobs and were keen to regain their health and return to flying. This was impossible to answer; since the aviation industry continues to deny any link between contaminants in cabin air and chronic ill health, no long-term outcome or treatment studies have ever been commissioned. Some pilots were so desperate to return to flying they agreed to pay large sums of money to private healthcare providers who offered treatments with no or limited evidence base (e.g., vitamin injections).
- Those who had retired were not only devastated to have lost the job they loved and trained so hard for, but they also suffered financially. Without an agreed diagnosis, they were unable to claim income protection insurance or critical illness cover and many had to sell their homes, remove children from schools, and cash-in investments to survive.

Conclusion

Clearly there is an urgent need to resolve the debate about aerotoxic syndrome to reduce suffering and for obvious flight safety reasons. Unfortunately, it does not look like this will happen any time soon. Sadly, neurotoxic conditions are often controversial because exposure frequently occurs in the workplace where an admission of chemical poisoning might have health and safety implications for the employer and result in litigation.

To complicate matters further, few healthcare professionals in the United Kingdom receive training in toxicology unless they specialize in occupational medicine, which means neurotoxic conditions are frequently misdiagnosed or not diagnosed at all. Failure to diagnose results in patients being referred to multiple specialists (often over many years) based on symptom clusters rather than on a clear diagnosis. This is costly for the health service and distressing for patients.

There is an urgent need for increased awareness and understanding of neurotoxic conditions, and neuropsychologists have an important role to play in both clinical and research settings in detecting and evaluating the effects of toxic substances. Neurotoxic conditions can be difficult to diagnose because routine medical investigations and brain imaging frequently fail to identify abnormalities (Hartman, 1995).

Neuropsychological assessment has been described by Muriel Lezak as the most sensitive means of examining the effects of toxic exposure, of monitoring for industrial safety, and of understanding the complaints and psychosocial problems of persons exposed to toxins (Bowler & Lezak, 2015; Lezak, 1984). It is also useful for differential diagnosis, whereby alternative causes of cognitive impairment are explored and ruled out. The author has examined pilots who reported cognitive impairment that they attributed to contaminated air, but that the author considered more likely to be due to other factors. In one particularly memorable case, the author's suspicion a pilot was showing signs of early dementia, not toxic poisoning, was subsequently confirmed.

Considerable scientific uncertainty still surrounds this issue, and given the limited number of high-quality research studies undertaken over the past two decades, further research is warranted. What is needed is a prospective epidemiological survey of a large and representative randomly recruited sample of aircrew, in which symptoms are described and qualified in exposed and unexposed groups and compared with rates in other clinical and general populations. However, such an exposure–health outcome study will require airline participation and facilitation, which has not been forthcoming to date.

References

Ackland, C.A., Molesworth, B.R.C., Grisham, J.R., & Lovibond, P.F. (2022). Pilot mental health, methodologies, and findings: A systematic review. *Aerospace Medicine and Human Performance, 93*(9), 696–708. https://doi.org/10.3357/AMHP.6043.2022

Anderson, J. (2021). Sources of onboard fumes and smoke reported by U.S. airlines. *Aerospace, 8*(5), Article 122. https://doi.org/10.3390/aerospace8050122

BBC Panorama. (2008). *Something in the air* [Video file]. https://www.youtube.com/watch?v=3dsDznr4z5w

Bendtsen, K.M., Bengtsen, E., Saber, A.T., & Vogel, U. (2021). A review of health effects associated with exposure to jet engine emissions in and around airports. *Environmental Health, 20,* Article 10. https://doi.org/10.1186/s12940-020-00690-y

Boeing. (2016). *Boeing response to query: Cabin air & bleed air contaminants.* Cabin-Air-Contaminants-Boeing-backgrounder (newairplane.com)

Bowler, R.M., & Lezak, M.D. (2015). Neuropsychological evaluation and exposure to neurotoxicants. In M. Lotti & M.L. Bleeker(Eds.), *Handbook of clinical neurology* (Vol. 131, pp. 23–45). Elsevier.

Burdon, J., Budnik, L.G., Baur, X., Hageman, G., Howard, C.V., Roig, J., Coxon, L., Furlong, C.E., Gee, D., Loraine, T., Terry, A.V., Jr., Midavaine, J., Peterson, H., Bron, D., Sosklone, C.L., & Michaelis, S. (2023). Health consequences of exposure to aircraft contaminated air and fume events: A narrative review and medical protocol for the investigation of exposed aircrew and passengers. *Environmental Health, 22*, Article 43. https://doi.org/10.1186/s12940-023-00987-8

Chen, R., Fang, L., Liu, J., Herbig, B., Norrefeldt, V., Mayer, F., Fox, R., & Wargocki, P. (2021). Cabin air quality on non-smoking commercial flights: A review of published data on airborne pollutants. *Indoor Air, 31,* 926–957. https://doi.org/10.1111/ina.12831

Committee on Toxicity of Chemicals in Food Consumer Products and the Environment. (2007). *Statement on the review of the cabin air environment, ill health in aircraft crews and the possible relationship to smoke/fume events in aircraft* [Final report]. https://cot.food.gov.uk/Statement%20on%20Aircraft%20Cabin%20Air%20Quality#executive-summary

Committee on Toxicity of Chemical in Food Consumer Products and the Environment. (2013). *Position paper on cabin air.* https://cot.food.gov.uk/Statement%20on%20Aircraft%20Cabin%20Air%20Quality#executive-summary

Cox, L., & Michaelis, S. (2002). A survey of health symptoms in BAe 146 aircrew. *Journal of Occupational Health and Safety (Australia & New Zealand), 18,* 305–312.

Coxon, L. (2002). Neuropsychological assessment of a group of BAe 146 aircraft crew members exposed to jet engine oil emissions. *Journal of Occupational Health and Safety (Australia & New Zealand), 18,* 313–319.

Coxon, L. (2014). Delayed cognitive impairment and pilot incapacitation following contaminated air inhalation. *Journal of Biological Physics and Chemistry, 14,* 107–110. https://doi.org/10.4024/13CO14M.jbpc.14.04

Crump, D., Harrison, P., & Walton, C. (2011). *Aircraft cabin air sampling study: Part 1 of the final report.* Institute of Environment and Health, Cranfield University.

de Boer, J., Antelo, A., van der Veen, I., Brandsma, S., & Lammertse, N. (2015). Tricresyl phosphate and the aerotoxic syndrome of flight crew members – current gaps in knowledge. *Chemosphere, 119,* S58–S61.

de Ree, H., van den Berg, M., Brand, T., Mulder, G.J., Simons, R., van Zanten, B.V., & Westerink, R.H. (2014). Health risk assessment of exposure to TriCresyl Phosphates (TCPs) in aircraft: A commentary. *Neurotoxicology, 45,* 209–215. https://doi.org/10.1016/j.neuro.2014.08.011

European Aviation Safety Agency (EASA). (2017). *Final report EASA_REP_RESEA_2014_4. Research Project: CAQ Preliminary cabin air quality measurement campaign.* https://www.easa.europa.eu/en/document-library/research-reports/easarepresea20144

Federal Aviation Administration. (2020). *Cabin air quality.* https://www.faa.gov/newsroom/cabin-air-quality

Fushimi, A., Saitoh, K., Fujitani, Y., & Takegawa, N. (2019). Identification of jet lubrication oil as a major component of aircraft exhaust nanoparticles. *Atmospheric Chemistry and Physics, 19,* 6389–6399. https://doi.org/10.5194/acp-19-6389-2019

Gold, J. (2011, October 6). Boeing suit settlement stirs jetliner air safety debate. *NBC News.* https://www.nbcnews.com/id/wbna44777304

Guan, J., Gao, K., Wang, C., Yang, X., Lin, C-H., Lu, C., & Gao, P. (2014). Measurements of volatile organic compounds in aircraft cabins. Part 1: Methodology and detected VOC species in 107 commercial flights. *Building and Environment, 72,* 154–161. https://doi.org/10.1016/j.buildenv.2013.11.002

Hageman, G., Pal, T.M., Nihom, J., Mackenzie Ross, S.J., & van den Berg, M. (2020). Three patients with probable aerotoxic syndrome. *Clinical Toxicology, 58*(2), 139–142. https://doi.org/10.1080/15563650.2019.1616092

Harper, A. (2005). A survey of health effects in aircrew exposed to airborne contaminants. *Journal of Occupational Health and Safety (Australia & New Zealand), 21*(5), 433.

Hartman, D.E. (1995). *Neuropsychological toxicology: Identification and assessment of human neurotoxic syndromes* (2nd ed.). Plenum Press.

Hayes, K., Megson, D., Doyle, A., & O'Sullivan, G. (2021). Occupational risk of organophosphates and other chemical and radiative exposure in the aircraft cabin: A systematic review. *Science of The Total Environment, 796,* Article 148742. https://doi.org/10.1016/j.scitotenv.2021.148742

Heuser, G., Aguilera, O., Heuser, S., & Gordon, R. (2005). Clinical evaluation of flight attendants after exposure to fumes in cabin air. *Proceedings of the BALPA Air Safety and Cabin Air Quality International Aero Industry Conference* (pp. 107–112). Imperial College, London.

High Court of Australia. (2010). *Transcript of proceedings* [HCATrans 238]. https://jade.io/article/238302

Hirtz, D., Thurman, D.J., Gwinn-Hardy, K., Mohamed, M., Chadhuri, A.R., & Zalutsky, R. (2007). How common are the "common" neurologic disorders? *Neurology, 68,* 326–337. https://doi.org/10.1212/01.wnl.0000252807.38124.a3

House of Lords Science and Technology Committee. (2007). *First report of session 2007–2008. Air travel and health: An update.* The Stationery Office.

Houtzager, M.M.G., Havermans, J.G.B.A., & Bos, J.G.H. (2013). *Investigation of presence and concentration of tricresylphosphates in cockpits of KLM Boeing 737 aircraft during normal operational conditions* (TNO report 2013, TNO2013 R11976).

Howard, C.V., Michaelis, S., & Watterson, A. (2017). The aetiology of aerotoxic syndrome – a toxico-pathological viewpoint. *Open Access Journal of Toxicology, 1*(5), Article 555575. https://doi.org/10.19080/OAJT.2017.01.555575

Howard, C.V., Johnson, D.W., Morton, J., Michaelis, S., Supplee, D., & Burdon, J. (2018). Is a cumulative exposure to a background aerosol of nanoparticles part of the causal mechanism of aerotoxic syndrome. *Nanomedicine and Nanoscience Research, 1,* Article 139. https://doi.org/10.29011/JNAN-139

Howard, C.V. (2020). Inappropriate use of risk assessment in addressing health hazards posed by civil aircraft cabin air. *Open Access Journal of Toxicology, 4*(2), 65–71.

International Air Transport Association. (2023). *Travel and safety.* https://www.iata.org/en/programs/safety/

Lambert-James, E., & Williams, N. (2014, February 26). *Fume events: The current position* [Online]. Clyde & Co LLP. http://www.lexology.com/library/detail.aspx?g=cdfb2845-fa16-48d4-a25d-85f8e4d0b911

Lezak, M.D. (1984). Neuropsychological assessment in behavioral toxicology – developing techniques and interpretative issues. *Scandinavian Journal of Work, Environment & Health, 10,* 25–29. http://www.jstor.org/stable/40965024

Mackenzie Ross, S. (2008). Cognitive function following exposure to contaminated air on commercial aircraft: A case series of 27 pilots seen for clinical purposes. *Journal of Nutritional & Environmental Medicine, 17,* 111–126. https://doi.org/10.1080/13590840802240067

Mackenzie Ross, S. (2017). Assessing cognitive function in airline pilots: The importance of neuropsychological assessment. In R. Bor, C. Eriksen, M. Oakes, & P. Scragg (Eds.), *Pilot mental health assessment and support: A practitioner's guide* (pp. 116–131). Routledge.

Mackenzie Ross, S. (2023). Aerotoxic syndrome: Are passengers and aircrew breathing toxic cabin air? In J. Fish, S. Betteridge, & B. Wilson (Eds.), *Rare conditions, diagnostic challenges, and controversies in clinical neuropsychology. Out of the ordinary* (pp. 191–205). Routledge Taylor & Francis Group. https://doi.org/10.4324/9781003228226-15

Mackenzie Ross, S., Harper, A., & Burdon, J. (2006). Ill health following exposure to contaminated aircraft air: Psychosomatic disorder or neurological injury? *Journal of Occupational Health and Safety (Australia & New Zealand), 22,* 521–528.

Mackenzie Ross, S., Harrison, V., Madeley, L., Davis, K., Abraham-Smith, K., Hughes, T., & Mason, O. (2011). Cognitive function following reported exposure to contaminated air on commercial aircraft: Methodological considerations for future researchers. *Journal of Biological Physics and Chemistry, 11*(4), 180–191. https://doi.org/10.4024/41111/11-4-abs7.jbpc.11.04

Michaelis, S., Burdon, J., Howard, C.V. (2017). Aerotoxic syndrome: A new occupational disease. *Public Health Panorama, 3*(1), 141–356.

Michaelis, S. (2003). A survey of health symptoms in BALPA Boeing 757 pilots. *Journal of Occupational Health and Safety (Australia & New Zealand), 19*(3), 253–261.

Michaelis, S. (2011). Contaminated aircraft cabin air. *Journal of Biological Physics and Chemistry, 11,* 132–145. https://doi.org/10.4024/41111/11-4-abs1.jbpc.11.04

Michaelis, S., Loraine, T., & Howard, C.V. (2021). Ultrafine particle levels measured on board short-haul commercial passenger jet aircraft. *Environmental Health, 20,* Article 89. https://doi.org/10.1186/s12940-021-00770-7

Montgomery, M.R., Wier, G.T., Zieve, F.J., & Anders, M.W. (1977). Human intoxication following inhalation exposure to a synthetic jet lubricating oil. *Clinical Toxicology, 11,* 423–426. https://doi.org/10.3109/15563657708988205

Murawski, J. T. L., & Supplee, D. S. (2008). An attempt to characterize the frequency, health impact, and operational costs of oil in the cabin and flight deck supply air on US commercial aircraft. *Journal of American Society for Testing & Materials International, 5*(5), 1–15. https://doi.org/10.1520/JAI101640

Parliament of the Commonwealth of Australia. (2000). *British aerospace: Evidence to the Senate Rural and Regional Affairs and Transport References Committee. Air safety and cabin air quality in the BAe 146 aircraft.* https://www.aph.gov.au/binaries/senate/committee/rrat_ctte/completed_inquiries/1999-02/bae/report/report.pdf

Reneman, L., Schagen, S. B., Mulder, M., Mutsaers, H. J., Hageman, G., & de Ruiter, M. B. (2016). Cognitive impairment and associated loss in brain white microstructure in aircrew members exposed to engine oil fumes. *Brain Imaging and Behavior, 10,* 437–444. https://doi.org/10.1007/s11682-015-9395-3

Schindler, B. K., Weiss, T., Schütze, A., Koslitz, S., Broding, H. C., Bünger, J., & Brüning, T. (2013). Occupational exposure of air crews to tricresyl phosphate isomers and organophosphate flame retardants after fume events. *Archives of Toxicology, 87,* 645–648. https://doi.org/10.1007/s00204-012-0978-0

Schuchardt, S., Koch, W., & Rosenberger, W. (2019). Cabin air quality-Quantitative comparison of volatile air contaminants at different flight phases during 177 commercial flights. *Building and Environment, 148,* 498–507. https://doi.org/10.1016/j.buildenv.2018.11.028

Shehadi, M., Jones, B., & Hosni, M. (2016). Characterization of the frequency and nature of bleed air contamination events in commercial aircraft. *Indoor Air, 26,* 478–488.

Solbu, K., Daae, H. L., Olsen, R., Thorud, S., Ellingsen, D. G., Lindgren, T., Bakke, B., Lundanes, E., & Molander, P. (2011). Organophosphates in aircraft cabin and cockpit air-method development and measurements of contaminants. *Journal of Environmental Monitoring, 13,* 1393–1403. https://doi.org/10.1039/c0em00763c

Somers, M. (2005). Assessing over thirty flight crew who have presented as a result of being unwell after exposure to fumes on the BAe 146 jets. *Proceedings of BALPA Air Safety and Cabin Air Quality International Aero Industry Conference* (pp. 131–145). Imperial College, London.

UK Civil Aviation Authority. (2024a). *Our role. Information on our work and strategic objectives.* https://www.caa.co.uk/Our-work/About-us/Our-role/

UK Civil Aviation Authority. (2024b). *Aircraft fume events. Information for health professionals on aircraft fume events.* https://www.caa.co.uk/passengers-and-public/before-you-fly/am-i-fit-to-fly/guidance-for-health-professionals/aircraft-fume-events/

Wang, C., Yang, X., Guan, J., & Gao, K. (2014). Source apportionment of volatile organic compounds (VOCs) in aircraft cabin. *Building and Environment, 81,* 1–6. https://doi.org/10.1016/j.buildenv.2014.06.007

Wang, C., Yang, X., Guan, J., Gao, K., & Li, Z. (2014). Volatile organic compounds in aircraft cabin: measurements and correlations between compounds. *Building and Environment, 78,* 89–94. https://doi.org/10.1016/j.buildenv.2014.04.016

Winder, C., & Balouet, J. C. (2000). Aerotoxic syndrome: Adverse health effects following exposure to jet oil mist during commercial flights. *Proceedings of the International Congress on Occupational Health,* 196–199.

Winder, C., & Balouet, J. C. (2002). The toxicity of commercial jet oils. *Environmental Research, 89,* 146–164. https://doi.org/10.1006/enrs.2002.4346

Wolkoff, P., Crump, D. R., & Harrison, P. T. C. (2016). Pollutant exposures and health symptoms in aircrew and office workers: Is there a link? *Environment International, 87,* 74–84. https://doi.org/10.1016/j.envint.2015.11.008

Section V

Specialist Aspects of Aviation Neuropsychology

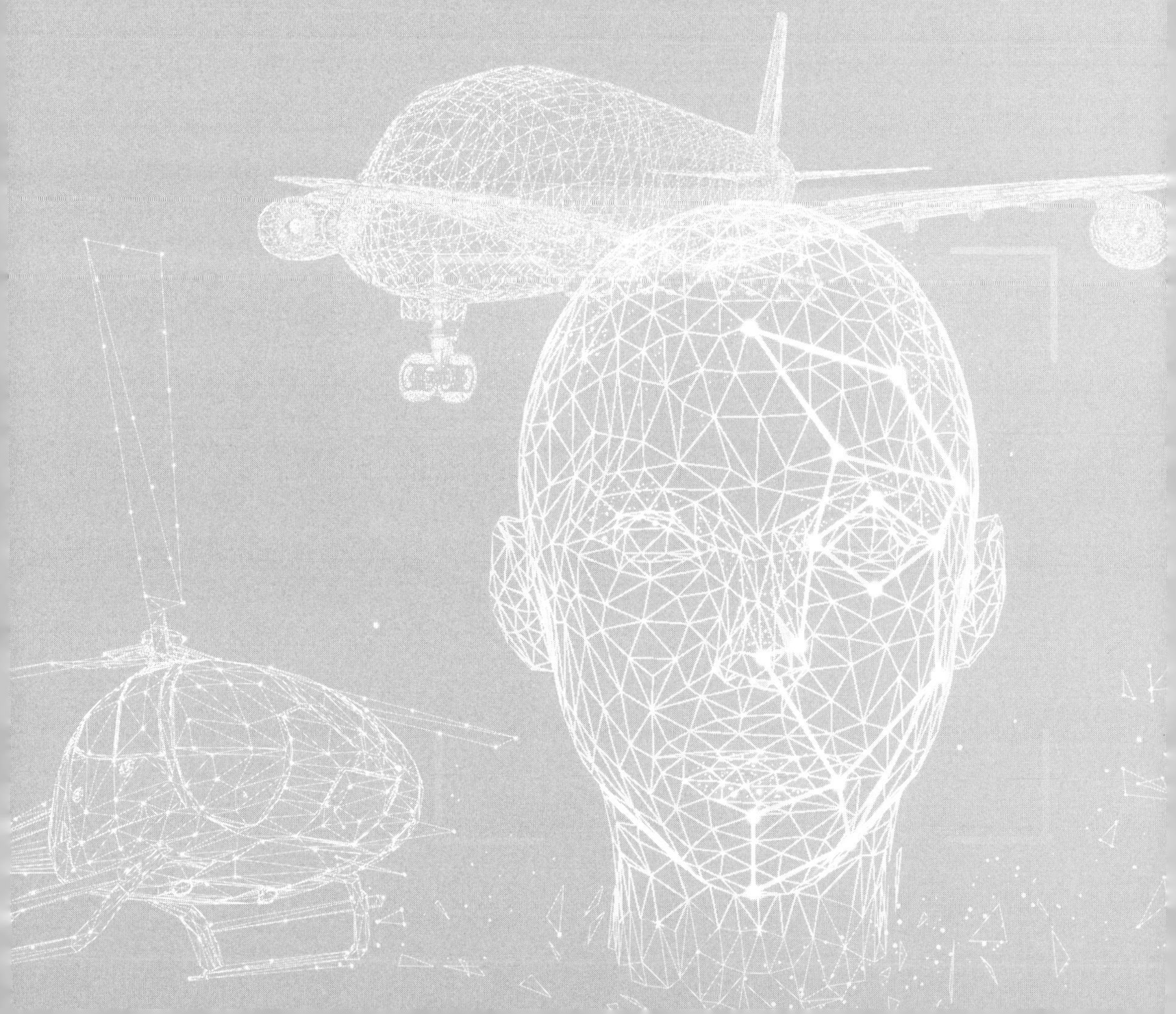

Chapter 24
Conditions Common in Aviation and Their Neuropsychological Implications

Lauren Drag

Introduction

Over the span of just a few months during the winter of 2022/2023, there were several well-publicized mishaps and near-misses in commercial aviation. In December 2022, an aircraft lost altitude shortly after take-off, entering a steep dive before recovering less than 800 ft above the ocean (Shepardson, 2023a). In February 2023, a departing passenger jet and an incoming cargo plane came within 100 ft of colliding (Shepardson, 2023b). In March 2023, two planes clipped wings while taxiing (Andersen, 2023). The common thread among these incidents is that they were all suspected to be due to human error.

Thus, even in the current era of groundbreaking advances in aircraft technology, aviation safety continues to be dependent on the pilots flying the plane. Pilots, just like other individuals outside of the aviation world, are susceptible to a range of mental health and psychosocial issues. Some of these will be covered in this chapter, to include sleep problems, fatigue, depression, anxiety, stress, and burnout. These factors may be unrelated to the condition or circumstances that bring a pilot in for neuropsychological testing but can nevertheless affect a pilot's cognitive and overall functioning. Across most workplaces, such issues can significantly impact an employee's productivity, level of engagement, and performance. However, unlike in many other occupations, the well-being of the pilot can also have significant implications for the lives and safety of others.

Sleep and Fatigue in Pilots

Aircrew fatigue has consistently been identified as a significant issue for the aviation industry. Understanding the potentially disastrous impact of fatigue on aviation safety, regulatory bodies and airlines have strict requirements in place to minimize fatigue. For example, the Federal Aviation Administration (FAA) has set maximums for flight duty periods (FDP), ranging from 14 to 19 hr depending on the number of pilots in the flight crew (an FDP typically starts when pilots report for duty and ends when the aircraft is parked). Similarly, the FAA has set upper limits for total flight times (between 9 and 17 hr) and cumulative flight hours (100 hr per month and 1,000 hr per year). Some regulators such as the FAA also require airlines to establish fatigue risk management systems, including education and awareness training for crewmembers. Such programs outline route-specific requirements, including the number and types of pilots in the flight crew, allowable FDP start times, allowable flight departure times, minimums for pre-flight rest periods, minimum durations of in-flight sleep opportunities, and minimum layover rest periods.

Despite these mitigations, fatigue continues to be a problem for many pilots. For example, an open letter from the Southwest Airlines Pilot Association (SWAPA) in 2022 cited an increase in fatigue-related callouts. Concerns were raised that "fatigue, both acute and cumulative, has become Southwest Airlines' number-one safety threat ... Our primary job as Pilots is identifying and capturing errors in order to break the error chain, but our ability to do so is compromised when we are fatigued" (SWAPA Board of Directors, 2022, paragraphs 4–5).

The Impact of Job Demands on Sleep

Commercial pilots are at an increased risk of fatigue, sleep disruption, and sleep disorders, which is not surprising given the unique demands of their job. Inherent to their jobs are flights across multiple time zones, irregular and changing work hours, extended work hours, shift work (i.e., working outside of the normal 9 a.m. to 5 p.m. schedule), and frequently changing sleep environments (whether it be the plane bunk, a hotel room, a crash pad, or the airport itself).

Pilots often work long hours. Commercial pilots are commonly paid hourly wages, with a typical pilot flying around 75–80 hr per month. It is important to keep in mind that these work hours typically start when the aircraft brake is released to leave the gate and stop when the cabin door opens for passengers to deplane. These work hours do not include time spent on administrative work, weather look-ups, traversing airports, pre-flight briefings, and commuting to and from home. Thus, a 9-hr flight might involve a total work time of 12 hr or more. The probability of an accident increases as duty time increases for commercial pilots (Goode, 2003).

Long duty periods can impact sleep in different ways, depending on the timing and the duration of the flight (i.e., short-haul vs. long-haul schedules). For short-haul pilots flying shorter but more frequent flights, fatigue can occur due to sleep deprivation, long duty days, and high workloads. Reduced sleep is associated with early morning starts (Hartzler, 2014), which are common for short-haul pilots flying domestic routes. It has been estimated that for every hour that a duty period starts before 9 a.m., total sleep time is reduced by 15 min (Roach et al., 2012). This means a pilot can lose approximately 1 hr of total sleep when assigned a 5 a.m. start time. One less hour of sleep may not be a significant problem on an infrequent basis. However, chronic sleep restriction has significant ramifications, as discussed in the following sections.

Conversely, long-haul pilots often cross multiple time zones on long international flights, and their sleep can be impacted by limited sleep quantity, sustained wakefulness, circadian disturbances, and time zone changes/jet lag. Many long-haul pilots have duty times that start between 12 a.m. and 6 a.m., resulting in conflicts with both circadian rhythms as well as the natural sleep drive that increases at night. Specifically, the high demand for alertness during night flights contradicts the progressively increasing sleep drive that is associated with the body's circadian low and sustained wakefulness at night. Additionally, there can be inconsistencies between the physiological body clock and the local time zone, such as when a California-based pilot's body clock is set to 4 a.m. Pacific Standard Time despite it being bright and sunny upon their 1 p.m. arrival in Germany. In general, nighttime work has a greater impact on fatigue and cognitive performance compared to daytime work (Arsintescu et al., 2022; Kazemi et al., 2016). For this reason, FAA regulations prohibit aircrew from working more than three consecutive FDPs that infringe on the window of circadian low. Given the nature of their schedules, it is not surprising that long-haul pilots often experience reduced sleep, reduced sleep efficiency, and changes in sleep architecture; these sleep changes do not fully return to normal during layovers (Caldwell et al., 2004).

To combat fatigue, pilots flying with augmented crews (i.e., more than the minimum of two pilots) have opportunities for rest during long-haul flights, sleeping on average 3–5 hr during flight (Gander et al., 2013; Rempe et al., 2022; van den Berg et al., 2015). However, the amount of sleep obtained during flight can depend on factors such as whether pilots are on an outbound (i.e., leaving their home airport) versus inbound flight, the time of day (e.g., sleep may not come easily to a pilot who is given rest during the middle of their biological day), and the in-flight timing of the rest break. Sleep dysregulation is particularly worse with eastward flights (Caldwell, 2005), and there are higher rates of fatigue and lower amounts of sleep at the end versus the beginning of long-haul flights (Petrilli et al., 2006). Further, in-flight sleep is less restorative than ground-based sleep (Roach et al., 2010).

Fatigue and Sleep Problems

Sleep disruptions and fatigue are common in pilots and have significant safety ramifications; it has been estimated that over 20 % of aviation incidents are related to fatigue (Marcus & Rosekind, 2017).

Across studies, a high percentage of pilots report high levels of fatigue, daytime sleepiness, and poor sleep quality, even on rest days (Pellegrino et al., 2019; Reis et al., 2016; Venus, 2021). In a recent survey of Saudi Arabian pilots, nearly half of respondents reported insomnia, and over one-third reported impaired sleep quality. Furthermore, 17% of pilots were determined to be at risk of sleep apnea (Alzehairi et al., 2021).

A number of factors can impact the risk of fatigue. Across studies, high rates of sleep complaints and fatigue in pilots have been associated with the following risk factors: early morning starts, a higher number of hours worked per month, working more than three flights per day, finish times after 10 p.m., working both day and night shifts, moderate alcohol consumption, an evening chronotype (i.e., "night owls"), lower rates of physical activity, working more than six consecutive days, working more than four consecutive nights, frequent operational flight delays, and problems commuting between home and domicile (i.e., the airport where their work trips originate; Alzehairi et al., 2021; Bourgeois-Bougrine et al., 2003; Pellegrino et al., 2019; Reis et al., 2016; van Drongelen et al., 2017).

Findings regarding aging and sleep in pilots have been mixed. For example, some studies have shown that older long-haul pilots are more susceptible to sleep fragmentation, sleep loss, and cognitive difficulties during night shifts compared to their younger counterparts, suggesting that adaptation to jet lag may become increasingly difficult with age (see Gander & Signal, 2008). Age has also been shown to be a risk factor for fatigue in pilots (van Drongelen et al., 2017). Conversely, other studies have found an increased risk of sleep problems in younger pilots (Alzehairi et al., 2021). This is not entirely surprising, as older (and presumably more senior) pilots may be better adapted to flight schedules and have higher seniority and priority for selecting favorable flight schedules.

Sleep problems and fatigue can impact flight safety. Pilots report that their fatigue is associated with reduced alertness and attention, increased response times, and minor mistakes (Bourgeois-Bougrine et al., 2003). In one study, 80 % of pilots reported feeling tired enough that their judgment was affected while flying (Jackson & Earl, 2006). While over one-quarter of pilots reported having nodded off during a flight (Gregory et al., 2010), there are likely many more instances of dozing that pilots are not aware of. Lapses in vigilance (also known as microsleeps) during flights are evident on electroencephalography and are nine times more likely to occur during night flights as opposed to day flights. Pilots average 1.9 microsleeps per hour on night flights. Microsleeps are also most common during periods of low workload, such as during the cruise portion of long-haul flights. These microsleeps are not always noticeable to pilots, who may believe they stayed alert when in fact, they repeatedly dozed off in the cockpit (Caldwell et al., 2004).

The Cognitive Impact of Sleep Problems

Sleep deprivation (i.e., a prolonged period of wakefulness without sleep) has a significant impact on cognition. Continued wakefulness beyond 16 hr has been associated with reduced performance across multiple cognitive domains. The largest effects are seen on measures of vigilance with moderate effects on complex attention and working memory and smaller (but still significant) effects on processing speed and learning and memory (Killgore, 2010; Lim & Dinges, 2010; Lopez et al., 2012; O'Hagan et al., 2020). It has been hypothesized that tasks associated with prefrontal functioning are particularly vulnerable to sleep deprivation; this is supported by functional neuroimaging findings (see Lim & Dinges, 2010, for review). Tasks involving reasoning and crystallized intelligence tend to be less sensitive to the effects of sleep deprivation. Studies have shown that 20–24 hr of wakefulness can have the equivalent impact on cognitive and psychomotor coordination tasks as a blood alcohol level of 0.10 (Dawson & Reid, 1997; Lamond & Dawson, 1999). For pilots, these cognitive deficits can directly impact operational skills; impairments are seen in flight simulators following prolonged wakefulness (Caldwell, 2005; Lopez et al., 2012).

The clear impact of sleep deprivation on cognition has obvious implications for a pilot who is attempting to maintain high levels of alertness and cognitive effort in the cockpit while in a prolonged period of wakefulness. However, pilots are also faced with the more chronic problem of sleep restriction, which is the reduction of sleep below baseline amounts. Sleep restriction can be cumulative; for example, multiple consecutive days of early start times can compound over time and can have potent neurocognitive effects. Chronic sleep restriction even to as much as 7 hr of sleep per night has been shown to negatively impact working memory, sustained attention, learning and memory, processing speed, reaction times, response inhibition, verbal fluency, planning, psychomotor vigilance, psychomotor coordination, divided attention, risk-taking, inhibitory control, and emotional processing (Banks & Dinges, 2007; Belenky et al., 2003; Hartzler, 2014; Lowe et al., 2017; Tempesta et al., 2020; Van Dongen et al., 2003). The largest effect sizes are seen in processing speed and attention/vigilance, with complex tasks being more vulnerable to the effects of sleep restriction than simple tasks (Waters & Bucks, 2011). It is also common to see significant intraindividual variability in individuals with sleep problems, both within a task and across a testing session due to fluctuating levels of vigilance. Dysregulated sleep has less of an effect on crystallized abilities, such as retrieval of acquired knowledge, reading comprehension, and visual reasoning. The cumulative impact of chronic sleep restriction on cognition can reach the equivalent of two nights of full sleep deprivation. Not surprisingly, there is a dose-dependent relationship with cognitive performance declining as sleep restriction is prolonged; however, self-ratings of sleepiness do not increase with ongoing sleep restriction (Van Dongen et al., 2003). Thus, pilots who are in a chronic state of sleep restriction may underestimate their fatigue and overestimate their performance readiness.

Sleep problems can have implications beyond cognition. Dysregulated sleep has been associated with acute physiological changes such as reduced glucose tolerance, elevated cortisol levels, slowed metabolism, increased oxidative stress, increased blood pressure, and increased inflammatory markers, as well as longer-term health impacts such as diabetes, metabolic syndrome, increased all-cause mortality, weight-related issues, hypertension, arrhythmia, stroke, dyslipidemia, and cardiovascular disease (Banks & Dinges, 2007; Faraut et al., 2012; Hartzler, 2014; Medic et al., 2017; Özdemir et al., 2013; Waters & Bucks, 2011). There can also be implications for mental health; pilots who report experiencing fatigue or sleep disturbances are three to five times more likely to also report depression and anxiety (O'Hagan et al., 2017)

The effects of chronic sleep restriction can persist for days (and possibly weeks) even after sleep has returned to normal (Belenky et al., 2003; Ruskin et al., 2015). For example, sleep restriction results in measurable immune and inflammatory changes even after one to two nights of recovery sleep (Faraut et al., 2012). Studies have also found that following sleep restriction of 7 hr per night or less, cognitive performance continues to be impacted after several (and even up to seven) nights of restorative sleep (Axelsson et al., 2008; Ruskin et al., 2015).

Following a prolonged recovery period, there do not appear to be more long-term effects of shift work and sleep dysregulation, as cognitive sequelae can eventually resolve following a normal sleep schedule (see Leso et al., 2021, for review). Long-term studies have failed to show persistent cognitive effects of sleep dysregulation following the resumption of normal sleep patterns (Bokenberger et al., 2017; Devore et al., 2013; Thomas et al., 2019), although recovery of cognitive functioning after chronic shift work may take up to 5 years (Marquié et al., 2015).

In addition to the transient effects of dysregulated sleep, pilots are at increased risk for sleep apnea, which has significant neuropsychological implications (Alzehairi et al., 2021). Sleep apnea is associated with deficits in attention, working memory, vigilance, memory, psychomotor performance, and executive functioning; verbal abilities are typically unaffected (Vanek et al., 2020). These cognitive changes can be attributed to a combination of both sleep fragmentation as well as chronic hypoxemia. While some cognitive deficits can resolve with treatment, aspects of cognitive dysfunction (most notably executive functioning) can persist even with use of continuous positive airway pressure (Sforza & Roche, 2012; Vanek et al., 2020). Thus, cognitive deficits associated with sleep apnea should not be assumed to be reversible with treatment.

Implications for the Neuropsychological Evaluation

It is important for neuropsychologists to understand the typical sleep patterns of the pilots they are seeing for evaluation. Neuropsychologists should be aware of the potential impact of sleep disruption related to both chronic sleep problems as well as more acute dysregulation in the days leading up to the evaluation. To mitigate possible sleep issues, the neuropsychologist should stress to the pilot the importance of being well-rested for the evaluation, especially for those pilots who may be traveling from a distance and across time zones for the evaluation. Particular caution should be taken when scheduling actively flying pilots, who may be eager to complete the evaluation as soon as possible and/or fit the evaluation in during a window of days off. As noted in the previous section, the effects of sleep restriction can persist for several days following the resumption of normal sleep patterns, and this should be taken into account when scheduling the testing. It is also recommended that pilots be encouraged to reschedule the testing if there is any indication that fatigue or sleep problems are impacting the accuracy of the test data.

As with any evaluation, screening for possible sleep apnea and other sleep disorders is important. This can include inquiring about the number of hours slept on average, the number of hours slept the night prior to the evaluation, daytime fatigue, a history of sleep disorders, difficulties falling or staying asleep, snoring and apneic events, unusual movements during sleep, and feeling rested upon awakening. Use of alcohol or other substances can be important to consider, as this can impact sleep quality and exacerbate (or be used to self-medicate) underlying sleep problems. There are several formal sleep inventories, such as the STOPBANG (Chung et al., 2012) or the Pittsburgh Sleep Quality Index (Buysse et al., 1989) that can be used. To understand more chronic sleep patterns for active pilots, information about their commute to their domicile, the airframe flown, and the typical nature of their flight schedule can be helpful.

Finally, the neuropsychologist should inquire about the use of any sleep aids and be aware of any potential impact on test findings. Use of prescription sleep aids may be allowed for pilots, typically with minimum wait times between the last dosage and the start of operational responsibilities. For example, the FAA requires a minimum of 24 hr between the last dose of Ambien and the resumption of pilot duties. A meta-analysis of Ambien use indicated that Ambien can have significant effects on attention and verbal memory with smaller effects on psychomotor speed on average 9 hr after ingestion (Stranks & Crowe, 2014). Other studies have also found acute cognitive impairments associated with Ambien use that resolved by the morning after ingestion (Kleykamp et al., 2012).

Depression and Anxiety in Pilots

Per the World Health Organization (WHO), there is between an 18%–36% lifetime prevalence of mental health disorders in the general population (Kessler et al., 2007). Anxiety is the most common disorder (with a lifetime prevalence of 14%) followed by mood disorders (with a lifetime prevalence of 11%). Not surprisingly, pilots are not immune to these conditions. For example, prevalence rates of depression in commercial airline pilots have been estimated to range from 2%–13% (Pasha & Stokes, 2018), although in some survey-based studies, 14%–25% of pilots reported significant levels of depression, even while actively flying (Omholt et al., 2017; Venus, 2021; Wu et al., 2016). In a survey of 330 commercial pilots (Cahill et al., 2019), nearly half of the respondents reported having a close colleague who experienced a mental health issue, and 13% of respondents reported a clinically significant level of depression themselves. The vast majority of pilots indicated that the environment in which they work could contribute to the onset of or worsening of an existing mental health issue.

There have been multiple aviation accidents and incidents that have been attributed to mental health issues, including acute psychotic episodes in the cockpit, stress from negative life events (e.g., impending demotion or termination, financial losses, marital problems), and panic (see Mulder & de Rooy, 2018, for review). In particular, the potential risk of aircraft-assisted pilot suicides was thrust into the spotlight following well-publicized incidents such as Germanwings Flight 9525 and Malaysia Flight 370. Survey-based studies have indicated that 4%–8% of pilots reported experiencing suicidal thoughts in the 2 weeks prior (Cahill et al., 2019; Wu et al., 2016). Fortunately, aircraft-assisted pilot suicides are rare. According to National Transportation Safety Board accident investigations, there were a total of 12 fatal aviation accidents caused by pilot suicide from 1996 through 2004 (Vuorio et al., 2018).

Beyond these rare suicidal acts, there is concern that emotional distress can have a more subtle but still aeromedically significant impact on a pilot's cognitive and operational ability. Even mild psychological disorders can impact functioning; per a WHO report, individuals with even mild mental health disorders report experiencing 12–69 days per year when they are unable to carry out their usual activities because of their mental health (Kessler et al., 2007).

Factors that have been associated with psychological disorders in pilots include alcohol use, fatigue, sleep disturbance, use of sleep medication, high workload, low physical activity, lack of autonomy at work, long duty hours, and lack of social support (O'Hagan et al., 2017; Pasha & Stokes, 2018). Female pilots are more likely to report depression and anxiety than their male counterparts (O'Hagan et al., 2017). It has also been suggested that short-haul pilots and pilots for low-cost carriers have higher levels of depression and lower levels of well-being than their long-haul and legacy counterparts (Venus, 2022). Job-specific factors can also contribute to depression and anxiety in pilots, including erratic schedules, social isolation (due to work schedules), poor sleep, and poor diet.

There is likely a reluctance to seek help due to both the stigma of mental health issues as well as the career consequences that can arise when pilots self-disclose a potentially medically disqualifying condition, as this can result in a temporary or sometimes permanent loss of a medical certificate. In one study, over three quarters of pilots stated that they would not disclose a mental health issue to their employer, and over half stated that if they were unfit for duty due to a mental health issue, they would give their employer a different reason (Cahill et al., 2019).

The aviation community recognizes the importance of mental health issues for pilots, and there has been a push to include mental health issues in standard training. For example, in 2014 the European Aviation Safety Agency proposed a change to their crew resource management (CRM) training, adding training on resilience development, stress management, and workload management. Similarly, in 2015 an expert working group from the Aerospace Medical Association encouraged increased education and global recognition of the importance of mental health in aviation safety. Recommendations included the inclusion of mental health in CRM training and specific mental health training for physicians performing aeromedical assessments. Many major carriers such as American Airlines (Project Wingman), Delta (Pilot Assistance Network), and FedEx (Pilot Assistance Team Helpline) have pilot assistance programs that provide mental health support for their pilots.

The Cognitive Impact of Depression and Anxiety

From a neuropsychological perspective, it is well documented that psychological disorders can be associated with measurable cognitive changes.

Depression is associated with cognitive deficits across multiple domains, including attention, processing speed, learning and memory, and executive functioning (e.g., working memory, verbal fluency, inhibition, and set-shifting; Ahern & Semkovska, 2017; Goodall et al., 2018). In fact, impairments in concentration and decision-making are a core diagnostic criterion for major depressive disorder. Some of these cognitive changes, particularly in attention, memory, and executive functioning, can persist even following remission of depressive symptoms (Hasselbalch et al., 2011; Reppermund et al., 2009). This raises questions about whether cognitive dysfunction in depression is secondary to trait-related factors (i.e., a stable, underlying vulnerability in individuals predisposed to depression), state-related factors (i.e., the transient effects of a depressive episode), and/or scar (i.e., the development of neural changes associated with the duration and/or number of depressive episodes; Ahern & Semkovska, 2017).

Individuals with anxiety often complain of problems staying focused, and concentration problems are a core diagnostic criterion for generalized anxiety disorder. Anxiety at the chronic (i.e., trait) level is associated with cognitive deficits in attention and executive functioning, to include working memory, inhibition, attentional control, and set-shifting; researchers have suggested that weaknesses in these cognitive processes most likely predispose individuals to pathological levels of worry (Eysenck & Derakshan, 2011; Hirsch & Mathews, 2012; Hopko et al., 2005).

Findings are less clear regarding the cognitive impact of anxiety at the state level (e.g., test anxiety). It is possible that test anxiety can impact cognitive performance as it diverts attentional resources that would otherwise be allocated to the task at hand. For example, one study found that anxiety surrounding testing, math, and/or fears of negative evaluation was associated with performance on measures of working memory (digit span), response inhibition (Stroop test), and dual-tasking (the Paced Auditory Serial Addition Test; Hopko et al., 2005). Other studies have found no negative effects (and in some cases positive effects) of state anxiety/arousal on test performance, although this depends on many characteristics including the cognitive complexity of the task and the test environment (e.g., neutral vs. high-stakes environments; Cavuoto et al., 2021; Chaudhry & Ready, 2012; Gass & Curiel, 2011; Lukasik et al., 2019; Potvin et al., 2013). However, these null research findings may not necessarily translate to the pilot population. The impact of test anxiety is often studied using artificial test environments and/or questionnaires to assess levels of state anxiety in healthy individuals. The testing circumstances for those research volunteers can be very different from the circumstances for pilots, who can enter testing with the belief that their medical certificate (and ultimately their careers) may be in jeopardy. The level of perceived pressure and test anxiety that some pilots may experience during a neuropsychological evaluation is unlikely to be captured adequately in most research paradigms.

Implications for the Neuropsychological Evaluation

It is well-established that depression and anxiety can be associated with cognitive dysfunction and poor performance on neuropsychological testing, particularly in the domains of attention, learning and memory, processing speed, and executive functioning. Thus, careful assessment of depression, anxiety, and other mental health disorders is a critical part of the aeromedical neuropsychological evaluation. It is noteworthy that cognitive difficulties can sometimes persist even in the remitted state. Pilots may be reluctant to openly report any emotional distress for many reasons, including the stigma associated with mental health disorders as well as the potential consequences on their medical certificate and career. Underreporting of symptoms is common and can limit the interpretability of self-reported information. Information from collateral sources can be helpful, including a review of medical records and interviews with individuals who know the pilot well (such as any treating mental health providers). Given the likelihood of underreporting of symptoms, it is valuable to utilize psychological inventories with symptom validity scales such as the Minnesota Multiphasic Personality Inventory (with use of norms specifically derived from a sample of airline pilot applicants; Butcher, 1994).

As noted earlier, test anxiety is likely high for many pilots completing neuropsychological evaluations, although the research on the potential negative impact of test anxiety is mixed. Test anxiety is likely exacerbated, if not precipitated, by perceived failures during the testing process (Cavuoto et al., 2021). Thus, when determining the order of test administration, consideration should be given to the level of difficulty of certain tasks and the effects it can have on anxiety and confidence in the testing session. It can be helpful to avoid stress-inducing and/or cognitively taxing tasks at the start of testing and balance the distribution of these tasks across the testing session. Test anxiety can potentially be minimized by setting clear expectations for what the testing process will entail (e.g., the duration of testing), discussing the nature of the tests (e.g., all examinees get some answers wrong, tests may get harder as you go), and acknowledging that some level of normal variability is to be expected (e.g., Binder et al., 2009). In some cases, test anxiety that is severe enough to significantly impact test performance during the neuropsychological evaluation could raise concerns about whether performance anxiety could also impact operational performance in the cockpit. The neuropsychologist should use clinical judgment in considering and addressing this possibility.

Stress and Burnout in Pilots

As discussed earlier, there is a not insignificant proportion of pilots reporting depression and anxiety. In addition to these formal mental health conditions, pilots are at risk for high levels of stress and burnout, which can have equally significant impacts on their workplace performance.

There are many potential sources of stress for pilots, some of which are unique to aviation. Pilots are in the customer service field and are held to high degrees of professionalism while interacting closely with numerous other individuals, including copilots, flight attendants, gate agents, schedulers, and passengers, often for prolonged periods in very close quarters. Being in command of the aircraft, they must deal with any issues that may arise, including but not limited to aggressive and unruly passengers. Additionally, flight crews vary by flight, and thus pilots are required to interact closely with a large number of colleagues who are oftentimes strangers. In a research interview on pilot well-being, one pilot remarked that "due to lack of familiarity with colleagues, each day in work is like a first date" (Cullen et al., 2021, p. 5).

It is not uncommon for flight schedules to change or be extended at a moment's notice, and rest periods can be irregular or insufficient. Concerns have been raised regarding *pilot push-*

ing, a term used to describe pressures to fly faster or longer, change flight plans, and/or fly in potentially unsafe situations in order to maintain the carrier's schedule. While there are upper limits on the number of hours flown, this represents the total time in the air (e.g., the time from when the brake is released from the departure gate to the arrival at the arrival gate). This typically does not include any delays on the ground, time spent on layovers, any pre-flight preparations, and time spent commuting from home to the airport and back. Many pilots do not live close to their domicile and spend additional hours (if not days) commuting to and from work. This commute time is not factored into their work schedule, and thus an assigned 3-day work trip may actually result in 4 or 5 days away from home due to the commute. In most cases, the responsibility to find flights to commute to and from their domicile is the responsibility of the pilots, who rely on empty seats in the cockpit (i.e., jumpseating) or in the cabin (i.e., non-revenue travel) to make it to work on time. This can cut into a pilot's rest and sleep and add to commute-related stress.

Pilots' schedules nearly invariably result in them being separated for extended periods of time from family and friends, which can impact their ability to reliably engage in social and extracurricular activities and fulfill home and personal obligations. Schedules can result in increased and/or unequal domestic responsibilities for spouses. Birthday parties, holidays, sporting events, and other social and family activities may be missed. There may be little control over scheduling vacations and days off, particularly for junior pilots. When away on trips, communication with friends and family can be limited, and in some countries, access to email and the Internet can be restricted. In a survey of 1,059 commercial pilots, nearly half of pilots reported social isolation and marital/family discord due to their job (Cahill et al., 2019). Interestingly, despite the potential for marital strain, US pilots have an approximately 31% divorce rate, which is no greater than the average US divorce rate (Yau, 2017).

Additionally, pilots can be exposed to a range of physiological stressors, which include extreme temperatures; prolonged periods of sitting; difficulty maintaining a healthy diet while traveling; and a noisy, bright, and crowded work environment. Due to the nature of flying, there are often fluctuations between high levels of physical and mental demands (e.g., at take-off and landing) interspersed with periods of boredom (e.g., midflight on a long-haul flight).

Pilots sometimes have to deal with high levels of uncertainty. Salaries and benefits of pilots are often impermanent, as contracts may be negotiated and re-negotiated every few years. Pilots can be required to bid for the airframes they fly and the airports they are based out of (which can significantly impact schedules, routes, and commutes), and these can change unexpectedly based on carrier needs. There can also be uncertainty about financial and employment security. Many pilots lost their jobs or were furloughed following 9/11 and again in the economic downturn in 2008. One of the greatest periods of uncertainty came about with the COVID pandemic. COVID was associated with significant uncertainty regarding whether certain carriers could withstand the drastic decrease in travel and regarding the future of the airlines in general. The pandemic was also associated with reduced salaries, voluntary and involuntary furloughs, lost jobs, and early retirements for some airline employees. In addition to concerns about financial and job security, pilots continued to work even in the early days of the pandemic, resulting in potential stress regarding health and safety. In a survey of 1,523 aviation workers, nearly two thirds of workers agreed that their mental health had worsened since COVID (Cahill et al., 2021). Over half of workers surveyed had lost their jobs and 98% of the workers who were still employed had a reduction in salary. Over two thirds of these workers worried about meeting their financial obligations, and only 20% had confidence about their future employment in the aviation sector.

In another survey of pilots, nearly half of pilots reported experiencing psychological distress during the pandemic (Alaminos-Torres et al., 2022).

At the end of 2022, news coverage prominently featured an operational crisis at Southwest Airlines. Weather-related delays were exacerbated by problems with scheduling technology, leading to the cancellation of more than 60 % of flights in 2 days. Reverberations lasted for days, and overall, 16,700 flights were canceled over a 10-day period. In a personal communication, one Southwest captain remarked that this was by far the most stressful period of work in their over 15-year career. At one point, they had no way to get a hold of their scheduling department and were faced with aggressive and abusive passengers as they scrambled on their own to find a flight crew and a plane to fly. They observed this operational crisis to be a mental health breaking point for many flight crew.

Overall, there are many potential sources of job-related stress and burnout for pilots. In a sample of 1,147 European pilots, 40 % of respondents reported a very high level of burnout, which is higher than rates found in the general working population; burnout ratings were associated with happiness ratings (Demerouti et al., 2019). Similarly, in another survey of pilots, the majority of pilots reported work-related stress that impacted their performance (Cahill et al., 2021). Across surveys, top sources of stress and burnout in pilots were irregular work hours, antisocial work hours, long duties, a divergence of values between pilots and their management, pressure from management to fly with excessively shortened rest periods, severe weather conditions, and critical equipment problems (Cahill et al., 2019; Fanjoy & Harriman, 2010). Female (compared to male) pilots and pilots for low-cost (compared to legacy) carriers report higher levels of work-related stress (Douglas & Pittenger, 2020; Venus, 2022). High levels of work-related stress have been associated with reduced job satisfaction, reduced job performance, and higher rates of health complaints in aircrew (Omholt et al., 2017; Ozel & Hacioglu, 2021).

The Cognitive Impact of Stress and Burnout and Implications for the Neuropsychological Evaluation

Chronic levels of work-related stress can have a significant impact on a pilot's overall well-being as well as their neuropsychological test performance. Stress has been associated with disrupted sleep, subjective cognitive concerns, and reduced cognitive performance in domains including attention, reaction time, processing speed, executive functioning, working memory, and verbal learning and memory (Eskildsen et al., 2017; Jonsdottir et al., 2013; Linton et al., 2015; Österberg et al., 2014). Interestingly, one study found that the cognitive test most susceptible to work-related stress was the Paced Auditory Serial Addition Test (Eskildsen et al., 2015), which is a test of attention, dual-tasking, working memory and mental math that is commonly administered in aeromedical evaluations.

It is recommended that neuropsychologists inquire about potential sources of stress, which may be either acute or chronic; some of these may be common in the general population but others may be specific to aviation. Potential sources of stress to consider include job security, commute schedules, work schedules (e.g., short-haul vs. long-haul, typical routes, typical rest periods), contract negotiations with their employer, loss of their medical certificate, financial strain, medical disability, loss of company benefits while on leave, and family conflicts. Identifying support systems and coping mechanisms can provide important information regarding a pilot's ability to tolerate and manage stress.

Conclusion

It has become increasingly recognized that conditions such as sleep, fatigue, anxiety, depression, and stress are common in pilots and can have significant impacts on their well-being. These conditions can be initiated, exacerbated, and/or perpetuated by the unique demands of the job. Careful assessment and consideration of these issues are an important part of the neuropsychological evaluation of pilots as they can impact a pilot's psychological health, performance on neuropsychological testing, and overall functioning.

References

Ahern, E., & Semkovska, M. (2017). Cognitive functioning in the first-episode of major depressive disorder: A systematic review and meta-analysis. *Neuropsychology, 31*(1), 52–72. https://doi.org/10.1037/neu0000319

Alaminos-Torres, A., Martinez-Lorca, M., Sifre De Sola, I., López-Ejeda, N., & Dolores Marrodán, M. (2022). Psychological distress in Spanish airline pilots during the aviation crisis caused by the COVID-19 pandemic and psychometric analysis of the 12-item general health questionnaire. *Ergonomics, 65*(5), 741–752. https://doi.org/10.1080/00140139.2021.1984587

Alzehairi, A., Alhejaili, F., Wali, S., Alqassas, I., Balkhyour, M., & Pandi-Perumal, S. R. (2021). Sleep disorders among commercial airline pilots. *Aerospace Medicine and Human Performance, 92*(12), 937–944. https://doi.org/10.2257/AMHP.5809.2021

Andersen, T. (2023, March 6). Planes clip each other at Logan Airport, one week after close call on runway. *Boston Globe.* https://www.bostonglobe.com/2023/03/06/metro/planes-clip-each-other-logan-airport-one-week-after-close-call-runway/

Arsintescu, L., Pradhan, S., Chachad, R. G., Gregory, K. B., Mulligan, J. B., & Flynn-Evans, E. E. (2022). Early starts and late finishes both reduce alertness and performance among short-haul airline pilots. *Journal of Sleep Research, 31*(3), Article e13521. https://doi.org/10.1111/jsr.13521

Axelsson, J., Kecklund, G., Åkerstedt, T., Donofrio, P., Lekander, M., & Ingre, M. (2008). Sleepiness and performance in response to repeated sleep restriction and subsequent recovery during semi-laboratory conditions. *Chronobiology International, 25*(2–3), 297–308. https://doi.org/10.1080/07420520802107031

Banks, S., & Dinges, D. F. (2007). Behavioral and physiological consequences of sleep restriction. *Journal of Clinical Sleep Medicine, 3*(5), 519–528. https://doi.org/10.5664/jcsm.26918

Belenky, G., Wesensten, N. J., Thorne, D. R., Thomas, M. L., Sing, H. C., Redmond, D. P., Russo, M. B., & Balkin, T. J. (2003). Patterns of performance degradation and restoration during sleep restriction and subsequent recovery: A sleep dose-response study. *Journal of Sleep Research, 12*(1), 1–12. https://doi.org/10.1046/j.1365-2869.2003.00337.x

Binder, L. M., Iverson, G. L., & Brooks, B. L. (2009). To err is human: "Abnormal" neuropsychological scores and variability are common in healthy adults. *Archives of Clinical Neuropsychology, 24*(1), 31–46. https://doi.org/10.1093/arclin/acn001

Bokenberger, K., Ström, P., Dahl Aslan, A. K., Åkerstedt, T., & Pedersen, N. L. (2017). Shift work and cognitive aging: A longitudinal study. *Scandinavian Journal of Work, Environment and Health, 43*(5), 485–493. https://doi.org/10.5271/sjweh.3638

Bourgeois-Bougrine, S., Carbon, P., Gounelle, C., Mollard, R., & Coblentz, A. (2003). Perceived fatigue for short- and long-haul flights: A survey of 739 airline pilots. *Aviation, Space, and Environmental Medicine, 74*(10), 1072–1077.

Butcher, J. N. (1994). Psychological assessment of airline pilot applicants with the MMPI-2. *Journal of Personality Assessment, 62*(1), 31–44. https://doi.org/10.1207/s15327752jpa6201_4

Buysse, D. J., Reynolds, C. F., Monk, T. H., Berman, S. R., & Kupfer, D. J. (1989). The Pittsburgh sleep quality index: A new instrument for psychiatric practice and research. *Psychiatry Research, 28*(2), 193–213. https://doi.org/10.1016/0165-1781(89)90047-4

Cahill, J., Cullen, P., Anwer, S., & Gaynor, K. (2021). The impact of the COVID 19 pandemic on aviation workers and the aviation system. *International Symposium on Aviation Psychology, 28*, 164–171.

Cahill, J., Cullen, P., Gaynor, K., Cahill, J., Cullen, P., & Gaynor, K. (2019). Pilot wellbeing & work related stress (WRS). *20th International Symposium on Aviation Psychology*, 43–48. https://corescholar.libraries.wright.edu/isap_2019/8

Caldwell, J.A. (2005). Fatigue in aviation. *Travel Medicine and Infectious Disease, 3*(2), 85–96. https://doi.org/10.1016/j.tmaid.2004.07.008

Caldwell, J.A., Caldwell, J.L., Brown, D.L., & Smith, J.K. (2004). The effects of 37 hours of continuous wakefulness on the physiological arousal, cognitive performance, self-reported mood, and simulator flight performance of F-117A pilots. *Military Psychology, 16*(3), 163–181. https://doi.org/10.1207/s15327876mp1603_2

Cavuoto, M.G., Franzese, S., & Kinsella, G.J. (2021). Pre-test experience and memory performance in older adults: The impact of test anxiety and self-efficacy. *Archives of Clinical Neuropsychology, 36*(5), 791–800. https://doi.org/10.1093/arclin/acaa093

Chaudhry, M., & Ready, R. (2012). Differential effects of test anxiety & stress on the WAIS-IV. *Journal of Young Investigators, 24*(5), 60–66.

Chung, F., Subramanyam, R., Liao, P., Sasaki, E., Shapiro, C., & Sun, Y. (2012). High STOP-Bang score indicates a high probability of obstructive sleep apnoea. *British Journal of Anaesthesia, 108*(5), 768–775. https://doi.org/10.1093/bja/aes022

Cullen, P., Cahill, J., & Gaynor, K. (2021). A qualitative study exploring well-being and the potential impact of work-related stress among commercial airline pilots. *Aviation Psychology and Applied Human Factors, 11*(1), 1–12. https://doi.org/10.1027/2192-0923/a000199

Dawson, D., & Reid, K. (1997). Fatigue, alcohol and performance impairment. *Nature, 388*(6639), 235–235. https://doi.org/10.1038/40775

Demerouti, E., Veldhuis, W., Coombes, C., & Hunter, R. (2019). Burnout among pilots: Psychosocial factors related to happiness and performance at simulator training. *Ergonomics, 62*(2), 233–245. https://doi.org/10.1080/00140139.2018.1464667

Devore, E.E., Grodstein, F., & Schernhammer, E.S. (2013). Shift work and cognition in the nurses' health study. *American Journal of Epidemiology, 178*(8), 1296–1300. https://doi.org/10.1093/aje/kwt214

Douglas, S., & Pittenger, L.M. (2020). Adversity in aviation: Understanding resilience in the workplace for female pilots. *International Journal of Aerospace Psychology, 30*(3–4), 89–103. https://doi.org/10.1080/24721840.2020.1763175

Eskildsen, A., Andersen, L.P., Pedersen, A.D., Vandborg, S.K., & Andersen, J.H. (2015). Work-related stress is associated with impaired neuropsychological test performance: A clinical cross-sectional study. *Stress, 18*(2), 198–207. https://doi.org/10.3109/10253890.2015.1004629

Eskildsen, A., Fentz, H.N., Andersen, L.P., Pedersen, A.D., Kristensen, S.B., & Andersen, J.H. (2017). Perceived stress, disturbed sleep, and cognitive impairments in patients with work-related stress complaints: A longitudinal study. *Stress, 20*(4), 371–378. https://doi.org/10.1080/10253890.2017.1341484

Eysenck, M.W., & Derakshan, N. (2011). New perspectives in attentional control theory. *Personality and Individual Differences, 50*(7), 955–960. https://doi.org/10.1016/j.paid.2010.08.019

Fanjoy, R., & Harriman, S. (2010). Individual and environmental predictors of burnout among regional airline pilots. *International Journal of Applied Aviation Studies, 10*(1), 15–29.

Faraut, B., Boudjeltia, K.Z., Vanhamme, L., & Kerkhofs, M. (2012). Immune, inflammatory and cardiovascular consequences of sleep restriction and recovery. *Sleep Medicine Reviews, 16*(2), 137–149). https://doi.org/10.1016/j.smrv.2011.05.001

Gander, P., & Signal, L. (2008). Who is too old for shift work? Developing better criteria. *Chronobiology International, 25*(2–3), 199–213. https://doi.org/10.1080/07420520802077556

Gander, P.H., Signal, T.L., van den Berg, M.J., Mulrine, H.M., Jay, S.M., & Jim Mangie, C. (2013). In-flight sleep, pilot fatigue and Psychomotor Vigilance Task performance on ultra-long range versus long range flights. *Journal of Sleep Research, 22*(6), 697–706. https://doi.org/10.1111/jsr.12071

Gass, C.S., & Curiel, R.E. (2011). Test anxiety in relation to measures of cognitive and intellectual functioning. *Archives of Clinical Neuropsychology, 26*(5), 396–404. https://doi.org/10.1093/arclin/acr034

Goodall, J., Fisher, C., Hetrick, S., Phillips, L., Parrish, E.M., & Allott, K. (2018). Neurocognitive functioning in depressed young people: A systematic review and meta-analysis. *Neuropsychology Review, 28* (2), 216–231. https://doi.org/10.1007/s11065-018-9373-9

Goode, J.H. (2003). Are pilots at risk of accidents due to fatigue? *Journal of Safety Research, 34*(3), 309–313. https://doi.org/10.1016/S0022-4375(03)00033-1

Gregory, K.B., Winn, W., Johnson, K., & Rosekind, M.R. (2010). Pilot fatigue survey: Exploring fatigue factors in air medical operations. *Air Medical Journal, 29*(6), 309–319. https://doi.org/10.1016/j.amj.2010.07.002

Hartzler, B.M. (2014). Fatigue on the flight deck: The consequences of sleep loss and the benefits of napping. *Accident Analysis & Prevention, 62*, 309–318. https://doi.org/10.1016/j.aap.2013.10.010

Hasselbalch, B.J., Knorr, U., & Kessing, L.V. (2011). Cognitive impairment in the remitted state of unipolar depressive disorder: A systematic review. *Journal of Affective Disorders, 134*(1–3), 20–31. https://doi.org/10.1016/j.jad.2010.11.011

Hirsch, C.R., & Mathews, A. (2012). A cognitive model of pathological worry. *Behaviour Research and Therapy, 50*(10), 636–646. https://doi.org/10.1016/j.brat.2012.06.007

Hopko, D.R., Hunt, M.K., & Armento, M.E.A. (2005). Attentional task aptitude and performance anxiety. *International Journal of Stress Management, 12*(4), 389–408. https://doi.org/10.1037/1072-5245.12.4.389

Jackson, C.A., & Earl, L. (2006). Prevalence of fatigue among commercial pilots. *Occupational Medicine, 56*(4), 263–268. https://doi.org/10.1093/occmed/kql021

Jonsdottir, I.H., Nordlund, A., Ellbin, S., Ljung, T., Glise, K., Währborg, P., & Wallin, A. (2013). Cognitive impairment in patients with stress-related exhaustion. *Stress, 16*(2), 181–190. https://doi.org/10.3109/10253890.2012.708950

Kazemi, R., Haidarimoghadam, R., Motamedzadeh, M., Golmohamadi, R., Soltanian, A., & Zoghipaydar, M.R. (2016). Effects of shift work on cognitive performance, sleep quality, and sleepiness among petrochemical control room operators. *Journal of Circadian Rhythms, 14*(1), 1–8. https://doi.org/10.5334/jcr.134

Kessler, R.C., Angermeyer, M., Anthony, J.C., De Graaf, R., Demyttenaere, K., Gasquet, I., De Girolamo, G., Gluzman, S., Gureje, O., Haro, J.M., Kawakami, N., Karam, A., Levinson, D., Medina Mora, M.E., Oakley Browne, M.A., Posada-Villa, J., Stein, D.J., Adley Tsang, C.H., Aguilar-Gaxiola, S., ... Ustün, T.B. (2007). Lifetime prevalence and age-of-onset distributions of mental disorders in the World Health Organization's World Mental Health Survey Initiative. *World Psychiatry: Official Journal of the World Psychiatric Association (WPA), 6*(3), 168–176.

Killgore, W.D.S. (2010). Effects of sleep deprivation on cognition. *Progress in Brain Research, 185*, 105–129. https://doi.org/10.1016/B978-0-444-53702-7.00007-5

Kleykamp, B.A., Griffiths, R.R., McCann, U.D., Smith, M.T., & Mintzer, M.Z. (2012). Acute effects of zolpidem extended-release on cognitive performance and sleep in healthy males after repeated nightly use. *Experimental and Clinical Psychopharmacology, 20*(1), 28–39. https://doi.org/10.1037/a0025237

Lamond, N., & Dawson, D. (1999). Quantifying the performance impairment associated with fatigue. *Journal of Sleep Research, 8*, 255–262. https://doi.org/10.1046/j.1365-2869.1999.00167.x

Leso, V., Fontana, L., Caturano, A., Vetrani, I., Fedele, M., & Iavicoli, I. (2021). Impact of shift work and long working hours on worker cognitive functions: Current evidence and future research needs. *International Journal of Environmental Research and Public Health, 18*(12), 6540. https://doi.org/10.3390/ijerph18126540

Lim, J., & Dinges, D.F. (2010). A meta-analysis of the impact of short-term sleep deprivation on cognitive variables. *Psychological Bulletin, 136*(3), 375–389. https://doi.org/10.1037/a0018883

Linton, S.J., Kecklund, G., Franklin, K.A., Leissner, L.C., Sivertsen, B., Lindberg, E., Svensson, A.C., Hansson, S.O., Sundin, Ö., Hetta, J., Björkelund, C., & Hall, C. (2015). The effect of the work environment on future sleep disturbances: a systematic review. *Sleep Medicine Reviews, 23*, 10–19. https://doi.org/10.1016/j.smrv.2014.10.010

Lopez, N., Previc, F.H., Fischer, J., Heitz, R.P., & Engle, R.W. (2012). Effects of sleep deprivation on cognitive performance by United States Air Force pilots. *Journal of Applied Research in Memory and Cognition, 1*(1), 27–33. https://doi.org/10.1016/j.jarmac.2011.10.002

Lowe, C.J., Safati, A., & Hall, P.A. (2017). The neurocognitive consequences of sleep restriction: A meta-analytic review. *Neuroscience and Biobehavioral Reviews, 80*, 586–604. https://doi.org/10.1016/j.neubiorev.2017.07.010

Lukasik, K.M., Waris, O., Soveri, A., Lehtonen, M., & Laine, M. (2019). The relationship of anxiety and stress with working memory performance in a large non-depressed sample. *Frontiers in Psychology, 10*(4), 1–9. https://doi.org/10.3389/fpsyg.2019.00004

Marcus, J.H., & Rosekind, M.R. (2017). Fatigue in transportation: NTSB investigations and safety recommendations. *Injury Prevention, 23*(4), 232–238. https://doi.org/10.1136/injuryprev-2015-041791

Marquié, J.-C., Tucker, P., Folkard, S., Gentil, C., & Ansiau, D. (2015). Chronic effects of shift work on cognition: Findings from the VISAT longitudinal study. *Occupational and Environmental Medicine, 72*(4), 258–264. https://doi.org/10.1136/oemed-2013-101993

Medic, G., Wille, M., & Hemels, M. (2017). Short- and long-term health consequences of sleep disruption. *Nature and Science of Sleep, 9*, 151–161. https://doi.org/10.2147/NSS.S134864

Mulder, S., & de Rooy, D. (2018). Pilot mental health, negative life events, and improving safety with peer support and a just culture. *Aerospace Medicine and Human Performance, 89*(1), 41–51. https://doi.org/10.3357/AMHP.4903.2018

O'Hagan, A.D., Issartel, J., Nevill, A., & Warrington, G. (2017). Flying into depression. *Workplace Health and Safety, 65*(3), 109–117. https://doi.org/10.1177/2165079916659506

O'Hagan, A.D., Issartel, J., Wall, A., Dunne, F., Boylan, P., Groeneweg, J., Herring, M., Campbell, M., & Warrington, G. (2020). "Flying on empty" – effects of sleep deprivation on pilot performance. *Biological Rhythm Research, 51*(7), 1133–1154. https://doi.org/10.1080/09291016.2019.1581481

Omholt, M.L., Tveito, T.H., & Ihlebæk, C. (2017). Subjective health complaints, work-related stress and self-efficacy in Norwegian aircrew. *Occupational Medicine, 67*(2), 135–142. https://doi.org/10.1093/occmed/kqw127

Österberg, K., Skogsliden, S., & Karlson, B. (2014). Neuropsychological sequelae of work-stress-related exhaustion. *Stress, 17*(1), 59–69. https://doi.org/10.3109/10253890.2013.862615

Özdemir, P.G., Selvi, Y., Özkol, H., Aydin, A., Tülüce, Y., Boysan, M., & Beşiroğlu, L. (2013). The influence of shift work on cognitive functions and oxidative stress. *Psychiatry Research, 210*(3), 1219–1225. https://doi.org/10.1016/j.psychres.2013.09.022

Ozel, E., & Hacioglu, U. (2021). Examining the relationship between burnout and job satisfaction of flight crew. *International Journal of Business Ecosystem & Strategy (2687-2293), 3*(1), 1–20. https://doi.org/10.36096/ijbes.v3i1.246

Pasha, T., & Stokes, P.R.A. (2018). Reflecting on the Germanwings disaster: A systematic review of depression and suicide in commercial airline pilots. *Frontiers in Psychiatry, 9*, 86. https://doi.org/10.3389/fpsyt.2018.00086

Pellegrino, P., De Castro Moreno, C.R., & Marqueze, E.C. (2019). Aspects of work organization and reduced sleep quality of airline pilots. *Sleep Science, 12*(1), 43–48. https://doi.org/10.5935/1984-0063.20190053

Petrilli, R.M., Roach, G.D., Dawson, D., & Lamond, N. (2006). The sleep, subjective fatigue, and sustained attention of commercial airline pilots during an international pattern. *Chronobiology International, 23*(6), 1357–1362. https://doi.org/10.1080/07420520601085925

Potvin, O., Bergua, V., Meillon, C., Le Goff, M., Bouisson, J., Dartigues, J.F., & Amieva, H. (2013). State anxiety and cognitive functioning in older adults. *American Journal of Geriatric Psychiatry, 21*(9), 915–924. https://doi.org/10.1016/j.jagp.2013.01.029

Reis, C., Mestre, C., Canhão, H., Gradwell, D., & Paiva, T. (2016). Sleep complaints and fatigue of airline pilots. *Sleep Science, 9*(2), 73–77. https://doi.org/10.1016/j.slsci.2016.05.003

Rempe, M.J., Basiarz, E., Rasmussen, I., Belenky, G., & Lamp, A. (2022). Pilot in-flight sleep during long-range and ultra-long range commercial airline flights. *Aerospace Medicine and Human Performance, 93*(4), 368–375. https://doi.org/10.3357/AMHP.6023.2022

Reppermund, S., Ising, M., Lucae, S., & Zihl, J. (2009). Cognitive impairment in unipolar depression is persistent and non-specific: Further evidence for the final common pathway disorder hypothesis. *Psychological Medicine, 39*(4), 603–614. https://doi.org/10.1017/S003329170800411X

Roach, G.D., Darwent, D., & Dawson, D. (2010). How well do pilots sleep during long-haul flights? *Ergonomics, 53*(9), 1072–1075. https://doi.org/10.1080/00140139.2010.506246

Roach, G. D., Sargent, C., Darwent, D., & Dawson, D. (2012). Duty periods with early start times restrict the amount of sleep obtained by short-haul airline pilots. *Accident Analysis and Prevention, 45*, 22–26. https://doi.org/10.1016/j.aap.2011.09.020

Ruskin, K. J., Caldwell, J. A., Caldwell, J. L., & Boudreau, E. A. (2015). Screening for sleep apnea in morbidly obese pilots. *Aerospace Medicine and Human Performance, 86*(9), 835–841. https://doi.org/10.3357/AMHP.4163.2015

Sforza, E., & Roche, F. (2012). Sleep apnea syndrome and cognition. *Frontiers in Neurology, 3*, 87. https://doi.org/10.3389/fneur.2012.00087

Shepardson, D. (2023a, August 10). US NTSB cites United crew failure in Boeing 777 altitude loss incident. *Reuters*. https://www.reuters.com/business/aerospace-defense/us-ntsb-cites-united-crew-failure-boeing-777-altitude-loss-incident-2023-08-10/

Shepardson, D. (2023b, February 6). FedEx, Southwest planes believed under 100 feet apart -NTSB. *Reuters*. https://www.reuters.com/business/aerospace-defense/fedex-southwest-planes-believed-under-100-feet-apart-ntsb-2023-02-06/

Stranks, E. K., & Crowe, S. F. (2014). The acute cognitive effects of zopiclone, zolpidem, zaleplon, and eszopiclone: A systematic review and meta-analysis. *Journal of Clinical and Experimental Neuropsychology, 36*(7), 691–700. https://doi.org/10.1080/13803395.2014.928268

Southwest Airlines Pilot Association Board of Directors. (2022, April 12). *An open letter to SWA*. https://files.constantcontact.com/90a941aa001/4c29adfc-22d4-476d-ab57-e232264e98e2.pdf?rdr=true

Tempesta, D., Salfi, F., De Gennaro, L., & Ferrara, M. (2020). The impact of five nights of sleep restriction on emotional reactivity. *Journal of Sleep Research, 29*(5), e13022. https://doi.org/10.1111/jsr.13022

Thomas, J., Overeem, S., & Claassen, J. A. H. R. (2019). Long-term occupational sleep loss and post-retirement cognitive decline or dementia. *Dementia and Geriatric Cognitive Disorders, 48*(1–2), 105–112. https://doi.org/10.1159/000504020

van den Berg, M. J., Signal, T. L., Mulrine, H. M., Smith, A. A. T., Gander, P. H., & Serfontein, W. (2015). Monitoring and managing cabin crew sleep and fatigue during an ultra-long range trip. *Aerospace Medicine and Human Performance, 86*(8), 705–713. https://doi.org/10.3357/AMHP.4268.2015

Van Dongen, H. P. A., Maislin, G., Mullington, J. M., & Dinges, D. F. (2003). The cumulative cost of additional wakefulness: Dose-response effects on neurobehavioral functions and sleep physiology from chronic sleep restriction and total sleep deprivation. *Sleep, 26*(2), 117–126. https://doi.org/10.1093/sleep/26.2.117

van Drongelen, A., Boot, C. R. L., Hlobil, H., Smid, T., & van der Beek, A. J. (2017). Risk factors for fatigue among airline pilots. *International Archives of Occupational and Environmental Health, 90*(1), 39–47. https://doi.org/10.1007/s00420-016-1170-2

Vanek, J., Prasko, J., Genzor, S., Ociskova, M., Kantor, K., Holubova, M., Slepecky, M., Nesnidal, V., Kolek, A., & Sova, M. (2020). Obstructive sleep apnea, depression and cognitive impairment. *Sleep Medicine, 72*, 50–58). https://doi.org/10.1016/j.sleep.2020.03.017

Venus, M. (2021). Short and long haul pilots' rosters, stress, sleep problems, fatigue, mental health, and well-being. *Aerospace Medicine and Human Performance, 92*(10), 786–797. https://doi.org/10.3357/AMHP.5812.2021

Venus, M. (2022). Comparison of schedules, stress, sleep problems, fatigue, mental health and well-being of low cost and network carrier pilots. *International Journal of Aviation, Aeronautics, and Aerospace, 9*(3), 1–20. https://doi.org/10.15394/ijaaa.2022.1714

Vuorio, A., Laukkala, T., Junttila, I., Bor, R., Budowle, B., Pukkala, E., Navathe, P., & Sajantila, A. (2018). Aircraft-assisted pilot suicides in the general aviation increased for one-year period after 11 September 2001 attack in the United States. *International Journal of Environmental Research and Public Health, 15*(11), 1–10. https://doi.org/10.3390/ijerph15112525

Waters, F., & Bucks, R. S. (2011). Neuropsychological effects of sleep loss: Implication for neuropsychologists. *Journal of the International Neuropsychological Society, 17*(4), 571–586. https://doi.org/10.1017/S1355617711000610

Wu, A. C., Donnelly-McLay, D., Weisskopf, M. G., McNeely, E., Betancourt, T. S., & Allen, J. G. (2016). Airplane pilot mental health and suicidal thoughts: a cross-sectional descriptive study via anonymous web-

based survey. *Environmental Health: A Global Access Science Source, 15*(1), 1–12. https://doi.org/10.1186/s12940-016-0200-6
Yau, N. (2017, July 25). *Divorce and occupation*. Flowingdata. https://flowingdata.com/2017/07/25/divorce-and-occupation/

Chapter 25
Neurologic Conditions With Aeromedically Significant Cognitive Relevance

Roger R. Hesselbrock

Introduction

While reviewing the pre-landing checklist at the end of an otherwise routine flight, an experienced commercial pilot was repeatedly unable to correctly respond to required items, which meant the second pilot had to accomplish them and to assume aircraft control for the remainder of the flight. Subsequent administrative investigation from the air carrier indicated this pilot had marginal performance on recent check rides, with at least one check ride failure. A medical evaluation was requested, which revealed concerns from the pilot's spouse of slowly progressing cognitive decline over the past several years. The pilot was ultimately diagnosed with mild cognitive impairment and medical certification was withdrawn.

As this example illustrates, neurologic conditions may go unrecognized until a critical incident occurs, and they can significantly impact aviation safety. Neurologic conditions are routinely encountered in aerospace medicine and, as noted by Høva et al. (2017), are a common cause of medical disqualification. In general, prevalence of neurologic disorders in aviators is expected to be similar to the general population, as would be the cognitive sequelae, accounting for age and education. Evidence data of cognitive impacts from neurological disease in non-aerospace populations must often be applied to aviators, noting that aviator-specific studies rarely exist. However, some aerospace groups such as military aviators and astronauts are younger, more physically fit, have greater cognitive reserve, and do not have typical disease risk factors seen in the general population, making direct literature evidence correlation challenging. Lack of relevant evidence for medical conditions in the aeromedical population frequently results in necessarily conservative return-to-work recommendations. Risk assessment incorporates the frequency and severity of the condition and also any treatments, as effects of treatments may have aeromedically adverse consequences. Current and future risks of both sudden and subtle or unrecognized incapacitation are considered in aeromedical recommendation decisions. Another important consideration in aerospace medicine is potential augmentation of adverse clinical effects with stresses experienced in the aerospace environment. Clinical advances and evidential data allow for safe medical certification for many neurologic conditions that previously were considered permanently unfitting.

Functional-anatomic association with brain regions has been established in animals and humans from experimental and clinical data, as shown in Table 25.1. Many disease processes can affect cognitive function, and a comprehensive review is beyond the scope of this chapter. Major conditions that have potential aeromedically significant cognitive impact are listed in Box 25.1 and will be addressed separately. In some cases, discrete brain regions are affected, and resulting cognitive changes correlate well with the neurologic examination and cognitive assessments. In other situations, more than one brain region is affected, and some conditions globally impact brain function. This, along with individual variability in response to disease, limits the predictive value of localization from the clinical examination and neuropsychological assessment.

Table 25.1. Common cognitive deficits associated with brain regions

Region	Cognitive deficit
Dominant hemisphere	Language
Non-dominant hemisphere	Visuospatial (hemiagnosia/etc.)
Frontal	Executive function, expressive speech
Temporal	Memory, auditory processing
Parietal	Spatial relationships, receptive speech
Occipital	Visual perception
Thalamus	Attention, memory, speech
Basal ganglia	Multidomain
Cerebellum	Executive function, spatial cognition, language, affect
Brain stem	Executive function, attention, memory, visuospatial skills

Box 25.1. Major neurological conditions with aeromedically significant cognitive impairment concerns

Head injury
Stroke
Multiple sclerosis
Neoplasms
Parkinson disease
Central nervous system infections
Mild cognitive impairment
Dementias
Episodic conditions (epilepsy, migraine)
Systemic illness
Medications
Toxins
Treatment effects

Neuropsychological evaluations can identify current cognitive capability, abnormal behaviors, and provide a reference frame for future cognitive assessments. These assessments are but one facet of a comprehensive clinical evaluation. While very important, neuropsychological assessment findings should not be used in isolation for aeromedical disposition determinations, but rather should be considered in the entire evaluation context. Good communication between the referring physician and neuropsychologist is paramount to determine indicated testing and ensure adequate evaluation. Optimally, the referring physician should specify the underlying condition or concern that led to consultation, should note the particular area(s) of the brain affected by the condition, and should indicate any specific concerns identified in the history suggesting abnormal behavior, functioning or symptoms suggestive of specific cognitive domain concerns, e.g., executive function, short-term recall, etc. Since many referring physicians, including neurologists, are not well versed in interpreting neuropsychological evaluation test results, their focus will be on "bottom line" conclusions. The neuropsychologist should make every effort to clearly outline findings and concerns in their summary notes. When evaluating aviators, it is extremely useful to include a statement on whether there are any aeromedically significant abnormalities, as this will help the referring physician and reviewing authorities in their disposition recommendations.

Head Injury

A helmeted private pilot was riding his bicycle and sustained polytrauma when he was struck by a car. He was unconscious for 20 mins but had no neurologic symptoms or findings on initial medical assessment. Cranial imaging shortly after the accident showed a non-displaced skull fracture but no brain injuries. Follow-up imaging showed evidence of hemosiderin deposition in several regions. Neuropsychological evaluation 1 year post-injury showed no concerning findings. Continued observation until 5 years post-injury before medical certification consideration was advised due to increased seizure risk.

Head injures affect all age groups and are a major cause of morbidity and mortality, as noted by Capizzi et al. (2020). Centers for Disease Control and Prevention statistics (2023a) indicated traumatic brain injuries (TBIs) accounted for over 220,000 hospitalizations and over 64,000 deaths. These figures vastly underestimate prevalence, as cases of non-hospitalized patients with TBI were not included in these data. Head injury severity is graded as mild, moderate, or severe, with concussion generally used to define minor head trauma. Several different head injury severity classification schemes are available, each with slightly different inclusion criteria. The classification system currently used by the Federal Aviation Administration defines mild head injury as having less than 1 hr of unconsciousness, alteration of consciousness, or amnesia. Moderate head injury is defined as between 1 and 24 hr of unconsciousness, alteration of consciousness, or amnesia, or the presence of a non-depressed skull fracture. The definition of severe head injury includes over 24 hr of unconsciousness, alteration of consciousness, or amnesia; the presence of any type of intracranial bleeding; or a depressed skull fracture. Recommended post-head injury observation times typically range from at least 6 months for mild, at least 12 months for moderate, and 5 years for aeromedically severe head injuries. The presence of seizures is also considered and may incur additional post-injury observation time. The huge variety of mechanisms, locations, and clinical response to head injury make each case unique. Disparity between the degree of structural brain injury and clinical symptoms is not uncommon. For example, cases of significant structural damage with relatively mild clinical manifestations can be seen, and cases with little or no apparent structural brain injury can have functionally limiting cognitive symptoms. Repetitive head injuries can have cumulative cognitive effects, rarely including chronic traumatic encephalopathy (CTE), a neurodegenerative disease with progressively worsening cognition and motor dysfunction. Unsurprisingly, as outlined by Arciniegas et al. (2002), cognitive changes from head injury are not limited to one domain, but overall, attention, memory, executive function and behavior are most commonly affected, regardless of injury severity. Mood disorders frequently overlap with cognitive and behavioral manifestations of brain injury or neurologic disease. Depression is common after TBI, as is PTSD especially in the military and veteran population. The role of the neuropsychologist is often key in sorting out effects of underlying mood disorders from the effect of neurological damage, or in pointing out cases where a clear separation is impossible, which allows appropriate consideration to the possibility of other associated mood disorders. The role of the aeromedically sophisticated neuropsychologist cannot be undervalued. The case reported by Verde et al. (2022) highlights that subtle deficits after TBI and other neurological conditions that are important for safe performance in the demanding aviation environment may be missed by standard clinical providers. Proper timing of the neuropsychological assessment is essential to ensure valid results. Adequate recovery time from injury should occur before cognitive function testing. This can range from several months for milder injuries to 1 year or more for severe TBI cases. Follow-up testing should ideally incorporate different tests or test versions if performed very soon after initial assessment to minimize practice effects or other confounding factors.

Stroke

A military tanker pilot developed sudden-onset vertigo, nausea, and vomiting on final approach. The copilot immediately declared an in-flight emergency and had to assume all landing-related activities. Fortunately, the aircraft landed uneventfully. The pilot was expediently evaluated by the unit flight surgeon and was assessed as having peripheral vestibular dysfunction (labyrinthitis). Referral to otolaryngology was made, and the consultant requested a magnetic resonance imaging (MRI) study, which unexpectedly showed a small recent cerebellar infarct. Further evaluation revealed a large patent foramen ovale (PFO) with intracardiac shunting, which was felt likely the causative factor for the stroke, and the PFO was then percutaneously closed. No further symptoms were reported, and medical certification was granted after 2 years of observation.

While often considered a disease of older people, stroke can occur at any age, although risk increases with age. In the United States, according to Centers for Disease Control and Prevention statistics (2023b), almost 800,000 strokes occur annually, with about 25% being recurrent. Most strokes in adults occur from blockage of blood flow or ischemia, but a minority of strokes occur from bleeding or hemorrhage. Risk factors for stroke are similar to those of coronary heart disease. Clinical symptoms can range from silent or minimal to catastrophic depending on the location and size of the brain injury. Similar to head injury, cognitive effects from stroke are quite variable and often involve multiple cognitive domains. Premorbid cognitive dysfunction can be augmented by stroke. A recent study by D'Souza et al. (2022) indicated about 10% of stroke patients develop incident dementia following the first stroke and 30% will develop dementia with recurrent stroke. Cognitive effects from stroke are not confined to the older population, however. A systematic review and meta-analysis from Weterings et al. (2023) looked at younger stroke patients and found similar patterns of cognitive impairment to that in the general stroke literature, with 44% prevalence of cognitive impairment and 22% prevalence of aphasia. These sobering figures illustrate the importance of assessing cognitive function in virtually all aviators with stroke. As with head injury, adequate recovery time after stroke should be given before the individual undergoes neuropsychological assessment. The authors recommend at least 6 months after minor strokes and 12 months following major strokes prior to formal cognitive testing.

Neoplasms

Cognitive impairment is commonly seen with brain tumors and can be a presenting symptom, as Fox et al. (2006) reported. Any cognitive domain can be affected depending on tumor location. Cognition may be impaired by direct damage to brain structures from the tumor itself and also affected by any associated surrounding changes such as edema. Neoplasms involving the brain are broadly classified as primary (rising from brain cells) or metastatic (spread to the brain from neoplasms in other parts of the body). Histologically, neoplasms are classified as benign or malignant based on growth aggressiveness and propensity to metastasize. Anatomically, however, even histologically benign tumors can produce serious clinical symptoms when located in critical regions. For example, schwannoma (nerve sheath tumor) involving the vestibular nerve may expand outside the internal auditory canal and compress the brain stem. Tumor location and growth rate determine the timing and type of clinical symptoms. If not located in neurologically eloquent locations, slow-growing tumors such as meningiomas can grow quite large before overt clinical symptoms are noticed. In addition to tumor-associated cognitive changes, chemotherapy and radiation therapy treatment may also affect cognition, sometimes long after clinical remission or cure. The readers is referred to the "Treatment Effects" section of this chapter for more details on this aspect. Baseline cognitive screening should be obtained for virtually all patients with brain tumors but is not always accomplished. Formal neuropsychological evaluation is generally reserved for patients with a favorable mid- to long-term survival prognosis. The timing of evaluation in such cases is best deferred until sufficient recovery from treatment has occurred and clinical stability is established. Serial neuropsychological testing is recommended in cases of tumor growth or recurrence.

Multiple Sclerosis/Demyelinating Disease

Barkhof and Koeller (2020) noted that demyelinating diseases that affect the central nervous system include multiple sclerosis (MS), neuromyelitis optica spectrum disorder, acute disseminated encephalomyelitis, progressive multifocal leukoencephalopathy, and other conditions. Of these conditions, MS is the most common. MS is a dynamic condition with an unpredictable risk of exacerbations. Cognitive impairment was seen in 43%–70% of patients with MS in a review by Grzegorski and Losy (2017). Greater lesion burden correlates with the degree of cognitive involvement. Symptom manifestation aligns with the location of demyelinating lesions. Aeromedically concerning is the potential for subtle, unrecognized impairment that could adversely affect aviation safety. Formal neuropsychological testing is aeromedically indicated in aviators newly diagnosed with MS so as to establish a reference baseline, and serial assessments, usually at 1- to 2-year intervals, are recommended to ensure continued freedom from significant cognitive deficits.

Parkinson Disease

A 70-year-old pilot noted resting hand tremor and some muscle stiffness. Examination showed reduced facial expression, soft speech, pill-rolling right-hand tremor, decreased right arm swing when walking, and mild cogwheel rigidity. Parkinson disease (PD) was diagnosed, and treatment with carbidopa-levodopa was initiated. No side effects were reported and dramatic clinical improvement occurred. Neuropsychological testing was unremarkable and functional assessment showed no difficulties operating aircraft controls. A 12-month medical certification was granted, with annual reassessment required.

PD is the second most common age-related neurodegenerative condition in North America, as noted by Willis et al. (2022). Marras et al. (2022) furthermore noted that PD currently affects over 900,000 US individuals over age 45. This condition is inexorably progressive. There are no curative treatments, and currently available treatment modalities only provide temporizing symptom relief. While sudden incapacitation is uncommon in early and well-treated PD, potentially unrecognized subtle incapacitation is a significant concern. Cognitive involvement in PD is well known and was reviewed recently by Aarsland et al. (2021). Weintraub and Irwin (2022) noted that up to one third of PD patients have mild cognitive impairment and cognitive deficits that can be seen even in 10%–20% of newly diagnosed cases. Weintraub and Irwin (2022) also noted that cognitive impairment can involve a range of domains, especially attention, executive function, and visuospatial skills, and a particular aeromedical concern is the occurrence of unpredictable cognitive fluctuations. Such fluctuations should be considered carefully in aviators who may demonstrate improved performance after an unfavorable task or show inconsistency within a testing session. Detailed history may help identify individuals with cognitive fluctuations, which are often reported as intermittent functional difficulties or unpredictable daytime sleepiness. Medical certification in PD cases is only considered early in the disease course and, if granted, only for short terms and with close longitudinal monitoring. Formal neuropsychological testing to establish a cognitive baseline reference is aeromedically indicated in all aviators with PD who are felt potentially eligible for medical certification. In PD aviators who have been medically certificated, periodic neuropsychological retesting is required, generally on an annual basis, and may even be needed more often if unstable or fluctuating performance is suspected.

Central Nervous System Infections

Many infectious processes can adversely affect cognitive function, both through direct involvement of the brain or indirectly by systemic effects. Any portion of the brain can be affected. Susceptibility to nervous system infections can be increased by immune system compromise from underlying medical conditions such as cancer or by immunosuppressive medications such as corticosteroids. The list of potential infectious agents is extensive and encompasses bacteria, viruses, fungi, parasites, and prions. A comprehensive discussion is outside the scope of this chapter. For additional information, a review by Giovane and Lavender (2018) covers central nervous system infections in detail. Direct brain involvement is seen with encephalitis and brain abscess. Meningitis, as its name indicates, primarily affects the coverings of the brain and spinal cord, but can also involve brain tissue, in which case the term "meningoencephalitis" is used. Other secondary insults such as stroke or hemorrhage may occur in the course of infection. Many nervous system infections are self-limiting, but long-term or permanent damage may occur. Cognitive function is often affected, and unrecognized mild cognitive impairment has been reported by Sittinger et al. (2002) in fully recovered patients with viral meningitis with no sign of brain parenchymal involvement. Neurosyphilis is a prototypic example of central nervous infection that can produce permanent cognitive impairment. Herpes simplex encephalitis commonly damages the temporal lobes, with resulting memory impairment. HIV infects the brain early in the disease course but is often asymptomatic. Although not thought to directly infect brain tissue, SARS-CoV-2 infection has been associated with long-term neurocognitive symptoms, primarily in the areas of executive function, attention, and episodic memory, as noted by Tavares-Júnior et al. (2022). Please refer to Chapters 26 and 27 covering HIV and COVID, respectively, for additional information on these conditions. Obtaining formal neuropsychological evaluation is indicated in all cases of encephalitis and brain abscess. Neuropsychological assessment is also indicated in cases with persistent cognitive symptoms following other infections involving the nervous system and provides objective information on the degree of impairment. Ensuring adequate recovery time is necessary before formal evaluations and will vary depending on the specific infectious process.

Mild Cognitive Impairment

Cognitive function normally declines with age. While often annoying, normal subjective age-related changes do not cause functional impact or impairment. When cognitive difficulties rise to a level causing consistent symptoms or measurable decline without significant day-to-day functional impact, mild cognitive impairment (MCI) is often diagnosed, as noted in the first case vignette of this chapter. MCI is on the continuum of cognitive decline between normal age-related changes and frank dementia. A review from Jongsiriyanyong and Limpawattana (2018) noted an MCI prevalence of 6.7%–25.2% in adults over age 60 and a 5%–17% annual rate of progression to dementia. Due to this not-insignificant progression risk, a formal diagnosis of MCI generally preludes medical certification, and further neuropsychological evaluation is not aeromedically indicated. Furthermore, while MCI by definition does not impact day-to-day activities, it would be an unacceptable risk in the cognitively demanding aviation environment. However, since other medical conditions can mimic MCI clinically, some of which are potentially reversible, a clinical evaluation is necessary in suspected MCI cases, and neuropsychological assessment may be part of the diagnostic evaluation. See sections "Systemic Conditions" and "Medications" in this chapter for more information on these subjects.

Dementias

Dementia is an acquired loss of cognitive function of sufficient degree to impair occupational and/or social functioning. It is more of a symptom description than a specific disease process. Many different causes are possible, including primary degenerative conditions such as Alzheimer disease, Parkinson's disease, Lewy body disease, or frontotemporal dementia and cerebrovascular disease with infarctions. A recent review from Arvanitakis et al. (2019) addresses the various types of dementia and noted a US prevalence of Alzheimer disease in 5.8 million persons. As with MCI, medical conditions may clinically mimic dementia, and some of these conditions are potentially reversible. Evaluation for dementia should address these possibilities and may include neuropsychological assessment as part of the evaluation. A formal diagnosis of dementia preludes medical certification, and neuropsychological evaluation is therefore not aeromedically indicated in established dementia cases.

Episodic Disorders (Epilepsy, Migraine)

A military instructor pilot was leading a four-aircraft trainer formation flight and developed partial vision loss and light sensitivity as the formation emerged from clouds into sunlight. Immediate action was taken to break formation and a midair collision was narrowly avoided. On medical evaluation by the flight surgeon, the pilot was extremely shaken by this incident and then reported having experienced migraine headaches at least once monthly over the past several years, sometimes with transient visual disturbance, which had not previously been disclosed at annual flight physicals. Neurologic evaluation results were negative. The pilot was grounded from flying duties, subsequently incorporated healthy lifestyle changes, and remained symptom-free for over 1 year. Medical certification was then granted, initially with restrictions to dual-pilot aircraft.

Common episodic neurologic disorders that are not readily classified into other disease categories include epilepsy and migraine. These can have aeromedically significant associated cognitive effects, not only from the condition itself, but also from medications used for management.

Regarding epilepsy, etiologies widely range from genetically determined to posttraumatic, postinfectious, and poststroke to idiopathic. Neurocognitive impairment is frequently seen in epilepsy patients, as outlined by van Rijckevorsel (2006). Jobst (2020) noted that in focal epilepsies, affected cognitive domains align with seizure focus location; frontal lobe epilepsy would have more executive dysfunction and temporal lobe epilepsy would more commonly affect short- and long-term memory. Cognitive dysfunction in epilepsy may reflect underlying abnormal brain development and also anti-epileptic medications may also contribute to it. Anti-epileptic medication use is aeromedically incompatible. Aeromedically, long seizure-free and medication-free observation times are required before medical certification consideration. Formal neuropsychological evaluation should be considered on an individual basis in those cases of seizure or epilepsy that are felt potentially suitable for medical certification.

Concerning migraine, no definitive etiology is uncovered in most cases. Most attacks are self-limited and do not have persistent symptoms, although rarely migraine can produce stroke. Functional impairment is often seen during the acute migraine episode, but constitutional symptoms, including cognitive slowing, may occur as a prodrome to the migraine attack or continue in the postdromal migraine phase. Gil-Gouveia and Martins (2019) noted that reversible attack-related cognitive dysfunction occurs during migraine attacks and may persist in patients with frequent or complicated attacks, but evidence did not support an increased risk of long-term or persistent cognitive dysfunction. Formal neuropsychological evaluation is rarely indicated in migraine cases unless cognitive symptoms are endorsed or office screening tests show abnormally low scores.

Systemic Conditions

A wide variety of systemic medical conditions may produce cognitive dysfunction, as outlined in a journal issue coedited by Safdieh and Lewis (2020). Some common examples include disorders of sodium (hypo- and hypernatremia), disorders of glucose (hypo- and hyperglycemia), thyroid function disorders (hypo- and hyperthyroidism), localized infections (urinary tract, pneumonia), vitamin B_{12} deficiency, autoimmune disorders (sporadic or paraneoplastic encephalitis), sleep apnea, heart failure, and severe chronic obstructive pulmonary disease. Older adults are particularly susceptible to cognitive effects from local infections and electrolyte abnormalities. Systemic medical disorders can occur concomitantly with other primary neurologic conditions and worsen cognitive function. Metabolic disturbances more commonly result in delirium or encephalopathy, which are generally reversible once the underlying abnormality is corrected. However, aeromedically significant persistent cognitive changes can be seen with B_{12} deficiency, hypothyroidism, profound/prolonged hypoglycemia, autoimmune encephalitis, and too rapidly corrected hyponatremia (osmotic demyelinating syndrome). Abnormal brain MRI findings can be seen in some cases of persistent cognitive dysfunction. Global cognitive domains are typically affected with systemic illness. Formal neuropsychological evaluation in cases of systemic illness-associated cognitive dysfunction is best deferred until adequate time has elapsed once any acute abnormalities are corrected and clinical stability established.

Medications

Midway through a transcontinental flight, a young commercial pilot was found to be asleep during a routine air traffic control communication. The pilot was noted to be persistently groggy on awakening, and the second pilot assumed aircraft control for the remainder of the flight. Following the flight, the pilot indicated having seasonal allergy and congestion symptoms, and had taken Benadryl prior to the flight, assuming this was safe to use while flying since it was non-prescription.

The review by Nevado-Holgado et al. (2016) noted that almost any medication has potential to adversely affect mentation. The American Geriatrics Society (2023) updated AGS Beers Criteria for potentially inappropriate medication use in older adults is coincidentally quite helpful in identifying medication for which aeromedical cognitive concern may also exist, particularly Table 3 which lists central nervous system-active drugs, and Table 7, which lists anticholinergic medication (AGS, 2023). The impact of medications on mentation is quite variable and is influenced by underlying medical conditions, individual genetically determined metabolism, diet, simultaneous ethanol intake, and medication–medication interactions. In addition to adverse cognitive effects, medications may increase risk of injuries from falling, which is a significant cause of morbidity in the older population. Sorting out which medication or medications are responsible for cognitive changes is often challenging, especially in the setting of polypharmacy. Prototypic agents that adversely affect mentation include opioids, benzodiazepines, sedative/hypnotics, and first-generation antihistamines. The latter category is of particular aeromedical significance, as sedating antihistamines such as diphenhydramine (Benadryl) and doxylamine (Unisom) are non-prescription and ubiquitously available. As the case example illustrated, despite ongoing educational efforts to the contrary, some aviators assume that these medications can be safely used before or during flight since they can be obtained without prescription. Psychoactive medications such as antidepressants (especially first-generation tricyclic agents) and antipsychotics have aeromedically concerning cognitive effects. Dopamine agonists, used in the management of PD, restless leg syndrome, and pituitary tumors, have an increased risk of impulse-control disorders, as noted by Grall-Bronnec et al. (2018), and are generally contraindicated aeromedically. Anti-epileptic medications can adversely affect mentation and are also aeromedically contraindicated. Corticosteroids are well known to produce behavioral effects, including depression mania and frank psychosis, even at standard therapeutic dosages. Anti-retroviral agents used to suppress HIV can produce treatment-limiting neuropsychiatric side effects. In general, cognitive effects from medications are global, crossing many functional domains, can range in severity from subtle cognitive slowing to full-blown encephalopathy, and are reversible once the offending agent(s) is(are) discontinued. Persistent cognitive dysfunction after medication discontinuation is uncommon. Formal neuropsychological evaluation is indicated in cases of medication-induced persistent cognitive dysfunction and is best obtained after sufficient time has elapsed from discontinuing the offending agent(s) to establish clinical stability.

Toxins

A middle-age commercial pilot was observed to have a seizure during pre-flight cockpit activities and was immediately sent for medical evaluation. Cranial imaging showed age-inappropriate cerebral atrophy. Elevated mean corpuscular volume and hepatic transaminases were noted on laboratory studies. History was obtained that indicated previously unreported long-standing nearly daily heavy ethanol use, with limited consumption over the previous several days due to schedule disruptions. The diagnosis of alcohol-related seizure was made. Neuropsychological testing showed likely diminished performance in several cognitive domains, but these were not felt to be aeromedically significant by the consultant. After intensive rehabilitative treatment and observation, medical certification was eventually granted. Follow-up cranial imaging showed resolution of cerebral atrophy.

Many toxins can produce lasting cognitive dysfunction and, as noted in the review from de Oliveira et al. (2019), can result in abnormalities on brain imaging studies. Ethanol is a neurotoxin that can affect both the central and peripheral nervous systems. It is widely consumed recreationally and is well known to cause both acute and chronic cognitive changes. Alcohol use disorders also have significant aeromedically concerning behavioral factors that must be considered. Please refer to Chapter 11 for additional information on aeromedical concerns from ethanol use. Illicit drug use can produce long-term, sometimes permanent, cognitive dysfunction. In their book chapter, Caito and Aschner (2015) reviewed toxicity of heavy metals, and noted that metal exposures, including lead, mercury, arsenic, manganese, and aluminum, have potential neurotoxic effects. Chronic industrial or recreational exposure to organic and aliphatic hydrocarbons, including solvents, is associated with cognitive dysfunction, which may be permanent. Carbon monoxide poisoning can produce permanent brain damage with resulting cognitive deficits. Recreational inhalation of nitrous oxide is not uncommon and, as noted in the review by Xiang et al. (2021), can produce central and peripheral nervous system damage through interference with vitamin B_{12} metabolism. Formal neuropsychological evaluation is indicated in cases of toxin exposure with persistent cognitive dysfunction and is best obtained after sufficient time has elapsed to establish clinical stability.

Treatment Effects

In addition to aeromedically significant cognitive effects from underlying medical conditions, treatments used for their management can independently impact cognition. In some cases, adverse cognitive effects from treatments outlast primary effects from the underlying condition and are more aeromedically concerning. Immunosuppressive agents have an increased risk of causing opportunistic infections and secondary malignancies that can affect cognitive function. Surgical treatment can damage brain structures with resulting cognitive deficits. Foki et al. (2017) reported that deep brain stimulation, used in PD management, has been associated with cognitive decline. Perhaps the most widely recognized treatment-associated cognitive dysfunction is with cancer treatment, as Lange et al. (2019) noted in their review. Cognitive dysfunction in cancer patients is often multifactorial, without a single causative factor. Cognitive symptoms are common in long-term cancer survivors, especially pediatric cancers. The review from Santomasso (2020) indicated many anticancer drugs are directly toxic to central and peripheral nervous system tissue. Chemotherapy may produce long-term cognitive impairment, colloquially known as "chemo brain," as noted by Vega et al. (2022). Radiation therapy can cause cognitive changes, which, as noted by Saad and Wang (2015), may involve specific cognitive domains and have delayed manifestations. Neuropsychological evaluation is indicated in cases of suspected treatment-associated cognitive dysfunction and is best obtained after sufficient time has elapsed to establish clinical stability.

Conclusion

Neurologic conditions that can affect cognition are commonly encountered in aerospace medicine and are a major cause of morbidity. Impairments may be subtle and under-recognized by aviators and their treating providers alike. Recognition of aeromedically significant cognitive impairment potential from neurologic disorders is pivotal in guiding evaluation and management to determine medical certification suitability. Neurologic conditions rarely occur in isolation, and synergistic adverse cognitive effects from other medical conditions or treatments must always be considered in the overall aeromedical assessment. Clinical vigilance with a heightened index of suspicion for potential cognitive impairment is essential in medical evaluations. Neuropsychological evaluation findings are an important aspect of medical certification determinations. A low threshold should be maintained for obtaining formal cognitive function assessments in all aviators with neurologic disorders.

References

American Geriatrics Society (AGS) Beers Criteria Update Expert Panel. (2023). American Geriatrics Society 2023 updated AGS Beers Criteria for potentially inappropriate medication use in older adults. *Journal of the American Geriatrics Society, 71*, 2052–2081. https://doi.org/10.1111/jgs.18372

Arciniegas, D.B., Held, K., & Wagner, P. (2002). Cognitive impairment following traumatic brain injury. *Current Treatment Options in Neurology, 4*(1), 43–57. https://doi.org/10.1007/s11940-002-0004-6

Aarsland, D., Batzu, L., Halliday, G.M., Geurtsen, G.J., Ballard, C., Ray Chaudhuri, K., & Weintraub, D. (2021). Parkinson disease-associated cognitive impairment. *Nature Reviews: Disease, 7*(1), 47. https://doi.org/10.1038/s41572-021-00280-3

Arvanitakis, Z., Shah, R.C., & Bennett, D.A. (2019). Diagnosis and management of dementia: Review. *JAMA, 322*(16), 1589–1599. https://doi.org/10.1001/jama.2019.4782

Barkhof, F., & Koeller, K.K. (2020). Demyelinating diseases of the CNS (brain and spine). In J. Hodler, R.A. Kubik-Huch, & G.K. von Schulthess (Eds.), *Diseases of the brain, head and neck, spine 2020–2023: Diagnostic imaging* (pp. 165–176). Springer. https://doi.org/10.1007/978-3-030-38490-6_13

Caito, A., & Aschner, M. (2015). Neurotoxicity of metals. In M. Lotti & M.L. Bleeker (Eds.), *Handbook of clinical neurology* (Vol. 131, pp. 169–189). https://doi.org/10.1016/B978-0-444-62627-1.00011-1

Capizzi, A., Woo, J., & Verduzco-Gutierrez, M. (2020). Traumatic brain injury: An overview of epidemiology, pathophysiology, and medical management. *Medical Clinics of North America, 104*(2), 213–238. https://doi.org/10.1016/j.mcna.2019.11.001

Centers for Disease Control and Prevention. (2023a). *Traumatic brain injury and concussion: TBI data.* https://www.cdc.gov/traumatic-brain-injury/data-research/?CDC_AAref_Val=https://www.cdc.gov/TraumaticBrainInjury/data/index.html

Centers for Disease Control and Prevention. (2023b). *Stroke: Stroke facts.* https://www.cdc.gov/stroke/data-research/facts-stats/?CDC_AAref_Val=https://www.cdc.gov/stroke/facts.htm

de Oliveira, A.M., Paulino, M.V., Vieira, A.P.F., McKinney, A.M., da Rocha, A.J., dos Santos, G.T., da Costa Leite, C., de Souza Godoy, L.F., & Lucato, L.T. (2019). Imaging patterns of toxic and metabolic brain disorders. *RadioGraphics, 39*(6), 1672–1695. https://doi.org/10.1148/rg.2019190016

D'Souza, C.E., Greenway, M.R.F., Graff-Radford, J., & Meschia, J.F. (2022). Cognitive impairment in patients with stroke. *Seminars in Neurology, 41*(1), 75–84. https://doi.org/10.1055/s-0040-1722217

Foki, T., Hitzl, D., Pirker, W., Novak, K., Pusswald, G., Auff, E., & Lehrner, J. (2017). Assessment of individual cognitive changes after deep brain stimulation surgery in Parkinson's disease using the Neuropsychological Test Battery Vienna short version. *Wiener Klinische Wochenschrift, 129*(15–16), 564–571. https://doi.org/10.1007/s00508-017-1169-z

Fox, S.W., Mitchell, S.A., & Booth-Jones, M. (2006). Cognitive impairment in patients with brain tumors: assessment and intervention in the clinic setting. *Clinical Journal of Oncology Nursing, 10*(2), 169–176. https://doi.org/10.1188/06.CJON.169-176

Gil-Gouveia, R., & Martins, I.P. (2019). Cognition and cognitive impairment in migraine. *Current Pain and Headache Reports, 23*(11), Article 84. https://doi.org/10.1007/s11916-019-0824-7

Giovane, R.A., & Lavender, P.D. (2018). Central nervous system infections. *Primary Care, 45*(3), 505–518. https://doi.org/10.1016/j.pop.2018.05.007

Grall-Bronnec, M., Victorri-Vigneau, C., Donnio, Y., Leboucher, J., Rousselet, M., Thiabaud, E., Zreika, N., Derkinderen, P., & Challet-Bouju, G. (2018). Dopamine agonists and impulse control disorders: A complex association. *Drug Safety, 41*(1), 19–75. https://doi.org/10.1007/s40264-017-0590-6

Grzegorski, T., & Losy, J. (2017). Cognitive impairment in multiple sclerosis – a review of current knowledge and recent research. *Reviews in Neurosciences, 28*(8), 845–860. https://doi.org/10.1515/revneuro-2017-0011

Høva, J.K., Thorheim, L., & Wagstaff, A.S. (2017). Medical reasons for loss of license in Norwegian professional pilots. *Aerospace Medicine and Human Performance, 88*(2), 146–149. https://doi.org/10.3357/AMHP.4551.2017

Jobst, B.C. (2020). Epilepsy and cognition. *Practical Neurology,* 42–43. https://practicalneurology.com/articles/2020-oct/epilepsy-and-cognition

Jongsiriyanyong, S., & Limpawattana, P. (2018). Mild cognitive impairment in clinical practice: A review article. *American Journal of Alzheimer's Disease & Other Dementias, 33*(8), 500–507. https://doi.org/10.1177/1533317518791401

Lange, M., Joly, F., Vardy, J., Ahles, T., Dubois, M., Tron, L., Winocur, G., De Ruiter, M.B., Castel, H. (2019). Cancer-related cognitive impairment: An update on state of the art, detection, and management strategies in cancer survivors (2019). *Annals of Oncology, 30*(12), 1925–1940. https://doi.org/10.1093/annonc/mdz410

Marras, C., Beck, J.C., Bower, J.H., Roberts, E., Ritz, B., Ross, G.W., Abbott, R.D., Savica, R., Van Den Eeden, S.K., Willis, A.W., Tanner, C.M., & Parkinson's Foundation P4 Group. (2022). Prevalence of Parkinson's disease across North America (2022). *NPJ Parkinson's Disease, 4*, Article 21. https://doi.org/10.1038/s41531-018-0058-0

Nevado-Holgado, A.J., Kim, C.H., Winchester, L., Gallacher, J., & Lovestone, S. (2016). Commonly prescribed drugs associate with cognitive function: A cross-sectional study in UK Biobank. *BMJ Open, 6*(11), Article e012177. https://doi.org/10.1136/bmjopen-2016-012177

Saad, S., & Wang, T.J. (2015). Neurocognitive deficits after radiation therapy for brain malignancies. *American Journal of Clinical Oncology, 38*(6), 634–640. https://doi.org/10.1097/COC.0000000000000158

Safdieh, J.E. (Guest Ed.), & Lewis, S.L. (Series Ed.). (2020). Neurology of systemic disease. *Continuum (Minneap Minn.), 26*(3). https://journals.lww.com/continuum/toc/2020/06000
Santomasso, B.D. (2020). Anticancer drugs and the nervous system. *Continuum, 26*(3), 732–764. https://doi.org/10.1212/CON.0000000000000873
Sittinger, H., Müller, M., Schweizer, I., & Merkelbach, S. (2002). Mild cognitive impairment after viral meningitis in adults. *Journal of Neurology, 249*(5), 554–560. https://doi.org/10.1007/s004150200064
Tavares-Júnior, J.W. L., de Souza, A.C. C., Borges, J.W. P., Oliveira, D.N., Siqueira-Neto, J.I., Sobreira-Neto, M.A., & Braga-Neto, P. (2022). COVID-19 associated cognitive impairment: A systematic review. *Cortex, 152*, 77–97. https://doi.org/10.1016/j.cortex.2022.04
van Rijckevorsel, K. (2006). Cognitive problems related to epilepsy syndromes, especially malignant epilepsies. *Seizure, 15*(4), 227–234. https://doi.org/10.1016/j.seizure.2006.02.019
Vega, J.N., Albert, K.M., Mayer, I.A., Taylor, W.D., & Newhouse, P.A. (2022). Subjective cognition and mood in persistent chemotherapy-related cognitive impairment. *Journal of Cancer Survivorship, 16*, 614–623. https://doi.org//10.1007/s11764-021-01055-1
Verde, P., Guadagno, A.G., D'Angelo, A. Vitalone, R., Di Vita, A., & Piccardi, L. (2022). A controversial assessment of fitness to fly after a traumatic brain injury. *Aerospace Medicine and Human Performance, 93*(2), 116–122. https://doi.org/10.3357/AMHP.5978.2022
Weintraub, D., & Irwin, D. (2022). Diagnosis and treatment of cognitive and neuropsychiatric symptoms in Parkinson disease and dementia with Lewy bodies. *Continuum (Minneap Minn), 28*(5), 1314–1332. https://doi.org/10.1212/CON.0000000000001151
Weterings, R., Kessels, R., de Leeuw, F-E., & Piai, V. (2023). Cognitive impairment after a stroke in young adults: A systematic review and meta-analysis. *International Journal of Stroke, 18*(8), 888–897. https://doi.org/10.1177/17474930231159267
Willis, A.W., Roberts, E., Beck, J.C. Fiske, B., Ross, W., Savica, R., Van Den Eeden, S.K., Tanner, C.M., & Marras, C. (2022). Incidence of Parkinson disease in North America. *NPJ Parkinson's Disease, 8*, Article 170. https://doi.org/10.1038/s41531-022-00410-y
Xiang, Y., Li, L., Ma, X., Li, S., Xue, Y., Yan, P., Chen, M., & Wu, J. (2021). Recreational nitrous oxide abuse: Prevalence, neurotoxicity, and treatment. *Neurotoxicity Research, 3*, 975–985. https://doi.org/10.1007/s12640-021-00352-y

Chapter 26
COVID-19 – Initial and Chronic Neuropsychological Symptoms

Christopher F. Flynn

Introduction

The Coronavirus disease 2019 (COVID-19) became the first pandemic of the 21st century, officially lasting from March 11, 2020 to May 5, 2023. During the pandemic, SARS-CoV-2 infected over 767.5 million of the world's population. Despite 13.4 billion vaccine doses administered, it has caused more than 6.9 million deaths (World Health Organization, 2023). Highly transmissible, the initial infection by the SARS-CoV-2 typically creates a respiratory infection with cough and shortness of breath. Two prior coronaviruses created similar outbreaks that did not evolve into pandemics: severe acute respiratory syndrome coronavirus 1 (SARS-CoV) in 2002 and the Middle Eastern respiratory syndrome coronavirus (MERS-CoV) in 2012 (van Vuren et al., 2021). While the COVID-19 pandemic may be "officially" over, the damage from the pandemic continues.

World economies are striving to recover after a severe global economic downturn. The geographic isolation that reduced viral spread also collapsed countries' economies. Mass unemployment followed, including layoffs in the professional aviation business sector (International Civil Aviation Organization [ICAO], 2021). Families suffered from social isolation, financial loss from unemployment, and the grief from lost loved ones (Mousavi, 2020). Even without becoming infected by the virus, people's fear and uncertainty caused psychological distress to surge from 3.9 % (2018) to 13 % (2020) in the general population (McGinty et al., 2020). For those who survived a SARS-CoV-2 infection, about 10 %–15 % will have prolonged symptoms beyond 6 weeks (Nalbandian et al., 2023; Rubin, 2020). As many as 21 %–56 % of those patients with chronic symptoms suffer from ongoing cognitive difficulties (called "brain fog"; COMEBAC Group et al., 2021; Crunflí et al., 2021; Monje & Iwasaki, 2022; Toniolo et al., 2021;).

This chapter provides an overview of the biological and psychological problems of COVID-19 and SARS-CoV-2 infection. A comparison of symptoms across the three coronavirus outbreaks will add perspective when considering initial and chronic problems. Although multiple organs in the body are damaged by the SARS-CoV-2 viral infection, this chapter looks carefully at the virus's impact on the brain. Initial and chronic cognitive symptoms are identified, along with current concepts of how the infection creates these problems. Aviators who have persistent symptoms from a SARS-CoV-2 infection may improve, but (at this time) will have few evidence-based treatments to help them return to the cockpit.

COVID-19: Pandemic Psychosocial Symptoms

Whether an individual became infected by the virus or not, the COVID-19 pandemic generated tremendous psychological stress in the world population (van Vuren et al., 2021). Millions of individuals lost their jobs, leading to severe financial strain. As an example, by November 2020, 22 million US workers were unemployed and 10 million fewer jobs were available. Of those still working full time, 33 % had taken a pay cut (Work, 2020). Someone still employed felt the pressure of not losing the job at any costs (even risking exposure to illness). Children were unable to attend school, and usual social support (friends, extended family) often could not assist due to the required social isolation and travel restrictions. Families lost loved ones, affecting (on average) seven individuals with every death. Often, those grieving suffered without the healing power of connectedness at times of loss (Simon et al., 2020). Conflicting information about treatments, the use of masks, and social isolation made it difficult to find hope for an end to the pandemic. Moreover, each time infection rates began to drop, new (Delta and Omicron) variants seemed to create a new wave of suffering. The psychosocial strain for the world's population was enormous.

In a survey of US adults in 2020, one or more adverse mental health conditions were present in 41%; and 11% had seriously considered suicide in the past 30 days (Simon et al., 2020). In a meta-analysis of Southeast Asians, pandemic anxiety levels surged to 31 % and depression levels to 16 % (Pappa et al., 2022). Overall COVID-19 increased the point prevalence of anxiety and depression by 1.3–1.5 times the expected rate (Kessler et al., 2022). Yet, one meta-analysis of the general population disagreed, concluding that change estimates for anxiety and depression symptoms were not statistically significant (Sun et al., 2023).

With rare exceptions, individuals with a preexisting mental health condition experienced greater psychological burdens as well as higher rates of SARS-CoV-2 infection and mortality. (Bertolini et al., 2023) Individuals with substance use disorders appeared particularly affected. In one study, 19 % of those attempting abstinence experienced relapse, while 23 % of "regular drinkers" reported increased consumption (Sun et al., 2020). Worsening addictive behaviors caused alcohol-related deaths to increase by 25 % from 2019 to 2020 (White et al., 2022), and drug overdose deaths by 30 % for the same time period (Tanz et al., 2022). In a meta-analysis of pooled population studies, both suicidal ideation (clinical, prevalence ratio [PR] = 1.13) and suicide attempts (clinical, PR = 1.32) rose significantly during the pandemic in general and clinical populations. Conversely, death by suicide had a nonsignificant downward trend (rate ratio = 0.923; Yan et al., 2023). COVID-19 generated tremendous suffering and mental health burdens in individuals, even if they were never infected.

SARS-CoV-2 Infection: Initial Phase Symptoms

Initial Infection Susceptibility

Coronavirus infection and outbreaks (SARS 2002, MERS 2012, SARS-CoV-2 2020) share similar biological features and create similar damage in the human body (van Vuren et al., 2021). Although SARS-CoV-2 enters the body through the nose, throat, and lungs, it primarily invades cells through the angiotensin-converting enzyme 2 (ACE2) receptor. This receptor is present in the cells of most major human organ systems, including the brain

(Pyne & Brickman, 2021). Yet, SARS-CoV-2 is far more infectious than earlier coronaviruses. It is thought that its greater structural flexibility allowed it to generate a stronger bond to enter human cells (Wang et al., 2021). Once available, COVID-19 vaccinations provided time-limited reductions in patients' risk of, severity of, and death from infection (dos Santos et al., 2023). However, some individual factors seemed to increase the risk for a person to become infected.

Meta-analyses suggested that increased rates of infection, symptom severity, and death were present in individuals who had preexisting mental or neurological disorders (Bertolini et al., 2023; Castro et al., 2021; Frontera & Simon, 2022; Toubasi et al., 2021) In one meta-analysis of 16 studies, patients with a preexisting mental disorder had an increased risk for symptom severity and death (odds ratio [OR] =1.52). Another meta-analysis of nine studies found that patients with any mental disorder had an increased risk for infection (OR=1.71), severe illness course (OR=1.32–1.77), and death (OR=1.38–1.52) compared to the general population (Bertolini et al., 2023). Increased infection rate (but not mortality) was noted for patients with anxiety disorders, while increased mortality (but not illness severity) was found for patients with schizophrenia spectrum disorders (Bertolini et al., 2023). In a meta-analysis of 319,025 patients, those with autoimmune diseases were more likely to become infected (OR=2.19; Akiyama et al., 2021). After infection, older adults, men, and people of color were also more likely to have worse medical outcomes (Pyne & Brickman, 2021).

Preexisting cognitive problems also increased the negative impact of an individual's SARS-CoV-2 infection. In a UK Biobank study of 431,051 healthy individuals, low performance on verbal and numerical reasoning, as well as reduced reaction speed, increased the risk for infection (Chang et al., 2020). A US study found that preexisting dementia (OR=5.2) and preexisting Alzheimer's dementia (OR=7.7) increased infection risk (Batty et al., 2020). Researchers proposed that an inability to follow public health recommendations might have led to these patients' worse outcomes. Finally, some patients who carried dormant Epstein-Barr virus (EBV) in their cells developed worse symptoms from SARS-CoV-2 infection. For many, their EBV reactivated and produced a second infection. In a study of 217 COVID-19 patients, blood counts of cells fighting EBV were significantly higher in non-survivors than in survivors (Meng et al., 2022). This was not true for patients with other latent viruses, such as cytomegalovirus (CMV; Monje & Iwasaki, 2022). Taken together, there were multiple factors that appeared to make an individual more susceptible to SARS-CoV-2.

Biological Symptoms

SARS-CoV-2 is a respiratory virus that creates infection through inhaled viral particles. Yet, once the virus enters the bloodstream through the lungs, it can also harm the heart, liver, kidneys, and brain (Pyne & Brickman, 2021). Separately, SARS-CoV-2 is also thought to directly infect the brain's olfactory nerve that extends directly above the nose (Douaud et al., 2022). This direct viral damage to the olfactory neurons can lead to the loss of smell (anosmia) and to altered taste (ageusia), which were common initial symptoms in infected patients (Lukiw et al., 2022) The human body reacts to infection by generating inflammatory cells to fight the pathogen. However, SARS-CoV-2 appears to cause a much greater inflammatory response in some patients. Called a "cytokine storm," cells that react to fight infection over-react. Following the adage, there can be "too much of a good thing"; this overly aggressive response of immune cells and proteins causes additional complications of bleeding, organ failure, and (in one study) a 23 % death rate (Ramatillah et al., 2022). How this process becomes dysregulated is not clear, because measurements of typical infection biomarkers do not reliably predict the severity of SARS-CoV-2 organ damage and complications (Umesh et al., 2022).

While direct brain infection has been detected in patient autopsies (Monje & Iwasaki, 2022), the more likely route of entry to brain neurons comes from leaks through blood vessels. SARS-CoV-2 has been shown to damage two typically robust barriers that protect the brain from pathogens in the blood: the blood–brain barrier (BBB) and the blood–cerebrospinal fluid barrier (B-CSF-B). Injured blood vessels allow the virus, immune cells, and cytokines into the brain (Lee et al., 2022; Monje & Iwasaki, 2022; Pellegrini et al., 2020). Using the ACE2 receptor to enter the neuron, a variety of intracellular systems can then transport the virus to adjacent neurons (Chen et al., 2022; Monje & Iwasaki, 2022). Yet, in another confounding analysis, some patients with neurological symptoms were not found to have evidence of SARS-CoV-2 in the brain or CSF (Lee et al., 2021; Monje & Iwasaki, 2022; Song et al., 2021).

In a systematic review of 79 studies that examined the neurological symptoms of initial infection in COVID-19 patients, diagnoses included encephalitis (78 %), seizure (30 %), confusion (23 %), headache (21 %), disorientation (15 %), and altered mental status (12 %). Among these patients, abnormal results were found in their brain magnetic resonance imaging (MRI; 78 %), electroencephalogram (76 %), and CSF tests (64 %; Islam et al., 2022). Yet, severity of respiratory infection was not proportional to severity of brain injury in patients. Researchers found multiple areas of brain injury, even in milder respiratory cases (Fernández-Castañeda et al., 2022; Monje & Iwasaki, 2022). Additional causes for neurological symptoms in COVID-19 patients would include seizures, metabolites from organ failure, medications, fever, or low oxygen levels (see Table 26.1).

Psychological Symptoms

A review of past coronavirus data on early and prolonged psychological symptoms demonstrated a higher incidence of symptoms up to 6 weeks, but ongoing symptoms in many (Rogers et al., 2020; see Table 26.2). In one study of patients with severe COVID-19 infection, 30 % of patients developed psychiatric symptoms, including catatonia (Oh et al., 2023). Separately, among 125 hospitalized older UK patients, 39 (31 %) presented with altered mental status. Of those 39 patients, 21 (53 %) developed a new psychiatric diagnosis: 10 had psychosis, six had a dementia-like syndrome, and five had affective illness or catatonia (Varatharaj et al., 2020).

As discussed earlier, SARS-CoV-2 can damage the brain in multiple ways, including inflammation. Curiously, in a systematic review of 53 research studies on the role of low-grade inflammation in psychiatric illness, some patients with mood, anxiety-related, and psychotic symptoms had elevated inflammatory cytokine levels (Fitton et al., 2022). In a corollary finding, serotonin selective reuptake inhibitors (SSRI) medications, which are widely used in the treatment of anxiety and depressive disorders, also reduce inflammatory cytokines (Patel et al., 2023). Further, the SSRI fluvoxamine was proven to be effective in reducing the severity of COVID-19 illness, when early medication treatment options were very limited (Lenze et al., 2020). The ameliorative benefit of fluvoxamine is proposed to be its anti-inflammation effectiveness. As noted in Table 26.2, new-onset psychological symptoms are to be expected in all three coronavirus infections.

Table 26.1. SARS-CoV-2 biological factors affecting brain neurons

Entry into body and brain	Neurons damaged by	Neuron injury causes	Neuron injury creates
COVID-19 lung infection (Monje & Iwasaki, 2022)	Attack from autoimmune (anti-neuron, anti-interferon, anti-nuclear) antibodies (Su et al., 2022)	Glial cell dysregulation (Braga et al., 2023)	Brain circuit dysfunction (Monje & Iwasaki, 2022)
COVID-19 olfactory nerve infection (Douaud et al., 2022)	Attack from cytokines (interleukin-6, C-reactive protein, eotaxin-CCL11 (immune) (Fernández-Castañeda et al., 2022) Direct viral infection (Pellegrini et al., 2020) Leaking of BBB and B-CSF-B causing brain bleeding and clots (Lee et al., 2021) Loss of available oxygen (hypoxia) (Monje & Iwasaki, 2022) Metabolites from organ failure (Monje & Iwasaki, 2022) Medications (Monje & Iwasaki, 2022) Quiescent viruses (e.g., EBV, HSV, varicella) reactivating in the neuron (Wang et al., 2021)	Reduced neuronal health (Fernández-Castañeda et al., 2022)	Cognitive dysfunction (Tavares-Júnior et al., 2022)

Table 26.2. Patients' mental health symptoms after COVID-19, SARS, or MERS infection

Topic	COVID-19, up to 6 weeks	SARS, MERS, up to 6 weeks	COVID-19, 2 months or longer	SARS, MERS; 2 months to 12 years
Depressed mood	31% (Mazza et al., 2020) 48% (Frontera & Simon, 2022)	32.6% (Rogers et al., 2020)	3% (Frontera & Simon, 2022) 9% (Mazza et al., 2021) 18% (COMEBAC Group et al., 2021) 20% (Crunflí et al., 2021), (Frontera & Simon, 2022)	10.5% (Rogers et al., 2020)

Table 26.2. continued

Topic	COVID-19, up to 6 weeks	SARS, MERS, up to 6 weeks	COVID-19, 2 months or longer	SARS, MERS; 2 months to 12 years
Anxiety	33% (Frontera & Simon, 2022) 42% (Frontera & Simon, 2022), (Mazza et al., 2020)	35.7% (Rogers et al., 2020)	7% (Frontera & Simon, 2022) 23% (COMEBAC Group et al., 2021) 28% (Crunflí et al., 2021) 30% (Mazza et al., 2021) 46% (Frontera & Simon, 2022)	12.3% (Rogers et al., 2020)
Memory loss[b]	7% (Frontera & Simon, 2022) 55% (Frontera & Simon, 2022)	34.1% (Rogers et al., 2020)	4% (Frontera & Simon, 2022) 10% (Mazza et al., 2021) 24% (Becker et al., 2021) 28% (Crunflí et al., 2021) 34% (Garrigues et al., 2020) 47% (Frontera & Simon, 2022)	18.9% (Rogers et al., 2020)
Inattention			28% (Garrigues et al., 2020) 33% (Mazza et al., 2021)	
Processing speed			18% (Becker et al., 2021) 33% (Mazza et al., 2021)	
Executive dysfunction[b]			16% (Becker et al., 2021) 34% (Crunflí et al., 2021) 50% (Mazza et al., 2021) 56% (Crunflí et al., 2021)	
Insomnia	29% (Frontera & Simon, 2022) 40% (Mazza et al., 2020)	41.9% (Rogers et al., 2020)	3% (Frontera & Simon, 2022) 27% (Frontera & Simon, 2022) 30.8% (Garrigues et al., 2020)	12.1% (Rogers et al., 2020)

Table 26.2. continued

Topic	COVID-19, up to 6 weeks	SARS, MERS, up to 6 weeks	COVID-19, 2 months or longer	SARS, MERS; 2 months to 12 years
Any mental health diagnosis[b]	55% (Mazza et al., 2020)		5.8% (Taquet et al., 2021) 18.1% (Taquet et al., 2021) 24% (Mazza et al., 2021) 43% (Frontera & Simon, 2022)	14.8% (Rogers et al., 2020) 32.2% (Rogers et al., 2020)
Hospitalized, any mental health symptom (including fatigue)[b]	11% (Frontera & Simon, 2022) 46% (Frontera & Simon, 2022) 53.1% (Carfì et al., 2020)		5% (Frontera & Simon, 2022) 31% (COMEBAC Group et al., 2021) 55% (Garrigues et al., 2020)	
Long hauler's symptoms[a]			10% (Rubin, 2020) 15% (Nalbandian et al., 2023)	

Note. [a]Symptoms include fatigue, myalgias, SOB = shortness of breath, "brain fog" (i.e., poor memory or concentration). [b]This includes confusion caused by delirium.

Cognitive Symptoms

Given the considerable biological impact of COVID-19 infection on brain neurons, it is not unexpected that cognitive problems would occur (Monje & Iwasaki, 2022; Pandharipande et al., 2013) During the early phase of COVID-19 illness, 7%–56% of patients have cognitive complaints (Crunflí et al., 2021; Frontera & Simon, 2022). Cognitive function relies on the precise integration of neural circuits. Circuit interconnections are supported by brain microglial cells that maintain synaptic strength, synaptic connectivity, and myelination (Monje & Iwasaki, 2022). Microglial cell dysregulation is known to occur during an inflammatory response. At these times, rather than repairing damaged neurons, microglia can instead further damage brain cells. Damaged neurons and brain circuits are well established contributors to cognitive impairment (Monje & Iwasaki, 2022). In a meta-analysis of 22 studies where cognitive assessments were completed up to 12 weeks after COVID-19 infection, the most affected cognitive domains were executive function, attention, working memory, processing speed, and episodic memory. The incidence of impairment ranged from 2.6% (lowest in outpatients) to 81% (highest in hospitalized patients; Tavares-Júnior, 2022). In a French study of 45 COVID-19 patients requiring intensive care unit (ICU) treatment, 33% were found to have a dysexecutive syndrome at discharge (Toniolo et al., 2021). While not all patients will have ongoing cognitive symptoms, persistent cognitive symptoms will be discussed in the next section.

SARS-CoV-2 Prolonged Symptoms

Prolonged Symptoms Susceptibility

Approximately 10 %–15 % of patients who have suffered a SARS-CoV-2 infection experience ongoing symptoms (Nalbandian et al., 2023; Rubin, 2020). Reports on the prevalence and duration of individual symptoms have varied due to a lack of standardized research methods across studies, in addition to follow-up periods ranging from months to years (Braga et al., 2023; Frontera & Simon, 2022). Most data support the conclusion that the risk for prolonged symptoms is independent of age, employment or exercise status, or whether hospitalization (or ICU care) was required – during the initial infection (Douaud et al., 2022; Garrigues et al., 2020; Nalbandian et al., 2023). Yet, other studies suggest that several factors may increase the risk for continued symptoms: higher intensity of initial SARS-CoV-2 symptoms (data are mixed), diabetes, SARS-CoV-2 initial viral load, EBV reactivation and increased auto-antibody (anti-interferon, anti-nuclear) levels (Frontera & Simon, 2022; Monje & Iwasaki, 2022; Su et al., 2022).

Continuing the conflicting views, a study of 215 long-COVID patients found no evidence for elevated levels of auto-antibodies (Klein et al., 2022). Three corollary studies identified that patients with long-COVID symptoms showed elevated levels of inflammatory proteins (interleukin-6, C-reactive protein, eotaxin-CCL11; Fernández-Castañeda et al., 2022; Ferrando et al., 2022; Klein et al., 2022), and low cortisol levels (Klein et al., 2022). Having pre-existing respiratory, neurological, or psychiatric illness and female sex have also been implicated as factors increasing the risk of developing long-COVID symptoms (Frontera & Simon, 2022; Nalbandian et al., 2023; Thurner & Stengel, 2023).

Vaccination may reduce the risk for long-COVID. In a study of 33,940 vaccinated individuals compared with 113,474 unvaccinated, the risk of long-COVID was reduced by 15 % in the vaccinated group (Al-Aly et al., 2022). A second meta-analysis found vaccination was associated with reduced odds of long-COVID, identifying also that two doses were more effective than one (Notarte et al., 2022). A separate study of 455 vaccinated patients with long-COVID compared with 455 unvaccinated COVID patients found a small reduction in both severity and duration of long-COVID symptoms in the vaccinated group (Taylor, 2023). Twice as many vaccinated patients reported their long-COVID symptoms to be in remission, while unvaccinated patients reported that their social, professional, and family lives were more negatively impacted (Taylor, 2023). These data suggest that vaccination before COVID-19 infection is a protective factor for long-COVID symptoms. However, data are mixed on whether vaccination after long-COVID symptoms exist will reduce these symptoms (Notarte et al., 2022). While these retrospective studies have proposed some potential risk factors of long-COVID symptoms, no prospective study has confirmed any predictors.

Prolonged Physical Symptoms

Common persisting physical symptoms in COVID-19 patients include body aches, insomnia, elevated heart rate, and shortness of breath – in up to 31 % of patients (Garrigues et al., 2020; Nalbandian et al., 2023; Rogers et al., 2020; Rubin, 2020). When considering ongoing neurological symptoms, a meta-analysis of 18,258 patients showed a neurological manifestations pooled prevalence of 23 % (Mahdizade Ari et al., 2022). In persons with severe initial COVID-19 symptoms that led to death, a proliferation of microglial and/or astroglial cells (called “gliosis”) were noted in half of postmortem studies (Braga et al., 2023). Gliosis is identified as a causal mechanism for neuropsychiatric disease (Braga et al., 2023).

Compared with COVID-19-negative outpatients in the 12 months following a respiratory infection, those with survived SARS-CoV-2 had an increased risk of Alzheimer’s disease (relative risk [RR] = 3.5), Parkinson’s disease (RR = 2.6), ischemic stroke (RR = 2.7), and intracerebral hemorrhage (RR = 4.8; Taquet et al., 2022; Zarifkar et al., 2022). In those who died, autopsies identified brain blood vessel injury and neuron damage from low oxygen levels (called “hypoxia”) in 20–30 areas of those patients’ brains (Thakur et al., 2021). While low oxygen levels will damage all brain cells, even mild hypoxia is particularly damaging to hippocampal pyramidal neurons that are instrumental in memory function (Monje & Iwasaki, 2022).

Long-COVID patients may continue to have a dysregulated immune response. Prolonged increases in IgG reactivity to latent viruses (EBV, herpes simplex, varicella zoster) have been described. Similarly, elevated levels of cytokines (interleukin 6, C-reactive protein) were more frequently noted in long-COVID patients than controls (Monje & Iwasaki, 2022; Zhou et al., 2020). Overall, the duration of long-COVID physical symptoms is highly individualized and patients can experience ongoing symptoms for months to years.

Prolonged Psychological Symptoms

Persistent psychological complaints have occurred in all three coronavirus infections, causing depression, fatigue, and anxiety symptoms in 3 %–55 % of patients. Table 26.2 reflects a combination of studies of outpatients, inpatients, and ICU patients – with assessments occurring from 21 days to 12 years after coronavirus infection. Some COVID-19 patients became ill pre-vaccines, while others had completed available vaccinations (Braga et al., 2023; COMEBAC Group et al., 2021; Crunflí et al., 2021; Garrigues et al., 2020). In comparing these rates of psychological symptoms with the general population, researchers have conflicting opinions: that COVID-19 patients have a higher rate (Frontera et al., 2022) or no significant difference (Sun et al., 2023). In a 2-year follow-up study of 1,487,712 COVID-19 patients compared with patients with other severe respiratory diseases, rates of prolonged depression or anxiety were not significantly different between the two groups; however, there were more cases of psychosis in the COVID-19 group (Taquet et al., 2022). In this study, the risk for depression or anxiety was initially elevated, but then dropped to general population levels at 2 months post-infection (Taquet et al., 2022). These data suggest that the timing when research cohorts complete their surveys may be one explanation for the conflicting opinions. While the overall rate of psychological symptoms in long-COVID patients might match a general population rate, it does not reduce the negative impact of the symptoms on these patients’ lives.

Prolonged Cognitive Symptoms

As noted earlier, SARS-CoV-2 infection may damage the brain and diminish cognitive function by multiple causes (see Table 26.1). At least one in five long-COVID patients (18 %–87 %) will have cognitive difficulties with memory (10 %–47 %), inattention (10 %–33 %), processing speed (18 %–33 %), concentration (28 %), and executive function (16 %–56 %; Becker et al., 2021; COMEBAC Group et al., 2021; Crunflí et al., 2021; Garrigues et al., 2020; Mazza et al., 2021; Monje & Iwasaki, 2022; Rogers et al., 2020; Tavares-Júnior et al., 2022). In a meta-analysis of 81 studies of COVID-19, the overall proportion of patients with cognitive symptoms persisting 12 weeks past the initial infection was 22 % (Ceban et al., 2022). These symptoms have collectively become known as "brain fog."

Two meta-analyses (25 and 22 studies) found memory, attention, and executive functions were the most likely domains to be affected (Bertuccelli et al., 2022; Tavares-Júnior et al., 2022). Delayed recall and learning were the most impaired domains, while language and visuospatial abilities were rarely affected (Bertuccelli et al., 2022). Although neuropsychological tests were sometimes the basis of identifying cognitive deficits, in one meta-analysis 50 % of the studies relied primarily on the Montreal Cognitive Assessment (MoCA; Nasreddine et al., 2005; Tavares-Júnior et al., 2022).

Some patients with persisting cognitive symptoms demonstrate continuing elevations of cytokine proteins (CCL11, C-reactive protein) and proinflammatory biomarkers (Ceban et al., 2022; Fernández-Castañeda et al., 2022; Zhou et al., 2020). Consistent with this inflammatory cause of neuron damage (and therefore cognitive deficits), autopsies have shown distributed (not plaque-like) areas of demyelination (Fernández-Castañeda et al., 2022). A reduction in immature hippocampal cells in COVID-19 patients may also be due to inflammatory attacks on these neurons (Soung et al., 2022). Considering initial SARS-CoV-2 infection severity as a risk factor for hyper-inflammation, inpatients at initial diagnosis had an increased (OR=1.8–3.0; Becker et al., 2021) chance of developing prolonged cognitive symptoms. Yet, outpatients at initial diagnosis were not spared (hazard ratio [HR]=1.7; Xu et al., 2022).

MRI data from patients with long-COVID gathered on average 141 days after diagnosis revealed widespread structural abnormalities in the olfactory system, limbic system (including the hippocampus), cerebellum, and major white matter tracts (fimbria and superior fronto-occipital fasciculus). There was also a small but significant global decrease in brain volume (Douaud et al., 2022). Authors have suggested that long-COVID patients' difficulties in learning, memory, and executive function could be due to damage in the frontal–subcortical neural networks and the hippocampus (Newhouse et al., 2022).

Against the inflammation theory causing ongoing cognitive symptoms is a single positron emission tomography (PET) study that measured an inflammatory-related brain protein. Researchers found no correlation between heightened activity of this protein in the hippocampus and cognitive function scores (Braga et al., 2023). In addition, not all patients experiencing persistent cognitive complaints had severe initial COVID-19 symptoms, either; a likely cause for inducing a hyper-inflammatory state (Bertuccelli et al., 2022; Douaud et al., 2022; Tavares-Júnior et al., 2022; Toniolo et al., 2021). Therefore, while many "leads" suggest inflammation is a key factor in long-COVID-19 cognitive symptoms, data are not yet conclusive.

Other potential causes for long-COVID cognitive changes include physical illness, exhaustion, and psychological distress. In one study, a logistical regression analysis predicted worse cognitive testing scores when using factors of current depression scores, number of medical comorbidities, subjective cognitive complaints, and initial COVID-19 infection severity (Ferrando et al., 2022). Another study of COVID-19 patients also found a significant correlation between poor cognitive performance and higher mood/anxiety symptom scores (Whiteside et al., 2022).

Evidence-based conclusions regarding the causes of long-COVID cognitive symptoms must await further studies. Yet, it is reasonable to expect that about one in five long-COVID patients will have cognitive complaints. Poor performance in memory, attention, concentration, processing speed, executive function, and learning was a common finding, while current data suggest that language function and visuospatial skills were less effected. Multiple investigations have suggested a range of biological attacks on brain neurons could be the primary cause for ongoing cognitive symptoms (see Table 26.1). However, physical illness and psychological symptoms have also been shown as contributory. There are currently no predictors of the duration of a patient's "brain fog," as each recovery is patient specific.

Aviator Impact, Regulatory Response, and Treatment

COVID-19 created a deadly infection pandemic as well as a surge of psychosocial distress due to fear, grief, unemployment, and isolation requirements. During the pandemic, both international and domestic airline travel plummeted, reducing international passenger travel by 74 % and domestic passenger travel by 50 % (ICAO, 2021). In the first year of the pandemic, 51 % of aviation professionals surveyed (38 % were professional pilots) had lost their jobs (Cahill et al., 2023). In 2020, 67 % of pilots reported the pandemic had worsened their mental health, with 10 % having passive suicidal thoughts in the previous 2 weeks (Cahill et al., 2023) When confronting elevated stress levels, pilots appear to benefit from choosing strategies such as exercise (Cahill et al., 2021), mindfulness (Li et al., 2020) proactive coping (Guo et al., 2017), and cognitive flexibility (Sung et al., 2019). COVID-19 (both from the pandemic and/or infection) can create prolonged physical, psychological, and cognitive symptoms, preventing an aviator's return to work (Garrigues et al., 2020; Toniolo et al., 2021).

Several strategies may help reduce the likelihood of persistent symptoms from COVID-19 infection:

- Reducing the chance of COVID-19 infection by following public health recommendations
- Reducing the severity of infection by maintaining up-to-date COVID-19 variants vaccination (Al-Aly et al., 2022; Notarte et al., 2022; Taylor, 2023)
- (When infected) seeking evidence-based medical treatments quickly

Treatment is essential not only against the SARS-CoV-2, but also against (if present) a secondary re-activation of latent (EBV, herpes simplex, or varicella zoster) viruses (Thakur et al., 2021).

When there is persistent psychological distress, a pilot may use psychotherapy or an approved mental health medication (Federal Aviation Administration [FAA], 2023). A curious intersection of psychiatry and COVID-19 treatment is that SSRI medication has been shown to reduce inflammation (cytokine) markers in patients. After 12 weeks of antidepressant treatment (sertraline, venlafaxine, citalopram, or mirtazapine) in patients with newly diagnosed, major depression, blood inflammatory protein (cytokine) levels dropped. Further, patients with depression who demonstrated a favorable clinical response to treatment had the greatest reduction in cytokine levels (van Vuren et al., 2021). Fluvoxamine (another SSRI medication) was found in two randomized controlled trials to reduce the severity of COVID-19 infection, with the most plausible explanation being that it worked as an anti-inflammatory drug (Lenze et al., 2020; Lenze et al., 2023). Therefore, the use of a regulatory-agency-approved SSRI medication may be favorable treatment in an aviator for multiple reasons.

If an aviator develops ongoing cognitive symptoms, no current studies confirm an optimal treatment strategy. Caution is advised when using nootropic supplements that are advertised to enhance cognition. These supplements have variable ingredients and can be unpredictable when interacting in a long-COVID brain state (Zaami et al., 2020). Cognitive training (rather than cognitive rest) has been proposed as advantageous (Windsor, 2021). With multiple studies suggesting inflammation as a possible etiology of neuronal damage causing cognitive problems, FDA-approved medications that reduce inflammatory cells (such as pexidartinib) may be used in the future (van Vuren et al., 2021; Venkataramani & Winkler, 2022), possibly even considering an SSRI medication (Braga et al., 2023).

When considering medical recertification of an aviator post-SARS-CoV-2 infection, the initial concerns are the pilot's physiological strength and cognitive focus to maintain performance in a high-workload environment (Gilad et al., 2021). If there are lingering physical, psychological, or cognitive symptoms, these must be evaluated following the regulatory requirements of the certifying authority. For pilots with a history of SARS-CoV-2 infection, the FAA allows medical certification, unless there are residual signs and symptoms or there was an ICU hospitalization (FAA, 2022). The European Union Aviation Safety Agency (EASA) allows medical certification, unless there were significant pulmonary symptoms or there are ongoing symptoms (EASA, 2021). In the UK, aviators may receive medical certification, unless they required hospitalization or continue with unresolved symptoms (UK Civil Aviation Authority, 2024). When an aviator has long-COVID cognitive or mental health symptoms, these regulatory agencies will not consider medical re-certification without an appropriate behavioral health specialist assessment.

Two studies suggest that for many patients, their long-COVID symptoms are greatly diminished by 1 year post-infection (Havervall et al., 2021; Nalbandian et al., 2023). If confirmed by further studies, this timeline could give hope to aviators with prolonged symptoms. Based upon individual assessment, the aviator with ongoing problems may benefit from psychological therapies, cognitive remediation, and/or regulatory approved anti-inflammatory medications (possibly including SSRI medications). Once symptoms are resolved and behavioral health consultations are favorable, the pathway back to duty appears promising.

Conclusion

The current COVID-19 pandemic is the third serious coronavirus outbreak within the last 20 years, following SARS-CoV in 2002 and MERS in 2012 (van Vuren et al., 2021). SARS-CoV-2 infection attacks multiple organ systems, including the brain. However, persistent symptoms (long-COVID) occur in 10 %–15 % of infected patients, including cognitive difficulties known as "brain fog" (Nalbandian et al., 2023; Rubin, 2020).

Likely biological causes for ongoing cognitive problems include (1) damage to neurons by latent virus reactivation, (2) autoimmune cells attacking neurons, (3) overactivation of cytokine inflammatory cells that disrupt neuronal circuitry, (4) artery and vein leaks into the brain that cause clots and/or low oxygenation damage to neurons, and (5) direct infection of neurons by the coronavirus (Lee et al., 2021; Lee et al., 2022; Monje & Iwasaki, 2022; Pellegrini et al., 2020; Song et al., 2021). Psychological and physical symptoms also appear to be causes of long-COVID cognitive symptoms.

Although several factors may increase the risk for long-COVID physical, psychological, and cognitive symptoms, even patients with relatively mild initial COVID-19 infections can have persistent symptoms that last for years (Douaud et al., 2022; Garrigues et al., 2020; Nalbandian et al., 2023). No evidence-based treatments for long-COVID symptoms have been identified at this time. Therefore, treatment of persisting COVID-19 psychological and/or cognitive problems may include psychotherapies, cognitive remediation, and/or regulatory approved anti-inflammatory medications (possibly, even SSRI antidepressants).

Aviators with hospitalization and/or ICU treatment, very severe initial symptoms, or current long-COVID symptoms require symptom resolution prior to regulatory consideration for a return to aviation duties. Depending upon the length and severity of cognitive or psychological symptoms, an aviator may require an evaluation with a behavioral health specialist. Although data on recovery from long-COVID symptoms are very limited, early data suggest that many long-COVID patients appear to improve by 1 year from the time of infection (Havervall et al., 2021; Nalbandian et al., 2023). Our hope is that many of our aviators will fall into this recovery timeline.

References

Akiyama, S., Hamdeh, S., Micic, D., & Sakuraba, A. (2021). Prevalence and clinical outcomes of COVID-19 in patients with autoimmune diseases: A systematic review and meta-analysis. *Annals of the Rheumatic Diseases, 80*(3), 384–391. https://doi.org/10.1136/annrheumdis-2020-218946

Al-Aly, Z., Bowe, B., & Xie, Y. (2022). Long COVID after breakthrough SARS-CoV-2 infection. *Nature Medicine, 28*(7), 1461–1467. https://doi.org/10.1038/s41591-022-01840-0

Batty, G.D., Deary, I.J., Luciano, M., Altschul, D.M., Kivimäki, M., & Gale, C.R. (2020). Psychosocial factors and hospitalisations for COVID-19: Prospective cohort study based on a community sample. *Brain, Behavior, and Immunity, 89*, 569–578. https://doi.org/10.1016/j.bbi.2020.06.021

Becker, J.H., Lin, J.J., Doernberg, M., Stone, K., Navis, A., Festa, J.R., & Wisnivesky, J.P. (2021). Assessment of cognitive function in patients after COVID-19 infection. *JAMA Network Open, 4*(10), Article e2130645. https://doi.org/10.1001/jamanetworkopen.2021.30645

Bertolini, F., Witteveen, A.B., Young, S., Cuijpers, P., Ayuso-Mateos, J.L., Barbui, C., Cabello, M., Cadorin, C., Downes, N., Franzoi, D., Gasior, M.E., Gray, B., John, A., Melchior, M., van Ommeren, M., Palantza, C., Purgato, M., Van der Waerden, J., Wang, S., & Sijbrandij, M. (2023). Risk of SARS-CoV-2 infection, severe COVID-19 illness and COVID-19 mortality in people with pre-existing mental disorders: An umbrella review. *BMC Psychiatry, 23*(1), Article 181. https://doi.org/10.1186/s12888-023-04641-y

Bertuccelli, M., Ciringione, L., Rubega, M., Bisiacchi, P., Masiero, S., & Del Felice, A. (2022). Cognitive impairment in people with previous COVID-19 infection: A scoping review. *Cortex, 154*, 212–230. https://doi.org/10.1016/j.cortex.2022.06.002

Braga, J., Lepra, M., Kish, S.J., Rusjan, P.M., Nasser, Z., Verhoeff, N., Vasdev, N., Bagby, M., Boileau, I., Husain, M.I., Kolla, N., Garcia, A., Chao, T., Mizrahi, R., Faiz, K., Vieira, E.L., & Meyer, J.H. (2023). Neuroinflammation after COVID-19 with persistent depressive and cognitive symptoms. *JAMA Psychiatry, 80*(8), 787–795. https://doi.org/10.1001/jamapsychiatry.2023.1321

Cahill, J., Cullen, P., Anwer, S., Wilson, S., & Gaynor, K. (2021). Pilot work related stress (WRS), effects on wellbeing and mental health, and coping methods. *The International Journal of Aerospace Psychology, 31*, 87–109. https://doi.org/10.1080/24721840.2020.1858714

Cahill, J., Cullen, P., & Gaynor, K. (2023). The case for change: Aviation worker wellbeing during the COVID 19 pandemic, and the need for an integrated health and safety culture. *Cognition, Technology & Work (Online), 25*(1), 75–117. https://doi.org/10.1007/s10111-022-00711-5

Carfì, A., Bernabei, R., & Landi, F. (2020). Persistent symptoms in patients after acute COVID-19. *JAMA, 324*(6), 603–605. https://doi.org/10.1001/jama.2020.12603

Castro, V. M., Gunning, F. M., McCoy, T. H., & Perlis, R. H. (2021). Mood disorders and outcomes of COVID-19 hospitalizations. *The American Journal of Psychiatry, 178*(6), 541–547. https://doi.org/10.1176/appi.ajp.2020.20060842

Ceban, F., Ling, S., Lui, L. M. W., Lee, Y., Gill, H., Teopiz, K. M., Rodrigues, N. B., Subramaniapillai, M., Di Vincenzo, J. D., Cao, B., Lin, K., Mansur, R. B., Ho, R. C., Rosenblat, J. D., Miskowiak, K. W., Vinberg, M., Maletic, V., & McIntyre, R. S. (2022). Fatigue and cognitive impairment in post-COVID-19 syndrome: A systematic review and meta-analysis. *Brain, Behavior, and Immunity, 101*, 93–135. https://doi.org/10.1016/j.bbi.2021.12.020

Chang, T. S., Ding, Y., Freund, M. K., Johnson, R., Schwarz, T., Yabu, J. M., Hazlett, C., Chiang, J. N., Wulf, A., UCLA Health Data Mart Working Group, Geschwind, D. H., Butte, M. J., & Pasaniuc, B. (2020). *Prior diagnoses and medications as risk factors for COVID-19 in a Los Angeles Health System.* medRxiv. https://doi.org/10.1101/2020.07.03.20145581

Chen, Y., Yang, W., Chen, F., & Cui, L. (2022). COVID-19 and cognitive impairment: neuroinvasive and blood–brain barrier dysfunction. *Journal of Neuroinflammation, 19*(1), Article 222. https://doi.org/10.1186/s12974-022-02579-8

COMEBAC Group Writing Committee for the COMEBAC Study Group. (2021). Four-month clinical status of a cohort of patients after hospitalization for COVID-19. *JAMA, 325*(15), 1525–1534. https://doi.org/10.1001/jama.2021.3331

Crunflí, F., Carregari, V. C., Veras, F. P., Vendramini, P. H., Gazzola Fragnani Valença, A., Saraiva Leão Marcelo Antunes, A., Brandão-Teles, C., da Silva Zuccoli, G., Reis-de-Oliveira, G., Silva-Costa, L. C., Monteiro Saia-Cereda, V., Campos Codo, A., Lorencini Parise, P., Toledo-Teixeira, D. A., Fabiano de Souza, G., Primon Muraro, S., Santos de Castro, I. M., Silva Melo, B. M., Almeida, G. M., ...& Martins-de-Souza, D. (2021, February 07). SARS-CoV-2 infects brain astrocytes of COVID-19 patients and impairs neuronal viability. medRxiv. https://www.medrxiv.org/content/10.1101/2020.10.09.20207464v3

dos Santos, C. V. B., Valiati, N. C. M., de Noronha, T. G., Gomes Porto, V. B., Pacheco, A. G., Picinini Freitas, L., Codeço Coelho, F., Ferreira da Costa Gomes, M., Soares Bastos, L., Gonçalves Cruz, O., Martins Lana, R., Mendes Luz, P., Fagundes de Carvalho, L. M., Loureiro Werneck, G., Struchiner, C. J., & Antunes Maciel Villela, D. (2023). The effectiveness of COVID-19 vaccines against severe cases and deaths in Brazil from 2021 to 2022: A registry-based study. *Lancet Regional Health Americas, 20*, Article 100465. https://doi.org/10.1016/j.lana.2023.100465

Douaud, G., Lee, S., Alfaro-Almagro, F., Arthofer, C., Wang, C., McCarthy, P., Lange, F., Andersson, J. L. R., Griffanti, L., Duff, E., Jbabdi, S., Taschler, B., Keating, P., Winkler, A. M., Collins, R., Matthews, P. M., Allen, N., Miller, K. L., Nichols, T. E., & Smith, S. M. (2022). SARS-CoV-2 is associated with changes in brain structure in UK Biobank. *Nature, 604*(7907), 697–707. https://doi.org/10.1038/s41586-022-04569-5

European Union Aviation Safety Agency. (2021, July 1). Guidelines in relation to the COVID-19 pandemic. *Guidelines for Aero-Medical Centres and Aeromedical Examiners regarding the examination and assessment of applicants*, Issue 01. https://www.easa.europa.eu/en/document-library/general-publications/guidelines-aero-medical-centres-and-aeromedical-examiners#group-easa-downloads

Federal Aviation Administration. (2022, October 26). COVID-19 infections disposition table. *AME Guide.* https://www.faa.gov/ame_guide/media/COVID-19_disposition_table.pdf

Federal Aviation Administration. (2023, June 28). Item 47. Psychiatric conditions –use of antidepressant medications. *AME Guide.* https://www.faa.gov/ame_guide/app_process/exam_tech/item47/amd/antidepressants

Fernández-Castañeda, A., Lu, P., Geraghty, A. C., Song, E., Lee, M., Wood, J., O'Dea, M. R., Dutton, S., Shamardani, K., Nwangwu, K., Mancusi, R., Yalçın, B., Taylor, K. R., Acosta-Alvarez, L., Malacon, K., Keough, M. B., Ni, L., Woo, P. J., Contreras-Esquivel, D., ... Monje, M. (2022). Mild respiratory COVID can cause multi-lineage neural cell and myelin dysregulation. *Cell, 185*(14), 2452–2468. https://doi.org/10.1016/j.cell.2022.06.008

Ferrando, S.J., Dornbush, R., Lynch, S., Shahar, S., Klepacz, L., Karmen, C.L., Chen, D., Lobo, S.A., & Lerman, D. (2022). Neuropsychological, medical, and psychiatric findings after recovery from acute COVID-19: A cross-sectional study. *Journal of the Academy of Consultation-Liaison Psychiatry, 63*(5), 474–484. https://doi.org/10.1016/j.jaclp.2022.01.003

Fitton, R., Sweetman, J., Heseltine-Carp, W., van der Feltz-Cornelis, C. (2022). Anti-inflammatory medications for the treatment of mental disorders: A scoping review. *Brain, Behavior, & Immunity – Health, 26*, Article 100518. https://doi.org/10.1016/j.bbih.2022.100518

Frontera, J.A., & Simon, N.M. (2022). Bridging knowledge gaps in the diagnosis and management of neuropsychiatric sequelae of COVID-19. *JAMA Psychiatry, 79*(8), 811–817. https://doi.org/10.1001/jamapsychiatry.2022.1616

Garrigues, E., Janvier, P., Kherabi, Y., Le Bot, A., Hamon, A., Gouze, H., Doucet, L., Berkani, S., Oliosi, E., Mallart, E., Corre, F., Zarrouk, V., Moyer, J. Galy, A., Honsel, V., Fantin, B., & Nguyen, Y. (2020). Post-discharge persistent symptoms and health-related quality of life after hospitalization for COVID-19. *The Journal of Infection, 81*(6), e4–e6. https://doi.org/10.1016/j.jinf.2020.08.029

Gilad, D., Gabbai, D., Tehori, O., Nakdimon, I., Bar-Shai, A., Shapira, S., & Ben-Ari, O. (2021). Return to aviation duty after recovery from COVID-19. *Journal of Military Veteran and Family Health, 7*(2), 116–120. https://doi.org/10.3138/jmvfh-2020-0041

Guo, Y., Ji, M., You, X., & Huang, J. (2017). Protective effects of emotional intelligence and proactive coping on civil pilots' mental health. *Aerospace Medicine and Human Performance, 88*(9), 858–865. https://doi.org/10.3357/AMHP.4799.2017

Havervall, S., Rosell, A., Phillipson, M., Mangsbo, S.M., Nilsson, P., Hober, S., & Thalin, C. (2021). Symptoms and functional impairment assessed 8 months after mild COVID-19 among health care workers. *JAMA, 325*(19), 2015–2016. https://doi.org/10.1001/jama.2021.5612

International Civil Aviation Organization. (2021, March 23). *Effects of novel coronavirus (COVID-19) on civil aviation: Economic impact analysis*. https://www.icao.int/sustainability

Islam, M.A., Cavestro, C., Alam, S.S., Kundu, S., Amjad Kamal, M., & Reza, F. (2022). Encephalitis in patients with COVID-19: A systematic evidence-based analysis. *Cells, 11*(16), Article 2575. https://doi.org/10.3390/cells11162575

Kessler, R.C., Chiu, W.T., Hwang, I.H., Puac-Polanco, V., Sampson, N.A., Ziebrowski, H.N., & Zaslavsky, A.M. (2022). Changes in prevalence of mental illness among US adults during compared with before the COVID-19 pandemic. *The Psychiatric Clinics of North America, 45*(1), 1–28. https://doi.org/10.1016/j.psc.2021.11.013

Klein, J., Wood, J., Jaycox, J., Lu, P., Dhodapkar, R.M., Gehlhausen, J.R., Tabachnikova, A., Tabacof, L., Malik, A.A., Kamath, K., Greene, K., Silva Monteiro, V., Peña-Hernandez, M., Mao, T., Bhattacharjee, B., Takahashi, T., Lucas, C., Silva, J., Mccarthy, D., Breyman, E., ...& Iwasaki, A. (2022). *Distinguishing features of long COVID identified through immune profiling*. medRxiv. https://doi.org/10.1101/2022.08.09.22278592

Lee, M.H., Perl, D.P., Nair, G., Li, W., Maric, D., Murray, H., Dodd, S.J., Koretsky, A.P., Watts, J.A., Cheung, V., Masliah, E., Horkayne-Szakaly, I., Jones, R., Stram, M.N., Moncur, J., Hefti, M., Folkerth, R.D., & Nath, A. (2021). Microvascular injury in the brains of patients with Covid-19. *The New England Journal of Medicine, 384*(5), 481–483. https://doi.org/10.1056/NEJMc2033369

Lee, M.H., Perl, D.P., Steiner, J., Pasternack, N., Li, W., Maric, D., Safavi, F., Horkayne-Szakaly, I., Jones, R., Stram, M.N., Moncur, J.T., Hefti, M., Folkerth, R.D., & Nath, A. (2022). Neurovascular injury with complement activation and inflammation in COVID-19. *Brain, 145*(7), 2555–2568. https://doi.org/10.1093/brain/awac151

Lenze, E.J., Mattar, C., Zorumski, C.F., Stevens, A., Schweiger, J., Nicol, G.E., Miller, J.P., Yang, L., Yingling, M., Avidan, M.S., & Reiersen, A.M. (2020). Fluvoxamine vs placebo and clinical deterioration in outpatients with symptomatic COVID-19: A randomized clinical trial. *JAMA, 324*(22), 2292–2300. https://doi.org/10.1001/jama.2020.22760

Lenze, E.J., Reiersen, A.M., Zorumski, C.F., & Santosh, P.J. (2023). Beyond "psychotropic": Repurposing psychiatric drugs for COVID-19, Alzheimer's diseases, and cancer. *Journal of Clinical Psychology, 84*, Article 22414494. https://doi.org/10.4088/JCP.22r14494

Li, Y., Chen, H., Xin, X., & Ji, M. (2020). The influence of mindfulness on mental state with regard to safety among civil pilots. *Journal of Air Transport Management, 84*, Article 101768. https://doi.org/10.1016/j.jairtraman.2020.101768

Lukiw, W.J., Pogue, A., & Hill, J.M. (2022). SARS-CoV-2 Infectivity and Neurological Targets in the Brain. *Cellular and molecular neurobiology, 42*(1), 217–224. https://doi.org/10.1007/s10571-020-00947-7

Mahdizade Ari, M., Mohamadi, M.H., Shadab Mehr, N., Abbasimoghaddam, S., Shekartabar, A., Heidary, M., & Khoshnood, S. (2022). Neurological manifestations in patients with COVID-19: A systematic review and meta-analysis. *Journal of Clinical Laboratory Analysis, 36*(5), Article e24403. https://doi.org/10.1002/jcla.24403

Mazza, M.G., De Lorenzo, R., Conte, C., Poletti, S., Vai, B., Bollettini, I., Melloni, E.M.T., Furlan, R., Ciceri, F., Rovere-Querini, P., COVID-19 BioB Outpatient Clinic Study Group, & Benedetti, F. (2020). Anxiety and depression in COVID-19 survivors: Role of inflammatory and clinical predictors. *Brain, Behavior, and Immunity, 89*, 594–600. https://doi.org/10.1016/j.bbi.2020.07.037

Mazza, M.G., Palladini, M., De Lorenzo, R., Magnaghi, C., Poletti, S., Furlan, R., Ciceri, F., COVID-19 BioB Outpatient Clinic Study Group, Rovere-Querini, P., & Benedetti, F. (2021). Persistent psychopathology and neurocognitive impairment in COVID-19 survivors: Effect of inflammatory biomarkers at three-month follow-up. *Brain, Behavior, and Immunity, 94*, 138–147. https://doi.org/10.1016/j.bbi.2021.02.021

McGinty, E.E., Presskreischer, R., Anderson, K.E., Han, H., & Barry, C.L. (2020). Psychological distress and COVID-19-related stressors reported in a longitudinal cohort of US adults in April and July 2020. *JAMA, 324*(24), 2555–2557. https://doi.org/10.1001/jama.2020.21231

Meng, M., Zhang, S., Dong, X., Sun, W., Deng, Y., Li, W., Li, R., Annane, D., Wu, Z., & Chen, D. (2022). COVID-19 associated EBV reactivation and effects of ganciclovir treatment. *Immunity, Inflammation and Disease, 10*, Article e597. https://doi.org/10.1002/iid3.597

Monje, M., & Iwasaki, A. (2022). The neurobiology of long COVID. *Neuron, 110*(21), 3484–3496. https://doi.org/10.1016/j.neuron.2022.10.006

Mousavi, S.F. (2020). Psychological well-being, marital satisfaction, and parental burnout in Iranian parents: The effect of home quarantine during COVID-19 outbreaks. *Frontiers in Psychology, 11*, Article 553880. https://doi.org/10.3389/fpsyg.2020.553880

Nalbandian, A., Desai, A.D., & Wan, E.Y. (2023). Post-COVID-19 Condition. *Annual Review of Medicine, 74*, 55–64. https://doi.org/10.1146/annurev-med-043021-030635

Nasreddine, Z.S., Phillips, N.A., Bédirian, V., Charbonneau, S., Whitehead, V., Collin, I., Cummings, J.L., & Chertkow, H. (2005). The Montreal Cognitive Assessment, MoCA: A brief screening tool for mild cognitive impairment. *Journal of the American Geriatrics Society, 53*(4), 695–699. https://doi.org/10.1111/j.1532-5415.2005.53221.x

Newhouse, A., Kritzer, M.D., Eryilmaz, H., Praschan, N., Camprodon, J.A., Fricchione, G., & Chemali, Z. (2022). Neurocircuitry hypothesis and clinical experience in treating neuropsychiatric symptoms of post-acute sequelae of severe acute respiratory syndrome coronavirus 2. *Journal of the Academy of Consultation-Liaison Psychiatry, 63*(6), 619–627. https://doi.org/10.1016/j.jaclp.2022.08.007

Notarte, K.I., Catahay, J.A., Velasco, J.V., Pastrana, A., Ver, A.T., Pangilinan, F.C., Peligro, P.J., Casimiro, M., Guerrero, J.J., Gellaco, M.M.L., Lippi, G., Henry, B.M., & Fernadez-de-las-Penas, C. (2022). Impact of COVID-19 vaccination on the risk of developing long-COVID and on existing long-COVID symptoms: A systematic review. *EClinicalMedicine, 53*, Article 101624. https://doi.org/10.1016/j.eclinm.2022.101624

Oh, J., Sahota, P.C., Mohammadi, T., Pradhan, B.K., & Koola, M.M. (2023). COVID-19 and catatonia: Prevalence, challenges, pathophysiology, and treatment. *Annals of Clinical Psychiatry, 35*(2), 118–130. https://doi.org/10.12788/acp.0109

Pandharipande, P.P., Girard, T.D., Jackson, J.C., Morandi, A., Thompson, J.L., Pun, B.T., Brummel, N.E., Hughes, C.G., Vasilevskis, E.E., Shintani, A.K., Moons, K.G., Geevarghese, S.K., Canonico, A., Hopkins, R.O., Bernard, G.R., Dittus, R.S., & Ely, E.W. (2013). Long-term cognitive impairment after critical illness. *The New England Journal of Medicine, 369*(14), 1306–1316. https://doi.org/10.1056/NEJMoa1301372

Pappa, S., Chen, J., Barnett, J., Chang, A., Kechen Dong, R., Xu, W., Yin, A., Chen, B.Z., Delios, A.Y., Chen, R.Z., Miller, S., Wan, X., & Zhang, S.X. (2022). A systematic review and meta-analysis of the mental health symptoms during the Covid-19 pandemic in Southeast Asia. *Psychiatry and Clinical Neurosciences, 76*(2), 41–50. https://doi.org/10.1111/pcn.13306

Patel, S., Keating, B.A., & Dale, R.C. (2023). Anti-inflammatory properties of commonly used psychiatric drugs. *Frontiers in Neuroscience, 16*, Article 1039379. https://doi.org/10.3389/fnins.2022.1039379

Pellegrini, L., Albecka, A., Mallery, D.L., Kellner, M.J., Paul, D., Carter, A.P., James, L.C., & Lancaster, M.A. (2020). SARS-CoV-2 infects the brain choroid plexus and disrupts the blood-CSF barrier in human brain organoids. *Cell Stem Cell, 27*(6), 951–961. https://doi.org/10.1016/j.stem.2020.10.001

Pyne, J.D., & Brickman, A.M. (2021). The impact of the COVID-19 pandemic on dementia risk: Potential pathways to cognitive decline. *Neurodegenerative Diseases, 21*(1-2), 1–23. https://doi.org/10.1159/000518581

Ramatillah, D.L., Gan, S.H., Pratiwy, I., Sulaiman, S.A.S., Jaber, A.A.S., Jusnita, N., Lukas, S., & Bakar, U.A. (2022). Impact of cytokine storm on severity of COVID-19 disease in a private hospital in West Jakarta prior to vaccination. *PloS one, 17*(1), Article e0262438. https://doi.org/10.1371/journal.pone.0262438

Rogers, J.P., Chesney, E., Oliver, D., Pollak, T.A., McGuire, P., Fusar-Poli, P., Zandi, M.S., Lewis, G., & David, A.S. (2020). Psychiatric and neuropsychiatric presentations associated with severe coronavirus infections: A systematic review and meta-analysis with comparison to the COVID-19 pandemic. *The Lancet Psychiatry, 7*(7), 611–627. https://doi.org/10.1016/S2215-0366(20)30203-0

Rubin, R. (2020). As their numbers grow, COVID-19 "long haulers" stump experts. *JAMA, 324*(14), 1381–1383. https://doi.org/10.1001/jama.2020.17709

Simon, N.M., Saxe, G.N., & Marmar, C.R. (2020). Mental health disorders related to COVID-19-related deaths. *JAMA, 324*(15), 1493–1494. https://doi.org/10.1001/jama.2020.19632

Song, E., Bartley, C.M., Chow, R.D., Ngo, T.T., Jiang, R., Zamecnik, C.R., Dandekar, R., Loudermilk, R.P., Dai, Y., Liu, F., Sunshine, S., Liu, J., Wu, W., Hawes, I.A., Alvarenga, B.D., Huynh, T., McAlpine, L., Rahman, N., Geng, B., ... Farhadian, S.F. (2021). Divergent and self-reactive immune responses in the CNS of COVID-19 patients with neurological symptoms. *Cell Reports Medicine, 2*(5), Article 100288. https://doi.org/10.1016/j.xcrm.2021.100288

Soung, A.L., Vanderheiden, A., Nordvig, A.S., Sissoko, C.A., Canoll, P., Marianai, M.B., Jiang, X., Bricker, T., Rosoklija, G.B., Arango, V., Underwood, M., Mann, J.J., Dwork, A.J., Goldman, J.E., Boon, A.C. M., Boldrini, M., & Klein, R.S. (2022). COVID-19 induces CNS cytokine expression and loss of hippocampal neurogenesis. *Brain, 145*(12), 4193–4201. https://doi.org/10.1093/brain/awac270

Su, Y., Yuan, D., Chen, D.G., Ng, R.H., Wang, K., Choi, J., Li, S., Hong, S., Zhang, R., Xie, J., Kornilov, S.A., Scherler, K., Pavlovitch-Bedzyk, A.J., Dong, S., Lausted, C., Lee, I., Fallen, S., Dai, C.L., Baloni, P. ... Heath, J.R. (2022). Multiple early factors anticipate post-acute COVID-19 sequelae. *Cell, 185*(5), 881–895. https://doi.org/10.1016/j.cell.2022.01.014

Sun, Y., Li, Y., Bao, Y., Meng, S., Sun, Y., Schumann, G., Kosten, T., Strang, J., Lu, L., & Shi, J. (2020). Brief report: Increased addictive internet and substance use behavior during the COVID-19 pandemic in China. *The American Journal on Addictions, 29*(4), 268–270. https://doi.org/10.1111/ajad.13066

Sun, Y., Wu, Y., Fan, S., Dal Santo, T., Li, L., Jiang, X., Li, K., Wang, Y., Tasleem, A., Krishnan, A., He, C., Bonardi, O., Boruff, J.T., Rice, D.B., markham, S., Levis, B., Azar, M., Thombs-Vite, I., Neupane, D., Agic, B., Fahim, C., Martin, M.S., Sockalingam, S., Turecki, G., Benedetti, A., & Thombs, B.D. (2023). Comparison of mental health symptoms before and during the covid-19 pandemic: Evidence from a systematic review and meta-analysis of 134 cohorts. *BMJ (Clinical Research Ed.), 380*, Article e074224. https://doi.org/10.1136/bmj-2022-074224

Sung, E., Chang, J.H., Lee, S., & Hyun Park, S. (2019). The moderating effect of cognitive flexibility in the relationship between work stress and psychological symptoms in Korean Air Force Pilots. *Military Psychology, 31*(2), 100–106. https://doi.org/10.1080/08995605.2018.1556083

Tanz, L.J., Dinwiddie, A.T., Snodgrass, S., O'Donnell, J., Mattson, C.L., & Davis, N.L. (2022, August). A qualitative assessment of circumstances surrounding drug overdose deaths during the early stages of the COVID-19 pandemic. *SUDORS Data Brief, 2*. https://www.cdc.gov/overdose-prevention/media/pdfs/SUDORS-Data-Brief-2.pdf

Taquet, M., Luciano, S., Geddes, J.R., & Harrison, P.J. (2021). Bidirectional associations between COVID-19 and psychiatric disorder: retrospective cohort studies of 62 354 COVID-19 cases in the USA. *The Lancet Psychiatry, 8*(2), 130–140. https://doi.org/10.1016/S2215-0366(20)30462-4

Taquet, M., Sillett, R., Zhu, L., Mendel, J., Camplisson, I., Dercon, Q., & Harrison, P.J. (2022). Neurological and psychiatric risk trajectories after SARS-CoV-2 infection: An analysis of 2-year retrospective cohort studies including 1284437 patients. *The Lancet Psychiatry, 9*(10), 815–827. https://doi.org/10.1016/S2215-0366(22)00260-7

Tavares-Júnior, J.W.L., de Souza, A.C.C., Borges, J.W.P., Oliveira, D.N., Siqueira-Neto, J.I., Sobreira-Neto, M.A., & Braga-Neto, P. (2022). COVID-19 associated cognitive impairment: A systematic review. *Cortex, 152*, 77–97. https://doi.org/10.1016/j.cortex.2022.04.006

Taylor L. (2023). Covid-19: Vaccination reduces severity and duration of long covid, study finds. *BMJ (Clinical Research Ed.), 380*, Article 491. https://doi.org/10.1136/bmj.p491

Thakur, K.T., Miller, E.H., Glendinning, M.D., Al-Dalahmah, O., Banu, M.A., Boehme, A.K., Boubour, A.L., Bruce, S.S., Chong, A.M., Claassen, J., Faust, P.L., Hargus, G., Hickman, R.A. Jambawalikar, S., Khandiji, A.G., Kim, C.Y., Klein, R.S., Lignelli-Dipple, A., Lin, C., ... Canoll, P. (2021). COVID-19 neuropathology at Columbia University Irving Medical Center/New York Presbyterian Hospital. *Brain, 144*(9), 2696–2708. https://doi.org/10.1093/brain/awab148

Thurner, C., & Stengel, A. (2023). Long-COVID syndrome: Physical-mental interplay in the spotlight. *Inflammopharmacology, 31*(2), 559–564. https://doi.org/10.1007/s10787-023-01174-4

Toniolo, S., Scarioni, M., Di Lorenzo, F., Hort, J., Georges, J., Tomic, S., Nobili, F., Frederiksen, K.S., & The Management Group of the EAN Dementia and Cognitive Disorders Scientific Panel. (2021). Dementia and COVID-19, a bidirectional liaison: Risk factors, biomarkers, and optimal health care. *Journal of Alzheimer's Disease, 82*(3), 883–898. https://doi.org/10.3233/JAD-210335

Toubasi, A.A., AbuAnzeh, R.B., Tawileh, H.B.A., Aldebei, R.H., & Alryalat, S.A. S. (2021). A meta-analysis: The mortality and severity of COVID-19 among patients with mental disorders. *Psychiatry Research, 299*, Article 113856. https://doi.org/10.1016/j.psychres.2021.113856

Umesh, M., Singaravelu, V., Daulatabad, V., Kamble, P., Singhal, A., John, N.A., & John, J. (2022). An overview of prognostic value of neurologic and cardiac biomarkers in patients with COVID-19 sequelae. *Hormone Molecular Biology and Clinical Investigation, 43*(4), 475–484. https://doi.org/10.1515/hmbci-2022-0015

UK Civil Aviation Authority. (2024, July 22). *Infectious Respiratory Illness: Guidance for community acquired pneumonia, COVID-19 and other respiratory infections.* https://www.caa.co.uk/aeromedical-examiners/medical-standards/pilots/medical-conditions/infectious-disease/infectious-respiratory-illness/

van Vuren, E.J., Steyn, S.F., Brink, C.B., Möller, M., Viljoen, F.P., & Harvey, B.H. (2021). The neuropsychiatric manifestations of COVID-19: Interactions with psychiatric illness and pharmacological treatment. *Biomedicine & Pharmacotherapy, 135*, Article 111200. https://doi.org/10.1016/j.biopha.2020.111200

Varatharaj, A., Thomas, N., Ellul, M.A., Davies, N.W.S., Pollak, T.A., Tenorio, E.L., Sultan, M., Easton, A., Breen, G., Zandi, M., Coles, J.P., Manji, H., Al-Shahi Salman, R., Menon, D.K., Nicholson, T.R., Benjamin, L.A., Carson, A., Smith, C., Turner, M.R., ... Michael, B.D. (2020). Neurological and neuropsychiatric complications of COVID-19 in 153 patients: A UK-wide surveillance study. *The Lancet Psychiatry, 7*(10), 875–882. https://doi.org/10.1016/S2215-0366(20)30287-X

Venkataramani, V., & Winkler, F. (2022). Cognitive deficits in long Covid-19. *The New England Journal of Medicine, 387*(19), 1813–1815. https://doi.org/10.1056/NEJMcibr2210069

Wang, B., Zhong, C., & Tieleman, D.P. (2021). *The supramolecular organization of SARS-CoV and SARS-CoV-2 virions revealed by coarse-grained models of intact virus envelopes.* bioRxiv. https://doi.org/10.1101/2021.09.16.460716

White, A.M., Castle, I.P., Powell, P.A., Hingson, R.W., & Koob, G.F. (2022). Alcohol-related deaths during the COVID-19 pandemic. *JAMA, 327*(17), 1704–1706. https://doi.org/10.1001/jama.2022.4308

Whiteside, D.M., Basso, M.R., Naini, S.M., Porter, J., Holker, E., Waldron, E.J., Melnik, T.E., Niskanen, N., & Taylor, S.E. (2022). Outcomes in post-acute sequelae of COVID-19 (PASC) at 6 months post-infection Part 1: Cognitive functioning. *The Clinical Neuropsychologist, 36*(4), 806–828. https://doi.org/10.1080/13854046.2022.2030412

Windsor, M. (2021, February 22). *Trial studying technique to clear 'brain fog' after COVID-19*. University of Alabama Reporter. https://www.uab.edu/reporter/patient-care/advances/item/9410-trial-studying-technique-to-clear-brain-fog-after-covid-19

Work, H. A. J. (2020, December 17). *The US still has 10 million fewer jobs now than before the pandemic*. CNBC. https://www.cnbc.com/2020/12/08/the-us-has-10-million-fewer-jobs-now-than-before-the-pandemic.html

World Health Organization. (2023, July). *Coronavirus (COVID-19) dashboard*. https://covid19.who.int/

Xu, E., Xie, Y., & Al-Aly, Z. (2022). Long-term neurologic outcomes of COVID-19. *Nature Medicine, 28*(11), 2406–2415. https://doi.org/10.1038/s41591-022-02001-z

Yan, Y., Hou, J., Li, Q., & Yu, N. X. (2023). Suicide before and during the COVID-19 pandemic: A systematic review with meta-analysis. *International Journal of Environmental Research and Public Health, 20*(4), Article 3346. https://doi.org/10.3390/ijerph20043346

Zaami, S., Rinaldi, R., Bersani, G., Del Rio, A., Ciallella, C., & Marinelli, E. (2020). Nootropics use in the workplace: Psychiatric and ethical aftermath towards the new frontier of bioengineering. *European Review for Medical and Pharmacological Sciences, 24*(4), 2129–2139. https://doi.org/10.26355/eurrev_202002_20393

Zarifkar, P., Peinkhofer, C., Benros, M. E., & Kondziella, D. (2022). Frequency of neurological diseases after COVID-19, influenza A/B and bacterial pneumonia. *Frontiers in Neurology, 13*, Article 904796. https://doi.org/10.3389/fneur.2022.904796

Zhou, H., Lu, S., Chen, J., Wie, N., Wang, D., Lyu, H., Shi, C., & Hu, S. (2020). The landscape of cognitive function in recovered COVID-19 patients. *Journal of Psychiatric Research, 129*, 98–102. https://doi.org/10.1016/j.jpsychires.2020.06.022

Chapter 27
Neurocognitive Functioning in People With HIV

Implications for Pilots and Air Traffic Controllers

Andrew Levine

NeuroHIV: A Brief History and Current Status

History and Definitions

Soon after the first cases of acquired immunodeficiency syndrome (AIDS) were identified in the early 1980s, it became evident that a rapidly progressing dementia was a common consequence of the disease. The dementia syndrome associated with advanced human immunodeficiency virus-1 (HIV) infection, characterized by cognitive impairment, behavioral changes, and central motor abnormalities, was first systematically described and termed *AIDS dementia complex* by Navia and colleagues in 1986 (Navia et al., 1986). AIDS dementia complex affected between 20 % and 30 % of people living with HIV (PWH), often in the final stages of life (Brew, 1999). Diagnostic criteria published in 1991 by the AIDS Task Force of the American Academy of Neurology identified two levels of cognitive impairment: (1) HIV-associated dementia, or HAD; and (2) minor cognitive motor disorder, characterized by milder cognitive deficits and mild difficulties with activities of daily living (ADLs) ("Nomenclature and research case definitions," 1991).

In the years after the widespread implementation of combination anti-retroviral therapy in 1996, the incidence of AIDS dementia complex decreased. However, into the new millennium, researchers were identifying subtler "asymptomatic" or "subsyndromal" cases, in which study participants' scores were below expectations yet they did not report difficulties with ADLs. With these cases in mind, updated research criteria were published in 2007, establishing HIV-associated neurocognitive disorder, or HAND, as a syndrome that captured the spectrum of HIV-related neurocognitive deficits (Antinori et al., 2007). These "Frascati" criteria established three levels of severity under HAND criteria: (1) asymptomatic neurocognitive impairment (ANI), defined as one standard deviation below the mean on two or more cognitive domains in the absence of ADL impairment; (2) mild cognitive disorder (MCD), defined as one standard deviation below the mean on two or more cognitive domains with concomitant and mild ADL impairment; and (3) HAD, defined as two standard deviations below the mean on two or more cognitive domains with marked impairment in ADLs. Importantly, the group that developed the Frascati criteria were aware of the confounding influence of comorbidities when determining the cause of neurocognitive deficits.

In the years since the introduction of the Frascati criteria, several shortcomings have been identified, leading to a growing chorus of researchers and clinicians calling for a more effective framework. The weaknesses of the HAND construct are considered in the following sections and, later in this chapter, novel approaches for the clinical assessment of PWH are discussed.

Prevalence

Estimates of the prevalence of HAND are considerably varied. However, an oft-cited figure is 50 %, most often based on case-control studies (Heaton et al., 2011; Heaton et al., 2015; Robertson et al., 2007). The vast majority of the HAND diagnoses in these studies, around 70 %, have ANI and, by definition, are free of self-reported functional (i.e., ADL) impairments despite scoring low on standardized testing as compared to published normative data. A controversy of particular relevance to the current context is that the inclusion of ANI in current diagnostic schemas may have had the unintended consequence of high rates of false-positive diagnoses, thereby inflating HAND prevalence estimates (Gisslen et al., 2011; Meyer et al., 2013; Nightingale et al., 2021). This is primarily due to the low threshold required to be considered neurocognitively impaired, resulting in a significant percentage of healthy, uninfected individuals with no known neurologic or psychiatric illness meeting criteria for ANI, save for the fact that they are not HIV-infected (Binder et al., 2009; Gisslen et al., 2011; Meyer et al., 2013; Nightingale et al., 2021; Schretlen et al., 2008; Wang et al., 2021; Wang et al., 2019a). These observations underscore the questionable utility of the 2007 HAND criteria within research and clinical contexts, and call into question the oft-cited prevalence rates of HAND.

A critical examination of the research literature reveals that study design has a substantial influence on estimates of HAND prevalence. Two general types of study design used in neuroHIV research are case-control and cohort. Briefly, in the former design, individuals with a condition of interest (e.g., HIV or HAND) are recruited and may be compared with a control group that does not have the condition. In the latter design, individuals at risk for a condition of interest (e.g., HIV or HAND) are recruited, allowing analysis of the differences between those who develop the condition during the study and those who do not. The cohort study typically has the advantage of a more suitable comparison group and is better for estimating incidence and prevalence of the condition of interest. In addition, case-control studies can result in a biased sampling, as recruitment may attract those with the condition of interest (e.g., HAND). In the neuroHIV research literature, case-control studies, such as those cited above, have typically reported a high prevalence of HAND (e.g., 50 %), whereas cohort studies have generally reported that HIV-uninfected participants have near similar rates of cognitive impairment to the HIV-infected participants (Sacktor et al., 2016; Wang et al., 2019b). This discrepancy appears to be due in large part to poorly matched controls in the aforementioned case-control studies (Heaton et al., 2011) or to no controls at all (Heaton et al., 2010). Another cause for the discrepancy, as indicated earlier, is the false-positive rate inherent in the approach used to classify HAND. This is best illustrated in studies utilizing multivariate normative comparison (MNC) methods, which reduces the influence of intercorrelation among cognitive domains. As an example, recent studies of the Multicenter AIDS Cohort Study (MACS), a decades-long study of gay and bisexual men, compared several diagnostic methods. Using MNC, it was found that 6.3 % of seronegative men and 7.5 % of seropositive men had cognitive impairment(Wang et al., 2019a). Using the Frascati criteria, the rates were 24.5 % and 25.7 %, respectively. Importantly, in neither method did they find HIV serostatus to be associated with cognitive impairment. Comparable findings were reported from another cohort study, the Women's Interagency HIV

Study (WIHS; Vance et al., 2016). As reported in that review of several WIHS analyses, although female PWH had greater NCI than uninfected females, HIV infection itself was a relatively minor contributor to neurocognitive impairment compared to age-related medical comorbidities or psychiatric and demographic characteristics.

As discussed further in a later section, another cause for the discrepant findings is non-HIV intraindividual factors that better explain the cognitive deficits, such as demographic and historical differences between PWH and their HIV-seronegative counterparts(Nightingale et al., 2023; Wei et al., 2020), some of which have not been considered, or may not be easily controlled for, in statistical analyses.

In summary, while some studies have found high prevalence rates of neurocognitive dysfunction in PWH, substantially lower rates are indicated in studies that employed a cohort design with better-matched controls as well as statistical approaches that consider the inter-correlation between neurocognitive domains.

Pathogenesis

The pathogenesis of HAND remains unclear. Relevant to the current context, evidence suggests that at least the mild and moderate forms of HAND (i.e., ANI and MND) are due to a chronic neuroinflammatory state (Kraft-Terry et al., 2009; McArthur, 2004). Beyond that, decades of research have led to the identification of a dizzying number of cellular and molecular factors associated with HIV-related neuropathology and neurocognitive dysfunction (Achim & Wiley, 1996; Anthony & Bell, 2008; Borjabad et al., 2010; Boven et al., 2000; Cysique & Brew, 2009; Everall et al., 2005; Fox et al., 1997; Gelman, 2007; Kallianpur et al., 2018; Khanlou et al., 2009; Levine et al., 2009; Masliah et al., 2000; Pemberton & Brew, 2001; Roberts et al., 2004; Rubin et al., 2018; Woods et al., 2009; Zheng & Gendelman, 1997; Zhou et al., 2009), yet no reliable biomarkers have been identified. Similarly, several pharmaceutical trials targeting putative neuropathogenic factors have failed to produce results beyond the preclinical stage (Kolson, 2022). Therefore, it may be that HAND is not caused by a single pathogenic process, but is instead the culmination of a range of pathogenic processes resulting in systemic dysregulation and dysfunction. In fact, accumulating evidence suggests that HAND may not be a singular syndrome, but instead represents any form of cognitive impairment found in PWH, regardless of the cause (Nightingale et al., 2023).

Studies investigating the pathogenesis of HAND are complicated by myriad factors not directly related to the infection, including substance abuse, history of traumatic head injury, psychiatric comorbidities, neurotoxicity of combination antiretroviral therapy (cART), and hepatitis C co-infection, among several others, all of which may have more profound effects on neuropsychological functioning than the virus itself (Cohen & Gongvatana, 2010; Cysique et al., 2016; Desquilbet et al., 2011; Kirk et al., 2013; Lanman et al., 2021; Lucas et al., 2007; Richardson et al., 2005; Silverberg et al., 2009; Silverberg et al., 2011; Sulkowski & Thomas, 2003; Wendelken & Valcour, 2012; Womack et al., 2011; Yu et al., 2019). This is especially important in the current context, in which pilots, air traffic controllers (ATCs), and applicants are generally high functioning and lack substantial histories of these risk factors. However, one notable risk factor for HAND that is particularly relevant in the current context is the burden of medical comorbidities.

Medical Comorbidities and HAND

HIV infection is associated with an increased risk for a number of diseases and medical conditions typically associated with aging, including cardiovascular disease, several cancers, kidney disease, and liver disease, among others (Deeks, 2011; Desquilbet et al., 2011; Grinspoon & Carr, 2005; Lucas et al., 2007; Martin & Volberding, 2010; Silverberg et al., 2009; Silverberg et al., 2011; Triant et al., 2007; Womack et al., 2011). Indeed, among PWH, the incidence of such HIV-associated non-AIDS (HANA) conditions increased after the widespread implementation of cART (Greene et al., 2013). Findings from the Veterans Administration Cohort Study indicated that the prevalence of HANA conditions is 60%–63% (Goulet et al., 2007). These conditions often occur together, creating multimorbidity that increasingly affects quality of life and life expectancy (Rodriguez-Penney et al., 2013) and adversely impacts neurocognitive functioning in PWH, perhaps via vascular and degenerative brain changes (Lake et al., 2017; McIntosh et al., 2021). While there is little question that HIV alone can have deleterious effects on the brain (Alvarez-Carbonell et al., 2019; Ances & Hammoud, 2014; Kallianpur et al., 2018), the relative contribution of those effects to neurocognitive impairment in PWH, as compared to HANA, appears small, since recent findings from both cohort and case–control studies implicate HANA conditions as the major driving force behind neurocognitive deficits in PWH (Lake et al., 2017; Saloner et al., 2019; Vance et al., 2016; Yu et al., 2019).

A mechanism underlying this increased comorbidity incidence may be alterations to the epigenome that accelerates the aging process. Since the first reports that HIV infection accelerates the aging process in peripheral blood mononuclear cells and brain tissue (Gross et al., 2016; Horvath & Levine, 2015; Shiau et al., 2021), additional studies from various independent groups have demonstrated the clinical relevance of accelerated aging in PWH. This includes accelerated aging in the brains of deceased adults diagnosed with HIV-associated neurocognitive disorder within 1 year of death (Levine et al., 2015), neuropsychological aberrations in perinatally HIV-infected adolescents (discussed in the next section), and neuroimaging abnormalities in adults and adolescents (Heany et al., 2023; Hoare et al., 2022; Lew et al., 2021). Importantly, accelerated aging itself may be the result of chronic inflammation common among PWH, with some more vulnerable due to genetic predispositions (Sundermann et al., 2019).

For aviation neuropsychologists assessing the HIV-infected applicant, pilot, or ATC, the takeaway is that rather than the virus itself, comorbidities and lifestyle factors are more likely to result in neurocognitive impairment among individuals who have effectively managed the infection.

Neuropsychological Functioning in PWH

Perinatal HIV Infection

Individuals who become infected with HIV perinatally (PHIV) are at increased risk of neurodevelopmental abnormalities and poorer neurocognitive outcomes later in life, due to aberrant myelination and inflammation in developing brains (Hoare et al., 2015), as well as morphological abnormalities (Hoare et al., 2018). A recent meta-analysis comparing PHIV with behaviorally acquired HIV among adolescents found that the former was more likely to result in executive dysfunction, although there was a dearth of studies in the latter group(Rowe et al., 2021). A meta-analysis identified executive function, working memory, and processing speed as the most affected cognitive domains in PHIV (Phillips et al., 2016), but others have also reported deficits in virtually every domain (Hoare et al., 2016; Malee et al., 2016). Over time, neurocognitive functioning may improve relative to adolescents who were perinatally exposed but did not become infectious; however, gains in processing speed were not seen among the PHIV group (Robbins et al., 2020). In addition, as with adults, a history of greater disease burden (e.g., high viral load or AIDS) limits gains over time (Nichols, 2022).

As with adult PWH, this process also appears to be driven in part by accelerated biological aging. PHIV is associated with biologically older blood by adolescence. For example, in a cross-sectional study that included 180 PHIV-positive children aged 9–12 years, mean DNA methylation age (16.01 years) was notably greater than mean chronological age (10.77 years), and epigenetic age acceleration contributed more to regional alterations of brain volumes, cortical thickness, cortical surface areas, and neuronal microstructure as compared to chronological age. Age acceleration was also found to be correlated with measures of executive functioning, working memory, and processing speed (Horvath et al., 2018). A subsequent study, in which 60 PHIV-positive adolescents and 36 age-matched controls who were aged 9–12 years old at baseline were re-examined after 36 months, epigenetic age was still greater among the PHIV group, was positively associated with viral load, and was negatively associated with CD4 T-cell ratio. In addition, epigenetic age acceleration was positively associated with whole-brain gray matter volume and alterations in whole-brain white matter integrity.

Considering the consistency of findings from the PHIV literature, applicants with the condition may find it especially challenging to meet the neurocognitive requirements for a special issuance medical certificate. However, it is important to consider the historical context for each examinee, as those who have PHIV are also disproportionately affected by lower childhood socioeconomic status and education quality, among other adversities. These considerations are touched on in the section discussing an emerging diagnostic approach to neurocognitive dysfunction in PWH.

Neurocognitive Function in Adults With Horizontally Acquired HIV

HAND was once conceived of as a subcortical-type syndrome(Price et al., 1991), with deficits generally involving processing speed, motor functioning, and executive functioning, while visuospatial abilities, language, and memory encoding were relatively spared. More recently, a far-reaching review of the literature reported evidence for deficits in virtually every cognitive domain (Woods et al., 2009). Importantly, there is considerable variation of findings across studies, and considering the significant influence of comorbidities, a HAND-specific cognitive profile is not discernable. Still, some have proposed psychomotor slowing and cognitive control over mental operations as the primary cause of deficits in other cognitive domains, and that this could be due to the disruption of fronto-striatal circuits essential to cognitive functions(Woods et al., 2009), a proposal that is supported by several neuroimaging studies (Becker et al., 2011; Ipser et al., 2015; Israel et al., 2019; Kuhn et al., 2019). In addition, a longitudinal study of older PWH in the international HIV Neuroimaging Consortium found progressive volume loss localized to subcortical structures

(Nir et al., 2019). Note, however, that the participant sample consistent of individuals with history of advanced HIV disease, making the findings less generalizable to individuals typically seen in the aviation neuropsychology setting.

As with the varied neurocognitive findings, neuroimaging studies have not provided consistent findings. For example, some have reported differences in cortical association and primary sensory areas (Chiang et al., 2007; Wilson et al., 2015), while findings from the Enhancing Neuro Imaging Genetics Through Meta-Analysis (ENIGMA) consortium identified limbic structures as most affected in relation to virologic factors (Nir et al., 2021). Still others have reported differences in the corpus callosum (Thompson et al., 2006), non-frontal-striatal white matter bundles (Kuhn et al., 2019), cerebellum (Klunder et al., 2008), and other non-striatal subcortical structures (Wade et al., 2015). Importantly, the extent to which these studies included well-matched HIV-seronegative controls and considered confounding factors such as medical comorbidities varied considerably, making interpretation difficult. However, it is notable that in a series of studies from the MACS cohort, what was initially interpreted as HIV-associated morphologic changes as determined through brain magnetic resonance imaging (Becker et al., 2012) was later found to be due to medical comorbidities, including hypertension, diabetes mellitus, higher body mass index, and elevated visceral fat (Lake et al., 2017; Wu et al., 2018). That is, once these medical comorbidities were considered in the analyses, the effects of HIV became nonsignificant.

To summarize in relation to the current context, there is no reliable neurocognitive profile in PWH, nor consistent pathophysiology, that would enable the aviation neuropsychologist to differentiate between HIV-related cognitive deficits and those due to other factors.

Longitudinal Changes in Neurocognitive Functioning in PWH

Concerning the progression of cognitive deficits over time, recent data from the CNS HIV Antiretroviral Therapy Effects Research (CHARTER) study, which does not include uninfected controls, indicate that PWH declined at a faster rate than would be expected due to typical aging. Consistent with the discussion above, cognitive decline was not related to HIV disease or treatment characteristics, but rather to medical comorbidities including diabetes, hypertension, chronic pulmonary disease, and depression, prompting the authors to suggest that more focus be paid to comorbidities when seeking to prevent cognitive decline (Heaton et al., 2023). Offering a different perspective from a nonsimilar cohort, a recent study from the MACS, which does include uninfected controls, looked at individual-level outcomes over a 5-year period (Oliveira et al., 2021). The authors did not find that HIV status conferred risk for cognitive decline. Instead, it was AIDS and/or baseline infection with hepatitis B or C that conferred risk. Similar findings were reported in a MACS sample utilizing the MHC method (Wang et al., 2021).

Still, others have reported decline over time. Examining cognitive trajectories over 4 years among participants in the Women's Interagency HIV Study, Rubin and colleagues reported that virally suppressed PWH had poorer baseline functioning compared with demographically similar uninfected participants, particularly in attention/working memory, learning, memory, fluency, and executive functioning (Rubin et al., 2017). Further, those discrepancies persisted over 4 years; however, only motor functioning, as assessed with the Grooved

Pegboard, declined in the HIV-positive participants. Importantly, the most robust predictor of better cognitive test performance was the proportion of time without detectable viral load. In addition, a lifetime diagnosis of AIDS, lower nadir CD4 count, and plasma viral failure were all associated with poorer performance. Findings such as these, which have been fairly consistent, underscore the likelihood of a "legacy effect" in HAND; that is, advanced illness and/or immunosuppression can result in brain injury that will continue to manifest after the individual becomes healthier. Also, it should be noted that the WIHS population may not be representative of the typical applicant for a special issuance medical certificate. For example, in the study just discussed, a large proportion of the sample reported depression (26%–34%), recent cannabis use (14%–25%), and past or current cocaine use (54%–61%) across the groups examined.

Declining cognitive functioning was also implicated in recent results from a case–control study of 155 PWH who had been taking cART for at least 15 years. That study found that, compared with well-matched HIV/seronegative control participants, the PWH scored lower on several tests of attention/working memory, motor functioning, and information processing speed (McMahan et al., 2023). However, as many as 70% of the PWH may have been infected prior to the availability of cART, raising the possibility of the legacy effect in the sample. In addition, the score differences, while statistically significant, may not have been clinically meaningful (e.g., 30.2 vs. 32.2 on the Symbols Search test). Finally, and perhaps most important, medical comorbidities were not considered in the study.

Focusing on HAND stage rather than specific cognitive abilities, with the intent of determining whether ANI represents a prodromal stage for more severe HAND, a study from the CHARTER cohort found that individuals diagnosed with ANI at baseline progressed to symptomatic impairment faster than neurocognitively normal participants, as determined via self-report or performance-based measures of everyday functioning (Grant et al., 2014). Specifically, they found that 50% of the ANI and 22% of a neurocognitively normal group progressed to symptomatic HAND (MND or HAD). While such findings suggest that ANI may be prodromal for more severe HAND in many cases, it does not quell the likelihood that many cases are misdiagnosed, because the study lacked HIV-seronegative controls. Furthermore, those who declined were older, less educated, were more likely to have had AIDS and hepatitis C, and were more likely to have a lifetime history of substance use disorder. In addition, 45% of those in the ANI group had contributing comorbidities, compared to 23% in the neurocognitively normal group. Clearly, these groups were not similar to begin with, and the myriad factors associated with progression make it difficult to discern causality. Finally, that study did not report how many of those with ANI recovered to a neurocognitively normal status. This is important, as change in HAND status is common in both directions (recovery and worsening; Sacktor et al., 2016). Despite this, there appears to be a bias in neuroHIV publications of reporting the data that suggest worsening cognitive functioning. For example, a study of 197 seropositive individuals enrolled in the MACS revealed that, over the 4-year study, 77% remained at their same HAND stage, with 13% showing deterioration and 10% showing improvement, and that a diagnosis of ANI was associated with a twofold increased risk of symptomatic HAND (MND or HAD) compared with a diagnosis of normal cognition (Sacktor et al., 2016). That study, which did not examine HIV-seronegative individuals, is often cited as evidence for decline over time. However, in the Methods section of the paper, the authors report the result of a Monte Carlo analysis in which, after applying the HAND criteria to 100,000 random datasets, they found that 23% of individuals in a random dataset of persons from the general population would be classified with cognitive impairment. As noted above, other studies using MACS data that did include HIV-seronegative individuals indicate that they are just as likely to have cognitive impairment both cross-sectionally and across time (Wang et al., 2019b; Wang et al., 2021). The bidirectionality of cognitive trajectories in PWH is further supported by data from other studies, including the Hawaii Aging with HIV (Antinori et al., 2007).

The explanation for the variability in intraindividual HAND severity across visits remains incomplete. However, until recently, one unexplored factor in fluctuating HAND severity and inflation of HAND prevalence is the influence of inadequate effort on psychometric testing outcomes. Such *suboptimal effort* occurs when research participants perform below their potential on neurocognitive tests; that is, due to one or a combination of several potential factors (e.g., fatigue, apathy, distraction, boredom, intoxication), participants' scores do not reflect their true ability. If a significant portion of individuals enrolled in case-control or cohort studies fail to put forth adequate and/or consistent effort on neurocognitive testing, erroneous findings can result. Indeed, there is evidence in other research populations of such suboptimal effort (e.g., college students seeking course credit; An et al., 2012; DeRight & Jorgensen, 2015; Ross et al., 2016). Such suboptimal effort may have substantial downstream effects on HAND prevalence estimates and, subsequently, public policy. The author's research on this subject found support for such suboptimal effort among participants in the MACS (Levine et al., 2017), with a negative correlation between self-reported effort and HAND severity. Such findings could help to explain the conspicuous discrepancy between the prevalence of HAND as reported by large case-control studies versus the very low frequency of HIV-related referrals to the various neuropsychological clinics (Ferretti et al., 2018) as well as the wide variation in intraindividual severity seen across time.

Finally, in a recent comprehensive summary of longitudinal studies of HAND, the authors concluded that cognitive stability was the most consistent finding in the majority of studies (Cysique et al., 2021). However, the authors estimated that 14 %–30 % of individuals do decline over the study periods (6–36 months), and that a history of AIDS, lower nadir CD4 count, and more severe viral load are the most common predictors of decline; that is, it is the legacy effect of previous severe HIV illness that can affect future cognitive abilities. In the current context, considering the outsized influence of a history of advanced HIV illness, it behooves the aviation neuropsychologist to obtain a detailed history of viral, immunologic, and HIV-related disease history in their evaluation.

Functional Impairment in PWH

Whether or not PWH also evince impairment in day-to-day functioning (i.e., functional impairment) has been a topic of interest due to the inclusion of functional impairment as a diagnostic criterion for MND and HAD (but not ANI). Generally, case-control and cohort studies have employed self-report measures, such as the Lawton–Brody (Lawton & Brody, 1969) and Patient's Assessment of Own Functioning Inventory (Chelune et al., 1986). However, self-report measures are lacking due to the bias of self-report and the fact that many study participants do not engage in the activities queried by the questionnaire. To address this, several studies have looked at the association between neurocognitive tests and functional performance measures. For example, the CHARTER study has used the Medication Management Test (Grant et al., 2014; Heaton et al., 2004). Vocational functioning has also been assessed through various instruments (Grant et al., 2014). Further studies from the CHARTER suggest that performance-based measures have stronger associations with objective functional status, such as employment, and that self-report measures are biased by depressed mood (Blackstone et al., 2012); however, the generalizability of those findings is limited, considering that 63% of the participants were significantly immunologically suppressed (CD4 count <200) or had AIDS-defining illness. In addition, while the CHARTER has published some of the most influential and oft-cited publications in the neuroHIV field, its lack of an HIV-seronegative control group has greatly limited the interpretability of its findings.

For the interested reader, a recent review paper highlights the inconsistent findings, in particular the lack of replicability when associating neurocognitive tests scores with ADL measures or employment status (Ripamonti & Clerici, 2021). As with the other areas of neuroHIV research discussed in this chapter, the impact of HIV on functional abilities is limited by the methodologies and participant samples used to produce the data. However, recently proposed consensus criteria, discussed in the next section, provide a possible way forward in clinical settings.

Current FAA Guidelines for PWH

Since 1997, PWH are eligible for special issuance medical certificate under FAR Part 67.401. Those with history of AIDS, however, remained ineligible until August 2001. In 2003, neurocognitive screening (CogScreen-AE) and supplemental testing was integrated into special issuance consideration for all three medical classes. In May 2015, the FAA began allowing HIV-uninfected applicants taking pre-exposure prophylaxis to qualify for medical certification by their aviation medical examiner (R. Georgemiller, personal communication December 10, 2023).

Currently, several criteria need to be met, and these differ depending on whether or not the individual has had AIDS. Concerning those with no history of AIDS, firstly, any antiretroviral medication they are taking must be approved by the US Food and Drug Administration and used in accordance with current guidelines (Gibert, 2016). Secondly, they require a current report from a physician knowledgeable in the treatment of PWH that includes a medical history detailing symptoms and treatment referable to the immune system. Thirdly, current CD4, lymphocyte, complete blood count with differential, and viral load values; results of current liver function tests; and blood, urea, nitrogen (BUN) and creatine values are required. The requirements are more stringent for those who have a history of AIDS. Such applicants are required to obtain CD4 and viral load measures twice, 1 month apart, to ensure immunologic stability and viral suppression.

Neuropsychological Assessment of HIV-Positive Applicants for Special Issuance

All HIV-positive applicants will also require neuropsychological evaluation. The most recent test specifications for PWH were released in February 2021. The specifications state that testing should be administered when the applicant is immunologically stable with full viral suppression; that is, their CD4+ T-cell count is within the normal range and they have an undetectable viral load according to polymerase chain reaction (PCR) testing. The initial evaluation requires administration of a full neuropsychological battery. Follow-up evaluations consist of the CogScreen-AE, with re-administration of the full battery in the event of failed screening. For ATCs and first- and second-class aviators, follow-up testing is conducted annually, whereas for third-class aviators it occurs biannually.

It may be helpful at this juncture to review the history of requiring HIV-positive applicants to undergo neuropsychological testing. In 1993, Mapou et al. published two papers in which they argued that HIV-positive applicants should undergo regular neurocognitive testing with an emphasis on detecting subtle deficits and decrements in processing speed that would best be measured via computerized testing (i.e., CogScreen; Mapou, Kay, et al., 1993; Mapou, Rundell, et al., 1993). At the time, the Aerospace Medical Association recommended routine HIV testing of pilots and that seropositivity should result invariably in disqualification from flying duties ("HIV positivity and aviation safety," 1992). However, the FAA still forbade PWH from obtaining medical certification. Mapou et al. reviewed the existing, albeit scant, literature addressing neurocognitive functioning in HIV, with an emphasis on processing speed, and concluded that while most neurologically asymptomatic PWH do not evince significant deficits, a not insignificant percentage do, thus prompting their recommendation for comprehensive neuropsychological testing to include both traditional cognitive tests and computerized testing. Importantly, the authors also recommended that studies be conducted to determine how deficits detected via neurocognitive testing relate to CNS integrity and job-related performance. It is important to point out that the studies reviewed by Mapou et al. occurred in the era prior to widespread cART, which incorporated protease inhibitors beginning in late 1995. It was the implementation of cART that led to a reduction in the incidence of HAD and AIDS in general (https://archive.cdc.gov/#/details?url=https://www.cdc.gov/media/pressrel/aids-d1.htm).

From Data to Policy

In this edition *of Aviation Neuropsychology*, Norris et al. describe two studies of HIV-positive pilots, and how those studies have informed FAA policy in regard to PWH. Importantly, the analyses conducted by Norris, Skaggs, and Chidester (see Chapter 22) have real-world impacts. Most notably, their analysis on the cognitive effects of SSRI use led to the termination of routine CogScreen-AE administrations for individuals taking the restricted medications.

In their initial 2018 study, which is unpublished but described in more detail in this book, Skaggs et al. found that, had a 5-year neuropsychological evaluation interval been implemented, the 4.5% of HIV-positive examinees who failed cognitive screening would have been missed, although for only 1% (two cases) would the testing have affected their final certification outcomes. Importantly, a high attrition rate was noted in those data, but the reason(s) was(were) unclear. In their new analysis (Norris et al., 2023), also unpublished, they observed a remarkable attrition rate of 62.3% over 5 years and 82.4% over 10 years for all HIV-positive pilots who underwent medical examinations between January 1, 2007 and December 2020. While the 5-year rate was considerably higher than the overall pilot population (45%) and also higher than those with arrhythmia, hypertension, and brain disorders, it was less than that of active pilots with diabetes, atrial fibrillation, and myocardial infarct.

Concerning predictors of subsequent abnormal cognitive examination results, the authors found that the cumulative number of medications and medical conditions (a proxy for medical comorbidities) were not significant prognosticators. Nor did they find any risk associated with increasing age, once again underscoring the low rate of replicability in neuroHIV studies. Instead, they found that a history of "abnormal" CD4 and/or viral load and the duration of HIV infection increased the risk of cognitive decline, as captured by the subsequent cognitive examinations. Their findings were consistent with other longitudinal studies that reported immunologic dysfunction and virologic factors to be most predictive of decline, such as those from the WIHS (Rubin et al., 2017). If "abnormal" CD4 is synonymous with AIDS, their findings are also consistent with studies from the MACS (Oliveira et al., 2021; Wang et al., 2021). In both cases, the findings from Norris, Skaggs, and Chidester, as reported in Chapter 22 of this book, lend additional support for the legacy effect in later neurocognitive functioning among PWH and for the applicability of cohort studies to pilots with HIV.

What is unclear from their data is why HIV-positive applicants do not return for special issuance after a failed neurocognitive examination. The authors propose that the attrition is due to declining cognitive status. However, there are alternative explanations that should also be entertained, including the age of examinees, the extent of their personal and/or financial investment in being a pilot, and the stigma of HIV infection.

The Fairness of the Current Policy

Speaking to the appropriateness of the serial follow-ups required of HIV-positive pilots, the bulk of this chapter has called into question the impact of HIV as it pertains to cognitive functioning. As discussed, it appears that, at least among PWH who have maintained immunological functioning and sufficient viral suppression, and who lack a history of significant substance use and medical and psychiatric comorbidities, the likelihood of neurocognitive deficits due to HIV is quite low. At this point, it may be useful to draw comparisons between HIV and other infectious diseases with reported neurocognitive sequelae. Perhaps most relevant is severe acute respiratory syndrome coronavirus-2 (SARS-CoV-2), the virus that causes coronavirus disease 2019 (COVID-19). At present, it is still unclear whether or not there are lasting neuropsychological sequelae associated with COVID-19. However, particularly in individuals infected with the earlier strains (e.g., Alpha and Delta), there was a notable percentage that reported lasting "brain fog," anxiety, memory loss, and other neuropsychological symptoms. Morphologic changes in the brain of those infected with SARS-CoV-2 have been reported, including reduction in gray matter thickness and tissue contrast in the orbitofrontal cortex and parahippocampal gyrus and reduction of global brain size (Douaud et al., 2022), although the clinical significance of such changes remains unclear (Kremer & Jager, 2022). Still, a large volume of published studies indicates lasting neurocognitive deficits among previously SARS-CoV-2-infected individuals (Crivelli et al., 2022; Vanderlind et al., 2021). There are certainly parallels between the study of the neurocognitive effects of HIV and SARS-CoV-2, and cohort studies will be needed to elucidate and separate the effects of the virus versus other causes (Levine et al., 2020). While a comprehensive review of neuroCOVID research is beyond the scope of this chapter, when one considers the sheer numbers of individuals with a history of COVID-19 and post-acute sequelae of COVID-19 (PASC), even the small percentage with possible long-term sequelae would rival the number of individuals projected to have HAND. It is conceivable that most US citizens have been infected. Despite this, there are no FAA guidelines in place to require neuropsychological testing for people with a history of COVID-19 or PASC. The same is true of other viral infections that can affect cognitive functioning (Gascon et al., 2023; Thames et al., 2015; Yeoh et al., 2018).

Summary and New Directions

While it appears indisputable that HIV has deleterious effect on the brain (Kraft-Terry et al., 2009; Lew et al., 2021; Woods et al., 2014), recent studies indicate that, in the vast majority of PWH who have maintained sufficient virologic control and immunological health, the effect of comorbidities and lifestyle factors convey greater risk for neurocognitive impairment than HIV. However, given the role of HIV in accelerated onset of HANA conditions, many of which are the very medical comorbidities that increase risk of neurocognitive dysfunction in PWH, one could argue that the effects are due to HIV nonetheless. In any event, in performing evaluations on PWH, the aviation neuropsychologist has a relatively complex task for which the existing diagnostic guidelines are of questionable validity.

Recognizing the high false-positive rates inherent in the 2007 Frascati criteria, the inconsistency of findings from neuroHIV studies, and the incongruency of estimated prevalence rates with observations outside of research setting, an international group of neuroHIV researchers recently published a consensus statement for improving the determination of cognitive functioning in PWH in clinical and research settings (Nightingale et al., 2023). Proposing that HAND be replaced with a new construct, *HIV-associated brain injury* (HABI), the group developed six recommendations for the neuropsychological assessment of PWH: (1) that classification of cognitive impairment in PWH should consider multiple causes aside from HIV (e.g., medical comorbidities and substance misuse); (2) that one differentiates legacy HABI (i.e., due to brain injury sustained during a period of advanced HIV/AIDS) from active HABI (i.e., progression of brain injury over time despite apparent viral control due to, e.g., cerebrospinal fluid HIV RNA escape or CD8 encephalitis); (3) that clinical context be considered when interpreting low cognitive test scores (e.g., education, socioeconomic status, acculturation); (4) that one considers the false-classification rate when interpreting test data (more relevant in research settings when specific diagnostic criteria are applied); (5) that cognitive impairment be defined based on the presence of significant findings across at least two of three areas: neuropsychological assessment, self- or other-report of cognitive symptoms, and evidence of brain injury via neurologic or neurophysiologic examination; (6) that the examinee's report of cognitive symptoms, or that of a collateral informant, be considered in the diagnosis of HABI, whether or not those symptoms affect activities of daily living. Importantly, the consensus statement recommends that HABI not be considered when individuals and/or their collateral informants do not report cognitive symptoms, a significant departure from the Frascati criteria. Lastly, but equally as important, the consensus group points out that the label of cognitive impairment can not only adversely impact self-esteem and confidence, but it can also lead to discrimination (Low & Purwaningrum, 2020). As an acutely relevant example, the Civil Aviation Authority of the United Kingdom removed restrictions on HIV-positive pilots in 2022, following years of activism (UK Civil Aviation Authority, 2022). Also, notably, they ended mandatory neuropsychological testing of PWH. Such substantial policy changes have not spread beyond the United Kingdom, however, as the FAA and the European Union Aviation Safety Agency have maintained annual screening for commercial pilots (EASA, n.d.).

With the preceding review and the above recommendations from the International HIV-Cognition Working Group in mind, the following suggestions are provided to the aviation neuropsychologist for the assessment of PWH:

- Obtain a full history of HIV disease. This would include nadir CD4 T-cell count, highest viral load, history of AIDS-defining illness, and duration of antiretroviral treatment. History of severe illness (e.g., nadir CD4 T-cell <200 and/or AIDS-defining illness) would increase the likelihood of cognitive deficits via the legacy effect.
- Document medical and psychiatric comorbidities, as these would also increase the likelihood of cognitive deficits in PWH (e.g., depression, anxiety, history of significant substance use, hepatitis C co-infection). In some instances (e.g., age-related medical conditions), the presence of comorbidities might reflect an underlying accelerated aging process that can affect a range of organs, including the brain.
- Pay particular attention to psychosocial factors, such as socioeconomic status throughout the lifespan and quality and quantity of education, as these may affect cognitive testing performance regardless of HIV serostatus.
- Obtain permission to interview a collateral informant. If not possible, consider requesting performance evaluations or, if the applicant is a student, recent academic records in order to assess for functional deficits.

Several topics related to neuroHIV were not discussed in this chapter due to space limitations and, frankly, the incredibly broad-based literature extending back 40 years. The reader is pointed to papers covering the most relevant to the aviation neuropsychologist, including psychiatric changes associated with HIV (Mitra et al., 2022), sex differences in neurocognitive functioning among PWH (Rubin et al., 2019), neurocognitive functioning in resource limited countries (Mekuriaw et al., 2023; Saloner & Cysique, 2017), and the neurocognitive effects of antiretrovirals (Al-Khindi et al., 2011; Gao et al., 2020).

References

Achim, C. L., & Wiley, C. A. (1996). Inflammation in AIDS and the role of the macrophage in brain pathology. *Current Opinion in Neurology, 9*(3), 221–225. https://doi.org/10.1097/00019052-199606000-00013

Al-Khindi, T., Zakzanis, K. K., & van Gorp, W. G. (2011). Does antiretroviral therapy improve HIV-associated cognitive impairment? A quantitative review of the literature. *Journal of the International Neuropsychological Society, 17*(6), 956–969. https://doi.org/10.1017/S1355617711000968

Alvarez-Carbonell, D., Ye, F., Ramanath, N., Garcia-Mesa, Y., Knapp, P. E., Hauser, K. F., & Karn, J. (2019). Cross-talk between microglia and neurons regulates HIV latency. *PLoS Pathogen, 15*(12), e1008249. https://doi.org/10.1371/journal.ppat.1008249

An, K. Y., Zakzanis, K. K., & Joordens, S. (2012). Conducting research with non-clinical healthy undergraduates: Does effort play a role in neuropsychological test performance? *Archives of Clinical Neuropsychology, 27*(8), 849–857. https://doi.org/10.1093/arclin/acs085

Ances, B. M., & Hammoud, D. A. (2014). Neuroimaging of HIV-associated neurocognitive disorders (HAND). *Current Opinion in HIV and AIDS, 9*(6), 545–551. https://doi.org/10.1097/COH.0000000000000112

Anthony, I. C., & Bell, J. E. (2008). The neuropathology of HIV/AIDS. *International Review of Psychiatry, 20*(1), 15–24. https://doi.org/10.1080/09540260701862037

Antinori, A., Arendt, G., Becker, J. T., Brew, B. J., Byrd, D. A., Cherner, M., Clifford, D. B., Cinque, P., Epstein, L. G., Goodkin, K., Gisslen, M., Grant, I., Heaton, R. K., Joseph, J., Marder, K., Marra, C. M., McArthur, J. C., Nunn, M., Price, R. W., ... Wojna, V. E. (2007). Updated research nosology for HIV-associated neu-

rocognitive disorders. *Neurology, 69*(18), 1789–1799. https://doi.org/10.1212/01.WNL.0000287431.88658.8b
Becker, J.T., Maruca, V., Kingsley, L.A., Sanders, J.M., Alger, J.R., Barker, P.B., Goodkin, K., Martin, E., Miller, E.N., Ragin, A., Sacktor, N., & Selnes, O. (2012). Factors affecting brain structure in men with HIV disease in the post-HAART era. *Neuroradiology, 54*(2), 113–121. https://doi.org/10.1007/s00234-011-0854-2
Becker, J.T., Sanders, J., Madsen, S.K., Ragin, A., Kingsley, L., Maruca, V., Cohen, B., Goodkin, K., Martin, E., Miller, E.N., Sacktor, N., Alger, J.R., Barker, P.B., Saharan, P., Carmichael, O.T., & Thompson, P.M. (2011). Subcortical brain atrophy persists even in HAART-regulated HIV disease. *Brain Imaging and Behavior, 5*(2), 77–85. https://doi.org/10.1007/s11682-011-9113-8
Binder, L.M., Iverson, G.L., & Brooks, B.L. (2009). To err is human: "Abnormal" neuropsychological scores and variability are common in healthy adults. *Archives of Clinical Neuropsychology, 24*(1), 31–46. https://doi.org/10.1093/arclin/acn001
Blackstone, K., Moore, D.J., Heaton, R.K., Franklin, D.R., Jr., Woods, S.P., Clifford, D.B., Collier, A.C., Marra, C.M., Gelman, B.B., McArthur, J.C., Morgello, S., Simpson, D.M., Rivera-Mindt, M., Deutsch, R., Ellis, R.J., Hampton Atkinson, J., Grant, I., & Group, C.H.A.T.E.R. (2012). Diagnosing symptomatic HIV-associated neurocognitive disorders: self-report versus performance-based assessment of everyday functioning. *Journal of the International Neuropsychologcial Society, 18*(1), 79–88. https://doi.org/10.1017/S135561771100141X
Borjabad, A., Brooks, A.I., & Volsky, D.J. (2010). Gene expression profiles of HIV-1-infected glia and brain: toward better understanding of the role of astrocytes in HIV-1-associated neurocognitive disorders. *Journal of Neuroimmune Pharmacology, 5*(1), 44–62. https://doi.org/10.1007/s11481-009-9167-1
Boven, L.A., Middel, J., Verhoef, J., De Groot, C.J., & Nottet, H.S. (2000). Monocyte infiltration is highly associated with loss of the tight junction protein zonula occludens in HIV-1-associated dementia. *Neuropathology and Applied Neurobiology, 26*(4), 356–360. https://doi.org/10.1046/j.1365-2990.2000.00255.x
Brew, B.J. (1999). AIDS dementia complex. *Neurologic Clinics, 17*(4), 861–881. https://doi.org/10.1016/s0733-8619(05)70170-5
Chelune, G., Heaton, R., & Lehman, R. (1986). Neuropsychological and personality correlates of patients' complaints of disability. In T.R. Goldstein G (Ed.), *Advances in clinical neuropsychology*. (Vol. 3, pp. 95–126). Plenum Press. https://doi.org/10.1007/978-1-4613-2211-5_4
Chiang, M., Dutton, R., Hayashi, K.M., Lopez, O.L., Aizenstein, H.J., Toga, A.W., Becker, J.T., & Thompson, P.M. (2007). 3D pattern of brain atrophy in HIV/AIDS visualized using tensor-based morphometry. *Neuroimage, 34*, 44–60. https://doi.org/10.1016/j.neuroimage.2006.08.030
Cohen, R.A., & Gongvatana, A. (2010). The persistence of HIV-associated neurocognitive dysfunction and the effects of comorbidities. *Neurology, 75*(23), 2052–2053. https://doi.org/10.1212/WNL.0b013e318200d833
Crivelli, L., Palmer, K., Calandri, I., Guekht, A., Beghi, E., Carroll, W., Frontera, J., Garcia-Azorin, D., Westenberg, E., Winkler, A.S., Mangialasche, F., Allegri, R.F., & Kivipelto, M. (2022). Changes in cognitive functioning after COVID-19: A systematic review and meta-analysis. *Alzheimer's & Dementia, 18*(5), 1047–1066. https://doi.org/10.1002/alz.12644
Cysique, L.A., & Brew, B.J. (2009). Neuropsychological functioning and antiretroviral treatment in HIV/AIDS: A review. *Neuropsychology Review, 19*(2), 169–185. https://doi.org/10.1007/s11065-009-9092-3
Cysique, L.A., Casaletto, K.B., & Heaton, R.K. (2021). Reliably Measuring cognitive change in the era of chronic HIV infection and chronic HIV-Associated neurocognitive disorders. In L.A. Cysique & S.B. Rourke (Eds.), *Neurocognitive complications of HIV-infection*. Springer. https://doi.org/10.1007/7854_2019_116
Cysique, L.A., Dermody, N., Carr, A., Brew, B.J., & Teesson, M. (2016). The role of depression chronicity and recurrence on neurocognitive dysfunctions in HIV-infected adults. *Journal of NeuroVirology, 22*(1), 56–65. https://doi.org/10.1007/s13365-015-0368-5
Deeks, S.G. (2011). HIV infection, inflammation, immunosenescence, and aging. *Annual Review of Medicine, 62*(1), 141–155. https://doi.org/10.1146/annurev-med-042909-093756
DeRight, J., & Jorgensen, R.S. (2015). I just want my research credit: Frequency of suboptimal effort in a non-clinical healthy undergraduate sample. *Clinical Neuropsychology, 29*(1), 101–117. https://doi.org/10.1080/13854046.2014.989267

Desquilbet, L., Jacobson, L.P., Fried, L.P., Phair, J.P., Jamieson, B.D., Holloway, M., & Margolick, J.B. (2011). A frailty-related phenotype before HAART initiation as an independent risk factor for AIDS or death after HAART among HIV-infected men. *The Journals of Gerontology Series A: Biological Sciences and Medical Sciences, 66A*(9), 1030–1038. https://doi.org/10.1093/gerona/glr097

Douaud, G., Lee, S., Alfaro-Almagro, F., Arthofer, C., Wang, C., McCarthy, P., Lange, F., Andersson, J.L.R., Griffanti, L., Duff, E., Jbabdi, S., Taschler, B., Keating, P., Winkler, A.M., Collins, R., Matthews, P.M., Allen, N., Miller, K.L., Nichols, T.E., & Smith, S.M. (2022). SARS-CoV-2 is associated with changes in brain structure in UK Biobank. *Nature, 604*(7907), 697–707. https://doi.org/10.1038/s41586-022-04569-5

EASA. (n.d.). *Review of recent scientific publications to support a decision on a change in the aeromedical certification of applicants for a commercial pilot license living with HIV.* https://www.easa.europa.eu/en/document-library/general-publications/review-recent-scientific-publications-support-decision-change

Everall, I.P., Hansen, L.A., & Masliah, E. (2005). The shifting patterns of HIV encephalitis neuropathology. *Neurotoxicity Research, 8*(1–2), 51–61. https://doi.org/10.1007/BF03033819

Ferretti, F., Mora-Peris, B., Underwood, J., Waldman, A., Everitt, A., & Winston, A. (2018). Cognitive impairment in a clinical setting. *Journal of Acquired Immune Deficiency Syndrome, 77*(1), e10–e13. https://doi.org/10.1097/QAI.0000000000001547

Fox, L., Alford, M., Achim, C., Mallory, M., & Masliah, E. (1997). Neurodegeneration of somatostatin-immunoreactive neurons in HIV encephalitis. *Journal of Neuropathology and Experimental Neurology, 56*(4), 360–368. https://doi.org/10.1097/00005072-199704000-00004

Gao, C., Meng, J., Xiao, X., Wang, M., Williams, A.B., & Wang, H. (2020). Antiretroviral therapy improves neurocognitive impairment in people living with HIV? A meta-analysis. *International Journal of Nursing Sciences, 7*(2), 238–247. https://doi.org/10.1016/j.ijnss.2020.03.007

Gascon, M.R.P., de Oliveira, G.S., Laurence, P.G., Gualqui, C.F., de Oliveira, A.C.P., Smid, J., Fonseca, L.A. M., Casseb, J., & Macedo, E.C. (2023). Neuropsychological profile of patients with infectious disease: Characterization and comparison of patients with HIV, HTLV, and HCV. *Journal of NeuroVirology, 29*(1), 27–34. https://doi.org/10.1007/s13365-022-01108-w

Gelman, B.B. (2007). The neuropathology of HIV. *Handbook of Clinical Neurology, 85*, 301–317. https://doi.org/10.1016/S0072-9752(07)85018-4

Gibert, C.L. (2016). Treatment guidelines for the use of antiretroviral agents in HIV-Infected adults and adolescents: An update. *Federal Practitioner, 33*(Suppl. 3), 31S–36S.

Gisslen, M., Price, R.W., & Nilsson, S. (2011). The definition of HIV-associated neurocognitive disorders: Are we overestimating the real prevalence? *BMC Infectious Diseases, 11*, 356. https://doi.org/10.1186/1471-2334-11-356

Goulet, J.L., Fultz, S.L., Rimland, D., Butt, A., Gibert, C., Rodriguez-Barradas, M., Bryant, K., & Justice, A.C. (2007). Aging and infectious diseases: Do patterns of comorbidity vary by HIV status, age, and HIV severity? *AClinical Infectional Diseases, 45*(12), 1593–1601. https://doi.org/10.1086/523577

Grant, I., Franklin, D.R., Jr., Deutsch, R., Woods, S.P., Vaida, F., Ellis, R.J., Letendre, S.L., Marcotte, T.D., Atkinson, J.H., Collier, A.C., Marra, C.M., Clifford, D.B., Gelman, B.B., McArthur, J.C., Morgello, S., Simpson, D.M., McCutchan, J.A., Abramson, I., Gamst, A., ... Group, C. (2014). Asymptomatic HIV-associated neurocognitive impairment increases risk for symptomatic decline. *Neurology, 82*(23), 2055–2062. https://doi.org/10.1212/WNL.0000000000000492

Greene, M., Justice, A.C., Lampiris, H.W., & Valcour, V. (2013). Management of human immunodeficiency virus infection in advanced age. *JAMA, 309*(13), 1397–1405. https://doi.org/10.1001/jama.2013.2963

Grinspoon, S., & Carr, A. (2005). Cardiovascular risk and body-fat abnormalities in HIV-infected adults. *New England Journal of Medicine, 352*(1), 48–62. https://doi.org/doi:10.1056/NEJMra041811

Gross, A.M., Jaeger, P.A., Kreisberg, J.F., Licon, K., Jepsen, K.L., Khosroheidari, M., Morsey, B.M., Swindells, S., Shen, H., Ng, C.T., Flagg, K., Chen, D., Zhang, K., Fox, H.S., & Ideker, T. (2016). Methylome-wide analysis of chronic HIV Infection reveals five-year increase in biological age and epigenetic targeting of HLA. *Molecular Cell, 62*(2), 157–168. https://doi.org/10.1016/j.molcel.2016.03.019

Heany, S.J., Levine, A.J., Lesosky, M., Phillips, N., Fouche, J.P., Myer, L., Zar, H.J., Stein, D.J., Horvath, S., & Hoare, J. (2023). Persistent accelerated epigenetic ageing in a longitudinal cohort of vertically infected

HIV-positive adolescents. *Journal of NeuroVirology, 29*(3), 272–282. https://doi.org/10.1007/s13365-023-01130-6

Heaton, R.K., Clifford, D.B., Franklin, D.R., Jr., Woods, S.P., Ake, C., Vaida, F., Ellis, R.J., Letendre, S.L., Marcotte, T.D., Atkinson, J.H., Rivera-Mindt, M., Vigil, O.R., Taylor, M.J., Collier, A.C., Marra, C.M., Gelman, B.B., McArthur, J.C., Morgello, S., Simpson, D.M., ... Grant, I. (2010). HIV-associated neurocognitive disorders persist in the era of potent antiretroviral therapy: CHARTER Study. *Neurology, 75*(23), 2087–2096. https://doi.org/10.1212/WNL.0b013e318200d727

Heaton, R.K., Ellis, R.J., Tang, B., Marra, C.M., Rubin, L.H., Clifford, D.B., McCutchan, J.A., Gelman, B.B., Morgello, S., Franklin, D.R., & Letendre, S.L. (2023). Twelve-year neurocognitive decline in HIV is associated with comorbidities, not age: A CHARTER study. *Brain, 146*(3), 1121–1131. https://doi.org/10.1093/brain/awac465

Heaton, R.K., Franklin, D.R., Ellis, R.J., McCutchan, J.A., Letendre, S.L., Leblanc, S., Corkran, S.H., Duarte, N.A., Clifford, D.B., Woods, S.P., Collier, A.C., Marra, C.M., Morgello, S., Mindt, M.R., Taylor, M.J., Marcotte, T.D., Atkinson, J.H., Wolfson, T., Gelman, B.B., ... Grant, I. (2011). HIV-associated neurocognitive disorders before and during the era of combination antiretroviral therapy: Differences in rates, nature, and predictors. *Journal of NeuroVirology, 17*(1), 3–16. https://doi.org/10.1007/s13365-010-0006-1

Heaton, R.K., Franklin, D.R., Jr., Deutsch, R., Letendre, S., Ellis, R.J., Casaletto, K., Marquine, M.J., Woods, S.P., Vaida, F., Atkinson, J.H., Marcotte, T.D., McCutchan, J.A., Collier, A.C., Marra, C.M., Clifford, D.B., Gelman, B.B., Sacktor, N., Morgello, S., Simpson, D.M., ... Group, C. (2015). Neurocognitive change in the era of HIV combination antiretroviral therapy: The longitudinal CHARTER study [Research Support, N.I.H., Extramural]. *Clinical Infectional Diseases, 60*(3), 473–480. https://doi.org/10.1093/cid/ciu862

Heaton, R.K., Marcotte, T.D., Mindt, M.R., Sadek, J., Moore, D.J., Bentley, H., McCutchan, J.A., Reicks, C., & Grant, I. (2004). The impact of HIV-associated neuropsychological impairment on everyday functioning. *Journal of the International Neuropsychological Society, 10*(3), 317–331. https://doi.org/10.1017/S1355617704102130

HIV Positivity and Aviation Safety. (1992). *Aviation, Space, and Environmental Medicine, 63*(5), 375–377.

Hoare, J., Fouche, J.P., Phillips, N., Joska, J.A., Myer, L., Zar, H.J., & Stein, D.J. (2018). Structural brain changes in perinatally HIV-infected young adolescents in South Africa. *AIDS, 32*(18), 2707–2718. https://doi.org/10.1097/QAD.0000000000002024

Hoare, J., Fouche, J.P., Phillips, N., Joska, J.A., Paul, R., Donald, K.A., Thomas, K.G., & Stein, D.J. (2015). White matter micro-structural changes in ART-naive and ART-treated children and adolescents infected with HIV in South Africa. *AIDS, 29*(14), 1793–1801. https://doi.org/10.1097/QAD.0000000000000766

Hoare, J., Phillips, N., Joska, J.A., Paul, R., Donald, K.A., Stein, D.J., & Thomas, K.G. (2016). Applying the HIV-associated neurocognitive disorder diagnostic criteria to HIV-infected youth. *Neurology, 87*(1), 86–93. https://doi.org/10.1212/WNL.0000000000002669

Hoare, J., Stein, D.J., Heany, S.J., Fouche, J.P., Phillips, N., Er, S., Myer, L., Zar, H.J., Horvath, S., & Levine, A.J. (2022). Accelerated epigenetic aging in adolescents living with HIV is associated with altered development of brain structures. *Journal of NeuroVirology, 28*(2), 208–216. https://doi.org/10.1007/s13365-021-00947-3

Horvath, S., & Levine, A.J. (2015). HIV-1 infection accelerates age according to the epigenetic clock. *The Journal of Infectious Diseases, 212*(10), 1563–1573. https://doi.org/10.1093/infdis/jiv277

Horvath, S., Stein, D.J., Phillips, N., Heany, S.J., Kobor, M.S., Lin, D.T.S., Myer, L., Zar, H.J., Levine, A.J., & Hoare, J. (2018). Perinatally acquired HIV infection accelerates epigenetic aging in South African adolescents. *AIDS, 32*(11), 1465–1474. https://doi.org/10.1097/QAD.0000000000001854

Ipser, J.C., Brown, G.G., Bischoff-Grethe, A., Connolly, C.G., Ellis, R.J., Heaton, R.K., Grant, I., & Translational Methamphetamine, A.R.C.G. (2015). HIV infection is associated with attenuated frontostriatal intrinsic connectivity: A preliminary study. *Journal of the International Neuropsychological Society, 21*(3), 203–213. https://doi.org/10.1017/S1355617715000156

Israel, S.M., Hassanzadeh-Behbahani, S., Turkeltaub, P.E., Moore, D.J., Ellis, R.J., & Jiang, X. (2019). Different roles of frontal versus striatal atrophy in HIV-associated neurocognitive disorders. *Human Brain Mapping, 40*(10), 3010–3026. https://doi.org/10.1002/hbm.24577

Kallianpur, A.R., Gittleman, H., Letendre, S., Ellis, R., Barnholtz-Sloan, J.S., Bush, W.S., Heaton, R., Samuels, D.C., Franklin, D.R., Jr., Rosario-Cookson, D., Clifford, D.B., Collier, A.C., Gelman, B., Marra, C.M., McArthur, J.C., McCutchan, J.A., Morgello, S., Grant, I., Simpson, D., ... Group, C.S. (2018). Cerebrospinal fluid ceruloplasmin, haptoglobin, and vascular endothelial growth factor are associated with neurocognitive impairment in adults with HIV infection. *Molecular Neurobiology, 56,* 3808–3818. https://doi.org/10.1007/s12035-018-1329-9

Khanlou, N., Moore, D.J., Chana, G., Cherner, M., Lazzaretto, D., Dawes, S., Grant, I., Masliah, E., & Everall, I.P. (2009). Increased frequency of alpha-synuclein in the substantia nigra in human immunodeficiency virus infection. *Journal of Neurovirology, 15*(2), 131–138. https://doi.org/10.1080/13550280802578075

Kirk, G.D., Mehta, S.H., Astemborski, J., Galai, N., Washington, J., Higgins, Y., Balagopal, A., & Thomas, D.L. (2013). HIV, age, and the severity of hepatitis C Virus-related liver disease. A cohort study. *Annals of Internal Medicine, 158*(9), 658–666. https://doi.org/10.7326/0003-4819-158-9-201305070-00604

Klunder, A.D., Chiang, M.C., Dutton, R.A., Lee, S.E., Toga, A.W., Lopez, O.L., Aizenstein, H.J., Becker, J.T., & Thompson, P.M. (2008). Mapping cerebellar degeneration in HIV/AIDS. *Neuroreport, 19*(17), 1655–1659. https://doi.org/10.1097/WNR.0b013e328311d374

Kolson, D.L. (2022). Developments in neuroprotection for HIV-associated neurocognitive disorders (HAND). *Current HIV/AIDS Reports, 19*(5), 344–357. https://doi.org/10.1007/s11904-022-00612-2

Kraft-Terry, S.D., Buch, S.J., Fox, H.S., & Gendelman, H.E. (2009). A coat of many colors: neuroimmune crosstalk in human immunodeficiency virus infection. *Neuron, 64*(1), 133–145. https://doi.org/10.1016/j.neuron.2009.09.042

Kremer, S., & Jager, H.R. (2022). Brain changes after COVID-19 – how concerned should we be? *Nature Reviews Neurology, 18*(6), 321–322. https://doi.org/10.1038/s41582-022-00661-6

Kuhn, T., Jin, Y., Huang, C., Kim, Y., Nir, T.M., Gullett, J.M., Jones, J.D., Sayegh, P., Chung, C., Dang, B.H., Singer, E.J., Shattuck, D.W., Jahanshad, N., Bookheimer, S.Y., Hinkin, C.H., Zhu, H., Thompson, P.M., & Thames, A.D. (2019). The joint effect of aging and HIV infection on microstructure of white matter bundles. *Human Brain Mapping, 40*(15), 4370–4380. https://doi.org/10.1002/hbm.24708

Lake, J.E., Popov, M., Post, W.S., Palella, F.J., Sacktor, N., Miller, E.N., Brown, T.T., & Becker, J.T. (2017). Visceral fat is associated with brain structure independent of human immunodeficiency virus infection status. *Journal of NeuroVirology, 23*(3), 385–393. https://doi.org/10.1007/s13365-016-0507-7

Lanman, T., Letendre, S., Ma, Q., Bang, A., & Ellis, R. (2021). CNS neurotoxicity of antiretrovirals. *Journal of Neuroimmune Pharmacology, 16*(1), 130–143. https://doi.org/10.1007/s11481-019-09886-7

Lawton, M.P., & Brody, E.M. (1969). Assessment of older people: Self-maintaining and instrumental activities of daily living. *The Gerontologist, 9*(3), 179–186. https://doi.org/10.1093/geront/9.3_Part_1.179

Levine, A., Sacktor, N., & Becker, J.T. (2020). Studying the neuropsychological sequelae of SARS-CoV-2: Lessons learned from 35 years of neuroHIV research. *Journal of NeuroVirology, 26*(6), 809–823. https://doi.org/10.1007/s13365-020-00897-2

Levine, A.J., Martin, E., Sacktor, N., Munro, C., & Becker, J. (2017). Predictors and impact of self-reported suboptimal effort on estimates of prevalence of HIV-associated neurocognitive disorders. *Journal of Acquired Immune Deficiency Syndrome, 75*(2), 203–210. https://doi.org/10.1097/QAI.0000000000001371

Levine, A.J., Quach, A., Moore, D.J., Achim, C.L., Soontornniyomkij, V., Masliah, E., Singer, E.J., Gelman, B., Nemanim, N., & Horvath, S. (2015). Accelerated epigenetic aging in brain is associated with pre-mortem HIV-associated neurocognitive disorders. *Journal of NeuroVirology, 22,* 366–375. https://doi.org/10.1007/s13365-015-0406-3

Levine, A.J., Singer, E.J., & Shapshak, P. (2009). The role of host genetics in the susceptibility for HIV-associated neurocognitive disorders. *AIDS and Behavior, 13*(1), 118–132. https://doi.org/10.1007/s10461-008-9360-x

Lew, B.J., Schantell, M.D., O'Neill, J., Morsey, B., Wang, T., Ideker, T., Swindells, S., Fox, H.S., & Wilson, T.W. (2021). Reductions in gray matter linked to epigenetic HIV-associated accelerated aging. *Cerebral Cortex, 31*(8), 3752–3763. https://doi.org/10.1093/cercor/bhab045

Low, L.F., & Purwaningrum, F. (2020). Negative stereotypes, fear and social distance: a systematic review of depictions of dementia in popular culture in the context of stigma. *BMC Geriatrics, 20*(1), 477. https://doi.org/10.1186/s12877-020-01754-x

Lucas, G.M., Mehta, S.H., Atta, M.G., Kirk, G.D., Galai, N., Vlahov, D., & Moore, R.D. (2007). End-stage renal disease and chronic kidney disease in a cohort of African-American HIV-infected and at-risk HIV-seronegative participants followed between 1988 and 2004. *AIDS, 21*(18), 2435–2443. https://doi.org/10.1097/QAD.0b013e32827038ad

Malee, K.M., Smith, R.A., Mellins, C.A., & Pediatric, H.I.V.A.C.S. (2016). Brain and cognitive development among U.S. Youth with perinatally acquired human immunodeficiency virus infection. *Journal of Pediatric Infectious Diseases Society, 5*(Suppl. 1), S1–S5. https://doi.org/10.1093/jpids/piw041

Mapou, R.L., Kay, G.G., Rundell, J.R., & Temoshok, L. (1993). Measuring performance decrements in aviation personnel infected with the human immunodeficiency virus. *Aviation, Space, and Environmental Medicine, 64*(2), 158–164.

Mapou, R.L., Rundell, J.R., Kay, G.G., & Tramont, E.C. (1993). Relating cognitive function to military aviator performance in early HIV infection. *Vaccine, 11*(5), 555–559. https://doi.org/10.1016/0264-410x(93)90231-l

Martin, J., & Volberding, P. (2010). HIV and premature aging: A field still in its infancy. *Annals of Internal Medicine, 153*(7), 477–479. https://doi.org/10.7326/0003-4819-153-7-201010050-00013

Masliah, E., DeTeresa, R.M., Mallory, M.E., & Hansen, L.A. (2000). Changes in pathological findings at autopsy in AIDS cases for the last 15 years. *AIDS, 14*(1), 69–74. https://doi.org/10.1097/00002030-200001070-00008

McArthur, J.C. (2004). HIV dementia: An evolving disease. *Journal of Neuroimmunology, 157*(1–2), 3–10. https://doi.org/10.1016/j.jneuroim.2004.08.042

McIntosh, E.C., Tureson, K., Rotblatt, L.J., Singer, E.J., & Thames, A.D. (2021). HIV, vascular risk factors, and cognition in the combination antiretroviral therapy era: A systematic review and meta-analysis. *Journal of the International Neuropsychological Society, 27*(4), 365–381. https://doi.org/10.1017/S1355617720001022

McMahan, C., Dietrich, D.K., Horne, E.F., Kelly, E., Geannopoulos, K., Siyahhan Julnes, P.S., Ham, L., Santamaria, U., Lau, C.Y., Wu, T., Hsieh, H.C., Ganesan, A., Berjohn, C., Kapetanovic, S., Reich, D.S., Nair, G., Snow, J., Agan, B.K., Nath, A., & Smith, B.R. (2023). Neurocognitive dysfunction with neuronal injury in people with HIV on long-duration antiretroviral therapy. *Neurology, 100*(24), e2466–e2476. https://doi.org/10.1212/WNL.0000000000207339

Mekuriaw, B., Belayneh, Z., Teshome, W., & Akalu, Y. (2023). Prevalence and variability of HIV/AIDS-associated neurocognitive impairments in Africa: A systematic review and meta-analysis. *BMC Public Health, 23*(1), Article 997. https://doi.org/10.1186/s12889-023-15935-x

Meyer, A.C., Boscardin, W.J., Kwasa, J.K., & Price, R.W. (2013). Is it time to rethink how neuropsychological tests are used to diagnose mild forms of HIV-associated neurocognitive disorders? Impact of false-positive rates on prevalence and power. *Neuroepidemiology, 41*(3–4), 208–216. https://doi.org/10.1159/000354629

Mitra, P., Jain, A., & Kim, K. (2022). HIV and AIDS in older adults: Neuropsychiatric changes. *Current Psychiatry Reports, 24*(9), 463–468. https://doi.org/10.1007/s11920-022-01354-z

Navia, B.A., Jordan, B.D., & Price, R.W. (1986). The AIDS dementia complex: I. Clinical features. *Annals of Neurology, 19*(6), 517–524. https://doi.org/10.1002/ana.410190602

Nichols, S.L. (2022). Central nervous system impact of perinatally acquired HIV in adolescents and adults: An update. *Current HIV/AIDS Reports, 19*(1), 121–132. https://doi.org/10.1007/s11904-021-00598-3

Nightingale, S., Ances, B., Cinque, P., Dravid, A., Dreyer, A.J., Gisslen, M., Joska, J.A., Kwasa, J., Meyer, A.C., Mpongo, N., Nakasujja, N., Pebody, R., Pozniak, A., Price, R.W., Sandford, C., Saylor, D., Thomas, K.G.F., Underwood, J., Vera, J.H., & Winston, A. (2023). Cognitive impairment in people living with HIV: Consensus recommendations for a new approach. *Nature Reviews Neurology, 19*, 424–433. https://doi.org/10.1038/s41582-023-00813-2

Nightingale, S., Dreyer, A.J., Saylor, D., Gisslen, M., Winston, A., & Joska, J.A. (2021). Moving on from HAND: Why we need new criteria for cognitive impairment in persons living with human immunodeficiency virus and a proposed way forward. *Clinical Infectional Diseases, 73*(6), 1113–1118. https://doi.org/10.1093/cid/ciab366

Nir, T.M., Fouche, J.P., Ananworanich, J., Ances, B.M., Boban, J., Brew, B.J., Chaganti, J.R., Chang, L., Ching, C.R.K., Cysique, L.A., Ernst, T., Faskowitz, J., Gupta, V., Harezlak, J., Heaps-Woodruff, J.M., Hinkin,

C.H., Hoare, J., Joska, J.A., Kallianpur, K.J., ... Jahanshad, N. (2021). Association of immunosuppression and viral load with subcortical brain volume in an international sample of people living with HIV. *JAMA Network Open, 4*(1), Article e2031190. https://doi.org/10.1001/jamanetworkopen.2020.31190

Nir, T.M., Jahanshad, N., Ching, C.R.K., Cohen, R.A., Harezlak, J., Schifitto, G., Lam, H.Y., Hua, X., Zhong, J., Zhu, T., Taylor, M.J., Campbell, T.B., Daar, E.S., Singer, E.J., Alger, J.R., Thompson, P.M., Navia, B.A., & Consortium, H.I.V.N. (2019). Progressive brain atrophy in chronically infected and treated HIV+ individuals. *Journal of NeuroVirology, 25*(3), 342–353. https://doi.org/10.1007/s13365-019-00723-4

Nomenclature and research case definitions for neurologic manifestations of human immunodeficiency virus-type 1 (HIV-1) infection. Report of a Working Group of the American Academy of Neurology AIDS Task Force. (1991). *Neurology, 41*(6), 778–785. https://doi.org/10.1212/WNL.41.6.778

Norris, A., Skaggs, V., & Chidester, T. (2023). *Assessing potential risk factors of abnormal cognitive function among HIV-positive airmen - an updated analysis* [Unpublished internal AAM report].

Oliveira, N.L., Kennedy, E.H., Tibshirani, R., Levine, A., Martin, E., Munro, C., Ragin, A.B., Rubin, L.H., Sacktor, N., Seaberg, E.C., Weinstein, A., Becker, J.T., & Neuropsychology Working Group of the Multicenter, A.C.S. (2021). Longitudinal 5-year prediction of cognitive impairment among men with HIV disease. *AIDS, 35*(6), 889–898. https://doi.org/10.1097/QAD.0000000000002827

Pemberton, L.A., & Brew, B.J. (2001). Cerebrospinal fluid S-100beta and its relationship with AIDS dementia complex. *Journal of Clinical Virology, 22*(3), 249–253. https://doi.org/10.1016/S1386-6532(01)00196-2

Phillips, N., Amos, T., Kuo, C., Hoare, J., Ipser, J., Thomas, K.G., & Stein, D.J. (2016). HIV-associated cognitive impairment in perinatally infected children: A meta-analysis. *Pediatrics, 138*(5). https://doi.org/10.1542/peds.2016-0893

Price, R.W., Sidtis, J.J., & Brew, B.J. (1991). AIDS dementia complex and HIV-1 infection: A view from the clinic. *Brain Pathology, 1*(3), 155–162. https://doi.org/10.1111/j.1750-3639.1991.tb00655.x

Richardson, J.L., Nowicki, M., Danley, K., Martin, E.M., Cohen, M.H., Gonzalez, R., Vassileva, J., & Levine, A.M. (2005). Neuropsychological functioning in a cohort of HIV- and hepatitis C virus-infected women. *AIDS, 19*(15), 1659–1667. https://doi.org/10.1097/01.aids.0000186824.53359.62

Ripamonti, E., & Clerici, M. (2021). Living with chronic HIV disease in the antiretroviral era: The impact of neurocognitive impairment on everyday life functions. *Topics in Antiviral Medicine, 29*(3), 386–396.

Robbins, R.N., Zimmerman, R., Korich, R., Raymond, J., Dolezal, C., Choi, C.J., Leu, C.S., Nguyen, N., Malee, K., Wiznia, A., Abrams, E.J., & Mellins, C.A. (2020). Longitudinal trajectories of neurocognitive test performance among individuals with perinatal HIV-infection and -exposure: Adolescence through young adulthood. *AIDS Care, 32*(1), 21–29. https://doi.org/10.1080/09540121.2019.1626343

Roberts, E.S., Masliah, E., & Fox, H.S. (2004). CD163 identifies a unique population of ramified microglia in HIV encephalitis (HIVE). *Journal of Neuropathology and Experimental Neurology, 63*(12), 1255–1264. https://doi.org/10.1093/jnen/63.12.1255

Robertson, K.R., Smurzynski, M., Parsons, T.D., Wu, K., Bosch, R.J., Wu, J., McArthur, J.C., Collier, A.C., Evans, S.R., & Ellis, R.J. (2007). The prevalence and incidence of neurocognitive impairment in the HAART era. *AIDS, 21*(14), 1915–1921. https://doi.org/10.1097/QAD.0b013e32828e4e27

Rodriguez-Penney, A.T., Iudicello, J.E., Riggs, P.K., Doyle, K., Ellis, R.J., Letendre, S.L., Grant, I., Woods, S.P., & Group, H.I.V.N.R.P.H. (2013). Co-morbidities in persons infected with HIV: Increased burden with older age and negative effects on health-related quality of life. *AIDS Patient Care STDS, 27*(1), 5–16. https://doi.org/10.1089/apc.2012.0329

Ross, T.P., Poston, A.M., Rein, P.A., Salvatore, A.N., Wills, N.L., & York, T.M. (2016). Performance invalidity base rates among healthy undergraduate research participants. *Archives of Clinical Neuropsychology, 31*(1), 97–104. https://doi.org/10.1093/arclin/acv062

Rowe, K., Buivydaite, R., Heinsohn, T., Rahimzadeh, M., Wagner, R.G., Scerif, G., & Stein, A. (2021). Executive function in HIV-affected children and adolescents: A systematic review and meta-analyses. *AIDS Care, 33*(7), 833–857. https://doi.org/10.1080/09540121.2021.1873232

Rubin, L.H., Maki, P.M., Springer, G., Benning, L., Anastos, K., Gustafson, D., Villacres, M.C., Jiang, X., Adimora, A.A., Waldrop-Valverde, D., Vance, D.E., Bolivar, H., Alden, C., Martin, E.M., Valcour, V.G., & Women's Interagency, H.I.V.S. (2017). Cognitive trajectories over 4 years among HIV-infected women with optimal viral suppression. *Neurology, 89*(15), 1594–1603. https://doi.org/10.1212/WNL.0000000000004491

Rubin, L.H., Neigh, G.N., Sundermann, E.E., Xu, Y., Scully, E.P., & Maki, P.M. (2019). Sex differences in neurocognitive function in adults with HIV: Patterns, predictors, and mechanisms. *Current Psychiatry Reports, 21*, Article 94. https://doi.org/10.1007/s11920-019-1089-x

Rubin, L.H., Sacktor, N., Creighton, J., Du, Y., Endres, C.J., Pomper, M.G., & Coughlin, J.M. (2018). Microglial activation is inversely associated with cognition in individuals living with HIV on effective antiretroviral therapy. *AIDS, 32*(12), 1661–1667. https://doi.org/10.1097/QAD.0000000000001858

Sacktor, N., Skolasky, R.L., Seaberg, E., Munro, C., Becker, J.T., Martin, E., Ragin, A., Levine, A., & Miller, E. (2016). Prevalence of HIV-associated neurocognitive disorders in the Multicenter AIDS Cohort Study. *Neurology, 86*(4), 334–340. https://doi.org/10.1212/WNL.0000000000002277

Saloner, R., & Cysique, L.A. (2017). HIV-associated neurocognitive disorders: A global perspective. *Journal of the International Neuropsychological Society, 23*(9–10), 860–869. https://doi.org/10.1017/S1355617717001102

Saloner, R., Heaton, R.K., Campbell, L.M., Chen, A., Franklin, D., Jr., Ellis, R.J., Collier, A.C., Marra, C., Clifford, D.B., Gelman, B., Sacktor, N., Morgello, S., McCutchan, J.A., Letendre, S., Grant, I., Fennema-Notestine, C., & Group, C.S. (2019). Effects of comorbidity burden and age on brain integrity in HIV. *AIDS, 33*(7), 1175–1185. https://doi.org/10.1097/QAD.0000000000002192

Schretlen, D.J., Testa, S.M., Winicki, J.M., Pearlson, G.D., & Gordon, B. (2008). Frequency and bases of abnormal performance by healthy adults on neuropsychological testing. *J Int Neuropsychol Soc, 14*(3), 436–445. https://doi.org/10.1017/S1355617708080387

Shiau, S., Brummel, S.S., Kennedy, E.M., Hermetz, K., Spector, S.A., Williams, P.L., Kacanek, D., Smith, R., Drury, S.S., Agwu, A., Ellis, A., Patel, K., Seage, G.R., 3rd, Van Dyke, R.B., Marsit, C.J., & Pediatric, H.I.V.A.C.S. (2021). Longitudinal changes in epigenetic age in youth with perinatally acquired HIV and youth who are perinatally HIV-exposed uninfected. *AIDS, 35*(5), 811–819. https://doi.org/10.1097/QAD.0000000000002805

Silverberg, M., Chao, C., Leyden, W., Xu, L., Tang, B., Horberg, M., Klein, D., Quesenberry, C., Towner, W., & Abrams, D. (2009). HIV infection and the risk of cancers with and without a known infectious cause. *AIDS, 23*(17), 2337–2345. https://doi.org/10.1097/QAD.0b013e3283319184

Silverberg, M.J., Chao, C., Leyden, W.A., Xu, L., Horberg, M.A., Klein, D., Towner, W.J., Dubrow, R., Quesenberry, C.P., Neugebauer, R.S., & Abrams, D.I. (2011). HIV infection, immunodeficiency, viral replication, and the risk of cancer. *Cancer Epidemiology Biomarkers & Prevention, 20*(12), 2551–2559. https://doi.org/10.1158/1055-9965.epi-11-0777

Sulkowski, M.S., & Thomas, D.L. (2003). Hepatitis C in the HIV-infected person. *Annals of Internal Medicine, 138*(3), 197–207. https://doi.org/10.7326/0003-4819-138-3-200302040-00012

Sundermann, E.E., Hussain, M.A., Moore, D.J., Horvath, S., Lin, D.T.S., Kobor, M.S., Levine, A., & Group, H. (2019). Inflammation-related genes are associated with epigenetic aging in HIV. *Journal of NeuroVirology, 25*(6), 853–865. https://doi.org/10.1007/s13365-019-00777-4

Thames, A.D., Castellon, S.A., Singer, E.J., Nagarajan, R., Sarma, M.K., Smith, J., Thaler, N.S., Truong, J.H., Schonfeld, D., Thomas, M.A., & Hinkin, C.H. (2015). Neuroimaging abnormalities, neurocognitive function, and fatigue in patients with hepatitis C. *Neurol Neuroimmunol Neuroinflamm, 2*(1), Article e59. https://doi.org/10.1212/NXI.0000000000000059

Thompson, P.M., Dutton, R.A., Hayashi, K.M., Lu, A., Lee, S.E., Lee, J.Y., Lopez, O.L., Aizenstein, H.J., Toga, A.W., & Becker, J.T. (2006). 3D mapping of ventricular and corpus callosum abnormalities in HIV/AIDS. *Neuroimage, 31*(1), 12–23. https://doi.org/10.1016/j.neuroimage.2005.11.043

Triant, V.A., Lee, H., Hadigan, C., & Grinspoon, S.K. (2007). Increased acute myocardial infarction rates and cardiovascular risk factors among patients with human immunodeficiency virus disease. *The Journal of Clinical Endocrinology & Metabolism, 92*(7), 2506–2512. https://doi.org/10.1210/jc.2006-2190

UK Civil Aviation Authority. (2022). *UK CAA certification guidance for applicants living with HIV.* https://www.caa.co.uk/media/szlnkgq2/20240613-v2-1-guidance-for-applicants-living-with-hiv.pdf

Vance, D.E., Rubin, L.H., Valcour, V., Waldrop-Valverde, D., & Maki, P.M. (2016). Aging and neurocognitive functioning in HIV-infected women: A review of the literature involving the Women's Interagency HIV Study. *Current HIV/AIDS Reports, 13*(6), 399–411. https://doi.org/10.1007/s11904-016-0340-x

Vanderlind, W.M., Rabinovitz, B.B., Miao, I.Y., Oberlin, L.E., Bueno-Castellano, C., Fridman, C., Jaywant, A., & Kanellopoulos, D. (2021). A systematic review of neuropsychological and psychiatric sequalae of COVID-19: Implications for treatment. *Current Opinion in Psychiatry, 34*(4), 420–433. https://doi.org/10.1097/YCO.0000000000000713

Wade, B.S., Valcour, V., Busovaca, E., Esmaeili-Firidouni, P., Joshi, S.H., Wang, Y., & Thompson, P.M. (2015). Subcortical shape and volume abnormalities in an elderly HIV+ cohort. *Proceedings SPIE, 9417*. https://doi.org/10.1117/12.2082241

Wang, Z., Cheng, Y., Seaberg, E.C., Rubin, L.H., Levine, A.J., Becker, J.T., & Neuropsychology Working Group of the MACS (2021). Longitudinal multivariate normative comparisons. *Statistics in Medicine, 40*(6), 1440–1452. https://doi.org/10.1002/sim.8850

Wang, Z., Molsberry, S.A., Cheng, Y., Kingsley, L., Levine, A.J., Martin, E., Munro, C.A., Ragin, A., Rubin, L.H., Sacktor, N., Seaberg, E.C., Becker, J.T., & Neuropsychology Working Group of the Multicenter, A.C.S. (2019a). Cross-sectional analysis of cognitive function in the MACS with multivariate normative comparisons. *AIDS, 33*(14), 2115–2124. https://doi.org/10.1097/QAD.0000000000002312

Wang, Z., Molsberry, S.A., Cheng, Y., Kingsley, L., Levine, A.J., Martin, E., Munro, C.A., Ragin, A., Rubin, L.H., Sacktor, N., Seaberg, E.C., Becker, J.T., & Neuropsychology Working Group of the Multicenter, A.C.S. (2019b). Cross-sectional analysis of cognitive function using multivariate normative comparisons in men with HIV disease. *AIDS, 33*(14), 2115–2124. https://doi.org/10.1097/QAD.0000000000002312

Wei, J., Hou, J., Su, B., Jiang, T., Guo, C., Wang, W., Zhang, Y., Chang, B., Wu, H., & Zhang, T. (2020). The prevalence of Frascati-criteria-based HIV-associated neurocognitive disorder (HAND) in HIV-infected adults: A systematic review and meta-analysis. *Frontiers in Neurology, 11*, Article 581346. https://doi.org/10.3389/fneur.2020.581346

Wendelken, L., & Valcour, V. (2012). Impact of HIV and aging on neuropsychological function. *Journal of NeuroVirology, 18*(4), 256–263. https://doi.org/10.1007/s13365-012-0094-1

Wilson, T.W., Heinrichs-Graham, E., Becker, K.M., Aloi, J., Robertson, K.R., Sandkovsky, U., White, M.L., O'Neill, J., Knott, N.L., Fox, H.S., & Swindells, S. (2015). Multimodal neuroimaging evidence of alterations in cortical structure and function in HIV-infected older adults. *Human Brain Mapping, 36*(3), 897–910. https://doi.org/10.1002/hbm.22674

Womack, J.A., Goulet, J.L., Gibert, C., Brandt, C., Chang, C.C., Gulanski, B., Fraenkel, L., Mattocks, K., Rimland, D., Rodriguez-Barradas, M.C., Tate, J., Yin, M.T., Justice, A.C., & for the Veterans Aging Cohort Study Project, T. (2011). Increased risk of fragility fractures among HIV infected compared to uninfected male veterans. *PLoS One, 6*(2), Article e17217. https://doi.org/10.1371/journal.pone.0017217

Woods, S.P., Doyle, K.L., Morgan, E.E., Naar-King, S., Outlaw, A.Y., Nichols, S.L., & Loft, S. (2014). Task importance affects event-based prospective memory performance in adults with HIV-associated neurocognitive disorders and HIV-infected young adults with problematic substance use. *Journal of the International Neuropsychological Society, 20*(6), 652–662. https://doi.org/10.1017/S1355617714000435

Woods, S.P., Moore, D.J., Weber, E., & Grant, I. (2009). Cognitive neuropsychology of HIV-associated neurocognitive disorders. *Neuropsychology Review, 19*(2), 152–168. https://doi.org/10.1007/s11065-009-9102-5

Wu, M., Fatukasi, O., Yang, S., Alger, J., Barker, P.B., Hetherington, H., Kim, T., Levine, A., Martin, E., Munro, C.A., Parrish, T., Ragin, A., Sacktor, N., Seaberg, E., Becker, J.T., & Neuropsychology Working Group of the Multicenter, A.C.S. (2018). HIV disease and diabetes interact to affect brain white matter hyperintensities and cognition. *AIDS, 32*(13), 1803–1810. https://doi.org/10.1097/QAD.0000000000001891

Yeoh, S.W., Holmes, A.C.N., Saling, M.M., Everall, I.P., & Nicoll, A.J. (2018). Depression, fatigue and neurocognitive deficits in chronic hepatitis C. *Hepatology International, 12*(4), 294–304. https://doi.org/10.1007/s12072-018-9879-5

Yu, B., Pasipanodya, E., Montoya, J.L., Moore, R.C., Gianella, S., McCutchan, A., Ellis, R., Heaton, R.K., Jeste, D.V., Moore, D.J., & Marquine, M.J. (2019). Metabolic syndrome and neurocognitive deficits in HIV infection. *Journal of Acquired Immune Deficiency Syndrome, 81*(1), 95–101. https://doi.org/10.1097/QAI.0000000000001964

Zheng, J., & Gendelman, H.E. (1997). The HIV-1 associated dementia complex: a metabolic encephalopathy fueled by viral replication in mononuclear phagocytes. *Current Opinion in Neurology, 10*(4), 319–325. https://doi.org/10.1097/00019052-199708000-00007

Zhou, L., Rua, R., Ng, T., Vongrad, V., Ho, Y.S., Geczy, C., Hsu, K., Brew, B.J., & Saksena, N.K. (2009). Evidence for predilection of macrophage infiltration patterns in the deeper midline and mesial temporal structures of the brain uniquely in patients with HIV-associated dementia. *BMC Infectious Diseases, 9*, Article 192. https://doi.org/10.1186/1471-2334-9-192

Chapter 28
Attention-Deficit/Hyperactivity Disorder in Aviation Neuropsychology

Jason A. King and Daniel N. DaSilva

Introduction

Attention-deficit/hyperactivity disorder (ADHD) is a neurodevelopmental condition characterized by inattention, hyperactivity, and impulsivity. The symptoms of ADHD are evident during childhood and may persist to varying degrees into adulthood. Affected individuals experience a range of problems in their functioning, which may include difficulty concentrating, distractibility, deficient executive cognitive functions such as multitasking and planning, restlessness, difficulty tolerating boredom, poor emotional self-regulation, and tendencies to engage in impulsive behaviors that are not well-considered. Given the nature of the cognitive and behavioral symptoms associated with ADHD, this condition presents serious concerns regarding aviation safety. The importance of thorough assessment and aeromedical disposition of individuals who have been diagnosed with or treated for ADHD is recognized by civil and military aviation authorities. Because rates of ADHD diagnosis and treatment with medications such as psychostimulants have been rising considerably during recent years, ADHD represents an increasingly important topic in aviation neuropsychology.

Description of the Condition

Problematic symptoms of hyperactivity and inattention in children have been recognized in medicine since the early 20th century. The diagnosis of attention deficit disorder (ADD) initially appeared in the third edition of the American Psychiatric Association's *Diagnostic and Statistical Manual* (DSM-III) in 1980, and the condition has been further refined in subsequent editions of the DSM. Correspondingly, the World Health Organization's (WHO) *International Classification of Disease* (ICD) previously described a similar condition known as "hyperkinetic disorder," which has more recently been replaced by ADHD, with ADHD first appearing in the 10th edition (ICD-10) published in 2016, and hyperkinetic disorder no longer appearing in the 11th edition (ICD-11) published in 2019.

In the most recent version of the DSM, the text revision of the fifth edition (DSM-5-TR; American Psychiatric Association, 2022), ADHD is defined as a persistent pattern of inattention and/or hyperactivity-impulsivity that interferes with functioning or development. Diagnosis requires the presence of specific behavioral criteria including six or more symptoms of inattention and/or six or more symptoms of hyperactivity and impulsivity, present before the age of 12 years, present in two or more settings (e.g., home, school, work, or other activities), and resulting in negative effects on social, academic, or occupational functioning. Three subtypes of ADHD are recognized: predominantly inattentive presentation, predominantly hyperactive/impulsive presentation, and combined inattentive and hyperactive/impulsive presentation.

In addition to the core symptom domains of inattention and hyperactivity/impulsivity, many individuals with ADHD experience a range of maladaptive alterations in mood and behavior, even in the absence of comorbid psychiatric disorders, that have come to be known as *emotional dysregulation*. Children with ADHD are prone to irritability, temper tantrums, and disruptive behavior (Sobanski et al., 2010). Manifestations of emotional dysregulation often persist into adolescence and adulthood, with adults with ADHD also prone to irritability and temper outbursts, and additionally described as impatient, easily frustrated and overwhelmed, easily excited, having unstable mood, and tending to overreact (Asherson et al., 2016; Barkley, 2015). Notably, among adults with ADHD these symptoms of emotional dysregulation have been shown to contribute to impairment in multiple broad domains of life functioning (e.g., occupational, educational, criminal, driving, and financial outcomes) beyond the core symptom domains of inattention and hyperactivity/impulsivity (Barkley & Fischer, 2010).

Neurobiological Basis

While environmental factors (e.g., parenting style) are thought to influence manifestations of ADHD, there is a strong established neurobiological basis for the condition. Genetic studies have suggested that multiple genes are related to ADHD, with heritability estimated at roughly 70%–75% for both core symptom dimensions of inattention and hyperactivity (Nikolas & Burt, 2010). An extensive literature has documented abnormalities of brain structure and brain function/physiology among children, adolescents, and adults with ADHD. Findings from these studies have identified abnormalities in the frontal lobes of the brain and their connections with other brain regions (e.g., frontal-striatal; frontal-parietal-temporal; frontal-cerebellar; and frontal-limbic), which are networks that are involved in attention, executive functions, memory, and emotional regulation (Cortese et al., 2012; Rubia et al., 2014).

It has further been demonstrated that children with ADHD exhibit delays of several years in reaching normal thickness of brain cortex in regions of the frontal lobes, and persistence of ADHD symptoms into adulthood is associated with persistent cortical thinning, while improvement in ADHD symptoms has been associated with normalization cortical thickness (Shaw et al., 2013). Despite these findings, no neuroimaging or other biological markers have demonstrated sufficient sensitivity and specificity for clinical diagnosis at present, and ADHD remains a diagnosis based upon specific behavioral criteria at this time.

Comorbidity and Impairment in Functioning

Extensive research during the past several decades has revealed that ADHD is associated with significantly higher rates of other neurodevelopmental and psychiatric conditions as well as with significant impairment in functioning across a wide range of factors in life. Individuals with ADHD commonly experience co-occurring learning disorders (e.g., reading, math), various psychiatric disorders (e.g., oppositional, conduct, mood, and anxiety disorders), and increased rates of substance use disorders and personality disorders (especially antisocial personality disorder) in adolescence and adulthood (Klein et al., 2012; Wilens et al., 2018). ADHD is associated with impairment in academic performance and peer relationships; increased risk for accidental injury and death including suicide; poor health-related behaviors; and poorer long-term educational, occupational, and economic outcomes (Hinshaw & Scheffler, 2018; Klein et al., 2012).

Developmental ADHD Across the Lifespan

Originally conceptualized as a disorder of children primarily affecting school performance, more recent research has made clear that ADHD persists into adulthood for many affected individuals. With respect to prevalence, a meta-analysis of prospective studies following children with ADHD into adulthood (Faraone et al., 2006) indicated that at age 25, approximately 15 % of affected individuals continued to meet full diagnostic criteria for ADHD, and 65 % continued to experience clinically significant symptoms of ADHD associated with some degree of impairment in their functioning while no longer satisfying full diagnostic criteria for ADHD (i.e., met DSM-IV criteria for partial remission).

In the developmental course of ADHD, there are notable differences in symptom expression across the lifetime (Asherson et al., 2016). In early childhood, symptoms of hyperactivity are often pronounced, with inattention becoming more noticeable during school years. Among individuals experiencing persistent symptoms into adulthood, overt hyperactivity tends to subside and the overall severity of symptoms tends to diminish, but adults with ADHD often continue to experience difficulties with attention-related symptoms such as distractibility, difficulty planning, procrastination, and impulsive decision-making. With these general trends noted, there is considerable variability in the symptom expression of ADHD across the lifespan, and it is possible for an individual with ADHD to experience any combination of symptoms at any point in their lifetime (Asherson et al., 2018).

Prevalence

ADHD is a common condition, with meta-analysis reviews indicating prevalence rates of roughly 5 %-7 % among children, and the condition being more frequent among boys than girls (Polanczyk et al., 2007; Willcutt, 2012). Prevalence among adults has been estimated at 2.5 % based upon a systematic review and meta-analysis of studies primarily comprising young adult and middle-aged adult participants (Simon et al., 2009). Among older adults aged 60–94, a similar prevalence of 2.8 % has been reported, with 4.2 % of the sample experiencing some symptoms but not meeting full diagnostic criteria (Michielsen et al., 2012). The prevalence of ADHD has been reported as being similar in countries across the world, with some differences in prevalence attributable to variations in diagnostic practices and cultural differences in the threshold for considering symptoms pathological (Canino & Alegria, 2008; Polanczyk et al., 2007).

Treatment

Psychostimulant medications are generally considered the first-line treatment for ADHD, and a large body of research findings has demonstrated short-term effectiveness for psychostimulants in the treatment of core ADHD symptoms (Wolraich et al., 2019). Methylphenidate and amphetamine, in various preparations including short-acting and extended-release formulations, are used in the treatment of ADHD around the world (Hinshaw et al., 2011). Two classes of non-stimulant medications, including selective norepinephrine reuptake inhibitors (e.g., atomoxetine; viloxazine) and alpha-2 adrenergic agonists (e.g., guanfacine; clonidine), have also received regulatory approval for treatment of ADHD, although these medications generally tend to be less effective than psychostimulants (Dittmann et al., 2018). Non-medication interventions including cognitive-behavioral therapy (CBT), cognitive remediation or compensatory strategy training, and neurofeedback (i.e., EEG biofeedback) are also used to treat adults with ADHD, although findings regarding the effectiveness of these interventions have been mixed in the research literature.

Recent Trends and Controversy

There have been large increases in the rates of ADHD diagnosis and the number of individuals treated with stimulant medications during recent decades, and it appears that the rates of prescriptions for stimulant medications are continuing to increase over time. In their detailed analysis of trends in ADHD diagnosis and medication treatment between 2003 and 2011, Visser et al. (2014) reported significant increases in both diagnosis and medication treatment, with a remarkable finding that more than 1 in 10 school-aged children had received an ADHD diagnosis by a healthcare provider in 2011, with nearly 1 in 5 high school boys having had a diagnosis of ADHD at some point in their lifetime.

Correspondingly, large increases in the number of prescriptions for stimulant medications have been documented, with amphetamine surpassing methylphenidate, and stimulant prescriptions for adults surpassing those for youth (Safer, 2016). Notably, Safer (2016) indicated that off-label treatment with stimulant medications was reported to be 40 % or more of total use and appears to be more common in adults. The trend for increasing numbers of stimulant prescriptions has continued to the present, with the percentage of adults and adolescent females receiving prescription stimulant medications increasing during 2016–2021, particularly during 2020–2021 associated with the onset of the COVID-19 pandemic (Danielson et al., 2023).

Considerable controversy has accompanied the recent increases in ADHD diagnosis and treatment with stimulant medications. As reviewed above, there is clear evidence that ADHD is a real condition that results in significant impairment in functioning among affected individuals and that treatment improves symptoms and functioning. However, at the same time, there have been concerns that ADHD may be increasingly overdiagnosed and overtreated, including stimulant medications prescribed for individuals who do not have an adequately established diagnosis of ADHD (Hinshaw & Scheffler, 2014). Findings have suggested that clinicians may tend to overdiagnose ADHD, especially among males, due to failure to adhere to diagnostic criteria (Bruchmuller et al., 2012).

A range of additional factors have been linked to possible inappropriate diagnoses and excessive treatment with ADHD medications, including students or parents desiring enhancement of their academic performance through school accommodations and effects of stimulant medications, and diversion of stimulant medications with potential for recreational abuse (Hinshaw & Scheffler, 2014). More recent factors include self-diagnosis trends on social media, with a recent study determining that half of videos about ADHD on a popular social media platform were misleading (Yeung et al., 2022). Other factors have been associated with the COVID-19 pandemic, including increasing reports of ADHD-like symptoms among employees working at home rather than external workplaces, and increased ease of availability of controlled stimulant medications via telehealth providers (Danielson et al., 2023).

ADHD and Aviation Safety

Piloting an aircraft is a complex activity that requires a range of physical and mental abilities and learned skills. It has long been recognized that most aviation accidents are due to pilot error and that it is therefore essential that pilots possess intact cognitive abilities as a component of aeromedical fitness to safely operate an aircraft (Jensen, 1982). In their review of the literature including psychological task analysis, Banich et al. (1989) identified multiple cognitive abilities required for piloting: perceptual-motor abilities; spatial abilities; working memory; attention; planning and sequencing abilities; and processing flexibility (e.g., executive abilities including inhibition, selective attention, fluency, and conceptual reasoning/problem-solving).

Different stages of flight involve different cognitive demands. Extensive planning, preparation, and practice are necessary before flight. This includes thorough safety checks to prevent something from going wrong once in the air. Bursts of fast-paced activity and multitasking are required during takeoff and landing, as well as during other unexpected situations such as troubleshooting an in-flight emergency. By contrast, routine cruising places more demands on other cognitive abilities, such as maintaining vigilance and situational awareness, monitoring various systems on the aircraft, and managing boredom for hours at a time on long flights (Porges & Gropp, 2018).

Attention-related abilities and executive functions have been identified as critical cognitive abilities affecting all the core activities required to safely pilot an aircraft, summarized in the oft used adage "aviate, navigate, and communicate" (Fitzgerald et al., 2011; King et al., 2021). *Aviating* involves controlling the attitude and flight path of the aircraft. Operating a complex machine in three-dimensional space requires intact executive functions (e.g., planning, judgment, decision-making, prioritizing tasks, divided attention, allocating attention resources, impulse control, and emotional regulation). *Navigating* requires continuous determination of the aircraft's position and course and draws upon a range of cognitive abilities including executive functions such as planning, as well as math and visual-spatial abilities. *Communicating* involves making and receiving radio communications with air traffic controllers (ATCs) and others. While flying, pilots hear constant chatter of ATCs communicating with other aircraft. It is necessary for pilots to continuously monitor and detect when their identification number is called by ATCs, requiring sustained attention vigilance, selective attention, and auditory discrimination.

Compromises of pilot attention and executive functions have consistently been implicated in aviation accidents. Various specific aspects of attention and executive cognitive functions are closely associated with the key aviation safety concepts of *situational awareness*, *task sat-*

uration, and *aeronautical decision-making* that have been reported to be related to many accidents and incidents. The Australian Transport Safety Bureau (2006) conducted an analysis of aviation accidents and incidents involving pilot distraction and determined that distractions (i.e., misallocation of attention on nonessential targets resulting in failure of situational awareness) contribute to many accidents and incidents, can occur during all phases of flight including ground and in-flight phases, and commonly occur during periods of both high and low pilot workload. Numerous other analyses of have highlighted the importance of failures of attention, working memory, and executive functions in aviation accidents, flight crew errors, and poor aeronautical decision-making (Dismukes et al., 2018; Hoffmann et al., 1998; National Aeronautics and Space Administration, 2015).

Given the nature of the behavioral and cognitive symptoms associated with ADHD, the condition presents serious concerns regarding aviation safety. As a disorder that involves difficulty focusing attention, difficulty maintaining attention over time, being easily distracted by internal and external stimuli, making careless mistakes, lack of attention to details, making impulsive poorly considered decisions, restlessness, difficulty tolerating boredom, and being prone to unusual frustration and emotional outbursts, the core symptoms of ADHD directly overlap with numerous cognitive, emotional, and behavioral characteristics considered essential for flight safety. Moreover, ADHD may result in deficits of various cognitive abilities involving attention and executive functioning that are relevant to aviation safety, including focused attention, sustained attention, selective attention, working memory (auditory and visual), planning, set shifting/mental flexibility, inhibition, decision-making, ability to perceive and estimate time intervals, and excessive variability and inconsistency in response times. A comprehensive discussion of the cognitive deficits and maladaptive behavioral characteristics associated with ADHD is beyond the scope of this chapter. Interested readers are referred to thorough reviews of cognitive deficits (Coghill et al., 2018; Solanto, 2015) and emotional dysregulation (Barkley, 2015; Ryckaert et al., 2018).

It has been demonstrated that ADHD results in a considerably increased risk of automobile accidents (Curry et al., 2019), workplace injuries (Kessler et al., 2009), and other accidents and injuries (Brunkhorst-Kanaan et al., 2021). ADHD is also associated with increased mortality including suicide (Barbaresi et al., 2013). Recent research has documented that individuals with ADHD have a substantially increased risk of many different types of accidents and injuries throughout the lifespan and has highlighted the role risk-taking behavior plays in causing accidents and injuries among individuals with ADHD (Libutzki et al., 2023). Risk-taking and impulsive behaviors may be more related to accidents in novel settings, while deficits in sustained attention may play a greater role in more familiar settings or over longer periods of time (Groom et al., 2015).

Piloting an aircraft shares many similarities with driving an automobile, albeit with some critically important differences including that aircraft operate in three-dimensional space and that one cannot simply pull over to the side of the road if there is a problem. As such, the numerous studies demonstrating increased rates of traffic accidents among drivers with ADHD are particularly relevant to aviation safety. Curry et al. (2019) found that drivers with ADHD had higher rates of crashes, moving violations (e.g., speeding, seatbelt nonuse, distraction with electronic equipment), driver's license suspensions, and drug- and alcohol-related traffic violations, with the highest risk among adolescents and newly licensed drivers regardless of age. An analysis of factors related to road accidents among drivers with ADHD identified multiple potential causative factors, including risky, dangerous, and illegal driving behaviors; inattention; dysregulation of waking systems; distraction (e.g., social networking sites while driving); substance abuse; and aggressive behaviors (Romo et al., 2021). In a 2015 study, Groom et al. found that adults with ADHD reported significantly more traffic accidents, violations, and lapses and demonstrated higher rates of impaired performance in a driving simulator, characterized by difficulty regulating and controlling impulsive behaviors such as speeding, frustration with other users on the roadway, unsafe driving maneuvers, and resulting in greater likelihood of an accident following an unexpected event.

ADHD has been implicated as a potential causative factor in multiple fatal aviation accidents. Laukkala et al. (2017) identified nine fatal aviation accidents between the years 2000 and 2015 in the National Transportation Safety Board (NTSB) database possibly associated with ADHD or ADD. The NTSB identified a range of causative factors, including a student pilot improperly handling aircraft controls, pilot fatigue, failure to maintain adequate airspeed, decision to attempt a flight not qualified for, ignoring poor weather conditions, impairment due to prescription medication and alcohol, poor decision-making, decision to fly at a low altitude, pilot distraction (attention diverted to flying over a residence), pilot failure to maintain clearance from power line, pilot failure to maintain aircraft control and altitude, pilot failure to maintain aircraft attitude, and a non-instrument-rated pilot's decision to continue visual flight into instrument meteorological conditions resulting in loss of aircraft control. In the majority of these incidents, postmortem toxicology revealed the presence of stimulant medications used to treat ADHD (e.g., amphetamine, methylphenidate).

Stimulant medications used to treat ADHD are also associated with aviation safety risk. Commonly used stimulants (e.g., amphetamine, methylphenidate) have short half-lives, and these medications may need to be taken multiple times daily. This presents concerns for pilots on long trips when the timing and frequency of medication administration may be problematic (Fitzgerald et al., 2011). While stimulant medications are effective in temporarily ameliorating the behavioral symptoms associated with ADHD, underlying cognitive impairments persist among individuals with ADHD (Gualtieri & Johnson, 2008). Fitzgerald et al. (2011) further noted that treatment with stimulant medications may result in diminished ability to recognize fatigue, which may result in unrecognized deterioration in performance and poor decision-making.

Policies of Aviation Authorities on ADHD

Civilian and military aviation regulatory authorities have recognized the significant threat ADHD poses to aviation safety and successful mission completion. As noted by Laukkala et al. (2017), it is generally accepted by aviation regulatory authorities around the world that ADHD is a disqualifying medical condition for a pilot. Yet it is also recognized that some individuals with a history of ADHD diagnosis and/or treatment with stimulant medications experience full or nearly full remission of symptoms as they mature into adulthood, while others may have initially received an inadequate or inaccurate diagnosis of ADHD and probably never met full diagnostic criteria for the condition. Therefore, most civilian and military aviation authorities offer the possibility of waivers or other paths to issuance of aeromedical certification considered on a case-by-case basis.

In the United States, the Federal Aviation Administration (FAA) considers ADHD to be a medically disqualifying condition. The FAA's *Guide for Aviation Medical Examiners* provides guidance and aeromedical decision considerations for pilot applicants with a history of

ADHD diagnosis and/or treatment with ADHD medications and can be found on the FAA's website (https://www.faa.gov). The disease protocol notes that ADHD, formerly called "attention deficit disorder" (ADD), and medications used for treatment may result in cognitive deficits that would make an aviator unsafe to perform pilot duties. The FAA has developed detailed specifications for neuropsychological testing requirements for ADHD evaluations. Due to concerns regarding test security, the specifications are not available publicly and are provided only to qualified professional neuropsychology examiners.

Until recently, FAA ADHD specifications required all aeromedical certification applicants who had been deferred by their aviation medical examiner for a history of ADHD to have a neuropsychological evaluation by a qualified neuropsychologist. In 2023, new guidelines went into effect for the disposition of pilot applicants with a history of ADHD, with a "fast track" option for expedited review of applicants who are determined by a qualified psychologist or neuropsychologist examiner to satisfy the following four criteria: (1) not currently displaying any symptoms of ADHD; (2) demonstrated stable academic/occupational and social functioning during the past 4 years; (3) not taken ADHD medication for any reason during the past 4 years; and (4) do not have a history of any other psychiatric diagnosis or treatment. Applicants who do not satisfy all these criteria must proceed with the "standard track," which includes the neuropsychological evaluation.

For standard-track applicants, the neuropsychological evaluation consists of a relatively brief initial battery of neuropsychological tests, detailed clinical interview, and review of historical information. It is followed by a supplemental test battery if the initial battery indicates aeromedically significant deficits or additional testing is needed to clarify diagnosis, identify coexisting disorders, and/or to confirm or disconfirm the presence of aeromedically significant deficits. Prior to evaluation, the applicant must discontinue ADHD medication for a minimum of 90 days. Within 24 hr of the neuropsychological evaluation, the applicant must submit to urinalysis, including screening for both amphetamines and methylphenidate, to document they were not taking psychostimulant medication at the time of the evaluation to improve their performance on neurocognitive testing.

In the United States military, ADHD is considered aeromedically disqualifying. Different branches of the military have developed their own aeromedical standards regarding ADHD. A detailed review of US military standards and aeromedical waivers for psychiatric conditions and treatments, including ADHD, was conducted by Saitzyk et al. (2013). Saitzyk et al. (2013) indicated that aeromedical standards for ADHD for the US Army are contained in the Army Aeromedical Policy Letters. The US Air Force standards are contained in the *United States Air Force Aerospace Medicine Waiver Guide Compendium* (2023) and are available from the US Air Force Medical Service. The US Navy standards are contained in the *Aeromedical Reference and Waiver Guide* (2019) and are available from the Navy Bureau of Medicine and Surgery. Currently, each branch offers the possibility of a waiver considered on a case-by-case basis. Waivers may not be required if the initial diagnosis of ADHD was clearly inappropriate and there was only short-term medication treatment for less than 1 year (Army) or if the pilot candidate has not used medication and has not received special accommodations for occupational or academic performance in the last 4 years (Air Force).

Commonalities among the US military branches include an emphasis on examiners conducting a detailed clinical interview and review of background records to determine if the initial diagnosis of ADHD was accurate and was based upon an adequate evaluation. Current treatment with psychostimulant medications is considered aeromedically disqualifying across all branches of the military. The US Army considers waivers for pilots currently treated with non-stimulant medications for ADHD (e.g., Wellbutrin/bupropion or Strattera/atomoxetine), while the US Air Force and US Navy do not permit pilots to take non-stimulant medications for ADHD. The US Air Force and the US Navy require pilot candidates to be off ADHD medication for at least 12 months and to have demonstrated stable functioning as indicated by academic or occupational performance (Air Force) or absence of symptoms (Navy) before a waiver is considered. Each branch requires neuropsychological testing in certain circumstances, but none requires it routinely for all cases.

In the United Kingdom, the UK Civil Aviation Authority (CAA) provides guidance for aeromedical examiners including medical standards for pilot applicants with mental health conditions. The standards for ADHD can be found on the CAA website (https://www.caa.co.uk). The CAA notes that ADHD is diagnosed according to DSM-5 when an individual demonstrates inattention, hyperactivity, or impulsiveness sufficient to cause significant impairment in social, school, or work functioning. The impairment should have appeared in childhood for the diagnosis to be made and may improve with age. Therefore, anyone applying for pilot licensing who has been diagnosed with this condition must undergo neuropsychological assessment to assess the likelihood of them being able to perform safely as a pilot. An individual with ongoing ADHD will not, by definition, be able to complete pilot training. Medication used for this disorder is normally disqualifying.

In Australia, the Civil Aviation Safety Authority (CASA) provides guidance for aeromedical examiners assessing applicants with a history of ADHD. CASA previously required pilot applicants with a history of ADHD to undergo neuropsychological testing both on and off medication for the purpose of documenting ongoing cognitive deficits associated with ADHD and whether the applicant requires medication treatment. However, in recent years CASA has discontinued the requirement for routine neuropsychological testing and has developed a protocol with greater emphasis on current clinical assessment against DSM criteria and current psychosocial functioning (Fitzgerald et al., 2011).

Current CASA ADHD guidance, which can be found on the CASA website (https://www.casa.gov.au), notes that the condition has aeromedical implications due to inattention and its effect on multitasking in aviation, with implications for working memory, situation awareness, task prioritization, task accomplishment, and time management. It is specified that ADHD may result in premature and/or ill-considered actions, restlessness, and excess of movement causing distraction, impulsivity with excessive involvement in speech, or activities resulting in errors, and that associated emotional dysregulation or effect of comorbid mental health conditions may have adverse impact on pilot performance. Active ADHD not in remission and the need for medication are considered risk factors. Applicants in full remission without need for any safety-relevant medication such as stimulants and who demonstrate disease-free status or stability (i.e., absence of symptoms for a minimum of 6 months after treatment completed) may be considered for aeromedical certification. CASA's risk assessment protocol requires review of detailed historical information, including the following: medical records medical records from date of diagnosis to the present (medical consultations and prescription of medications); an up-to-date assessment by the treating pediatrician or psychiatrist if available; completion by the pediatrician/psychiatrist and the chief flying instructor of an ADHD instructor's questionnaire regarding symptoms in the context of aviation; copies of academic records and employment history; copies of traffic infringements and criminal records; copies of any special investigations performed such as QEEG or neuropsychological testing; follow-up plan; and previous specialist reports if available.

CASA's guidance indicates that pilots granted aeromedical certification may be subject to annual review by an appropriate specialist on a case-by-case basis. Unrestricted certification is possible if it is documented that the pilot is in full remission without medication. Favorable factors identified include ADHD having been diagnosed in childhood and treated with no persisting symptoms without medication for at least the past 6 months, and adults with ADHD not on any treatment for at least 6 months. Unfavorable factors identified include ADHD symptoms persisting in adulthood, which results in an increased likelihood of impairing performance, and applicants having continuing ADHD requiring treatment.

The European Union Aviation Safety Agency (EASA) is an agency of the European Union (EU) with responsibility for civil aviation safety (https://www.easa.europa.eu). EASA regulations include psychological standards for flight crew, including psychological assessment of flight crew, as well as systematic and random testing of psychoactive substances to ensure medical fitness of flight and cabin crew members. However, EASA offers no specific guidance on ADHD in aircrew.

Clinical Aeromedical Assessment of Pilots With ADHD

Because ADHD is a disorder whose diagnosis is based upon subjective symptom report without objective biomarkers and one that can vary considerably in severity and developmental course across the affected individual's lifetime, aeromedical assessment of the condition is complex. Yet adequate aeromedical assessment of pilots with a history of ADHD is crucial because continuing active symptomatic ADHD results in serious risks of compromised aviation safety. This is likely to be an increasingly important topic in aviation and aerospace medicine in coming years, due to the increasing rates of ADHD diagnosis and treatment with ADHD medications, including some individuals who receive inaccurate diagnoses and some who inappropriately use stimulant medications.

Aviation neuropsychologists and other aeromedical examiners who assess pilots with a history of ADHD must be familiar with the guidance and specifications for assessment from the relevant aviation regulatory authority. While there are some differences in assessment protocols across different jurisdictions, there are many aspects of assessment that are important for all aeromedical evaluations of individuals with a history of ADHD. Broadly speaking, the goals of such evaluations include determination of whether the initial diagnosis of ADHD was accurate and was based upon an adequate evaluation, and whether the affected individual continues to experience active behavioral symptoms and cognitive deficits associated with ADHD that would be considered aeromedically disqualifying. The methods used to collect relevant information may include review of background information and historical records, clinical interviews with the pilot applicant and collateral sources of information if available, current mental status examination, administration of standardized ADHD symptom questionnaires to the pilot applicant and collaterals if available, and in some cases administration of neurocognitive and psychodiagnostic testing (Fitzgerald et al., 2011; Laukkala et al., 2017).

Was the initial diagnosis of ADHD accurate and based upon an adequate assessment? Examiners should inquire when and by whom the initial diagnosis of ADHD was made. It is important to discuss and specify the individual's symptoms or concerns at the time and why they (or their parents/guardians) brought the concerns to medical attention. Various clinical healthcare professionals may make diagnoses of ADHD and prescribe medication treatments for ADHD, based upon a wide range of clinical assessment practices (Adler & Alperin, 2015). Diagnoses of ADHD may be made by non-mental health specialists, such as pediatricians and family medicine practitioners, and increasingly by mid-level practitioners such as nurse practitioners and physician assistants. In our experience as aviation neuropsychologists in the clinic, it is common to encounter pilot applicants who received a diagnosis of ADHD and initiated treatment with stimulant medications as a child based only upon a brief clinical discussion between their parents and their pediatrician. Other individuals may receive diagnoses of ADHD and start stimulant medications as older adolescents or adults on the basis of similar cursory assessments, primarily for the purpose of enhancement of academic or work performance. On the other hand, if the individual had a thorough diagnostic workup with a psychologist, psychiatrist, or other mental health specialist, including objective testing and adequate consideration of differential diagnoses, one can have more confidence in the accuracy of the diagnosis at the time. Examiners should review original records from the initial diagnostic assessment for ADHD and all records relating to subsequent treatment.

An issue of paramount importance is determination of the extent to which ADHD has continued to affect the individual's current and recent functioning. Noting that a considerable proportion of individuals with ADHD experience full remission or a substantial reduction in symptoms as they mature into adulthood, it is possible that the individual may have had clear well-documented symptomatic ADHD as a child but may no longer experience impairing symptoms of the condition as an older adolescent or adult. Examiners can rely upon several sources of information in making this determination. A key question is whether the individual has had ongoing recent medication treatment for ADHD, which suggests active symptoms of the condition. It is recommended that both medical treatment records and pharmacy records for at least the last 4 years should be reviewed.

If the individual has required accommodations or other modifications or limitations in their academic or occupational functioning during recent years, this also suggests active symptoms of ADHD at the time. It is recommended that examiners should review academic records (e.g., Section 504 plans, Individualized Education Programs [IEPs], or other academic plans; school-based psychoeducational evaluations; tutoring reports; disciplinary action; all academic transcripts/report cards through the highest level of education achieved). Because ADHD has been associated with increased motor vehicle accidents, traffic violations, other impulsive behaviors, and comorbid conditions such as antisocial personality disorder, driver's license records from all states where the individual has held a license and criminal records from all states where the individual has resided are important sources of documentation.

There are additional sources of information unique to the aviation environment. If the individual has had flight training, an important source of documentation is a report from their certified flight instructor (CFI) documenting the following: evidence of operational flight experience to include emergency procedures; communication with air traffic control; ability safely to manipulate aircraft controls; crew–cockpit communication; and aeronautical decision-making. In addition to pilot training records from flight school, Laukkala et al. (2017) suggested review of additional sources of information, including simulator and line performance records; feedback from coworkers regarding erratic behavior, carelessness in carrying out procedures, or following checklists; evidence of disregard for or "bending" of standard operating procedures and rules; indications of inattention or impulsivity in training or line operations; and observations of unusual increased levels of physical activity, restlessness, or fidgeting suggestive of hyperactivity or difficulty tolerating boredom.

While neuropsychological testing is not a requirement for routine clinical diagnosis of ADHD, it may be helpful in aeromedical assessment of pilots with a history of ADHD and may be required by the relevant aviation regulatory authority depending upon the specifics of the case. Neuropsychological testing in such cases is useful in providing a standardized measurement of various cognitive abilities that may be affected by ADHD (e.g., focused and sustained attention, auditory/verbal and visual working memory, planning, mental flexibility, verbal and nonverbal fluency, and other executive functions). These domains are also relevant to aeromedical examinations for determining medical certification and have been implicated in aviation accidents, as discussed earlier. The goal of conducting neuropsychological testing is to identify any neurocognitive deficit or impairment that is aeromedically significant. Where available, use of appropriate pilot norms for neurocognitive tests is recommended, in addition to standard demographically corrected norms. Further, Kay (2013) noted that older pilots do not have the benefit of landing on "age-corrected runways" (i.e., all pilots must use the same equipment and perform the same tasks regardless of age). Therefore, it is helpful to compare the pilot's performance with both age-corrected and non-age-corrected pilot norms where available.

Finally, examiners should conduct a thorough differential diagnosis and assessment for comorbid conditions. The FAA notes that many applicants who disclose the diagnosis of ADHD and/or use of medication treatment for the condition may have a comorbid condition or a different condition that accounts for their symptoms (e.g., learning disability or another developmental disorder, traumatic brain injury, sleep disorder, psychiatric disorder, other behavior disorder) that may or may not be aeromedically disqualifying. There is a high rate of comorbidity between ADHD and substance use disorders (i.e., alcohol and other intoxicating substances, both illicit drugs and inappropriate use of pharmaceuticals). Therefore, special attention should be paid to a careful and detailed review of the pilot's substance use habits.

References

Adler, L.A., & Alperin, S. (2015). Diagnosing ADHD in adults in the primary care setting. In R.A. Barkley (Ed.), *Attention-deficit hyperactivity disorder: A handbook for diagnosis & treatment, fourth edition* (pp. 501–509). The Guilford Press.

American Psychiatric Association. (1980). *Diagnostic and statistical manual of mental disorders* (3rd ed.).

American Psychiatric Association. (2022). *Diagnostic and statistical manual of mental disorders* (5th ed., text revision). https://doi.org/10.1176/appi.books.9780890425787

Asherson, P., Buitelaar, J., Faraone, S.V., & Rohde, L.A. (2016). Adult attention-deficit hyperactivity disorder: Key conceptual issues. *The Lancet Psychiatry, 3*(6), 568–578. https://doi.org/10.1016/S2215-0366(16)30032-3

Asherson, P., Ramos-Quiroga, J.A., & Young, S. (2018). Adult ADHD clinical presentation and assessment. In T. Banaschewski, D. Coghill, & A. Zuddas (Eds.), *Oxford textbook of attention deficit hyperactivity disorder* (pp. 178–189). Oxford University Press. https://doi.org/10.1093/med/9780198739258.001.0001

Australian Transport Safety Bureau. (2006). Dangerous distraction: An examination of accidents and incidents involving pilot distraction in Australia between 1997 and 2004. *ATSB Aviation Research Investigation Report B2004/0324.* https://www.atsb.gov.au/publications/2005/distraction_report

Banich, M.T., Stokes, A., & Elledge, V.C. (1989). Neuropsychological screening of aviators: a review. *Aviation, Space, and Environmental Medicine, 60*(4), 361–366.

Barbaresi, W.J., Colligan, R.C., Weaver, A.L., Voigt, R.G., Killian, J.M., & Katusic, S.K. (2013). Mortality, ADHD, and psychosocial adversity in adults with childhood ADHD: A prospective study. *Pediatrics, 131*(4), 637–644. https://doi.org/10.1542/peds.2012-2354

Barkley, R.A. (2015). Emotional dysregulation is a core component of ADHD. In R.A. Barkley (Ed.), *Attention-deficit hyperactivity disorder: A handbook for diagnosis & treatment, fourth edition* (pp. 81–115). The Guilford Press.

Barkley, R.A., & Fischer, M. (2010). The unique contribution of emotional impulsiveness to impairment in major life activities in hyperactive children as adults. *Journal of the American Academy of Child & Adolescent Psychiatry, 49*(5), 503–513. https://doi.org/10.1016/j.jaac.2010.01.019

Bruchmuller, K., Margraf, J., & Schneider, S. (2012). Is ADHD diagnosed in accord with diagnostic criteria? Overdiagnosis and influence of client gender on diagnosis. *Journal of Consulting and Clinical Psychology, 80*(1), 128–38. https://doi.org/10.1037/a0026582

Brunkhorst-Kanaan, N., Libutzki, B., Reif, A., Larsson, H., McNeill, R.V., & Kittel-Schneider, S. (2021). ADHD and accidents over the life span – a systematic review. *Neuroscience & Biobehavioral Reviews, 125*, 582–591. https://doi.org/10.1016/j.neubiorev.2021.02.002

Canino, G., & Alegria, M. (2008). Psychiatric diagnosis – is it universal or relative to culture? *Journal of Child Psychology and Psychiatry, 49*, 237–250. https://doi.org/10.1111/j.1469-7610.2007.01854.x

Coghill, D., Toplak, M., Rhodes, S., & Adamo, N. (2018). Cognitive functioning in ADHD: inhibition, memory, temporal discounting, decision-making, timing and reaction time variability. In T. Banaschewski, D. Coghill, & A. Zuddas (Eds.), *Oxford textbook of attention deficit hyperactivity disorder* (pp. 94–102). Oxford University Press. https://doi.org/10.1093/med/9780198739258.001.0001

Cortese, S., Kelly, C., Chabernaud, C., Proal, E., Di Martino, A., Milham, M.P., & Castellanos, F.X. (2012). Toward systems neuroscience of ADHD: A meta-analysis of 55 fMRI studies. *American Journal of Psychiatry, 169*, 1038–1055. https://doi.org/10.1176/appi.ajp.2012.11101521

Curry, A.E., Yerys, B.E., Metzger, K.B., Carey, M.E., & Power, T.J. (2019). Traffic crashes, violations, and suspensions among young drivers with ADHD. *Pediatrics, 143*(6), 2018–2305. https://doi.org/10.1542/peds.2018-2305

Danielson, M.L., Bohm, M.K., Newsome, K., Claussen, A.H., Kaminski, J.W., Grosse, S.D., Siwakoti, L., Arifkhanova, A., Bitsko, R.H., & Robinson, L.R. (2023). Trends in stimulant prescription fills among commercially insured children and adults – United States, 2016-2021. *Morbidity and Mortality Weekly Report (MMWR), 72*(13), 327–332. https://doi.org/10.15585/mmwr.mm7213a1

Dismukes, R.K., Kochan, J.A., & Goldsmith, T.E. (2018). Flight crew errors in challenging and stressful situations. *Aviation Psychology and Applied Human Factors, 8*, 35–46. https://doi.org/10.1027/2192-0923/a000129

Dittmann, R., Hage, A., Pedraza, J.D., & Newcorn, J.H. (2018). Non-stimulants in the treatment of ADHD. In T. Banaschewski, D. Coghill, & A. Zuddas (Eds.), *Oxford textbook of attention deficit hyperactivity disorder* (pp. 293–401). Oxford University Press. https://doi.org/10.1093/med/9780198739258.001.0001

Faraone, S., Biederman, J., & Mick, E. (2006). The age-dependent decline of attention deficit hyperactivity disorder: A meta-analysis of follow-up studies. *Psychological Medicine, 36*(2), 159–165. https://doi.org/10.1017/S003329170500471X

Fitzgerald, D.J.P., Navathe, P.D., & Drane, A.M. (2011). Aeromedical decision making in attention-deficit/hyperactivity disorder. *Aviation, Space, and Environmental Medicine, 82*(5), 550–554. https://doi.org/10.3357/ASEM.2889.2011

Groom, M.J., van Loon, E., Daley, D., Chapman, P., & Hollis, C. (2015). Driving behaviour in adults with attention deficit/hyperactivity disorder. *BMC Psychiatry, 15*(175), 1–11. https://doi.org/10.1186/s12888-015-0566-y

Gualtieri, C.T., & Johnson, L.G. (2008). Medications do not necessarily normalize cognition in ADHD patients. *Journal of Attention Disorders, 11*(4), 459–469. https://doi.org/10.1177/1087054707305314

Hinshaw, S.P., & Scheffler, R.M. (2018). ADHD in the twenty-first century: Biology, context, policy, and the need for integrative perspective. In T. Banaschewski, D. Coghill, & A. Zuddas (Eds.), *Oxford textbook of attention deficit hyperactivity disorder* (pp. 9–15). Oxford University Press. https://doi.org/10.1093/med/9780198739258.001.0001

Hinshaw, S. P., & Scheffler, R. M. (2014). *The ADHD explosion: Myths, medication, money, and today's push for performance.* Oxford University Press.
Hinshaw, S. P., Scheffler, R. M., Fulton, B. D., Aase, H., Banaschewski, T., Cheng, W., Mattos, P., Holte, A., Levy, F., Sadeh, A., Sergeant, J. A., Taylor, E., & Weiss, M. D. (2011). International variation in treatment procedures for ADHD: Social context and recent trends. *Psychiatric Services, 62*(5), 459–464. https://doi.org/10.1176/ps.62.5.pss6205_0459
Hoffmann, C. C., Hoffmann, K. P., & Kay, G. G. (1998). The role that cognitive ability plays in crew resource management (CRM). In *The Research and Technology Organization (RTO) of the North Atlantic Treaty Organization (NATO): RTO-MP-4.* https://www.researchgate.net/publication/267402686_37-l_THE_ROLE_THAT_COGNITIVE_ABILITY_PLAYS_IN_CRM
Jensen, R.S. (1982). Pilot judgment: Training and evaluation. *Human Factors, 24*(1), 61–73. https://doi.org/10.1177/001872088202400107
Kay, G. G. (2013). Aviation neuropsychology. In C. H. Kennedy & G. G. Kay (Eds.), *Aeromedical psychology* (pp. 239–268). Ashgate. https://doi.org/10.1201/9781315565811
Kessler, R., Lane, M., Stang, P., & Van Brunt, D. (2009). The prevalence and workplace costs of adult attention deficit hyperactivity disorder in a large manufacturing firm. *Psychological Medicine, 39*(1), 137–147. https://doi.org/10.1017/S0033291708003309
King, J. A., Georgemiller, R. J., & Kay, G. G. (2021, October 8–10). *Introduction to aviation neuropsychology* [Virtual conference presentation]. 19th Annual Conference of the American Academy of Clinical Neuropsychology.
Klein, R. G., Mannuzza, S., Olazagasti, M. A. R., Roizen, E., Hutchison, B. A., Lashua, M. A., & Castellanos, X. (2012). Clinical and functional outcome of childhood attention-deficit/hyperactivity disorder 33 years later. *Archives of General Psychiatry, 69*(12), 1295–1303. https://doi.org/10.1001/archgenpsychiatry.2012.271
Laukkala, T., Bor, R., Budowle, B., Sajantila, A., Navathe, P., Sainio, M., & Vuorio, A. (2017). Attention-deficit/hyperactivity disorder and fatal accidents in aviation medicine. *Aerospace Medicine and Human Performance, 88*(9), 871–875. https://doi.org/10.3357/AMHP.4919.2017
Libutzki, B., Neukirch, B., Kittel-Schneider, S., Reif, A., & Hartman, C. A. (2023). Risk of accidents and unintentional injuries in men and women with attention deficit hyperactivity disorder across the adult lifespan. *Acta Psychiatrica Scandinavica, 147*(2), 145–154. https://doi.org/10.1111/acps.13524
Michielsen, M., Semeijn, E., Comijs, H., Van de Ven, P., Beekman, A., Deeg, D., & Kooij, J. (2012). Prevalence of attention deficit hyperactivity disorder in older adults in the Netherlands. *The British Journal of Psychiatry, 201*(4), 298–305. https://doi.org/10.1192/bjp.bp.111.101196
National Aeronautics and Space Administration. (2015). *Effects of acute stress on aircrew performance: Literature review and analysis of operational aspects.* (NASA STI Program Reort). https://ntrs.nasa.gov/citations/20190002685
Nikolas, M. A., & Burt, S. A. (2010). Genetic and environmental influences on ADHD symptom dimensions of inattention and hyperactivity: A meta-analysis. *Journal of Abnormal Psychology, 119*(1), 1–17. https://doi.org/10.1037/a0018010
Polanczyk, G., de Lima, M. S., Horta, B. L., Biederman, J., Rohde, L. A. (2007). The worldwide prevalence of ADHD: A systematic review and metaregression analysis. *American Journal of Psychiatry, 164,* 942–948. https://doi.org/10.1176/ajp.2007.164.6.942
Porges, C., & Gropp, T. (2018, September 21–24). *Airline pilots: Relevant cognitive and personality variables* [Conference presentation]. Aeromedical Psychology Seminar, Denver, Colorado, USA.
Romo, L., Sweerts, S., Ordonneau, P., Blot, E., & Gicquel, L. (2021). Road accidents in young adults with ADHD: Which factors can explain the occurrence of injuries in drivers with ADHD and how to prevent it? *Applied Neuropsychology: Adult, 28*(3), 372–377. https://doi.org/10.1080/23279095.2019.1640697
Rubia, K., Alegria, A., & Brinson, H. (2014). *Imaging the ADHD brain: disorder-specificity, medication effects and clinical translation, Expert Review of Neurotherapeutics, 14*(5), 519–538. https://doi.org/10.1586/14737175.2014.907526
Ryckaert, C., Kuntsi, J., & Asherson, P. (2018). Emotional dysregulation and ADHD. In T. Banaschewski, D. Coghill, & A. Zuddas (Eds.), *Oxford textbook of attention deficit hyperactivity disorder* (pp. 103–117). Oxford University Press. https://doi.org/10.1093/med/9780198739258.001.0001

Saitzyk, A.R., Alfonzo, C.A., Greydanus, T.P., Reaume, J.R., & Parsa, B.B. (2013). U.S. military standards and aeromedical waivers for psychiatric conditions and treatments. In C.H. Kennedy & G.G. Kay (Eds.), *Aeromedical psychology* (pp. 125–158). Ashgate. https://doi.org/10.1201/9781315565811

Safer, D.J. (2016). Recent trends in stimulant usage. *Journal of Attention Disorders, 20*(6), 471–477. https://doi.org/10.1177/1087054715605915

Shaw, P., Malek, M., Watson, B., Greenstein, D., de Rossi, P., & Sharp, W. (2013). Trajectories of cerebral cortical development in childhood and adolescence and adult attention-deficit/hyperactivity disorder. *Biological Psychiatry, 74*(8), 599–606. https://doi.org/10.1016/j.biopsych.2013.04.007

Simon, V., Czobor, P., Balint, S., Meszaros, A., & Bitter, I. (2009). Prevalence and correlates of adult attention-deficit hyperactivity disorder: Meta-analysis. *The British Journal of Psychiatry, 194*(3), 204–211. https://doi.org/10.1192/bjp.bp.107.048827

Sobanski, E., Banaschewski, T., Asherson, P., Buitelaar, J., Chen, W., Franke, B., Holtmann, M., Krumm, B., Sergeant, J., Sonuga-Barke, E., Stringaris, A., Taylor, E., Anney, R., Ebstein, R.P., Gill, M., Miranda, A., Mulas, F., Oades, R.D., Roeyers, H., Rothenberger, A., Steinhausen, H.C., & Faraone, S.V. (2010). Emotional lability in children and adolescents with attention deficit/hyperactivity disorder (ADHD): Clinical correlates and familial prevalence. *Journal of Child Psychology and Psychiatry, 51*, 915–923. https://doi.org/10.1111/j.1469-7610.2010.02217.x

Solanto, M.V. (2015). Executive function deficits in adults with ADHD. In R.A. Barkley (Ed.), *Attention-deficit hyperactivity disorder: A handbook for diagnosis & treatment* (4th ed., pp. 256–266). The Guilford Press.

United States Air Force. (2023). *United States Air Force aerospace medicine waiver guide compendium.* https://www.afrl.af.mil/Portals/90/Documents/711/USAFSAM/Air%20Force%20Waiver%20Guide_230101.pdf

United States Navy. (2019). *Aeromedical reference and waiver guide.* https://www.med.navy.mil/Navy-Medicine-Operational-Training-Command/Naval-Aerospace-Medical-Institute/Aeromedical-Reference-and-Waiver-Guide/

Visser, S.N., Danielson, M.L., Bitsko, R.H., Holbrook, J.R., Kogan, M.D., Ghandour, R.M., Perou, R., & Blumberg, S.J. (2014). Trends in the parent-report of health care provider-diagnosed and medicated attention-deficit/hyperactivity disorder: United States, 2003–2011. *Journal of the American Academy of Child & Adolescent Psychiatry, 53*(1), 34–46. https://doi.org/10.1016/j.jaac.2013.09.001

Wilens, T.E., Isenberg, B.M., Kaminski, T.A., Lyons, R.M., & Quintero, J. (2018). Attention-deficit/hyperactivity disorder and transitional aged youth. *Current Psychiatry Reports, 20*, 100. https://doi.org/10.1007/s11920-018-0968-x

Willcutt, E.G. (2012). The prevalence of DSM-IV attention-deficit/hyperactivity disorder: A meta-analytic review. *Neurotherapeutics, 9*, 490–499. https://doi.org/10.1007/s13311-012-0135-8

Wolraich, M., & Subcommittee on Children and Adolescents with Attention-Deficit/Hyperactive Disorder. (2019). Clinical practice guideline for the diagnosis, evaluation, and treatment of attention-deficit/hyperactivity disorder in children and adolescents. *Pediatrics, 144*(4), Article e20192528. https://doi.org/10.1542/peds.2019-2528

World Health Organization. (2016). *International statistical classification of diseases and related health problems* (10th ed.). https://icd.who.int/browse10/2016/en

World Health Organization. (2019). *International statistical classification of diseases and related health problems* (11th ed.). https://icd.who.int/

Yeung, A., Ng, E., Abi-Jaoude, E. (2022). TikTok and attention-deficit/hyperactivity disorder: A cross-sectional study of social media content quality. *Canadian Journal of Psychiatry, 67*(12), 899–906. https://doi.org/10.1177/07067437221082854

Chapter 29
Dreaming to Fly and the Neuropsychological Reality

Case Studies in ADHD and ASD

Alastair L. Gray

Introduction: Borderline Cases

This chapter will focus on three very different case studies. All are desperate to fly, either as a private pilot or commercially. All present with symptomatology that could be problematic in the safety-critical environment that is a cockpit and all have diagnoses that reflect a presentation that could be disqualifying. In such cases, the stakes are high; should the report present favorable conclusions, the pilot is more likely to be allowed to pursue their dream, but should the report present a less favorable outcome, dreams are shattered (but aviation and the wider public remain protected). Borderline cases such as these therefore present the aviation psychologist with some of the most challenging circumstances to consider. No assessment is ever based solely on data, but in these cases the importance of considering both the data obtained but also the circumstances in which they were collected, the history of the case in question, and how the diagnosis may play out under the stress of modern-day aviation should not be underestimated. Given that an individual's future rests (maybe not entirely on the outcome of the neuropsychological assessment, but substantially so) on the data obtained at assessment and presented in an aviation neuropsychology report, the importance of submitting compelling evidence that stands up to scrutiny cannot be overstated. Such borderline cases have dreams to fly and escape the humdrum existence of their day-to-day lives, but the obstacles that stand in their way are the regulatory requirements associated with cognitive assessment as a result of their diagnoses. This could be the last roll of the dice. They know this and so should the aviation neuropsychologist.

The Context: Post-COVID

Following the COVID-19 pandemic, many of us have re-evaluated our lives. The way we work, consume, and socialize has changed from pre-pandemic days. A quick look at how we now use office space, the rise in cost of domestic holiday destinations, and the profits being made by online retail point to fundamental changes in society that may very well not be reversible. From my own perspective as a part-time aviation psychologist and part-time clinical psychologist working in neuropsychological rehabilitation for people with traumatic brain injury, one of the biggest changes that I have encountered is the sudden and marked lack of available individuals willing to work as support workers or rehabilitation assistants. Prior to the onset of the COVID-19 pandemic, it was usually the case that a support worker could be identified within a couple of months of an advert being placed in relevant agencies. Today, waits of over 12 months are not uncommon, and while this could be expected in more rural locations where the pool of suitable candidates is understandably shallower, given that we are also finding this shortage to be evident in the United Kingdom's two biggest cities, something more fundamental is clearly afoot. While the flow of cheaper eastern European labor has been affected by both the war in Ukraine and the United Kingdom's departure from the European Union (also known as Brexit), the COVID-19 pandemic has indirectly resulted in significant changes in the labor market.

In 2022, the UK Government's Economic Affairs Committee reported (in an uncharacteristically whimsically entitled report, "Where have all the workers gone?") that, in combination with the COVID-19 pandemic, UK citizens are part of an aging population that is retiring early. The report states that in October 2022, there were 565,000 more economically inactive 16- to 64-year-olds than before the start of the pandemic (Economic Affairs Committee, 2022). Amid the vast uncertainty following the pandemic, a recent survey of more than 9,000 UK workers reported that 65% of individuals looking for employment now prioritize a better work–life balance over pay and benefits (Randstad, 2021). In a more recent article, a drift away from office-based employment toward more flexible roles was reported with particular growth evident in transportation and logistics (Reuters, 2023), while another report indicates that changes in the labor market are associated not only with the COVID-19 pandemic, but also the fact that Generation Z (those born between 1995 and 2010) are now entering the workforce and have very different expectations and demands than their predecessors (Fernandez et al., 2023). As one commentator noted, "all over the world, the pandemic highlighted to workers that something had to change. And they started resigning from their jobs in droves. They were tired of being underpaid, overworked and treated as disposable" (Randstad, 2022, p. 2). Unfortunately, this latter quote referred to the recruitment challenges facing the aviation industry in a post-pandemic landscape that saw a massive loss of workers from an industry that was already experiencing a skills shortage. The Randstad report indicates the need for the aviation industry to start "appealing to young people from an early age," and this seems to be happening, with airlines offering added benefits, paying large signing on bonuses, and even offering cash rewards to current workers who recommend a friend (Edwards, 2022). In short, the global labor market has shifted seismically after the COVID-19 pandemic and aviation has not been immune. Indeed, it was one of the biggest casualties. Having been brought to its knees by nationally imposed COVID lockdowns and international travel restrictions, airlines continue to try to fill vacancies by targeting individuals who are new to the job market (Woods, 2022). A quick Internet search will bring up pages of news articles that talk about how desperate airlines are for new air and cabin crew and what opportunities await those individuals who wish to take to the skies.

From the perspective of an aviation neuropsychologist, I have noted (so far only on an anecdotal basis) an increase in the referral of individuals who are now seeing these new opportunities in aviation as a personal opportunity to turn a lifelong interest in aviation into a viable career. These same individuals come to our attention as a result of requiring psychological and neuropsychological assessments as a result of a preexisting conditions, such as an autistic spectrum disorder (ASD) or attention-deficit/hyperactivity disorder (ADHD). Interestingly, all such referrals could be considered as belonging to Generation Z, and it is tempting to speculate that the recent traumatizing effects of the COVID-19 pandemic detailed in previous paragraphs have reinforced the desire for a positive work–life balance whereby people seek employment in an area that coincides with a passion rather than taking a more "mundane" career path. This is of course speculative, and it is probably too soon to be making judgments regarding changes in applicants to airlines on a post-pandemic basis, but it is an interesting hypothesis for future research and one that may be relatively easily underpinned by data from airline human resource departments. It is also a hypothesis that is underpinned by the fact that, prior to the COVID-19 pandemic, referrals such as those described here were very thin on the ground.

From a regulatory perspective in terms of ASD, the UK's Civil Aviation Authority (CAA) note that as a result of potential conflicts between symptoms associated with ASD and the crew resource management environment of the modern professional airline cockpit, it is essential that applicants with ASD undergo psychological assessment before embarking upon a career in aviation. Similarly, for ADHD the CAA states that anyone applying for a license who has been diagnosed with this condition must undergo neuropsychological assessment to evaluate the likelihood of a candidate being able to perform safely as a pilot, with medication used for this disorder being normally disqualifying (UK Civil Aviation Authority, 2023).

The following case studies describe three typical referrals that fit the above conditions and criteria. All three present as cases with ASD, with one presenting with concurrent ADHD. Interestingly, while all present in slightly different ways, clear similarities are evident, although outcomes in all three are very different. A background to each case is provided alongside an outline of the report's conclusions and recommendations. Given that neuropsychological assessment test tools must remain confidential and not be disseminated into the wider public domain, no mention will be made of specific tests used, but broad outline descriptions of areas of cognitive functioning will be provided.

Case A: 22 Years Old at Assessment

Case A was referred to our clinic on the advice of the patient's aeromedical examiner, who recommended psychological and neuropsychological assessment following a diagnosis of ASD. Case A told me that they had received a diagnosis of ASD in 2011 with a number of follow-up appointments that, to use their words, "narrowed down the diagnosis to Asperger's syndrome." Following this revised diagnosis, Case A was reviewed routinely 1 year later, but was then discharged from the specialist service and no further follow-ups were offered or sought. Unfortunately, due to the passage of time (12 years), no paperwork concerning the assessment or diagnostic process followed was available, although Case A's family doctor was able to confirm what the patient described at assessment. Case A did not report any other particular difficulties other than being briefly prescribed an antidepressant at the point where their parents were separating. Case A described that time as very difficult but that over subsequent years, their relationship with their parents returned to normal and Case A had discontinued antidepressant medication well before the current assessment took place. No other mental or physical health issues were recorded.

From a personal perspective, Case A told me that their current job as a telecommunications engineer was very enjoyable and they had been in the post for approximately 3 years. Case A told me that they enjoy the customer-facing role of their job, and although occasionally they found that they misinterpreted what was being said to them, they reported no difficulties at work. Case A told me that the management style of the company that they work for is "quite intense," but that Case A managed potentially stressful engineering situations by ensuring that "it is done right first time." From what Case A was saying, there seemed to be some evidence of communication issues, with them admitting that occasionally they misunderstood what was being said to them, and a certain adherence to the rules regarding telecommunication engineering and getting things "done right first time." Both observations would be consistent with the diagnosis, but certainly as far as the latter is concerned, not necessarily a negative!

From an educational perspective, Case A attended college until 18 years of age, studying engineering, and had originally wanted to work in aerospace engineering, but instead followed an alternative interest in electronics. Case A continued to follow their interest in aviation outside of work and came for assessment as a result of wanting to obtain their private pilot's license with a view to possibly working part-time in a commercial setting if the opportunity arose. At the time of the assessment, Case A had clocked up 29 hr in a light aircraft at a local flying club, and I understand that there were no difficulties or concerns being expressed by the flying school.

Away from telecommunications engineering and aviation, Case A reported that they had just returned from a holiday with friends from high school, they enjoy socializing with them, attend the local gym regularly, are a light drinker, and smoke up to 10 cigarettes per day (although they expressed an intention to quit). Case A reported no particular difficulties in terms of cognition, and day-to-day functioning was completed without any reports of difficulty. This was backed up somewhat by background information provided by Case A's family doctor and a brief report from their flying club.

In terms of general observations at assessment, Case A's presentation was entirely unremarkable in that they were attentive, cooperative, and pleasant throughout the assessment. In terms of the assessment itself, evaluations of intelligence, memory, language, attention, and executive functioning were all completed. Case A's performance on assessments of intelligence indicated high levels of functioning with the exception of some slower processing styles under certain circumstances. In particular, where scores were lower, Case A's performance was characterized by a failure to develop a strong response strategy, which then hindered their ability to give relatively quick responses. While accuracy was not significantly affected, with many of the slow responses being as accurate as fast ones, the overall pace at which they were delivered was more pedestrian than would have been ideal. That said, the issues identified were not statistically significant and could be reasonably characterized as a trait or a trend in the data collected.

It is of note that the CAA specifically state that a candidate with ASD may be able to acquire the skills necessary to function safely as a pilot or air traffic controller, and this report concluded that Case A was one such individual. In terms of recommendations, the report suggested that Case A would benefit from some support in the development of cognitive strategies to aid ongoing revision for flying exams and overall flight training that could major upon their methodical response style, without significantly impacting upon their ability to learn to fly, or impact upon the future ability to safely operate an aircraft at a private pilot's license level. In terms of recommendations, the report suggested that Case A would benefit from some support in the development of cognitive strategies to aid ongoing revision for flying exams and overall flight training that could major upon their methodical response style, without significantly impacting upon their ability to learn to fly, or impact upon the future ability to safely operate an aircraft at a private pilot's license level. Whether the slow and/or more methodical response style is compatible with the requirements of commercial aviation remains open for debate and represents a different question for further down the line. Overall, the report concluded that Case A should be considered for medical certification upon receipt of a report from their flying instructors, commenting specifically on the candidate's ability to process information both on the ground and in the cockpit. The report concludes that should there be any suggestion of difficulties, this would be consistent with some aspects of the current neuropsychological assessment and it would then be up to the aeromedical examiner to conclude as to whether or not the candidate is appropriate for medical certification. I later learned that the candidate had been cleared by their flying school and no difficulties have been noted, with them subsequently gaining medical certification.

In this case, I suspect that Case A will probably not progress to commercial aviation, (although in discussions with them, they were entirely happy to fly as a private pilot) but what this case highlights is the fact that a potentially problematic diagnosis does not necessarily result in the ending of the dream to fly. This is in contrast to Case B.

Case B: 23 Years Old at Assessment

I suspect that most readers of this chapter, if they are in patient-facing roles, will be familiar with a scenario where they receive a referral and, no matter what information accompanies the referral in terms of background or is provided as a result of further enquiries, the initial gut feeling is that something is "off." While I am not in the habit of relying upon gut feeling, generally speaking if my gut tells me that something isn't right, it usually isn't. In Case B, the initial referral came on the patient's aeromedical examiner's advice. Unusually, much of the background investigation that had been completed prior to a referral to us had been completed in another country, making it more difficult to obtain certain aspects of Case B's medical history. Despite significant pre-assessment attempts to obtain additional information from Case B, only the briefest of outlines was available prior to offering an assessment appointment, and as the individual concerned was not a UK national, they were also not well known to their aeromedical examiner, who could provide little more by way of background. In conversation with the CAA, they were similarly finding a somewhat patchy medical history, and if a government department could have a gut reaction, reading between the lines of their communications they were having a negative one.

What was understood was that Case B had been diagnosed with ASD by a psychiatrist in their home country (date unspecified), and that this diagnosis meant that they required further psychological assessment. In pre-assessment emails, Case B was very clear in their desire to fly commercial aircraft and when we responded by advising that their diagnosis may mean that they were unable to pursue their chosen career path, Case B very reasonably pointed out that they would like to ascertain one way or the other as to whether or not their diagnosis limited future career options. Consequently, an assessment appointment was offered.

At assessment, Case B stated that they had had a long-standing interest in aviation and that their aim was to, firstly, obtain their private pilot's license with a view to, secondly, becoming a commercial pilot in the future. Interestingly, Case B had identified the aircraft types that they would like to fly commercially and had also identified the airline that they would like to fly for. At the time of the assessment, however, Case B was living in the north of England where they described their day-to-day activity as being consumed by "studying aviation." When asked about what else they were doing with their time (e.g., as far as employment was concerned), Case B stated that they were considering a part-time job as a bus or truck driver. I understand that day-to-day living expenses were covered by family members in the patient's home country, but Case B stated that they had been advised that this was not going to be an ongoing arrangement and that they needed to gain paid employment in the relatively near future. Observationally, this employment plan (fly for a major international airline or drive a bus) felt somewhat chaotic and possibly unrealistic in nature and potentially inconsistent with a role in a safety-critical environment.

In terms of background health history, Case B told me that they had been diagnosed with ASD by a psychiatrist in their home country (date unspecified) and that they no longer had the paperwork to go with this diagnosis. Case B also told me that when they were younger (approximately 10 years old, but again date unspecified), they had been assessed as a result of some behavioral issues that their parents were noting. When asked what these behavioral issues consisted of, Case B stated that they related to their behavior at school and in particular difficulties concentrating in class. In conjunction with the somewhat haphazard approach to potential future employment, I started to wonder if there were particular issues relating to attention or more broadly ADHD. I asked if there were any further assessments that Case B had not yet shared with us, the aeromedical examiner, or the CAA, and the patient admitted that they had also been diagnosed with ADHD in their home country and had been prescribed methylphenidate. Unfortunately, Case B could not recall who had completed the ADHD assessment and that they had been unable to find a copy of the report relating to this diagnosis. In 2020, Case B stated that they had a further assessment relating to ADHD, and that methylphenidate was again prescribed. It was unclear as to why Case B had stopped taking methylphenidate in their childhood, but that they restarted on the advice of a consultant psychiatrist, who assessed Case B in 2020. Upon disclosing this information, Case B was asked if they were still taking methylphenidate, and they replied that they only take it when they "have a lot of work on." The patient was asked why they thought that varying the dose was an appropriate course of action, given the drug's very clear prescribing guidelines, and Case B answered that taking it on a regular basis was "too heavy" for them. Upon pressing further, Case B admitted that they had taken 10 mg of methylphenidate (despite the prescription being for 60 mg daily) before our appointment. When asked how often Case B took methylphenidate, they replied that they took it possibly 75 % of the time, but that they tended to vary the dose as they saw fit. Given that Case B had described the prescribed dose as "too heavy," I asked whether this dose had ever been reviewed, and Case B stated that they did not see the need as they were able to vary the dose according to what they needed. I stated that methylphenidate is a drug that would probably mean that they could not gain medical certification to learn to fly, and Case B stated that they would therefore manage without it. We went on to discuss what it felt like when the patient did and did not take their medication (either as prescribed or on some other arbitrary basis), and Case B stated that when they do not take the medication, impacts on memory are noticeable. Specifically day-to-day matters are forgotten and concentration is affected. Case B was very clear that they did not think their medication or diagnosed conditions would affect their ability to fly and insisted on proceeding with the neuropsychological assessment.

Case B denied any other health conditions or difficulties, but given the problems experienced in obtaining a reliable and consistent health history and the possibly evasive approach taken to providing pre-assessment information to either our clinic or the CAA, confidence in this statement was low.

During the assessment phase of the appointment, elements of impulsivity were very evident in terms of response style. By way of example, it was noted that Case B had a tendency to start responding to a question or a test item before task instructions had been concluded, and on one occasion started helping themselves to test items when these had not been provided for them. Impulsivity was also present on other assessments, which hindered the patient's ability to take in all information before responding, and where impulsivity was not an issue, concentration was, with difficulties in focusing upon the task in hand also being evident. In short, Case B presented as either easily distracted or very impulsive and this was backed up by the data obtained in testing. In several areas of evaluation, data indicated that the patient was presenting with significant attentional difficulties that would be consistent with a diagnosis of ADHD. Certain memory tests exhibited an extremely inconsistent response style, which was consistent with the lack of concentration on the assessments in question and this was consistent with what was noted anecdotally during testing. Other subtests indicated a marked lack of attention to detail where any assessment requiring a written or drawn response were characterized by a careless and hastily executed answer that often failed to meet basic criteria for a "full answer." Additional poor processing of information provided at the start of each assessment contributed to what was a cognitive profile that would be inconsistent with any role that required concentration, even at its most basic level.

As part of the conclusion to this case, the report noted that the patient had a current prescription for methylphenidate. Case B had admitted to choosing when they did and did not take this medication and when taken, the dose was varied according to what the patient thought was appropriate. Not following prescription guidance suggests, at the very least, poor judgment and should the patient have believed that the dose was not correct for them, an entirely reasonable course of action would be to expect the patient to seek a follow-up appointment for review. No such follow-up had taken place, and not engaging in any follow-up appointments concerning conditions such as ADHD, when they are as poorly controlled as in this case, is a source of serious concern. The haphazard approach to medication adopted by this patient cannot maximize anyone's chances of doing themselves justice in a cognitive assessment, but the lack of judgment, both in the run-up to this assessment and also in managing day-to-day health issues, is also of concern.

The assessment noted that there were a number of question marks over the cognitive profile obtained (more accurately, one big question mark over the whole thing), and in conjunction with the behavior observed during testing and the background information received regarding medication and diagnosed conditions, it would be concerning if this client was issued with any class of medical certification. In short, Case B presented with no convincing evidence to suggest that they should be considered for a role in a safety-critical environment. Indeed, I would be concerned if they were offered any role that fell within the vague proximity of a safety- critical environment.

Case C: 21 Years Old at Assessment

Case C was an interesting referral in that it appeared to represent a situation when expected procedures had not been followed prior to the case being referred to our clinic. Specifically, Case C contacted us following a recommendation made by their current aeromedical examiner indicating that they required psychological and neuropsychological assessments due to a diagnosis of ASD being made. From the information that Case C gave us, this diagnosis had been disclosed when they were applying for their Class 2 medical certificate a number of years ago, but despite this disclosure, no further investigation into the diagnosis was made and the Class 2 medical certificate was granted. Initially, it was believed that the diagnosis of ASD had been made after the Class 2 medical certificate had been granted, but it transpired that the diagnosis was made when Case C was approximately 3 years of age. Given that the CAA state very clearly that it is essential for an applicant with ASD to undergo an assessment by a psychologist, it is unclear how this case initially slipped through the net with a Class 2 medical certificate being granted without the necessary assessments completed.

At the initial assessment, Case C stated that they had held a Class 2 medical certificate for some years and in total had 100 hr solo flight time. Their Class 2 medical certificate has expired but given that they were wanting to transition into commercial aviation, they were forgoing the renewal of their Class 2 in favor of seeking Class 1 certification.

In terms of background to Case C, from a cognitive perspective they told me that they did not think that they had any particular difficulties, although they did state that they tend to take what people say very literally. Clearly, this could be a difficulty in the safety-critical environment of a cockpit, and when we discussed this in assessment, Case C stated that they were not aware of any difficulties in their current workplace environment as a member of cabin crew for a major European carrier, although they did state that they still tend to take what other people say at face value. Case C stated that they were very conscious of this difficulty, and consequently were aware of the potential issues surrounding communication. No other communication processing or cognitive issues were reported in the assessment by Case C.

From a health perspective, Case C told me that they were diagnosed with ASD at the age of 3 years, and although initially requiring significant levels of support in school, it was understood at assessment that they transitioned to mainstream schooling at the age of approximately 5 years where minimal, and ultimately no further, input or support was required. Case C progressed through their school career and in 2021 completed their A levels where grades A through D were acquired. Case C then took 1 year off to focus on flying, and it is during this time that they gained considerable experience in aviation (although they had gained their Class 2 medical certification in 2018).

In terms of their current career path, Case C stated that they were currently working for a major European carrier as a member of cabin crew on short- and medium-haul flights. Case C told me that they currently enjoyed this work and also stated that they really enjoyed the perks that came with the job. In addition to the cabin crew role, Case C told me that they also work as the operations controller for their flight school.

Away from aviation, Case C told me that they enjoy music (in particular piano and music production, which they release on apps such as SoundCloud and YouTube), enjoy spending time with former school friends, and had recently traveled to Iceland with this same friendship group. Case C told me that they try to remain fit and healthy by going to the gym on a weekly basis, and I understand that Case C was in a relationship at the time of the assessment. In terms of observations during assessment, Case C's presentation was entirely unremarkable and they engaged appropriately throughout the assessment phase of our appointment.

From the perspective of data obtained from our neuropsychological evaluations, Case C presented with relative strengths in a number of cognitive domains, both in terms of general intelligence and aspects of verbal memory. Executive functioning screening tests were good and in line with both estimates of cognitive functioning, but also in line with their performance on other assessments that were presented verbally. This was in contrast to Case

C's performance when information was presented visually, where functioning was lower than would be expected. While it would be unfair to say that visually presented information was always interpreted inaccurately, there were more inaccuracies in visually processed information than in verbally processed information. It was also noted that where measures could be derived, there was a processing speed issue associated with visually based assessments. From an observational perspective, it was noted that when Case C was completing visually based assessments, they did so in an often-idiosyncratic way, which meant that information was missed or was not affectively processed in the first place. The slow pace at which this information was often accurately processed meant that not only were fewer items completed on some subtests, but accuracy rates were variable under other subtests and overall response rates were lower than when information was presented verbally.

In any safety-critical environment, information needs to be processed in a timely manner, data need to be assimilated effectively, and appropriate courses of action need to be implemented without undue delay. It is difficult to see how these processes can be supported when significant levels of impairment, such as those described in this case, have been identified. In particular, the data obtained through visually presented subtests may indicate that significant issues could arise if Case C found themselves at a time-sensitive, safety-critical decision point. The recommendations from this case suggested that the candidate should carefully consider their next career steps in relation to the cognitive profile obtained, and that the aeromedical examiner makes the findings of the neuropsychological assessment known should the candidate revert to renewing their Class 2 medical certification instead of proceeding with their Class 1 application. This case highlights potential issues associated with the sometimes fragmented circumstances of aeromedical assessment in the United Kingdom when compared with other jurisdictions. In this case, it is clear that the requirements of the CAA were either not followed or not recognized at the time of the initial Class 2 application. Although no serious fallout from the decision to grant a Class 2 medical certificate had resulted, not following the very clear recommendations made by the CAA illustrates how easy it is for cases to fall through the recommendation net.

Conclusion

The preceding sections have described three cases that fall under broadly similar diagnostic umbrellas but at assessment presented with markedly different conclusions as a result of the data obtained alongside the differing backgrounds, histories, and observations during testing. All three cases presented with ASD, and while underlying expected themes (such as speed of processing or communication issues) were identified, the assessments summarized in this chapter highlight a number of observations. Specifically, while the diagnosis can be the same, the presentation can be very different from individual to individual, with very different conclusions drawn and consequences for the individual concerned. Case A presented with a neuropsychological profile that was broadly unremarkable, but where additional information concerning in-flight performance would be desirable before the aeromedical examiner drew conclusions. Case B highlighted the importance of any form of mental health assessment in marginal cases such as this where confidence in the candidate's ability to function within a safety-critical environment without threat to themselves or others is low, while Case C highlighted the need for procedures to be adhered to so that individuals presenting with potentially problematic symptomatology are identified at the earliest opportunity, thereby protecting both themselves and the wider public.

In addition, all three cases highlight why the importance of gaining clear histories and outlines of current presentations is vital. Where there is a lack of clarity, the aviation neuropsychologist needs to ask why and whether or not this person is an appropriate individual to be considering a flying career. The bar is set necessarily high in aviation, and if neuropsychological assessment leads to doubt that an individual can function in the safety-critical environment that is aviation, then there is no doubt; subsequent conclusions will almost certainly ground them.

In terms of broader conclusions concerning whether we are seeing a different type of referral emerging that reflects a post-pandemic landscape, I suspect that an "N" of 3 can only provide the start of a conversation. What can be concluded is that we are receiving more of these referrals than we did prior to the COVID-19 pandemic. Additionally, given that it is well documented that the UK public have changed the way that they are prepared to work, what working environments they are willing to accept, the benefits that they see as holding value, and the industries that they are willing to work in, is the airline industry able to effectively tap into these new pools of labor? While recent recruitment drives by airlines appear to be doing just this, is this a response (by the airline) and a reaction (by working age adults) that represents a post-pandemic blip or does it represent a longer-term trend? If it is the latter, the airline industry will need to be sufficiently agile to adapt to and survive in this significantly different post-pandemic recruitment landscape.

References

Economic Affairs Committee. (2022, December). *Where have all the workers gone?* House of Lords, UK Government. https://www.parliament.uk/business/lords/media-centre/house-of-lords-media-notices/2022/december-2022/where-have-all-the-workers-gone/

Edwards, J. (2022, June 22). Air New Zealand offers cash incentives to attract workers after Covid exodus. *The New Zealand Herald*. https://www.nzherald.co.nz/business/air-new-zealand-offers-cash-incentives-to-attract-workers-after-covid-exodus/7UPGCWU5VS7UEBTYTGSJPSB2P4/

Fernandez, J., Landis, K., & Lee, J. (2023, January 18). Helping Gen Z employees find their place at work. *Harvard Business Review*. https://hbr.org/2023/01/helping-gen-z-employees-find-their-place-at-work

Randstad. (2021). *Employer brand research: 2021 global report*. https://workforceinsights.randstad.com/hubfs/REBR%202021/Randstad-Employer-Brand-Research-Global-Report-2021.pdf

Randstad. (2022). *The recruitment challenges in the aviation industry post-pandemic*. https://www.randstad.co.uk/market-insights/aviation/recruitment-challenges-aviation-industry-post-pandemic/

Reuters. (2023). *The post-pandemic workforce*. https://www.reuters.com/graphics/USA-ECONOMY/OCCUPATIONS/znpnbrlwjpl/

UK Civil Aviation Authority. (2023). *Neurodevelopmental conditions: Dyslexia, Aspergers syndrome and attention deficit hyperactivity disorder*. https://www.caa.co.uk/aeromedical-examiners/medical-standards/pilots/conditions/mental-health/dyslexia-asperger-syndrome-and-adhd/

Woods, B. (2022, November 11). How airlines plan to create a new generation of pilots at time of crisis. *CNBC*. https://www.cnbc.com/2022/11/11/how-airlines-plan-to-create-new-generation-of-pilots-at-time-of-crisis.html

Chapter 30
Learning Disabilities in Aviation Neuropsychology

Daniel N. DaSilva and Jason A. King

Introduction

Although the impact of specific learning disabilities (SLDs) and their impact on the academic functioning of children and adolescents has been broadly and extensively researched, their impact on adults and more specifically in aviation are far less understood. For example, much is known of SLDs and their manifestations in both adaptive functioning and their presentations in formal assessment (Fletcher & Grigorenko, 2017). Similarly, aerospace neuropsychology continues to develop a broader understanding of neurocognitive functioning and its relationship to operational demands in aviation (Kay, 2013; Taylor et al., 2000;) Yet, the nexus between SLDs and aviation neuropsychology has not been well studied.

Importantly, these disabilities represent levels of functioning well below expectation for the individual's age and, with some exceptions, often manifest during the early elementary school years. In the most recent edition of the *Diagnostic and Statistical Manual of Mental Disorders* (DSM-5-TR; American Psychiatric Association, 2022), an SLD is a clinical diagnosis of a neurodevelopmental disorder that interferes with the individual's ability to acquire and apply academic skills. The diagnosis is further refined by identifying specific subtypes including dyslexia, dysgraphia, and dyscalculia. Dyslexia manifests in difficulties with spelling, reading/decoding, and comprehension. Dysgraphia presents as difficulties with letter formation/handwriting, use of proper grammar and punctuation, and written expression. Finally, dyscalculia can manifest as difficulties with number sense, mathematical reasoning, and difficulties applying mathematical concepts in problem-solving.

Alternatively, the *International Classification of Diseases 10th Edition* (ICD-10; World Health Organization [WHO], 2016) included "Specific developmental disorders of scholastic skills" with ICD-10 and subtypes of specific reading disorder, specific spelling disorder, disorder of arithmetical skills, and mixed types. The diagnostic category was renamed "Developmental learning disorder" in the more recent ICD-11 (WHO, 2019). This classification system specifies four subtypes including impairments in reading, written expression, mathematics, and other specified impairment of learning.

Incidence

The incidence of learning disabilities varies greatly and depends largely on classification systems and methodologies in assessment and identification. However, the United States' National Health Interview Survey, 2016–2018 (National Center for Health Statistics, 2018) found 13.8 % of children in the 3–17 years age range had been diagnosed with either ADHD or learning disability. That national survey also showed that non-Hispanic Black children were more likely to be diagnosed with either disorder (16 %) versus non-Hispanic White (14.7 %) or Hispanic (11.9 %) children. That said, it is generally accepted that the incidence of learning disabilities among school-age children can range from 5 % to 15 % of young learners. Furthermore, 32 % of children receiving special education services in the United States were identified with SLD as the primary disability (National Center for Education Statistics, 2023).

According to the US National Center for Education Statistics (NCES, 2023), there were 7.3 million students receiving special education and related services during the 2021–2022 period, representing a rebound to pre-pandemic levels. SLDs accounted for 32 % of all students receiving services followed by speech or language impairment (19 %), other health impairment (15 %), and autism (12 %). This analysis also identified some racial disparities, with the highest incidence among American Indian/Alaska Native students (19 %) and Black students (17 %). The lowest rate was noted among Pacific Islander (11 %) and Asian (8 %) students (NCES, 2023).

In a large group of school-based special education administrators, significant differences between US regions and school districts were found (Lockwood et al., 2022). Differences in methodologies of identification included curriculum-based methodologies, particularly in districts that use a response to intervention (RTI) approach (Lockwood et al. 2022). It is also important to note that while most learning disability research emerges from English-speaking cultures, disorders of reading and written expression extend across cultures and orthographies (Brunswick, 2010; Pugh et al., 2006).

Among the predominant SLD categories, dyslexia is estimated to be present in 7 %–16 % of the population, depending on assessment cutoffs. For a variety of developmental and statistical reasons, there is a slightly greater predominance of males versus females with dyslexia (Pennington et al., 2019). On the other hand, prevalence rates of math disabilities have ranged from 3 % to 6 %, with some indications that sensitivity under newer DSM-5 criteria will increase the prevalence (Pennington et al., 2019). However, it has been pointed out that most (85 %) individuals identified with a learning disability have a reading disability and upwards of 20 % of the population have dyslexia (Shaywitz et al., 2021). Nevertheless, the overall ranks of students receiving special education services for math disabilities remains far lower than reading disabilities, as those students are less likely to be referred for services.

Given the narrow scope of this chapter focusing on aeromedically significant conditions, only the more widely accepted disorders of reading and mathematics will be reviewed. Other conditions such as non-verbal disabilities and disorders of written expression may be considered in the future.

Identification

As already noted, significant variability among diagnostic methodologies and systems of identification exist. For example, some identifications are based solely on a brief medical examination and history, while others are based on a more extensive psychoeducational assessment or even more elaborate and probing neuropsychological assessments. As one would expect, the definitions of both the presence and severity of the identified disorder will vary depending on the assessment methodology. In some corners, the largely discredited achievement-ability discrepancy model is still utilized, a method that fails to capture some of the more subtle and atypical learning disorders. Nevertheless, that commonly used method yields a reading disability rate of about 7% of the general population. The different methodologies can also fail to account for severity with the milder presentations resolving prior to adulthood.

The identification of SLD has moved beyond the long-standing discrepancy model of lower academic achievement relative to intellectual functioning (Taylor et al., 2017). In fact, the identification of a learning disability presumes the presence of overall normal-range intelligence. Moreover, learning disability is not necessarily limited to the early education/elementary school years but can manifest in secondary and post-secondary years as well as in the occupational setting (Scanlon, 2013). Those later manifestations often impact higher-level processing and skills (Scanlon, 2013).

The US 2020 re-authorization of the Individuals With Disabilities Education Act (IDEA, 2018, Sec. 300.8 [a]) defines learning disability as:

> A disorder in one or more of the basic psychological processes involved in understanding or in using language, spoken or written, that may manifest itself in the imperfect ability to listen, think, speak, read, write, spell, or to do mathematical calculations, including conditions such as perceptual disabilities, brain injury, minimal brain dysfunction, dyslexia, and developmental aphasia.

The act specifically excludes, "learning problems that are primarily the result of visual, hearing, or motor disabilities, of intellectual disability, of emotional disturbance, or of environmental, cultural, or economic disadvantage."

There is strong consensus among practitioners that individuals with SLDs present with a pattern of psychological processing weaknesses and strengths (Hale et al., 2010). Furthermore, it is important to underscore that low achievement alone is not indicative of SLD nor are SLDs by necessity associated with intellectual disability. In fact, as noted, SLDs commonly present in the context of overall normal intellectual abilities. Moreover, assessment approaches should also account for comorbid conditions such as attention-deficit/hyperactivity disorder (ADHD), other learning disabilities, and other conditions that would preclude an SLD diagnosis such as sensory impairments, intellectual disability, or environmental and cultural factors.

Reading Disabilities/Dyslexia

The diagnosis of dyslexia for the purposes of educational classification often encompasses the broad range of reading-related disorders including word decoding and recognition, reading fluency, and the higher-level function of reading comprehension. The widely accepted phonological theory of dyslexia is based on the notion that the development of phonological awareness and the eventual development of sound-symbol relationship awareness underlies the accurate decoding of written words. In turn, the development of word recognition and reading fluency is facilitated. However, as summarized by Peterson and Pennington (2022), this theory fails to account for individuals who exhibit phonological deficits but do not exhibit a reading disorder and, conversely, those who do not have the related deficits but do exhibit deficiencies in reading.

Shaywitz and Shaywitz (2007) summarized that students with dyslexia exhibit a failure of the left occipitotemporal or word form region. While this region continues to develop normally in typical readers, individuals with dyslexia develop a region somewhat more posterior medial and associated with a more memory-based system of learning. This in turn suggests that dyslexic individuals develop a mechanism of memorization of words in their printed form rather than mechanisms based on phonology (Shaywitz & Shaywitz, 2007).

Regardless of the underlying process, the individual with dyslexia struggles with single-word reading/decoding. Reading fluency is also disrupted and the overall core challenges can, in turn, disrupt reading comprehension. However, it is important to underscore that weaknesses in reading comprehension are not a necessary component of dyslexia but can manifest as a secondary deficiency.

As a neurodevelopmental disorder, early signs of dyslexia and reading disability can emerge early during the preschool and kindergarten years. Those learners will often exhibit the initial struggles in establishing sound-symbol (letter-sound) relationships. These children often exhibit broader challenges with speech and language that emerge earlier in development. Delays in first words, short phrases, and full sentences are common precursors that may be detected early on by parents, pediatricians, and daycare and preschool teachers. If identified early enough, the child may be eligible for Early Intervention Program (IEP) services available up to the age of 36 months. These services can include developmental, speech, occupational, and physical therapy services.

By elementary school age, teachers may express concerns regarding word decoding and recognition skills, which, in turn, often lead to recommendations for formal assessment. In the United States, school-based assessments can determine eligibility for special education and related services as per IDEA. While beyond the scope of this chapter, intervention services often include research-based, multimodal, and multisensory techniques, many of which focus on word-attack techniques (Ritchey & Goeke, 2006). By the early to late teen years, reading fluency can remain weak and struggles with reading can become more apparent especially if there are comorbid, higher-level language disturbances.

Into adulthood, multiple studies have focused on a variety of topics including job satisfaction, employment earnings, social adjustment, and self-concept as well as factors related to "success" in the young adult years (Katz et al., 2001). The review pointed out that while the effects of reading disorders can persist into later life, the severity and impact can lessen over time. On the other hand, long-term social/emotional outcomes may also be significant with some indications that outcomes may be more problematic for women than for men.

As already discussed, early challenges with phonological knowledge and phonological manipulation represent one aspect of weak neurocognitive functioning in dyslexia and can be a particularly strong predictor of reading ability. Additional neurocognitive deficiencies may include rapid naming and automaticity, higher-level language and vocabulary, auditory comprehension, nonverbal processing speed, short-term memory, and deficiencies in the attention/executive matrix (Fletcher & Grigorenko, 2017; Pennington et al., 2019).

Math Disorders/Dyscalculia

Although the body of learning disability research focuses predominantly on reading disorders, the focus on math disabilities is increasing. It also stands that math disabilities are less frequently identified as the majority of referrals for learning disability assessments are for the reading/language-based disorders. In general, math disabilities typically comprise deficits in computation or problem-solving or both. From the developmental perspective, the emergence of basic math skills and reasoning follows the developmental stages theorized by Piaget. The process follows the progression of concrete, numerical concepts and abilities and culminates in abstract and metacognitive skills (Ojose, 2008). The progression of math skills development in accordance with Piaget's theory has also been shown to coincide with the development of related neuroanatomical regions (Houdé et al., 2011). Implicated regions include bilateral parietofrontal networks specifically involved in numerical and executive functions.

More recent research has identified reduced white matter coherence and shorter tract length of the left superior longitudinal/arcuate fasciculus and left anterior thalamic radiation in a group with developmental dyscalculia. These findings were then associated with the lower math performance (Ayyıldız et al., 2023). The authors concluded that learning, memory, and language-related pathways in the left hemisphere might be related to developmental dyscalculia in children. Numerous other regions have been implicated in math abilities including the bilateral inferior parietal lobules and areas of bilateral prefrontal cortex (Arsalidou & Taylor, 2011; Dehaene, 2003).

In terms of manifestations in adaptive functioning, math deficiencies present as performances that fall significantly below age expectations on standardized assessments. Because early instruction focuses predominantly on numerical knowledge and basic math facts and concepts, initial deficiencies are more evident in computational math and numerical operations. As development progresses into adolescence and young adulthood, math demands become increasingly abstract with a shift to mathematical reasoning and problem-solving, with greater demands on executive and visuospatial abilities.

In adulthood, Katz et al. (2001) describe that the more problematic presentations of devel opmental math disabilities emerge when the cognitive demands of mathematics courses exceed the student's limited capability. As such, it is common for the disorder to first be identified later in life such as college age. Vocational challenges can also emerge for the first time when adults transition to occupations placing greater demands on math abilities (Katz et al., 2001). Associated cognitive deficiencies include general intellectual abilities, working memory, processing speed, and general language abilities (Pennington et al., 2019).

Any discussion of math disability should include mention of nonverbal learning disability (NVLD; Rourke, 1989). A syndrome that, while not specifically listed in formal diagnostic systems, is recognized by many clinicians as a syndrome comprised of poor social perception, difficulties with abstraction, and impairments in spatialization abilities, poor spatial problem-solving, and academic deficits in mathematics. Conversely, these individuals typically present with intact reading and writing skills, despite initial lags, and intact rote learning skills. The syndrome implicates non-dominant, right hemisphere deficits and can have both acquired and developmental etiologies (Rourke, 1989).

Comorbidities

As with most developmentally based disorders, comorbidities are common. For example, there is a high rate of comorbidity of learning disorders with ADHD in adolescence and adulthood (Jakobson & Kikas, 2007; Klein et al., 2012; Sexton et al., 2012). Math disabilities also frequently co-occur with primary language impairments. The SLDs also frequently co-occur with each other (Archibald et al., 2013).

Cognitive Demands of Flying

As has been discussed in other chapters, operation of aircraft is a complex activity that requires a range of physical and mental abilities and learned skills. It has long been recognized that most aviation accidents are due to pilot error and that it is therefore essential that pilots possess intact cognitive abilities as a component of aeromedical fitness to safely operate an aircraft (Jensen, 1982). In their review of the literature including psychological task analysis, Banich et al. (1989) identified multiple cognitive abilities required for piloting: perceptual-motor abilities; spatial abilities; working memory; attention; planning and sequencing abilities; and processing flexibility (e.g., executive abilities including inhibition, selective attention, fluency, and conceptual reasoning/problem-solving).

Taylor et al. (2000) generated a series of composite scores derived from the CogScreen-Aeromedical Edition (Kay, 1995), a computerized battery to assess aeromedically relevant cognitive functions, which they related to flight simulator performance. Using a regression analysis, they found four strong predictors of simulator performance. The strongest predictor was a combined cognitive speed and working memory factor, which accounted for 33 % of the variance in flight performance. The other factors included motor coordination, visual association memory, and tracking. A second study added an attribute identification factor. Predicted flight parameters included maintaining course, communications, traffic avoidance, cockpit monitoring, and approach.

As suggested by the Taylor et al. (2000) study, the correlated flight parameters place different demands on cognitive functioning. All pilots are familiar with the adage, "aviate, navigate, and communicate." Aviating involves controlling the attitude and flight path of the aircraft. Operating a complex machine in three-dimensional space requires intact executive functions (e.g., planning, judgment, decision-making, prioritizing tasks, divided attention, allocating attention resources, impulse control, and emotional regulation). Navigating requires continuous determination of the aircraft's position and course and draws upon a range of cognitive abilities including executive functions such as planning as well as math and visual-spatial abilities. Communicating involves making and receiving radio communications with air traffic controllers (ATC) and others. In active air spaces, pilots hear constant communications of ATC with other aircraft. Pilots continuously monitor frequencies and detect when their identification number is called by ATC, requiring working memory, sustained attention vigilance, selective attention, and auditory discrimination.

Dismukes et al. (2018) studied 12 airline accidents and identified 212 errors that were then categorized into eight groups, which included inadequate comprehension/interpretation/assessment, poor management of competing task demands, inadvertent omission of required actions, inadequate or improper communication, inadequate/improper execution of tasks, inadequate physical execution of action, and failure to acquire information. Performance degradation in the presences of increased stress was a component, and implicated cognitive functions included decision-making, working memory, auditory comprehension, and verbal communication.

Automation and computer-assisted flight have become an integral part of aviation from small recreational and general aviation aircraft to the most sophisticated airliners and military aircraft. However, for the foreseeable future, there will continue to be demands that draw on core academic achievement areas and cognitive abilities.

Most math demands have been vastly reduced in aviation due to automation, flight management systems (FMS), and even handheld devices (e.g., tablets, calculators, electronic E6Bs). However, the failure of any of these aides may require the modern pilot to draw on mathematical computation and even reasoning skills during flight. For example, the need to calculate descent and fuel consumption rates may certainly arise. The reading of checklists particularly under stress may also arise, as well as reading output from the FMS. That said, typical major, regional, and small carrier pilot demands can include operating the "glass" cockpit itself, the FMS, in addition to the ubiquitous checklists and radio communications. These associated demands can increase exponentially in single-pilot operations where all demands fall on the one pilot thereby increasing the need for multitasking. In the world of general/recreation flight there can be an ever-widening array of available aides and instruments, and as in single-pilot commercial operations, the general aviation pilot also faces the increased working memory and multitasking demands associated with ATC communications and other concurrent task management.

Every pilot is familiar with the ever-present checklists associated with his or her aircraft. Familiarity with and repetition of checklists as well as standard memory items certainly reduce the load on reading fluency and comprehension. The computational demands are less frequently called upon due to automation but are, nevertheless, taught to every pilot in the ground school training. However, certain situations (i.e., in-flight emergencies) may present increased cognitive loads in a pilot with limited "bandwidth" for processing information. It is in these situations in which more limited psychological processes associated with learning disabilities may emerge, interfering or limiting the pilot's ability to process critical information in a critical situation.

According to 14 CFR, § Part 61.96, US pilots must be able to read, speak, write, and understand the English language (Aeronautics and Space, 2023). These requirements must be met for student, private, sport, recreational, commercial, and airline transport pilot certifications. Reading with varying comprehension demands for all pilots include reading FAA regulations, flight plans, aircraft operating manuals, flight evaluation reports, preflight checklist, FAA notices (NOTAMS), aircraft gauges and instruments, maintenance logs, and weather charts.

Beyond those routine demands, Robert Elliott examined the reading level of selected manuals and tests using the Flesch–Kincaid reading grade-level formula (Kincaid, et al. 1975). In a survey of basic and common reading requirements, grade level requirements spanned the 8th to 11th grades. For example, the recreational pilot examination and private pilot examinations have reading grade-level requirements of 8.1 and 9.3, respectively. The Cessna 172 Operating Handbook has a reading grade level requirement of 11.2 and commercial aircraft documents span the 8th to 10th grade levels (Elliott & DaSilva, 2021).

On the other hand, math problem-solving and computational demands can also be quite varied. Pilots may be required to perform calculations, computations, and to "think mathematically," which can involve flight-related functions such as calculating weights and balances; operating a calculator or mechanical E6B flight computer; estimating sizes, distances, quantities, time, and costs; calculating fuel consumption; analyzing charts and graphs, the effects of wind on performance, and altitude; calculating angles; performing corrections to heading; and even converting units between different measurement systems.

Policies of Aviation Authorities on Learning Disabilities

Federal Aviation Administration (FAA) Order 8080.6H (2017) specifies the conduct of the Airman Knowledge Test and presents specific guidelines for applicants with learning or reading disabilities. Specifically, applicants are allowed one of three available accommodations. Pilots can request one and a half times the standard allotted time for completion of the test. Alternatively, if the applicant chooses not to use one of these two accommodations, they can elect to use a member of the testing site to assist in reading specific words or terms, without additional explanations, from the test questions. In order to avail themselves of these accommodation options, the applicant must provide physician documentation verifying that the applicant has a learning or reading disability. Beyond these provisions, the FAA specifies no other disqualifications or necessary waivers associated with SLDs. However, aside from ADHD, the US federal regulations have no specific procedures in assessments to address SLDs in flight crew other than consideration of possible co-occurring disabilities in individuals with ADHD or other neurodevelopmental disorders.

With regard to mandated reporting, the FAA's standard application for airman medical certification (FAA Form 8500-8; FAA, 1999), Item 18 (medical history), Part m (mental disorders) of the 8500-8 is the only opportunity for an applicant to report any condition such as SLD, ADHD, or other developmental disorder. However, many applicants do not recognize the need to endorse that item as they often fail to recognize ADHD as a mental disorder. As such, it becomes incumbent on the aviation medical examiner (AME) to properly query the applicant regarding the presence of possible disqualifying conditions not reported on the form.

US military service branches recognize and address SLDs somewhat differently. For example, the US Air Force presumes that individuals with learning disabilities, which typically manifest in childhood and require remedial services, are unlikely to be able to successfully complete rigorous military aviation training. As such, learning disabilities are considered disqualifying for Flying Class One (FC1). On the other hand, the individual can be considered for FC1 if the prospective pilot can demonstrate passing academics without medication or strong job performance off medication for a period of no less than 12 months. The US Air Force requires documentation of the severity and nature of the disorder as well as comorbid psychiatric conditions made during childhood recognizing that some disorders are unfounded or unsubstantiated following careful review of the history (United States Air Force, 2023).

The US Navy, on the other hand, considers waivers for learning disorders under the category of neurodevelopmental disorders (2021). The US Navy recognizes that SLDs may be associated with abnormalities in cognitive processing, such as deficiencies in academic abilities, visual processing, or language processing. Associated aeromedical significance can depend on the severity of the condition which can, in turn, "jeopardize both safety and mission execution in the highly dynamic aviation environment" (US Navy, 2022, Psychiatry-4, first paragraph). However, while not specifically disqualifying, the severity and nature of the SLD needs to be documented and any residual challenges or history of persistent SLD requires neuropsychological assessment. As with the US Air Force standard, the US Navy requires a careful review of history including a review of grades and transcripts. However, the US Army also considers SLDs to be disqualifying but provides no waiver process at present (Department of the Army, 2019).

In the United Kingdom, the UK Civil Aviation Authority (CAA, 2023; https://www.caa.co.uk) specifically addresses dyslexia, recognizing it is a "long-term impairment" that can exert adverse effects on the individual's day-to-day functioning. The CAA further recognizes that individuals with dyslexia are entitled to "reasonable adjustments." However, the CAA does not consider accommodations or modifications to be reasonable for pilots meeting flight operations. Therefore, if an individual can complete training including the required written work, that person will be considered to have demonstrated reading and writing ability sufficient to safely perform the duties of pilot. On the other hand, if the pilot cannot demonstrate those abilities without assistance, the CAA concludes that there is no reasonable adjustment with current technology that would enable the individual to safely pursue aviation duties.

Although the Australian Civil Aviation Safety Authority (CASA) provides specific guidance for aeromedical examiners regarding ADHD, CASA lists no specific policy regarding SLDs. Pilots with a history of ADHD were previously required to undergo neuropsychological testing. However, the current CASA standard discontinues the requirement for routine neuropsychological testing and follows a protocol of detailed examination of presenting history and clinical assessment of current symptoms (CASA; https://www.casa.gov.au).

The European Union Aviation Safety Agency (EASA; https://www.easa.europa.eu), the regulatory aviation agency of the European Union offers no specific guidance on SLDs in aircrew. While EASA regulations include psychological standards for flight crew, it specifies general psychological assessment requirements of flight crew as well as systematic and random testing of psychoactive substances to ensure medical fitness of flight and cabin crew members.

While there is considerable variability between agencies on how the issue of SLDs is addressed, there are some common themes. Among several agencies, there is recognition that the manifestation of challenges associated with SLDs in aircrew is disqualifying for the safe operation of aircraft. The US military services, in particular, specify the need for the absence of symptoms at the time of certification and, in some cases, for a period of time preceding consideration for medical certification. In addition, the absence or resolution of symptoms is demonstrated by the absence of need for accommodations or modifications while maintaining adequate academic achievement. Formal assessment, although less common, may also be conducted in order to satisfy certification requirements. A thorough clinical review of the academic and developmental history may also be required.

Clinical Aeromedical Assessment of Pilots With SLDs

As noted previously, there is no mandated reporting of SLDs on the FAA form 8500-8, other than the voluntary request for accommodations on the written examinations as per FAA Order 8080.6H. Similarly, there is no mandated reporting among the other civil authorities. Given the vague reporting requirements across the civil agencies and military organizations, the deleterious impacts of SLDs may more typically arise during the selection, routine testing, and training of aircrew. However, it would stand to reason that SLD-related performance or training failures would account only for the more pronounced and persisting SLDs. This leaves the more subtle manifestations of SLDs secondary to the underlying neurocognitive deficiencies in pilots and pilot applicants. These more subtle presentations may represent the gradual maturation and spontaneous accommodation to the adaptive demands of the SLD while still possessing the psychological processing weaknesses associated with their SLD.

Given these circumstances, the identification of SLDs and associated psychological processing weaknesses is often left to the AME or other evaluators. Often in the course of assessing other reportable conditions, such as ADHD, traumatic brain injury, or substance use disorders, or even in assessing flight performance or training issues, a history of learning disorder may come to light. The history may become known during the course of a clinical interview with an AME or with an evaluating psychologist. In such instances, additional records may be requested, in order to review academic performance and grades, as well as diagnostic tests to shed light on the possible severity of the preexisting SLD.

In other instances, the presence of an SLD may come to light as a result of diagnostic test performance for an already-reported condition such as ADHD. Furzer et al. (2022) found that children who were young for their grade are more likely to be incorrectly diagnosed with ADHD. In addition, the high degree of co-occurrence of reading disorder and ADHD (estimated to be between 15% and 45%) raises the possibility that a given individual identified with one of these disorders could be experiencing comorbidity with both disorders present.

Careful interview and, more so, review of records at the time of the aeromedical ADHD assessment may yield indications of an SLD warranting further investigation. Evidence of an SLD may also emerge in the course of formal assessment for ADHD or one of the other reportable conditions. For example, weaknesses on measures of math reasoning or computation may yield evidence of a preexisting math disorder that, in turn, may be associated with language, executive, or working memory deficits. Similarly, performance on measures of phonological fluency, difficulties comprehending math word problems, and rapid naming may hint at the possible presence of latent reading/decoding, fluency, and comprehension issues. In fact, several subtests of the CogScreen-AE (Kay, 1995) are particularly sensitive to the deleterious effects of SLDs including subtests tapping math problem-solving, visual matching of letter and number sequences, visuomotor letter sequencing, and the reading and execution of simple instructions. Associated measures of traditional neuropsychological batteries are similarly sensitive to those deficits.

Should it become necessary to further explore the possibility of SLDs and associated psychological processes based on interview, history, or other incidental findings, a proper assessment of aeromedically significant domains should be considered. Since a discussion of the relative merits or weaknesses of specific measures is beyond the scope of this chapter, only areas and domains to be assessed will be discussed.

As already suggested, a clear accounting of the pilot's early history is necessary. As much as possible, that history should include an examination of early developmental factors. Risk factors can include challenges in the acquisition of approximate and symbolic number systems, automaticity, and number sense. Additional general cognitive risk factors can include general intelligence, early language functioning, processing speed, and working memory – all of which are, in and of themselves, potentially aeromedically significant. Other early risk factors include difficulties in development of phonological awareness, rapid naming, verbal and nonverbal processing speed, short-term memory, vocabulary, verbal fluency, and early speech/sound disorders. While some of this information may be available in existing records of prior evaluations, the use of collateral informants such as parents may also be particularly helpful.

In the US education system, special education and related services may be provided, particularly in the government-funded public school systems. Students in those settings may receive special education services as provided in Individualized Education Plan (IEP) or an accommodation plan under Section 504 of the IDEA (2018/2020). Those documents will delineate the needs of the student as well as the services, accommodations, and modifications provided at varying points in the educational process. Those services will often be based on standardized educational and cognitive/psychological assessments performed either by the school district or by outside, private clinicians. Over the course of the educational process, a student may undergo several triennial evaluations as mandated by code (IDEA, 2018/2020). A review of these documents will show evidence of the severity of the presenting condition as well as its trajectory in terms of resolution of accommodation. Collection of academic records should include transcripts of grades and report cards, which may include valuable teacher comments and input.

In terms of formal assessment, a comprehensive neuropsychological battery to assess for aeromedically significant deficiencies is necessary. Evaluation should include assessment of auditory and visual working memory functions, sustained attention, processing speed, and verbal output modulation and fluency. Executive functions including deductive and abstract reasoning and cognitive flexibility, as well as core language and visuospatial abilities, should be assessed. Visual and verbal memory functions including semantic and rote memory functions may also be assessed. Additionally, general intellectual functioning as well general psychological functioning should be part of a complete battery.

With regard to educational assessment, a comprehensive battery will adequately assess reading, writing, and math skills. With regard to reading, necessary components include word reading/recognition, phonological decoding, reading comprehension, and reading fluency. Assessment of math skills necessarily assesses automaticity and fluency, computational math skills, and math reasoning/problem-solving.

Aviation neuropsychologists and other aeromedical examiners who assess pilots with a history of possible neurodevelopmental disorders must be familiar with the guidance and specifications for assessment from the relevant aviation regulatory authority. While there are some differences in assessment protocols across different jurisdictions, there are many aspects of assessment that are important for all aeromedical evaluations of individuals with possible neurocognitive impairment.

In general, the records review and standardized testing will be the cornerstones of the determination in most settings.

Ultimately, the task of the aviation neuropsychologist is to determine the extent to which the SLD in and of itself or the associated psychological processes are still present and to what extent they represent a risk, if any, to aviation safety. As with many neurodevelopmental conditions (i.e., autism, ADHD, speech/language disorders), attenuation of functional challenges may come about as a function of the maturation process. It is also possible that the individual may have had well-documented challenges as a child but may no longer experience impairing symptoms of the condition as an older adolescent or adult. An essential question in the evaluation process is the extent to which the applicant has continued to utilize academic assistance later in schooling, suggesting the persistence of active symptoms of the condition. One caveat is the student who continues to rely on accommodations long after their need for those accommodations has passed. More contemporaneous and timely information may also be given by the applicant's certified flight instructor (CFI), provided that flight training has started. The CFI may be able to provide documentation of operational flight experience to include emergency procedures, communication with air traffic control, ability to safely manipulate aircraft controls, crew-cockpit communication, and aeronautical decision-making.

While neuropsychological testing is not a requirement for routine clinical diagnosis of SLDs, assessment may be necessary in the aeromedical assessment of pilot applicants with significant histories and may be required by the relevant aviation regulatory authority depending on the specifics of the case. Where available, use of appropriate pilot norms for neurocognitive tests is recommended, in addition to standard demographically corrected norms. Further, Kay (2013) noted that older pilots do not have the benefit of landing on "age-corrected runways" (i.e., all pilots must use the same equipment and perform the same tasks regardless of age). Therefore, it is helpful to compare the pilot's performance with both age-corrected and non-age-corrected pilot norms where available.

Conclusion

Finally, with increasing awareness of neurodiversity in the workplace (Chambers, 2022) and increasing identification of SLDs and co-occurring conditions, it is expected that the aviation neuropsychologist will encounter more applicants who present with significant histories warranting further assessment before consideration for medical certification. At the same time, with increasing focus of SLDs in adults, more research examining the presence of SLDs among certified air crew and related performances may become increasingly necessary as more individuals enter the pilot ranks.

References

Aeronautics and Space, 14 C.F.R., § 61.96 (2023). https://www.ecfr.gov/current/title-14

American Psychiatric Association. (2022). *Diagnostic and statistical manual of mental disorders* (5th ed., text revision). https://doi.org/10.1176/appi.books.9780890425787

Archibald, L.M.D., Oram Cardy, J., Joanisse, M.F., & Ansari, D. (2013). Language, reading, and math learning profiles in an epidemiological sample of school age children. *PloS One, 8*(10), Article e77463. https://doi.org/10.1371/journal.pone.0077463

Arsalidou, M., & Taylor, M.J. (2011). Is 2+2=4? Meta-analyses of brain areas needed for numbers and calculations. *NeuroImage (Orlando, Fla.), 54*(3), 2382–2393. https://doi.org/10.1016/j.neuroimage.2010.10.009

Ayyıldız, N., Beyer, F., Üstün, S., Kale, E.H., Mançe Çalışır, Ö., Uran, P., Öner, Ö., Olkun, S., Anwander, A., Witte, A.V., Villringer, A., & Çiçek, M. (2023). Changes in the superior longitudinal fasciculus and anterior thalamic radiation in the left brain are associated with developmental dyscalculia. *Frontiers in Human Neuroscience, 17,* Article 1147352. https://doi.org/10.3389/fnhum.2023.1147352

Banich, M.T., Stokes, A., & Elledge, V.C. (1989). Neuropsychological screening of aviators: A review. *Aviation, Space, and Environmental Medicine, 60*(4), 361–366.

Brunswick, N. (2010). Unimpaired reading development and dyslexia across different languages. In N. Brunswick, S. McDougall, & P. de Mornay Davies (Eds.), *Reading and dyslexia in different orthographies* (pp. 131–154). Taylor & Francis Group. https://doi.org/10.4324/9780203858462

Chambers, B. (2022, May 27). Neurodiversity is diversity: Why companies should hire more neurodivergent employees. *Forbes.* https://www.forbes.com/sites/forbescommunicationscouncil/2022/05/27/neurodiversity-is-diversity-why-companies-should-hire-more-neurodivergent-employees/

Dehaene, S. (2003). Acalculia and number processing disorders. In T.E. Feinberg & M.J. Farah (Eds.), *Behavioral neurology and neuropsychology* (2nd ed., pp. 207–215). McGraw-Hill.

Department of the Army. (2019). *Army regulation 40-501, standards of medical fitness.* https://armypubs.army.mil/epubs/DR_pubs/DR_a/ARN37720-AR_40-501-002-WEB-4.pdf

Dismukes, R. K., Kochan, J. A., & Goldsmith, T. E. (2018). Flight crew errors in challenging and stressful situations. *Aviation Psychology and Applied Human Factors, 8*(1), 35–46. https://doi.org/10.1027/2192-0923/a000129

Elliott, R., & DaSilva, D. (2021). *FAA aviation psychology seminar* [Virtual seminar]. Federal Aviation Administration. https://faavideo.zoomgov.com/j/16045711094

Federal Aviation Administration. (1999). *Form 8500-8 – Application for Airman Medical Certificate or Airman Medical & Student Pilot Certificate.* https://www.faa.gov/forms/index.cfm/go/document.information/documentID/185786

Federal Aviation Administration. (2017). *Order 8080.6H – conduct of airman knowledge tests.* https://www.faa.gov/documentLibrary/media/Order/FAA_Order_8080.6H.pdf

Fletcher, J. M., & Grigorenko, E. L. (2017). Neuropsychology of learning disabilities: The past and the future. *Journal of the International Neuropsychological Society, 23*(9–10), 930–940. https://doi.org/10.1017/S1355617717001084

Furzer, J., Dhuey, E., & Laporte, A. (2022). ADHD misdiagnosis: Causes and mitigators. *Health Economics, 31*(9), 1926–1953. https://doi.org/10.1002/hec.4555

Hale, J., Alfonso, V., Berninger, V., Bracken, B., Christo, C., Clark, E., Cohen, M., Davis, A., Decker, S., Denckla, M., Dumont, R., Elliott, C., Feifer, S., Fiorello, C., Flanagan, D., Fletcher-Janzen, E., Geary, D., Gerber, M., Gerner, M., & Yalof, J. (2010). Critical issues in response-to-intervention, comprehensive evaluation, and specific learning disabilities identification and intervention: An expert white paper consensus. *Learning Disability Quarterly, 33*(3), 223–236. http://www.jstor.org/stable/25701450

Houdé, O., Pineau, A., Leroux, G., Poirel, N., Perchey, G., Lanoë, C., Lubin, A., Turbelin, M.-R., Rossi, S., Simon, G., Delcroix, N., Lamberton, F., Vigneau, M., Wisniewski, G., Vicet, J.-R., & Mazoyer, B. (2011). Functional magnetic resonance imaging study of Piaget's conservation-of-number task in preschool and school-age children: A neo-Piagetian approach. *Journal of Experimental Child Psychology, 110*(3), 332–346. https://doi.org/10.1016/j.jecp.2011.04.008

Individuals with Disabilities Education Act (IDEA), 20 U.S.C. § 300.8 (2018). https://sites.ed.gov/idea/regs/b/a/300.8/a

Jakobson, A., & Kikas, E. (2007). Cognitive functioning in children with and without attention-deficit/hyperactivity disorder with and without comorbid learning disabilities. *Journal of Learning Disabilities, 40*(3), 194–202. https://doi.org/10.1177/00222194070400030101

Jensen, R. S. (1982). Pilot judgment: Training and evaluation. *Human Factors, 24*(1), 61–73. https://doi.org/10.1177/001872088202400107

Katz, L. J., Goldstein, G., & Beers, S. R. (2001). *Learning disabilities in older adolescents and adults: Clinical utility of the neuropsychological perspective.* Springer. https://doi.org/10.1007/b108001

Kay, G. G. (1995). *CogScreen: Professional manual.* Psychological Assessment Resources.

Kay, G. G. (2013). Aviation neuropsychology. In C. H. Kennedy & G. G. Kay (Eds.), *Aeromedical psychology* (pp. 239–268). Ashgate. https://doi.org/10.1201/9781315565811

Kincaid, J. P., Fishburne, R. P., Rogers, R. L., & Chissom, B. S. (1975). Derivation of new readability formulas (automated readability index, fog count, and Flesch reading ease formula) for Navy enlisted personnel. *Research Branch Report, 8-75.* Chief of Naval Technical Training, Naval Air Station Memphis. https://doi.org/10.21236/ADA006655

Klein, R. G., Mannuzza, S., Olazagasti, M. A. R., Roizen, E., Hutchison, B. A., Lashua, M. A., & Castellanos, X. (2012). Clinical and functional outcome of childhood attention-deficit/hyperactivity disorder 33 years later. *Archives of General Psychiatry, 69*(12), 1295–1303. https://doi.org/10.1001/archgenpsychiatry.2012.271

Lockwood, A. B., Farmer, R. L., Winans, S., & Sealander, K. (2022). Specific learning disability identification practices in the USA: A survey of special education administrators. *Contemporary School Psychology, 26*(4), 535–544. https://doi.org/10.1007/s40688-021-00375-4

National Center for Education Statistics. (2023). *Students with disabilities. Condition of education.* U.S. Department of Education, Institute of Education Sciences. https://nces.ed.gov/programs/coe/indicator/cgg

National Center for Health Statistics. (2018). *Survey description. National Health Interview Survey.* https://www.cdc.gov/nchs/nhis/nhis_2018_data_release.htm

Ojose, B. (2008). Applying Piaget's theory of cognitive development to mathematics instruction. *The Mathematics Educator, 18*(1), 26–30.

Pennington, B.F., McGrath, L.M., & Peterson, R.L. (2019). *Diagnosing learning disorders: From science to practice* (3rd ed.). The Guilford Press.

Peterson, R.L., & Pennington, B.F. (2022). Speech, language, and reading disabilities. In M.H. Beauchamp, R. Peterson, M.D. Ris, H.G. Taylor, & K.W. Yeates (Eds.), *Pediatric neuropsychology: Research, theory and practice* (pp. 254–278). The Guilford Press.

Pugh, K.R., Sandak, R., Frost, S.J., Moore, D., & Mencl, W.E. (2006). Examining reading development and reading disability in diverse languages and cultures: Potential contributions from functional neuroimaging. *Journal of American Indian Education, 45*(3), 60–76.

Ritchey, K.D., & Goeke, J.L. (2006). Orton-Gillingham and Orton-Gillingham-based reading instruction: A review of the literature. *The Journal of Special Education, 40*(3), 171–183. https://doi.org/10.1177/00224669060400030501.S2CID16132344

Rourke, B.P. (1989). *Nonverbal learning disabilities: The syndrome and the model.* Guilford Press.

Scanlon, D. (2013). Specific learning disability and its newest definition: Which is comprehensive? and which is insufficient? *Journal of Learning Disabilities, 46*(1), 26–33. https://doi-org.proxy.libraries.rutgers.edu/10.1177/0022219412464342

Sexton, C.C., Gelhorn, H., Bell, J., & Classi, P. (2012). The co-occurrence of reading disorder and ADHD: Epidemiology, treatment, psychosocial impact, and economic burden. *Journal of Learning Disabilities, 45*(6), 538–564. https://doi.org/10.1177/0022219411407772

Shaywitz, S.E., & Shaywitz, B.A. (2007). The neurobiology of reading and dyslexia. *ASHA Leader, 12*(12), 20–21. https://doi.org/10.1044/leader.ftr7.12122007.20

Shaywitz, S.E., Shaywitz, J.E., & Shaywitz, B.A. (2021). Dyslexia in the 21st century. *Current Opinion in Psychiatry, 34*(2), 80–86. https://doi.org/10.1097/YCO.0000000000000670

Taylor, J.L., O'Hara, R., Mumenthaler, M.S., & Yesavage, J.A. (2000). Relationship of CogScreen-AE to flight simulator performance and pilot age. *Aviation, Space, and Environmental Medicine, 71*, 373–380.

Taylor, W.P., Miciak, J., Fletcher, J.M., & Francis, D.J. (2017). Cognitive discrepancy models for specific learning disabilities identification: Simulations of psychometric limitations. *Psychological Assessment, 29*(4), 446–457. https://doi.org/10.1037/pas0000356

UK Civil Aviation Authority. (2023). *Dyslexia, Asperger syndrome and ADHD.* https://webarchive.nationalarchives.gov.uk/ukgwa/20230116022452/https://www.caa.co.uk/aeromedical-examiners/medical-standards/pilots/conditions/mental-health/dyslexia-asperger-syndrome-and-adhd/

United States Air Force. (2023). *United States Air Force aerospace medicine waiver guide compendium.* https://www.airforcemedicine.af.mil/

United States Navy. (2022). *Aeromedical reference and waiver guide.* https://www.med.navy.mil/Navy-Medicine-Operational-Training-Command/Naval-Aerospace-Medical-Institute/Aeromedical-Reference-and-Waiver-Guide/

World Health Organization. (2016). *International statistical classification of diseases and related health problems* (10th ed.). https://icd.who.int/browse10/2016/en

World Health Organization. (2019). *International statistical classification of diseases and related health problems* (11th ed.). https://icd.who.int/

Chapter 31
The Impact of Age on Cognitive Performance at Work

A Focus on Pilots and Air Traffic Controllers

Mickaël Causse, Damien Mouratille, Marc Baumgartner, and Jean-Paul Imbert

Introduction

The aging of the working population is the natural consequence of the demographic evolution of Western countries. Managing this change is a real challenge for society and it raises the issue of the retirement age extension. Beyond economic considerations, it is imperative to explore strategies for preserving performance and safety at work with older individuals. This is naturally true for physical jobs, but also for critical and cognitively demanding fields of activity involving a rapid pace of decision-making such as piloting (van Drongelen et al., 2017) and air traffic control (ATC; Heslegrave, 1998). In 2023, the CEO of the Regional Airline Association stated that approximately 50 % of the commercial airline workforce will retire within the next 15 years. The shortage of aviation professionals is thus a major issue for local and national authorities and companies in the coming years. This retirement trend is anticipated also for air traffic controllers (ATCOs), although the specific numbers may vary from country to country. In this chapter, we describe the effects of aging on the cognitive performance of aviation professionals, and the way in which the authorities regulate its potential consequences for safety. We then present the biological basis of age effects, with an emphasis on the CRUNCH (compensation-related utilization of neural circuits hypothesis) model. A number of studies on aging in the fields of piloting and ATC are presented. Finally, we outline some prospects for objective measurements of aging using physiological measures.

Aging and Regulations

Not only does aging make individuals more sensitive to fatigue, but above all, it has been established that aging causes cognitive slowing (Salthouse, 1996), a decrease in short-term memory performance (Anders et al., 1972), and more generally a disturbance of executive functions (Buckner, 2004; Nyberg et al., 2020). Naturally, numerous studies have highlighted the effects of age on piloting performance (Booze, 1977; Harkey, 1996; Kay, 2001; Taylor et al., 2007) and on the ability to adapt to new generations of aircraft (Pelegrin et al., 1995). However, these findings are to be tempered by the fact that the experience gained during a career can compensate for the detrimental effects of age on cognitive performance (G. Li et al., 2003). Also, aging effects on cognitive functions can be very heterogeneous among individuals (Cabeza et al., 2018), due to complex interactions between the cerebral structures underlying cognition (Buckner, 2004), sociocultural background (Chan et al., 2018), genetic factors (Nagel et al., 2008), or lifestyle (Yu et al., 2019).

Contrary to other fields of activity that have benefited greatly from scientific studies aiming at better understanding the effects of aging on performance, as is the case for piloting, relatively few studies have investigated the impact of aging on ATCOs. However, human errors in this field can also have serious consequences and some research results highlight the harmful effects of aging on a controller's performance and therefore on air safety (Becker & Milke, 1998). Like for piloting, it is now clearly established that work experience accumulated during life can compensates for age-related cognitive deficits. For example, a study by Nunes and Kramer (2009) showed that even if the compensatory effects of experience do not concern all dimensions of the ATC activity, its beneficial effects are particularly visible in the most complex tasks. In agreement with other studies on piloting (Causse, Dehais, Arexis, et al., 2011; Causse, Dehais, & Pastor, 2011; LG. Li et al., 2003), Nunes and Kramer (2009) highlighted the fact that it is quite possible for older operators to maintain acceptable performance at work. In other words, *chronological age,* measured in years, may be a less relevant factor than *biological age*, namely, the actual physical and mental functions (Causse, Dehais, & Pastor, 2011).

The retirement age of pilots and ATCOs is governed by local and national authorities, although the influence of the International Civil Aviation Organization (ICAO) plays a significant role. As the institution responsible for regulating international air traffic and establishing guidelines such as retirement age, ICAO holds considerable sway. While local authorities retain the right to challenge ICAO regulations, they typically tend to adopt them. In 2007, ICAO adopted Amendment 167 to Annex 1 (Standards and Recommended Practices adopted by ICAO as the minimum standards for personnel licensing), which allowed commercial pilots from ICAO member states (193 countries) to continue flying until the age of 60 for single-pilot operations and 65 for multi-crew operations (Cornell et al., 2007); no age limit was set for general aviation (GA). In the United States, the Federal Aviation Administration (FAA) follows the ICAO regulation: Commercial airline pilots working for airlines operating under multi-crew operations must retire at 65. In addition, pilots over the age of 60 must undergo a medical examination every 6 months. Due to the shortage of pilots, there are discussions in the US congress to raise the retirement age to 67, but this is strongly opposed by the unions (e.g., ALPA or IFALPA).

In Europe, the European Union Aviation Safety Agency (EASA) also applies ICAO regulation: The age limit is also 60 for single pilot operations and 65 for multi-crew operations (Regulation No. 1178/2011). In 2018, the EASA funded a study to assess the possible need to mitigate the risk for flight safety resulting from pilots aged over 60 (Simons et al., 2018). They conducted a systematic review about incapacitation and age and found that the rate of incapacitation may increase moderately with age. The study proposed raising the age limit of commercial pilots flying single-pilot operations to 65 years with additional measures to reduce the likelihood of pilot incapacitation: the medical screening of all aircrew above the age of 40 as well as proficiency and simulator checks for single-pilot operations above 60. For multi-crew operations, they recommended that the retirement age should remain at 65.

Regarding ATCOs, the retirement age can vary as there is no regulation determined by the ICAO. For instance, in the United States, the FAA sets the retirement age for ATCOs at 56 (Public Law 92-297). In France, the retirement age was 59 for ATCOs working in en-route centers or major airports and 65 for smaller airports. In accordance with the recently implemented French social protocol, all ATCOs are now required to retire at the age of 59. In Belgium, the retirement age is set at 55, making it the lowest in Europe, whereas the majority of European countries have a retirement age of 60. In 2009, the International Federation of Air Traffic Controllers' Associations (IFATCA), the international organization representing air traffic controller associations, published a paper on the retirement policy in which they proposed that the retirement age should be closer to 50 than 55 (IFATCA, 2009). However, most air navigation service providers (ANSPs) are currently increasing the retirement age and several countries are considering or have already raised the retirement age between 59 and 65.

Biological Aging

Understanding how we can adapt working conditions to advance in age would benefit from a greater understanding of how time alters brain functioning, the seat of our intellectual activity. Functional neuroimaging has highlighted anatomical and physiological changes that affect the brain (Cabeza et al., 2002; Cabeza et al., 2018; Nyberg et al., 2020). A growing body of evidence points to early deterioration of prefrontal networks compared to other cortical regions (Morcom & Henson, 2018; Moscovitch & Winocur, 1995; Tisserand & Jolles, 2003). This early deterioration of prefrontal lobes could be a major cause of early cognitive changes (West, 2000) and for disorders in executive functions in particular (Raz, 2000). It seems that this degradation mainly occurs in the dorsolateral prefrontal cortex (DLPFC) rather than the ventromedial part of the prefrontal cortex (MacPherson et al., 2002). Changes in the DLPFC during aging lead to deficits that concern various executive functions such as working memory (Yaple et al., 2019), mental flexibility (Wecker et al., 2005), or inhibition (Zuber et al., 2019).

From a biological perspective, one of the possible mechanisms of cognitive decline is that inefficient electron transport through the mitochondrial respiratory complexes leads to reduced adenosine triphosphate (ATP) synthesis and the generation of superoxide radicals as a byproduct (Nilsson & Tarnopolsky, 2019; Yankner et al., 2008). Mitochondria are protected against endogenously generated reactive oxygen species by antioxidant defenses; however, it seems that these defenses are reduced (and thus overwhelmed) during aging, resulting in local oxidative damage to mitochondrial proteins and DNA. These damages persisting in the aged brain may result in the silencing of genes – that is, reduction of their expression and production, and thus of the physiological mechanisms that depend on them – involved in synaptic plasticity, mitochondrial function, and protein trafficking, potentially contributing to a variety of cognitive declines (Yankner et al., 2008).

During normal aging, amyloid plaques (aggregates of misfolded proteins that form in the spaces between nerve cells) can appear in the neocortex and hippocampus (Saha & Sen, 2019). Also, neurofibrillary tangles (NFTs), abnormal accumulations of tau proteins within the cell bodies of affected neurons, can accumulate predominantly in the entorhinal cortex (Sengoku, 2020; Yankner et al., 2008). The entorhinal cortex plays a crucial role in memory processing, in particular the perforant path (Witter, 2007) that is involved in the encoding of recently acquired information (Kordower et al., 2001). It is not surprising that memory decline is among the main symptoms of normal aging. It must be noted that this memory decline concerns primarily short-term and working memory, linked to the capacity to store and manipulate information and to acquire new knowledge/memories. Long-term memory (and thus old previous knowledge) is largely unaffected, except in the case of neurological disorders such as Alzheimer disease, in which a large set of cortical regions including ones involved in long-term memory are severely impacted (Yankner et al., 2008).

A crucial point of brain aging concerns the way the central nervous system reorganizes itself to cope with age-related degradation. Numerous studies have revealed structural and functional (e.g., hypo-activation, hyper-activation) changes. These modifications have been interpreted as deficits or compensations. The observation of cerebral hypo-activation during tests involving executive functions (Johnson et al., 2004) corresponds well to a model of the brain degraded by age. For example, the alteration of the prefrontal regions, the hippocampus, and the cerebellum (Resnick et al., 2003; Salat et al., 2004) or the loss of white matter, particularly in the prefrontal cortex (Bartzokis et al., 2004), can easily lead to the hypothesis of a diminished contribution of specialized brain areas, which, being atrophied, will be less able to engage the appropriate neuronal circuitry. In turn, weaker brain activation in older individuals compared with younger ones can be observed, and these alterations would produce a decline in efficiency of various cognitive abilities such as attention or memory (Craik & Rose, 2012; Kane et al., 1994).

Yet, one of the most singular findings in functional neuroimaging is that aging is sometimes accompanied by additional (and not weaker activations) brain activations in a contralateral hemisphere, or by greater brain activation of the regions involved in the task, compared with younger individuals who activate the same regions during the task, but less intensely. Thus, given these surprising results, it has been established that there is a tendency for older individuals to recruit brain regions, in particular the prefrontal cortex, in a less asymmetric manner than younger persons. These findings have been labeled the "HAROLD model," for hemispheric asymmetry reduction in older adults (Cabeza et al., 2002). This phenomenon can either reflect a difficulty in recruiting specialized brain regions (dedifferentiation) or be interpreted as a compensatory measure against neurocognitive decline.

In the first conception, aging would be associated with a phenomenon of dedifferentiation, which can be defined as a decrease in the specialization of the central nervous system region (Koen & Rugg, 2019; S.-C. Li & Lindenberger, 1999). The additional cerebral activities (in particular in the contralateral hemisphere) would reflect a reduced capacity to use specialized neural networks. In the second conception, the recruitment of additional regions would serve to compensate for the reduced efficiency of the regions involved in the task (Reuter-Lorenz & Cappell, 2008). This compensation hypothesis is also made plausible by the presence of neural activity in additional (including contralateral) regions in brain-damaged patients after recovery of certain cognitive functions such as language (Cao et al., 1999).

A study by Cabeza et al. (2002) attempted to decide between dedifferentiation and compensation. Participants performed two different memory tasks: a recall condition and a contextual condition. In both conditions, participants learned a list of items before being placed in a scanner. Memory performance was then tested in the scanner. For the recall condition, participants had to first remember 24 pairs of semantically unrelated words (e.g., lawyer–window), then during the scan, the first word (e.g., lawyer) was presented to them and they had to recall the second (e.g., window). For the contextual condition, participants studied lists of 12 words presented auditorily or visually; then during the scan, they read each of these words and had to specify whether it had been read or heard during the learning phase (contextual recall). The authors measured the regional cerebral blood flow of 12 young and 16 older participants during the contextual recall test. This test tends to elicit brain activation in the right hemisphere. The older participants were subdivided into two groups according to their performance (comparable to or lower than that of the young participants). According to the compensation hypothesis, a reduction in the asymmetry of the activations in the prefrontal regions should be observed only in the older participants with a performance equivalent to that of the young. On the other hand, according to the dedifferentiation hypothesis, this reduction in asymmetry could be expected in older participants with poor performance. The results obtained were in favor of the compensation hypothesis. Indeed, a right-lateralized prefrontal activity was observed during the task in young participants while a bilateral activity was observed in older participants with a performance comparable to that of young participants. By contrast, prefrontal activity was more diffuse and localized in the right hemisphere only in older participants with low performance. Given these results, it appears that the older participants with the poorest performance engaged a network similar to that of the young participants, but used it less efficiently, whereas the older participants with performance equivalent to that of the young participants compensated for the age-related neural decline through recruitment of the contralateral hemisphere.

Reuter-Lorenz and Cappell (2008) proposed that, due to lower efficiency, older individuals would recruit more intensively the brain regions involved in a task, as if the level of difficulty was artificially higher for them. This overactivation would occur in older participants able to compensate for the effects of aging, thus achieving higher cognitive performance than other participants of the same age but with lower performance. This model has been called "CRUNCH," for compensation-related utilization of neural circuits hypothesis. It predicts that declining neural efficiency leads older adults to engage more neural circuits than young adults in order to meet task demands (Reuter-Lorenz & Cappell, 2008). At low levels of load, older adults' brain activity may match that of younger adults or be slightly higher. At intermediate and high levels of load, older people exceed their processing capacity and show less brain activity than younger people (see Figure 31.1); performance may decline at this point.

Results supporting the CRUNCH hypothesis were found recently in a study by Toepper et al. (2014) and Causse et al. (2019). Toepper et al. (2014) assessed the working memory performance of 18 young and 18 old participants. They were assessed with the Corsi block

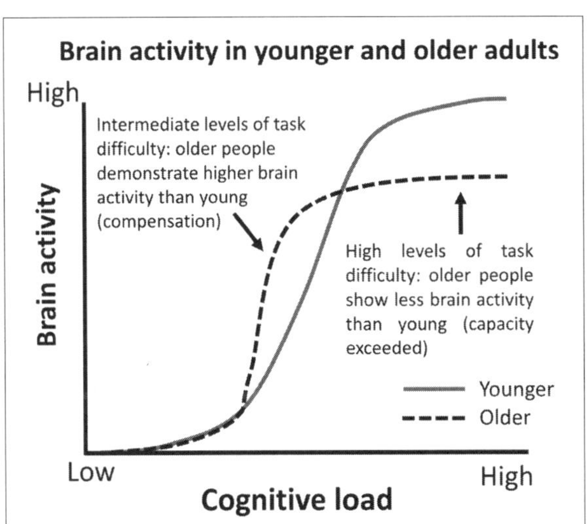

Figure 31.1. CRUNCH model and task difficulty. The "CRUNCH point" is defined as the point where difficulty exceeds older adults' processing capacity: Older adults' task performance declines and they start to show less activity than younger adults. Image inspired from Jamadar, 2020.

test, which measures the visuospatial component of working memory and involves reproducing, in the same or reverse order, a sequence of pointing movements to different cubes previously shown to the participant. The researchers compared brain activations between young and old individuals, but also between young high/low performers and old high/low performers. Compared with young participants, older individuals showed lower activations of the right inferior DLPFC. By contrast, old high performers showed greater activations of the superior region of the right DLPFC and anterior cingulate cortex compared with old low performers. These results suggest a decrease in the activity of crucial brain regions with aging but also a possible compensation of performance by an increased mobilization of these regions. In the work of Causse et al. (2019), older individuals demonstrated a drastic increase in error committed during a spatial working memory task when difficulty was high, and this was concomitant with a plateau of brain activity. By contrast, younger individuals were able to maintain correct performance and to continue to increase brain activations until the most difficult levels of task difficulty. It should be noted that some authors have challenged the CRUNCH model, sometimes producing opposite results to those predicted by the model, for example, during a visuospatial task (Jamadar, 2020).

Scientific Studies on Aging of Pilots and Air Traffic Controllers

A number of studies have been carried out to better understand the effects of aging on piloting. For example, Taylor et al. (2000, 2007) have highlighted a decline in psychomotor skills, working memory, and problem-solving in older pilots. Other studies also indicated a decline in time-sharing efficiency (Tsang & Shaner, 1995), processing speed (Hardy & Parasuraman, 1997), attention and executive ability, verbal and visual learning, and memory (Hardy et al., 2007). Van Benthem and Herdman (2016) showed that speed and working memory, visual attention, and cognitive flexibility performance mediate the relation between age and flight path maintenance in private pilots. This poorer performance in older pilots has been found recently in flight tasks performed in virtual reality (Audu et al., 2021).

According to a study conducted by Bazargan and Guzhva (2011), which examined 40,000 GA accidents in the United States (82% of all air transport accidents), there is no correlation between age or gender and the likelihood of accidents for pilots up to the age of 60. However, beyond 60, pilots are more susceptible to being involved in fatal accidents. Simons et al. (2018) studied the link between incapacitation rate and aging with a systematic review and accident analysis. Overall, 50%–70% of medical incapacitations are not directly dependent on brain aging. The most prevalent cause are cardiovascular accidents and mental health conditions. However, cognitive impairment was not really studied in this report, and the focus was mainly on medical impairment examined for loss of license. Furthermore, it seems likely that incidents and accidents linked to cognitive deficits are more difficult to detect than medical causes. Accordingly, Simons et al. (2018) suggest considering more individual cognitive and sensory performance in order to generate a more complete picture of the pilot's ability to fly safely during aging. Thus, identifying the cognitive functions both involved in piloting and affected by aging is an important aviation safety objective.

The CogScreen-AE battery has been designed primarily to detect subtle changes in cognitive functioning and thus has been largely studied in the field of pilot aging. Taylor et al.

(2000) showed that the aggregation of four CogScreen-AE scores (speed/working memory, visual associative memory, motor coordination, and tracking) predicted 45% of the performance in flight simulators. Moreover, age improved prediction by 6%. These results were obtained from a cohort of 100 pilots aged between 50 and 69 years. The incremental validity of age means that age still has an influence on flight performance even when controlling for cognitive abilities. In GA, where the accident rate has been estimated to be 92 times the rate for air carriers (G. Li et al., 2005), the effects of aging are a particularly sensitive issue since no age limit is defined. Based on a database of over 300,000 GA pilots, Li et al. (2005) showed that the risk of crash involvement is maximum after 65.

Another study by Taylor et al. (2007) specifically investigates the effects of aging on the GA pilot population, while taking flight experience into account. Unlike conventional cross-sectional studies, this longitudinal research followed a cohort of 118 pilots (aged 40–69) over 3 years in order to observe the effects of aging within the same population. The results showed that pilots with the greatest experience, defined according to qualification level (VFR, IFR Instructor, etc.), achieved a better flying performance than those with less experience. Further analysis showed that the most experienced pilots had a slower decline in performance over the 3 years of the study, illustrating the protective effects of experience.

Some of the tasks that pilots must perform have been linked to specific cognitive functions. For example, the effect of age on communication tasks has been attributed to working memory performance (Taylor et al., 2005). Yesavage et al. (2011) found that processing speed and executive function performance predicted the rate at which flight simulator performance declined over time. Pilots with the highest scores on tests of these abilities were less affected by the aging effect on flight performance. Finally, it is worth noticing that the impact of aging is sex-dependent (Armstrong et al., 2019), and with the increasing proportion of women in commercial aviation (Ferla & Graham, 2019), it will be desirable to study the specific consequences of aging on women, such as menopause, which is thought to affect cognitive functions (Conde et al., 2021; Sochocka et al., 2023).

Because of the 1981 strike and the dismissal of more than 10,000 ATCOs, a large number of new recruits were needed. Since all these ATCOs recruited at the same time retired at the same time, aging has been an important issue for the FAA since the mid-2000s. In the Heil study (1999), the cognitive abilities of 1083 en-route controllers were assessed using the AT-SAT battery (selection battery used by the FAA for several years). Hierarchical polynomial regression revealed a curvilinear relationship between age and several cognitive tests (mainly fluid reasoning). Performance on these tests increased slightly with age until controllers reached their mid to late 40s. However, beyond this age range, there was a slight decline in performance. Some limitations have been raised by the authors. Participation was voluntary, and thus ATCOs uncomfortable with their level of performance would choose not to participate. Also, since it was not a longitudinal study and participants of different ages were compared, a follow-up would be interesting.

During 2005–2006, several papers were published on age-performance relationships (Broach, 2005; Broach & Schroeder, 2006). A comprehensive analysis involved the extraction of 3,054 en-route operational errors that occurred during the period from 1997 to 2003. Age was not significantly related to these errors when controlling for experience. Broach (2005) suggested that administrative decisions about ATCO retirement age should be based on firm scientific results with appropriate methods and statistics. For Eißfeldt and Gayraud (2015) and Goeters et al. (2004), some cognitive functions are more critical than others for ATC. Indeed, the central aspect of ATC is the dynamic process of acquiring, processing, and sharing information from multiple sources. A great amount of information must be integrated in real time to keep situation awareness updated. In the studies by Goeters et al. (2004) and Eißfeldt and Gayraud (2015), participants had to rate the importance of cognitive functions used during ATC work. Six cognitive functions were rated as important by 16 graduating students and 12 experienced ATCOs (Goeters et al., 2004) and by 227 ATCOs with an average experience of 6 years (Eißfeldt & Gayraud, 2015). These six functions are divided attention, selective attention, monitoring, listening comprehension, vigilance, and perceptual speed. Recently, mainly based on the work by Broach (2013), a review paper from Wium and Eaglestone (2022) highlighted the importance of visuospatial processing, fluid reasoning, working memory, speed of processing, and long-term memory for ATC operations.

A few studies have been carried out to examine the interaction between aging and experience on ATC performance. A study conducted by Eurocontrol confirmed that experience is a moderating effect of aging among ATCOs (Straeter, 2003). Six European control centers participated in the study and 76 ATCOs were surveyed (mean age = 49 years, mean experience = 26 years). Their professional opinion on aging effects and retirement was collected. According to them, the main problems due to aging are the adaptation to changes and the job demand (night shifts). Learning, multitasking and complexity also appeared more difficult to deal with for aged ATCOs. The majority of respondents stated that experience allowed them to partially compensate for the negative effects of aging. Indeed, with accumulating years of experience, ATCOs can rely on the recollection of applicable solutions developed through the myriad situations they have encountered. Overall, 42 ATCOs reported better situational awareness and 28 reported better knowledge of conflicts resolution.

In the work of Nunes and Kramer (2009), 18 older (53–64 years old) and 18 younger (25–38 years old) Canadian ATCOs were recruited. The same number of age-matched civilians were used as control participants. The battery of tests used included both domain-relevant abilities (inhibition, set-shifting, visuospatial processing, working memory, attention) and less relevant measures of different aspects of cognition (reasoning and processing speed). Analyses revealed age-related declines in all cognitive tasks both for ATCOs and for civilians, with evidence of experience-based compensation in inhibition and visuospatial abilities. In addition to cognitive abilities, the researchers used ATC simulations to assess problem-solving. They found that experience mitigated age effects specifically on the more complex ATC tasks, suggesting that older ATCOs may be able to perform at high level due to the accumulation of experience. Finally, aging can also have worsening effects on the level of fatigue, to the point that fatigue is sometimes considered an early indicator of the aging process (Avlund, 2010). Thackray and Touchstone (1982) studied the effect of rest periods on the performance of 40 middle-aged participants (40–50 years old). During a 2-hr radar monitoring task, a break of 5 min every 30 min allowed the middle-aged participants to perform at the same level as younger participants (18–29) who did not have any break. This result showed that reducing fatigue levels may help older individuals to reach nominal performance.

Physiological Measurements to Better Understand Aging Effects?

While cognitive performance tests are routinely used to assess the impact of aging on performance or for selection purpose (Mouratille et al., 2022), physiological measures are rarely used to get cues on how aging affects cognitive performance across varying levels of task difficulty. Recently, Baumgartner et al. (2024) were commissioned by Skyguide, the Swiss Air navigation service provider (ANSP), and HELVETICA, the Swiss association representing all Skyguide ATCOs, to study the impact of aging on cognitive performance and ATC abilities. The authors hypothesized that controllers might encounter greater challenges with complex tasks, aligning with the CRUNCH model. In addition to performance, the researchers also sought to analyze physiological activity, hypothesizing that older ATCOs should mobilize more mental resources to perform complex tasks and therefore demonstrate increased physiological activity, such as a higher heart rate, in comparison with younger ATCOs. ATCOs were divided into four age groups (28–36, 37–44, 45–54, and 55–59) and

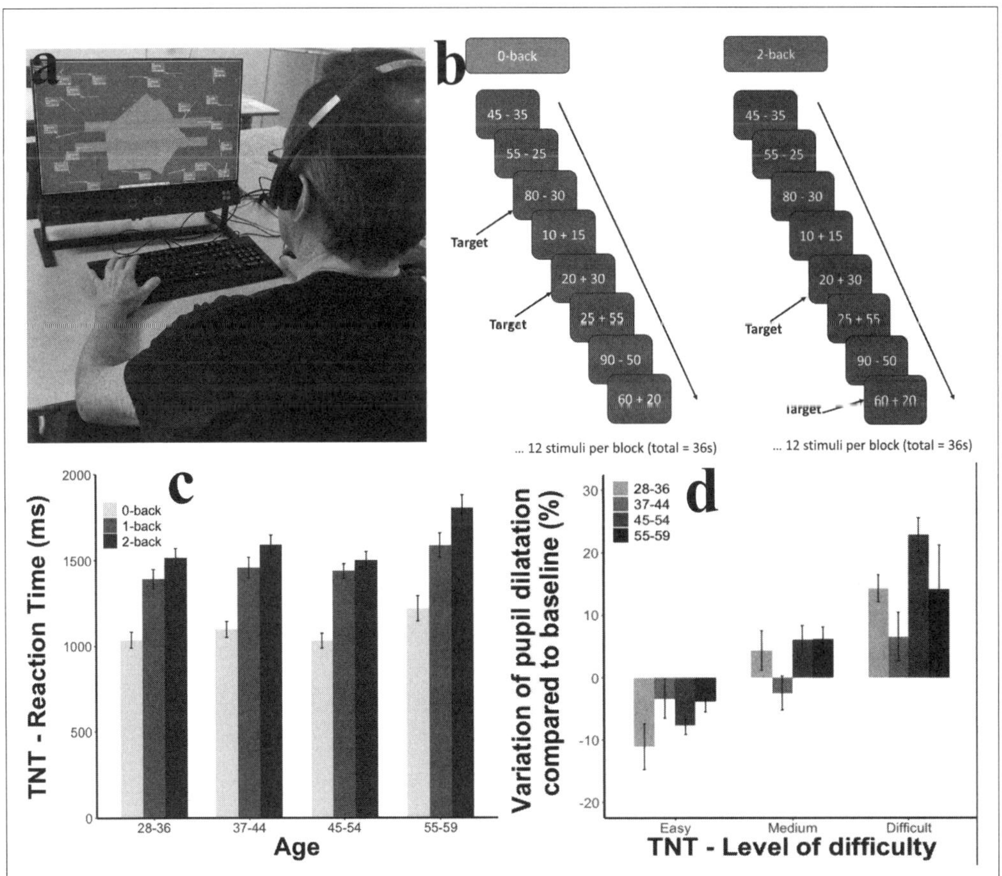

Figure 31.2. Illustration of the study funded by Skyguide and HELVETICA. **a** An ATCO performing the LABY test, a low-fidelity ATC simulation. **b** The Toulouse N-back Task that assesses working memory and mental calculation. **c** Reaction times during the Toulouse N-back Task according to age group and level of difficulty. **d** Pupil diameter variation according to age and level of difficulty of the Toulouse N-back Task.

several cognitive functions were assessed: short-term memory, working memory, fluid reasoning, vigilance, attention, inhibition, cognitive flexibility, and processing speed. A low-fidelity ATC simulation (see Figure 31.2a) was also employed to evaluate ATC performance and establish correlations with cognitive performance. A working memory task designed to be very complex (Toulouse N-back Task) was used (see Figure 31.2b). In the physiological aspect of the study, pupil diameter, heart rate, and oximeter measures were utilized. Interestingly, there was almost no significant effect of age on accuracy in the cognitive tests. However, reaction times were affected by age in most of the tests. Both accuracy and reaction times were affected only in the two most difficult tests: the ATC simulation and the Toulouse N-back Task (see Figure 31.2c for reaction times according to the level of difficulty and age). Physiological data were not affected by aging, but successfully indicated the level of difficulty of the tasks, for example, higher pupil diameter when level of difficulty increased (see Figure 31.2d).

Conclusion

Undeniably, aging has a significant impact on pilots' and ATCOs' activities. As they age, these aviation professionals may face physical challenges that can potentially compromise their performance and flight safety. Cognitive abilities such as memory, processing speed, and decision-making can be affected. It is important that aviation regulators and airlines are aware of these effects and have policies and procedures in place to mitigate the risks associated with aging pilots and ATCOs. Regular medical assessments, including cognitive tests and thorough health examinations, can help identify potential problems and take appropriate preventive measures. At the same time, ongoing training and awareness programs must be put in place to help aviation professionals maintain their skills and keep abreast of the latest technological and regulatory advances. Finally, an open and transparent safety culture is essential to encourage pilots and ATCOs to report any cognitive problems that may affect their performance. Confidential reporting mechanisms and information-sharing between aviation stakeholders must be implemented to promote a safe working environment for all. Ultimately, it is important to strike a balance between the experience and expertise of aging aviation professionals and the need to ensure flight safety. By adopting a proactive approach based on rigorous policies, continuous training, knowledge transfer from the most experienced, and a strong safety culture, we can continue to benefit from the expertise of experienced pilots and ATCOs while ensuring the highest levels of safety in modern aviation.

References

Anders, T.R., Fozard, J.L., & Lillyquist, T.D. (1972). Effects of age upon retrieval from short-term memory. *Developmental Psychology, 6*(2), 214–217. https://doi.org/10.1037/h0032103

Armstrong, N.M., An, Y., Beason-Held, L., Doshi, J., Erus, G., Ferrucci, L., Davatzikos, C., & Resnick, S.M. (2019). Sex differences in brain aging and predictors of neurodegeneration in cognitively healthy older adults. *Neurobiology of aging, 81*, 146–156. https://doi.org/10.1016/j.neurobiolaging.2019.05.020

Audu, O., Van Benthem, K., & Herdman, C.M. (2021). Validation of virtual reality cognitive assessment for pilots across the lifespan. In D. Harris & W.C. Li (Eds.), *Engineering psychology and cognitive ergonomics. HCII 2021. Lecture notes in computer science* (Vol. 12767). Springer. https://doi.org/10.1007/978-3-030-77932-0_1

Avlund, K. (2010). Fatigue in older adults : An early indicator of the aging process? *Aging Clinical and Experimental Research, 22*, 100-115. https://doi.org/10.1007/BF03324782

Bartzokis, G., Sultzer, D., Lu, P.H., Nuechterlein, K.H., Mintz, J., & Cummings, J.L. (2004). Heterogeneous age-related breakdown of white matter structural integrity : Implications for cortical "disconnection" in aging and Alzheimer's disease. *Neurobiology of Aging, 25*(7), 843–851. https://doi.org/10.1016/j.neurobiolaging.2003.09.005

Baumgartner, M., Cabon, P., Drogoul, F., Causse, M., Imbert, J., & Mouratille, D. (2024). Scientific evaluation of the impact of an increase in the retirement age on the cognitive functions and well-being of air traffic controllers (ATCOs). In G. Praetorius, C. Sellberg, & R. Patriarca (Eds.), *Advances in human factors of transportation. AHFE (2024) International Conference* (Vol 148). AHFE International. http://doi.org/10.54941/ahfe1005189

Bazargan, M., & Guzhva, V.S. (2011). Impact of gender, age and experience of pilots on general aviation accidents. *Accident Analysis & Prevention, 43*(3), 962–970. https://doi.org/10.1016/j.aap.2010.11.023

Becker, J.T., & Milke, R.M. (1998). Cognition and aging in a complex work environment : Relationships with performance among air traffic control specialists. *Aviation, Space, and Environmental Medicine, 69*(10), 944–951.

Booze, C.F., Jr. (1977). *An epidemiologic investigation of occupation, age, and exposure in general aviation accidents.* Federal Aviation Administration Washington DC Office of Aviation Medicine.

Broach, D. (2005). ATCS age and en route operational errors: A re-investigation. *2005 International Symposium on Aviation Psychology*, 88–92. https://corescholar.libraries.wright.edu/isap_2005/143

Broach, D. (2013). *Selection of the next generation of air traffic control specialists : Aptitude requirements for the air traffic control tower cab in 2018.* Civil Aerospace Medical Institute.

Broach, D., & Schroeder, D.J. (2006). Air traffic control specialist age and en route operational errors. *The International Journal of Aviation Psychology, 16*(4), 363–373. https://doi.org/10.1207/s15327108ijap1604_2

Buckner, R.L. (2004). Memory and executive function in aging and AD: Multiple factors that cause decline and reserve factors that compensate. *Neuron, 44*(1), 195–208. https://doi.org/10.1016/j.neuron.2004.09.006

Cabeza, R., Albert, M., Belleville, S., Craik, F.I., Duarte, A., Grady, C.L., Lindenberger, U., Nyberg, L., Park, D.C., & Reuter-Lorenz, P.A. (2018). Maintenance, reserve and compensation : The cognitive neuroscience of healthy ageing. *Nature Reviews Neuroscience, 19*(11), 701–710. https://doi.org/10.1038/s41583-018-0068-2

Cabeza, R., Anderson, N.D., Locantore, J.K., & McIntosh, A.R. (2002). Aging gracefully : Compensatory brain activity in high-performing older adults. *Neuroimage, 17*(3), 1394-1402. https://doi.org/10.1006/nimg.2002.1280

Cao, Y., Vikingstad, E.M., George, K.P., Johnson, A.F., & Welch, K. (1999). Cortical language activation in stroke patients recovering from aphasia with functional MRI. *Stroke, 30*(11), 2331–2340. https://doi.org/10.1161/01.STR.30.11.2331

Causse, M., Chua, Z.K., & Rémy, F. (2019). Influences of age, mental workload, and flight experience on cognitive performance and prefrontal activity in private pilots : A fNIRS study. *Scientific Reports, 9*(1), 1–12. https://doi.org/10.1038/s41598-019-44082-w

Causse, M., Dehais, F., Arexis, M., & Pastor, J. (2011). Cognitive aging and flight performances in general aviation pilots. *Aging, Neuropsychology, and Cognition, 18*(5), 544–561. https://doi.org/10.1080/13825585.2011.586018

Causse, M., Dehais, F., & Pastor, J. (2011). Executive functions and pilot characteristics predict flight simulator performance in general aviation pilots. *The International Journal of Aviation Psychology, 21*(3), 217–234. https://doi.org/10.1080/10508414.2011.582441

Chan, M.Y., Na, J., Agres, P.F., Savalia, N.K., Park, D.C., & Wig, G.S. (2018). Socioeconomic status moderates age-related differences in the brain's functional network organization and anatomy across the adult lifespan. *Proceedings of the National Academy of Sciences, 115*(22), E5144–E5153. https://doi.org/10.1073/pnas.1714021115

Conde, D.M., Verdade, R.C., Valadares, A.L., Mella, L.F., Pedro, A.O., & Costa-Paiva, L. (2021). Menopause and cognitive impairment : A narrative review of current knowledge. *World Journal of Psychiatry, 11*(8), 412–428. https://doi.org/10.5498/wjp.v11.i8.412

Cornell, A., Baker, S.P., & Li, G. (2007). Age-60 rule: The end is in sight. *Aviation, Space, and Environmental Medicine, 78*(6), 624–626.

Craik, F.I., & Rose, N.S. (2012). Memory encoding and aging : A neurocognitive perspective. *Neuroscience & Biobehavioral Reviews, 36*(7), 1729–1739. https://doi.org/10.1016/j.neubiorev.2011.11.007

Eißfeldt, H., & Gayraud, K. (2015). Shifts in ability requirements as perceived among aviation operators. *Procedia Manufacturing, 3*, 2543–2549. https://doi.org/10.1016/j.promfg.2015.07.549

Ferla, M., & Graham, A. (2019). Women slowly taking off : An investigation into female underrepresentation in commercial aviation. *Research in Transportation Business & Management, 31*, Article 100378. https://doi.org/10.1016/j.rtbm.2019.100378

Goeters, K.-M., Maschke, P., & Eißfeldt, H. (2004). Ability requirements in core aviation professions : Job analysis of airline pilots and air traffic controllers. In K.-M. Goeters (Ed.), *Aviation psychology: Practice and research* (pp. 99–119). Routledge.

Hardy, D.J., & Parasuraman, R. (1997). Cognition and flight performance in older pilots. *Journal of Experimental Psychology: Applied, 3*(4), 313.

Hardy, D.J., Satz, P., D'Elia, L.F., & Uchiyama, C.L. (2007). Age-related group and individual differences in aircraft pilot cognition. *The International Journal of Aviation Psychology, 17*(1), 77–90. https://doi.org/10.1080/10508410709336938

Harkey, J.A. Y. (1996). Age-related changes in selected status variables in general aviation pilots. *Transportation Research Record, 1517*(1), 37–43. https://doi.org/10.1177/0361198196151700105

Heil, M.C. (1999). *An investigation of the relationship between chronological age and indicators of job performance for incumbent air traffic control specialists.* Federal Aviation Administration Washington DC Office of Aviation Medicine. https://rosap.ntl.bts.gov/view/dot/8733

Heslegrave, R. (1998). Fatigue : Performance impairment, sleep and ageing in shiftwork operations. In L. Hartley (Ed.), *Managing fatigue in transportation: Proceedings of the 3rd Fatigue in Transportation Conference.* (pp. 167–185). Elsevier Science.

International Federation of Air Traffic Controllers'' Associations. (2009). *WP No. 163. Review of retirement policy.* 48th Annual Conference, Dubrovnik, Croatia.

Jamadar, S.D. (2020). The CRUNCH model does not account for load-dependent changes in visuospatial working memory in older adults. *Neuropsychologia, 142*, 107446. https://doi.org/10.1016/j.neuropsychologia.2020.107446

Johnson, M.K., Mitchell, K.J., Raye, C.L., & Greene, E.J. (2004). An age-related deficit in prefrontal cortical function associated with refreshing information. *Psychological Science, 15*(2), 127–132. https://doi.org/10.1111/j.0963-7214.2004.01502009.x

Kane, M.J., Hasher, L., Stoltzfus, E.R., Zacks, R.T., & Connelly, S.L. (1994). Inhibitory attentional mechanisms and aging. *Psychology and Aging, 9*(1), 103–112. https://doi.org/10.1037/0882-7974.9.1.103

Kay, G. (2001). Effects of aging on aviation-related cognitive function in commercial airline pilots. *Aviation Space Environmental Medicine, 72*, 241.

Koen, J.D., & Rugg, M.D. (2019). Neural dedifferentiation in the aging brain. *Trends in Cognitive Sciences, 23*(7), 547–559. https://doi.org/10.1016/j.tics.2019.04.012

Kordower, J.H., Chu, Y., Stebbins, G.T., DeKosky, S.T., Cochran, E.J., Bennett, D., & Mufson, E.J. (2001). Loss and atrophy of layer II entorhinal cortex neurons in elderly people with mild cognitive impairment. *Annals of Neurology, 49*(2), 202–213. https://doi.org/10.1002/1531-8249(20010201)49:2<202::AID-ANA40>3.0.CO;2-3

Li, G., Baker, S.P., Grabowski, J.G., Qiang, Y., McCarthy, M.L., & Rebok, G.W. (2003). Age, flight experience, and risk of crash involvement in a cohort of professional pilots. *American Journal of Epidemiology, 157*(10), 874–880. https://doi.org/10.1093/aje/kwg071

Li, G., Baker, S.P., Qiang, Y., Grabowski, J.G., & McCarthy, M.L. (2005). Driving-while-intoxicated history as a risk marker for general aviation pilots. *Accident Analysis & Prevention, 37*(1), 179–184. https://doi.org/10.1016/j.aap.2004.04.005

Li, S.-C., & Lindenberger, U. (1999). Cross-level unification : A computational exploration of the link between deterioration of neurotransmitter systems and dedifferentiation of cognitive abilities in old age.

In L.G. Nilsson & H.J. Markowitsch (Eds.), *Cognitive neuroscience of memory* (p. 103–146). Hogrefe & Huber.

MacPherson, S.E., Phillips, L.H., & Della Sala, S. (2002). Age, executive function and social decision making : A dorsolateral prefrontal theory of cognitive aging. *Psychology and Aging, 17*(4), 598–609. https://doi.org/10.1037/0882-7974.17.4.598

Morcom, A.M., & Henson, R.N. (2018). Increased prefrontal activity with aging reflects nonspecific neural responses rather than compensation. *Journal of Neuroscience, 38*(33), 7303–7313. https://doi.org/10.1523/JNEUROSCI.1701-17.2018

Moscovitch, M., & Winocur, G. (1995). Frontal lobes, memory, and aging. *Annals of the New York Academy of Sciences, 769*, 119-150. https://doi.org/10.1111/j.1749-6632.1995.tb38135.x

Mouratille, D., Amadieu, F., & Matton, N. (2022). A meta-analysis on air traffic controllers selection : Cognitive and non-cognitive predictors. *Journal of Vocational Behavior, 138*, Article 103769. https://doi.org/10.1016/j.jvb.2022.103769

Nagel, I.E., Chicherio, C., Li, S.-C., Von Oertzen, T., Sander, T., Villringer, A., Heekeren, H.R., Bäckman, L., & Lindenberger, U. (2008). Human aging magnifies genetic effects on executive functioning and working memory. *Frontiers in Human Neuroscience, 2*, Article 1. https://doi.org/10.3389/neuro.09.001.2008

Nilsson, M.I., & Tarnopolsky, M.A. (2019). Mitochondria and aging – the role of exercise as a countermeasure. *Biology, 8*(2), Article 40. https://doi.org/10.3390/biology8020040

Nunes, A., & Kramer, A.F. (2009). Experience-based mitigation of age-related performance declines : Evidence from air traffic control. *Journal of Experimental Psychology: Applied, 15*(1), 12–24.

Nyberg, L., Boraxbekk, C.-J., Sörman, D.E., Hansson, P., Herlitz, A., Kauppi, K., Ljungberg, J.K., Lövheim, H., Lundquist, A., & Adolfsson, A.N. (2020). Biological and environmental predictors of heterogeneity in neurocognitive ageing : Evidence from Betula and other longitudinal studies. *Ageing Research Reviews, 64*, Article 101184. https://doi.org/10.1016/j.arr.2020.101184

Pelegrin, C., Maho, V., & Amalberti, R. (1995). Pilot age and training performance. In N. Johnston, R. Fuller, & N. McDonald (Eds.), *Aviation psychology: Training and selection. Proceedings of the 21st Conference of the European Association for Aviation Psychology (EAAP)* (Vol. 2, pp. 354–363). Ashgate.

Raz, N. (2000). Aging of the brain and its impact on cognitive performance: Integration of structural and functional findings. In F.I.M. Craik & T.A. Salthouse (Eds.), *The handbook of aging and cognition* (2nd ed., pp. 1–90). Lawrence Erlbaum Associates Publishers.

Resnick, S.M., Pham, D.L., Kraut, M.A., Zonderman, A.B., & Davatzikos, C. (2003). Longitudinal magnetic resonance imaging studies of older adults : A shrinking brain. *Journal of Neuroscience, 23*(8), 3295–3301. https://doi.org/10.1523/JNEUROSCI.23-08-03295.2003

Reuter-Lorenz, P.A., & Cappell, K.A. (2008). Neurocognitive aging and the compensation hypothesis. *Current Directions in Psychological Science, 17*(3), 177–182. https://doi.org/10.1111/j.1467-8721.2008.00570.x

Saha, P., & Sen, N. (2019). Tauopathy : A common mechanism for neurodegeneration and brain aging. *Mechanisms of Ageing and Development, 178*, 72–79. https://doi.org/10.1016/j.mad.2019.01.007

Salat, D.H., Buckner, R.L., Snyder, A.Z., Greve, D.N., Desikan, R.S.R., Busa, E., Morris, J.C., Dale, A.M., & Fischl, B. (2004). Thinning of the Cerebral cortex in aging. *Cerebral Cortex, 14*(7), 721–730. https://doi.org/10.1093/cercor/bhh032

Salthouse, T.A. (1996). The processing-speed theory of adult age differences in cognition. *Psychological Review, 103*(3), 403–428. https://doi.org/10.1037/0033-295X.103.3.403

Sengoku, R. (2020). Aging and Alzheimer's disease pathology. *Neuropathology, 40*(1), 22–29. https://doi.org/10.1111/neup.12626

Simons, R., Van Drongelen, A., Roelen, A., Maire, R., Brouwer, O., van Dijk, H., & Valk, P. (2018). *Age limitations commercial air transport pilots.* https://publications.tno.nl/publication/34635096/X6rWMm/TNO-2018-age.pdf

Sochocka, M., Karska, J., Pszczołowska, M., Ochnik, M., Fułek, M., Fułek, K., Kurpas, D., Chojdak-Łukasiewicz, J., Rosner-Tenerowicz, A., & Leszek, J. (2023). Cognitive decline in early and premature menopause. *International Journal of Molecular Sciences, 24*(7), Article 6566. https://doi.org/10.3390/ijms24076566

Straeter, O. (2003). *Age, experience and automation in European air traffic control.* EUROCONTROL. https://skybrary.aero/sites/default/files/bookshelf/5557.pdf

Taylor, J.L., Kennedy, Q., Noda, A., & Yesavage, J.A. (2007). Pilot age and expertise predict flight simulator performance : A 3-year longitudinal study. *Neurology, 68*(9), 648–654. https://doi.org/10.1212/01.wnl.0000255943.10045.c0

Taylor, J.L., O'Hara, R., Mumenthaler, M.S., Rosen, A.C., & Yesavage, J.A. (2005). Cognitive ability, expertise, and age differences in following air-traffic control instructions. *Psychology and Aging, 20*(1), 117–133. https://doi.org/10.1037/0882-7974.20.1.117

Taylor, J.L., O'Hara, R., Mumenthaler, M.S., & Yesavage, J.A. (2000). Relationship of CogScreen-AE to flight simulator performance and pilot age. *Aviation, Space, and Environmental Medicine, 7*, 373–380.

Thackray, R.I., & Touchstone, R.M. (1982). *Performance of 40-to 50-year-old subjects on a radar monitoring task : The effects of wearing bifocal glasses and interpolated rest periods on target detection time.* Civil Aerospace Medical Institute.

Tisserand, D.J., & Jolles, J. (2003). On the involvement of prefrontal networks in cognitive ageing. *Cortex, 39*(4–5), 1107–1128. https://doi.org/10.1016/S0010-9452(08)70880-3

Toepper, M., Gebhardt, H., Bauer, E., Haberkamp, A., Beblo, T., Gallhofer, B., Driessen, M., & Sammer, G. (2014). The impact of age on load-related dorsolateral prefrontal cortex activation. *Frontiers in Aging Neuroscience, 6*, Article 9. https://doi.org/10.3389/fnagi.2014.00009

Tsang, P.S., & Shaner, T.L. (1995). Age, expertise, structural similarity, and time-sharing efficiency. *Proceedings of the Human Factors and Ergonomics Society Annual Meeting, 39*(2), 124–128. https://doi.org/10.1177/154193129503900201

Van Benthem, K., & Herdman, C.M. (2016). Cognitive factors mediate the relation between age and flight path maintenance in general aviation. *Aviation Psychology and Applied Human Factors, 6*(2), 81–90. https://doi.org/10.1027/2192-0923/a000102

van Drongelen, A., Boot, C.R., Hlobil, H., Smid, T., & van der Beek, A.J. (2017). Risk factors for fatigue among airline pilots. *International Archives of Occupational and Environmental Health, 90*, 39–47. https://doi.org/10.1007/s00420-016-1170-2

Wecker, N.S., Kramer, J.H., Hallam, B.J., & Delis, D.C. (2005). Mental flexibility: Age effects on switching. *Neuropsychology, 19*(3), 345–352. https://doi.org/10.1037/0894-4105.19.3.345

West, R. (2000). In defense of the frontal lobe hypothesis of cognitive aging. *Journal of the International Neuropsychological Society, 6*(6), 727–729. https://doi.org/10.1017/S1355617700666109

Witter, M.P. (2007). The perforant path : Projections from the entorhinal cortex to the dentate gyrus. In H.E. Scharfman (Ed.), *Progress in brain research* (Vol. 163, p. 43–61). Elsevier. https://doi.org/10.1016/S0079-6123(07)63003-9

Wium, J., & Eaglestone, J. (2022). Job analysis for air traffic control. *Aviation Psychology and Applied Human Factors, 12*(1), 31–49. https://doi.org/10.1027/2192-0923/a000218

Yankner, B.A., Lu, T., & Loerch, P. (2008). The aging brain. *Annual Review of Pathology, 3*, 41–66. https://doi.org/10.1146/annurev.pathmechdis.2.010506.092044

Yaple, Z.A., Stevens, W.D., & Arsalidou, M. (2019). Meta-analyses of the n-back working memory task : fMRI evidence of age-related changes in prefrontal cortex involvement across the adult lifespan. *NeuroImage, 196*, 16–31. https://doi.org/10.1016/j.neuroimage.2019.03.074

Yesavage, J.A., Jo, B., Adamson, M.M., Kennedy, Q., Noda, A., Hernandez, B., Zeitzer, J.M., Friedman, L.F., Fairchild, K., Scanlon, B.K., Murphy, G.M., Jr., & Taylor, J.L. (2011). Initial cognitive performance predicts longitudinal aviator performance. *The Journals of Gerontology: Series B, 66B*(4), 444–453. https://doi.org/10.1093/geronb/gbr031

Yu, J., Collinson, S.L., Liew, T.M., Ng, T.-P., Mahendran, R., Kua, E.-H., & Feng, L. (2019). Super-cognition in aging : Cognitive profiles and associated lifestyle factors. Applied Neuropsychology. *Adult, 27*(6), 497–503. https://doi.org/10.1080/23279095.2019.1570928

Zuber, S., Ihle, A., Loaiza, V.M., Schnitzspahn, K.M., Stahl, C., Phillips, L.H., Kaller, C.P., & Kliegel, M. (2019). Explaining age differences in working memory: The role of updating, inhibition, and shifting. *Psychology & Neuroscience, 12*(2), 191–208. https://doi.org/10.1037/pne0000151

Chapter 32
Putting It Into Words – Neuropsychological Report Writing in Aviation

Alastair L. Gray

Introduction

Neuropsychological report writing holds a crucial position within the aviation industry, serving as a vital tool for assessing the cognitive and psychological fitness of pilots and crew members. Such reports are central in assessing performance in the safety-critical environment that is aviation. Through such a central role, neuropsychology in aviation protects those in the aircraft but also those on the ground. By providing insights into an individual's neurocognitive functioning, mental health, and overall suitability for functioning in aviation-related occupations via the evaluation of different aspects of cognitive neuropsychological functioning, such assessments and the reports that they generate contribute to ensuring the safety and efficiency of aviation operations.

The aviation environment places unique demands on individuals, necessitating optimal cognitive functioning. Neuropsychological reports in aviation are therefore required to detail such cognitive functioning, thereby helping to identify any potential impairments or limitations that may impact upon their performance within this high-stakes field. Additionally, such reports may also explore mental health factors such as mood, anxiety, and stress levels, as these can significantly influence an individual's capacity to function effectively in aviation settings. Accurate and comprehensive neuropsychological report writing is therefore essential for aviation professionals to make informed decisions regarding an individual's fitness to fly. Reports need to use robust and well-validated assessment measures and be reported in the context of an objective interpretation. Moreover, such reports need to be accessible to aviation personnel, who may not possess the specialized knowledge in, or vocabulary of, neuropsychology. In short, reports need to be clear, concise, and relevant to aviation regulations and requirements. The following paragraphs detail the general report-writing requirements needed when producing a report that fulfils the aforementioned criteria. This chapter also details the aviation-specific issues that report authors need to be aware of and, where necessary, incorporate into their work. Given that reports concerning inaccurate assessments are rare, where inaccuracies do occur, whether that be as a result of inaccurate evaluation, (mis)interpretation, or misunderstanding, their implications can be far reaching. A case study highlighting the potential unfortunate consequences of inaccurate data leading to inaccurate conclusions and recommendations is included at the end of the chapter.

Format

Considering the readership is probably the best place to start when authoring a neuropsychological report within an aviation setting. Asking questions such as whether or not readers will understand specific technical information or terminology regarding neuropsychological assessment is key in ensuring that your report is as accessible as possible. Writing in simple and clear terms is a skill that few of us are born with and it only comes with practice. It is, however, a vital skill in writing neuropsychological assessments both in and outside of aviation. It is especially important within aviation, given not only the number of different professions that will potentially see your report, but also the need for clear and unambiguous communications in the context of a safety-critical environment. Establishing who the report is going to will also drive how you address referral questions: Are you writing to the regulator and therefore must consider your region's specific requirements? Are you writing to the aviation medical examiner (AME) in response to specific questions that relate to aspects of a fitness-to-fly case? Are you writing to the airline or their human resources team, in which case, are you happy that they are going to understand what may very well be a highly technical report? Or are you writing to the pilot themselves? Considering who will read your report is vital. It is also important to recognize that a neuropsychological report may have far-reaching implications for the crew member involved with regard to their ongoing employment. It is therefore critical to ensure that any ambiguities are absent from neuropsychological assessment. This can only be achieved through the use of clear and simple terms that the readership will comprehend (Bowden, 2011; Canavor, 2017; Gray, 2020).

It is important to establish whether or not there are specific formats that are expected when completing a report detailing neuropsychological evaluations. Such formats vary from region to region, and it is imperative that authors establish the correct format expected either via the aviation regulator or their country's professional body (or preferably, both). Establishing the expected format will also aid the author in guiding what sort of language should be used. While such reports are clearly professional and technical, as previously noted they must also be clear and accessible. In short, authors of neuropsychological reports are required to make sure that the readership immediately recognizes the structure of the report, thereby ensuring that the reader does not turn off at the first paragraph. By following a standardized report format, neuropsychological assessments in aviation can effectively communicate assessment results, inform decision-making processes, and thereby ensure the safety and well-being of aviation personnel and passengers. Once authors have established an overall format, they will then need to identify the sources of information available to them and, most importantly, the question(s) to be answered.

Background Information and Referral Questions

There are clear established elements of any neuropsychological assessment, but as far as aviation neuropsychology is concerned, there are specific sources of information that should also be considered as part of background information required prior to the assessment taking place. The specific reason for requiring background information prior to assessment is that any neuropsychological assessment should be tailored to the specific presentation while satisfying statutory requirements for neuropsychological assessment structure. Many regulatory authorities use a standardized approach to neuropsychological assessment, but this does not mean that additional specific neuropsychological assessments cannot be included in an evaluation. It is especially important to consider these additional neuropsychological evaluations, as they will provide further information regarding a pilot's presentation, but it is only possible to set up a tailor-made neuropsychological assessment if appropriate background information is provided beforehand.

The first element of the vital background information is a clear and concise referral question. Like establishing who the likely readership is going to be, identifying what question or questions the report will be answering will inform the overall approach that the author will be taking. Unclear or diffuse referral questions will result in, at best, unclear or diffuse conclusions and, at worst, erroneous or misleading ones. It is therefore essential that referral questions are clear, focused, and succinct, and if they are not, authors should seek immediate clarification before proceeding any further. Once the author has a specific referral question, that question should be treated as the report's "brief." Adhering to answering, and opinion relating, specifically to the referral question will ensure that the report remains "on message" throughout. It will also make conclusions much easier to write and clearer to understand, as they will have a context that is present throughout the report. The referral questions should also be treated as the boundaries for any report written in aviation; including additional or peripheral material within a report simply serves to confuse matters and potentially irritates the reader (leading to the significant risk of the reader disengaging from important central messages). Where an author believes that additional or potentially peripheral information is necessary, providing a clear justification will ensure that the readership understands the relevance of inclusion.

From the initial referral question, it should then be only a matter of routine to start bringing together sources of information that the author will use in putting the report together. Background information concerning the referral question should, at the very least, include details concerning the incident or condition that the pilot or crew member is being referred for further investigation in, alongside any contemporaneous assessments completed by other professionals. If it is a medical condition that is notifiable, the pilot or crew member should have access to historical reports or diagnoses, and having sight of such paperwork will aid in structuring your assessment and guiding your report toward its appropriate conclusions. It is clear that background information is essential before embarking upon a neuropsychological assessment, and the author does not need to include large amounts of unnecessary detail in an introduction, but having the information to hand provides the basis for a summary that will drive the context of the report. It is important to remember that the report needs to be capable of standing on its own without any subsequent explanatory documentation; therefore background context is vital in the preparation of a clear and accessible assessment.

In addition to background information concerning the incident or condition, and alongside any third-party reports from other professionals, the airline's human resources or personnel department may be able to provide information such as training records that can also offer appropriate background, informing the interpretation of neuropsychological assessment.

Language

Identifying who will be reading the report, alongside identifying appropriate background information, will help clarify what language to use and where to pitch the narrative of the report. In aviation, it is likely that the majority of people reading a neuropsychological report will not be from a neuropsychological background. It is highly likely that conclusions drawn from a neuropsychological assessment will be enacted upon by non-neuropsychologists. It is therefore obvious that any report is written in a way as to ensure that ambiguities are kept to a minimum with the opportunity for misinterpretations being entirely absent. This is a tall order.

Assuming little in the way of preexisting knowledge concerning neuropsychological assessment should be the starting point of any neuropsychological assessment in aviation, and while writing in a "dumbed down" style will not win friends, it is entirely possible to ensure that a report contains suitable explanatory paragraphs that detail the basic premise or hypotheses that the report is generating. If it is not immediately clear why the author used certain assessment tools or approaches, explaining why specific choices have been made will provide the necessary underpinnings to conclusions drawn later in the report. Such explanations should not be written in the style of an exhaustive justification, but more simply a couple of lines to explain the background and to justify the chosen course of action. Using everyday language will be something that the readership will thank the author for and, at all possible costs, it is recommended that authors avoid the use of jargon and acronyms, where at all possible. If the author cannot stop themselves, they should provide a glossary of terms used. And although it is entirely possible to tie oneself up in knots while trying to second-guess what the readership may or may not comprehend, a more "do-able" approach may be to ask, "will a professional outside of neuropsychology understand this concept or this assessment?" while reading it back. If the answer is "no," a clear and succinct revision will be required. Strive to apply plain language principles by using simple and straightforward sentence structures while breaking down complex concepts into more easily understandable terms. By following this basic principle, authors will avoid sacrificing accuracy while maintaining appropriate levels of readability.

While planning the report, it is also important that the author keeps in mind what the central purpose of the assessment is. If the report is to inform the reader regarding specific conditions or presentations, the author will require enough information to support the central findings from the assessment. This is where context is vitally important and assembling the evidence to support conclusions and recommendations will enable the report to stand on its own two feet. Expressing that in accessible language will ensure that the report is understood and recommendations are, if not acted upon, at least considered (Bowden, 2011; Canavor, 2017; Gray, 2020).

Information Sources

If the author is following the structure described in previous paragraphs, they should now have an idea of what the referral questions are, who the intended audience or recipient will be, how the structure of the report will be formatted, and what language to adopt. From this point onwards, the report should adopt a narrative style. In other words, the report needs to tell a clear story with an introduction, details of the assessment, results, and then conclusions and recommendations. At all times, authors must ensure that they are sticking to a clear narrative that follows on from the initial ideas generated by the referral question. As previous paragraphs have indicated, the referral question should dictate the direction of the narrative all the way through to the conclusion, where the aim is to answer the referral question and detail the basis for any recommendations. Unfortunately, such a narrative approach is easier described than achieved, but constant reference back to the referral question will maximize the chances of keeping the report focused and within boundaries. The next stage is to start to collect information from assessment sources. In the current context, this is neuropsychological cognitive assessment data, and while it is beyond the scope of this chapter to go through specific tests for specific assessments of cognitive functioning, this should not detract from the fact that the central information sources will continue to guide your narrative report. It is helpful to think of such information sources as the "meat" in the center of the report sandwich, and in locating sources of information, the neuropsychologist has the advantage of knowing a little bit about the area in which the assessment is taking place. If this is not the case, they should probably be asking themselves whether or not the requested assessment is within their professional capability! Assuming that it is, it is back to the referral question(s) to understand how to best answer the question, using the neuropsychological tools available. It should be noted that different jurisdictions have different requirements concerning neuropsychological assessment, with some regulatory authorities requiring specific batteries of assessments to be completed while other jurisdictions simply require a clear demonstration of an understanding of the possible underpinnings to the pilot's presentation, alongside justifications regarding what assessments have been used. It is therefore clear that the author establishes what neuropsychological approaches are appropriate under the circumstances dictated by their jurisdiction and regulatory authority. In the United Kingdom, for example, neuropsychological assessment choices are broadly down to the individual neuropsychologist, who will base assessment choice on the presenting condition, without the need to follow a specific template of neuropsychological tests. In practice, neuropsychologists will tend to focus on certain core assessments and then add appropriate refinements to the battery to reflect the unique circumstances of each presentation. This contrasts with other jurisdictions, that may require baseline data from specific defined batteries of assessments and where deviation from the stipulated requirements would result in, at the very least, a time-consuming and costly additional assessment. This difference highlights the importance of establishing what the local jurisdiction or regulatory authority will require.

Once the author has established local jurisdiction and regulatory authority expectations, putting together the overall assessment is the next step in the process of adequately assessing the candidate. If you are using a battery of assessments that are of your own choosing, it is important to state why you are choosing the assessment, what it assesses, and what data that assessment can provide. The neuropsychologist will also need to ensure that they are qualified to deliver the individual assessments. The importance of adhering to the structure as set out by the administration requirements of the assessment is of clear importance in any neuropsychological assessment, but in a high-stakes situation such as aviation it is even more so. To deviate from the established administration requirements of a test runs the risk of generating invalid results, unsubstantiated conclusions, and an unrepeatable assessment. In the safety-critical environment that is aviation, it is of utmost importance that tests are repeatable and robust, especially given that possible conclusions drawn from such neuropsychological evaluations may significantly and negatively impact upon a pilot's ongoing future career and earnings potential. Neuropsychologists therefore need to ensure that they are reporting on results that are within their professional competency, and that where they are unsure as to conclusions that could or should be drawn, that they have access to appropriate supervision and mentorship. In terms of the specific tests themselves, they must be assessing what the author claims they are assessing, as, again, incorrect conclusions can easily be drawn from inappropriately utilized evaluations.

On the subject of tests, it should also be emphasized that assessments need to be appropriately used and only repeated according to the test's paradigm. If parallel versions of assessments are available, they should be used where repeat testing is indicated, although it is important to state that even where parallel versions are used, overall practice effects could still potentially occur (in a worst-case scenario this could result in data that show an apparent improvement where no such improvement exists). Where different parallel versions are used, authors should make sure that they cite sources of information to back up their use and why they are appropriate to ensure that any report stands up to analysis. Showing how results were obtained in the assessment phase will demonstrate to the readership that they can be confident in the knowledge that what they are reading is a credible and thoughtful response to their referral query. In short, as far as information sources are concerned, assessments need to be robust and well validated, if only so that the assessment can be repeated in the future. As far as tracking the potential path of a neurodegenerative condition or progressive mental health issue, or demonstrating recovery from multiple different presentations, robust repeatability is of central importance.

In addition to formal neuropsychological assessment, a significant source of further information will be the clinical interview. It is beyond the remit of this chapter to detail specific areas that should be covered in any clinical interview before neuropsychological assessment takes place. This is partly because the nature of this chapter is to provide the appropriate background information from which a structure can be derived for a neuropsychological assessment, but also because a clinical interview needs to reflect the individual referral questions. Again, the importance of having a clear indication of what the referrer is asking of the assessment should be obvious, but for the purposes of obtaining the correct information when interviewing aircrew, it is important that the clinical interview is guided by both the referral question and pre-assessment information as previously described. Therefore, the format of the clinical interview will be dependent on several preexisting factors. There are, however, a number of "givens" that should be adhered to when completing the clinical interview part of an assessment.

The first of these is to consider what is and what is not said by the person being assessed. How have they presented when they arrived at the clinic? How do they appear now sitting in the assessment room, awaiting the pre-assessment phase of the appointment? Do they appear nervous or talkative or are their responses monosyllabic? Are they comfortable in the formal setting of the clinic or are they unable to sit still and contain their nerves? While any such assessment is clearly going to be stressful for the individual on the receiving end, neuropsychologists need to ask themselves if the member of aircrew is managing the stress well. So much of neuropsychological assessment is about observations made before, during, and after testing, and it is such observations that will also inform the interpretation of the more formal element of neuropsychological assessment. In short, it is not all about the numbers, and a few lines detailing the patient's presentation at assessment can be as relevant to answering the referral question as the more formal neuropsychological data. For the curious reader, the author has included his own checklist that he uses in neuropsychological assessments in the form of an appendix at the end of this chapter. This is by no means an exhaustive list and the reader is encouraged to adapt and add to the checklist as appropriate.

Notes on the Psychologist

In terms of how the neuropsychologist conducts both the clinical interview and the neuropsychological assessment, while it may be stating the obvious, the approach adopted needs to be friendly but professional; assessors will gain a lot more information from an interviewee when they are "on side." Neuropsychologists need to ensure that not only do they keep an open mind regarding the member of aircrew sitting in front of them, but they also remember that questions should be open rather than closed to facilitate conversation and disclosure. At all times, the neuropsychologist needs to be supportive while not giving assistance, and this is especially important in the testing phase of the neuropsychological assessment where neuropsychologists need to be mindful of the feedback that they can give while maintaining assessment boundaries. If there are specific instructions or limitations regarding a particular test, it is good practice to inform the member of aircrew being assessed that instructions may vary from assessment to assessment, and while they should feel free to ask any questions that they have, the neuropsychologist may be limited in what information they can provide, due to the specific instructions associated with each evaluation.

The neuropsychologist also has a responsibility to maintain test confidentiality. At no point should they allow test material to leave the clinic, and it goes without saying that test information should not be provided under any circumstances. This includes the names of individual tests to be utilized. Unfortunately, there have been reports of neuropsychological test schedules circulating within pilot populations and this means that the utility of these tests is compromised. In the same way that the over-prescription of antibiotics renders the antibiotic in question less effective, the more familiar a population is with a certain neuropsychological assessment or procedure, the less robust that assessment becomes. It is therefore of utmost importance that test confidentiality is respected and followed at all times.

Tests and Scoring

It is important to say from the outset that neuropsychological assessments do not definitively say if someone is or is not safe to fly. Instead, they measure specific cognitive processes that are used in the safe operation of the aircraft. A neuropsychological assessment is obviously excellent for assessing the presence and/or impact of possible medical conditions or mental health presentations but does not represent a "real-world assessment" of flying ability; an assessment in a stationary ground-based office is going to be a somewhat different prospect when compared with a situation where the office is cruising at 560 mph, some 43,000 ft off the ground. Additionally, it is important to recognize that the neuropsychological assessment does not necessarily reflect how a pilot would respond in a cockpit environment. Having included these caveats, what neuropsychological assessments can do is evaluate the basic building blocks of cognitive functioning that are necessary to function effectively in a safety-critical environment. The fact that neuropsychological assessments could be seen as somewhat detached from the process of flying stresses the importance of ensuring that the data obtained from said assessments are viewed in the context of aviation.

Clearly, in the safety-critical environment that is aviation, ensuring that neuropsychological data are accurate, as far as is possible, is essential. Potential areas of error can include scoring errors at the point of testing and scoring errors at the point of processing data. The former can be guarded against in two ways; firstly, the use of robust task instructions that are followed to the letter will ensure that responses are accurately recorded as far as possible, and secondly, through the use of computer- or tablet-based neuropsychological evaluations. The use of computer- or tablet-based neuropsychological assessment has increased over recent years with many core assessments now available on systems such as Q Interactive from Pearson. While the use of such computerized batteries often requires an upfront financial commitment in terms of the purchase of hardware, the advantages of having a computerized assessment record of client responses rather than relying entirely on the neuropsychologist is advantageous in that it eliminates (or, depending on the specific battery, vastly reduces) the opportunity for operator error to occur. The other significant advantage associated with computer-based neuropsychological assessment is that the system scores the raw data. Again, this significantly reduces issues relating to clerical errors committed by the neuropsychologist and therefore contributes to confidence in the conclusions drawn.

It is beyond the scope of this chapter to deal in any detail with the thorny issue of normative data and cultural differences in neuropsychological testing. It is, however, worth mentioning that the neuropsychologist needs to be aware of issues relating to normative data in aviation-related assessment. Given the international nature of commercial aviation, it is essential that neuropsychologists ensure that the normative data used in assessment interpretation are appropriate for the population that the pilot hails from. A clear starting point in this endeavor is to ensure that the normative data that you use for your assessments are appropriate for your region and that potential cultural differences between different sources of normative data are minimized. From an assessment point of view, studies have indicated that significant differences can exist between the validity of certain test items when administered to, for example, UK versus US populations, and it is therefore essential that the neuropsychological assessment identifies the most appropriate for the pilot's background and circumstances. In practice, this is not always possible, with some assessments not having aviation normative data and others not having general population normative data based upon an appropriate international region. It can therefore be difficult for assessors to identify the most appropriate assessment, but ensuring that "mainstream" commercially available (or at the very least widely published and well-validated) assessments are prioritized will maximize the chances of a robust set of conclusions being drawn.

A Basic Layout

So far, this chapter has provided outlines concerning the format of the neuropsychological assessment, indicated the background information and referral questions required to be able to structure the format appropriately, and detailed the importance of appropriate language to be used and broad sources of information to be identified. Notes on how the psychologist should conduct themselves alongside a summary of scoring assessments have also been included to this point. The following section recommends a basic layout and is taken from the author's previously published outline on the subject.

As previously stated, an assessment in neuropsychology requires a structure that supports a clear narrative. At the very least, a report requires an introduction, a main body where findings and data are presented, and a conclusion where all the threads of the narrative are drawn together to answer referral questions and provide recommendations for ongoing support or input. The following structure is a basic expansion of the above. It should not be seen as a fixed template but instead as more of a guide that should be adapted according to the pilot's presentation.

Introduction

- The introduction should include setting of the scene that indicates the source of the referral and an acknowledgement of the referral questions being asked
- Dates of appointments and interviews should be provided.
- A summary of previous assessments, especially the case if your assessment represents a re-referral of the assessment of an ongoing issue, should be included (Bowden, 2011; Canavor, 2017; Gray, 2020).

Main Body

- Includes a description of the results from the clinical interview and neuropsychological assessments.
- Details of the tests and assessments that have been utilized should be provided, but attention should be paid to maintaining test confidentiality in any descriptions.
- Descriptions of what particular tests were appropriate and what they have been able to provide by way of further information can also be useful in highlighting the relevance to the referral question(s).
- A brief description of the methodology regarding test administration may also be useful in indicating how it is relevant to the initial referral question.
- This section should present and explain all findings that are then used in the following conclusions and recommendations section (Bowden, 2011; Canavor, 2017; Gray, 2020).

Conclusions and Recommendations

- This section is where the findings of neuropsychological assessment are drawn together, and all conclusions should flow naturally from the findings and information presented previously.
- No new data should be presented in the conclusion section.
- Summaries of data described in the main body of the report should back up and highlight why particular conclusions and recommendations have been drawn.
- All conclusions and recommendations should be based on fact and supported by the data obtained. Overstating or exaggerating the importance of specific findings runs the risk of stretching the credibility of both the report and the author.
- Data that present a counter-argument should be considered, as the author is required to be objective in all interpretations.
- Conclusions may be appropriate from a clinical perspective, but consideration should be given to whether or not they are realistic (Bowden, 2011; Canavor, 2017; Gray, 2020).

Context: A Case Study

This chapter has made reference to the unique circumstances of aviation neuropsychological assessment. Specifically, the outcome of any neuropsychological assessment may ultimately result in a pilot or member of the crew being unable to work in their chosen profession. For many pilots, this would be the worst outcome; being grounded and unable to do something that they love would represent the ultimate loss and it is this outcome that neuropsychologists need to consider when drafting a neuropsychological report. Mercifully, there have been relatively few reported situations where assessments or investigations have resulted in the permanent grounding of pilots, but when it does happen, the consequences can be significant and far reaching. The following example, while not related to neuropsychological inaccuracies, more than adequately illustrates the potential impact of reports that are based on inaccurate data and conclusions.

G-ALZU was one of a 20-strong fleet of Elizabethan class Airspeed Ambassadors introduced by British European Airways (BEA) during 1952. The airline referred to them as the "Elizabethan" class in honor of the newly crowned Queen Elizabeth II and the first scheduled flight of an Elizabethan was from Heathrow to Paris Le Bourget on March 13, 1952. The type proved to be a particularly popular aircraft with the flying public due to its overall levels of comfort and good soundproofing, but unfortunately the aircraft's popularity did not last long ("Airspeed Ambassador," 2024). By 1958, BEA was starting the process of withdrawing the aircraft in favor of the faster Vickers Viscount. G-ALZU was still with BEA in 1958 when it crashed at Munich-Reim Airport instantly killing 20 passengers with a further three dying at Munich's Rechts der Isar Hospital. One of the two captains in the cockpit died as a result of the accident, and one of the three members of cabin crew also lost their lives. At the time of the crash, G-ALZU was operating a charter flight transporting the Manchester United football team back from a European Cup match in Belgrade. This made the accident of significant interest to the British press at the time.

G-ALZU had stopped at Munich-Reim Airport to refuel en route to Manchester. The February weather was cold with a mixture of rain and snow falling over the airfield, but Captains James Thain and Kenneth Rayment were experienced former RAF pilots used to inclement conditions such as this. After refueling, the Elizabethan taxied back out to the runway and Captain Thain commenced the first take off at 15:30 hr. At approximately 105 knots, Captain Rayment noticed that the boost on both engines was fluctuating and abandoned take-off. The Elizabethan received permission to backtrack and return to the start of the runway, and at 15:34 hr it commenced a second run. Opening the throttles more slowly, it was noted that the starboard engine boost was steady, but that the port boost gauge started to fluctuate significantly. Captain Thain again ordered the take-off to be abandoned and returned to the apron for consultation with the Station Engineer. The Station Engineer reported that boost surging was not uncommon on Elizabethan aircraft at Munich, owing to the airfield height. The normal way of dealing with this relatively common issue was to throttle back slightly as soon as boost surging was noted, although this would mean that the aircraft would take longer to become airborne. Given the generous length of the runway at Munich-Reim, the pilots decided that this was not a problem and at 15:56 hr, G-ALZU was cleared to taxi to the runway. At 16:03 hr, G-ALZU reported "Zulu uniform rolling" on its third and final attempt at take-off. It never became airborne. At 85 knots, the port engine began to surge again and the throttle was pulled back marginally before being pushed forward again. V1 was reached at 117 knots (the point at which a take-off cannot be safely aborted) but V2 (take-off speed) never arrived. Instead, the Elizabethan started to slow despite throttle input. G-ALZU left the end of the runway and crashed into the fence surrounding the airfield. It skidded across the road before the port wing was torn off as it hit a house, with part of the aircraft's tail coming away before the left side of the cockpit hit a tree (Ministry of Transport and Civil Aviation, 1959, 1960; "The Munich Air Disaster," 2024).

Captain Kenneth Rayment suffered multiple injuries and died later in hospital as a result of a traumatic brain injury, with 22 others dying either at the scene or later as a result of their injuries. Initial accident investigation reports pointed the finger of blame at Captain Thain, with the German Commission of Enquiry concluding that he had taken off without de-icing the aircraft. The basis of the German authorities' report was that observations made some time after the accident indicated ice on the wings with a photograph of G-ALZU taken shortly before the third take-off attempt seemingly confirming the presence of snow or ice on the upper wing surfaces. Throughout the German Commission of Enquiry investigation, Captain Thain protested his innocence and stated that there was no ice or snow on the wings of his aircraft. Despite these protestations, the accident report stated that the captain was to blame for both the accident and subsequent loss of life. BEA dismissed him from his post and he never flew again ("The Munich Air Disaster," 2024).

For the next 10 years, Captain Thain and the British Airline Pilots' Association (BALPA) challenged the findings of the German Commission of Enquiry stating that the cause of the crash was due to the prevailing weather conditions at the time of the third take-off attempt leaving the runway not fit for use. Due to the longer take-off distances required as a result of throttling back on over-boosting engines, G-ALZU required the full length of the runway at Munich-Reim. Unfortunately, the final quarter of the runway had not been cleared of slush and subsequent investigations in 1968 (ordered by the then UK Prime Minister Harold Wilson) found that the Airspeed Ambassador was particularly prone to decelerate in slushy conditions. Additionally, a review of the photograph taken just before take-off revealed nothing of note on the wings, with the report concluding that what had previously been reported as ice build-up was in fact the reflection of light on the surface of the wing. Ultimately, the UK authorities cleared Captain Thain of responsibility for the accident, and instead placed the blame on airport authorities who had not ensured that the runway was fit for use. Despite these findings, Captain Thain was not reinstated by BEA, never flew again, and became a farmer until his death at the age of 54. In a newspaper interview (Manchester Evening News, 2010), Captain Thain's daughter described the negative publicity and death threats that her father and her family endured following the publication of the initial incorrect report, and detailed how the outcome of the investigations left him "crushed by his ordeal." She believes that the experience contributed to his early death. Government papers released in 2001 show that the disagreement between UK and German authorities led to a cooling of diplomatic relations (Evans, 2001). The German authorities did not reopen their investigation.

While not as a result of a neuropsychological assessment, the sad tale of the Munich air crash and subsequent investigation indicates the far-reaching ripples that incorrect conclusions, based on incorrect data, can create. From the loss of a man's livelihood, to the death threats that his family received, through to a cooling of diplomatic relations between the United Kingdom and Germany, this may be one of the most extreme examples of the potential consequences of incorrect conclusions being drawn from inappropriately interpreted information, but it serves to highlight two things: Firstly, the stakes are much higher in a safety-critical environment such as commercial aviation and, secondly, report authors need to be doubly sure that data and subsequently derived conclusions are sufficiently robust to stand up to intense scrutiny.

Conclusion

Writing any report in a clear and succinct way is a skill that needs to be practiced. Avoiding the use of jargon or buzzwords will always ensure that a report is as accessible as possible to the widest possible readership. It is also important to think about all of the sources of information that a report should be drawing upon, and where conclusions are drawn that they are based on the most robust data available. Neuropsychological assessment should always be an objective reporting of the facts, whether that be based on the neuropsychological data derived from cognitive assessments, from observations made before or during testing, or from information provided prior to the valuation appointment. Additionally, the author should always consider including an indication of the sources of information that they are drawing upon. In conclusion, making complex concepts appear simple is a skill that needs practice; the more reports that a neuropsychologist writes, the better the reports will be, but appropriate supervision and mentorship are an essential part of this process. Following the steps detailed in this chapter will also help avoid inaccurate data being drawn upon in the formation of inaccurate conclusions and recommendations.

References

Airspeed Ambassador. (2024, July 2). In *Wikipedia*. https://en.wikipedia.org/wiki/Airspeed_Ambassador

Bowden, J. (2011). *Writing a report* (9th ed.). How To Books Ltd.

Canavor, N. (2017). *Business writing for dummies*. John Wiley & Sons.

Evans, R. (2001, August 26). Munich air crash inquiry clouded by diplomacy. *The Guardian*.

Gray, A. L. (2020). Assessment report preparation in pilot selection. In R. Bor, C. Erikson, T. P. Hubbard, & R. King (Eds.), *Psychological principles and practice* (pp. 219–231). CRC Press.

Manchester Evening News. (2010, April 20). Pilot's daughter pays tribute. *Manchester Evening News*.

Ministry of Transport and Civil Aviation. (1959). *Report by the Federal Republic of Germany, relating to the inquiry into the accident, to G-ALZU AS 57 Ambassador (Elizabethan) on the 6th of February 1958 at Munich-Reim Airport*. Her Majesty's Stationary Office.

Ministry of Transport and Civil Aviation. (1960). *Report of the reviewing body appointed to considering reports on certain matters connected with the accident to the Elizabethan Aircraft G-ALZU at Munich on 6 February 1958*. Her Majesty's Stationary Office.

The Munich Air Disaster. (2024, July 24). In *Wikipedia*. https://en.wikipedia.org/wiki/Munich_air_disaster

Appendix

This appendix contains a checklist of background information collected in the clinical interview phase of an aviation neuropsychology assessment, prior to the cognitive neuropsychological aspects of the evaluation. It is by no means exhaustive or complete and is broader than just an aviation focus, thus the reader is encouraged to adopt, adapt, and add to as necessary. It is *not* a script; instead, it should be seen as an aide-mémoire for the assessing neuropsychologist with each question being viewed as a potential starting point for conversation.

1. Purpose of the investigation – discussion with pilot
2. Demographic variables
   a) Age
   b) Handedness
   c) Education
   d) Professional background
   e) Family/home life circumstances
3. Results of any previous investigations – discussion and review of available documentation
   a) Medical investigations (e.g., general practitioner/family doctor, specialist assessments such as neurology, psychiatry, neuroimaging etc.)
   b) Previous psychological assessments
   c) Discussion relating to previous and/or current diagnoses
   d) Review of documentation relating to previous and/or current diagnoses
   e) Other medical issues (e.g., blood pressure, cholesterol etc.)
   f) Current medication
4. History of presenting condition(s)
   a) Onset and chronology since
   b) Details of injury or conditions (i.e., medical or psychiatric history)
   c) Circumstances surrounding current onset (medical, personal life circumstances, life events etc.)
   d) Any history of seizures, anoxia, posttraumatic amnesia, posttraumatic unconsciousness, traumatic brain injury
   e) History of any cognitive issues
   f) Reports from any surgical procedures
5. Factors affecting testing
   a) Current medication
   b) Anxiety, mood, and motivation
   c) Other deficits that might affect testing
6. Additional background questions – general circumstances
   a) How have your current circumstances affected your life?
   b) How are you different now compared to before injury/condition development?
   c) What problems do you now have on a day-to-day basis?
7. Work
   a) How is work? How have your current circumstances affected your employment?
   b) How are you coping with the demands of your current role?
   c) How do you find learning new tasks?
   d) Dealing with pressure/stress at work
   e) Decision-making
   f) Have colleagues/managers made any comments about your work standards?

8. Social
   a) What do you do in your spare time to relax?
   b) Interacting with family, friends, any social difficulties?
   c) Ask about social anxieties
9. Personality and emotion
   a) Ask about the enjoyment of activities
   b) Check mood
   c) Ask about fatigue and lack of energy
   d) What sort of person are you, and how do others see you?
   e) New worries
   f) Tolerance level - anger/aggression
   g) Emotional lability
10. Language
    a) Understanding what is said to you, or finding the correct words with which to express yourself
    b) Observe expressive language during neuropsychological phase
11. Memory and attention
    a) We all forget things from time to time - what sort of things do you forget?
    b) Does this happen more often?
    c) Under what circumstances is it worse?
    d) How are you at remembering new things?
    e) Has anybody else commented upon your memory functioning?
    f) Mental slowing
    g) Concentration
    h) Following a narrative
    i) Completing everyday tasks
12. Other issues or difficulties
    a) Fitness and exercise levels
    b) Alcohol use
    c) Drug use
    d) Sleep/appetite/weight
    e) Activities such as driving
    f) Last time "old self"

Contributors

Editors

Robert Bor, DPhil, CPsychol, CSci, FBPsS, HonFRAeS, EuroPsy, is Director and, with Aedrian Bekker, co-founder of the Centre for Aviation Psychology (https://www.centreforaviationpsychology.com), which provides well-being support to thousands of pilots. Professor Bor is a registered and practicing clinical, counseling, and health psychologist in the United Kingdom. He is also a certified aviation psychologist in Europe and a board member of the European Association for Aviation Psychology, civilian psychologist to the Royal Air Force, on the International Civil Aviation Organization Mental Health Working Group, Aerospace Medical Association Mental Health Group, and European Pilot Peer Support Initiative Committee. He was the Lead Consultant Clinical Psychologist at the Royal Free Hospital National Health Service Foundation Trust, London, until 2023, working in critical care and high-risk settings. He has published more than 35 textbooks and 200 academic papers and chapters in books, including three key textbooks in aviation psychology. He received the highest award in aviation in 2017, an honorary fellowship of the Royal Aeronautical Society. He is Liveryman of the Honorary Company of Air Pilots and holds the Freedom of the City of London. Rob is a Churchill Fellow (presented by HM The Queen) and together with the AsMA mental health group has recently received the Boothby–Edwards award from the Aerospace Medical Association.

Carina Eriksen, MSc, Dip Psych, DPsych, CPsychol, FBPsS, BABCP, is a UK Health and Care Professions Council registered and British Psychological Society (BPS) chartered consultant psychologist with an extensive London-based private practice for young people, adults, couples, and families. She is a fellow of the BPS, a registered aviation psychologist, and an accredited member of the British Association for Behavioural and Cognitive Psychotherapies, having specialized at the Institute of Psychiatry. She has managed a team of clinical and counseling psychologists in the National Health Service for several years, and she used to be an external supervisor for the Priory Group. She has extensive experience consulting in clinical and organizational settings in the United Kingdom and Europe. Dr. Eriksen is a consultant at the Centre for Aviation Psychology and has, along with her colleagues, developed and implemented pilot peer support programs for major UK airlines. She is a committee member of the BPS specialist group in aviation psychology, and she has experience as a trainer/presenter of the BPS Continuing Professional Development Course for Aviation Mental Health. Dr. Eriksen has taught at several London universities. She is an author and coauthor of several books, and her work has been published in prestigious scientific journals. She has also contributed to various widely recognized textbooks on topics including pilot mental health, pilot assessment and selection, fear of flying, psychology health and medicine, counseling and health, clinical supervision, aviation psychology, anxiety disorders, mental health in the workplace, relationship issues, and mood disorders, to name a few.

Randy J. Georgemiller, PhD, ABPP, is a board-certified licensed clinical psychologist who is the recently retired Supervisory Psychologist for Aviation Psychology and Chief Neuropsychologist in the Office of Aerospace Medicine at the Federal Aviation Administration (FAA) headquarters. In these roles he oversaw the execution of psychology and neuropsychology case reviews for pilots and air traffic control specialists, and he provided expert advice and technical support to the Federal Air Surgeon and the Medical Specialties Division Director. Prior to coming to work full-time for the FAA, he was appointed as a neuropsychology consultant to the Federal Air Surgeon during his tenure of 20+ years as the president of a group psychology practice. On the national level, professional activities include positions as past president of the American Psychological Association (APA) Division 44 (Society for the Psychology of Sexual Orientation and Gender Diversity), the APA's Committee for Lesbian Gay Bisexual and Transgender Concerns, Council of Representatives, and Commission for the Recognition of Specialties in Professional Psychology. Leadership at the statewide level includes service as past president of the Illinois Psychological Association. He is a fellow of the American Psychological Association and Illinois Psychological Association: diplomate of the American Board of Professional Psychology; and member of the Aerospace Medical Association, European Association for Aviation Psychology, International Neuropsychological Society, and National Academy of Neuropsychology. He has published and presented before national and international professional organizations on the topics of military psychology, LGBTQ psychology, aerospace neuropsychology, and geropsychology.

Alastair L. Gray, BSc, PhD, D Clin Psych, PG Dip Neuropsych, C Psychol, AFBPS, gained a degree in psychology from the University of Leeds, before moving to Newcastle University to complete a PhD in neuropsychology. He then trained at the world-renowned Institute of Psychiatry, King's College London, where he gained his doctorate in clinical psychology and his postgraduate diploma in neuropsychology. He initially worked with the National Health Service in adult mental health and assessment, and then later for his own private practice. Dr. Gray now delivers neuropsychological assessment and opinion for both private and commercial pilots in the United Kingdom as an accredited aviation psychologist (through the European Association for Aviation Psychology). Working both independently through Eastern Aviation Psychology and as an associate with the Centre for Aviation Psychology in London, Dr. Gray provides specialist neuropsychological evaluations for conditions ranging from stress and burnout through to attention-deficit/hyperactivity disorder and autistic spectrum disorders. Additionally, he teaches on the British Psychological Society's Clinical Skills for Working With Air Crew course and has presented at both European Association of Aviation Psychology and Federal Aviation Administration events. He has also provided psychological support for display pilots who are not necessarily covered by employer-sponsored programs and is a civilian psychologist for the Royal Air Force. In his non-aviation roles, Dr. Gray works for Meridian Psychology Cambridge, primarily supporting patients who have sustained serious traumatic brain injuries, typically through road traffic accidents.

Authors

Corrie Anna Ackland, PhD: Clinical Psychologist and the Clinical Director of the Sydney Phobia Clinic, Australia

Mathias Basner, MD, PhD, MScEpi: Professor and Director of the Behavioral Regulation and Health Section in the Department of Psychiatry at the University of Pennsylvania Perelman School of Medicine, Philadelphia, PA, USA

Marc Baumgartner: Operational Air Traffic Controller and Center Supervisor at Geneva ACC, Switzerland

Nadine Belser, PhD: Psychologist at Hamburg Police, Hamburg, Germany

Eilis Boudreau, MD, PhD: Professor in the Department of Medical Informatics and Clinical Epidemiology, Department of Neurology, at Oregon Health & Science University and in the Department of Neurology, VA Portland Health Care System, OR, USA

Thomas R. Carretta, PhD: Senior Research Psychologist at the Air Force Research Laboratory, Wright-Patterson Air Force Base, OH, USA

Anthony Carter, MA: Practicing Lawyer and Acting Branch Manager of Litigation, Investigations, and Enforcement with the Civil Aviation Safety Authority, Australia

Mickaël Causse, PhD: Professor of Neuroergonomics at ISAE-SUPAERO in Toulouse, France

Michael Chafetz, PhD, ABPP: Board-Certified Clinical Neuropsychologist working in independent practice in New Orleans, LA, USA

Thomas Chidester, PhD: Deputy Director of the Federal Aviation Administration's Civil Aerospace Medical Institute (CAMI) Oklahoma City, OK, USA

Monique Crane, PhD: Founder of Resilience Research and Training Systems at Macquarie University, Australia

Jerry Crutchfield, PhD: Engineering Research Psychologist at the FAA Civil Aerospace Medical Institute, Oklahoma City, OK, USA

Daniel N. DaSilva, PhD: Aerospace Neuropsychologist in private practice in Parsippany, NJ, and Faculty at Rutgers University, Graduate School of Education, New Brunswick, NJ, USA

Lauren Drag, PhD, ABPP: Board-Certified Clinical Neuropsychologist with clinical and faculty appointments at Stanford Medicine and a private practice in Los Gatos, CA, USA

Kelene A. Fercho, PhD: Senior Aviation Research Psychologist at the FAA Civil Aerospace Medical Institute, Oklahoma City, OK, USA

Christopher F. Flynn, MD: Board-Certified Psychiatrist and Assistant Chief Psychiatrist for the Federal Aviation Administration Washington, DC, USA

Ryan Green, PhD, ABPP: Former US Army Active Duty Major and Chief of Aeromedical Psychology, Board-Certified Clinical Psychologist and Human Intervention Motivational Study (HIMS) Neuropsychologist with an aerospace neuropsychology-focused private practice in Salt Lake City, UT, USA

Ruben C. Gur, PhD: Professor in Psychiatry, Neurology, and Radiology and Director of the Brain Behavior Lab, Department of Psychiatry, University of Pennsylvania Perelman School of Medicine, Philadelphia, PA, USA

Roger R. Hesselbrock, MD: Board-Certified Neurologist and Aeromedical Neurology Consultant at the Federal Aviation Administration (FAA) Medical Specialties Division, Washington, DC, USA

Tammy T. Ho, BSc: Psychology Technician at the Federal Aviation Administration, Civil Aerospace Medical Institute (CAMI), Oklahoma City, OK, USA

Jean-Paul Imbert, PhD: Research Engineer in the ACHIL team at the National School of Civil Aviation (ENAC), Toulouse, France

Farzin Irani, PhD, ABPP: Human Intervention Motivational Study (HIMS)-trained, multilingual, Board-Certified Neuropsychologist in private practice in the greater Philadelphia area, PA, USA

Mi-Yeoung Jo, PsyD, ABPP: Board-Certified Clinical Neuropsychologist and Board-Certified Subspecialist in Pediatric Neuropsychology with an independent practice in Los Angeles, CA, USA

Robert L. Kane, PhD, ABPP-CN: Board-Certified Clinical Neuropsychologist and CEO and President of Cognitive Consults and Technology, LLC, in Washington, DC, USA

Jason A. King, PhD: Board-Certified Clinical Neuropsychologist with a private practice in Atlanta, GA, USA

Raymond E. King, PsyD, JD: Licensed Clinical Psychologist and Chief Clinical Psychologist at the Federal Aviation Administration (FAA), Medical Specialties Division, Washington, DC, USA

Hunter T. Klevgard, MA, MS: Statistician for the National Airspace System (NAS) Human Factors Safety Research branch (AAM-520) within the Civil Aerospace Medical Institute (CAMI), Oklahoma City, OH, USA

Andrew Levine, PhD, ABPP: Board-Certified Clinical Neuropsychologist and Adjunct Professor in the Department of Neurology at the David Geffen School of Medicine at UCLA, CA, USA

Sarah V. Ligda, PhD: Engineering Research Psychologist at the Federal Aviation Administration's Civil Aerospace Medical Institute (CAMI), Oklahoma City, OK, USA

Sarah Mackenzie Ross, MA, MPhil, DPsychol, PhD: Consultant Clinical Neuropsychologist, Clinical Psychologist, Honorary Professor at University College London, and Lecturer at the University of Glasgow and Canterbury Christ Church University, UK

John Milanovich, PhD: Founder and Lead Investigator of Optimal Aviation: Brain Fitness for Pilots, Ann Arbor, MI, USA

Brett Robert Charles Molesworth, PhD: Professor in Human Factors and Aviation Safety at UNSW Sydney, Australia

Damien Mouratille, PhD: Researcher in human factors and neuroergonomics at the National School of Civil Aviation (ENAC) in Toulouse, France

David G. Newman, AM, MBBS, DAvMed, MBA, PhD: Aerospace Medicine Specialist and Visiting Professor of Aerospace Medicine at King's College London, UK

Ann Norris, PhD: Safety Management Systems Epidemiologist at the Federal Aviation Administration's Civil Aerospace Medical Institute (CAMI) in Oklahoma City, OK, USA

Viktor Oubaid, PhD: Head of Industry relation and Deputy Head of the Department of Aviation and Space Psychology of the German Aerospace Center in Hamburg, Germany

Raymond Padua, BSc, MSc, PhD, CCFP, FRCPsych, Dip Av Med: Aeromedical Psychiatrist with the Canadian Armed Forces and an Aeromedical Psychiatrist for Transport Canada, Winnipeg, MB, Canada

Forest Pavel, PsyD, LP, HSP: Psychologist for Aviation Psychology in the Office of Aerospace Medicine at the Federal Aviation Administration (FAA), Aeromedical Psychologist and Major in the US Army Reserves, and Licensed Clinical Psychologist (Health Services Provider), Kansas City, MO, USA

Asha Pook, BSc, MSc, MBBS, FRCPsych, PG Dip (CAT): Consultant Psychiatrist and Consultant Advisor to the UK Civil Aviation Authority

Carlos Porges, PsyD, ABPP: Board-Certified Aviation and Clinical Neuropsychologist, and also a B-787 pilot for United Airlines, Key Biscanye, FL, USA

Sanjiv Sharma, MB, BS, MD (Aerospace Medicine): Senior Medical Officer at the Civil Aviation Safety Authority, Australia

Laurie Shaw is an A350/A330 Captain with Fiji Airways, based in Nadi, Fiji

Delia Silva, PsyD, ABPP: Board-Certified Neuropsychologist and Human Intervention Motivational Study (HIMS)-trained, in full-time private practice in San Diego, CA, USA

Valerie Skaggs, PhD: Biostatistician at the Federal Aviation Administration's Civil Aerospace Medical Institute (CAMI), Oklahoma City, OK, USA

Quay Snyder, MD, MSPH: FAA/ALPA HIMS Program Manager and President and CEO of Virtual Flight Surgeons (Aviation Medicine Advisory Service), Englewood, CO, USA

Gary Strangman, PhD: Associate Professor in the Department of Psychiatry at Harvard Medical School, Director of the Neural Systems Group at Massachusetts General Hospital, and Science Lead for the Translational Research Institute for Space Health, Charlestown, MA, USA

Brett S. Torrence, PhD: Engineering Research Psychologist for the National Airspace System (NAS) Human Factors Safety Research Laboratory of the Aerospace Human Factors Research Division (AHFRD) at the Civil Aerospace Medical Institute (CAMI), Oklahoma City, OK, USA

Annette M. Totten, PhD, MPA: Professor in the Department of Medical Informatics and Clinical Epidemiology, Co-Director of the Pacific Northwest Evidence-Based Practice Center at Oregon Health & Science University in Portland, OR, USA

Anthony Tvaryanas, PhD: Manager of the Aerospace Medical Research Division at the Federal Aviation Administration's Civil Aerospace Medical Institute (CAMI), Oklahoma City, OK, USA

Thomas A. Van Dillen, PhD: FAA Aerospace Human Factors Safety Research Manager (AAM-520) within the Civil Aerospace Medical Institute (CAMI), Oklahoma City, OK, USA

Lea Sophie Vink, PhD: Head of Human Performance and Human Factors at Austro Control, Vienna, Austria; Chairwoman CANSO Human Performance Group; Co-Chair European Commission Expert Group on Human Dimension in Aviation, Brussels, Belgium

Alpo Vuorio, MD, PhD: Specialist in Occupational Medicine and an Aviation Medical Examiner at Helsinki Vantaa Airport, Finland

Mark W. Wiggins, PhD: Professor of Organisational Psychology at Macquarie University, Australia

Peer Commentaries

The editors of this handbook suggest that their audience should take the time to read it from cover to cover. They are absolutely right in doing so because your knowledgeability about what neuropsychology is, how it applies to aviation, and how it may impact aviation safety will grow with each single chapter. Put this title at the top of your list of books to buy – there is a fair chance this comprehensive and well-written handbook will become a true companion to you in your practice, career, or study in aviation.

André Droog, MSc Psychology, MSc Aerospace Engineering; Past President of the European Association for Aviation Psychology (EAAP)

In the ever-evolving realm of aviation, the Handbook of Aviation Neuropsychology *is a landmark and monumental contribution to the field of aviation psychology and neuropsychology. Knowledge of the content of the edited publication by Bor, Eriksen, Georgemiller, and Gray is crucial for ensuring the safety and effectiveness of aviation operations. This comprehensive volume delves into a wide array of topics that are essential and relevant for practitioners and researchers involved in aviation psychology, aviation neuropsychology, and aviation medicine.*

The book's chapters meticulously cover the historical development of the field of aviation psychology and neuropsychology, offering a context for current practices and advancements. The publication provides an insightful exploration focused on pilot and air traffic controller selection processes and the critical role of military aeromedical psychology.

The handbook provides comprehensive content regarding the psychiatrist's role in pilot assessments and the intricate issues surrounding pilot mental health. With detailed discussions on cognitive training, substance abuse, and cognitive challenges in aviation, it addresses the multifaceted aspects of pilot performance and safety. Notably, the book also emphasizes the importance of neuropsychological and psychological test results and their implications in aviation mental health, neurocognitive, and fitness for duty settings.

The volume goes further by addressing language and cultural considerations in neuropsychological evaluations, a crucial aspect in today's diverse aviation workforce. The exploration of neurological and neurodevelopmental conditions, including ADHD, HIV, learning disabilities, Asperger's, and other conditions, underscores the book's commitment to a holistic view of aviation physical and mental health and safety. Additionally, it tackles the impact of age on cognitive performance and offers guidance on neuropsychological report writing, making it a practical resource for clinicians, researchers, and others involved in aviation medicine, safety, and performance.

The Handbook of Aviation Neuropsychology *is an indispensable resource that brings together leading experts and provides a thorough, evidence-based perspective on the neuropsychological, mental health, and human factor dimensions in aviation. It is a must-read for anyone involved in the field of aviation psychology or neuropsychology, offering foundational knowledge, cutting-edge insights, and scholarly rigor with practical relevance.*

Robert W. Elliott, PhD, ABPP (CN), ABN, Aerospace Health Institute, Los Angeles, CA

Optimum cognitive abilities and mental health are essential to the safe performance of aviation duties. It is therefore important that psychologists and aeromedical doctors consider the neuropsychological conditions that may lead to decrements of performance. This handbook offers much-needed guidance and knowledge as it provides an up-to-date and complete overview of all facets of neuropsychology. This long-desired handbook is a must for psychologists and medical doctors engaged in evaluations of neuropsychological conditions that can affect performance of pilots and other safety-critical staff.

Dr. Ries Simons, Chair of the Advisory Board of the European Society of Aerospace Medicine (ESAM)

This groundbreaking handbook introduces aviation neuropsychology as a new sub-specialty within aviation psychology, offering profound insights into human behavior in aerospace environments and making a significant contribution to advancing flight safety. The expertise and dedication of the editors, along with the collective wisdom of all the contributors, have been instrumental in shaping this essential resource. We are especially proud that so many of them are esteemed members and ambassadors of the European Association for Aviation Psychology (EAAP).

Gunnar Steinhardt, President of the European Association for Aviation Psychology (EAAP)

With our growing appreciation of the psychiatric risk in aviation, this compendium of aviation neuropsychology brings together a growing body of knowledge that will be invaluable resource for those involved in the care or safety assurance of the human in aviation.

Dr. Michael J. A. Trudgill, Chief Medical Officer, Safety and Airspace Regulation Group, UK Civil Aviation Authority

